Past Forgetting

Past Forgetting

My Love Affair with Dwight D. Eisenhower

Kay Summersby Morgan

COLLINS
St James's Place, London
1977

William Collins Sons & Co Ltd
London · Glasgow · Sydney · Auckland
Toronto · Johannesburg

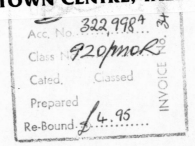
First published 1977
© 1976 by the estate of Kay Summersby Morgan
ISBN 0 00 211645 6
Set in Monotype Bembo
Made and Printed in Great Britain by
William Collins Sons & Co Ltd Glasgow

'Why will the foolish tears
tremble across the years?'

'I'll see you again
whenever spring breaks through again.
Time may lie heavy between,
but what has been is past forgetting.'

FROM *Bittersweet*

Acknowledgments

'I'll See You Again' by Noël Coward
© 1929 Chappell & Co Ltd
Reproduced by permission of the Noël Coward Estate and
Chappell & Co Ltd

Excerpt from *Plain Speaking* by Merle Miller
© 1973 by Merle Miller
Reproduced by permission of Victor Gollancz Ltd

Photographic Acknowledgments
US Army: Nos. 2, 7, 9, 10, 11, 12, 13, 14, 15, 16, 20, 22, 26, 27, 28
U.P.I.: Nos. 3, 18, 25   Black Star: No. 4
Wide World: Nos. 8, 30   Bourke-White/Time: No. 19
Time/Life: No. 29   Columbia Collection, Columbia University:
Nos. 31, 32

From the Publisher

Kay Summersby Morgan wrote this book under a death sentence. In late 1973, her doctors gave her six months to live, but Kay stretched it into more than a year – and lived every day until the very last with her customary gaiety and relish. 'There's no point in dwelling on it,' she would say.

She kept on working. Her last job was as fashion consultant for the film *The Stepford Wives*. On weekends she drove her beat-up second-hand Volkswagen to the Hamptons, where she played bridge and an occasional few holes of golf with old friends. And she wrote. She wrote this book because she wanted the truth to be known.

'I was always extremely discreet,' she said. 'But now the General is dead. And I am dying. Once I am dead, then I would like this book to speak for me. I would like the world to know the truth of the Eisenhower affair.'

Two weeks before Kay died, she moved from New York City to a tiny cottage in Southampton. 'I don't want to die in the city,' she said, and mustered her strength to make the move and to set out her autographed pictures of Dwight D. Eisenhower, Prime Minister Winston Churchill, and President Franklin D. Roosevelt – all men who had appreciated Kay's special gallantry and integrity.

She spent two January weeks delighting in the winter-fresh salt air of Long Island. It reminded her, she told friends, of the salt breezes of the Atlantic that blew across the meadows surrounding Innis Beg, her family's square old stone house in County Cork. The day came when she had to go to the hospital. The following day, she died.

Kay's ashes have been scattered over the Irish acres where she was

9

born and grew up. But her book remains, and we are proud to present it. We salute her as a loving and courageous woman; 'an officer and a lady' – to twist the phrase in a way that we suspect would have made her laugh and say, 'Oh, that's gorgeous!' Kathleen Helen McCarthy-Morrogh Summersby Morgan always made people feel good about themselves.

Chapter 1

More than half my life I have felt like the girl in the hair-colouring advertisement, the one that asks the question, 'Does she . . . or doesn't she?' In my case, they were not speculating about my hair colour.

It used to distress me enormously, but as time went by, emotional scar tissue formed over the raw nerve ends, and eventually 'Did she . . . or didn't she?' became a curiously old-fashioned speculation. If, through some time warp, I were to be in my early thirties again, serving as driver, secretary and confidante to the stalwart and utterly charming Supreme Commander of the Allied Forces in Europe, General Dwight David Eisenhower, no one would wonder 'Did they . . . ?' Today people would simply assume that we did – and given modern mores, forget the whole thing.

But that was not the way it was. It took years and years, decades, for people to forget. And just when I thought the whole issue had disappeared from people's minds, it was raised again – this time with a vengeance that ripped open that emotional scar tissue – in *Plain Speaking: An Oral Biography of Harry S. Truman* by Merle Miller. Late in the autumn of 1973, even before the book was officially published, the few paragraphs in it about General Eisenhower and me made the front pages of newspapers all over the world.

It was absolutely unbelievable. The General had been dead for four years. And I had not seen him – except from a determinedly anonymous distance – for more than a quarter of a century. It was ancient history. Or so I had thought. But the world did not agree. As Lloyd Shearer wrote in *Parade* magazine, 'Journalists began an intensive search for Kay Summersby. But Kay Summersby could be found nowhere.'

There was a reason for that. I had been on the operating table when the story broke. But journalists are a persistent breed. An Englishman finally tracked me down. He had looked up the old newspaper clippings and called a friend of mine who had been mentioned in one of them.

'Mrs P——?' he had asked. 'I'm calling from London. Weren't you present when Kay married Reginald Morgan?'

She was quite unsuspecting. 'I certainly was,' she replied. 'They were married right here in my apartment.'

'I'm an old friend of Kay's,' he said, 'and I've been trying to get in touch with her. Can you tell me where she is?'

This was a lie. I had never heard of him, but there was no way for her to know that. She told him, 'Kay's in New York Hospital. She has had some surgery.'

So there I was, barely out of the recovery room, with an intravenous solution dripping through a tube into my arm and another tube threaded through my nostril, and the hospital switchboard was calling to say that it had an overseas call for me. Did I feel up to taking it? I did not, but I took it anyway, positive that it was my brother, Seamus, calling me from Johannesburg, eight thousand miles away. Instead, it was this man.

'I'm calling from London,' he said. 'What about all this?'

Only someone who has had major surgery can understand the state I was in. The effects of the anaesthetic had not worn off completely, and I was drained, just terribly fatigued by the shock of surgery. Talking was an immense effort.

'What about all what?' I asked feebly.

'About you and Ike,' he said. 'Is it true or isn't it?'

I did not know what he was talking about. I thought he was just one more person raking up that old did-they-or-didn't-they speculation. I have had my share of middle-of-the-night calls from drunkards wanting to settle a bet and sick-sick people spilling vituperation into the telephone, but pursuing me into the hospital to ask about my relationship with General Eisenhower was just about the worst.

'No comment,' I said. And hung up. But he had his story. 'Kay Summersby Morgan, convalescing from surgery in New York City, refused to comment on report she and Ike planned to marry.'

The mischief had been done. Now the world knew where I was. Telephone calls and wires came into the hospital from all over the globe. I quickly learned what had prompted that call, of course, and one of my dearest friends brought me a copy of the book – complete with a bookmark flagging the pages with President Truman's revelations about General Eisenhower.

It was no secret that Harry S. Truman did not care for Dwight D. Eisenhower, but I had liked President Truman when he and his Secretary of State James Byrnes visited General Eisenhower's headquarters in Frankfurt at the time of the Potsdam Conference in 1945. The Big Three had had serious matters to discuss at Potsdam, including America's new weapon, the atomic bomb. (When I had heard Ike discussing the military and political implications of the Bomb with his top staff members several weeks before its existence was revealed, I remember thinking, Oh, oh! It's time to leave the room. This is something I don't want to know about.)

Towards the end of the conference, Truman came to Frankfurt to inspect the 84th Infantry Division (there were a lot of men from Missouri in it), and after driving through the dusty German countryside on that hot July day and talking to scores of American soldiers, he came back to headquarters. As he walked in, he said to General Eisenhower that it reminded him of the Pentagon, it was so big, and Eisenhower told him it used to be the hub of the huge I. G. Farben industrial complex. After the President and the General had concluded their talk, Ike called me in and introduced me to the President. I thought him extremely friendly and straightforwardly natural. A very appealing man.

My office diary, in which I often jotted down personal notes as well as the General's appointments, contains this entry for that day:

> *E. leaves office early to meet the President . . . Unexpectedly Ike brings the President and Secretary of State Byrnes into the office at 2:30. Ike talked to the President about my wanting to become an American citizen.*

That had truly been a red-letter day for me, and about three months later, as a result of that conversation, I flew to Washington to take out my first papers for American citizenship.

Now, twenty-eight years later, I sat cranked up to a half-sitting position in my hospital bed reading and rereading a story that I could hardly believe. President Truman had told his biographer, Merle Miller, that 'right after the war was over, he [Eisenhower] wrote a letter to General Marshall saying that he wanted to come back to the United States and divorce Mrs Eisenhower so that he could marry this Englishwoman'.

His request was brutally denied. Even outspoken President Truman seems to have been shocked at the harshness of the denial.

'Marshall wrote him back a letter,' said the President, 'the like of which I never did see. He said that if he . . . if Eisenhower even came close to doing such a thing, he'd not only bust him out of the Army, he'd see to it that never for the rest of his life would he be able to draw a peaceful breath . . . and that if he ever again mentioned a thing like that, he'd see to it that the rest of his life was a living hell.'

President Truman then said, 'One of the last things I did as President, I got those letters from his file in the Pentagon and I destroyed them.'

I would have liked to stay quietly in my spartan hospital cot, well away from the world, and have time to think about those long-ago days with Ike. These few paragraphs had shaken me. I needed to get my emotions in order.

But that kind of peace was unattainable. Even though the hospital no longer put calls through to me, it was impossible to escape the reporters. They were incredibly persistent. I returned from my first walk down the hall – ten paces to the bathroom and ten paces back on the arm of a nurse – to find an attractive girl sitting at the foot of my bed. I thought she must be the daughter of one of my friends who had grown, so that I did not recognize her. She was a reporter from *The Philadelphia Inquirer*. She had walked into my hospital room and plunked herself down. I was indignant.

'How can you come in here like this?' I asked. 'I have had serious surgery and I am not feeling at all well.' As a matter of fact, this was the day that the full report had come back from pathology, and yes, it was cancer. Liver cancer. And no, there was no hope. I had understood what my doctor had told me, and I was upset, but I had not really absorbed what it meant. It was literally weeks before I registered the finality of what he had told me. But even so, I was unable to cope with my own feelings that day, let alone cope with a reporter.

'I'm sure your editor would not approve of what you are doing,' I said.

She just sat there.

'Will you please leave? Or do I have to call for someone to remove you?' I asked.

At that she got up. 'You won't say anything?' she asked.

I wouldn't. I didn't. Not even goodbye. I simply turned my face away. I was shaking with weakness and frustration. My feet were cold, and I had beads of perspiration on my forehead.

There were dozens of others who invaded the hospital. 'No comment,' I would say, and they would go away. The nurses teased me about it. 'Unseal your lips,' one used to tell me; 'it's time for your medication.' As soon as I could muster the strength, I fled the hospital, despite the nervous protests of my doctor, to stay with friends who promised tranquil anonymity.

For the record, I swear that I had no idea that the General had written such a letter to General Marshall. Absolutely no idea at all. Not at the time that he was supposed to have written it. And not later.

I was interested to read that Major General Harry Vaughan, who had been President Truman's aide in the White House, told reporters that there had been rumours about those letters as early as 1952. 'Before the Republican National Convention,' he said, 'Senator Robert Taft of Ohio and Eisenhower were jockeying for position to get the Presidential nomination. The Taft boys heard about Ike's letters to Marshall and wanted to get copies. Truman heard about that. He ordered the Pentagon to send him the letters. He didn't want the Taft gang spreading them all over the country. But I don't think he destroyed them. I think he sent them to General Marshall with a covering note that said, "These belong in your personal files. I don't think they should be used for dirty politics." '

I had heard none of those 1952 rumours.

I *had* been given a hint later on that some such letters existed, but I had not believed it. A few years ago – it must have been four or five years ago – David Susskind called and said, 'Kay, I want you on my TV programme.'

'Oh, lovely!' I said. 'What do you want me to talk about?'

'The letter, of course,' David said.

'What letter?' I asked, truly mystified. 'I don't have an inkling of what you're talking about.'

And he said, 'Oh, come on, Kay. You know what I'm talking about. The Eisenhower letter. The letter Ike wrote telling Marshall that he wanted to divorce Mamie and marry you.'

For a moment I was stunned, and then I thought, Oh, that's nonsense. David's just trying to dredge up something sensational for his programme.

'David,' I said, 'I never heard of any such thing. Somebody's been feeding you a story. It's no good my going on your programme. I have nothing to say.'

And that was that. I forgot all about it. I never heard another word about the letters until I was in the hospital in 1973 – more than twenty years after the rumours presumably started. I myself have no way of knowing whether or not Ike really wrote such a letter. But I have great faith in Harry Truman's integrity. I do not believe that he would have said such a thing if it were not true. Nor would Harry Vaughan have said what he said if the letters did not exist.

I confess that I hope with all my heart that Ike did write to General Marshall. I believe that he did. And it is my belief that has given me the strength and the courage to write this book.

The public reaction to the disclosure of these letters startled me. Who would ever have believed that one Irishwoman's (I was born in County Cork and am not an 'Englishwoman' as President Truman described me) relationship with an American general, a relationship that began more than thirty-five years ago and was abruptly terminated three years later, could still be of interest to anyone at all? I suppose the whole thing stayed alive because Ike was not only a war hero and a two-term President of the United States, he was above all a man who had captured the heart of America. The heart of the world. And my heart, too.

So for those who are interested, here is the story of a general and his Irish driver. I feel free to talk about it now. The General is dead. I am dying. When I wrote *Eisenhower Was My Boss* in 1948, I omitted many things, changed some details, glossed over others to disguise as best I could the intimacy that had grown between General Eisenhower and me. It was better that way. And when Captain Harry C. Butcher, USNR, wrote his book, *My Three Years with Eisenhower*, he did the same thing for the same reason. Butch mentioned me only in passing, often simply referring to me as 'the driver'. We were both intent on keeping the General's private life private. In those days anything that could have been construed as a shadow on the General's character would have been seized upon as a political weapon. But times have changed. I do not believe that anyone today will construe our relationship as shameful. It certainly can cast no shadow on the General's character. I believe that truth makes for better history than evasions. And someday – perhaps – my truth will serve as a small, clarifying footnote to history.

The story I am about to tell happened a long time ago. I ask the reader to be lenient. My sources are my memory, my old blue leather diary – and my heart. If an occasional time sequence is twisted or a fact misplaced, it is only because of the tricks that memory plays as one grows older. The conversations in this book ring true to my ear and my heart, but it must be understood that they have been reconstructed from my memories. The events that I am writing about meant so much to me, however, and I have lived them over to myself during so many long nights, that I think my story is as close to reality as if it were only last night that I said my unsuspecting goodbye to the General, to Ike, to the man I loved.

Chapter 2

You never know when something important is going to happen, and when it does, you often don't realize that it did until long after. That is the way it was when I met General Eisenhower. He was Major-General Eisenhower then, and he had two stars – and they did not impress me one bit.

I was a member of Britain's Motor Transport Corps. This was *the* volunteer corps that the débutantes and post-débutantes flocked to when war was declared. I knew many of them. We had gone to the same dances, watched polo at Hurlingham together, spent long weekends in Scotland together, but there was a difference between them and me. Most of them were wealthy. I was not.

I had recently separated from my husband Gordon Summersby, a young publisher, and was earning my living modelling for Worth of Paris. Worth represented the cream of the couture and dressed – with superb materials and elegantly understated style – generations of the solid rich from débutante to dowager. There was a Winterhalter painting in the salon of a beautiful young woman who had sat for her portrait, half a century before, wearing a Worth ball gown. It was quite usual for me to go to one of the great balls in London in a new Worth design lent to me for the evening (it was good advertising, and the directress of the salon would often arrange to borrow jewellery for me to wear) and see one of the girls who would later join the Motor Transport Corps fox-trotting by in a gown that I had modelled for her approval earlier in the season. We would tell each other how absolutely marvellous we looked.

But Worth gowns were now a thing of the past. I had left the salon on 4 September 1939, the day after Prime Minister Neville Chamberlain told us we were at war with Germany. 'It is the evil things that we shall be fighting against,' he had said. He was right. They were evil things. To actually be at war was a thudding shock, even though we had all sensed it must come. The world changed overnight. My sister Evie had joined the Motor Transport Corps a few weeks earlier, and I decided to follow her example.

I was assigned to Post Number One, an old schoolhouse in the East End, near London's great maze of docks. Our Cockney neighbours there used to jeer at the 'society girls playing war'. Who could blame them? Many of them were heart-breakingly poor, and there we were with our smart uniforms, our Mayfair chatter and very little to do. There was an eerie few months of quiet after war was declared. Some called it a phony war. Then Norway and Denmark became captive nations, and the Nazis blitzed their way through Holland and through Belgium, forcing our troops to the very edge of the Continent, the beaches at Dunkirk.

There was a nightmare week in early June 1940 when a makeshift rescue armada had set out from English ports and brought back several hundred thousand soldiers from Dunkirk. It was a kind of miracle. The Germans bombed the helpless troops on the beaches. They bombed the destroyers and troop carriers and ferryboats scurrying back to England with their precious loads of husbands and fathers and brothers and sons. They even strafed the little cockleshell pleasure boats that had valiantly bobbed their way across the Channel to do their bit. Just a few days later, Paris fell. It was no phony war.

But all that was still in the future. The first order of business in the Corps was to get oneself properly outfitted. Our uniforms were very smart, almost exactly like the British Army officers' uniforms, except that we wore skirts. They had the same Sam Browne belt and everything. We bought them at an Army supply store, and they cost the earth – something like fifty pounds, a staggering sum of money in those days. It was for me, anyway, since the Corps was a voluntary outfit, which meant we weren't paid twopence. Eventually they did pay us. Two pounds ten a week it was, and barely enough to keep us in tea and stockings (on the black market – without ration coupons – a pair of silk stockings cost nearly eight shillings).

Of course, when the time came that the women of the Motor Transport Corps were doing their part in the Battle of Britain, uniforms could not have mattered less. At the height of the Blitz, when German bombers were making nightly sorties, my 'uniform' consisted of an old pair of corduroy pants, an Army shirt and a sweater that belonged to my brother Seamus. I topped this with a tin hat, slung my gas mask (where I kept my lipstick and compact) over my shoulder and was ready for duty. So much for uniforms. When the bombs were dropping and I was driving my MTC ambulance around the dock area in the East End, no one made us stand inspection.

The Battle of Britain had started early in September of 1940 – it was a year almost to the day after I had joined up – with a daylight bombing raid. The Germans sent a thousand planes over London and blanketed the city with bombs. The worst damage was in our area. Hundreds of people were killed that day, and thousands wounded.

After that, most of the raids were by night. There was a nasty little traitor – we called him Lord Haw-Haw – who broadcast from Germany. He would come on the radio and chant, 'There's *going* to *be* a *bomb*ing. There's *going* to *be* a *bomb*ing,' in the same cadence in which a child might chant, 'I'm *going* to *tell* your *moth*er. You're *going* to *get* a *spank*ing.' And he was always right. Some nights it was as if London were being shaken the way one shakes out a rug. It trembled and reeled from end to end. I remember one night in particular – it was just after Christmas – when the Germans dropped tens of thousands of incendiary bombs. It seemed as if all London were burning. The sky was red, with vast gusts of black smoke streaming across it like clouds in hell. Even the December-cold water of the Thames was warm as it spurted out of the fire-fighters' hoses. It was the most terrifying night of my life. I will never forget one of the men in my ambulance crew saying over and over, 'Hitler didn't ought to do this. He didn't ought to *do* it.'

Despite the horror, life went on. Our MTC ambulances picked up the dead and dying. The Cockneys, now our staunch supporters, trudged off to the tube every night with their children, their blankets, their playing cards and their Thermoses of tea to wait out the bombing hours hundreds of feet underground. Londoners looked terrible. No one had enough sleep. Many people had lost their homes. Rationing promised everyone fair shares, but it was fair shares of starchy foods for the most part. We all craved meat and butter and fresh fruit. Our clothes became shabbier each day from diving into trenches or flinging ourselves flat when the sirens' banshee screams sounded warning. But everyone kept going. There was no panic. We queued for food, for newspapers, for cigarettes, for buses. We grumbled. We were scared. We were tired. And bored. But no one ever thought of giving in to Hitler.

For me, it was a time of personal turmoil as well. Gordon and I had decided to take the next step after separation. Divorce. It was not easy. My whole world seemed to be disintegrating.

The Blitz stopped suddenly in May 1941. It was an uneasy pause, rather like waiting for the second boot to drop. There was nothing for my Motor Transport Corps unit to do once the bombing stopped. All of us were sitting around, bored and gossiping. Then I met an American colonel at a cocktail party who became very attentive when I told him that we were out of our minds with boredom. 'Hmm,' he said, 'you give me an idea.' I can't even remember that colonel's name now, but I have always been grateful to him. Within a week, the American Embassy had requested the Motor Transport Corps to lend it a couple of drivers who knew their way around London.

The Americans were not yet in the war, but their embassy was full of Special Observers who kept forgetting they were in civilian clothes and would salute each other all the time. Groups of American brass were constantly being shepherded around England and Scotland. Some went to see airfields; others inspected coastal defences; others filled their days – and nights – conferring with British military and government leaders. The embassy needed drivers to get these visitors where they wanted to go – and on time. This was not an easy job.

London, indeed the whole of England, was under the tightest security. There were no street signs, no highway route markers, nothing. Nothing that could possibly aid or enlighten a German parachutist. (A German invasion was a very real fear at that time.) At night, there was a total blackout. Any cars that were on the roads were allowed only the merest pin-point of light from their headlamps. Add the infamous London fogs to this and it was easy to see why the Americans never got to an evening engagement on time. They did very little better in the daylight. The American Army drivers, who did not know London at all, were constantly getting lost. And the blood pressures of their high-ranking military passengers climbed to dangerous highs.

I was delighted to be chosen as one of the drivers. I had known a few Americans before, but now at Number 20 Grosvenor Square, I was surrounded by them. In the days before Pearl Harbour, I think I knew every American officer in London. I liked their informality and their warmth and their energy. My social life became all-American, and soon it focused on one American in particular. Captain Richard Arnold. He was a West Pointer. Very handsome. And, I was told, a brilliant engineer.

Dick was one of the 'commuters'. He would be in London for three days, then fly to Washington for five, then back for two weeks or two days. I never knew when he would arrive or when he would have to leave. But we both knew that something special was going on between us. After a few months, Dick came back from Washington and told me that he had asked his wife for a divorce and that she had agreed. 'When I'm free, Kay,' he asked, 'would you – ' I did not even wait for him to finish before accepting his proposal.

Our engagement did not change things much. We still had to steal an hour here, an evening there. It did not matter. We knew we were going to get married – sometime. Sometime when we were free. Sometime when the war permitted. Sometime. Somehow. And in the meantime, we just had to muddle along the best we could.

Then the American tempo changed. Pearl Harbour was the precipitant. The United States was finally at war. There was an air of near-frantic urgency. One spring day our Motor Transport group – there were now several of us driving for the Americans – was alerted that a very important group of American generals was expected. I made up my mind that by sheer right of seniority I would drive the top man. Any Army man will understand how I felt. It was a matter of rank by association.

As it turned out, however, I got just about the lowest-ranking man –

a two-star general – and I almost got off on the wrong foot with him. I was late. On the other hand, if I had not been late in the beginning, I would probably never have got to know General Eisenhower.

It happened this way. The day the assignments were made, I had nothing to do, so I trotted off to the hairdresser, who took forever. When I got back to Grosvenor Square, the other girls had skimmed the cream of the lot. The second lieutenant in charge of handing out assignments to the motor pool said apologetically, 'Kay, you don't mind, I hope. This Eisenhower? He's the only one left.' He knew I wanted a crack at the top general, not a two-star nonentity. I made a face and said, 'Okay.'

After that it was days before the generals arrived. Their plane had been weathered in at Prestwick. Forty-eight hours later, they decided to come down from Scotland by train. That was late, too. But finally, one bright May morning, they were here, closeted with Ambassador John Winant at Grosvenor Square. Our instructions were to await instructions. The cars were lined up in a khaki-coloured parade out front. We waited and waited. The lunch hour passed. I became so hungry I could not bear it. So hungry I risked ducking out for a sand-wich.

When I came sauntering back, I was appalled to see the other embassy cars driving away, leaving one lone khaki Packard by the kerb. There were two American officers standing beside it. I cast lady-like dignity aside and ran as if my life depended on it. Skidding to a stop and trying to salute at the same time, I asked if one of them was General Eisenhower. One was. The short one.

'I'm your driver, sir,' I panted. 'Here's your car, sir.' I opened the door and stood at attention as General Eisenhower and General Mark Clark settled themselves in the back seat.

'We'd like to go to Claridge's, please,' Eisenhower told me. I could have screamed. All that for a two-block drive.

Later that afternoon, one of the Americans at headquarters asked, 'How did you like Ike?'

'Ike?'

'General Eisenhower,' he said.

I shrugged my shoulders. 'He's all right. I only saw him for a few minutes.'

'There are a lot of rumours about him,' he said. 'They say he's going to be in charge of the whole shooting match.'

I knew better than that. My father had been an Army man. Two-star generals are never in charge of anything important. Fortunately, I kept my mouth shut.

Chapter 3

Now I was to learn what a working day really meant.
The next morning I met my two generals in front of Claridge's on the
dot of nine and delivered them back there some sixteen hours later. As
I held the door, Eisenhower turned to me and said, 'We'll expect you
at nine, Miss Summersby.'

The following days were more of the same. It was obvious that
there were great projects afoot. I remember one day very well. It was
common knowledge that Field-Marshal Sir Bernard Law Montgomery, that character with the beret and the swagger stick, was – to
put it mildly – a thorn in Eisenhower's side throughout the war. There
was friction between the two of them from the very first moment they
met.

I had driven Clark and Eisenhower to a base outside London to
observe Monty in action. He was just a lieutenant-general then, with a
reputation for being very able. On the way back to London late in the
afternoon, the two American generals discussed their day and the
military exercise Monty had conducted. I usually paid very little
attention to backseat conversations, but Eisenhower's voice caught my
attention. It had turned harsh. I heard something about 'that son of a
bitch' and started listening. He meant Monty. Within minutes of
meeting chain-smoker Eisenhower, nonsmoker Montgomery had
stated crisply that he did not permit smoking in his headquarters. The
General had obediently stubbed out his cigarette, but he was furious –
really steaming mad. And he was still mad. It was my first exposure to
the Eisenhower temper. I sneaked a look in the rear-view mirror. His
face was flaming red, and the veins in his forehead looked like worms.

The relationship between the two men never got any better; in fact, as the war progressed, Monty's self-righteousness and rigidity often had the General actually gasping in anger.

Situations that might make another man angry, however, often did not perturb the General at all. For instance, Eisenhower was tremendously impressed by the total security-consciousness of the English. One day when I was not quite sure which way to go, I stopped to ask directions from a group of soldiers.

'I've got General Clark and General Eisenhower in the car,' I said, 'and I'm not sure which fork to take for the base. Can you tell me?'

Not one of them would give me directions. 'We don't know,' they said. And that was that. They were quite right, of course. In those days no one had ever heard of General Eisenhower. All they saw was a military car with a woman driver. And at that time there were all kinds of stories going around about audacious German spies and infiltrators. This changed later when England was crammed full of American soldiers asking how to get here or there. Then the English reverted to their naturally courteous ways and would give directions in the most minute detail. (One American GI told me that what he remembers best about the English penchant for detailed directions was that 'After five minutes of telling you to bear left at the second meadow and right at the third pub, they'd end up saying, "You cawn't miss it." That always gave me a kick,' he said.) But in 1942 these soldiers were not going to tell anyone anything. I was furious, but Eisenhower was not upset in the least. 'Goddamnit,' he said to General Clark, 'that's the spirit.'

Another day I drove the two generals to Dover, site of those famous white cliffs, where they inspected the defences that had been thrown up against a German invasion. Afterwards both men stood for a long time peering through high-powered glasses at the Continent, only a few miles across the English Channel – and distant as the moon.

'In 1928,' Eisenhower said, 'I made a tour of the battlefields of the last war, and I remember standing over there one afternoon looking at these white cliffs over here.' He was in a reminiscent mood and told a number of stories about French villagers he had met during that trip.

'I'd certainly like to look some of them up again,' he told Clark, 'when we get over there.' *Over there!* It sounded like a dream. I truly did not believe I would ever again sit in a sidewalk café on the Champs-Élysées or go riding in the Bois de Boulogne.

As we started back to London, I mentioned that the London-Dover highway was known as Bomb Alley. It had got the name during the Blitz when the Germans jettisoned their left-over bombs along this stretch as they lumbered back to the Continent pursued by the RAF in their Spitfires and Hurricanes. General Eisenhower asked me what I had done during the Blitz.

'Me? Oh, I drove,' I said. 'I drove an ambulance in the East End.'

That started the questions. Eisenhower wanted to know about the part women had played in the Battle of Britain. I told him that my sister and almost all the women I knew were in uniform. And that my mother and many of her contemporaries had served as incendiary-bomb spotters. Incendiary bombs were about a foot long. They would drop on the street or the roof. All you would hear was a thud or a bump. After a certain amount of time, the incendiary would ignite and there would be a big blaze. Mummy's job was to pick them up as soon as they were dropped and take them to a depot where they could be dealt with. It was really quite dangerous work. Eisenhower was a persistent interviewer. By the time he finished, he knew everything I knew about women's roles in the defence of Britain.

As the days went by, the two American generals lost their bounce. Their faces were drawn, their eyes bloodshot from lack of sleep. It seemed to be a real effort for them to get out of the car and stride briskly into yet another conference. I was beginning to droop myself. One day they announced happily that they were going to take the afternoon off.

'The war can get along without us for a few hours,' Eisenhower said. 'Now, where is a good place to have lunch, Kay? You should know. Some place where they won't feed us cabbage.'

It took me a moment to gather my wits. All the other Americans called me Kay, but Clark and Eisenhower had always been very correct and called me Miss Summersby. I was thrown by the new informality.

I knew what the General meant when he vetoed cabbage so firmly. One afternoon I had overheard him mutter to General Clark that 'this must be the fartingest war in history'. I had stared right ahead and never let on that I had caught this particular remark. Almost every base they visited served them boiled cabbage or brussels sprouts, and the result often kept the generals rolling down the car windows.

'The Connaught,' I said finally. 'That's a very good place. You'll have an excellent meal there.'

'The Connaught it is, then,' said General Eisenhower, and off we went to Mount Street. I let them out and started to get back into the car.

'Come on, Kay,' said Eisenhower. 'You'll join us, won't you?'

Never had such a thing happened to me. Generals don't ask their drivers to lunch with them. But it appeared that American generals did. At least some American generals. I accepted with pleasure, and the three of us walked into the Edwardianly elegant Connaught under the scandalized eyes of the doorman, who believed people should know their places – and this applied to American generals as well as to their drivers.

It was the first time that I had ever looked General Eisenhower in the face for more than a fleeting moment as I said, 'Good morning, General', or held the door for him. Now I had a good look across the table. Brilliant blue eyes. Sandy hair – but not very much of it. A fair, ruddy complexion. A nice face – not conventionally handsome, but strong and, I thought, very American. Certainly very appealing. And I succumbed immediately to that grin that was to become so famous.

He and General Clark were happy truants at that lunch, and they entertained me with all kinds of stories from their Army past. We laughed and had a glorious time. The lunch was superb. I can remember it as if it were last week. General Eisenhower ordered a bottle of white wine. We had poached salmon and green salad. Salad, believe it or not, was even more of a luxury than salmon in London those days. For dessert there were little strawberry tarts that were so beautiful that one hesitated to break into them with a fork. We devoured them in two bites and asked for seconds. There were no seconds. That was the only blot on the day.

For that hour or two, the war did not seem to exist. We were in another world. But it is the laughter that still rings in my memory. A long time afterwards – we were in Versailles, I think – Ike asked me, 'Do you remember that first time we went out together? That lunch at the Connaught? I'll never forget it,' he said. 'I had never laughed so much in my life.'

It was that kind of day.

After lunch, General Eisenhower said, 'Kay, how about taking us sight-seeing? We'd like to see a little something of England besides the military installations.'

'Yes, sir,' I said happily, and suggested that we drive up-country towards Oxford. 'It's awfully pretty there,' I told them.

'Whatever you say. You're in command this afternoon. Isn't that right, Wayne?' And General Clark – Ike always called him Wayne – nodded agreeably.

So off we went. Both men were fascinated by the picturesque little villages. They asked me to stop in one – West Wycombe, I think it was – so they could have a closer look at the quaint shops and thatched cottages with flowers at the windows.

'How old would you say that house is?' General Eisenhower would ask.

'Three hundred years old, perhaps,' I would hazard, and he would shake his head. We had a wonderful time wandering about aimlessly and staring like tourists. It was almost June, and England was at its best – all green and gold and perfumed with roses.

Eventually we piled back into the car. It was warm, and I was parched. Without thinking how outrageous I was being, I pulled up in Beaconsfield and said, 'You absolutely must visit an English pub.' Obviously just as warm and thirsty as I was, the two of them were out of the car before I could run around and open the door for them. (It may seem strange that on such an occasion I would hold the door, but it must be remembered that this was wartime and we were in uniform. Door-holding, saluting and such were all part of that way of life. Although General Eisenhower still insisted on some of the peacetime courtesies, such as letting a woman precede him through the door, he accepted the rest as part of very necessary military discipline.)

It was a gin-and-tonic kind of day. As we sat there and sipped our drinks, the late-spring afternoon slipped into evening. The nightingales were singing. It was high time for the three truants to get back to London.

The next morning we were back in our routine, but when I picked up my generals at Claridge's, I was pleased to see that some of their bounce was back and their faces no longer so drawn. In a few days, their mission was over. My last assignment was to drive them to the airport. One can always count on English weather. That day it was so bad that their departure was postponed for twenty-four hours.

On impulse I called Claridge's. If I'd stopped to think, I would never have done it, but I had come to feel so comfortable with these two Americans that it seemed natural.

'General, this is Kay,' I said. 'I wondered, since you can't leave today, if you would like to do some more sight-seeing. I'd love to show you around.' Suddenly I was horrified at my brashness and held on to the receiver expecting a curt military 'No, thanks.'

'Just the thing,' he said, sounding pleased. 'We're at loose ends.'

That day I showed them all the traditional sights – and others not so traditional, such as Threadneedle Street, which is the home of the Bank of England, and Fleet Street, the heart of the London journalistic world. I also showed them the Guildhall, but none of us was psychic enough to sense that this ancient building would one day be the scene of one of Eisenhower's greatest triumphs.

I showed them the Tower of London and even drove by Bryanston Court, where Mrs Simpson had lived when the Prince of Wales was courting her. Eisenhower shook his head. 'A shame,' he said. 'The King lost sight of duty.' I remember thinking that this General Eisenhower was not a man who would ever lose sight of duty. I told them that it was in a house on Grosvenor Square that Mrs Simpson was first introduced to the Prince of Wales. 'That house used to stand right where your headquarters is,' I told them. 'They tore it down when they built 20 Grosvenor.' Eisenhower was really very much interested. Turning to General Clark, he said, 'You know, I met the Duke of Windsor last year. He was visiting the States with his wife and touching all the bases in Washington, including the War Department. I was there in the War Room when he came in. Everyone was kow-towing and pointing at maps, but I realized that he was being told nothing whatsoever. They didn't trust him. This man who had once been King. It was shocking how the man had gone down.'

As I drove about, they kept up a running comment on the way whole blocks of buildings had been levelled in one spot while on the other side of the street only one building might have been demolished. I told them how one morning during the Blitz when I had just got off duty, I had decided to drop in on my mother at Warwick Court for breakfast. As I turned the corner, I stopped. Half of her house was torn away. My knees began to shake. I had never felt so weak in my life. Then I started running towards the house. My mother was safe, thank God; she had gone to the shelter.

'Would you like to see where I was stationed then?' I asked. Without waiting for their answer, I turned the big Packard towards the East End, and soon we were driving down the streets where a year ago I had been piloting an ambulance through bombs and fires and collapsing buildings. We walked around the blasted warehouses and skeletons of tenements that still remained. 'Some call it Hitler's slum-clearance project,' I said.

Eisenhower shook his head. 'You must have been frightened during the bombings,' he said.

'General, it was like hell must be,' I blurted out. 'There would be all those buildings on fire. I would be driving and then we'd hear a bomb. I never knew what to do – stop, go back or go on. I always elected to press on. And my crew always backed me. "That's right, lady," they would say. "Press on. That's best." The men would bring the bodies out. Usually they were burned. All black and twisted. Sometimes there was no body. Just bits and pieces. They had these big canvas bags to put them in. The smell was so bad that we would wear gauze masks.

'The very worst thing,' I remembered, 'was to have the ambulance crammed full of bodies, so many bodies that we ran out of shrouds and there would be these arms and legs sticking out with tags tied to them – and then there would be no place to leave them. I would drive from mortuary to mortuary only to be told, "No room", and have to drive off again. I remember one night when the bombing was particularly brutal. I finally found a mortuary with room for more bodies. I sat at the wheel, as I always did while the crew unloaded. One of the attendants came out and said, "Better come in. It's bad out tonight."

'It was an old warehouse. There were two double beds off to one side, and a sort of bomb shelter had been built around them. We all sat there on those beds. The five men in the ambulance crew. The three mortuary men. Me. And all the bodies stacked high in their shrouds just a few feet away. They passed a bottle of whisky around and we all took a swig – right from the bottle. It was just what I needed. It burned that taste of dead flesh out of my mouth. That horrible taste! It was in the very air we breathed. And . . .'

I stopped. I was embarrassed to have made such a dramatic fool of myself running on like that.

There was silence. General Clark looked acutely uncomfortable, and that embarrassed me even more. 'Poor Kay,' he said.

'Poor people. Poor London,' Eisenhower added. Then he patted me on the back as if I were a child with hiccups. 'You were very brave,' he said.

The next morning I drove them to Northolt Airport. They were really off this time. General Clark shook my hand and thanked me for driving them about. General Eisenhower shook my hand too, then reached back into the car and brought out a box.

'This is from both of us, Kay,' he said.

'Chocolates!' In rationed England, sweets were a magnificent present. I broke into such a smile that they both laughed.

'If I'm ever back this way,' General Eisenhower said, 'I hope you will drive for me again.'

'I'd like that, sir,' I replied. And I meant it. I liked that man they called Ike. But I never expected to drive for him or even see him again.

Chapter 4

It was a let-down, going back to the motor pool after the generals had left, but within a few days I was driving another two-star general – Carl Spaatz, familiarly known as Tooey, who was in charge of the Eighth Air Force. He had been suffering – and not quietly – from his American sergeant driver's unfamiliarity with London.

'Ike says you're tops,' he told me the first morning I reported. I was startled and flattered to think that these generals had found time to discuss my merits as a driver.

General Spaatz had been in London all through the Blitz. It was well known that he had never taken shelter. Instead, he would station himself on a rooftop and make notes on the bombings. He was a serious man, serious to the point of grimness, and certainly the hardest-working man in the whole US Army Air Force.

Despite his rather dour personality, there was a party in his suite at Claridge's practically every night. The Air Force had the reputation of being the glamorous service, and his staff worked hard at maintaining that reputation. His aides entertained all the top English theatre people as well as the Hollywood stars who passed through London to entertain the troops. Liquor and food were dispensed on a lavish scale.

When General Spaatz and I would walk in at the end of a long day spent at Bushey Park, the Air Force headquarters outside London, it was like entering a crowded cocktail lounge – lots of people, lots of smoke, lots of chatter, lots of flirtations – but the General would not even break his stride as he made his way through the living-room nodding briskly right and left, I tagging along behind him carrying his briefcase. He would go straight to his study and close the door. Then the fatigue of the day was allowed to show. His shoulders slumped; his ramrod spine seemed to crumple, and he would sit in his big chair at the desk silently staring into space.

At the beginning I felt uncomfortable, not knowing quite what he expected from me, but I soon got into the habit of bringing along a book, and I would read while the General either stared into space or sighed and attacked the paperwork that had piled up. Some nights he would sit there for half an hour and then he'd say, 'Time to be off. How long will it take us to get to Hornchurch?' or some such destination.

'Oh, twenty minutes,' I might say.

'You'll have to do better than that,' he would instruct me. 'You've got exactly fifteen minutes to get me there.'

'Yes, sir.' And I would rush down to bring the car around.

Far more demanding than Eisenhower had been, General Spaatz always made me estimate the time it would take me to reach where he was going – and then would shave a few minutes off my estimate. I began to feel more like a fighter pilot than a driver as I careered through London, my gas pedal constantly pressed to the floor, thanking God for the absence of civilian traffic.

Then there were nights when the General made a command decision to relax. Sometimes he and his staff would settle in for an all-night poker game. They all loved to play cards with the boss – he usually lost. Other nights, he would bring out his guitar. I used to adore those evenings. The American Officers were like boys – sitting around, their heads thrown back, singing rackety old songs they had learned at West Point. One of their favourites that they would absolutely bellow out was 'I want to be, I want to be/I want to be away on furlough . . .' sung to the tune of 'Dixie'. They also loved the sentimental old songs from the last war like 'There's a long, long trail awinding/Into the land of my dreams' and 'Pack up your troubles in your old kit bag/And smile, smile, smile'. Another favourite was 'Over There'. There weren't many songs from the present war that caught their fancy the way the old ones did except for 'Lili Marlene'. I used to join in occasionally, and I would help with the drinks and answer the telephone and feel as much at home as if it were one of the after-the-hunt parties we used to have at home in Ireland.

I settled down happily into Air Force life. When I heard that General Eisenhower had been appointed Commander of the European Theatre and was back in London, I did not give it a second thought. I had enjoyed driving him, but I liked General Spaatz, too. One evening, just about a month after I started driving for him – it was rather late but still bright, since we were on double summer time – I pulled up in front of Claridge's and General Spaatz jumped into the car.

'Hendon Airport,' he said. 'And don't spare the horses.'

There was an impressive array of brass at Hendon. This must be someone extra special, I thought. The plane taxied up. The door opened. The brass stood at attention. And General Eisenhower came down the stairs.

After he had greeted the brass, Eisenhower came over to me. 'Kay, where have you been?' he said. 'I've been looking all over London for you.'

He looked at Spaatz. 'Tooey, you've been hiding her in the Air Force,' he accused.

'Now, don't you take Kay away from me,' Spaatz growled. 'She's the only driver who knows her way around.'

'We'll see,' Eisenhower said. He turned to me again. 'Kay, I brought some fruit back from the States for you, but it won't keep forever.'

'Fruit!' I exclaimed. 'I'd love some! Could I come get it tomorrow?'

General Spaatz laughed and said, 'Stop trying to bribe my driver.'

When I walked into General Eisenhower's headquarters on Grosvenor Square the next day, I discovered that he really had been looking for me. One of his aides said, 'Kay Summersby! Where have you been? I've been turning London upside down trying to get in touch with you. Didn't you get my note?'

Indeed I had, but I had thrown it away. There had been a note tucked under the windshield wiper of General Spaatz's car asking me to stop by 20 Grosvenor and see a Colonel Lee. But I did not know any Colonel Lee and I was not about to stop by anyone's office unless General Spaatz told me to. I had not the slightest idea that this Lee was one of General Eisenhower's aides. The General made time to see me immediately, and on his desk was a box of fruit: oranges and grapefruit – rarer than emeralds in England. I was truly deeply touched that the General had remembered me and impressed by the thoughtfulness of the gift.

'I can't thank you enough, General,' I said. 'I just can't tell you what a treat these will be.'

'I don't want any thanks,' he said. 'All I want to know is if you are willing to come back and drive for me. For good this time.' And he smiled.

I didn't know what to say. I liked Tooey Spaatz, but it would be silly to turn down the opportunity to drive for the top commander, so I murmured something stupid about I would like to if it was all right with General Spaatz.

Within two days, I was back driving General Eisenhower.

Chapter 5

Eisenhower was back for the long pull towards victory. His responsibilities as the commanding general were truly crushing, and he set about organizing his life in the most efficient manner to accomplish his mission. This included establishing a family for himself.

More than most men in public life, Eisenhower relished the comforts of home and hearth. His work and his home were the two great poles of his life during the war, and despite the fact that he was tremendously sought after by London hostesses, he became almost as much of a recluse as Greta Garbo. Not that he particularly wanted to be alone; in fact, he usually detested being alone; but he was impatient with anything that took his time or energy away from the war. He had very little sympathy with what he called 'all that la-di-da' – the airs and pretensions of London's social upper crust. I remember him getting into the car after one reception grumbling, 'I don't think my blood pressure can take it if one more silly woman calls me "My deeaaah General". I'm nobody's goddamned "deeaaah General", and I'm not fighting this war over teacups.'

In ordinary circumstances, General Eisenhower was probably more gregarious than most people, but these were not ordinary times. Shortly after he arrived in London, he established a policy of refusing all invitations that were not directly connected with his work. Three incidents had prompted the decision.

The first was Ambassador John Winant's Fourth of July reception, where Eisenhower shook so many hands in the course of the afternoon that the next morning his right hand was terribly swollen, all puffy and black and blue. He complained that even his fingernails hurt, and he

37

was literally not able to initial memos with his right hand.

The second was a luncheon with King Haakon of Norway. I had been instructed to pick up the General shortly after two. I was there right on time, but it was hours before the General appeared – in a fury of exasperation. Protocol prohibits anyone from leaving a social gathering before royalty, and King Haakon had been having such a royal good time that it was practically teatime before he left.

The only kind of protocol Eisenhower had any patience with was Army protocol, and he often complained about that. Some of the English customs and traditional courtesies might have been expressly designed to enrage him. One morning after he had attended a formal dinner party given by Ambassador Winant, there was a call from the Ambassador asking if the General could spare him a few minutes.

I was in the outer office when the Ambassador walked in. Winant was quite handsome, a very courteous, gentle and very, very shy man. That day he was twisting his hands together as if he were some great schoolboy about to get caned. When he left the General's office five minutes later, he looked even more distressed. I heard about what had happened behind the closed doors later that day when I was driving the General back to the hotel. Eisenhower told the story with a mixture of righteous indignation and impish little-boy glee.

The Ambassador had come to the point immediately. 'General,' he had said rather uncomfortably, 'in this country it is the custom not to smoke at a dinner party until after the toast to the King.' The General, who was never without a cigarette, had automatically lit up the moment he sat down at the dinner table.

'Now, how could I have known that?' Eisenhower asked. 'Of all the goddamned silly customs!' To a chain-smoker like the General, this not only seemed silly, it was intolerable. 'I told Winant that I was sorry,' he said, 'and that I'd certainly never offend in that way again. I also told him that last night was the last time I will ever attend a formal dinner in London.'

It was not, of course, but it did mark the end of purely social dinner parties. Invitations to luncheons, dinners, dances, drinks, weekends in the country continued to pour in – and were all declined. Lady Astor insisted that the General come to dinner and meet George Bernard Shaw. Lady Cunard dangled Noël Coward as social bait. The General sent his regrets. Any social event that was not directly associated with his job – like his weekly lunch and dinner with Prime Minister Winston Churchill – was out.

He knew what he needed, and it was not a glittering social life; it was a home and a family and all the warmth and laughter and sympathy that a family generates. He had put together his immediate wartime family in Washington. It was a tight little group: Butch and Tex and Mickey.

Butch – Harry Butcher – was the sparkler. Eisenhower had known him for years. Their families were so close that Mrs Eisenhower and Mrs Butcher were sharing an apartment in Washington and Butch had moved into the General's hotel suite in London. Butch was utterly charming, very handsome, with a captivating smile and a million friends. A former vice-president of the Columbia Broadcasting System, he handled public relations for Ike. And, more important, he helped the General keep his sanity. Time and again, I heard Eisenhower tell people, 'There are days when I just want to curl up in the corner like a sick dog, but Butch won't let me. That's why I need him. To keep me from going crazy.' He really loved Butch. Butch was comfortable, merry, trusted – and someone from home. He had grown up in a small town in Iowa not all that far in miles or outlook from the small town in Kansas where Eisenhower grew up. Both of them loved to play bridge and golf, and they had a lot of friends in common. I always thought of Butch as playing the role of a favourite younger brother – full of admiration, but with enough brash confidence to speak up when he disagreed with the General.

Tex – Colonel Ernest Lee from Texas – was the other aide and a very different character. He resembled a worried bloodhound and was incredibly efficient. Tex was the one who ran the office and saw to it that everything worked. He could untangle red tape faster than the Army could tangle it. He never relaxed and was uneasy if he had to be away from the headquarters office routine for even a day. Eisenhower's seven-day week suited him to the bottom of his shiny Army boots. Some people thought Tex was cold, but the truth was that he was very shy, despite the fact that he had been a salesman before the war. He was extremely reticent and quiet – except (and this was a big except) for his voice. He had a big, booming voice that used to drive us crazy. Tex was never as close to the General as Butch, but still, he was part of the family – something like a brother-in-law who was never on quite the same wavelength as anyone else.

Then there was Mickey – Sergeant Michael McKeogh, who was Eisenhower's orderly, and living proof that the saying about no man's being a hero to his valet is incorrect. Mickey polished the General's shoes, shined his brass, ironed his shoe-laces, changed his razor blades, squeezed the paste on to his toothbrush, helped him dress and undress, packed for him, unpacked for him, worried about him – and felt privileged to do it.

His hero worship sometimes struck the rest of us as funny. I remember one morning in Algiers when the General came downstairs all buffed and pressed and brushed and polished, and Mickey looked at him and sighed, 'He's better looking than Gary Cooper.' The General burst out laughing, and the rest of us joined in. Mickey could not understand what was so funny.

As I list Mickey's duties, I have to smile when I think of his helping Eisenhower dress and undress. During the General's first trip to London, the orderly who had been temporarily assigned to him confided in a burst of democratic exasperation that he was even expected to help Eisenhower on with his underpants in the morning. I went into peals of laughter at the thought of that nice, unassuming American being helped on with his underwear. I could not believe it. Later I learned it was true. The General had learned to enjoy being waited on hand and foot when he served under General Douglas MacArthur in the Philippines, where servants were plentiful. 'When I came back from Manila,' he told me once, 'General Marshall asked if I had learned how to put my pants on again now that I was back in the States. I told him I'd never lost the knack. It was tying my shoelaces that bothered me.'

Mickey was no mere pants-holder. He could never do enough for the Boss. He saw to it that his bedside table was well supplied with chocolate bars, chewing gum and cigarettes, and he made it his business to see that the General had a steady supply of new Westerns, his favourite – and almost only – reading matter apart from official papers.

Mickey also wrote a weekly report to Mrs Eisenhower. There were times when this self-imposed assignment of his made Butch and me a little nervous.

1. Kay Summersby as a member of Britain's Motor Transport Corps, 1941

2. Major Dwight D. Eisenhower, shortly before World War II

3. The General's driver: Kay adjusts the flag of Eisenhower's car

4. The General speaks his mind to Kay in an unguarded moment!

5. Kay and dog

6. Kay at her desk, with Telek

7. Eisenhower at work

The last thing that I had expected when I left General Spaatz to return to General Eisenhower was to become a member of his little family, but as each day went by I found myself being included more and more until I felt like one of the charter members. It could not have come about more naturally. When I was not driving the General, I had very little to do, so I would pitch in and answer the telephones and help with the mail and make appointments for him. I probably spent more time with General Eisenhower than anyone else did. I would pick him up early in the morning, drive him here and there, work at this and that at the office and get him back to his hotel whenever he decided to call it a day.

The General was fiercely protective of us and made it clear that Butch, Tex and I were responsible to him and him alone. 'That goes for you especially, Kay,' he said meaningfully. He knew that some officers at headquarters often asked me to run errands and do this or that. He would have none of this. We were his staff, his personal staff, and no one was to take advantage of us.

The more I did for the General, the more we had to talk about and the better we got to know each other. At one point, he said, 'Kay, I've heard so much about your mother. I'd really like to meet her. Why don't you ask her to have dinner with us some evening?'

It was like the time he and General Clark had invited me to lunch at the Connaught. Unprecedented. My mother to dine with the General! 'Oh, I'm sure she'd love to, General. Thank you,' I said.

We had a wonderful evening. Eisenhower wanted to know about every member of the family, and my mother was more than willing to tell him. She told him about my sister Evie and her husband; about our youngest sister, Sheila, who died. (Poor baby, she died at seven from the same rotten disease that is killing me. I wonder if it is hereditary.) And she told him about my brother, Seamus, an engineer, who was fighting with Wingate.

'Shaymus?' the General said. 'That's an odd name. It's what we call detectives.'

'It's not odd at all, General,' my mother said indignantly. 'It is the Irish of James. We spell it S-E-A-M-U-S.'

'If it's S, why does it sound like S-H?' he asked.

'Oh, that's the Irish of it,' she laughed. 'In Ireland, everything is S-H.

It's like Innis Beg. We say Innish.'

'And what's Innis Beg the Irish for?'

'That's our home,' I interrupted eagerly. 'Innis Beg means Little Isle. Our house is all by itself on an island in a river that flows into the Atlantic. It's a beautiful place.'

At the end of the evening, the General took my mother's hand in both of his. 'This won't be the last evening we'll be spending together,' he told her. 'I want to hear more of your stories of Ireland.' Mummy was captivated by him. 'A very intelligent man,' she said, 'and so warm and charming. I liked him, Kathleen,' she told me. After that dinner, I truly felt as if I were a member of the family, or the General a member of mine.

Chapter 6

The General hated hotel living, and Claridge's was too rich for his taste. His sitting-room in that home away from home for potentates and multimillionaires was decorated in black and gold like some Hollywood set, and although I always felt that Fred Astaire might come tap-tap-tapping along at any minute, the General disagreed. 'It looks like a goddamned fancy funeral parlour to me,' he stated. The bedroom made him even more uncomfortable. 'Whorehouse pink' was the way he described the colour scheme. 'Makes me feel as if I'm living in sin,' he complained.

He moved to the Dorchester – still elegant and luxurious, but somewhat noisier, somewhat shinier; somewhat, in fact, American. He felt a bit more at home here, especially after Butch moved in with him, but the four walls kept closing in on him.

'I'm a captive,' he complained. 'I can't even go for a walk without starting a parade.' Unknown a few weeks ago, he found that his name and face had become familiar to Londoners. Every morning when he stepped out of the elevator at the side entrance of the hotel and crossed the sidewalk to the car, there were people staring – even at seven in the morning. This had never happened to him before, and he did not like it. The General even came to resent room service as an intrusion, with the result that Butch added cooking to his other duties. In the morning, Butch brewed coffee on a little spirit stove. It was never strong enough for the General. 'I use two tablespoons of coffee for every cup,' Butch told me, 'and then Ike says, "How do you expect me to drink this dishwater?"' When the General had no official dinner scheduled, Butch would make soup by adding boiling water to a little packet of powder. This, together with bread and butter and chocolate bars, was supper, a meal I often shared if I had to drive the Boss to an evening appointment.

General Eisenhower actually spent very little time at the Dorchester. Six or seven hours' sleep was all he allowed himself – and often he got less. Ten to twelve hours out of every twenty-four were spent at Grosvenor Square. His days were filled with meetings. Meetings to resolve the political conflicts that arose between the British and the Americans. Meetings to resolve the personality conflicts. Meetings to work out the details for the operation called Torch aimed at the liberation of North Africa. (Although it is not within the realm of this book, or indeed within the scope of my abilities, to reconstruct the campaigns and intrigues of the Second World War, it is a fact that after what seemed like insurmountable – and unending – political problems, it had been agreed that the first order of Allied business was to liberate North Africa, and all the General's energies were directed towards preparing the invasion – an enormous task made even more agonizing by the difficulties of setting up a workable and unified Allied command. The General's book *Crusade in Europe* tells about all this far better than I could ever hope to.) And there were countless meetings with the Prime Minister for war-gaming sessions in which the PM and the General went over and over all possible eventualities like two chess players with the world at stake. Usually these sessions would be held after dinner at 10 Downing Street or in the bombproof underground shelter off St James's Park where the PM spent a lot of time, but on weekends they would be at Chequers, the PM's country residence. The General detested going there, because – even in full summer – it was cold. He called it a 'damned icebox', and when he had to go there he always wore two suits of underwear. Part of Chequers was more than five hundred years old, and of course, there was no central heating. Quite often the PM and Mrs Churchill would wear their coats to the dining table when Ike was there, but he did not feel that he should follow their example. Harry Hopkins, President Roosevelt's special emissary to the PM, probably hated going to Chequers even more than the General did. Once when I drove the two of them out there, I heard Mr Hopkins complain that there was only one bearable room in the house – the downstairs lavatory. Later on, Eisenhower told me a story about that. It seems that the PM wanted to talk to Mr Hopkins, but nobody could find him. He was not in his bedroom. Not in the library, nor in the great gallery. Finally he was discovered in that little lavatory. He was wearing his overcoat, gloves, muffler and hat, perched on the toilet reading the newspaper.

The pressure never seemed to let up. There were times when the Boss would look up from his desk at 20 Grosvenor at four or five in the afternoon and say wearily, 'Kay, get me out of here. I'm going stir crazy.'

'Certainly, General,' I'd say and tear down to get the car. Then I would drive him about until the last glimmering of twilight. Sometimes Butch would come along and amuse him with bits of gossip he had picked up, but usually it was just the two of us. One of his favourite drives, when he had time, was the run to Windsor. 'It's like a storybook,' he said once, looking at the big grey stone castle sprawling above the town. He always liked to see the Eton schoolboys wandering about in their traditional top hats and never failed to say what he would have done if anyone had ever forced him to wear such a getup when he was a youngster. Once we drove to Beaconsfield, where we had spent a stolen couple of hours over gin and tonics just two months before. Now it was impossible for the General to drop into a pub. He would have been recognized immediately.

Sometimes as I was driving along, he would lean forward and say, 'This looks pleasant here, Kay. Why don't you stop and we'll walk a bit.' He really enjoyed those walks. Sometimes we would chat about this and that, but he usually stepped right out at a pace that kept me next to breathless, and we would march along in silence until the General would say, 'Well, I guess we'd better be getting back.'

Once in a while he would fall asleep in the back seat. I always knew his appointment schedule, so I would drive about, choosing the smoothest roads, until it was time for him to be back at the Dorchester. Then, shortly before we arrived, I would hit a few bumps so that he would be awake when I drew up to the door. He would shake his head, blink his eyes, pull at his tie and put his hat back on. 'I must have dozed off,' he would say.

There were not enough of these respites, however, to alleviate the General's very deep – and deepening – fatigue. His temper erupted at the least provocation, and he was a three-star bundle of nervous tension. (He had received that gratifying third star very shortly after returning to London.) Butch reported that there were many nights when Eisenhower just could not sleep and that he would get out of bed and sit by the window staring out into the dark for hours. He was losing weight, and the wrinkles on his face were suddenly much too deep for a man of fifty-two.

One night when I was driving him and Butch back to London after an inspection trip, the General said, 'There ought to be some place where I could get away and have some peace. Some place in the country.'

'Why not rent a place outside London?' Butch asked. 'You could get some fresh air and exercise without feeling as if a spotlight were on you every second if you had a house of your own.'

'Sounds good to me,' the General said.

That was enough of a go-ahead for Butch, and one afternoon in August, he walked into headquarters looking like the cat who swallowed the canary. 'I've got it!' he said. 'Ike, I've found you a dream house.'

He was right. Everything about Telegraph Cottage was right. It was in Kingston, a very pleasant suburb less than a half-hour drive from Grosvenor Square and only minutes from Bushey Park, then the US Army Air Force headquarters. Set in ten acres of woods and lawns amidst flowering shrubs, Telegraph Cottage was like an adorable Tudor doll-house, with a slate roof and a chimney that almost always had a plume of woodsmoke curling up into the sky. It looked as if it belonged on a Christmas card.

And it was blessedly private. A winding driveway with a white pole across the entrance led up to the house, which was completely invisible from the road. I used to curse that pole when I drove the General home at night. I would have to stop the car, hop out and swing the pole aside, drive the car through and then hop out again to put that blasted pole back. During the day a one-armed gatekeeper – a veteran of the last war – was there to swing the pole aside, but at night it was my detested job. It seems strange when one thinks back on it in these violent times, but that white pole was all that was needed in England, even in wartime, to keep unwelcome visitors away.

Naturally, no one knew that the General was there. The fact that he had a hideaway outside London was top secret then. And with wartime security, it was easy to keep the secret. This made Telegraph Cottage a true oasis of privacy and calm. There was only one telephone, a direct line to headquarters, which was in the General's bedroom.

The cottage was so secret that very few people knew it existed and even fewer knew where it was. The first time Averell Harriman was there – for a very important dinner meeting with Robert Murphy, the head of the American underground network in North Africa – Butch picked up Mr Harriman in London after dark and drove him to the cottage and then back to his hotel after the meeting. Mr Harriman had been instructed to tell his daughter Kathy that he was going to inspect a factory that was turning out supersecret devices for aeroplanes. With blackout conditions what they were, it was certain that Mr Harriman would never be able to pinpoint the cottage's location. Not that he was not trusted: it was simply that the existence of Telegraph Cottage and its whereabouts were confided on a need-to-know basis. Later on, things became somewhat more relaxed, but the cottage was never common knowledge.

The house had five tiny bedrooms and a really old-fashioned bathroom (when anyone pulled the chain, one would have thought it was the cataracts of the Nile, it was so noisy). Each bedroom had its own basin and pitcher and, yes, commode. There was no central heating but between the fireplace in the living-room and the big old stove in the kitchen, we were always very comfortable.

The little living-room had french doors that opened out on to a small terrace, where we would sit with our drinks on the rare evenings when it was warm enough, but usually we were happy to be in front of the fire. The living-room itself was furnished nicely if rather shabbily. There was just about room for two comfortable chairs by the fireplace and a quite uncomfortable sofa with a mahogany coffee table in front of it. In one corner there was a bookcase and a game table; in another corner, an old chest. One day Butch bought four pillows to make the sofa a bit kinder to the human anatomy, but then Eisenhower spotted the bill. 'What's this?' he exclaimed. 'Forty dollars for cushions! They must have solid-gold fringe!' He was quite angry, and Butch had to return them. If the truth must be told, the General did have a tendency to be just a little stingy.

The dining-room had a round oak table that sat six comfortably, eight elbow to elbow, and there were evenings when we squeezed ten people around it. Against the wall was a sideboard that we turned into a bar.

And that was it. It was a very simple little house, but it could not have been cosier or happier. From the very first time we drove out there, the General felt at home and so did the rest of us. It is hard to explain just how important the hours we spent there were. It was not a weekend house in any sense of the term, since Eisenhower worked a seven-day week and so did the rest of us. But it did represent an escape, and whenever we could escape we did. As time went by, the General spent three or four nights a week there.

One evening, early on, when I drove the General out to Kingston to spend the night, he said, 'Kay, you'd better wait and have a bite before you go back to London.' I was only too pleased to accept. By the time I got back to my little flat in Kensington Close, I knew I would be too tired to even boil water for tea.

'Mickey!' the Boss shouted. 'We're starving and we're cold and we're tired. Light the fire and rustle us up something to eat.' Mickey was in his element at Telegraph Cottage. He and the two soldiers, John Moaney and John Hunt, who did the cleaning, cooking and serving saw to it that everything was spotless, that the kitchen and the little bar were always well supplied and a fire always laid in the fireplace. Usually a fire would be burning when we arrived, but this evening Eisenhower had decided to come out on the spur of the moment, with no advance notice. No matter. Mickey had everything under control in minutes.

The General went straight to his sideboard bar and made us each a Scotch and water. By the time the drinks were poured, Mickey had the fire blazing away and plates of salted peanuts – the General's favourite – set out on the little table beside the armchairs. We sat sprawled by the fire. Two tired people, feeling absolutely relaxed and comfortable with each other. I loosened my tie, and Mickey helped the Boss off with his coat and into his old brown woolly cardigan. We sat and sipped and sighed in total relaxation. I don't exactly know how to describe this quality Eisenhower had, but he was a very comfortable man to be with.

He was easy to talk to, and what is to my mind even more important, he was one of those people who know how to make a silence companionable. I don't think I have ever in my life felt so much at ease with any other human being or felt so much at home as I did at Telegraph Cottage.

In due course Mickey brought two trays so we could eat in front of the fire. I can't for the life of me remember what we ate, but I know that it was something warm and tasty. What with the drinks, the fire and the food, I was as cosy as a cat.

'You know something, Kay?' the General said. 'We don't have enough fun in our lives. What should we do to make life a bit pleasanter? I know how hard it must be on you to work seven days a week. And don't think I don't realize that you rarely get to see Dick these days.'

I was touched that the Boss had taken time to think of my personal problems when he had so many of his own. More important and burdensome problems. 'Oh, Dick and I are managing,' I said. 'It's wartime, after all. We have to do what we have to do.'

Actually Dick, although very busy and harassed himself, was somewhat unhappy about my new life. I never asked the General for a day off. It just would not have been right. Dick would complain, 'Now that I'm permanently based in London, I don't see you as much as I did when I was only here a few days a month.'

'What can I do?' I would ask. 'The General drives himself even harder than he drives his staff. And he depends on me. I can't let him down. We have to wait. Some day our divorces will be final, and then things will be better.' Life was very different in those days. I would no more have suggested that Dick move into my little flat in Kensington Close before we were married than I would have walked down Piccadilly naked.

But this was nothing I felt I should talk to the General about. Instead I addressed myself to his question. 'I know what we could do for fun,' I said. 'Remember what a good time we had with General Gruenther?'

General Alfred Gruenther, who was an old friend of Eisenhower's and working with him on the planning for Torch, also happened to be one of the world's truly great bridge players. He and Butch had played General Eisenhower and me the previous week at the Dorchester, and it had been a hard-fought game. While we were playing cards, we had forgotten all about where we were and why. The game completely absorbed us. And afterwards the Boss had said, 'Goddamnit, we should do this more often.'

I have loved to play bridge ever since I was a child. My brother and sister and I used to sit around the schoolroom on the third floor at Innis Beg and play – auction bridge it was then – for hours at a time. We would shout at each other and fight and do a lot of cheating. Our games usually ended with our throwing our cards at each other and running out. We must have been little barbarians, but we had a lot of fun.

'Only one thing,' I said to the General, 'we shouldn't have any post mortems. Once my husband and I did not say one syllable to each other for three days after a post mortem.'

'Okay, that's it. Bridge. And no post mortems,' Eisenhower said. He really brightened up. I could tell he liked the idea. 'We'll start to-morrow night.'

That was the beginning of a nightly routine that lasted throughout the war wherever we were – in North Africa and in Italy, in France and in Germany. Whenever the Boss was free in the evening, we played bridge. And we played seriously, concentrating fiercely on our hands. There was no chatter at the card table. The General rarely spoke, and he discouraged newcomers who displayed a tendency towards conversation. When he had a good hand or a slam or something like that, he would chuckle and say, 'Oh, that's great!' but that was the extent of it. He would smoke one cigarette after another, and Mickey would be in the background busy emptying ashtrays, filling the peanut dishes – and the glasses – and putting fresh logs on the fire.

We never lacked for a foursome. Butch liked to play, and he would often bring along a friend for dinner and bridge. General Mark Clark was one of the steadies, and so was General T. J. Davis, an old friend of the General's. Once in a blue moon we would be very lucky and General Gruenther would take a hand. He was such a good player that people would call him up from all over the European Theatre to ask advice or have him settle a dispute over some fine point.

Harry Hopkins usually took a hand when he was around. He was quite a good player, although he preferred gin rummy to bridge. I was always nervous when he played, because he was so thin. So thin that his clothes looked as if they had been thrown on to a skeleton. I would look at him and think, My goodness, that man is going to fall over if anyone breathes too hard. He was quite tall and seemed terribly frail, although he worked like a demon.

We always played for money – threepence a hundred points. The General refused to keep score or involve himself with the book-keeping. 'I'm pulling rank,' he'd say with a grin. 'I've got enough aides here to keep score for me.' He insisted on the losers' paying promptly. He was prompt himself. If he lost, someone, usually I, would figure out how much he owed and then he would reach into his pocket very slowly, drawling out, 'I just happen to have a little money here.' It was always very little. The General's pay cheque went directly to his wife, and he never had more than a few dollars of spending money. There were times when he would make his little announcement and reach into his pocket only to find he had no money at all. Mickey would have forgotten to give the General his pocket money when he dressed that morning – or the General would have spent his daily allowance on cigarettes and chocolate bars. Then he would bellow, 'Mickey-ey-ey! Money-ey-ey!' even if Mickey was at his elbow, and Mickey would run upstairs and come back with a handful of small change so that the General could settle his bridge debt.

Bridge was not our only game. 'The frosting on the cake,' as Butch put it, was the fact that Telegraph Cottage was next to a golf course. A path led from the back of the house through the woods to a gate in a high wooden fence that marked the edge of the property. When we walked through the gate, we were at the thirteenth hole.

We got to know that thirteenth hole very well. If the General left headquarters early on a Saturday or Sunday, he would head straight for Telegraph Cottage and the thirteenth hole. Occasionally we would play three or four holes. I don't believe we ever visited the clubhouse, and I know that we never played the full eighteen holes. Many an evening we contented ourselves practising chipping and putting. But the situation was absolutely made to order for the General. The course could not have been more private. Most of the golfers we saw were elderly ladies, playing through with placid determination.

And just off the path that wound between the house and the golf course, we discovered a little rustic bench hidden behind some shrubbery. Later on, when we wanted to be completely alone, we would sit there and talk, away from everybody and everything.

We set up a badminton net and dragooned visitors into playing fast, sweaty games. And the General, Butch and Tex or Mark Clark would toss a football around, playing a childish game with rules they changed every time they played. It was always two against one, and the odd man tried to intercept the ball as the other two threw it back and forth to each other while they ran around in circles.

Moaney and Hunt used to save tin cans for pistol practice. Butch, the General and I would take turns shooting cans off the top of a stake driven into the ground. Later we got a regular target and set it up on the lawn. When the General learned that I did not have a gun, he went rummaging through his trunk and came up with one for me to use.

A few days later, he called me into his office at Grosvenor Square and said, 'I've got something for you.' He reached into the desk drawer and took out a small Beretta.

'I want you to get familiar with this,' he said. 'It's yours. When we're overseas, you never know what might happen. I'd prefer to see you dead rather than a prisoner of the Germans,' he added grimly.

This was the first hint I had had that he was considering taking me overseas with him. I knew that once the planning for Torch was completed, he would be off to North Africa, and I supposed I would be back in the motor pool waiting for another assignment. He did not say any more about it, but from that time on I spent hours potting away at those old tin cans with my Beretta. Fortunately, I had done a lot of shooting when I was growing up, so it did not take long before I could ping away pretty accurately.

When the General really wanted to get his mind off things, he would ask Mickey to get out his drawing paraphernalia and would make sketch after sketch of Telegraph Cottage. He could never capture it to his satisfaction. He would rip the pages off his pad and tear them up, and one could just see his blood pressure mounting. It got so that when he called Mickey to get out his sketch pad and set up a chair for him on the lawn, we would all roll our eyes at each other and try to distract him by suggesting that we go for a walk or something. We never succeeded – and neither did the General. Later, when he was in the

White House, I was always surprised by how much he had improved when I saw his paintings reproduced in a newspaper or magazine. But one thing can certainly be said for his early efforts: they did get his mind off the war.

After the first few evenings at Telegraph Cottage, Eisenhower decided that it was too much for me to drive back to London on the nights he decided to sleep over and then come back to pick him up in the morning, so he requisitioned a billet for me at Bushey Park, which was very close, so that I could get more sleep. This worked out very well. I would arrive at the cottage shortly before seven in the morning. Moaney and Hunt would be bustling around the kitchen getting breakfast. There would be bacon or a piece of ham and eggs. There was usually real butter, and there were always hot biscuits with lots of jam. We ate better – our supplies came from the Army mess – than almost anyone else in England; I am convinced of that. And there were gallons, or so it seemed, of blistering-hot black coffee. If the coffee was not as black as midnight and one degree short of boiling, the General would blow his top. Mickey would rush out to the kitchen and bring in a fresh pot that had obviously been boiling when he snatched it off the stove. 'It's hot, General. Watch your tongue,' he would say.

I remember one morning when Eisenhower had a breakfast guest, a high-ranking British officer, who was quite obviously taken aback by the bustling informality of this little household – and particularly by the idea of a batman's presuming to tell a general to watch out and not burn his tongue and by a woman driver's arriving for breakfast with a very unprofessional salute and a cry of 'Eggs! Oh, General, that's smashing!' It was not what one would call your ordinary general's household. But it was just what this American general wanted, needed and got.

As soon as the General had had his final cup of coffee and gone upstairs for Mickey to help him on with his coat and give him a final brushing, we would be off to Grosvenor Square.

Wartime is much more concentrated than peacetime. It was only a matter of days until our little family felt as if we had been leading this kind of life together for years. In the middle of a vast world war, the commanding general had managed to establish a happy home in that precarious calm of the eye of the storm.

Chapter 7

The General had been as good as his word, and my mother was often invited to the Dorchester and Telegraph Cottage. She and the General hit it off beautifully. They were both history buffs. My mother had been well educated – far better than I had been – in convents in France and Belgium where the nuns drilled their pupils in history and languages as well as needlework and etiquette, since these young ladies were expected to marry into important Catholic families, not to espouse land-poor cavalry officers as my mother had. She was insatiably curious about the American Civil War, and the General loved to refight the battles for her at the dinner table.

I have fond memories of the two of them, both smoking one cigarette after another over their coffee cups, engrossed in setting up battles between the Confederate and Union forces. The General used coins to represent soldiers, and Mickey often had to rush down to the lobby of the Dorchester and change a pound note to provide troops for my mother and the General.

The two of them became really good friends and used to chat and laugh together as if they had known each other for ages. In some ways they were remarkably alike. They had the same magnetic warmth and could establish almost instant rapport with people.

Mummy had separated from my father when I was sixteen or seventeen and come with me and my sister Evie to London, where she found a post as office manager. In those days I hated my father and was sure I knew why Mummy had left him: he was angry, cantankerous, impossible to live with. He was the villain. I was convinced of it. But now, looking back, I imagine it was a bit more complicated a relationship.

My father had his gentle, loving side as well as his black Irish furies. He loved his land. Those hundreds of green Irish acres that had belonged to his father and his father's father before him meant the world to him. He loved his flowers. His gardens were famous in southern Ireland. There were always two or three gardeners trundling wheelbarrows of manure about, staking the rosebushes, clipping the shrubbery and all that.

He loved his son, Seamus, and took a stern pride in the fact that he had an heir – strong, handsome and intelligent. And Seamus loved Innis Beg as much as our father did.

And my father loved his beautiful, vivacious and opinionated English wife. Today I am sure of that. But there was a disparity in their ages and in their background. And they were both wilful, stubborn souls. My father had spent much of his Army life in West Africa – 'the white man's grave' they called it then – and when he came back home and married, I suspect that he was not prepared for his young bride's dismay when she was introduced to the lonely old house that he loved so much.

Southern Ireland could be bitterly cold and damp. I remember that all of us children always had chilblains in the winter – raw, red, itching knuckles and ankles. We thought nothing of it. Chilblains were a way of life, part of winter, as were our streaming eyes and runny noses. Those chillingly damp Irish winters, when the smoke from open fires swooped through the house and billowed down the halls, driven by the wet Atlantic winds gusting in from the west, were probably responsible for Mummy's getting the touch of tuberculosis that prompted my father to pack her off to visit one of her friends in Italy to get her health back in the Mediterranean sun. That long separation coupled with unrealized expectations and sullen frustrations on both sides may have triggered the final separation.

Whatever the reason or reasons, she finally left my father. Ostensibly she was simply giving Evie and me a season in London, but she never returned to Innis Beg to live. Mummy told me, 'You can either be presented at Court or have a trip. I think it would be far more interesting for you to travel, but you have the choice.' It did not take me a minute to make that choice. I would travel. Who wanted all that non-sense of curtsies and ostrich feathers when it was possible to see the world instead? Also, to tell the truth, the thought of curtsying to the austerely regal Queen Mary rather daunted me. I was still a raw country girl fresh from County Cork.

Mummy arranged for me to visit one of her old schoolmates in Helsinki. It was a marvellous experience. I travelled all over Finland, and I think I met every important person in the country at my hostess's dinner table – including Field-Marshal Mannerheim, the famous statesman. I went to Oslo next, then to Brussels and Paris. I would stay with friends of Mummy's, and then other friends would come by and say, 'Oh, you must come visit with us too.' So every place I went, there were several families to take me around.

When I came back to London after six months, Mummy told me that I now had to learn how to earn my own living. 'There will be no money for you girls when your father dies,' she said. 'The property will go to Seamus. I want you to be self-supporting so you won't have to marry to get a roof over your head.'

So off I went to school. Not too eagerly. In the mornings I went to business school and learned how to type and write proper business letters. In the afternoon, I went to art school. But my social life soon turned into such an exciting whirl that I neglected my studies. Then I had a chance to work as an extra in a film that was being made at Elstree and stopped going to classes altogether. I was flirting with the idea of becoming an actress when I met Gordon Summersby.

It was love at first waltz. The party was in one of those wonderful old houses on St James's Square with a wide staircase curving up to a ballroom that probably was not used more than twice a year, if that. I wonder if any London houses today still boast ballrooms. They were part of a far different day, a more romantic one. After Gordon and I were introduced, we danced almost every dance with each other, drank champagne, which we were not used to, and talked a lot of nonsense. Finally we drifted back down that beautiful staircase and walked out into the sunrise. We were married within months.

Marriage was a hectic round of partying. We went out almost every night and would spend weekends at this place and that in the country visiting friends who, like us, were mad about racing and everything to do with horses. All play and no work turned out to be a very dull way of life, and eventually Gordon and I drifted apart. I started working as a model at Worth, the first job that was offered to me. The pay was peanuts, but it seemed a lot to me, because I had never earned any money before. I enjoyed the glamour, and I was fascinated by the process of artistic creation. Fashion became a living, breathing art to me. To be able to observe the creation of a design from the first sketch to the final fitting – quite often on me – was a privilege I would have been willing to pay for.

I had told the General all this in bits and pieces as I drove him around and in the evenings we spent chatting at Telegraph Cottage. He often said that he felt as if he had known my family for years. When I told him that Seamus was in London on leave, he said, 'Well, I've got to meet him. Why don't you ask your brother to come over for dinner tonight?'

'Oh, that would be lovely,' I said, and when Seamus came by the office, I told him that General Eisenhower had invited us to have dinner with him that evening.

He looked at me disbelievingly. I can still see his face. 'What's that you said?'

'You heard me,' I laughed. 'The General wants to meet you. I've told him all about you.'

'I can just imagine,' Seamus said.

We had a marvellous evening. It was completely informal. In the office and in public I was always careful to give the General every mark of formal respect. I never overstepped. I always saluted and was absolutely punctilious. But in private, that was different. I now saw him as a man and a friend, not just a general and a boss, and I had begun to call him Ike as the others did. That evening with Seamus was one of an absolutely at-home kind of fun for the three of us. It was ages since I had seen Seamus, and we started reminiscing about things we had done when we were children. It reached the point where we were clutching at our stomachs because we laughed so much. And the General laughed just as hard as Seamus and I did.

One of the funniest bits I remember was our telling the General about all the governesses – mostly young Englishwomen, although there was one elderly mademoiselle – that my mother managed to entice to Innis Beg. They never stayed long. And who could blame them? Seamus, of course, went off to school in Cork when he was eight or nine, but until then he was taught at home; and we girls were always taught at home, with the result that we did not learn much except how to ride and sail and dance and play bridge, all of which we taught ourselves or learned from our parents and their friends.

Seamus remined me of the time we offered to show a new governess around in our pony cart. We were barely out of sight of the house when Seamus whipped the poor fat pony, who toddled off as fast as his stubby legs could carry him, which was not very fast. Seamus, after making sure that there was no one who could hear him, shouted, 'Runaway! Runaway horse!' Evie and I joined in shrieking, 'Help! Help! Runaway horse!' and the poor governess just sat there hanging on for dear life and looking scared to death. Finally the pony got tired of exerting himself and ambled to a stop. The new governess hugged Seamus and called him a brave young hero.

Seamus and I flung ourselves about the living-room of the General's suite at the Dorchester as we told him the story, interrupting each other with freshly remembered details.

Then Seamus told the story of how I smashed my father's shotgun. I had been nine or maybe ten at the time and, quite disobediently, had taken one of my father's precious Purdeys out of the enormous glass-fronted gun case in the hall to go shooting. Scrambling over the fields, I dropped the shotgun – and cracked the stock!

I was ready to run away from home. His Purdeys were more precious than jewels to my father, certainly more precious than I was, or so I was convinced. I was so frightened that I hid in the stables. Seamus brought me a sandwich after supper, but I was too terrified to eat.

'What shall I do?' I quavered. 'He'll beat me until I'm dead.' I think I really believed that he would.

'You have to tell him,' Seamus said. He considered for a moment and added, 'You can't run away from home. You are not old enough to take care of yourself.'

'All right,' I decided. 'I'll tell him.' I marched into the house and knocked on the door of the library, where my father spent his evenings. He was going over papers at his desk and was very much surprised to see me. Surprised and obviously not pleased. I told him what had happened.

He looked at me. I suppose that what he saw must have appalled him. A bedraggled girl child. We all looked like urchins. Our day-in, day-out costumes had been devised by our mother for freedom and practicality. They consisted of floppy brown corduroy bloomers with tight elastic at the knee and sweaters that my mother knitted of a particularly horrid porridge-coloured wool. I used to wear my bloomers pulled way up to the crotch, where the elastic would cut into my legs with circulation-stopping cruelty, or pulled way down so that they looked like knickers, or so I hoped. With them we wore long woollen stockings that were more or less held up by suspenders that buckled around our waists – miserable contraptions that were always getting twisted.

There I was – dirty, guilty and snivelling – in this dismal outfit. Poor Father. It took me years to understand how bewildered he must have felt to have produced these strange, noisy, undisciplined offspring so late in life – especially after a career in the cavalry, where men were men and horses were horses and each performed properly or else. (He had been lieutenant-colonel of the Royal Munster Fusiliers, an Irish regiment, now disbanded.)

He surprised me. He did not beat me. He did not even shout at me. 'Go wash your face, Kathleen,' he said, 'and then come back.'

I came back, dragging my sleeve over my face to dry it. 'Come here,' father said. He put his arm around me and said, 'You know that you should not have taken my gun. That was wrong. But you were right to tell me about it. That was brave. We'll hear no more about it.'

When I listened to Seamus telling that old story, I had a feeling of sympathy and respect for my father. It suddenly dawned on me that perhaps he had loved me, but had not known how to express his feelings.

With all this talk about old times, Seamus and I were having a glorious reunion. And Ike was having fun too. He even told a story of his own about one of his uncles who had been a preacher on the prairie. His Uncle Abraham (I *think* that was his name) would stand on the seat of his wagon in the middle of a tiny village and shout, 'This way to

Heaven! This way to Heaven!' In no time at all, he had gathered fifteen or twenty people and launched into his sermon.

'I always thought there was a lesson in that,' Ike said, 'but I'm damned if I have ever been able to figure out what it is. I know the old man was mighty proud of himself the way he could raise an audience out of the dust, so to speak.'

The next morning he told me that he had had a fine time. 'Those stories you and Seamus told are almost as good as my Westerns,' he said with a smile, knowing my scorn for his favourite reading matter.

But evenings like this became increasingly rare as the preparations for North Africa neared completion. We were constantly on the go, and whenever the General had an evening to himself, all he wanted was to retreat to Telegraph Cottage and relax. There were nights when he was so bone-tired that he would fall asleep by the fire. He always asked us to wake him up when he did, because afterwards he would have trouble getting to sleep at night. The tensions were building up, and he would lie awake for hours going over problem after problem. All of us tried to think of ways to distract him and get his mind off the war for at least a few hours, but it became increasingly difficult.

As it turned out, an addition to our little family proved to be far more effective in helping the General relax than anything Butch and Beetle (General Walter Bedell Smith, Ike's chief-of-staff) and I had been able to dream up. The new member of the family was a perfect gentleman who was to be my almost constant companion, forever faithful and loving. His name was Telek, and he was a coal-black Scottie who deserves a chapter all his own.

Chapter 8

One lovely sunny October day when I was driving the General back from Cheltenham, our road lay among the rolling green hills of the Cotswolds with tiny villages of grey stone cottages and farmhouses surrounded by their barns and pens dotted here and there on the landscape. 'One of these days I'm going to have a farm,' Ike told me. 'Cows, horses, maybe some sheep. A kitchen garden. Nothing too big. But I want to have a real home. I've never had one since I was a youngster, you know. I've always gone from Army post to Army post. Telegraph Cottage is more of a home than most of the places I've lived in.'

'It's the homiest place I've ever known,' I agreed. 'When I walk into Telegraph Cottage, it's like coming home.'

'That's the way I feel about it,' Ike said. 'All it needs is some youngsters running around playing ball and climbing trees.'

'And a few dogs,' I added, entering into the spirit of the thing. 'I miss having a dog. We always had dogs around the house. My favourite was a Scottie, MacTavish. He was really adorable. Tavvy was so spunky you had to laugh.'

'Kay, would you like a dog? Another Scottie?' Ike asked.

I braked the car sharply. 'Would I like a dog? Oh, General, having a dog would be heaven!'

'Well,' he grinned, 'if you want one, we'll get one. I think I can manage that. I'd like to do something for you for working all these crazy hours and everything.'

I had no idea of the proportions Operation Dog would assume. The moment the word got out that the Commander wanted a dog, you should have seen the scurrying. The first thing I knew, Butch asked, 'Have you heard the latest? The Boss wants a dog for his birthday.'

'Oh,' I said very carefully. 'He does, does he?'

'He certainly does. He wants a Scottie. I told him he should get a Dandie Dinmont. That's a great little dog. But no, he wants a Scottie.'

'Well then,' I said, 'we certainly will have to get him a Scottie.'

The whole headquarters staff was out combing London and the suburbs for the finest Scottie to be had. Beetle and I joined forces and found two Scotties that were close to perfect. Of course, our notions of perfection differed.

One dog was about a year old, very sweet but without much spirit. Beetle liked him because he was already housebroken. The other, my favourite, was just a puppy, a three-month-old ball of black fur. I loved him. We decided to let the General choose, and in we went to his office carrying the dogs in our arms. The older dog just sat there quietly, but the puppy was adorable. The first thing he did was make a puddle in the exact centre of the rug; then he pranced around looking very proud of himself. 'Come here, fella,' the General said, and that little puppy went right over to him.

Ike looked at me. 'What do you think? Do you like him?'

'Oh, General, I love him,' I said.

He grinned. 'This is the one, Beetle.' As far as the world knew, this was the General's dog. 'You understand, don't you?' he asked me concernedly. 'There would be such a rumpus if it got out that I was getting a dog for my driver. God knows what people would say – or think.'

'Oh, I understand perfectly,' I assured him. And I did.

'That's good,' he said, 'because I'm the one who is going to name him.'

'Oh? And what is his name?'

'Telek.'

'Telek?'

'T-E-L-E-K,' he spelled it out. 'It's a combination of Telegraph Cottage and Kay,' he said. 'Two parts of my life that make me very happy.'

The formal presentation was on 14 October, the General's birthday, and it was one of the greatest birthday parties I have ever attended. It was at the cottage, of course. Mickey produced a marvellous cake frosted in white with three red frosting stars and a candle in the centre of each star. And there was champagne. As soon as Ike had blown out the candles and we had toasted him with champagne, Telek trotted out – a red ribbon around his neck, a wag to his tail and all the charm in the world. He saluted Ike with another puddle, and someone suggested that Ike change the puppy's name from Telek to Puddle, and Butch said Piddle would be even better. The General shook his head. 'Telek it is and Telek it's going to be,' he said firmly.

'Telek.' Butch shook his head disgustedly. 'It sounds like the name of a toothbrush.'

'Could be,' the General said mysteriously. 'His tail looks a bit like a toothbrush.'

'But it's a ridiculous name for a dog,' Butch persisted. 'Why not call him Blackie or Rover or something like that? What does Telek mean, anyway?'

'That would be telling,' Ike said. 'It's top secret. Just like Telegraph Cottage. Maybe when the war is over I'll explain it.'

The party broke up early, and the General and I had a last drink in front of the fire. Telek fell asleep in my lap. Ike came over and scratched the puppy's ears, and Telek opened his eyes, gave one little wag of his tail and went back to sleep. We smiled at each other. 'Thank you, Kay,' Ike said, 'for bringing so much gaiety into my life. I don't know what I'd do without you.'

The next morning Telek accompanied us to Grosvenor Square, sitting in front with me. He behaved like a perfect gentleman. From that time on, we were three. Telek went almost everywhere the General and I went. In the office he had his own little box with a pillow, where he snoozed most of the day. He even accompanied the General to Buckingham Palace when he went to pay his farewell call on the King before leaving for Gibraltar and North Africa. Telek did not go inside, of course. He stayed with me; but he did manage to leave his signature on a few inches of the Palace courtyard in a most disrespectful manner.

Telek had a pedigree a mile long. He was a true aristocrat. He was also spoiled rotten – and utterly, endearingly lovable. Once Admiral J. H. D. Cunningham of the Royal Navy took Ike to task for not training Telek properly. Not normally the kind of person who would venture to tell someone else how to train his dog, the Admiral simply could not refrain from speaking up when he noticed that Ike was feeding Telek bits from his plate at the luncheon table.

'That dog is spoiled,' the Admiral said. 'It's a mistake to feed dogs at the table. Gets them to thinking it should happen all the time.'

'It does, Admiral. It does,' Ike assured him.

The Admiral, who was really a very nice old boy, frowned but Ike simply grinned and shook his head.

'If you want me to train Telek, someone has to train me first,' he said. 'There isn't very much I can do that's fun, but I can spoil this dog, and he enjoys it as much as I do.'

When Telek was still a puppy, Ike would often say, 'Hand that little black tramp over to me. I think he needs a little man-to-man talk.' And he would hold him and talk nonsense to him and scratch his ears and his fat little stomach until Telek would curl up and go to sleep snuggled up to the General. Many a night we would lie on the floor in front of the fire, our drinks on the floor beside us, and roll a golf ball back and forth for Telek to chase. He would pounce on it as if he had captured a tiger. Another game he loved was tug-of-war. Ike would hold one end of the old leather belt he had donated to Telek's toy box and Telek would give a baby growl and grab the other end between his teeth. He used to shake the belt as if he were shaking a rat and growl ferociously all the time.

We were like two children with Telek – or perhaps doting parents might be closer to the truth. All we had needed to complete our little wartime family and make Telegraph Cottage a real home was a child. And Telek, for us, was a reasonable facsimile. Every dog lover will know how we felt.

Chapter 9

Men and women who are immersed in a creative process, whether it be waging war or making love or painting a picture or carrying a child in the womb or what I have come to think of as the ultimate creative process – dying – exist in their own special dimension. Their preoccupation is so great, their commitment so complete, their energies so all-absorbed that it is as if their days were being lived out in a tunnel. A transparent invisible tunnel.

They seem just like their neighbours – eating and sleeping, walking and talking, catching colds in their heads and losing fillings in their teeth – but they are people apart. The invisible tunnel encloses them as surely as the medieval convent held its nuns or the amber its fly. The fervour of commitment has the same high-tension euphoria as a butterfly-brief love affair. For all tunnels come to an end. Wars are won. Orgasm is achieved; a vision captured. A child is born. The gates of death open – and close. Then one must emerge. Into what?

General Eisenhower and I were embarked on a voyage through a tunnel of war. It was a just war, a crusade against 'the evil things'. Never did we have to question the righteousness of our cause, nor did we consider ourselves as noble or self-sacrificing. We had a job to do. That was all. A war to win.

Like any job, war had its own routine. The General's responsibilities seemed to be a mishmash of this and that, but no matter how his day was splintered into a thousand little and big responsibilities, the Boss's only real concern was the war. And again as with any job, there were parts of it that he disliked. More and more he was having to grapple with the political as well as the military aspects of Torch, something that did not appeal to him at all. 'Christ on the mountain,' he burst out one night on the way home, 'I'm a military man, not a politician!' He spent the rest of the drive to Kingston telling me how he had been taught at West Point that the military should not get involved with politics. 'It's as important as the separation of church and state,' he explained earnestly.

He was openly shocked at the country-club atmosphere at 20 Grosvenor. 'Some of these fellows have been in London too long,' he said darkly. Long lunches, early cocktail hours and three-day weekends had been taken for granted. But all that ended almost overnight. The General put an end to late arrivals and early departures by letting it be known that he expected everyone to report to work when he did – shortly before eight – and that he considered it very poor form for anyone to leave before the Old Man left.

Another problem was trying to establish harmony between the American and British soldiers. England is such a small country that the hundreds of thousands of Americans pouring off the troopships presented serious problems. There were all kinds of incidents that exacerbated the war-weary English, and the General spent hours smoothing these out. I remember one case well. An American officer, much the worse for drink, called a British officer a son of a bitch. The General ordered the American sent back to the States. The British officer asked the General to reconsider. 'He only called me a son of a bitch, sir,' he told the General. 'We have learned that this is an American expression that should not be taken too seriously, that it is often a term of affection.'

'I have been informed,' Ike said, 'that he called you a *British* son of a bitch. That is different. My ruling stands.'

The General used the term often enough himself. I remember when he heard about an American officer who was boasting that his men would show the British what fighting men really were. Eisenhower's voice came blistering through the walls of his office. 'I'll make that son of a bitch *swim* back to the States!' he shouted.

It was not only the officers who struck the wrong note. The English used to say that the trouble with the GI's was that 'They are over-sexed, overpaid – and over here.' The Americans were paid nearly three times as much as their British counterparts, and many girls were swept off their feet by the attractive, free-spending Yanks. Eisenhower sent out several memos urging the men to save their money, buy bonds or send it home, but he was never able to make much of a dent in their extravagant ways.

He also worked hard at turning his draftee army into proud fighting men. He started at the top, with the commanding officers, demanding that they insist on spit and polish, on salutes and military discipline. If a soldier did not behave in a disciplined manner, he would not make a good fighter. But he was not content with simply issuing orders. One afternoon he said, 'Kay, get the car. We're going to take a little ride.' Before he got into the big Packard, he said, 'Uncover the stars.' The three silver stars on a red plate attached to the Army licence plate were usually concealed by a little canvas slipcover, since Eisenhower did not care to call attention to himself. But this day the stars were shining silver bright, and his flag flew from the radiator cap, as he directed me to drive slowly down Audley Street past the Officers' Club and an enlisted men's canteen. The General sat erect and observant in the back.

'Around again,' he ordered. So around I went past the club again at something like ten miles an hour; then we cruised into and out of the other West End streets around Grosvenor Square, passing hundreds of officers and enlisted men, until he ordered, 'Back to headquarters.' His face was turkey red. In twenty minutes only one man had saluted – and he was a British officer. Ike stalked into 20 Grosvenor, his jaw thrust out and his eyes cold in anger. He marched up and down his office dictating a memo for distribution to all commanding officers. From now on, he told them, whenever he spotted any laxity in saluting, he himself would ask the name of the offender – and that of his commanding officer. He would hold the commanding officer responsible. He got his point across. A week later we made another test drive along Audley Street. This time there was a satisfactory flurry of salutes.

There were also great flurries of VIP conferences. General Marshall came to London. And so did Admiral Ernest King, his Navy counterpart. Harry Hopkins and Steve Early seemed to be continually flying back and forth between London and Washington. Even Eleanor Roosevelt came to see things for herself. And scores of top American politicians followed her example. There were meetings at the War

Office, at 10 Downing Street, at Chequers, at 20 Grosvenor. The olive-drab official cars shuttled back and forth with their important passengers.

It was truly a star-spangled time. I was meeting people I would never have expected to meet, let alone be on friendly terms with. The most impressive was Prime Minister Churchill himself. The General met with him at least twice a week – once for lunch and once for dinner – and usually more. One day I was sitting in the car waiting for the General in front of the building near St James's Park where he often met with the PM, when I looked up to see him walking towards the car accompanied by a familiar figure. The PM! I hopped out and stood at attention. Churchill looked just like all the photographs and cartoons – that same baby bulldog face, with eyes as blue as Eisenhower's. He wore his famous siren suit. This was his own wartime uniform and of his own design. The best way I can describe it is to say that it was very similar to a baby's one-piece sleeping suit. He liked it because he could thrust his stubby legs into it, pull it up, push his arms into the sleeves – and zip, he was dressed. He usually wore slippers with it when he was indoors.

The General introduced us, and the PM was absolutely charming. He told me that he had heard what a good driver I was and said, 'Now, I want you to take good care of your general. We need him.'

I could hardly believe it. The Prime Minister telling me to take good care of the Commander. I managed a weak 'Yes, sir.' This was the beginning of a long acquaintance. One day I was asked along with Ike to lunch at 10 Downing Street. It was far more informal than one would have thought. The Churchills were living in the basement, because a bomb that had exploded down the street had damaged the upper floors. But it was cosy, with chintz-covered chairs and sofas. There were a number of paintings, and fresh flowers everywhere. That made a great impression on me, because flowers were one of the casualties of wartime, one of those pleasures you don't realize you miss until you are reminded. Mrs Churchill was there, and so was their daughter Mary, who was in the ATS (Auxiliary Territorial Service – the women's branch of the British Army). There were a couple of young men, I think, but for the life of me I can't recall who they were. That is not so surprising, because the PM was such a spellbinder that he was always the centre of attention. He was more like a guest than a host, but Mrs Churchill was extremely gracious and charming. We had sherry and chatted for a bit before we went into the dining-room. I can't remember what was served for luncheon, but there was a great deal of liquid refreshment.

The General made a practice of introducing me to all his friends and many of his British military associates. It was very heady stuff. I could tell that he was pleased with – and possibly even proud of – me. At one point he said, 'I want you to know all these people, Kay. That way you can be even more helpful. I need someone to talk to and sort out my ideas with. Someone who knows the people and problems involved.'

I thought I understood what he meant. There were times when Beetle and Butch and Mark Clark and Tooey Spaatz and the others were inclined to push their own ideas instead of listening to Ike formulate his and following his lead. So just the fact of my knowing all these people and a little bit of how they would react to situations was useful. Ike knew I was utterly discreet, and he had slowly got into the habit of talking things over with me in the car or over a drink when we arrived at Telegraph Cottage after work. My contribution to these conversations was very limited. I rarely said anything more than, 'Hmm, yes, I see. Is that so? Oh, that *is* a problem, isn't it?' Noncommittal, sympathetic sounds, so that he had the feeling that there was someone responding to his thoughts. But I never disagreed. I never made suggestions. I was just there – like a hum in the background.

Our life was quite different from other people's lives – even though everyone was concerned with the war in some way. We worked seven days a week, and often twelve hours a day, in a quickening rhythm, on a task whose climax would affect the whole course of the war. The North African operation had to be successful. When you work this way with someone, no matter in what capacity, nothing else seems to matter.

No one outside the handful of people at headquarters, the top generals and statesmen and the members of the 'family' could share our world. It seemed calm, but only because the General imposed a calm on his surroundings. Although Butch and I and the rest of the little family shared only part of the General's crushing responsibilities, we were closer to his concerns, his moods, his physical ups and downs than we were to those of any other person.

The complete absorption of my time and energy disturbed my fiancé. Dick felt left out in the cold. 'My God,' he said one day, 'you know all those top generals, the ones the rest of us only hear about. And Winston Churchill calls you Kay.'

'It's only because of my job. It has nothing to do with me.'

Dick sighed. He was really upset. 'You know,' he said, 'when the war is over and we are living in the States, you won't be associating with prime ministers and three-star generals.'

'Well, that will be another phase,' I said. 'Naturally I wouldn't expect to be popping in on General Eisenhower for breakfast or playing cards with General Gruenther when we are in America. The circumstances will be completely different.'

The fact was that at this time I simply could not imagine leading any other life. I was completely caught up in the moment. I loved Dick. I really did. But at the moment, I felt closer to Ike. This was not a time for love, I felt. We all had a mission that was far more important than our personal lives and desires.

This knowledge was something that the General and I shared. His own family was far away. He rarely mentioned them. This was not through lack of caring. It was simply that we were in another world. And one could not share it with outsiders. The war was an irresistible catalyst. It overwhelmed everything, forced relationships like a hothouse so that in a matter of days one would achieve a closeness with someone that would have taken months to develop in peacetime.

Our nightly bridge games did a lot to bring Ike and me together. We had an almost telepathic relationship. From the very beginning we played well together, and we soon became so attuned to each other's thinking that we were a very effective team. I had never experienced such intuitive communication with anyone. Being bridge partners helped us transcend the boss-and-chauffeur relationship. One morning driving into London, I remarked on how uncannily we seemed to be able to read each other's minds at the bridge table. 'That's strange,' Ike said. 'I was thinking the same thing. You know, even if you hadn't ruled out post mortems after a game, I doubt if we would ever have had any problems. We never disagree.'

He was right. I could not imagine us disagreeing. The discovery that there was someone who could share my thoughts and feelings made me feel secure, just the way one feels crawling apprehensively into bed on a cold, damp night – only to discover that someone has tucked a couple of hot-water bottles between the sheets. You immediately relax and bask in the unexpected warmth.

By this time we had travelled deep into that invisible tunnel that separated us from others. Other people's ways, other people's lives were different from ours. We had a job to do. A crusade to make. And we were already very close to each other.

Chapter 10

Four buzzes. That was my signal. The secretary was one buzz, Tex two and Butch three.

'Sit down,' said Ike. 'I've been meaning to talk to you.'

Meaning to talk to me, I thought. What else has he been doing every day? What else was he doing on the way to work this morning? We'd reached Grosvenor Square only half an hour earlier. It must be something unpleasant. I rather suspected he was going to tell me that I would be transferred back to the motor pool when he left for North Africa. He had never followed up on that earlier hint that I might be going along.

'You know we'll be packing up and leaving for North Africa one of these days,' he said. There was a pause. He put his hands on the desk and leaned forward a bit. 'Kay, would you like to come along?'

I was practically jumping up and down in my chair. I wanted to go along. Badly. I would have felt simply terrible if I were left behind – although I would have understood.

'I'd give anything to go,' I said.

'It's settled, then.' He slapped his hands on the desk and leaned back. 'You'll be following us. It will probably be a month or so before the situation is stabilized. And Kay, you don't have to be told this is top secret. Not one word to anybody.'

'No, sir.' I stood. 'Thank you, sir,' I said, 'for asking me.' I saluted.

'And one other thing,' he said.

'Yes, sir?'

'You've got the sloppiest salute in the whole Army.'

I laughed. 'But General, you forget. I'm a civilian.'

And I was. The uniform did not mean a thing. And that added to the red tape, because I had to have a passport to go to North Africa and passports were not being given out freely in those days. Tex finally pulled all the right strings and I got one, good 'for one journey only'. From that time on, I felt as if there were clouds under my feet instead of pavements or a gas pedal.

There was still the here and now to cope with, including the business of throwing the press off the scent of the coming invasion of North Africa. We indulged in all sorts of subterfuges. I kept an old guide to Finland on my desk. Butch tacked a huge map of Norway on his wall. When a journalist would look at it questioningly, Butch would lean back, puff on his cigar and say, 'Great country, Norway. I understand they have some of the best fishing in the world.' I don't know if Butch ever convinced anyone that our first thrust would be to the north, but he had a great time trying.

The real business of headquarters proceeded at its usual gruelling pace. The General, who had tried to visit every military installation in Britain, scheduled one last inspection tour before taking off for Gibraltar and North Africa: an expedition to Scotland, where the First Division was practically disembarking and storming the beaches, capturing 'enemy' positions and grouping inland prior to embarking for North Africa.

We went up to Scotland in the General's private railroad car, *Bayonet*. It was quite elegant, panelled in teak, with a little sitting-room, a private office for the General and sleeping quarters. Ike and I settled down in the office to catch up with some paperwork, and then we spent the rest of the day playing bridge and napping. Midnight found us deep in Scotland – and it was Scotland at its most typical. Abominable. It was not only cold but wet, not only wet but windy. And it was dark, dark, dark. A car was waiting. I drove as close to where the practice landings were being made as I could; then the General and Butch would get out in the rain and tramp across fields, down cart tracks and on to the rugged beaches to talk to the men and the officers. Ike not only wanted to show himself and demonstrate his concern for American soldiers; he also wanted to brief himself on the level of competence of these troops, most of whom had never taken part in any military action in their lives. He would stay at each position for half an hour or so, then plod back to the car, and we would go on to the next manœuvres area.

The driving was sheer hell. Not only were blackout conditions rigidly observed, but on those rural Scottish roads there were no white lines painted in the centre. In London, blackout driving was feasible because except in the densest fog one could follow the white line. Here I could see nothing. I pushed ahead, daring to go only ten or twelve miles an hour, not even that. Ike was impatient at my snail's pace, but there was nothing else for it. Finally, the sombre grey dawn found us in Inveraray at Admiralty House, where we were given breakfast.

The General was disturbed by the lack of experience and leadership that he had observed during the night. 'They'll be sitting ducks if they don't sharpen up,' he said. It was a very weary and worried man who got back on the train at midday. We were all tired. Five minutes after *Bayonet* was under way, we were all stretched out on bunks, where we stayed until we pulled into London. We were a sad-looking group. Ike had a cold. Butch had a cold. Mickey had a cold. And I felt absolutely terrible.

It was a time when a million little things – and a number of big things – seemed to be going wrong. Everything became much worse when Ike's fantastically competent and hard-working chief-of-staff, Beetle Smith, fell ill. An old ulcer kicked up, and he looked like a ghost, he was so pale. He looked so awful, in fact, that one night when Ike and Beetle had dinner with the PM, Churchill took Ike aside and told him that he thought Beetle was going to die on his feet, right then and there. Ike immediately ordered Beetle to bed and then ordered Butch to find a nurse for him. Butch found the most beautiful nurse in the whole European Theatre, Ethel Westermann. She looked like a Madonna, with big dark eyes and lovely skin. She was not only gorgeous, she was bright and funny – and an excellent bridge player. We soon were seeing as much of Ethel as we did of Beetle.

The pressures were getting to Ike. He was impatient, tired and nervous, his temper at the ready. Butch reported that the Boss was not sleeping – not even at the cottage, where it was usually easy for him to relax. The General was worried about himself. 'I've got to get in shape,' he kept saying, 'before North Africa.' But he was drinking more coffee, smoking more cigarettes and getting less sleep than ever. He could not stay still for a moment. And when he did, his fingers would be tapping on the table.

One afternoon Butch got him to leave early to play a little golf, but that did not help much. Ike walked into the house and said, 'I've had it. Butch just beat me. That duffer beat me.' They had played the thirteenth hole and Butch had taken eleven strokes, the General sixteen.

'Oh, that's bad,' I said sympathetically.

'Let me tell you something,' he snapped. 'That's not bad. That's disastrous.' It was the kind of incident that he would have laughed about normally, but now it got under his skin.

Finally it was time. Everything that we had been working towards since the first of July was ready. This was it. It was hard to realize that one phase was over and another beginning. We had a final dinner at Telegraph Cottage, just family and friends. The eve of battle is an eerie time. There were a few toasts drunk to a successful operation, but no one felt like talking. We did not even play bridge, but simply sat around the living-room making remarks now and then, almost like courteous strangers in a waiting-room.

Butch turned on the radio, and my mood brightened immediately. A whole string of Noël Coward's songs was being broadcast, including my very favourite, 'I'll See You Again.'

'Oh, I love that song,' I said.

'It's pretty,' Ike agreed.

'Pretty!' I exclaimed. 'It is the most romantic song in the world.' I had seen *Bittersweet* the season it opened, and that song had been the hit. All London used to hum it, dance to it, sing it.

'What's *your* favourite song?' I asked Ike.

Butch answered for him: ' "The Beer Barrel Polka".'

'Not at all,' Ike said indignantly. 'My favourite's the one I hum all the time, "One Dozen Roses" ' – and he started singing it.

'It's nice,' I said, 'but it's not as romantic as mine.' And I started singing 'I'll See You Again'. And that was the way the evening ended. We sat around and sang a few songs and then said good night.

The next evening, after a day crammed with conferences and last-minute paperwork, Ike came out of his office and said, 'Well, let's go.' I drove him, General Clark and Butch to the out-of-the-way railroad spur where *Bayonet* was waiting to take them to Bournemouth. From

Bournemouth they would fly to Gibraltar in the General's B-17.

'Well, Sunday's the day,' Ike said.

'Good luck. And please take care of yourself.' I meant it. I had grown tremendously attached to this man.

'Don't worry. It's going to be all right. I'll be seeing you soon. Take care of the little fellow.' He gave Telek one last scratch under the chin and boarded *Bayonet*. I stood there waving, Telek in my arms, as the train chugged out of the freight spur and disappeared.

Forty-eight hours after General Eisenhower arrived in Gibraltar, the invasion was on. It had been scheduled for one o'clock in the morning of Sunday 8 November. And it went according to schedule. I spent all that night and the next day wrapped around my radio. It was so exciting that I could not sleep. There was a message from President Roosevelt, then a proclamation by General Eisenhower (but in such beautiful French that I knew it was not the General speaking), the stirring strains of the 'Marseillaise' and reports of the assault on the beaches. The invasion was on. The Torch had been lit.

I can't say that I felt triumphant or relieved. Mostly I felt worried. What about Ike? Was everything going according to the plans he had made? According to his hopes? When would he join the troops in North Africa? I also felt sorry for myself. I wanted to be there too, sharing the danger.

Chapter 11

Now it was my turn. The departure date had been set and I was packing for North Africa; in truth, I thought of it more as packing for the rest of my life. I had heard from Dick. He had been in the North African invasion. He was fine, he wrote, and was temporarily stationed in Oran. And there was good news: he had received word that his divorce had gone through. 'It's signed, sealed and delivered,' he wrote. My own divorce would be granted in a couple of months, and then we would be free to marry. Dick, of course, had no idea that I was going to Algiers. It would have been breaking security for me to tell him.

I was light-heartedly packing for the future in two Vuitton cases that had been part of my mother's trousseau. She had given them to me years ago when I went on my European tour. They were terribly elegant, with gleaming brass corners and locks that I polished just as carefully as I polished the buckle on my Sam Browne belt. I could never afford such luggage today.

Two cases were more than enough. It was wartime, and my trousseau was nothing like the one I had accumulated for my first marriage; in fact, it was practically nonexistent. Before I married Gordon, I had spent weeks shopping. I had bought nightgowns that were all lace and froth, and the most romantic, crazily impractical negligees I could find. One was white velvet trimmed with marabou, if you can imagine; another was of the palest green silk chiffon, so light that it floated behind me as I walked. My wartime trousseau was a bit different. An old blue flannel robe with white piping was the closest thing to a negligee, but there was a bit of luxury all the same. My old friends in the workroom at Worth had hand-stitched me a gorgeous wedding present: two satin nightgowns and three sets of marvellous silk crêpe de chine undies. I cannot convey how creamily smooth good silk satin used to be. It seemed to melt on the body. There is nothing like it today. As I was tucking sachets scented with Je Reviens into the silken folds, I could not resist. I stripped and slipped into one of the nightgowns. It was breathtaking. It could have been an evening gown. It slithered down to my ankles, outlining my body in what I considered a very seductive way. I took out the two barrettes that held my hair back and brushed my hair until it was loose and bouncy, just touching my shoulders, and admired myself in the mirror. I have to smile – sadly – when I think of myself posturing in front of the mirror in that fantastic gown, smoothing the creamy satin down over my hips and twisting about. Smiling into the mirror, pretending I was smiling at my lover. Flirting. Turning my head. Lifting my chin.

Suddenly I was embarrassed at such nonsense. I was no tremulous virgin, but a woman about to enter into her second marriage. I should have acquired a certain sophistication. But the truth was that I had not. I was still a harum-scarum Irish girl. Forget my London gloss. Forget those years of modelling at Worth. I was still Kathleen in her corduroy bloomers with a runny nose and chilblains – finding it hard to believe that I was really the glamorous woman posing in the mirror.

I took off my satin nightgown, folded it in tissue paper with a perfumed sachet and got back into the old sweater and tweed skirt that I wore around my flat. Wisdom comes with age, they say. God knows if it is really true, but one thing I do know now is that one should always indulge those foolish fancies. If I had not had those romantic, slightly ridiculous moments in front of the mirror, I would never have enjoyed the silken luxury of my capsule trousseau stitched by loving - and very skilled - fingers. One has to savour every moment. But I did not know that then. I just thought that I was a terrible idiot to carry on that way.

I packed my few bits and pieces of jewellery. The pearl necklace that had been my sixteenth-birthday present. A pair of diamond earrings my grandmother had left me. A few gold bangles. I packed dozens of snapshots of my family. I packed my new summer uniforms and all my woollies. I was very proud of my store of woollen underwear, odd as that may seem today. For the last three years, every

English house and office had been freezing cold in winter, since there was practically no fuel available. Most women wore woollies a good nine months of the year. Mine were what they called combinations. When I joined the Motor Transport Corps, I had refused to buy the regulation under-pinnings. They could not have been uglier – a seasick green – or scratchier. I rushed out instead and bought half a dozen combinations in lacy blue wool with pink ribbons and another half dozen in pink with blue ribbons. When you get up day after day and month after month and put on the same uniform every blessed morning, it is a great morale booster to know that you have something on underneath which is pretty and soft and feminine. I knew that Algiers was not all sunshine and orange blossoms. At headquarters we were hearing a lot about the raw climate and the mud.

Mummy dropped by that afternoon. 'Oh, you're packing,' says she. 'Yes,' says I. And we hugged each other and cried a bit. Nothing more was said. She had been a soldier's wife and knew better than to ask questions.

It was only a matter of hours now. I was packed and ready. I had been desperately lonely in London these last few weeks; although I had a lot of friends and had gone out almost every night to talk and drink and dance until dawn, I was not in the mood to be part of the gaiety as I might have been a year earlier. I missed Dick. I missed the General and Butch. I missed being part of things – and I missed Telek. It had been decided at the last moment that a dog had no place on a crowded troopship and that there might be some unpleasant publicity, so Telek had been flown to Gibraltar, where Mickey took care of him in Ike's subterranean headquarters deep under the Rock of Gibraltar, and now he was in Algiers.

The next day I boarded a troop train for the overnight trip to Scotland. It was a far cry from the luxurious journey in *Bayonet*, with Mickey there to take care of our every need; but when we arrived at Greenock on the Clyde the next morning, it was the same Scottish weather – grey, cold, rainy – that had met us on the first trip. We were queued up for hours in the drizzle waiting our turn for the tender that chugged back and forth between the dock and the ship – the *Strathallen*, a hideous tub that had been converted to a troopship – at anchor in the harbour.

Life aboard ship was so awful that it was funny. Fortunately, two good friends were sharing the cabin with me: Ethel Westermann, the nurse, and Jean Dixon, an American. When the three of us crowded into the cabin with our baggage, it was like fitting sardines into a can. The first morning when we tried to get dressed, it was something straight out of a Marx Brothers comedy. Three women trying to put on stockings. Six legs waving in the air.

No sooner had we squeezed ourselves into the cabin than the alarm sounded for lifeboat drill. The commander wanted us to get used to the procedure before we hit the rolling troughs of the December Atlantic. The next thing we were instructed to do was prepare our torpedo bags. This· became a nightly, before-bed chore. These musette bags were to be filled with essentials – official papers, medications, warm clothing, et cetera – just in case. The three of us were rather frivolous, however, when it came to packing our torpedo bags. I for one would not dream of abandoning ship without such necessities as my nylons, my grandmother's diamond earrings or my little silken trousseau. Those were my essentials, along with a few cosmetics and a clean shirt.

It was strange travelling in convoy. As we steamed away from Scotland, two ships accompanied us, but later as we ploughed through the stormy grey Atlantic, other ships loomed up out of the fog and took their positions. There were ten or twelve, I believe, when the convoy was complete. The *Strathallen* was the only ship with women aboard. There were WACs, nurses and a few civilians like me. On our first day out, Ethel and I discovered to our great joy that Margaret Bourke-White, the famous *Life* magazine photographer, was on board. Peg had taken pictures of the General and the headquarters staff just a few months before, and we had liked each other. The four of us turned the voyage into one continuous bridge game. There was really very little else to do – eat, sleep, gossip or play bridge. Besides queueing, that is. Queueing was the principal shipboard activity. It was so crowded that there were three sittings for each meal and we had to line up for them. We also had to line up for the toilets.

It was a very rough trip, but there came a night when the winds died down, the ship stopped rocking and we all ran on deck to get some fresh air. Then we heard a cry: 'Lights!' And there were. In the distance was something I had not seen for years: the starry lights of a city spread out along the coast like clusters of diamonds. After three years of blackout, this was something to exclaim over. Lights! There were still places in the world where the lights had not been pinched out.

It was dawn when we realized what it meant to be in the Mediterranean. The sun came up rosy and bright. The sky was blue. The sea was blue. It was intoxicating. And very rough. German submarines had been reported in the area, and the *Strathallen*, like its sister ships in the convoy, dropped a succession of depth charges, which frothed up the blue seas like a giant bubble. But after the winter gales we had been through, bouncing about in the sunshine seemed a minor irritation. In twenty-four hours we would be landing.

All that night there were last-night parties. In our joy at the prospect of landing, we forgot the crowding, the petty gossip, the discomfort and the dreary boredom of life on a troopship. It was close to one-thirty when we got back to the cabin, which looked almost shipshape for once. Before starting our round of partying, we had prepared for the morning. I had unpacked my torpedo bag for the last time and carefully tucked my treasures back into the Vuitton cases. All that had to be done was to get some sleep. We would start disembarking at dawn.

I perched on the edge of the bunk, kicked off my shoes, loosened my tie and was about to start polishing my shoes and buttons for the morning when a tremendous explosion threw me off the bunk. Ethel and Jean had fallen on the floor too. Then the lights flickered and went out. The ship was shivering as if it had a monstrous chill and then began rocking ominously back and forth. 'This is it,' Ethel said. 'Let's get going.'

I can't die now, I thought, and grabbed my shoes, my life preserver and my handbag. Ethel and I followed Jean, who had a flashlight, to our lifeboat station. We had done this drill every day, every single day, three times a day, and it had become second nature, just as it had become second nature to wear one's life preserver everywhere, even to the loo. We clambered into our lifeboat, I still clutching my shoes.

Everyone in our boat started leaning over the edge looking down. 'Don't do that!' I shouted. 'Sit still in the middle, goddamnit, or we'll all drown!' It was pure Eisenhower language – and it worked. I can still hear myself shouting, 'Goddamnit, sit still!' But someone had to. The crew, mostly lascars, did not know what to do. And I had been in boats all my life. The boat was lowered safely over the side, and there we were – adrift in the moonlight on the Mediterranean. Not as romantic as it sounds. Not romantic at all when the sea around you is filled with soldiers and nurses swimming about trying to find something to hang on to. Not every group had been as fortunate as we had. Several lifeboats had capsized. We pulled a good number of people into our boat, and Ethel went straight to work. Several had broken legs or arms. The boat was bobbing madly about as depth charges exploded far below. We could see the convoy silhouetted against the sky, our sister ships steaming past, seemingly aloof and uncaring. I felt very much alone. The *Strathallen* was in the distance now, settling lower and lower into the water.

Very soon, I thought, it's all going to be at the bottom of the sea. My little trousseau, the precious diamond earrings, the snapshots of my family. A British destroyer came up, and a megaphone voice told us that we would all be picked up in the morning. It was too chancy to try rescuing us at the moment because there was a pack of German submarines in the area. The sun eventually rose and helped dry us off and raise our spirits. Peg immediately went to work photographing the survivors and the other lifeboats surrounding us. Two cameras slung about her neck and a bag of film over her shoulder, Peg was oblivious of everything except her work. Many months later I saw one of her photographs. It brought the whole experience back very vividly. We were all sitting there, handkerchiefs over our heads as protection from the sun.

The destroyer steamed back in midmorning and started picking us up. Climbing that rope ladder and finally feeling a solid deck under my feet – well, it was then that I realized how terrified I had been. I began to cry, but I stopped immediately when I realized I had nothing to blow my nose on. The handkerchief that I had used to cover my head had disappeared in the scramble up the ladder.

They landed us at Oran. We had been so trim, so pressed and polished, during the trip out; now we were waifs. My stockings were in tatters. My shoes were an utter disaster. My hair was hanging down. Fortunately, I had a lipstick and comb. They helped a bit. I decided the thing to do was report to headquarters in Oran. Ethel went along with me. One thought was going through my head: Dick was in Oran – or

he had been when he wrote me. Wouldn't it be wonderful if . . . ?
When we got to headquarters, I went in and asked for Lieutenant-
Colonel (he had had a promotion) Arnold. The guard looked at me
rather oddly, then admitted that there was such an officer there and
agreed to call him for me.

I stood and waited. And waited. The soldiers looked at me as if I
were very, very peculiar. I could understand why. My uniform skirt was
stained from the salt water and terribly wrinkled. My shirt was torn.
I had thrown away my stockings. And my hair was a mess. Suddenly I
realized that my first order of business was to let the General know that
Ethel and I were safe. I asked the guard if I could telephone Algiers.
He looked uncomfortable and called a lieutenant, who came out to take
a look at me. The lieutenant called a major, who also took a look. And
the major summoned a colonel. By that time I was fed up with being
treated like some strange exhibit in the zoo. My Irish temper was up.

'Look here,' I told the colonel. 'I was on the *Strathallen*, the troopship that was torpedoed last night. I am a member of General Eisenhower's personal staff. I want to call him and tell him we're safe. I want
to get his orders as to what to do next.' I was blazing with fury, clipping
my words as if they were machine-gun bullets. But it was not my anger
that got results; it was Eisenhower's name. Suddenly I was ushered
into an office. Suddenly coffee was being offered. Suddenly I was
shown a washstand where I could tidy up. Suddenly the operator
announced that she had Algiers on the line. And suddenly there was
dear, dull Tex's voice booming over the phone as if he were in the
next room.

'Tex,' I said, 'we're here.' It was a bit inadequate, I suppose, but it
was all I could get out.

'Oh, that's great,' he shouted. 'We heard about the *Strathallen*. We
have all been worried sick. I'm going to put you on to the General. He
wants to talk to you.'

The next voice was Ike's. 'Thank God you're safe,' he said. 'Are you
all right?' I told him I was fine, although a trifle out of uniform.
'Great,' he said. 'Now you tell headquarters to find a place for you to
spend the night and I'll send a plane for you and Ethel tomorrow.'

I felt a lot better when I hung up the phone. Just hearing Ike's voice
was comforting.

Chapter 12

When I turned, there was a tall, dark-haired lieutenant-colonel standing in the doorway looking at me as if I were some apparition.

'It's me, Dick!' I cried. 'I'm here! I've been torpedoed!'

He almost fell over. He was in such a state of shock that I will never forget it. Absolutely stunned. He had not the least idea that I was coming to North Africa. Now, seeing me this way, my hair in tangles and my clothes in tatters – well, it was hardly what he had expected when the guard had summoned him, saying merely that he had a visitor.

'Kay!' In one step he was beside me and I was in his arms. He held me so close it hurt, but it felt good. Even those brass buttons sticking into me. After a minute he held me away, took a long look at me and said, 'Good God! Are you really all right?'

'I'd be all right if I had something to eat,' I said, feeling rather faint suddenly. I had not had anything to eat for what seemed like a very long time.

'Wait here,' Dick ordered, and I sat obediently while he loped down the hall. He was back in seconds with a chocolate bar – one of those wonderful American bars with nuts.

'I have to find a place to stay tonight,' I said between bites.

'What do you mean? You're staying with me. You need someone to take care of you.' In no time at all I was soaking in a hot bath in the apartment Dick was sharing with another officer. When I got out, all scrubbed and shampooed, there was a strange wardrobe laid out on the bed: a T-shirt, a pair of Dick's pyjamas, some socks. Everything miles too big. I rolled up the sleeves and pant legs and made do.

'You look like a refugee from a Charlie Chaplin movie,' he said when I emerged in my makeshift outfit. No matter how I looked, I felt marvellous. Clean and dry and terribly, terribly hungry. Dick rummaged around to provide a meal: rations, some cheese his mother had sent him and a bottle of local red wine. It was delicious. I do believe, though, that even my water-sodden shoes would have tasted good.

Then we talked. And talked. And talked. That is, I talked. I had so much to tell him. How the General had asked me if I wanted to go to Algiers, how I hoped we might be able to get married in North Africa, how I had packed my little trousseau and how it had gone to the bottom of the sea. He let me talk myself out, and whenever I paused for breath, he would say that he could not believe I was there. He just could not believe it.

I was with Dick. I was safe. I was well fed – and well wined. It was all I could ask for, except just possibly a few hours' sleep. It was agony to keep my eyes open, but I fought to stay awake. This was just about the longest time I had ever spent with Dick. Our time together had always been terribly limited. I saw more of the General in most weeks than I had seen of Dick in all the time I had known him. I yawned. I couldn't help it. Dick picked me up and tucked me into his bed. 'Go to sleep, precious. I'll be in the next room if you want anything.'

When I woke up, I found a note from Dick and a musette bag on the bedside table. The General's plane had arrived and I was to leave for Algiers at noon, Dick wrote. He would be back to drive me to the plane – and the musette bag held some things I might need.

Sitting up in bed, I dug into the bag and discovered a treasure trove. A toothbrush. And toothpaste. Two handkerchiefs. A uniform tie. Cold cream. A cake of soap. A nail file. It was one of those times when one could say, 'Just what I wanted', and mean it. When Dick arrived to pick me up, I was back in uniform – what was left of it. The only thing that looked decent was my new tie.

I hated to leave, but the General's B-17 was waiting. There were tears in my eyes when the plane took off. On the way to the airfield, Dick had told me he was doing everything he could to get transferred to the front. He wanted a regimental command. This terrified me, but naturally I did not say so. What could I do? Dick was a career man, a

West Pointer, doing what he had been trained to do, and war was the big proving ground. It did not occur to me for one moment to protest.

That afternoon I walked into headquarters in Algiers. The General's office was in the St-Georges Hotel, one of the oldest and most elegant hotels in North Africa – or so I was informed; the elegance had to be taken on faith. The sprawling structure was cold and dreary. The bright mosaics of the lobby floor were hidden under the mud that everyone tracked in. In Algiers, I soon discovered, it was either mud or dust.

I reported to Tex, who told me that the General and Butch had left for the front that morning to spend Christmas with the troops, so there was really nothing for me to do. 'Why don't you do some shopping?' Tex suggested. 'You look a mite untidy. I'll get some ration coupons for you and Ethel.'

My billet was about five minutes away from the St-Georges in what appeared to be a very large, gleaming white villa set in spacious grounds. What it was – and I laughed when I saw the name on the entrance – was a maternity hospital, the Clinique Glycine. It was a pretty place. Glycine means wisteria, and there were great vines of it everywhere. The quarters were what one might expect – white, bare, utilitarian – but for the moment it was heaven.

Within a few days, at Ike's suggestion, I was to move to a small house shared by five WAC officers* whom I had known in London. We called ourselves the Powerhouse, because we all worked for top brass. These women became my very close friends, and from then on we shared living quarters throughout the war – in London, in France and in Germany.

After a good night's sleep, Ethel, who was also billeted in the Clinique Glycine, and I set off on a shopping spree. It was not much of a spree. The Germans had occupied Algiers and left nothing behind. The cupboards were bare.

---

* One was Ruth Briggs from Rhode Island, a witty, brilliant woman and a superb bridge player, so good that when Ike returned to Europe after the war to head SHAEFE, he would send a plane to wherever Ruth was stationed to bring her to Paris for an evening of bridge. Once she was flown in from Turkey, she told me. Mattie Pinette, Ike's secretary-stenographer, was from Maine and a very pleasant, bright woman with whom I worked closely. Then there was Martha Rogers, a beauty from Mississippi, Louise Anderson from Colorado and Arlene Drexel from Minnesota.

In one shop we thought for a moment that we had struck it rich. The proprietress assured us that she had some *magnifique* brassieres. And indeed they were. They were for a woman with a *poitrine magnifique*, someone along the lines of a super Jane Russell. Neither of us filled the bill – or the cup. Finally we found a boutique with some stock – enough so that we could buy two pairs of panties and two bras apiece. But such underpinnings! They had obviously been designed for ladies of a certain calling. Ethel and I giggled when we saw them and asked to see something else, but when the very charming saleswoman told us that there was nothing else, we did not hesitate for a moment. We bought. The panties were black mesh with a satin vine leaf strategically placed. The brassieres, also black, were cut out at the nipples. Ethel whispered. 'How did they know we were at the Clinique Glycine?' I assure you, however, that these were not for nursing mothers.

I seem to be dwelling at quite some length on the matter of underwear, but there are times when it is very important. To finish with the subject once and for all, I would say that of all my torpedoed treasures, I probably missed my woollies the most. Algiers was hellishly cold and damp most of the winter. I was able eventually to get replacements from the States – delivered courtesy of a very high-ranking officer. He would have been more than disconcerted, I suspect, if he had known that the package he dropped off at General Eisenhower's office contained half a dozen snuggies with matching vests – in blue.

Headquarters, when I came back from shopping, was all doom and gloom. Admiral Darlan had just been assassinated. I no longer remember all the ins and outs of the Darlan affair, but its political repercussions had been enormous. The General had appointed the Admiral head of the French military forces in North Africa. Although Darlan had been a German sympathizer, even a collaborator, the General had thought him the best choice under the circumstances. It was a choice, however, for which he was bitterly criticized by many people. Now Darlan was dead, shot by a young Algerian, and even more problems loomed. Ike was rushing back from the front.

When the General arrived at the office late the next day after something like thirty hours of nonstop driving through rain and sleet, his face wore that familiar grey pall of exhaustion. He was in a dismal state of mind. At the front he had seen for himself that mud was as brutal an

enemy as the Germans. Torrential rains had turned the ground everywhere into mud, immobilizing the big tanks and even the jeeps so that
attack was impossible. Now he had this Darlan affair to handle.

Only the inner circle was allowed to see how depressed he really was.
To the rest of the world, he was his usual brisk, charming and confident
self – just a bit weary, that was all. Now that he was back, headquarters
seemed to become electric. Cables were coded and shot off to Washington and London. The switchboards were constantly lit up. Memos were
dictated and rushed to various commanding officers, both British and
American. Consultations were set up. It was the same frantic pace I had
become accustomed to at Grosvenor Square.

Along about eight or nine, Ike slapped his hands on his desk and
said, 'Well, I've done all I can do here. Kay, get the car.'

'Where is it?' I asked.

That did it. He leaned back in his chair and laughed. 'My God,
welcome home, Kay. It seemed so natural to have you here and I had
so much on my mind that I forgot you just arrived. Let me take a look
at you.'

He stood up, put his hands on my shoulders and turned me around.
'Well, no damage that I can see. You're here. And you're safe. When
the news came through that the *Strathallen* had been hit, well, I don't
mind telling you I never did get to sleep that night.

'Now, let's forget this mess for a few hours. Even a general is allowed
to celebrate Christmas.'

Christmas! I had not realized what day it was. 'Merry Christmas,' I
said, and the two of us walked out of the St-Georges. Ike wished all
the guards a Merry Christmas and he returned their salutes. He seemed
to have cast off his fatigue.

'Come on, Beetle is holding dinner for us,' he said. 'He's having a
real American Christmas dinner – roast turkey and the fixings. Georgie
Patton sent him two live turkeys. God only knows where he liberated
them.'

Suddenly Ike was in great spirits. Five minutes later, we walked into
Beetle's villa and Ike started carolling, 'God rest ye merry gentlemen,
let nothing you dismay . . .' Everyone was there, and we all hugged and
kissed each other. It was great to see them again. Beetle's villa was
gorgeous – practically a palace, with gardens and terraces and two vast

8. Ike and Prime Minister Churchill   9. Ike with King George VI

10. Ike and his Commander in Chief, Franklin D. Roosevelt

left hand page:

11. Ike at headquarters with General Mark W. Clark

12. Ike stands between Bradley and Patton in the ruins of a liberated continent

13. Ike is greeted by a jubilant George S. Patton, as Generals Omar Bradley and Courtney Hodges look on

right hand page:

14. Ike and General George C. Marshall

15. Ike in conversation with Field Marshal Sir Bernard Montgomery

16. Ike in France, conferring with General Omar Bradley, Commander of the US First Army

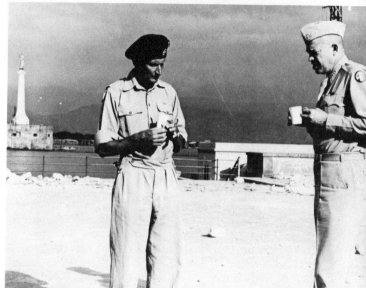

17. Telek poses on Ike's desk

18. Kay poses on her arrival in the United States with Telek beside her

drawing-rooms. Some of the floors were covered with mosaics of intricate design. There were lots of Oriental rugs and paintings.

Christmas dinner was just as it should have been: turkey and plum pudding and champagne. Beetle was a marvellous host. He was really at his best on occasions like this. At headquarters he was often a cold curmudgeon. He had to be. He was the Boss's other self. While Ike exerted his charms, Beetle played the role of villain – tough, obsessed with his job, driving others to the same point of exhaustion that he drove himself to. But at Telegraph Cottage and now here in his own villa in Algiers, the real Beetle was allowed to surface – witty, thoughtful, kind and with as much charm as Ike.

It was like being home again after all those weeks. Tex was there. Butch was there. Ethel was there. And best of all, the General was there. We talked a mile a minute, busy trying to catch up with all that had happened. Ethel and I described how it felt to be torpedoed, and we heard how Ike had caught a terrible cold in Gibraltar because his headquarters, deep inside the Rock, was cold and damp. 'The walls dripped so that there were puddles everywhere,' Butch said.

And that brought us to the subject of Telek. 'You should see that scamp,' Ike said. 'He's not housebroken yet.'

'Not housebroken yet!' I yelped. 'He was perfectly trained when he went off with Mickey. Well, almost perfectly. You just haven't been paying attention to him.'

Ike defended himself. 'I've had a couple of other things on my mind, you know.'

I felt like an idiot. I had not really expected the Boss, who had a war on his hands, to concern himself with the walking of a very small black Scottie. I apologized. Ike laughed. 'Don't worry. Now that you're here, Telek will straighten out.'

'I'm dying to see your house,' I told Ike. 'Is it as splendid as this one of Beetle's?'

'God, no!' he said. 'But it's still too splendid for my taste. You will see it tomorrow. You'll be over for breakfast, won't you?'

It all felt so right, so natural. 'Yes, thanks. I'll be over for breakfast,' I said happily. I was back where I belonged.

Chapter 13

Life in Algiers was not too much different from life in London. It was only the landscape that was different, and at that we still had those familiar barrage balloons dotting the sky. The weather was much like that of a late December or January in London – raw, grey, rainy – although there were occasional bright blue Mediterranean days when the breezes were deceptively balmy. Headquarters routine was almost exactly the same. The General still had to spend much of his time and energy forging a unified command. He was still inundated with paperwork. He still made constant inspection tours – of battlefronts now, rather than training camps. And my job was still the same. The only difference was that in the car's glove compartment I not only kept the usual maps and supply of cigarettes and a Western in case of delays; I also had a bottle of paregoric – the panacea for Algerian tummy.

But the first morning I drove up the long palm-lined driveway to Villa dar el Ouad, the most modest house in a compound of luxurious villas, it seemed as if I had been transferred to some exotic paradise. The villa was high on a hill above the city. Far below, the Mediterranean stretched sparkling blue to the horizon. There were sentries on the terrace who saluted smartly as I walked in. Unlike the Dorchester or Telegraph Cottage, this residence was heavily guarded. One had to show a pass before being allowed to enter the compounds. There were guards patrolling the driveway and the grounds. Anti-aircraft guns were dug in here, there and everywhere.

The moment I walked through the door all this was forgotten as a ball of black fur came rocketing at me, barking furiously and wagging his tail with joy. Telek! He remembered me! Breakfast was a long and

happy party that day. Telek sat in my lap and had half my bacon.
Moaney and Hunt told me that I had better get cracking and start house-
breaking him. I cheerfully scolded everyone, including Mickey, for
having spoiled Telek. Ike growled that he would like it if just one
morning he could get his coffee the way he liked it. Hot, goddamnit!
Butch said all he wanted for breakfast was a bowl of cold aspirin. He
had gone out for a second Christmas celebration after we had left
Beetle's the night before. It was nearly nine before Ike said, 'Well, we
better get going. We've got a war to win.' I could not have been
happier as I drove off with Telek at my side.

By the time I drove the Boss home that evening, I felt as if I had been
in Algiers for months. 'You're staying for supper tonight,' he told me.
'We've got a lot of bridge to play.' Before supper Butch gave me a tour
of the villa. Villa dar el Ouad, he informed me, meant Villa of the
Family. The name was appropriate, I agreed, but the house had no
family feeling about it. It lacked the cosiness of Telegraph Cottage on
the one hand, and on the other it seemed drearily middle class compared
with Beetle's beautiful place. When I mentioned this to Butch, he
groaned dramatically. 'If you only knew,' he said. 'I had a terrible time
getting Ike to go this high. He kept barking at me that he wanted
something small and simple. I kept telling him that this was not London.
He had to have a place that was compatible with his rank.'

Just as we finished dinner, we heard the old familiar air-raid noises.
German planes were bombing the harbour. We rushed out to the
terrace. It was like some giant fireworks display. Streamers of lights
streaking the sky, arcing up at the planes overhead; monster explosions below. We had snatched up our helmets as we went out, but
when the shrapnel started clattering down on the terrace helmets did
not seem like much protection, and we retreated inside, where Telek,
the wisest of us all, had stayed whimpering under the sofa.

Our retreat was only as far as the bridge table, which had been set up
in the small sitting-room as close to the fireplace as possible. Ike had the
place of honour in front of the fire, and although he complained that
his backside was getting roasted, he was obviously glad of the warmth.
He was developing another of his colds. Sometimes it seemed as if his
colds had colds. The night before at Beetle's, he had been sneezing and
complaining of a raw throat. Tonight he was a disaster area. His nose

was running and so were his eyes. There were great puffy bags under his eyes. He was obviously feverish. But woe to the person who dared mention his condition or suggest he might be better off in bed with a hot toddy and some aspirin.

Ike detested being ill, and he detested even more having anyone comment on his health. Every once in a while, Butch would take his life in his hands and tell the Boss that he should get some rest. Ike would practically bite his head off. This particular cold turned into the flu, and Ike was really miserable, miserable enough to stay in bed for four days before crawling back to the office, still sick and ashen pale. There was no point in even hinting that he go home. I knew just how he felt – there was so much at stake and he was responsible for all of it.

The North African operation was not going well. In fact, things were very bad. There were defeats – and glum expectations of more defeats. The walls of Ike's office were covered with big maps showing our positions and those of the Germans. Time after time during the past week I had gone into the office to find Ike sitting in his chair in front of the smoky fireplace, the only source of heat in the whole office, a long pointer in his hand, staring at situation maps. Sometimes he would lift the pointer and trace a tentative shift of position, then impatiently tap it on the floor as he dismissed the idea and slump back again in his chair.

'It's bad, Kay,' he would say. 'We weren't prepared for these rains, this mud.' He would fret about the quality of the leadership at the front. 'Our officers don't have the experience. Don't know how to handle their men or their weapons.' These were not criticisms, just statements of facts. Facts that had to be faced. The British complained that the American soldiers were green – 'apple green' was the way one general described them.

On top of that, the Boss was involved in the preparations for the Casablanca Conference. As the 'guest list' firmed up, I got very much excited. The PM and President Roosevelt would be there. So would General Marshall, Admiral Lord Louis Mountbatten and just about all of the top Western statesmen and military brass (Stalin had sent his regrets). The security arrangements alone were staggering. It was easy to understand why Ike did not want to sit home by the fire with hot lemonade and take care of his health.

I was far more interested in the conferees than I was in the agenda. I have never been politically minded, and in those days I was more than a trifle star-dazzled. Working with great men, men whose actions affected people's lives all over the world, has a very seductive glamour about it. The men themselves were very seductive. I don't mean that in a sexual sense, but they would not have had the power they possessed if they did not also possess this magnetism. And the great men I met while working for the General all possessed it. Even untidy, unprepossessing Harry Hopkins, who seemed to be President Roosevelt's unofficial envoy to almost everyone and every place; even cool, aristocratic Mountbatten – and most definitely President Roosevelt and the PM. They had what people today refer to as charisma – lots of it.

Tex stopped by my desk one morning and said, 'The General laughed twice. Guess that means he feels better.' Tex adored Ike, but somehow he always managed to rub him the wrong way – mostly through his eagerness to do a perfect job. His overwhelming pre-occupation with detail made him seem officious, but it was the very quality that made him indispensable, if a bit of a pest. Whenever Ike did not feel up to snuff, it was always Tex who got the brunt of it, and he could never understand why. He would have done anything to lighten the Boss's load. But nobody could. There was nothing any of us could do. Ike's blood pressure went up so sharply during this difficult January that we were very much worried. It wavered between 175 and 185. He was working long hours, looked ghastly – and there was absolutely nothing we could do to help him.

His healthy constitution and his determination pulled him through, but the Casablanca Conference did not do much for his state of mind. The war news was bad, and the top leaders, while not criticizing Ike openly, were not praising him either. 'The Boss's neck is in the noose. If anything more goes wrong, he's had it,' Butch said. But the General's neck was not the chief item on the agenda. Casablanca was the place where President Roosevelt and Prime Minister Churchill agreed that they would accept nothing less than unconditional surrender from the Germans.

There was one participant in the Casablanca Conference who was absolutely wholeheartedly behind Eisenhower, and that was General

George Catlett Marshall, Chief-of-Staff of the United States Army – Ike's boss. He terrified me. He was cold and austere and terribly, terribly formal. He came to visit Ike in Algiers after the conference, and Telek and I immediately got off on the wrong foot with him. I had driven the two men to Ike's villa, where Marshall was going to spend the night. When we arrived, Eisenhower said, 'Come on in, Kay. I know you're dying to see Telek.' I followed the generals in, and Telek came running. He had just discovered that he had a tail, and his favourite game was to chase it around and around. I soon got the very strong impression that General Marshall was not as charmed by his antics as Ike and I were, so I disappeared into the little sitting-room with Telek while the generals adjourned to the drawing-room.

Soon I overheard Ike say, 'Let me show you to your room.' The two men started up the stairs, and Telek, who never wanted to be left out of any excitement, jumped out of my lap and followed them. Butch told me the the rest of the story when he came downstairs, red-faced, Telek firmly under his arm.

'You know what this beast just did?'

I lifted my eyebrows.

'He peed on the General's bed.'

'I don't believe it,' I said.

'He did. Ike was leaning over, pushing down on the mattress to show Marshall how comfortable it was, and Telek jumped up on the bed. He went right there on the spread, and then before I could grab him, he trotted up to the head of the bed and lifted his leg on the pillow.'

'Oh, my dear God!' I said. 'What did Ike say?'

' "Get that goddamned dog out of here" – that's what he said.'

Telek was in deep disgrace for a few days. I took him home with me and did not allow him to show his nose at the villa until General Marshall was safely out of Algiers.

I don't know whether this incident had anything to do with it, but I always had the distinct impression that General Marshall would have been just as happy if I did not exist. He always shook hands when we met, but there was never any indication that he saw me as a person. Certainly he never addressed a personal word to me. This was not at all out of character. He was the only person I ever knew who worked closely with the General and never, ever, once called him Ike. It was always General Eisenhower. I thought Marshall was a cold fish.

Butch insisted that I did him an injustice, that while Marshall had a stiff exterior, he was very fond of the Boss. I snorted, but he may have been right. I know that Marshall spent an afternoon with Butch discussing the Boss's health. Marshall did not approve of Ike's regimen. He was working too hard, spending too much time in the office. Four hours a day should be sufficient, according to Marshall. 'I'm charging you with seeing that General Eisenhower cuts down,' he told Butch.

When Butch told me about this, he said, 'How am I going to persuade Ike to work a four-hour day? And how in holy hell am I going to get him to have a daily massage?' That had been another of General Marshall's orders. Butch was really in a funk. 'Why don't *you* tell Ike he has to have a massage?' he suggested. I begged off. Eisenhower could not have been more charming and kindly towards us, but he was not the commanding general for nothing. He was tough and he was in charge. No one was going to tell him what to do. Not Butch. And certainly not Kay Summersby.

We decided that the only thing to do was report General Marshall's instructions to the Boss and then see what happened. As it turned out, General Marshall had told Ike himself that he should use a masseur. Butch managed to come up with one and even managed to pin Ike down to a time and place for his first massage – his bedroom at six in the evening. Afterwards, Ike came down to supper saying that it had been very relaxing indeed – but that first massage turned out to be the only one. Somehow he never managed to be able to find the time again. Ike would faithfully carry out any of General Marshall's orders concerning the conduct of the war, but when it came to what he considered 'sissy stuff', Ike simply dug his heels in.

He was willing to concede that he needed some exercise to work off his nervous tension. 'I need another Telegraph Cottage,' he said longingly one night. 'Well, that's easy enough,' Butch said. And it must have been, because it was only a few days later that we drove ten miles outside the city to inspect the new secret hideaway. This one was a white stucco farmhouse with a red-tiled roof – rather shabby, but quite comfortable, and there were tennis courts and stables on the property. It had its charm, including a view of the sea, and it was private. Butch informed us that it was called Sailor's Delight (I'm inclined to think that the General's naval aide christened it himself).

It was at Sailor's Delight that Ike and I went riding together for the first time. Ike was an excellent horseman. 'West Point,' he told me when I remarked on it. 'I used to ride farm horses bareback when I was a boy in Kansas, but at the Point they taught us to ride like gentlemen.'

Butch had arranged for three magnificent Arab stallions to be put at the General's disposal. I had never been on anything like these beasts. They were chestnut in colour, with flowing manes, and truly beautiful. The only horses I have ever seen that were more impressive were those ridden by the spahis who guarded General de Gaulle's palace in Algiers. The spahis were mounted on pure white Arab stallions that looked like the horses one sees in a dream. Our horses were practically wild. If we allowed them to touch each other, they would rear and snort and go to it. You had to hit them with your riding crop as hard as you could to get them to obey you. The first time it happened, I was scared to death. My horse was dancing about on his hind legs, and I was not sure that I was strong enough to control him. What if one of those great hooves should strike the General in the head? I finally summoned every bit of strength I had and got the horse into a gallop across the fields. It was a good while before I dared to come up to Ike and his mount again that afternoon.

It was not the best riding country. It was stony underfoot, even in the wooded areas. The Army had cleared the area and there were guards posted – it seemed as if they were behind every bush – so we felt quite safe. We also felt as if we were on parade. There was always a security man riding discreetly behind us, in addition to the sharp-shooter guards. It is an eerie feeling, knowing that your every move is being watched. Ike often complained about it, not only while riding, but as it affected every phase of his life.

'I live in a goldfish bowl,' he said. 'There is never a moment when I don't feel that someone is peering at me.' He was right. Someone always was peering at him. And it had to be that way.

We were a strange couple. Ike was very correctly dressed, and he looked fabulous. I, on the other hand, had a hit-and-miss outfit: jodhpurs that had been sent from the States, Army shoes, a uniform shirt and a kerchief over my hair. We would leave the office in the middle of the afternoon several days a week, drive out to Sailor's Delight, ride for a couple of hours, shower, have a drink and supper and then drive back to Algiers. Once in a while we would spend Saturday night and all day Sunday, doing all the things we had done at Telegraph Cottage. We played bridge, sat outdoors when it was warm enough, knocked a few golf balls around on the grass and practised target shooting. My little Beretta had gone down with the *Strathallen*, but Ike had got me another, which he insisted I carry with me at all times. I used to sleep with it under my pillow.

While Sailor's Delight was never the real home that Telegraph Cottage had been, it did more for Ike than any number of massages ever could have done.

Chapter 14

One night as I was driving Ike home, there, standing in the drive, was a familiar figure in a familiar costume. Winston Churchill in his siren suit.

'Jesus Christ!' Ike said. 'What's he doing here?'

The General jumped out of the car, and after a moment's hesitation I followed. It was hard to know whether to behave as an impersonal driver or as a pleased and surprised acquaintance. Churchill settled that question promptly. He waved his big cigar at me and said, 'Well, Kay, I thought I might find you here. How do you like driving on the wrong side of the road?' It turned out that the PM had been meeting with President Roosevelt in Turkey and had decided to drop in on Ike on the way home. This was to be the first of many visits from the PM, who enjoyed what he referred to as 'lolling around' in Algiers. He definitely liked the warmth and the sun. Now that the season had changed, it was a far brighter world than that of grey, austerity-ridden London. Churchill and the General were always openly happy to be together, laughing and chatting like two old school chums.

Eisenhower immediately went to work planning a luncheon in the PM's honour. It turned out to be the luncheon of luncheons. As Ike worked out the guest list, he said, 'Do you realize, Kay, that almost all my guests will outrank me?' There were the Prime Minister; General de Gaulle; Sir Alan Brooke, who was Chief of the Imperial General Staff; Admiral Cunningham, who had been named Allied Naval Commander for the Mediterranean, and half a dozen others who boasted more stars and stripes than Ike. The protocol people were in a tizzy trying to work out a seating plan.

I don't know whether it was a result of this luncheon party or not – I suppose it really had nothing to do with it – but just a few days later Ike got his fourth star, the one that made him a full general. That night Ike broke out the champagne and we had an impromptu party just for our headquarters group. He was very, very happy that evening. I'll never forget the sheer pleasure that radiated from him. I remember thinking, There's a man who has never had very much fun in his life. The General was always very charming, always had that grin at the ready, but underneath it all he was a very serious and lonely man who worried, worried, worried. I used to feel that it was a real achievement whenever we were able to divert him so that he forgot his problems for a little while and was able to have fun.

Life in Algiers was not all promotions and parties. Not at all. I learned what life was like at the front. Miserably. My first combat drive was to Constantine, Tebessa and the Kasserine Pass. Things were very bad up there – so bad that just a few days after our visit, we suffered one of the great defeats of the war at the Kasserine Pass. The trek to the front was nothing like our carefree drives through the English countryside en route to a training camp or base. Now we travelled in convoy – a scout car leading, then the General's big car with the flag flying, a weapons carrier, a backup car in case something happened to the General's car and finally a second scout car bringing up the rear. The highway was two lanes wide, and the traffic was remorseless, all of it military. Trucks high-balling it up to the front with supplies; more trucks racketing back empty to pick up more supplies. Coping with those trucks on that narrow, pot-holed highway was an exhausting experience. The drivers were hard-boiled men, and the General's flag meant nothing to them. I was constantly terrified of being forced off the road and either being up to my axles in mud or tilted at a forty-five-degree angle in a ditch.

In addition to the driving problems, there was the ever-present danger of strafing attacks. I said to the General, 'If we're strafed, it's every man for himself. I'm going to stop and run as far away from this car as I can. Don't expect me to hold the door for you.'

'Fine,' said Ike. 'Agreed.' I looked up in my rear-view mirror and I could see the corners of his mouth twitching. It struck me how ridiculous I must have sounded, and I started to laugh. We got into one of those fits of laughter that children sometimes enjoy, when it is next to impossible to stop. There were laughter tears in my eyes by the time we finally sputtered into silence. After that, whenever we set off on one of these trips to the front lines, Ike would say, 'Now it's every man for himself. Right?' It was a bit silly, but silliness helps – especially when you are scared to death.

The truck drivers saluted me with whistles, wolf calls and all kinds of interesting proposals, completely uninhibited by the presence of my back-seat passenger. This used to make Ike absolutely livid. I assured him that it did not bother me in the least, but he still became very rigid and red when he heard the remarks that were tossed my way from the cabs of the trucks. I felt it was rather flattering, particularly considering that I was no longer the trim, tailored driver I had been in England. Driving in the combat zone, I wore boots, slacks, a man's battle blouse and an old Air Corps flying jacket that I had managed to scrounge. To top it all, I had a steel helmet. Ike used to tease me about trying to look like General Patton.

It took us about twenty-six hours to reach the front. At Tebessa we picked up a scout car to guide us to the command post. Ike went straight on up to the front to see conditions for himself and talk to the men. He always felt that it was very important for the men to see the commanding general and know that he did not spend all his time safely behind the lines.

I stayed at the command post. No one paid any attention to me as I watched and listened. The situation could not have been worse. There were bad casualties and talk of retreat. As the hours wore on I realized that they were all concerned about the General and that no one knew exactly where he was. The battle lines were fluid and it would have been very easy for his driver to mistake the enemy's patch of mud for our patch of mud. I decided to get some sleep so that if anything happened, I would be rested. They put me in the VIP tent, which differed from the others only in that it had a pebble flooring instead of the usual wall-to-wall mud. I spread out my sleeping bag on a cot and wriggled in completely dressed – boots and all. At one point I woke up and heard the General's voice outside. He was back safe, then. I heard him tell someone that he wanted to get a couple of hours' sleep before starting back.

'Your driver's in there,' someone said. 'We'll wake her.'

'Jesus Christ, don't do that. Let her sleep,' Ike growled. The next thing I knew, he was in the tent, spreading out his sleeping bag on another cot. In minutes he was snoring like a one-man artillery bombardment.

A few hours later we were ready to leave. Ike had on his heavy cold-weather gear and a wool hat pulled down over his ears, but he looked pinched with cold. He was very tired and very depressed. The commanding officer was anxious to get us out of there. A German breakthrough was expected within hours. He urged Ike to fly back to Algiers rather than risk driving into a German-occupied zone. Ike refused. We needed all our aircraft for fighting, he said, not for ferrying generals about.

There was a somewhat amusing sequel to this particular trip. When we were back in Algiers, Tex said, 'I think you ought to know, Kay, that there's a lot of gossip about you and the Boss. People are saying that you—uh—uh . . .' He was too embarrassed to continue. 'That we what?' I asked. 'That you, uh – well, that you sleep together when you go on trips.'

I stared at him and then burst out laughing. 'We did, Tex. We did!' Poor Tex looked completely bewildered until I told him what had happened. Then he shook his head. 'Don't worry, Tex. If anyone says anything more, just tell them that I'm engaged to be married and that the General and I are certainly not interested in each other that way. It's ridiculous,' I said. At the time I thought it was all very funny.

Sharing the hardships and the dangers of trips like this to the front actually did bring Ike and me closer together, although never as close as gossip would have it. His worries were my worries. Being at the front with him, seeing his utter frustration over losing a battle because of inexperience and weather increased my understanding of the pressures on him – including the pressures he put on himself. And he knew that I understood. He would often look over at me in the course of a conversation and say, 'Kay knows what I'm talking about.' And I did. I did indeed. I also recognized the emotional and physical toll these trips took of him.

I got my first grey hairs in Algiers, and Ike lost a lot of his hair there. People who think war is glamorous and exciting are people who believe what they see in the cinema. It is not. It is dirty, tiring, frightening. Ask the men who spent that war in the mud. They know. Eisenhower knew. And so did I.

Chapter 15

My divorce papers were on the way. In one of his typically thoughtful gestures, the General had instructed London that the documents were to be sent to Algiers by diplomatic pouch, which meant that they would arrive in a matter of days rather than weeks. The next time I saw Dick, who had just been promoted to full colonel, I was able to say, 'Now you're in for it. I'm a free woman.'

'Well you'll just have to hold your horses,' he laughed. 'I'm busy right now.' He was in Algiers for a few hours on his way to join his regiment. This was the first time I had seen him in months, and Ike had given me the day off. The fields outside Algiers were bright with poppies, and the air was filled with the scent of jasmine. We had a marvellous time at Sailor's Delight, swimming and playing tennis and making plans for the future. It would be a June wedding, we decided – if conditions permitted.

Things could not possibly have turned out any better, I thought. I no longer had to worry about Dick's being at the front. After the disastrous winter, spring had brought a change in Allied fortunes, and for all practical purposes the North African campaign was over. There had even been a victory parade in Tunis. The parade had been a terrible ordeal – hours in the blazing heat and smothering dust. I had thought I would pass out, but there had been one wicked pleasure that had kept me on my feet. General Montgomery was also on the reviewing stand. He deserved every salute that was flung at him. His Eighth Army had fought well. Monty was a shrewd, careful strategist, and his men were tough. But he was also a pain in the neck. Worse – he hated women. He was squirmingly uncomfortable in their company. My presence on the reviewing stand took the edge off his pleasure. And I was bitchy enough to be glad of it.

Monty was the only person in the whole Allied command whom I disliked. Not only was he a supercilious, woman-hating little martinet, but he did things that used to make me so indignant that I would say to the General, 'How can you stand it? Why don't you tell him off?'

Ike would shrug his shoulders. 'Don't let him bother you. He just can't help it,' he would tell me. I thought he jolly well could help it. He used to do mean, petty things. For example, when the General visited Eighth Army headquarters, Monty would ask him to bring along American cigarettes. He would also try to mooch the very last packet the General had in his pocket. Then Monty, the great non-smoker who would never allow Ike to smoke in his presence, would distribute the cigarettes to his men, never giving Ike or the Americans any credit. He was a perpetual thorn in Ike's side. That is exactly how the General used to describe him. 'He's a thorn in my side,' he would say wearily, 'a thorn in my side.' And he was to become even more infuriating after we left North Africa.

Apart from Monty, everything seemed to be coming up roses. Or orange blossoms. Every day was full of sunshine. Algiers gleamed, and the Mediterranean seemed to dance in the sun. Romance was in the air. Even Telek had been bitten by the love bug and become a husband and father. I was a bit jealous of Telek's romance. Butch had gone to Washington for a few days, and when he returned he had brought a surprise: a wife for Telek. A terrible little bitch, I thought. Her name was Caacie (for Canine Auxiliary Air Corps), pronounced 'Khaki', Butch announced. 'Stupid,' I said. 'Any stupider than Telek?' he asked. 'Much stupider,' I said firmly. But Caacie she was, and Caacie she remained.

Her first act on meeting Telek was to bite him, which did not endear her to me, but she soon accepted him, and he, the idiot, adored her. He was the very kindest of husbands, and she rewarded him with a litter of three of the most adorable jet black puppies I had ever seen. Telek was not one for humdrum domesticity, however. His idea of the good life was to go off to the office every morning with the Boss and me, sleep under my desk during the day and snuggle up to Ike for ear-scratching and stomach-rubbing when we drove back home again.

Headquarters routine continued at a somewhat less hectic pace, and despite the fact that Ike had started working on the invasion of Sicily in real earnest (the code name of this operation was Husky), there was a bit of time for bridge, for riding, for just sitting in the sun and talking. It was a time to catch one's breath before the next big push. One day I became very much concerned about Ike. He was all tied up in knots about something. As the day wore on, he became terribly withdrawn. I was truly worried when I drove him home from the office and he just sat there, slumped in the back seat. Ike was a master of small talk and always enjoyed chatting when we were going back and forth, but now he was silent. When we reached the villa, he got out heavily like an old man. I was positive that he was ill.

'Kay, come on in,' he said, just as he said it every night. We went into the little sitting-room. Ike lit a cigarette. I asked him if he would like me to make him a drink. 'That would be a good idea,' he said. 'Make one for yourself, too.' I was about ready to beg, 'Please, can't you tell me what's the matter?' when he said, 'Kay, I am just going to give this to you straight. Dick has been killed.'

I looked at him. I heard the words, but they had no impact. Very calmly I asked what had happened. 'It was a week ago,' he said, 'but the news just came through this morning. It got lost at the message centre. Dick was with another officer, inspecting a minefield. There was no danger; the mines had been marked. But the other man stumbled and caught his foot on a trip wire. Dick was killed. The other man was badly wounded.

'I am very, very sorry, Kay.'

I said nothing. I walked into the hall and paced up and down listening to my heels thud on the tiles in a mournful rhythm. 'Dick has been killed. Dick has been killed.' After a while I went back to Ike. 'It's all right,' I said. 'I'm all right.' And I burst into tears.

Ike put his arm around my shoulders and led me over to the sofa. 'Go ahead,' he said. 'Go ahead and cry. It's the only way. Just let it out.' And I did. I cried and cried. All the time Ike was there holding me, saying soothing things, not really saying anything, just making noises. 'There, there,' he'd say, and pat me. 'You'd better blow your nose,' he kept telling me, and would hand me a handkerchief. I would obediently stop for a moment, blow my nose and then start bawling again.

Finally Ike said, 'You'll make yourself sick. Come now, blow your nose again.' He was so kind, so gentle. I tried to do exactly as he told me. My sobs died down to sniffles. He handed me a fresh handkerchief. I looked at the pile of crumpled handkerchiefs on the floor and, curious, asked, 'Where did you get all those?'

'I called Mickey before we left headquarters,' Ike said. 'I told him to leave a dozen on the table.'

'I'll be back in a minute,' he told me, 'and then we can talk.' I stayed there huddled into a corner of the sofa, stunned. He came back with a cup of tea and spooned it into me as if I were a baby. And in between hiccups and sobs, I managed to get it down.

'Now let me tell you what I think,' he said. 'I think you ought to go out to Sailor's Delight for a few days. There's nobody there. You can be alone. Get yourself straightened out a bit. Go riding. Activity helps. I have learned that myself.'

That seemed like a good idea, and Butch drove me out there that night. I walked back and forth on the terrace for hours and finally went to bed. I lay there listening to the rustlings and chirpings around that rustic Algerian house, and when the sun rose I was still lying there listening. My love was dead. And I was alone.

This self-pity made me suddenly angry. Who was I to feel sorry for myself? I was alive. I should be thinking of Dick, not myself. And at this, I plunged even deeper into misery. I realized in the bright light of morning that I knew very little about Dick. I could think about the way his eyes crinkled when he laughed, the way he walked, about his devotion to the Army, the way he called me 'precious', but not much more. Ours had been a wartime romance. There had been weeks and months when we had not seen each other. Each time we met it had been as exciting as a first date, and probably for that very reason our knowledge of each other had not progressed much beyond the first-date stage. Ike knew more about me and had seen more of my family than Dick ever had. I knew very little of Dick's family. It was as if we had met and loved in a vacuum. Now when I tried to mourn him, I discovered that I did not really know the man I was grieving for.

I dressed hurriedly and had one of the stallions brought around. That day I rode until I was exhausted. I was full of the most immense sorrow – for Dick, for myself, for all that might have been. But I had touched bottom. The realization that I had never really known him was as shocking as the knowledge that now I never would.

Chapter 16

After a few days, I came back to Algiers. Ike had given me valuable advice the evening that he broke the news that Dick had been killed. 'Activity helps,' he had said. 'I have learned that myself.'

He did his best to keep me busy. When I think back on everything that he did for me in those first days, I wonder how he found the time to be so supportive. 'Kay, I've got a job for you,' he told me one morning. 'I know you can keep secrets, so I'm going to tell you a big one.' And he paused. Ike was always very good at leading up to something. He would have you sitting on the edge of your chair, holding your breath, waiting for him to come to the point. And he would sit there throwing out tantalizing little hints, building up to the climax.

'We're going to have a very important person visit us. The biggest VIP you can imagine.' He paused again. I was thinking furiously. The biggest VIP? Who could be bigger than the ones we had had? Bigger than Winston Churchill?

'The King of England!' he announced. 'King George the Sixth is coming to North Africa,' he said. Ike was always enchanted by royalty – kings and queens and princes and princesses, palaces and crowns. They had a fairy-tale aura for him. When I had told him once that I had met the then Prince of Wales at a dance during my first season in London, he was fascinated and asked all kinds of questions about him.

'I'd like you to drive me to meet His Majesty, Kay. If you feel up to it, that is,' the General said. 'The British will be escorting him about most of the time, but when he is in Algiers I will be his host. And I'd like you to be his driver.'

The King of England! That was exciting. In those days, there was still a tremendous amount of glamour attached to the throne. The then Duke of York had been forced on to a throne he had never wanted when his brother abdicated to marry Mrs Simpson. The shy new King had won the hearts and support of his subjects during these very difficult times by the example he set.

I had hero-worshipped the Prince of Wales. I made him into a superman – handsome, democratic and very wise – and I was not alone. The whole kingdom was charmed by him. But when as King Edward VIII he decided that he preferred one woman over all of us, we were hurt. I was, at least. It was terribly romantic, the idea of a King of England giving up his throne for the woman he loved, but what about the rest of us? As the General had said once, 'He lost sight of his duty.'

Oh, yes, I felt up to driving King George. There was no question about it. 'That would be smashing,' I said. 'Oh, I'd like that. I'd like that very much. Thank you so much.'

'Well, that's settled,' Ike said. 'You better go see the security people. You'll need to be briefed.' The security measures were fantastic, all designed so that no one would think that any extraordinary security measures were being taken. Algiers was teeming with spies and informers, so the whole operation had to be carried out as if nothing, absolutely nothing, out of the ordinary were going on.

The King was travelling as General Lyon. General Eisenhower would pick up General Lyon at the airport, welcome him and escort him to General Gale's villa, where he would be staying, in his big armour-plated Cadillac. I hated that car, and we rarely used it. The armour plating made it so heavy that not only did the tyres blow out all the time, but one had to really know the car in order to apply the brakes effectively. It was so heavy that the momentum would carry it three times beyond usual braking distance. But it was just the right automobile for the King. It was bulletproof and practically bomb-proof, barring a direct hit. I sighed when I realized that it was the logical car and prayed that my braking would have the necessary finesse. I practised for a couple of mornings in the compound to make sure I had the feel of the unwieldly vehicle.

When the day came, the Boss got into the car just a little more pressed and creased and polished than usual, if that was possible. Butch was going to accompany us. His job would be to hold the door for the King, who would sit in Ike's customary seat – on the right in back. After the King was comfortably settled, Ike would go around and get in on the left side of the car, where I would be holding the door. Then Butch and I would scramble into our seats in front, and off we would go.

We had rehearsed this, enlisting two of the sentries on duty at the villa to play the parts of King George and General Eisenhower. As we drove through Algiers, Butch said, 'I'm as nervous as if I were going to open on Broadway with only one rehearsal.' As we drove through the city, the customary two-motor-cycle escort rode ahead of us to clear traffic; there was absolutely nothing visibly different about this trip. Butch often accompanied the General on his trips here and there, and no one could possibly spot how extra clean and smart we all were. I had spent the night before washing my hair and polishing my shoes and buttons. I was squeaky clean – or as squeakily clean as it was possible to be in dusty, gritty Algiers.

Just as I drew up in the designated far corner of the airfield, there was the King's Lancaster dropping down out of the blue. It was one of the fastest landings I have ever seen. All the top British brass were there to greet the King, having come by different routes and in a variety of vehicles so that there would not be an obvious concentration of high-muck-a-mucks.

The plane door swung open. The King appeared, came rapidly down the steps, returned the salutes of the welcoming committee and smiled. Movie cameras were whirring away, salutes were being snapped off and there was an air of great, although sedate, excitement. Eventually Ike escorted the King to the Cadillac, and everything went just as we had rehearsed it with our sentry stand-ins. The King seemed very cheerful, even rather excited. He told the General that it was the first time he had been out of England in years. He remarked on the warmth and said that he was looking forward to spending some afternoons on the beach, swimming and soaking up the sun. He talked about his two daughters and said he wished he could give them the opportunity to get some of this sun.

All this time, as we wove our way back through Algiers, the King kept saluting as British soldiers would do a double take and snap to attention when they recognized the man in the car with General Eisenhower. The General also saluted. Butch muttered to me out of the side of his mouth, 'What do you think? Should *I* salute?' I whispered back, 'Of course – you're an officer. Go ahead.' So he did.

When we arrived at General Gale's villa, Butch rushed to open the door for His Majesty and I did the same for the General. Then, quite unexpectedly, 'Your Majesty,' said the General, 'I would like to present my naval aide, Captain Harry Butcher.' Butch got red in the face, but drew himself up stiffly and saluted. The King smiled and held out his hand.

Then Ike beckoned to me and presented me to His Majesty, saying that I was a British subject who was on loan to him. I was petrified. I did not know what to do. I was a civilian, so it would not have been correct for me to salute. On the other hand, I was in uniform, so I did not think it would be correct to curtsy. I would have given anything to have an Emily Post at my elbow to whisper instructions. I finally bobbed a half curtsy and stuck out my hand, saying, 'How do you do, sir?' but the King stood there like a statue. Whether he was struck speechless by my impudence or simply, like me, did not know what to do, I'll never know.

'Your Majesty,' Ike said, trying again. 'This is Miss Kay Summersby, who is a British subject and now on duty at my headquarters as my personal driver.'

The King nodded and turned to General Gale, and they started towards the house. I felt frustrated – and a little hurt.

When the King came back from his tour, I drove him on the return trip to the airfield. This time he was not the chatty, confiding, enthusiastic man we had picked up two weeks earlier, but utterly silent and glum. There was a reason. He had been stricken by Algerian tummy, sometimes known as the GI's – an undignified ailment that was no respecter of rank or royalty. We all carried paregoric to gentle its ravages.

I had hoped that as he left, he might shake my hand, bestow a smile or even a few words on me, but he departed without ever having recognized one of his most loyal subjects. I did not feel as crushed as I might have felt: during the ride to the airport, the King had not said one single, solitary word to the General either.

The summer rolled on. War has its own kind of accelerated time, and the sad days of early June began to fade into the past. Even the first precarious months in North Africa, now that we were involved with the Sicilian invasion, seemed ancient history. It was today that counted. The momentum increased, slackened, picked up again.

I was spending more time than ever with Ike. Even in London with our seven-day weeks, I occasionally visited Mummy and Evie, lunched with friends, went to the odd cocktail party. But now I trod a very narrow path. From breakfast to the final nightcap, I went where Ike went. Once when Omar Bradley was coming to dinner, Ike and I were a bit late. When we walked in, Brad said, 'Here they are. Ike and his shadow.' After that, whenever he saw Ike without me, he would ask, 'Where's your shadow?' When the General had an official engagement in the evening and did not need me, I would go straight home, wash my hair and go to bed. I never went out.

All of us in Ike's little wartime family felt very, very close. There was an intense quality to our relationships. And an idealism. There was no place in our group for pettiness or selfishness or any of the other less pleasant aspects of human nature. We all had a sense of working together for a better world. We were not the least bit cynical. We believed this, and we talked about it. Not that there was not a lot of savage political infighting, but that was on another level. In the little family that Ike had created, peace and trust and love prevailed. Our relationships seemed deeper, more meaningful and richer than any we had known before.

Butch and I were talking about this one day sitting on the terrace with our sundown drinks. We agreed that there was a sweetness about our relationships that was quite extraordinary. Ike came out and asked, 'What are you two being so serious about?' When we told him, he nodded. 'I know what you mean,' he said. 'There are times when we demand the best of ourselves,' I remember him saying. 'We're always better than we think.'

I was a better worker, at least, than I had ever believed I would or could be. Ike had recently given me a new responsibility: answering his mail from the public. 'I just can't keep up with this mail,' he complained. 'How would you like to take it over? How about it?'

'I'll have a crack at it,' I told him, 'and if you think I can handle it, I'll consider it a privilege.' I had occasionally helped him with some of his personal correspondence. One day he had asked apologetically if I would mind typing a letter to his wife for him. 'I've got so much on my desk that I'll never get to it today,' he said, 'and she gets upset if she doesn't hear from me.'

Naturally, I agreed. He told me briefly what he wanted to say, and I went back to my desk and typed it out. When I brought it in, he read it carefully and nodded. 'That's fine, Kay. Thank you. You sound more like me than I do myself.' He picked up a pen, added a few lines, folded the letter into the envelope I had prepared and sealed it carefully. I heard later that Mrs Eisenhower had taken exception to this. No more typewritten letters, she had informed him.

All kinds of people wrote to the General. There were letters with suggestions for horrible weapons that would end the war – and the world – promptly. From young mothers complaining that they had no place decent to live and bring up their children. From wives who had not heard from their husbands in weeks and were sick with worry. From mothers. Some letters reported injustices, family problems, all kinds of things that had to be investigated and then acted upon. Then there were the presents. Cookies and candy (lots of home-made fudge), games and books, just about everything that could be knitted or crocheted. The General insisted that every letter be answered and every gift acknowledged. 'They wouldn't take the trouble to write,' he said, 'if they didn't have something that seemed important to them to write about.' He had answered the letters himself up to this time, but now there were fifty or sixty a week and he just did not have the time.

I enjoyed my new chore. I would show Ike a few of the interesting letters, because he wanted to have a sense of what the writers were concerned about. If I read one and thought, Oh, this will amuse him or, This will make him feel good, I would set it aside for him to read. Most of the letters required nothing more than a courteous acknowledgement, but some required research and a final decision on some kind of action. I also saw that every present went to a hospital or rest centre or a local orphanage.

There were also hundreds of requests for the General's autograph, and I used to get him to sign his name thirty or forty times at a crack, but it became impossible to keep up with the demand. He insisted that I practise his signature so that I could sign the letters I wrote over his name. 'I'm damned if I'm going to sign them,' he said. 'I'll get writer's cramp.' Later on, I autographed most of the photographs he sent out too: *Dwight D. Eisenhower*, *DDE* or *DE*, depending on whether they were for GI's and their families or for personal friends.

Chapter 17

One morning when I went into the General's office at the St-Georges to consult him about something or other, he grinned and said, 'I have a surprise for you.'

'Oh,' said I. 'You do?'

'Yes,' said Ike. 'I do. How would you like a new uniform? Seems to me you could use a couple.'

He was right. I had been re-outfitted after my woebegone arrival in North Africa, but my two uniforms were now sadly worn. This was not the kind of life in which one came home from the office and changed into something comfortable. It was your uniform from the time you got up until you went to bed – seven days a week. My skirts were not only baggy, they had a shine on the seat, a shine polished to a high gloss from sliding in and out under the steering wheel. We had been at war for a long time now, and the 'wool' in our present uniforms was ersatz stuff for the most part, which did not wear well and did not hold its shape at all. My 'good' uniform was a far cry from the elegantly tailored outfit I had acquired for the Military Transport in 1939.

'I'm having some made for myself,' Ike went on, 'and I've told the tailor to measure you for a couple too. I think you deserve a little wardrobe freshening.'

'I'd absolutely adore a new uniform. Thank you.'

'Uniforms,' he corrected me. 'Plural.'

'That's too much,' I protested. 'You do so many nice things for me. How can I ever thank you?'

'You can't possibly know how much I would like to do for you,' he said. There was a strange quality to his voice. He was looking at me, his teeth clenched. That kind of look from which you cannot tell if a person is going to laugh or cry. Startled, I sat there at his desk looking at him. Neither of us said a word. Then Ike took off those reading glasses of his and stretched out his hand. 'Kay, you are someone very special to me.' I felt tears rising in my eyes. He was someone very special to me, too. I had never realized how special before. But he was. Very.

He laid his hand over mine. And he smiled. This was not the famous Eisenhower grin. This was a tender, almost tremulous smile, even a bit rueful. And full of love. I could not return it. I felt shaken, timid, almost as if I were undressing in front of him very slowly. In my face, in my eyes, there was nothing but absolute naked adoration. I could not hide it.

We just sat there and looked at each other. I felt overpoweringly shy. We were both silent, serious, eyes searching eyes. It was a communion, a pledging, an avowal of love.

And it was an absolutely shocking surprise.

So this is love, I thought. I had been in love before, but it had never been like this – so completely logical, so right. For over a year, Ike and I had spent more time with each other than with anyone else. We had worked, worried and played together. Love had grown so naturally that it was a part of our lives, something precious that I had taken for granted without ever putting a name to it.

Yes, I loved this middle-aged man with his thinning hair, his eyeglasses, his drawn, tired face. I wanted to hold him in my arms, to cuddle him, delight him. I wanted to lie on some grassy lawn and see those broad shoulders above me, feel the intensity of those eyes on mine, feel that hard body against mine. I loved this man.

No wonder I felt shy. This was all in my eyes as I looked helplessly at Ike. I don't know how long we sat there without speaking. Not too long. Tex burst in with a file of papers for the General. 'I'm next, Kay,' he boomed cheerfully. 'That's fine, Tex,' I told him. 'I was just going.' And I picked up whatever paper I had come in with and left the office.

Back at my desk, I pretended to sort out some papers, not knowing what I was doing, but trying desperately to appear busy. It would never do for anyone to note how moved I was. Oh yes, I loved Ike. I had loved him for a long time without ever being aware of it. Ike was the person around whom my world revolved and had been revolving for many months now. Ike was the person whom I admired more than any other. For whom I felt an aching tenderness and concern. With whom I always felt comfortable, at home.

I thought of all the times our eyes had met across the bridge table as we shared an unspoken comment on one of Butch's girl-friends or an instant of glee over a bluffing bid that had succeeded. Our communication was always instant and complete. I thought of how easy it was to work with him, knowing just what he wanted and how he wanted it. I thought of how unreservedly kind he had been to my mother and brother, how he had given me Telek, of the uncounted and uncountable ways he had befriended me, comforted me and involved himself in my life.

I thought, too, of the silly excuses we had made for touching each other all these weeks and months, excuses I had never admitted to myself before. A touch of the fingers as I handed him his appointment schedule for the day. His hand on my shoulder as he leaned over to look at some letter I had called to his attention. The occasional (was it really accidental?) touch of foot and knee at the dinner table. The times when, as we sat together on the sofa, our hands had slid together and touched without either of us seeming to notice – or moving them apart.

That morning, life took on a sweetness that was almost unbearable. I floated on a cloud of happiness, delighting in my secret, exploring the feelings I had hidden from myself for months. I felt peaceful and fulfilled.

I had no thought for the future, but went over and over exactly what had happened in that emotional interlude – what he had said, what he had done, how he had looked. But the daydreaming had to end. This was headquarters. There was a war. The General's mail was stacked on my desk, waiting to be read and answered. And in just a few minutes it would be time for me to drive him home for lunch.

I went into what I can only describe as a girlish panic. How was I going to face him? What should I say? What would he say? There was no time to think about it. Ike came striding out of his office with his usual 'Ready, Kay?' and I jammed my overseas cap on my head and ran for the car. It was a silent drive back to the villa. Usually we had so much to talk about that we were still chattering as we walked into the house. Today – not a word.

The sentries on the terrace saluted as we walked in. Mickey was at the door to take the General's hat, and he followed us to the dining-room, where Hunt and Moaney were waiting for the signal to put lunch on the table. This was the goldfish bowl that Ike was perpetually complaining about. Moaney came and went, serving lunch and clearing away. Mickey poured the coffee. Now that I was aching for privacy, I understood what a burden it was to live one's life under constant observation. There was not a moment, not one single moment when we could exchange a private word, a meaningful look. We sat there mute and poker-faced, completely caught up in thoughts and feelings that could not, should not be expressed. As we were leaving to go back to the St-Georges, Micky beckoned surreptitiously, and I stepped back into the dining-room.

'The General isn't himself today,' he whispered worriedly. 'Bad news this morning?'

'I don't know,' I whispered back. 'Hope not. I haven't heard any,' and I rushed after Ike. As we were driving out of the compound, Ike said, 'I'm sorry about this morning, Kay. That shouldn't have happened. I spoke out of turn. Please forget it.'

Forget it! Impossible. I was a woman caught up in a dream of love. This man was the centre of my existence. It had taken me long enough to realize it, but now – how could I forget it? I could not. Absolutely could not. If I cry, I thought, I will never be able to live with myself. I willed the tears to dry up. It was like willing the waves to stop breaking. One after another, the slow tears slid down my cheeks.

'Goddamnit!' Ike's voice crackled furiously into my ears. 'Don't you understand? It's impossible. I was a damn fool. I'm asking you to forget it.'

I did not say a word. There were no words.

'Goddamnit, stop crying,' he ordered.

I took a deep breath. Swallowed. Managed to say, 'I'm not crying. And furthermore, I do not understand what you are talking about.' I stuck my chin up in the air, clamped my lips shut and drew up at the side door of the St-Georges with a flourish. I would have given anything to be able to indulge in the old childish gesture of wiping my sleeve across my eyes to brush away the tears, but grown women in their thirties don't do that. I simply borrowed the General's favourite word and said, 'Goddamnit, I've got some of this bloody Algerian dust in my eyes.' If General Eisenhower regretted his words and his show of feeling, I regretted my reaction to them even more. I had made a fool of myself – a transparent, bloody fool of myself. That afternoon I applied myself to the typewriter with a vengeance.

Tex came out of Ike's office and warned, 'Watch out. He's a real bear this afternoon.'

Butch asked, 'What's up, Kay? Did he say anything at lunch? He was in a fine mood this morning.'

'No,' I answered honestly. 'He didn't say a word at lunch.'

Butch whistled. 'Hmmm – it's either Monty or the French. Can't imagine anything else that could have come up.' I could imagine something else, but I was not volunteering.

Suddenly, four buzzes. That was my signal. I took a firm clutch on my newfound poise, grabbed a pencil and pad and marched in.

'Just wanted to tell you that the tailor will be at the villa first thing tomorrow morning to take your measurements. Butch can drive me to the office and you can come along later when you're through.' The General did not look at me. He was flipping through a folder as he spoke.

'Oh, I think not,' I said coolly. 'What I've got will serve perfectly well. Thank you, but I think I should say no.'

He got so red in the face that I thought he would pop a blood vessel right then and there. He stood up and walked around his desk. 'You are a goddamned stubborn Irish mule,' he said between his teeth. 'You're going to get measured for those uniforms. And you're going to get measured tomorrow. That's an order.' He glared at me. I was just as angry as he was. We stood there like two fighters, each daring the other to make a move.

'Goddamnit, can't you tell I'm crazy about you?' he barked at me.

It was like an explosion. We were suddenly in each other's arms. His kisses absolutely unravelled me. Hungry, strong, demanding. And I responded every bit as passionately. He stopped, took my face between his hands. 'Goddamnit,' he said, 'I love you.'

We were breathing as if we had run up a dozen flights of stairs. God must have been watching over us, because no one came bursting into the office. It was lovers' luck, but we both came to our senses, remembering how Tex had walked in earlier that day. Ike had lipstick smudges on his face. I started scrubbing at them frantically with my handkerchief, worrying – What if someone comes in?

Ike put his hands on my shoulders. 'We have to be very careful,' he said. 'I don't want you to be hurt. I don't want people to gossip about you. God, I wish things were different.'

'I think things are wonderful,' I whispered. I knew what he was talking about. I understood the problems. And I did not believe for a moment that love conquers all. But still – everything *was* wonderful. I did not expect anything to be easy. But I was not one to deny love. I could see no reason to deny it. This is part of the business of living in that special dimension, in our case the tunnel of war, where all your feelings, all your energies are absorbed by one great purpose. Your world is different from that of other people, divorced from the world outside the tunnel. What was important here and now was that there was love – pulsating, irrepressible love.

When I came out of Ike's office, everyone looked up at me. I almost panicked, thinking that my hair was untidy or there was some other tell-tale sign. Then Tex asked, 'Well, how is he? Did he bite your head off too? Did you find out what was wrong?'

'No,' I said. 'He seems to be over whatever it was. He was cheerful enough.'

I wanted to stand in the middle of the office and laugh and say, 'Listen, everyone, we're in love. *Love!*' But as Ike had wanted, we had to be careful. Very, very careful. And until now, I have lived up to that bargain. I have lied and dissimulated to do it. But it's true. We were in love. And it was glorious.

Nothing had changed. Everything had changed. The acknowledgement of our love heightened the pleasure of every moment Ike and I spent together – and heightened the frustrations as well. As long as we were in Algiers, all we could hope for would be a few stolen moments of privacy – to talk. No more mad embraces. That initial passionate encounter could not be repeated. There were eyes and ears everywhere.

Many, probably most, of Ike's top staff officers had mistresses, but that was different. They were able to meet for assignations in hotel rooms, in rented or borrowed apartments or even in the officer's own villas, where there were always obliging, discreet orderlies to smuggle the lady out before dawn. But nothing and no one could slip discreetly into or out of Villa dar el Ouad. There were guards patrolling the grounds and sentries at the door twenty-four hours a day. Furthermore, this kind of liaison, this kind of behaviour was not possible for Ike. First of all, and most important of all, it was not in keeping with his character. Dwight David Eisenhower was a man of the utmost integrity. I have never known him to act with less than complete honour and fairness. He could not have acted otherwise. He did not possess the capability. And second, it simply would not have done for there to be gossip about the General. There were too many people who believed in him and looked up to him. He had caught the imagination of Europe and Great Britain as a man who represented all that was best about the American character. This was a tremendous responsibility for one man to carry, a man already burdened with staggering responsibilities. A man who was a man like all others – possibly more disciplined and more scrupulously honourable than some, but certainly no less human. Ike had always led a life that was above reproach – and it had to remain that way. I would not have had it otherwise. He *could* not have had it otherwise.

For all these reasons, love made no visible change in our lives; the change was all within. We picked up the threads of routine as if they had never been broken. The next morning when I arrived for breakfast, Ike was well into his first pack of cigarettes and badgering Mickey for more coffee – 'Hot, this time.' His coffee complaints were pure habit, just like brushing his teeth and polishing his spectacles.

'Go on upstairs,' he said. 'The tailor's waiting for you.'

There, spread out on Ike's big bed, was the material for my new uniform. Marvellous, gorgeous, wonderful real wool worsted. Simply beautiful fabric, the same cloth that Ike's uniforms were being cut from. I asked to have mine made just like the General's, with what we called the Eisenhower jacket. Actually, the jacket was borrowed from the British – Monty used to wear similar blouse-like jackets; but Ike was the one who started the fashion among the Americans. It was a neat, trim look and much more comfortable than the standard coat.

It was short – came to just below the waist, and gave you plenty of room to move. Every morning when I put on those uniforms I used to feel loved. I still have one of them. After the war I had it cleaned by the best cleaner in Washington; then I put it away in camphor. It has been in one of the packing cases that have followed me here and there for close on to thirty years.

As I went upstairs to be measured that morning, I overheard Butch saying, 'Well, what does one have to do around here to get a new tailor-made uniform?'

I stopped and listened for the reply. 'All you have to do,' Ike said brusquely, 'is work day and night, seven days a week, always be obliging and cheerful and get paid less than half of what the lowest-paid American clerk gets. That's all.'

Butch apologized. 'I shouldn't have said that, even joking. I keep forgetting that Kay's a civilian. She must have a hard time getting along.'

I didn't really. My pay was laughable, but there was nothing to spend it on. There was nothing to buy in Algiers and nowhere to go, so I always had money left over.

Ike tried hard to arrange his schedule so that we could go out to Sailor's Delight and ride every afternoon. This caused no comment, since it was known that Marshall had ordered him to get more exercise and spend less time in the office. Most of the time driving back and forth to the farm, we were alone, but the car was as much of a goldfish bowl as the villa or the office. The only difference was that it was on wheels. There was no stopping and parking by a secluded beach, no shifting of seating arrangements possible. Ike always sat in back on the right. Everyone knew the General's car with the big star stencilled on the side, the four-star plate and his flag.

I craved privacy now as I never had in my whole life. I said as much to Ike one day. 'I know. I know,' he said impatiently. 'So do I. But it's the one thing that I can promise you that we will never have.' It was relatively easy to find time to talk. It was hard to believe that there was anything about ourselves that we had not told each other already, but there were many things.

Ike was adept at small talk, but while seeming to be very candid, he rarely revealed much of the man within. He would tell fascinating stories about growing up in Kansas, about his mother and father, about his brothers, about how he used to work at a creamery. He was a delight at the dinner table and even his most aristocratic guests enjoyed his tales of an American boyhood. He never concealed his simple origins. 'I'm just a country boy,' he would say. 'I grew up poor.' And he seemed completely open. But he never discussed his feelings and one never knew what was going on inside this man.

One day when we were riding, I teased him about this. 'I know more about how you felt about the Belle Springs Creamery Company in Abilene than I do about how you feel about me.' I was half-serious, but I did not expect to raise the storm that I did. Ike hit his horse with his crop and they went tearing over the rocky fields as if ghosts were chasing them. He was back in minutes, coming around in a wide circle and slowly gentling his horse down to a sedate walk.

'I'm sorry,' he said. 'Let's stop and walk awhile.' We tethered the horses and walked along the cliff above the beach. 'I'm sorry,' he said again. 'It's hard for me to talk about things . . . about people . . . that mean something to me. I have always kept my feelings in check. Not talked about them. Not even thought about them much. I'm not used to talking about love. It makes me uncomfortable.'

This came out slowly, a few words at a time, as if he were trying to explain himself to himself as well as to me. We were walking along, both of us looking down at our feet. I would have given anything to be able to hold his hand, put my arm around him, pat his cheek – just touch him. I wanted to comfort him. He was upset, and he had always struck me as a man who had had very little comforting in his life. But I could not touch him. There were all those hidden eyes. We scuffed along silently. 'Your boots are getting dusty,' I said irrelevantly. He grunted. Eventually we turned back. He helped me mount, and we headed back towards Sailor's Delight. Every once in a while we would turn and smile at each other, but I was very thoughtful.

We stayed at the farm for supper that evening, sitting on the terrace during the long sunset, nursing a couple of drinks, not saying much, just enjoying the calm and the view until Mickey came out in exasperation to report that he could not keep our meal warm much longer. 'It will dry up,' he warned.

The cocktail hour was often a time we could count on for ourselves.

In Algiers we would sit on the high-backed sofa in the living-room, listen to some records, have a couple of drinks, smoke a few cigarettes and steal a few kisses – always conscious that someone might walk in at any moment. We were more like teen-agers than a woman in her thirties and a man in his fifties. We were certainly a curiously innocent couple – or perhaps it was simply the circumstances in which we found ourselves. But we were neither forlorn nor mopish. I was happy just to be with Ike. To be working with him and to know that he loved me. That was enough.

Telek and his offspring also gave us an excuse to be together. The three puppies he had sired were growing up to be fat little dumplings, full of mischief and personality. We would bring them into the living-room and get down on the floor and play with them, the way we had played with Telek when he was a puppy. Telek still liked to rollick around chasing balls and playing his old tug-of-war game. One afternoon in the car, Telek gave me the fright of my life. The windows were open, because it was blisteringly hot, and Telek saw a dog – one of those poor Arab mongrels, all skin and bones and sores. It must have been a female, because Telek got terribly excited and jumped out the window. Fortunately, I had been going very slowly. The road was rotten, and I didn't want to give Ike a bumpy ride. I jammed on the brakes and jumped out. Telek was lying there in the roadway perfectly still; then he got to his legs and shook himself in a very bewildered manner. He was a bit stunned, that was all. I picked him up in my arms and ran back to the car crying, 'He's all right! He's all right!' I had been terribly scared. Ike took him in the back seat. He checked him for broken bones and pronounced him whole. 'He'd better stretch out quietly for a bit,' he said, and he kept him quiet for the rest of the drive, scratching him behind his ears and telling him that he should not be such a woman chaser.

Later on, Ike said, 'When I saw your face, I felt sad. I don't think I could ever show as much feeling over a person as you did over a dog. I'm so used to concealing my feelings that there are times when I don't know what I feel – only what I think I ought to feel.

'And Kay, I don't think I'll ever change. I'm too old. It's too late. I've lived this way for a long time now. But I want you to know that I love you. There's nothing else that I can give you.' He sighed. 'If only things had been different,' he said. That was a phrase that he was to use over and over during our relationship.

'I've loved you for a long time,' he said huskily, 'and I'm going to tell you something so you'll never have to doubt my feelings. The night the signal came through that the *Strathallen* had been hit, I felt as if the ground had been taken away from under my feet.

'You don't know how much I was looking forward to seeing you again. I followed the progress of that convoy as I followed no other convoy. And then the bottom fell out of my world. I spent that night worrying about you, cursing myself for not having had you fly to Algiers. I went through hell that night.

'If there was ever any question in my mind as to how deeply I felt about you, that night answered it. I had never let myself realize quite how dear you were to me before. But for God's sake, I never thought that I would be talking to you like this. Never. I was never going to tell you how I felt. And sweet Jesus Christ, I don't know how I ever had the guts to.'

There was no mistaking his sincerity. Or that these words cost him a great effort. There was no reply possible.

'I'm very out of practice in love, Kay,' he said after a silence. I read no significance into this. For a man out of practise in love, Ike did many loving things.

One day he gave me a card with a four-leaf clover on it. 'I have two four-leaf clovers someone sent me from home,' he said. 'I'd like you to have one. They bring good luck, you know.' Ike believed in luck. He had some lucky coins that he used to rub during bridge games. He'd reach his hand into his pocket and smile and I would know that he was fingering his lucky coins. This day he told me, 'Maybe they'll bring us both good luck and happiness.' He had pasted the four-leaf clover on a little card, and on the back of it he had written, *Good luck to Kay*, and then, *Africa* and his initials, *D.E.* I have always carried that card in my wallet. For all these years. I have it still.

He liked to come up with little surprises. One night before dinner, he said, 'I've got some new records. Tell me what you think of them,' and he placed a couple on the turntable. They were all currently popular songs, but when the last record dropped down on to the turntable, he said, 'I think you may like this one.' It was 'I'll See You

Again', the waltz from *Bitter Sweet* that I had told him was my favourite song many months ago in England, just before he left for North Africa.

> When I'm recalling the hours we've had,
> Why will the foolish tears
> Tremble across the years?
> Why shall I feel so sad,
> Treasuring the mem'ry of these days
> Always?
>
> I'll see you again
> Whenever spring breaks through again.
> Time may lie heavy between,
> But what has been
> Is past forgetting.
> This sweet memory
> Across the years will come to me;
> Tho' my world may go awry,
> In my heart will ever lie
> Just the echo of a sigh,
> Goodbye.

The needle started spinning in the empty grooves. 'Oh, it's so beautiful, so romantic,' I sighed.

'It's pretty, but it's too sad,' Ike said. 'I don't like good-byes and sighs and all that.'

'But it *is* romantic,' I protested.

'Romantic,' he scoffed. 'Women!'

I didn't care. When a man carries the name of a song in his head for months and then produces it at the right moment, that is romantic. I felt wonderfully cherished. Perhaps it was because of this song that I always thought of these early days, when our love struck us like a kind of thunderbolt, as a kind of bittersweet honeymoon. Bitter only because unconsummated.

Chapter 18

General Eisenhower had much more than me, Kay Summersby, on his mind. World War II was an enormous enterprise. He not only had to work out strategies and determine priorities and make all the other decisions involved in waging war; he had to handle excruciatingly sensitive personnel problems. Probably no high executive is more of a prima donna by nature than a general. I say this as the daughter and sister of Army officers. The top brass tend to be a prickly, arrogant lot. Eisenhower's unassuming, considerate ways were most exceptional.

The most difficult man that Ike had to cope with – always excepting Montgomery, who was in a class by himself – was the flamboyant General George Patton. They were old, old friends, and Ike had great respect for Patton, but that man caused him a lot of grief.

I had met General Patton in London and driven him about occasionally. I'll never forget my first meeting with him. Ike had suggested that I give him 'the dock tour' – the same tour I had given Ike and Mark Clark when they first visited London. General Patton reacted very emotionally as I drove him around the East End dock area and showed him site after site that had been a grammar school, a warehouse, a cinema, a tenement or whatever and now was a heap of rubble. He would burst out with 'The bastards! The dirty mother-fucking bastards!' He would apologize immediately. 'Excuse me, Miss Summersby. I beg your pardon. My tongue ran away with me.' Seconds later he would be at it again. 'The sonsabitches! The bloody sonsabitches!' he would curse – and then apologize.

Despite his profanity, he was by no means coarse or crude. He was a gentleman, terribly courteous and very proper, with great respect for and consideration of women. I am not saying that the legendary 'blood and guts' George Patton did not exist. He most definitely did. But there was another side to the man, a rather sweet and affectionate side. He was very strange – and very endearing. He loved the Army. He loved pomp and spit and polish. He was always ramrod stiff, whether standing or sitting, and always a military fashion plate. I had never seen as many decorations as he used to wear. They stretched from armpit to armpit. He should have been a general in the time of the Romans when he could ride around in a chariot. And he had the world's most unfortunate voice, a high-pitched womanish squeak.

Georgie was amazingly childlike in some ways. One day he pulled out one of his guns and waved it under my nose. 'Look at that,' he commanded.

'It's very handsome,' I commented, wondering why he was showing it to me.

'People always talk about my pearl-handled revolvers,' he complained. 'That's not pearl. That's ivory. Good solid ivory,' he said with satisfaction. 'From an elephant,' he added a few seconds later.

We used to talk a lot about horses and polo. Patton had his own string of polo ponies in the States, he told me, and he had once been Master of Foxhounds of the Rappahannock Hunt in Virginia. A consummate horseman, he was always at ease with a fellow equestrian. When he learned that my father had been a cavalry officer, he was delighted. I remember his striding into Ike's office at 20 Grosvenor and demanding excitedly, 'Ike, did you know Kay's father was in the cavalry?'

Ike looked up at him and said, 'Seems to me I heard something to that effect.'

'Well?'

'Well what?' asked Ike. 'Are you suggesting I put her on a horse?'

'Well, no,' George squeaked. 'No, I just wanted to be sure you knew.'

'I know,' Ike said drily. I had no idea what had got Georgie so fired up about that bit of my background. It may simply have been that he felt a kinship to any horseman. But it was typical George Patton. You never knew what was coming next. Unfortunately.

Patton had played an important part in the fighting in North Africa;

19. Kay in a borrowed British Army Warm and checked headscarf,
after the sinking of the *Strathallen*

20. An angry Ike lays down the law to Admiral Darlan.
To the right, General Mark Clark looks on

21. Kay tries out an Army motor-cycle in the North African desert

22. Oujda, Morocco: Ike at the front observes machine gunners in action

and in Sicily, his Seventh Army had made Montgomery look like a cautious fuddy-duddy. Ike regarded him as one of his most valuable generals, and all the time we were in Algiers, he was a frequent guest. We always had a good time when he came to dinner. He was amusing and had an unending string of anecdotes. Ike used to tease him a lot. After Patton had finished telling some long, involved story, Ike would say, 'Come on, Georgie. I don't believe a word of it.' And Georgie would get all flustered and indignant.

After dinner, when the men started swapping off-colour stories, Patton would always shoo me out of the room as if I were his daughter, saying, 'Kay, it's time for you to leave. You tell one of those handsome aides of mine to play Ping-Pong with you.' Ike would wink. I'd excuse myself and off I'd go. I always appreciated his thoughtfulness. Georgie was really quite prudish. He could be very charming, and I liked him.

But now I was furious with him. Georgie had visited a field hospital just behind the lines in Sicily – one of the routine visits every commander makes. He chatted with the men, told some stories, and then he came upon a soldier who was sitting alone and shaking. Georgie asked what was wrong. The soldier told him that it was his nerves, that he could not stand the constant shelling any more. That set Patton off. He started ranting that there was no such thing as nerves, called the man a coward – and slapped him in the face. The incident had been kept under wraps for a while, but it was bound to get out, and it did. It was a terrible shocker.

Eisenhower wrote Patton a very severe reprimand and ordered him to make a public apology, but there were many people who criticized Ike for being too soft on the General. They thought that he should have court-martialed him or sent him back to the States in disgrace or both. The whole affair was very distressing. Ike did not condone Patton's behaviour for one moment, but on the other hand he did not want to lose a valuable general just because of one mistake. He lost many nights' sleep over this. Finally, 'I'm going to stand by Georgie,' he told us. 'I think we need him.' Patton was not abashed in the least when I talked to him about the incident a few weeks later. 'I always get in trouble with my goddamned mouth,' he said, 'but if this sort of thing ever comes up again, I'd do it again.'

One day when Georgie was lunching with us, he turned to me and

I

said, 'You should get Ike to bring you over to visit me next time he comes to Sicily. I'd love to show you around.' I said something about being sure that Georgie was too busy to entertain guests, but he insisted. 'It's only a hop, skip and jump from here. Ike,' he said, 'you bring Kay along. I owe her a sight-seeing trip.' Ike thought it was a good idea, and the visit was scheduled for the next day. Ruth Briggs, one of the Powerhouse WACS, went along with me.

Unlike Ike, General Patton believed in nothing less than the very best for himself. He was living in a palace that had once belonged to the King of Sicily. It suited Georgie's grandiose style very well. After lunch, he took us on the promised sight-seeing trip. He was an enthusiastic and well-informed guide. Our final stop was a medieval church just outside Palermo. He gave Ruth and me a short lecture on medieval architecture and then sank to his knees and prayed aloud for the success of his troops, for the health and happiness of his family and for a safe flight back for Ruth and me. He was completely unselfconscious and did not care who listened in on his prayers.

When I told Ike about our day, he smiled and shook his head. 'Georgie is one of the best generals I have,' he said, 'but he's just like a time bomb. You never know when he's going to go off. All you can be sure of is that it will probably be in the wrong place at the wrong time.'

Later on, when Patton's Third Army romped through France and Germany and across the Rhine, Eisenhower's decision to keep this master of military pursuit on his staff was amply vindicated. I think Patton, despite his bravado, was always truly appreciative of Eisenhower's forbearance. But he never did learn to keep his 'goddamned mouth' shut. And he caused Ike a lot of grief.

Chapter 19

It used to be said that if a person sat on the terrace of the Café de la Paix in Paris long enough, everyone he had ever known would pass by. North Africa was something like that in the autumn of 1943. Our life seemed to consist of a round of luncheons and dinners for the most important men in the Western World.

First and foremost, there was the PM. One never knew when Winston Churchill would pop in. Sometimes his visits were scheduled, and other times he just appeared – like a little boy who could not stay away from the action. Once he told Ike that the reason he came to Algiers was to take a bath. He revelled in long hot tub baths, which had become a delight of the past in England because of the stringent fuel rationing. The General would be invited to join the PM in the steamy bathroom for long talks, sitting on the toilet seat while Churchill soaked and smoked his cigars and discussed the state of the world. Ike would always have to change into a fresh uniform afterwards, because the steam was murder on trouser creases.

Ike really liked Churchill. They disagreed on a number of things, matters of strategy and military priorities, and had some very spirited arguments, but this did not affect their relationship. The only thing that Ike really deplored about the PM was his habit of staying up until all hours. By nature Ike was an early-to-bed, early-to-rise man; the PM was the opposite. He was at his best from dinnertime on and would keep a party going well into the wee hours without the slightest compunction for the other guests who would be in agony trying to stifle their yawns. Since the PM was always the ranking guest, no one could leave until he was ready to call it a night.

The PM was a menace at the dinner table in more ways than one. His table manners were atrocious, especially in contrast to Ike's, which were neat and unobtrusive, once I got used to the American way of handling a knife and fork. At the beginning, I used to say, 'Listen, I can't understand you. Here you are – cutting a piece of meat. After I cut mine, I simply raise my fork to my mouth. You have to switch your fork to your other hand. I thought Americans were supposed to be so efficient.'

I always used to think how shocked the PM's nanny would have been if she could see the way he behaved. He would slurp his soup, spill things, pick up food with his fingers. He would pick his nose while listening to the rare person who managed to get a word in edgewise and would quite uninhibitedly unzip his siren suit to scratch his crotch. I remember once at dinner he interrupted himself in mid-anecdote, banged his fist on the table and demanded, 'What happened, General? Did you run out of claret?' Mickey rushed to fill his glass. At that moment the PM, engrossed in his story again, made a sweeping gesture and knocked the glass to the floor. He paid no attention to what he had done. No attention whatsoever. Simply went on with his story. Ike and I exchanged a glance and a grin. Mr Churchill, you really had to acknowledge it, was adorable – but his manners were horrifying. The truth was that it did not matter. He was absolutely brilliant, and all these possibly purposeful gaucheries seemed trivial when he started talking. He had the most fabulous command of the English language. I could have listened to him forever.

Whenever he was coming to dinner, he would instruct Ike, 'Now, tell Kay to come. I want to see her.' And Ike would buzz me and say, 'You're invited to dinner. The PM wants you.' I don't know whether Churchill sensed the special feeling Ike and I had for each other or was just being gallant, but either way I appreciated his courtesy.

At one period, it seemed as if we had dinner parties almost every night. Ike entertained Lord Louis Mountbatten, whom he now knew well enough to call him Dicky, when he came by on his way to India. Then Averell Harriman, who had just been appointed American Ambassador to the Soviet Union, dropped in on his way to Moscow with his daughter Kathy. I had known Kathy in London, so this was a particularly welcome visit.

The Harrimans arrived on the General's birthday, and Ike said, 'Now, I don't want my birthday mentioned. You tell Butch that, too.'

'Fine,' said I. 'In that case you won't want your present, I suppose.'

He grinned. 'Well now, I don't remember saying anything about no presents.' So I whisked his birthday present out of my pocketbook – one of those dreadful Western magazines that he liked.

'You must have had to grit your teeth to buy this,' he said.

'You're right,' I told him. It was not much of a present, but there really wasn't anything to buy. It had been a toss-up between the magazine and a package of chewing gum.

Henry Morgenthau, the Secretary of the Treasury, and Cordell Hull, the Secretary of State, flew in while the Harrimans were there. This involved a series of back-to-back, high-level luncheons and dinner parties. And there were what seemed like a constant stream of American Congressmen, all of whom wanted to pay their respects to the General.

Then there were the theatre people and other entertainers who came to North Africa to perform for the troops. Whenever possible we would invite them to the villa for a buffet supper. I can't remember all the stars, but there was Vivien Leigh, who was even more beautiful in person than she had been on the screen as Scarlett O'Hara. There was Bob Hope, who was able to make the General double up with laughter. There were Kay Francis and her troupe. And Bea Lillie. The high point for me was Noël Coward's visit. The General told him that I had worn out his recording of 'I'll See You Again,' and Mr Coward said that it was probably the most popular song he had ever written. He told us that he had been in a traffic jam in New York City when the theme had come to him. I can remember just the way he described it – 'It was in the air waiting to be captured.' Just to convince the General that he was not planning to entertain the troops by singing romantic waltzes, Mr Coward sang that marvellously funny song, 'Mad Dogs and Englishmen Go Out in the Midday Sun,' doing a soft-shoe routine at the same time. Ike loved that. He slapped his knee and beamed and said, 'That's great. That's swell. That's the stuff.'

One day Ike asked me, 'Can you keep a secret?'

I was reproachful. 'I never breathe a word of anything,' I said. 'You know that.' And I never did.

'Well, do you want to know what I know?'

I was ready to wring his neck. Of course I did.

'President Roosevelt is going to visit us.'

Franklin D. Roosevelt. I had listened to his radio broadcasts and seen his pictures with that cigarette holder jutting out at a cocky angle. This was a man I would love to meet. He had been in North Africa at the time of the Casablanca Conference, but I had not gone to Casablanca. I was aware that he had been crippled by polio, but the image he projected – even in newspaper photographs – was so vital that one did not think of him as having any disability.

The King's visit and the frequent descents of the PM had not prepared us in any way for the security arrangements that prevailed for the President of the United States. They were incredible. The advance visits of the Secret Service people were responsible for several memorable eruptions of the Eisenhower temper. I wonder how he would have felt if he had suspected then that someday they would be performing the same services for him.

The Secret Service people were so powerful that they overruled the General's wishes – temporarily, at least – in the matter of who would drive the President. When the day came and I drew up beside the President's plane on the airfield in Tunisia, the Secret Service chief started shouting at me. I had met him earlier, when he was making the advance arrangements. His name was Mike Reilly, and he was as stubborn an Irishman as ever was born of Irishwoman. We almost got into an old-fashioned shouting match when he told me that 'No woman will ever drive the President.' He banged on the top of the car to make his point. 'No woman ever has – or ever will as long as I'm boss here,' he shouted.

The President and the General got into the car while all this fuss was going on – a far cry from the decorum that had obtained when we welcomed the King. The whole thing ended up with me driving Butch back to the villa just outside Tunis where the President was staying. When we got there, I jammed on the brakes. I'd never seen anything like it. The house was ringed with soldiers as if they expected an immediate attack in force. I was about to pull the car around in the driveway when one of President Roosevelt's aides came over and said, 'Miss Summersby, the President has asked to meet you.'

The President and General Eisenhower were in the library. Two of his sons, Elliot and Franklin, were with him. Ike walked over as I came in and took me to where the President was sitting in front of the big window. 'Mr President,' he said, 'this is Kay Summersby.' The first thing the President said was not 'How do you do?' or anything like that, but 'Why didn't you drive me? I'd heard you were going to be my driver and I was looking forward to it.'

'Mr President,' I said indignantly, 'your Secret Service wouldn't let me drive you.' Everyone laughed. There was no formality after that. The President said he would like it if I would drive him during his stay, and I said that there was nothing that I would like better.

As I left I ran into Reilly again and could not resist telling him that I had just been presented to the President and that he had asked me to drive him. Reilly scowled. I pointed out that the President would be safe with me. 'I'm as Irish as you are, Mike,' I told him. He looked at me disbelievingly. 'Now, are you?' he said. 'I wouldn't know with that Limey accent.' I convinced him, and peace was declared.

When Ike and I arrived the next day to take the President on a tour of the Tunisian battlefields, we were amazed at the scene that greeted us. They had assembled what seemed to be a small army – jeeps, weapons carriers, half-tracks, truckloads of armed MPs – to accompany us. The President was tucked into the car. Two men simply picked him up out of his wheelchair and set him down on the back seat with no to-do whatsoever. Our cavalcade got off with a roar of engines. A radio car led the way, then there were a couple of jeeps full of soldiers and then our car. Besides all those military vehicles bristling with armed men, our group looked like a family on a Sunday outing. Telek was sitting in front between me and a very quiet man in civilian clothes who was clutching a briefcase as if it contained the Crown Jewels. He was a Secret Service agent, and the briefcase held a machine-gun. The President and the General were chatting, very relaxed, in back when there was an unscheduled incident that not even the almighty Mike Reilly could have foreseen. Telek, who had made it clear that he did not care for the Secret Service agent, turned himself into a flying missile and launched himself directly at the President. Ike managed to grab Telek in midair before he landed on Roosevelt. The President just laughed. He took Telek on his lap, and as we drove along he scratched our bad Scottie under his chin and told us stories about Fala, his own Scottie.

Suddenly he broke off and said, 'Child.' He meant me. I discovered later that he called most young women 'child'. I liked it. Nobody else had ever called me that. 'Child,' he said. 'That's a pretty grove of trees there ahead. Let's have our picnic there.' That particular grove of trees was not on the schedule. Reilly had given me a programme that called for the President to have his lunch forty-five minutes later in a completely different locale. But I decided the President was boss and turned off the road on to a track leading into the trees. It was a pretty place, rather like an oasis in the barren country we had been driving through. I braked and started opening the picnic basket.

'No, let me do that, Kay,' Ike said. 'I'm very good at passing sandwiches around.'

All the time there was a grinding of gears and the noise of engines in the background as our escort vehicles lumbered after us. Soldiers jumped out and completely circled the car, elbow to elbow, their backs to us, bayonets fixed.

The President said, 'Won't you come back here, child, and have lunch with a dull old man?' Tremendously flattered, I got in back and sat beside him while Ike took over the front seat and the picnic basket. The Secret Service man had disappeared. 'I have a delicious chicken sandwich here that I can let you have,' he told the President as he peeked between the slices of bread. Roosevelt asked how he knew it was delicious and Ike said it was because of all the Sunday-school picnics he had gone to as a child. 'I got to know who made the best sandwiches pretty fast,' he said.

Roosevelt was enjoying himself immensely, laughing and telling stories. He had the gift of putting a person completely at ease, and I soon got over my awe of him and was chatting away as if I had known him all my life. I told him about London in the early days of the war, about the trips the General and I had taken to the front. I told him about the WAC officers with whom I shared the villa in Algiers and how much I liked them.

'It seems to me that you might like to join the WACs,' he said.

'There's nothing I'd like more, sir,' I told him. 'But it's impossible.

I'm a British subject and I'd have to become an American citizen to be a WAC.'

'Well, who knows? Stranger things have happened,' he said.

It is hard for me to imagine it now, but it seemed completely natural for me to be sitting in the back seat of a car parked in a grove of trees in Tunisia eating chicken sandwiches with the President of the United States – and having those sandwiches served to us by a four-star general who was in love with me – and I with him.

Chapter 20

There had been a reason for the flurry of VIP visitors. Two major conferences took place that autumn – the Cairo Conference, starring President Roosevelt, Prime Minister Churchill and Generalissimo Chiang Kai-shek, and the Teheran Conference, where Roosevelt and Churchill met with Stalin.

When General Marshall informed Ike that he was to attend the Cairo Conference, Ike said to me, 'Well, here's a chance for a little holiday. How about coming along?' I would love to, I told him, but how in the world could it possibly be arranged? 'No problem,' Ike said, 'I'll ask some of the other headquarters staff too. There's plenty of space in the plane.' And that's the way it worked. Ruth Briggs and Louise Anderson were delighted to have a chance to visit Cairo. Even ultra-conscientious Tex decided to go.

We all trooped into the big C-54 General Marshall had sent for Ike and settled down to a few rubbers of bridge just as if it were any other night. Mickey hovered about serving drinks and passing peanuts. After the game we all settled ourselves for the night. One by one the others dropped off to sleep, leaving Ike and me the only ones awake. Tex's snores drowned out our whispers, and we felt completely unobserved. I suppose it seems ludicrous to think of two adults necking in a darkened plane, but we were dreamily content. Reality took precedence over romance, however. We were dead tired and did not want to risk falling asleep in a compromising position. We moved apart and went to sleep. I kept waking up and looking over at Ike. Every time I turned my head and saw him there in the dim light, his mouth slightly open, his tie loosened, I felt a surge of tenderness. Even when the sun showed every

138

weary wrinkle and line, I could not imagine anything better than seeing that head on the pillow beside mine every morning. It was good just to have been close to him for those few hours.

Today, when sex seems to be so matter-of-fact, it may be hard to realize how wonderfully romantic and rather innocent people were only thirty years ago. To me, that night was as much an act of love as a more physically intimate encounter.

The appearance of three women with the General threw the welcoming group into a panic. Where would they put us up? 'That's no problem,' Ike said. 'They can stay with me.' There was plenty of room in the luxurious residence he had been assigned, and Ruth, Louise and I had our own private suite. It was a long time since we had lived in such comfort. We were all so used to our family-style life that the rank-conscious scruples of our conference hosts struck us as amusing and old-fashioned.

The General went off to his conference, and the three of us headed straight for the famous Shepheard's Hotel. After a marvellous lunch, we set out to sight-see and shop. Cairo was hot and dirty, but luxurious beyond belief. Store windows were full of fruit and clothing and jewellery. It was a whole other world. Unfortunately, almost everything was far too expensive for us. All I bought was some fruit.

That afternoon there was a huge cocktail party, and Ike was easily the most popular man there. That grin of his never faded as people kept pushing their way up so they could exchange a few words with him. I tried not to look in his direction too often. I was resolved that I would never give anyone reason to gossip.

Eisenhower dined with General Marshall that evening. Ruth and Louise went on to dinner from the cocktail party with a group of friends. I went home alone. Later that evening, Mickey knocked on the door. 'The General asks if you'd join him in a nightcap,' he said.

Ike was walking up and down the long drawing-room. 'Did I hear something about a drink?' I asked.

'Correct. Come on in. And Kay, close the door.' I closed the door softly and ran straight to him. We stood there, our arms around each other, his cheek on my hair. 'Oh, that's good,' he said. 'This is where you belong.' We stood there. Making cozy little noises. This was no passionate embrace. Just two people who ached to hold each other close and never got a chance.

After a few minutes, we drew apart and I opened the door again. There was no point in arousing anyone's curiosity. Ike sighed and reached for my hand. He sat there smoking one cigarette after another. He always smoked them right down to the stub. I used to say, 'You're very conservative. Just like me. You don't want to waste anything.'

'General Marshall has ordered me to go on vacation,' he said after a while.

My heart sank. In the last few weeks, rumours had been flying, rumours that struck panic into my heart – rumours to the effect that Ike would be recalled to Washington to serve as Chief of Staff and General Marshall would come to Europe to take over the Allied command of Overlord, the code name for the projected invasion of the Continent across the English Channel. In recent weeks one important personage after another had told Ike about these rumours. One day he exploded. 'Goddamnit, I've had a bellyful of every Tom, Dick and Harry coming here from Washington and telling me I'm about to be stuck behind a desk in the Pentagon.'

'What do you want me to do?' I asked. 'Gag every visiting fireman before he comes into your office?' But I did not feel at all flip. At head-quarters, the whole staff felt that such a move would be shabby recognition of the Boss's achievements in putting together a truly unified Allied command and conducting the successful Mediterranean campaigns. But like Ike, I did not want to hear about those rumours. As far as I was concerned, they were bad news. If Ike was recalled to Washington, there was not a chance in the world that I would ever see him again. He might be able to take other members of his personal staff with him, but there was no way that he would be able to bring a British civilian into the Pentagon as a member of his entourage. It was simply out of the question.

This was the first time I had ever had a glimmering that there would be an end to this wartime world of ours. I had come to think of it as a way of life; but now intimations of the future were being forced on me – and the future held changes that I did not want to face.

When Ike told me that General Marshall had ordered him to take a vacation, I caught my breath and very hesitantly asked, 'They're send-ing you back to Washington?'

'No, just a couple of days off. That's all. Damn it! I don't know. It may be a way of preparing me for the news. He didn't say. I didn't ask.' Ike shook his head. 'There's no point in worrying about it. They'll tell me when the time comes.'

I was not so sure. And no matter what he said, Ike was worried. I could tell. I remembered the typical Army snafu when he got his fourth star. The news had been on the BBC and the American radio hours before Ike had been notified. It did not seem inconceivable to me that they might send Ike away for a short vacation and announce that General Marshall would be the commander for Overlord in his absence. Not out of malice. No one held any bad feelings towards Ike, ever. Just out of the utter and incredible inefficiency of Army bureaucracy.

I said as much to Ike. 'No, there's too much involved,' he said. 'The British. The French. The Russians. It will be a big formal announcement when it comes.

'Don't look so upset,' he said. 'If it has to be Washington, I'll find a way. I'm never going to let you go.' I smiled a little trembly kind of smile. I knew he meant it. But I was a realist. There was no way he could ever manage to bring me to the United States.

'All we're talking about is a couple of days off,' Ike said. 'Marshall says I look tired. And I am. I'm very tired.' This was the first time I had ever heard him admit such a thing. He usually blew his top if anyone so much as intimated that he looked tired.

'I'm leaving tomorrow,' he said, 'and you're coming with me.'

'Me? I can't believe that's what the General ordered.'

Ike laughed. 'I thought I'd go take a look at the pyramids. I'll probably never have another chance. We could take the girls and Tex with us. What do you think? It would mean a lot to me to have you along.'

The next afternoon we were all in Luxor, a city built on the site of ancient Thebes. Elliot Roosevelt had come along too. That night we went out to view the crumbling temples, the huge statues of pharaohs and the rows of sphinxes in the moonlight. It seemed like a dream. This was such a tremendous experience that there was very little talk. Each person was concentrating on his own impressions. We wandered about quietly, separating, then coming back together. Ike pressed my hand.

'You have to know how much it means to me to be seeing this with you,' he said softly. Subdued and impressed, we eventually sauntered back to the hotel, the desert moon lighting our way. We had a drink and then said our good nights. Ike tucked a piece of paper into my hand as we walked down the hall. A few minutes later, alone in my room, I read, *You know what I am thinking. Good night. Sweet dreams.* I went to sleep thinking how much I loved him.

A caravan of decrepit cars awaited us the next morning to take us across the Nile to the famed Valley of the Kings. On the way we got a look at the very primitive life of the fellahin. Water buffalo plodded about in circles to pump water. Donkeys looked out of doorways. And everywhere there were hordes of grimy little children and flies, flies, flies. It was blazing hot, and the cars kept breaking down, but when we reached the desolate ravine that was the Valley of the Kings, we forgot about the discomforts. We spent the whole day exploring the tombs, learning about life in ancient Egypt as our very learned guide, a personal friend of Air Chief Marshal Tedder, explained the significance of some of the tomb paintings and translated the hieroglyphics. When we emerged from the last tomb in the late afternoon, we shook our heads as if we had jumped across hundreds of centuries.

Back in Luxor that evening, there was nothing any of us wanted except a cold drink, a warm bath and bed. It was a grand kind of tiredness. Ike went straight to bed and slept for fourteen hours. The next morning he looked like a different man.

General Marshall was so pleased when he saw how much better Ike looked after his two-day vacation that he insisted on his taking another short trip immediately. When Ike came back after meeting with General Marshall, he asked, 'Have you girls made any plans for today?' We had nothing special planned, but we were looking forward to more window-shopping and sight-seeing. 'Oh,' he said, feigning disappointment. 'I was thinking of going to Jerusalem for lunch. I'd hoped you would join me.'

'You are thinking of *what*?' I shrieked. 'Jerusalem! For lunch? We can go?' Ruth and Louise were equally enthusiastic, and Ike was highly pleased with the effect he had produced. At noontime we were lunching at the King David Hotel in Jerusalem, none of us quite believing it. After the pyramids, the Holy Land was a bit of a let-down. Nothing was the way we had imagined it. It was terribly commercial and not at all impressive. Even Bethlehem was a disappointment. We were going to visit the manger where Christ was born. I suppose it was utterly idiotic of me to expect to see a wooden manger filled with straw. It was an ornate hunk of marble, and I was absolutely repelled by it.

For me, and for Ike too, a stroll in the Garden of Gethsemane was the high point of the visit. None of Christ's long-ago agony communicated itself to us; it seemed, rather, more peaceful than the other religious landmarks we had visited, a place where meditation seemed natural. Our voices were hushed as we wandered along the paths. I felt that our visit was a form of prayer. And I was praying very hard. 'Please God,' I begged, 'don't let them send him back to Washington.'

Ike collected a lot of postcards, and when we were wandering through the bazaars in Jerusalem, I saw some good-looking sheepskin coats. I tried on one coat after another. There was one I liked particularly, and it cost only twenty dollars. I didn't have that much with me, but Ruth Briggs lent me a few dollars. 'You're crazy, you know,' she told me. 'You don't need that. When will you wear it?' 'After the war,' I said. 'I'll never find a good warm coat like this in England –not at this price.' I was very proud of my foresighted practicality.

Our next stop was the airport. We all agreed that we'd had enough of the Holy Land. We were playing cards on the way back when Ike wrinkled his nose. He sniffed and sniffed and then he said, 'What's that goddamn smell?'

'Smell? Smell?' I said. 'I don't smell anything.' And then I got it. The most disgusting rotten stink was wafting up from the back of the plane. 'Oh my dear God,' I said. 'It's my coat. It's my bargain.' As the interior of the plane warmed up, it had brought out the worst in my coat.

'For Christ's sake, you mean we're going to have to fly with that stink?' Ike was disgusted. It got worse and worse. Fortunately, it was a short flight. It was the only purchase of any size I made during the war, and it was a disaster.

Before we went to bed, Ike took the postcards he had been collecting out of his pocket. 'Here,' he said as he handed one to me. 'You liked the Garden of Gethsemane. This will be a little souvenir.' It was a postcard with its own envelope. On one side was printed, SOUVENIR FROM

THE GARDEN OF GETHSEMANE. And on the other side, Ike had written, *Good night – there are lots of things I could say – you know them. Good night.* I tucked it into my bag and said very briskly, 'Oh, thank you, General. Thank you so much. And thank you for a lovely day.' He spread the rest of the cards out on the table and said, 'Now Ruth, Louise, take what you want. You should have some remembrance of the trip besides that unholy stink from Kay's coat.'

Back in Algiers, headquarters was practically afloat with new rumours that Ike would be leaving for a post in Washington the first of the year. This really got him upset. He had come back rested, with a fresh perspective on things, and now, after just a couple of hours back at his desk, he was getting tied up in knots again.

'I don't see how they can send you back to Washington,' I told him. 'No one else can do the job you did in London and here. And Overlord will be the same job, the same kind of thing – just on a bigger scale. I don't know what they would do if anything ever happened to you.'

He gave a noncommittal grin – more of a grimace than a grin. 'Let me tell you something,' he said. 'There's no such thing as an indispensable man.'

'They couldn't get along without you,' I insisted stubbornly.

'Sure they could. Don't kid yourself. It might be difficult for a few days, even a week. But then everything would fall into place.'

There was nothing to do but wait. Not even Ike could make a guess as to how long it would be before the announcement was made. In the meantime, there was plenty to keep us all busy. Ike's mail had stacked up on my desk while we had been away, and I was working late every evening. We were setting up a trip to advance headquarters in Italy. The invasion there had bogged down badly, and Ike wanted to get over and 'light a fire under Monty'.

We were also preparing for the return visit of President Roosevelt on his way back to Washington from Teheran. This time we all took the Nervous Nellies of the Secret Service in our stride. We had become used to their ways. The President arrived on 7 December: a rather grim date, the anniversary of the attack on Pearl Harbour – but he was wearing that sparkling Roosevelt smile. On the way from the airfield, he congratulated Ike on his new appointment. It was definite, he told him.

23. At Ike's secret retreat outside London, Telegraph Cottage, Kay gets ready for their daily ride together

24. Ike takes a break with Kay on the Riviera, at the villa Sous le Vent near Cannes

25. Ike attends a theatre party in London, with Kay by his side (centre front) and his son, John (at far left)

26. June 5, 1944: Ike visits the paratroopers of General Maxwell Taylor's 101st Airborne Division just before their D-Day drop

27. Ike visits Hitler's retreat at Berchtesgaden in 1945, with Kay beside him

Ike would be named commander for Overlord. The announcement would be made as soon as the President got back to Washington. And Ike would have a new title: Supreme Allied Commander. The General was so happy I almost thought he would burst. That grin never left his face.

That night Elliott Roosevelt gave a dinner for his father. Ike and Butch and I were invited. It was rations, but lots of fun, the most informal meal you could imagine. There was a lot of joking and laughing, and everyone toasted Ike. He was beaming and looked fabulous. It was as if a load had rolled off his shoulders. It would be presumptuous of me to say that I was even happier than Ike, but I may have been. For him it was recognition of his professional abilities and achievements; for me, it was a reprieve.

It was a good thing that Ike had the prospect of Overlord to buoy him up, because our trip to Italy was pure misery. One never expected life at advance headquarters to be comfortable. It had been rugged enough in Tunisia – but in civilized Italy it was unspeakable. Ike's headquarters in Caserta were in a huge palace that was about the dirtiest place I have ever seen. We spent very little time there, however. Ike visited Montgomery at his headquarters and conferred with the other commanders at their command posts. He always made a point of talking to as many officers and men as he could. The men were always glad to see him. They would shout, 'Good old Ike!' and things like that. Despite the fact that the fighting was incredibly bitter, they were in good spirits. But Ike was depressed. The Germans were putting up an unexpectedly strong fight – and then there was Monty. He was never willing to take a chance. 'If I could only get Monty off his duff,' Ike complained over and over.

The lowest point of the trip was the night we spent in what had been Prince Umberto's hunting lodge in the mountains. Butch had wanted the General to have one day of rest during the trip and had set this up. In good weather the lodge might have been pleasant enough, but in the cold December rain it was utterly depressing. And cold. And dirty. Our spirits were pretty low after we inspected it. Then we heard Mickey shouting, 'There's a rat in the General's bathroom!'

Telek had been sniffing around, exploring his new quarters, and had flushed out a rat. All of us rushed to the bathroom. There was the rat. Sitting on his hind legs on the toilet seat.

'I can handle this,' Ike said. He put on his glasses, pulled out his gun and took aim. And missed. The rat jumped up and clung to a pipe. Ike fired again, and this time he got part of the poor rat's tail. He finally tumbled him on the third shot, but the rat was still alive. One of the sergeants came running in with a log and slammed it down on the poor thing. The rest of us were bent over with laughter. Butch congratulated Ike. 'Great marksmanship, Chief,' he said. 'Just what we'd expect from the Supreme Commander.'

That was the highlight of the stay. None of us got any sleep that night. The place was full of hungry Italian bugs. We left early the next morning – not even waiting for coffee – all of us scratching our bites.

It was Christmas Day when we got back to Algiers. We lunched at our desks and in the evening played a little bridge and went to bed early. We were so busy winding up affairs in Algiers that Christmas seemed beside the point. Ike was going back to the States for a couple of weeks and then would fly to London to set up SHAEF (Supreme Headquarters Allied Expeditionary Force). I would be leaving for London myself very shortly. I was beginning to feel homesick for the first time, now that I knew I was going home. It would be good to be back – no matter how cold or rationed or bleak it might be. It was home. And Ike would be there.

Ike had left for Washington and I was alone, left behind in Algiers. All the energy had gone out of headquarters like air out of a balloon. Some of us were preparing to join the General in London; others would go to other posts. It was a sad time. We had all been so close for so many months. Although I was going to London, I may have been the saddest of all.

I was also jealous. Ike and I had carefully avoided one topic. He rarely mentioned his wife in my presence, only when someone asked after her. I never mentioned her. But I thought about her. For one thing, I thought her a fortunate woman to have this man as her husband, the father of her son. I had other thoughts, too. Some rather graceless ones. I kept them all to myself. It was anguishing for me to think of Ike going home, home to his wife.

For the first time in my life I had trouble sleeping. What lay ahead for us? For me? When I tried to look at our relationship objectively, it seemed like a schoolgirl crush on my part. But I was no schoolgirl. And my feelings were reciprocated. I was serenely certain of that. Ever since Ike had told me – hesitant, mumbling, embarrassed and utterly, tenderly loving – about his night of torment when he heard that the *Strathallen* had been torpedoed, I had never doubted his love. And I did not doubt it now. But . . .

This was a strange love affair, if one could call it an affair. Whatever it was, I have never had such a perfect relationship with anyone else in my life. Ever. Not with anybody. We were absolutely in love with each other. If he took my hand and gave it a squeeze, I knew everything that was in his heart. He was like that. He was never able to come right out and say, 'I love you,' after that first time. His way of telling me would be to say, 'Kay, you know exactly what I would like to tell you. You have to understand.' And I would say, 'Yes, I understand.' And I did.

Tossing about in bed night after night, unable to get to sleep, I went over and over Ike's last hours in Algiers. After breakfast on the day he left – it was the last day of 1943 – we were drinking a last cup of coffee while elsewhere in the house Mickey attended to the packing. 'I'm going to miss you a lot,' I said. 'Two weeks seems like a long time. Especially when you are going to be so far away.'

'Twelve days,' he corrected me. 'You'll be with me all the time. Don't you know that, my darling? You know – you have to know – the things that are in my heart. You know what I want to say. I don't have the right. But think of me. I'll be thinking of you.' It was a long speech for Ike, the most taciturn of men when it came to sentiment.

He held my hand and looked at me for a long moment. Then we were on our way to the airport. We must have looked like a kennel on wheels. Telek was in front with me, and in back with Ike and Butch were Telek's son and daughter, Junior and Rubey. The men had decided the puppies were the perfect late-Christmas gifts for their wives. A small crowd was waiting to see the General off. I was grateful that he had arranged for those few private minutes for us to say goodbye. He shook hands with all his staff. I was the last one. He took a slip of paper out of his pocket and said, 'Kay, will you tend to this for me?' 'Certainly, General,' I told him. 'Have a safe trip.'

I stood on the ground watching until the plane disappeared into the haze on the horizon. Back in the car, I looked at the paper he had given me. *Think of me*, he had written. *You know what I will be thinking.* I cried. I simply could not help it. But that was a dangerous indulgence; someone might be watching. I sniffed and angrily scrubbed my fists into my eyes to wipe away the tears and turned the car around to head back to the St-Georges.

After days and nights of heart searching, playing over scene after scene in my head, starting from the very first day I had set eyes on the unknown major-general in Grosvenor Square, I finally became very calm and accepting. I loved Ike. That was all that mattered. I wanted nothing more. It was folly to think of the future. There was a war. If it had been peacetime, it would have been entirely different. An entirely different matter. Then, I believe, I might . . . after a certain time, I think I might . . . I might have said, 'Make up your mind.' But we were living in a different time. In wartime one has an entirely different approach to life, based on the here and now. After all, we were never sure that there would be a tomorrow. We had seen too much. Tomorrow would have to take care of itself.

I would follow my heart. And every one of my heartstrings led to Ike.

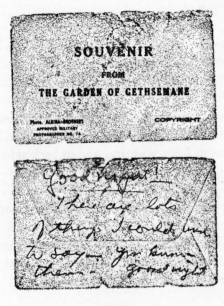

Chapter 21

I flew to London in General Eisenhower's brand-new B-17. It was a fantastically luxurious plane, with wood panelling and comfortable seats upholstered in blue leather. After hitching rides in cargo planes where you were lucky if there was a bench or a row of bucket seats bolted down (and the toilet facilities were also of the bucket variety), I thought this plane, with its carpeting and bunks and a washroom with a flush toilet, was like a Claridge's in the sky. This time I was not travelling with Vuitton cases and silken luxuries carefully wrapped in scented paper. All my belongings were easily stuffed into a duffel bag, and I did not feel the least bit underprivileged. I had learned how unimportant possessions are.

As we drove in from the airfield, everything said home to me: the grimy London buildings, the double-decker buses, the very way the English held themselves as they walked. I was in a rush to go around and see my mother. I was spilling over with all the experiences of the past year – but the most important, I kept to myself. I could not tell even my mother about my feelings for the General. She asked after him with great interest, and I told her all about the suspenseful time when we had not known whether he would be appointed commander for Overlord or be called back to a desk job in Washington. I told her how we had gone riding together at Sailor's Delight. I told her how he had been very ill with the flu. But I never mentioned a word of the love that had grown between us.

The next morning, the world was invisible. I stepped out into such a pea-soup fog, the kind that left your throat raw and your eyes red, as would have done credit to the days of Charles Dickens. One could barely see an arm's length ahead. When I walked into 20 Grosvenor, Tex told me excitedly, 'The Boss is on his way. You'll have to go get him.'

'Marvellous,' I said. 'Where is he coming in?' – getting ready to scramble for the car like a firehorse responding to the bell.

'He's in Scotland,' Tex said. 'He can't fly in because of the fog. They've sent *Bayonet* up for him and he'll be arriving around eleven tonight.' Tex looked concerned. 'Do you think you can drive in this fog? What should we do if it doesn't lift?' I assured him that I could find my way around London blindfolded. 'Don't worry,' I said. 'I'll be very careful. It will be a piece of cake.'

Once I had the car out on the street that night, however, I had my doubts. The fog was thicker. The buses were proceeding at a walk. Literally: most of them were being led by a man going ahead on foot carrying a lantern. I would have to stop every now and then, get out and scuffle around with my feet to find the kerb. I was scared silly of missing a turn and ending up miles out of the way. Even though I had allowed myself ample time, I began to wonder if I would reach the station before the train arrived. I did. Barely. I reached the platform just as the short train pulled in. There behind the engine was old, familiar *Bayonet*, the General's personal railroad car. And there was Butch. And Mickey. And the General. I felt like flinging my arms around him, but this was definitely not the time or the place.

'It's great to be back,' Ike said. Then he stepped out into the night. 'My God!' he exclaimed. 'This is the worst one I've seen. How did you ever get here?'

'No problem,' I said airily. 'I just muddled through.' I was praying that I would be able to muddle through again. I drove the return trip mostly by memory, but when I thought we must be close to 20 Grosvenor, there was no way to tell. The fog was that impenetrable. I stopped and got out, feeling for the kerb with my foot; then I got down and crawled across the sidewalk until I came up against a building wall. I started forward, shuffling so that I wouldn't fall into an open areaway, feeling for a door. I came to one within a few feet – and it was 20 Grosvenor. I had been right on target. It is impossible to describe my relief. 'Here it is!' I shouted. Ike insisted that we form a human chain reaching from the car to the door.

This was not the end of our travels that night. The General had only wanted to stop in at headquarters to check his messages. By the time I had washed the sidewalk grime off my hands, he was ready to go on. Because of his dislike for hotel living, they had found him a lovely town house just off Berkeley Square. Ike said, 'Come on in, Kay. Let's see where they've put me.' We went over the whole house from top to bottom. Ike even wanted to take a look at the basement. He liked the house. 'I don't need a big place like this,' he said, 'but it's very pleasant. Very pleasant. Still and all, I think I would rather be back in Telegraph Cottage.'

'Oh, my goodness,' I said. 'I don't think I could have found the cottage in the fog tonight.' He laughed.

We were all tired. The General had had a long plane trip and the train journey from Scotland on top of that. And I had had a nerve-racking couple of hours driving through fog. It was well after midnight. Butch said that he was going straight to bed, but the General was too wound up to settle down. 'Stay and have a nightcap, Kay,' he said. 'I'm too wide awake to go to bed.'

Mickey had a drink tray ready in no time at all, complete with a plate of cheese sandwiches. I realized that I was starving and gobbled two of them down one right after the other. Ike told Mickey that that would be all for the night, not to wait up for him.

We were alone – or practically. No one was going to come wandering into this living-room tonight. There were no peering eyes. This was no goldfish bowl.

'I've got a lot to tell you,' Ike said. 'Come here.' I sat down beside him, and he put his arm around me. 'I missed you,' he said. 'I missed you too.' We sat and talked. I told him how we had been grounded in Marrakech on the way back to London and spent a couple of days sun-bathing and sight-seeing. And he told me a bit about his stay in the States.

'After two days, I started getting itchy,' he said. 'I wanted to get back here and get to work. But Marshall insisted that I needed the whole twelve days as vacation. Some vacation. I spent as much of it as I could in the Pentagon.' He stopped and then said, 'Oh my God, I almost forgot. I saw the President while I was in Washington and he asked after you.'

'He did?'

'Yes, he did. He sent you his very best wishes and he gave me something for you.' Ike went out into the hall and yelled for Mickey. 'Where's that big envelope from the White House?' he asked when a sleepy Mickey came down the stairs. Mickey was back in a couple of minutes with the envelope. 'Will there be anything else?' he asked. 'No, no,' Ike said. 'Go to bed. Get some sleep.' And poor Mickey trudged upstairs again.

I opened the big envelope. It was a photograph of President Roosevelt inscribed to me. I was very flattered. Ever since the war, I have had my own photograph gallery of heroes – autographed pictures of General Eisenhower, Prime Minister Churchill and President Roosevelt. No matter where I have lived, they have always hung in the place of honour in my living-room.

Ike refilled our glasses several times and then, I suppose inevitably, we found ourselves in each other's arms in an unrestrained embrace. Our ties came off. Our jackets came off. Buttons were unbuttoned. It was as if we were frantic. And we were.

But this was not what I had expected. Wearily, we slowly calmed down. He snuggled his face into the hollow between my neck and shoulder and said, 'Oh God, Kay. I'm sorry. I'm not going to be any good for you.' I didn't know what to say except, 'You're good enough for me. What you need is some sleep.' It was a bit embarrassing struggling back into the clothes that had been flung on the floor. Finally we were dressed. Ike looked troubled. 'I don't want to let you go,' he said. 'But you can't stay here. God, I'm sorry. I can't even drive you home.'

'Don't worry,' I told him. 'I'll be fine. It's just around the corner.' We kissed good night. As he let me out the door, I saluted. 'Good night, General. I'll be here in the morning.' One never knew who might be lurking in the fog ready to catch an indiscreet word.

I was ready to go to sleep then and there with my head on the steering wheel. Or was I ready to bawl my head off? I did neither; simply drove another few blocks through the fog and got myself to bed. My last thought as I dropped off to sleep was to the effect that things are never the way you think they'll be.

I was back at the house at breakfast time. 'Come on, Kay,' Ike said. 'You better have an egg. We've got a big day ahead of us.' He and

Butch were very cheerful and energetic. The inner qualms I had had about seeing Ike this morning disappeared in the daylight. The fog had lifted. And life seemed bright again. Ike was discussing plans with Butch. He had decided to move SHAEF out of Grosvenor Square to Bushey Park, and take over the group of buildings where Tooey Spaatz's Eighth Air Force used to be headquartered. 'I'm going to move the whole shebang out to Kingston,' he told us. 'That way we won't get caught up in all that la-di-da London society stuff, and the officers will be thrown together so they'll get to know each other and each other's ways fast. I want to turn this command into a very close-knit group. It's the only way.'

I interrupted. 'Does that mean we can go back to Telegraph Cottage?'

'You're damned right it does.' Butch and I beamed at each other. 'When?' I asked. 'As soon as possible,' Ike said briskly. 'We'll keep this place for when I have to spend a night in London, but Telegraph Cottage is going to be home.' He said this last with great satisfaction.

After outlining his plans, Ike dispatched Butch to Bushey Park to start setting things up, and I drove Ike around to Grosvenor Square. We slipped right back into routine. That afternoon I drove the General out to Bushey Park. 'Let's make a detour,' he said. 'I'd like to take a look at the cottage. I've missed that little house.' Nothing could have pleased me more. I took the familiar turn and soon came to the driveway with the white pole across it.

'Goddamnit!' I said as I got out to swing the pole aside.

'What was that you said?' Ike asked, startled.

'It's that pole.'

'Oh,' he remarked. 'I just wondered where you picked up that kind of language.'

The house was just as we had remembered it. Adorable. 'Okay, let's go,' Ike said. I turned the car around to leave. Then he said, 'Just a minute.' I looked up at the rear-view mirror to see what he wanted.

His lips were grim and straight. 'I'm sorry about last night.' He was talking into the air over my shoulder. 'I told you a long time ago that I was out of practise in love.'

'I'm the one who should apologize,' I said. 'I should have known how exhausted you were. I should have known better.' I should have. It was not as if I did not know what he had been through in the last two weeks. Days crammed with family and military affairs. A long and exhausting air trip. On top of that, a twelve-hour train ride to London. He had been exhausted. Butch had been sensible and gone straight to bed. But we, the greedy lovers, had stayed up until after two in the morning. I was old enough to know better. I was sophisticated enough to know that a man in his fifties has only so much resilience.

'You're not terribly disappointed, then?'

'No, I'm not disappointed. Not a bit. Because now I know . . .' I hesitated. It was hard to say it. 'Now I know that someday we . . . well, you know . . . someday we're going to,' I ended rather incoherently.

'Maybe,' said Ike. He did not sound convinced. But I was not worried. I only wished that we did not have to have our very intimate emotional exchanges in the car. It is very difficult to respond to a voice coming over your shoulder, to a face you see only in the rear-view mirror.

Chapter 22

In no time at all, SHAEF was transferred to Bushey Park, and our little family along with it. Ike and Butch were back in Telegraph Cottage once again with Mickey and Sergeants Moaney and Hunt. I was about two minutes away, sharing a house with the five WACs. And Beetle flew in from Algiers to resume his duties as chief-of-staff, bringing Telek along with him.

Poor Telek had to go straight to a kennel for six months. The English quarantine laws are fantastically strict. They are not broken even for the Royal Family. The first time we went to visit him at the kennel, a crowd of journalists and photographers was lying in wait. Someone, probably the kennel people, had tipped off the press, and the result was a rash of cloying stories about Ike and Telek all over the London papers. Ike was boiling mad. In North Africa he had been well protected from the intrusions of the penny press, and he did not enjoy meeting up with them again.

The two of us sneaked back to the kennel the next day. I brought my old handbag for Telek so that he would not feel completely deserted. For the next six months, he always slept with his head on it. We went to see him at least twice a week, like visiting a prisoner. Telek would go wild with joy, but when we left, he sat there utterly dejected. Ike once said, 'This is terrible. I feel as if I have locked up part of my heart.' At first we saved all our beef bones for him, but this turned out to be a mistake. He got a stoppage, and the veterinarian told us very crossly, 'No more bones.'

Not everyone shared our love for Telek and his family. One evening I asked rather idly after Rubey and Junior. Were they thriving in

Washington? 'God only knows,' Ike growled. Both Mrs Eisenhower and Mrs Butcher had been dismayed at the sight of the puppies, he reported, and doubly dismayed when the poor things made a puddle on the living-room Oriental. Butch had had to spend a good part of his leave finding homes for the cuddly black waifs.

Ike made himself a drink and settled down in his favourite big chair by the fire. I was sitting across from him, my feet on the brass fender. It was cold and dark outside, warm and cosy within. 'There was the very devil to pay,' he said, 'from the moment we walked in with those two pups until I left. And it wasn't only the dogs.'

His lips twitched. He finally gave in and grinned. 'The big trouble was . . . I kept calling her Kay. That tore it.'

'What?'

'I kept calling her Kay. Every time I opened my mouth to say something to Mamie, I'd call her Kay. She was furious.'

I am ashamed to say that nothing could have pleased me more. No pity for Mrs Eisenhower spoiled my enjoyment. Today I feel great sympathy for her. It must have been a cruel shock to realize that another woman was uppermost in her husband's thoughts. But at that time, she was far away. And I was a woman in love.

'I'm sorry about that,' I said. 'It must have been a bit upsetting for her. And for you too.'

'Jesus Christ! You have no idea.' Ike was smoking one cigarette after another – lighting one from the tip of the last, then throwing the stub into the fire. 'I thought about you a lot,' he said. 'You know what I like to think about nights before I go to sleep?'

I shook my head.

'The first time I ever set eyes on you. I saw you walking along Grosvenor Square. You looked very glamorous. Beautiful. And all of a sudden, you started running straight towards me. It was as if you had read my mind. Then you stopped. All out of breath. And asked if one of us was General Eisenhower. Well! I thought I was dreaming. You would never believe how disappointed I was to discover that Claridge's was so close to headquarters. I wanted that drive to last forever.'

'You never told me that,' I said.

'You know me,' he protested. 'There are so many times I look at you and want to tell you how beautiful you are and how much you mean to me, but something always stops me. I suppose it's this stolid German-Swiss heritage of mine that makes me feel a man should not talk about such things. For God's sake, there were months when I could not let myself face how I felt about you. I used to think that if I had a daughter I would want her to be just like you. It took a disaster to ram the truth home to me. I had to nearly lose you before I could admit to myself that my feelings were more than paternal.

'And then there's something else. I just don't have the right to tell you what I want to tell you.'

When I think about the long talks we used to have at Telegraph Cottage, I am overwhelmed with nostalgia. Not that we were ever really alone. There was never once that the two of us had the house to ourselves – but we had privacy. We began to feel quite relaxed, sitting quietly in front of the fire, or on our favourite secluded bench hidden in the shrubbery, hand in hand, my head on his shoulder – talking our hearts out. Just enjoying being together.

I suspect that over the years – long before Ike and I ever set foot in Telegraph Cottage – many couples had sat in front of its fire and whispered confidences to each other. There was something about the atmosphere of that little house that bred intimacy and trust. It was easy to talk about all the things that one had never spoken of before. Of secret fears. Of past mistakes. Of withering sorrows.

It was in that living-room one sunny morning that Ike talked very seriously and at length about his relationship with his wife. There was deep hurt on both sides, hurt so deep that they were never able to re-capture their earlier relationship – although it was not for want of trying. Ike had applied to himself the wisdom he had shared with me that 'activity helps'; had thrown himself so completely into his work that there was room for nothing else. It was hard for him to tell the story, even in the benign atmosphere of Telegraph Cottage. He would say a few words, then halt. His voice was low. Most of the time he was leaning forward in his chair looking down at the floor.

'Kay, I guess I'm telling you that I'm not the lover you should have. It killed something in me. Not all at once, but little by little. For years I never thought of making love. And then when I did . . . when it had been on my mind for weeks, I failed. I failed with you, my dearest. Didn't I?'

I sat on the arm of his chair and cuddled his head against my breast. 'It's all right. It's all right,' I crooned to him the way my mother used to soothe me when I was a child. 'I love you. It's all right.'

He straightened up, took out his handkerchief and honked into it. His eyes were red. 'I'm sorry. I'm a damned fool. But you know that. God, I don't know what's the matter with me.'

'Nothing. Nothing at all,' I whispered.

'Somehow I just lost the way,' he said, standing with his back to me looking out the window.

'Some day things will be different,' I promised him. 'I'm not Irish and stubborn for nothing.'

It would be incorrect to think that the General and I spent most of our time exploring our emotions and feelings for each other. We were far too busy for that kind of introspective luxury. I was now acting as his appointments secretary. There could not have been a better job for me. I knew everyone the General knew and almost everything that was going on. And I knew the General – the people he liked, the people he tolerated and the people who drove him up the wall. I now had my own private office and my own secretary. I loved the job. It was a natural extension of our relationship.

No one could get in to see the General without going through my office first. I also took all his telephone calls. I would say, 'General Eisenhower's office. Miss Summersby speaking.' Then I would pop into his office and say, 'General So-and-So is on the line,' or 'The PM is calling you.' That way he was spared the jangling of the telephone and the irritation of the intercom buzzer. These were trivial annoyances, of course, but it was important to make his office life as smoothly efficient and pleasant as possible. He had enough problems without having to suffer avoidable irritation. When a visitor was staying too long or I thought that the General might want to cut a meeting short, I'd go into his office with a piece of paper in my hand and say, 'Excuse me, General. This message just came in.' Then whoever it was would usually say, 'Well, I've got to be going.' And if he didn't, Ike would say, 'I'm sorry. It looks as if we're going to have to cut this short,' and stand up so that his caller would have no choice but to rise to his feet as well. And that would be that.

Young officers who had been summoned to the Supreme Commander's office, usually to be congratulated on some achievement, would wait in my office. They would be nervous. Simply petrified. 'What should I say to him?' they would ask. 'What will I do when I'm in there?'

'Just be yourself,' I would say. 'Say what you have to say and you'll find out that you get along very well.'

Afterwards, when they came out of the General's office, their faces would be glowing. Ike always knew exactly how to put people at ease, and he liked talking to these young men. It was a bit of relaxation for him. He was really very, very busy in those months preceding the invasion of the Continent. A typical day would have a string of appointments that would read like this:

10:30	General Betts
11:30	Conference of the Commanders-in-Chief
12:30	General Prentice
1:30	Lunch with the PM
8:00	Dinner with Admiral Stark
10:00	General Spaatz

Each of these conferences would be on some vital aspect of mounting the invasion, and Ike was the only man who had all phases of the operation in his head. Then, for two or three days at a time, we would leave SHAEF and travel all over England and Scotland visiting different bases. Every time we came back from an inspection trip, Ike would have another cold. He wanted to visit every installation – including hospitals and certain factories – before the invasion: an almost impossible task. He would talk with the commanding officers, inspect the men's quarters, tour the mess and then talk to as many men as he possibly could. He wanted the men to know that the Supreme Commander was concerned about them.

He liked groups of three and four, where he could shake each man's hand and say a few personal words. Then he would move on to another group. He was awfully good at this, and the men liked him. They weren't just putting it on. You could tell that they really liked him. But when we got back to headquarters, he would be so hoarse that Ethel would be popping into and out of the office all day long, spraying his throat, taking his temperature and scolding him that he should be in bed.

His office was probably the worst place possible for a man with Ike's tendency to catch cold. It was unheated, as were all the offices. And although, in deference to his rank as Supreme Commander, there was a carpet on the floor, it was a very thin carpet and the damp chill of the concrete floor seeped right through it. We all wore long underwear when we worked there, and Ike often wore two pairs of socks to try to keep warm, but he suffered acutely from the cold. He developed a cough that lasted for months, and he was always getting little infections because he was so run down.

I still have my little blue leather appointment book for 1944. It is very shabby now and rather hard to read, because I scribbled everything down in a hurry and much of it is smudged. I used to jot down his appointments and add a word or two about the subject under discussion or Ike's comment on the meeting. One Friday, for instance, the most important entry was *Lunch with the King and Queen at Buckingham Palace, 1:30.* Later that day, I added Ike's report on the lunch: *Most enjoyable 2 hours.*

Little by little, the small blue book turned into a combination appointment book and diary. Ike would say, 'Bring the book in, Kay.' He would leaf through it – sometimes to check on what had been discussed the last time he saw a certain general, or sometimes just to relax. He would say, 'Oh, that was a great day. We had a good time, didn't we?' and laugh. Then he started writing in it himself. One Sunday he recorded the day's activities: *Office until 1:30 p.m. Home to lunch, then went for drive. Found very short way to kennels.* Another day he wrote: *Terribly busy at office. Had lunch at desk. Worked late, but saw Telek on way home. Beetle and Ethel came to dinner. To bed early.* I was the driver, of course, who found the short way to the kennels, and I was also there for dinner with Beetle and Ethel, but we never wrote such things down, even though the diary was kept safely tucked away.

I drew on the material in this little blue book when I wrote my first book a quarter of a century ago, but I was very careful about how I used it. In that book, for instance, I wrote: 'On an inspection trip to Scotland, he managed to get in an entire day of salmon fishing at the lovely estate of Colonel Ivan Cobbald.' A bland enough, non-gossip-provoking report. But what I had written in the diary at the end of that day in 1944 was: *Started fishing at Cobbald's place at 9:30. No luck at all. Beautiful weather though. I caught a baby salmon – three inches. E. got a kelt, which was bad luck as he had to throw it back in the river. We all had a lovely time, wish we could have stayed longer.*

Ike needed every possible diversion like this fishing trip that he could possibly get. He was as nervous as I had ever seen him and was extremely depressed. There were times when the problems that faced him seemed insurmountable. It is impossible to list them all. There was the problem of getting enough supplies to mount the invasion. He kept pleading for more landing craft. There were the inevitable problems arising from the fact that hundreds of thousands of American and Canadian soldiers were now tucked away all over England. It did not seem possible that one more man could fit on to this island – but every day, troopship after troopship unloaded new units. There were rapes, thefts, fights – the same problems that have bedevilled every army in history.

There was General de Gaulle, proud and prickly, who became so incensed at one point that he stalked out of a luncheon meeting, threatening the intricately woven fabric of Allied unity. There was General Montgomery, who resisted each and every directive of Eisenhower's and always wanted to do things in his own way at his own chosen time. Even the PM was a problem of sorts. An amateur of war, Mr Churchill had fresh ideas every day on how to conduct the invasion and insisted on imparting them to Ike himself. He often telephoned after midnight to discuss a new brainstorm. Ike could not simply tell the PM, 'That idea stinks.' He had to point out to him exactly why such and such an idea would not work or would not be politic. This took a lot of time and an awful lot of patience.

Telegraph Cottage became more important in maintaining the General's equilibrium than ever before. It was so close that it was easy for him to go home for lunch. That little break in the day helped him relax. Many days, if he had no afternoon appointments, he would not return to Bushey Park, but would stay home and go over his papers, then get some exercise.

We spent many afternoons riding in Richmond Park, just minutes away from the cottage. This is an absolutely delightful spot, with miles and miles of bridle paths winding through woods, along lakes and past some very beautiful houses, many of them royal 'grace and favour' dwellings in which relatives and friends live at the invitation of the Royal Family. We often rode past White Lodge, a royal residence that had been much favoured by Queen Victoria. It was not what one ordinarily thinks of as a lodge, but a big stone mansion. Ike had learned that the King and Queen had spent their honeymoon here and that the Duke of Windsor had been born here. That made the place interesting to him.

When the weather was bad, Ike indulged himself in a favourite hobby: cooking. Actually, I think anyone would enjoy cooking Ike's way. He had Hunt and Moaney to do all the dirty work. They did the chopping and measuring, set out all the ingredients – and, of course, they washed up afterwards.

His beef stew was really very tasty, but one had to know how to eat his fried chicken. I remember watching him make it one day. He always insisted on an audience. Butch and I and Tooey and Beetle and Ethel all stood around while Ike presided at the kitchen table. Hunt and Moaney followed his orders just like two nurses assisting a famous surgeon. Moaney cut the chicken up in pieces, and Hunt produced the ingredients for Ike's coating mixture.

Ike would say, 'Measuring spoon,' and Hunt would hand him the spoon. He would say, 'Chili powder,' and Hunt would open the little tin and pass it to him. Ike measured out each ingredient and dumped it into a bowl. When he was measuring out the chili powder, Butch groaned, 'There's not enough beer in England to put out that kind of fire.' Ike rolled the chicken pieces in the mixture and then started instructing Moaney as to just how hot the fat in the skillet should be. At that point, Tooey and Beetle intervened. They had been through this before and insisted that Ike join us in the living-room for a drink before dinner.

When we sat down to eat, Ike said, 'Now, isn't this great?' And we all agreed that it was. I discovered that if I scraped off the coating, which was throat-burning hot, the chicken was absolutely delicious. Moaney really knew how to fry chicken.

When the ground got dry enough in the spring, we played a little golf, and we played bridge every night that Ike was home. We had a lot of visitors. One I remember very well was Averell Harriman, who arrived from Moscow one day with a huge tin of caviar. We all sat around the table piling great gobs of it on Melba toast and washing it down with champagne. Butch looked at the caviar and the champagne bottles and said, 'Now I know what they mean when they say war is hell.'

Mummy joined us several times for dinner at the cottage. Georgie Patton was a guest one night that she was there, and I was a bit apprehensive about how she would react to his profanity, but the evening went by with only the mildest of outbursts from the usually incorrigible general, who put himself out to be gallant. Ike was always extremely thoughtful of my family. Once during this period he invited my brother to accompany him on a tour of air bases. When the photographers clustered around, as they did at every stop, Seamus quietly withdrew to the sidelines, but Ike said, 'Seamus, you have to be in this too,' and drew him into the group. It was gestures like this that showed Ike's truly deep consideration. He did everything he possibly could to make people feel good.

Ike still tried to sketch Telegraph Cottage, but was never satisfied with the results. One evening he had his sketch pad on his knee and was busy drawing. I looked over his shoulder and discovered that he was drawing floor plans, not a picture.

'What do you think?' he asked, holding out the pad. 'It struck me that if I owned this place, I'd want to make a few changes.' He had designed a little wing with a new kitchen and a little maid's room and bath. He thought that the present kitchen should be turned into a big dining-room and that another fireplace should be built where the old stove was. We had a lot of fun talking about the changes we'd like to make. After that, he would quite often pick up his pad and work out different floor plans for the cottage. He had a lot of very good ideas and would get completely absorbed in working them out. It was almost as much of an escape for him as playing bridge.

He also spent quite a bit of time planning the vegetable garden. He had some gorgeous seed catalogues sent to him from the States, and he would go through them and make lists of what he wanted to plant. When he came to some vegetable that he particularly liked, he'd stop and read the description to me. It was impossible to convince him that even though my father had been quite a noted gardener in County Cork, I knew less than nothing about sticking seeds into the ground and having them come up to be something one could eat. But he persisted. He would read things like ' "Lima beans, the finest, meatiest, most delicious beans. Strong plants." What do you think, Kay? Do you like lima beans? Here's another variety. "Very large flat beans with pink spots".'

'Oh,' I remember saying once, 'beans with pink spots. By all means. They should be very pretty.'

'That's not the point,' he snapped.

But there came a day when all this stopped abruptly. It was late May and the invasion was imminent. Everything we had been working for since the first of the year was about to be set in motion. The only major problem that still had to be resolved was – when? The invasion date had been narrowed down to a span of a few possible days when the moon and the tides would be on our side. Now everything depended on the weather. The General had the meteorologists on the telephone almost every hour, asking for the latest forecast. And at the end of May, we left Telegraph Cottage and moved to advance headquarters in the woods outside Portsmouth.

Chapter 23

Ike was bleakly depressed. And I reflected his mood. Our advance headquarters, hidden in the woods at Southwick about five miles north of Portsmouth, were dreary beyond belief. It was raining on and off, and the trees were dripping on to the roof of the trailer we used as an office. I kept thinking of Telegraph Cottage as we had left it. The sun had been shining, and every flower of spring had seemed to be blossoming in the garden. Here there was nothing but gloom.

The story of the D-Day decision and how much depended on the one thing man could not control – the weather – has been told and told again. There was a certain combination of moon, tide and sunrise needed for the attack on the Normandy beaches, and there were three days in early June that would provide the combination: the fifth, sixth and seventh. But without good weather the attack could not be mounted, and it would be some time before the moon and tide and sunrise would be properly synchronized again. This problem had been hanging over the General's head for months. He consulted with the meteorologists almost as often as he consulted with his top commanders. Hundreds of thousands of highly-trained soldiers, millions of tons of supplies, aircraft, ships – everything had been assembled for the invasion, all poised to go into action as soon as Ike gave the word. Sometimes it seemed as if Britain would sink under the weight of men and matériel. And everything hung on one unknown quantity: the weather.

On 4 June, the forecast for the following day was heavy clouds, high winds and rough seas. It would be impossible to land the men if waves were pounding on the beaches and equally impossible to provide air support without good visibility. The General postponed the invasion.

The long-range forecast was for more of the same. Ike could not have been more anxiety-ridden. There were smouldering cigarettes in every ashtray in the trailer. He would light one, put it down, forget it and light another. He was having blood-pressure headaches, and his stomach was giving him trouble too. Every once in a while he would bend over with a terrible gas pain.

He grumbled that military textbooks taught that the weather was neutral, but that in his experience – in North Africa, in Italy and now – the weather was always partisan, and on the side of the Germans. He marched up and down the trailer, stopping occasionally to stare out at the drizzle, his hands on his hips. Occasionally the sun would break through for a minute, and he would rush outside to look at the sky and tell me to get the weathermen on the telephone. He couldn't eat. He simply drank pot after pot of coffee and smoked.

At four o'clock in the morning of the next day, 5 June, the meteorologists phoned through a report that there would be a break in the weather. It very much looked as if 6 June would be a fine, clear day – and possibly 7 June as well. This did not give Ike much leeway. There was no assurance that the weather would not change suddenly, capriciously – faster than the weathermen had predicted. There were no guarantees. He listened. And then – fifteen minutes after he got that early-morning report – Ike made the decision that only he could make. The invasion was on. D-Day would be 6 June.

The General held a press conference that morning to brief the pool journalists who would cover the invasion. From then on, the pace was unrelenting. Orders were sent to ships already at sea and to those waiting in crowded harbours fringing the English Channel, to the commanding generals and to the Allied statesmen. The PM and his retinue arrived at the trailer. General de Gaulle came by. Field-Marshal Smuts of South Africa dropped in, and so did a dozen others. There were messages from Washington and London. Messages from commanders. From Monty. It was a frantic day. At one point Ike said, 'I hope to God I know what I'm doing. There are times when you have to put everything you are and everything you have ever learned on the line. This is one of them.'

'I know,' I told him, 'and if it goes all right, dozens of people will claim the credit. But if it goes wrong, you'll be the only one to get the blame.' I was wrong, as it turned out. Everyone gave Ike the credit he was due.

At six that evening he stopped everything. He had something important to do, something that turned out to be the most memorable event of the whole war for me. My little blue diary holds this entry: *6:30 p.m., start trip to visit Airborne troops in the Newbury area. Gen. Taylor. Visited 3 airfields. Morale of troops very high. Watched some of them take off. Wonderful sight.*

This conveys no idea of the drama of that evening. The 101st Airborne Division, commanded by General Maxwell Taylor, was the key to seizing Utah Beach and the eventual capture of Cherbourg. Not everyone agreed with this aspect of Ike's battle plan. Some British commanders thought that he was sending these men on a suicidal mission and that the casualties would be crushing, as high as eighty per cent. Ike never ignored dissenting opinions like this. He always sought and considered the views of his commanders, considered them very seriously. I think that was why he was so successful as Supreme Commander. He would not agree with the Americans just because he was an American. He would listen to the English, to the French, to the Czechs, to the Canadians, to the Poles. He would listen to the lot of them. And he was equally courteous to each. Then he would make up his own mind. Now he went over and over his battle plans. He spent hours alone in his tent checking every calculation he had made, taking everything that could possibly go wrong into account – and decided to stick to his plan. But he was worried.

And the night before D-Day, we dropped everything to make the long drive to Newbury and visit the 101st Airborne. They would be the first troops to land in Normandy behind the enemy lines. Some would be towed over in huge gliders that would settle down quietly in the darkness with their cargoes of young fighting men. Others would parachute down into this heavily fortified area. Ike's last task on the eve of D-Day was to wish these men well.

There was no military pomp about his visit. His flag was not flying from the radiator of the car, and he had told me to cover the four stars on the red plate. We drove up to each of the airfields, and Ike got out and just started walking among the men. When they realized who it was, the word went from group to group like the wind blowing across a meadow, and then everyone went crazy. The roar was unbelievable. They cheered and whistled and shouted, 'Good old Ike!'

There they were, these young paratroopers in their bulky combat kits with their faces blackened so that they would be invisible in the dark of the French midnight. Anything that could not be carried in their pockets was strapped on their backs or to their arms and legs. Many of them had packages of cigarettes strapped to their thighs. They looked so young and so brave. I stood by the car and watched as the General walked among them with his military aide a few paces behind him. He went from group to group and shook hands with as many men as he could. He spoke a few words to every man as he shook his hand, and he looked the man in the eye as he wished him success. 'It's very hard really to look a soldier in the eye,' he told me later, 'when you fear that you are sending him to his death.'

The good weather promised by the meteorologists had arrived, and all the time that Ike had been talking to the paratroopers there was the most spectacular sunset – deep glowing colours stretching across the sky. As it faded and the light started to go, the men began to embark. General Maxwell Taylor was the last to leave. Ike walked him to his plane and shook hands with him, and then we went over to the headquarters building of the 101st and climbed up to the roof.

The planes were taking off, roaring down the runways and climbing, climbing. Soon there were hundreds circling above us. By this time, it was dark and the moon had come up. It was a full moon, so brilliant that it cast shadows. The planes, wheeling like some immense flock of birds, blotted it out from time to time. It was such a gigantic moment! My heart was pounding, and I was practically crying. I knew I had never seen anything like it before and never would see anything like it again. We stayed on the roof for a long time watching the planes. Ike stood there with his hands in his pockets, his face tipped towards the sky. The planes kept circling, and then they began tailing off and headed towards Normandy. We sighed. A lot of those men, men whom Ike had just been walking with, shaking hands with, were going to their deaths.

The General turned and left the roof without saying a word to anyone. I hurried after him, but then I stopped. He was walking very slowly, his head bent. I could not intrude. He needed to be alone. Before he got into the car, he turned to me and said, 'Well, it's on. No one can stop it now.' There were tears in his eyes. We were silent as we drove back along the moonlit road to the trailer in the woods at Southwick.

For the next few hours, we just sat in the trailer waiting for the first reports. There was nothing Ike could do. Just wait. The hours went by. Like everyone else in England, we could hear the roar of planes, rising up from airfields all over the land, heading across the Channel. Every once in a while, I would stand behind Ike and massage his shoulders, trying to relax him just a trifle. He liked that. 'Um, that's good,' he'd always say, but in those tense pre-dawn hours, no matter how much strength I used, I could not undo the knots at the base of his neck. His eyes were bloodshot, and he was so tired that his hand shook when he lit a cigarette.

It is very hard to watch the man you love going through such a torture, waiting to find out the consequences of one of the gravest decisions that ever faced one man – a decision that, when you really face up to it, was nothing more nor less than a huge gamble, a gamble with hundreds of thousands of lives as the stake. You can't say, 'Don't worry.' That would be stupid. You can't say, 'Everything is going to be all right,' because there is a very good chance that everything may not be all right. All you can do is be there – and bite your tongue. It meant a lot to me that I was the person he chose to be with in those crucial hours. If Ike had wished, he could have been surrounded by top brass, by Churchill and De Gaulle, by any of the important personages who were gathered just a few miles away in Portsmouth. But he preferred to wait in solitude. And I was the one he permitted to share his solitude.

'What are your thoughts, Kay?' he asked at one point.

'I can't believe it,' I told him. 'After living here through the Blitz and everything . . . to be cut off for so long . . . just an island . . . and now to be landing on the Continent! After all these years of waiting and waiting and taking all the defeats from Dunkirk on . . . I just can't believe we've done it.

'I've been thinking of the first time you came to London and I drove you and Mark Clark to Dover. I heard you say something about "when we get over there", and I thought that we had a very slim chance of ever doing that. But now we have. You did it.'

'We'll see,' he said. 'We don't know yet whether we did it or not.'

It was quiet in the trailer except for the roaring of planes, as wave after wave of bombers streamed across the Channel to provide air support for the men landing on the beaches. The noise seemed to underline how remote and helpless we were at this moment. A couple of times I told him, 'Well, you know, I think you ought to go and lie down for a little while.' Around four in the morning, he finally agreed and said, 'You should do the same.' So we went back to quarters. We were all living in tents there at Southwick, and I thought it looked like some American Indian village.

The first reports were telephoned through to him a couple of hours later. Things were going well. The Germans had been caught unaware. 6 June was a beautiful sunny day. It was the beginning of the end of the war.

Chapter 24

There was a terrible let-down after D-Day. Everyone felt it. Ike was tired as if he had run out of steam. And he was very much depressed. Forty-eight hours after the attack had been mounted, he made a quick trip by destroyer to consult with his commanders and see what could be seen from the deck as the destroyer skirted the Normandy coastline, but most of the time we simply sat in the trailer in the woods waiting. Waiting for reports from the front. The Germans were fighting bitterly. We had a lot of casualties. But overall, the reports were encouraging. Ike always wanted to know more, however. We stayed late every night waiting for just one more report to come through. I would call up the mess and have them send over sandwiches for supper, and I would boil water on the little spirit stove for Ike's powdered coffee. He would sit there and smoke and worry. Every time the telephone rang, he would grab it.

When he had to go to London – and there were conferences in London and Bushey Park about every other day – he would insist on getting back to Portsmouth at night, even if it meant leaving London after midnight. Once he was able to set foot in France, some six days after D-Day, and talk to Monty, Bradley and some of the other commanders, he began to feel better. He was able to straighten out a lot of the logistics and communications problems on that visit.

There was something else that helped pull him out of his depression, and that was the knowledge that his son, John, would be in England very soon. Ike had told General Marshall that he was worried that he and his son were becoming almost like strangers. He had seen less of

John over the years than most fathers because of the demands of the military life. And during the past three years, he had seen practically nothing of him. Marshall had been extremely sympathetic and suggested that after John graduated from West Point in June, he might spend his leave in England with his father. Ike thought that was a grand idea, and during the spring he had often said things like 'When John gets here, we'll do this or that,' and 'When John gets here, we must be sure to go here or there.' He was always making plans for that visit. But then when D-Day was imminent, he told me rather dispiritedly, 'I'm afraid John's visit will have to be put off.'

'Oh?' said I.

'Yes,' he said. 'Graduation is on 6 June. With any luck, I should be in France then. And I'm not sure that I want the boy up at the front with me.'

General Marshall evidently did not share Ike's misgivings, because one of the messages that came into the trailer late on D-Day was to the effect that John would be arriving in Scotland on 13 June. Ike sent Tex up to Scotland in *Bayonet* to escort John to London, and late in the afternoon of 13 June, a tall, fresh-faced second-lieutenant walked into the office at SHAEF, put his arms around the Supreme Commander and kissed him. Ike was just one big grin. After giving John a quick tour of headquarters, we left for Telegraph Cottage. When I left around midnight, Ike and John were still talking a mile a minute trying to catch up with everything.

I was interested to observe that Ike was not a particularly doting father. He loved John very much and he was proud of him, but he was also critical. Sometimes I thought he was super-critical. John was a truly nice young man. He was intelligent, lots of fun, every bit as charming as his father and very simple and unassuming in manner. Not for one moment during his visit did he presume upon the fact that his father was Supreme Commander. He bent over backwards to observe protocol and be self-effacing. Nevertheless, his father saw room for improvement.

On the first evening at the cottage, John told us how excited he had been at the idea of coming to England, especially at such an important time. In order to leave West Point as soon as possible after the graduation ceremonies, he had done all his packing and turned in all his equipment, which included the mattress for his cot, the night before graduation. He reported that he had spent an uncomfortable, restless night on the bare springs of the cot.

I watched Ike's face become more and more closed as John was talking. He looked quite stern, although he said nothing. Later I asked him what had been going through his mind that made him look that way.

'What was going through my mind,' he said grimly, 'was that across the Channel there are thousands of young men sleeping in fox-holes – if they're lucky. And my son complains about a restless night on a cot without a mattress.'

'He wasn't complaining,' I said. 'He was just telling a story. What did you expect him to do? Go out and dig a foxhole?'

'I suppose not,' Ike grumbled, 'but I think he should toughen up.'

Then there were times when the brand-new second-lieutenant, eager to talk to his father about matters military as one military man to another, would venture some textbook observation only to have Ike snort, 'Oh, for God's sake!' Most of the time, however, Ike was the unabashedly proud and beaming father, and he had every reason to be. He enjoyed briefing John on what was going on in the most minute detail, and he took him along on a couple of inspection tours in Normandy.

Ike did his paternal best to teach John everything he knew during those two weeks, and that included bridge as well as military matters. He told John that his game needed sharpening up, so evening after evening we sat around the card table at the cottage while Ike analysed his son's game and told him what he was doing wrong. This was the only time the house rule about no post mortems was ever broken, and sometimes it got a bit uncomfortable, as Ike was as brusque with John as he was with any other young officer who needed to be pulled up a bit. But John took it all very good-naturedly. No matter how sharply Ike criticized him, it was obvious that he adored this son of his.

But not even John could distract his father's mind from the war. The invasion was still young, and the news was not always good. I remember one day – it was 19 June – when Ike heard that the weather over the Channel was so bad that all shipping was at a standstill. That meant that troops and supplies could not be landed. When the bad news was telephoned through to the cottage, Ike said, 'I need a drink.' This was the first and only time I ever heard him say that. I mixed him a Scotch and water. 'More Scotch,' he ordered, so I poured in a very healthy slug on top of his usual ounce-and-a-half jigger. 'That's good. I needed that,' he said as he gulped it down. The reason for his strong reaction was that if the invasion had been postponed earlier, 19 June would have been its next possible date. That storm turned out to be the most violent storm in fifty years, an actual hurricane, and was a real setback for the Allies – but nowhere near the disaster that it would have been if the invasion had been scheduled to take place at that time.

Before John arrived, Ike had worried about exposing him to danger at the front, but as it turned out, life in England had its own hazards. John's visit coincided with the first of the V-1 bombs. We called them buzz bombs. Something like small planes without pilots, they were launched from platforms in France. Usually, the first warning one got was a kind of drone that got louder and louder as the bomb approached. Then the engine would cut out. That was when you started holding your breath, because it meant the bomb was falling. It was impossible to tell where it would land until it exploded. You could see the falling bombs overhead like deadly black wasps. Many people felt these robot bombs were even worse than the Blitz. I never got over the creeps when I heard one, but Ike said their impact was more psychological than physical.

It was the buzz bombs that drove Ike to using the shelter at the cottage. Months earlier, when the PM had learned there was no bomb shelter on the grounds, he had peremptorily ordered one built. It was a rather unsightly mound, a quick scamper from the house. Ike had never used it, but now we were grateful for it. The second night of John's visit, we all slept in the shelter. We had been in it four or five times that evening. It must have been quite a sight as we all rushed out of the house and ran down the garden path. Finally Ike said, 'Well, we've got to get some sleep tonight. I guess the only place we'll get it is in the shelter.' There were plenty of cots, and Ike, John, Butch and I managed to squeeze in along with Moaney and Hunt and Mickey. It was very close quarters, but as the nights went by, we got used to sleeping there.

I was almost as sorry as Ike when John's visit drew to a close. It had really been nice having him around. But then Ike gave me the most glorious surprise. As we were going over the day's appointments in the office one early morning, he asked, right out of the blue, 'How would you like to go to Washington with John? Spend a few days there? Maybe go to New York?'

I opened my mouth, but could not get any sound out.

'I'm serious,' he said. 'I'm going to be in France all next week. There won't be much for you to do here. John is going back in the Fortress, so there will be plenty of room. What do you think?'

'I think it would be smashing,' I said. 'Thank you.'

And on the last day of June, Ike and John and I drove out to the airport together, drawing up next to the Supreme Commander's Flying Fortress, the same B-17 in which I had flown back from Algiers. Tex and Mattie, one of the Powerhouse WACs, and Sergeant Farr, one of the house staff, were there waiting for us. They were also going to Washington.

As we said our good-byes, Ike and I looked at each other. I really did not want to leave him. My face must have reflected this, because 'I want you to go,' Ike said softly. 'John will take care of you.' He shook my hand and sort of patted me on the shoulder. He looked over at John, who was talking to Tex, and then back at me. 'I'm putting all my eggs in one basket,' he said sombrely. 'Come back safe.' He was very serious. I nodded, gave him one of my untidy salutes and ran up the stairs into the plane.

Seconds later it started down the runway, then picked up speed, and we were in the air. As we circled the field, I could see Ike. He was still there standing beside the car. He looked very small. Small and very alone.

'I'm putting all my eggs in one basket,' he had said. I turned to John. 'Your father's going to miss you very much,' I told him. 'He's going to miss you too,' John said. 'Oh well, that's different,' I replied.

Flying in those days was no simple jet hop across the Atlantic between lunch and a late dinner. It took a full day and a half – from London to Prestwick to Iceland to Bangor to Washington. No one had prepared me for Washington. No one had warned me about the summer heat, the damp oppressiveness of it. No one had told me how dazzling a city it was. All the colours. All the lights. The women in pretty dresses. And the cars, all gleaming in different candy colours and shiny with chrome. And nobody had warned me that in the United States when you heard a siren, it was a fire engine or an ambulance or twelve o'clock noon. I had been in Washington less than three hours when I heard my first siren – and threw myself flat on the sidewalk. In England this was the automatic response to the wail of a siren when there was no shelter at hand.

My companions stared down at me. 'What's the matter? What happened? Are you ill?' their questions came as they helped me up. I brushed myself off and said, 'Well, that's one way to try to save your life when the bombs are falling. Aren't you glad you haven't had to learn it?'

Mrs Eisenhower had been at the airport and greeted me pleasantly before leaving with John. John called me the next morning to invite me to have drinks with his mother and a few friends that afternoon. I really did not want to go. I told John that I thought it was an imposition, but he insisted.

It was not much fun. I felt very stiff and foreign and military among these women in their fluttery light dresses. No other woman was in uniform. And certainly no other woman was being scrutinized as sharply as I was. As I sought out my hostess to say good-bye, John came up and told his mother that we were going to New York together and that he was going to take me to see *Oklahoma!*

She made a face. 'Oh, I'm sure Miss Summersby doesn't want to go to New York in all this heat.'

'Yes, she does,' said John. 'We're going to New York and do the town.'

I called him the next day and said, 'I don't think your mother approves of this trip to New York. And I can understand that. She wants to see as much of you as possible before you leave for Fort Benning. Why don't we cancel it?' I was quite serious.

'No,' said John. 'We're going.' And that was that.

I have always wondered if perhaps Ike had asked John to do this. I know that Ike would never have said much, but perhaps John might have asked him. 'Does she mean anything to you?' and his father might have said, 'Yes, she does.' Or Ike might simply have said, 'Kay has worked hard and been very conscientious. I'd appreciate it if you'd

28. Ike greets his new Commander in Chief, Harry S. Truman

29. Victory in Europe: Kay stands behind Ike as they celebrate the
surrender of the German Army. In some official versions of this photograph
Kay's presence has been removed

30. Ike, Telek and Secretary of the Navy Frank Knox

see that she has a good time. Take her to a show or something.'
John would have been scrupulous about doing anything his father
requested.

It was in Washington that I became aware of the gossip about Ike
and me. Of its virulence. No wonder the women at that little cocktail
party had been eyeing me so closely. Wherever I went, I began to feel
as if I were on display. I became increasingly sensitive to the whispers.
Ike must have been protecting me from a lot of this. Friends told me
that there had been several gossip-column mentions of the General's
glamorous driver and nastily-pointed insinuations about our relationship.

It is a pity that the gossip about the General and me was allowed to
persist. One general's wife handled a similar situation very wisely. Her
husband, whom Ike and I saw a great deal of, had been living openly
with a WAC officer. When the WAC came to Washington, the
General's wife gave a party in her honour and went around with her
arm in arm, introducing her to everyone and saying, 'I want you to
meet a marvellous girl. I don't know what the General would do without her. Or what I would do either, since she keeps me informed of
what he's up to when he's too busy to write.' All during the WAC's
stay, Mrs General saw to it that she was wined and dined and escorted
here and there by some of the handsomest officers at the Pentagon. She
treated her like a favourite niece, and the gossip died a sudden death.

It was a relief to get on the train for New York with John and get
away from the whispers and the side-glances. We did a lot of sight-
seeing and went to *Oklahoma!* I had never seen a musical like this before,
and I loved every minute of it. It was so American. I was completely
bedazzled. I had always been mad for the theatre, but this was a fantastically exciting experience. I fell in love with New York. I liked
everything about it. The skyscrapers, the people, the sense of vitality. I
found myself walking faster. And I promised myself that I would come
back after the war.

Washington and New York seemed to be bursting with luxury, and
at first I revelled in it. If anyone had told me before I left England that
I could have my fill of fresh fruit and chocolate, not to mention
delicacies like shrimp and those wonderful American hamburgers, I
would have told him he was crazy. But I did have my fill in just a few

days, and after that the plenty began to bother me. I was upset at the huge steaks that were served in restaurants, particularly when I observed that few people managed to finish what was on their plates. I kept thinking of what it was like at home, and how many soldiers were sitting at the side of a road or under a hedge in Normandy eating cold rations.

I was glad when the holiday was over. I had enjoyed most of it tremendously, and I had fallen in love with the United States, but now I longed to be back where I belonged. I had stepped out of that special dimension in which Ike and I had been living – and I did not like the world I found outside, a world where war was only incidental. Not a crusade against evil things, not a way of life that demanded the best one had to give – just an annoyance.

I was not the only one who wanted to get back. As the B-17 circled Washington to give us one last view of the city in the late-afternoon sun before heading north, Tex and Mattie also agreed that Washington was beautiful, but that they were eager to get back on the job. Thirty-three hours later I was back at Bushey Park. Although it was a Saturday, Ike was working, so I went straight to headquarters, took off my hat, combed my hair and opened the door to his office.

Ike looked up, rather annoyed, and then he saw it was I. When that grin flashed, I forgot how tired I was from the trip. The man who mattered was here. The time that mattered was now. I closed the door behind me. I had not felt his arms around me since before D-Day. It had been a long, long time.

'I'm so glad to be back,' I sighed.

'I'm so glad you're back,' he said. 'How was it?'

I told him all about the trip. All the good things. About how much fun John and I had had in New York. I told him about some of the parties I had gone to and the people I had met. But I said nothing, absolutely nothing, about the gossip.

'But I don't have to tell you about Washington,' I said finally. 'You know what it's like. What has been going on here?'

'The usual,' he said. 'I wrote everything down in the blue book. Why don't you catch up while I finish my messages, and then we can go home.'

I opened the little diary and saw that the General had made entries for every day while I had been away, starting with 30 June. That first entry in his neat handwriting had read: *John – Kay – Lee – Pinette – Farr started for US in my Fortress via Prestwick and Iceland. Lee* (that was Tex) *phoned from Prestwick, but neither J or K came to phone.* Other entries of the same day included *In shelter 5 times today on imminent danger,* and *Butch due back from Cherbourg this eve.,* and *Ethel and Mrs Perry coming to dinner – saw them in dispensary to get throat sprayed.*

I nodded as I read this. Good. He had had a foursome for bridge that night, so he could not have felt too lonely. But he had not said a word to me the day we left about having a sore throat. Typical.

He had left for Normandy on 1 July and stayed for five days. The diary showed he had inspected more than a dozen fighting units and conferred with Generals Gerow, Montgomery, Brooks and others. He had been very much disturbed to learn that Monty felt our Sherman tanks were not capable of taking on the German Panzers. He had inspected the very strong defences at Cherbourg, had worried that the attack was going very slowly, and he had gone up in a fighter plane to see what the country looked like from the air.

Back in England the afternoon of 5 July, he had written, *Buzz bombs chased us to cover about 6 times during the afternoon and 3 or 4 after going home.* (I was shocked to discover later on, when we got back to the cottage, that one buzz bomb had exploded so close that it had knocked down the ceiling in one of the bedrooms and broken several windows.) There was a later entry for 5 July that interested me very much: *Received message from Lee that he was still hanging about Wash. awaiting word from me on what to do about K and WACs. I made this plain before he left here, but I am irritated that message was not forwarded to me at Bradley's HQ.*

This was real news. I rushed into his office, diary in hand, and said, '*What* was Tex doing about me and the WACs?'

'I thought you might be interested in that,' he said with a big smile. 'Well, you've always said you'd like to join the WACs, and I decided to do something about it.'

'Me a WAC!'

'You a WAC,' he confirmed. 'There'll be no problem. Seems the President put in a good word for you.'

'Oh, my goodness' was all I could find to say. 'But what about – '

Ike interrupted me. 'I'm trying to plan ahead. We're winning this war, although I'm not always sure of it, and I'm not going to be in Europe forever. I told you once that I was never going to let you go. If you're a WAC, I can keep you on my staff later on.'

I went back to my office and continued reading, although my mind was darting about, considering all the implications of my becoming a WAC. On 7 July, there was a teasing entry that I knew was written with me in mind. *George brought a Countess and an 'Honourable' to lunch. Don't know names of either, but both were most attractive.*

Other entries read: *Butch's friends for dinner. Tried to play bridge. Awful!* and *Wish I could get time to see Telek.* Finally there was an entry for that very day: *Party from my office coming home today.*

The next morning I added one more entry for that Saturday. *Had a lovely evening at T* (Telegraph Cottage). *Champagne for dinner. Slept in shelter.* It had been a marvellous evening. Jimmy Gault, a terribly nice Guards officer who had been Ike's military aide for some time, was there with a couple of friends, so we had a festive little supper with champagne, a gift from a British admirer of Ike's. Afterwards, Jimmy went off with his friends and Ike and I sat out in the garden in the last of the light (with double summer time, it was light long into the evening hours), sipping more champagne and talking until the last of the sunset afterglow had disappeared. I was beginning to feel the fatigue from my long plane trip, but I was so happy to be with Ike that I refused to give in to it. He would reach out and squeeze my hand occasionally, and we would smile at each other. We were both very happy. It had been weeks since we had had a chance to really talk to each other.

I think that is what I remember best and miss most. We were always chattering away. We would talk about this and that and everything, leaping from subject to subject. We wanted very much to share all our experiences with each other. There was never any strain between us. That night was one of those nights when we talked, talked, talked. Finally, one of those rotten buzz bombs drove us into the shelter.

A few days later, we celebrated an important event: Telek's release from the kennels. I left the office early to pick him up. Ike had wanted to come, but after our previous experience he decided not to run the risk of more journalists and photographers avid to record the reunion of the Supreme Commander and his dog. Telek hopped into the car without a minute's hesitation, sitting beside me in the front seat, as if there had never been an interruption in his routine. Back at the cottage, he ran straight to Ike and rolled on his back, paws up in the air, a signal that he wanted his stomach scratched. We sat outside and watched Telek scurrying around, getting acquainted with his first home all over again.

'It's great to have that black scamp back home,' Ike said.

I agreed. 'It's like having a child come home after he's been away at school for the first time.'

We sat there for a while, and then Ike said something that shook me almost as if there had been an earth tremor. 'Kay,' he asked very quietly, 'would you like to have a child?' We had talked about how much we both liked children many times. Ike often said that he wished he had had a big family. Four children, he always said, would be ideal.

I couldn't be coy about this. 'Yes,' I said. 'I'd love to have a baby. Not *a* baby; *your* baby,' I corrected myself. Actually, I could think of nothing that I would like better. I had often day-dreamed about having a baby, Ike's child. I would love, absolutely love to have his child. I smiled thinking about it. I could see that baby – he was a boy and looked just like his father – toddling about on the grass, grinning a big grin when he fell down. I could see him later perched on the back of a horse, his father teaching him how to ride. And I could see us, when our son was eight or nine, the three of us galloping over the moors and then coming home and laughing and talking as we ate supper. The boy would fall asleep in front of the fire after supper, and Ike would carry him up to bed. We would sit there smiling at each other across his bed as he lay there, rosy-cheeked and deep in his child's sleep.

I sighed. 'It's impossible, you know.'

'I know,' said Ike. 'But maybe things will be different later. I'd like it, you know. I'd like it very much.'

We were quiet for a while. Then Ike asked, 'You don't think I'd be too old for the boy?'

He had decided it would be a boy too. 'No,' I said. 'You won't be too old. Not you. Not ever.'

We said nothing more about this, but every time our eyes met that evening, it was as if we had advanced into a new level of intimacy. That night after the buzz bombs had chased us to the shelter, Ike reached his hand out to me in the dark and we fell asleep holding hands between our cots.

Chapter 25

D-Day plus 335. That little sum added up to VE-Day – victory in Europe. That period from 6 June 1944, to 7 May 1945, was a frantic, topsy-turvy time with a pell-mell succession of advances and unexpected breakthroughs as well as equally unexpected setbacks, defeats and triumphs, culminating in a grimly matter-of-fact ceremony in the pre-dawn in Reims when the Germans signed the surrender papers.

Ike set up his advance headquarters in Normandy early in August, and after that the blessed privacy we had enjoyed at Telegraph Cottage was a thing of the past. Shellburst, which was the code name for all of Ike's advance headquarters in France, was in an apple orchard – all very pretty and bucolic. I lived in a tent pitched in a meadow close to where Ike's big wooden-floored office tent had been set up under the trees. It was so much calmer and more peaceful here just behind the front lines than it had been in England with the buzz bombs that we all slept like babies. The weather was fine, and it was almost like a lovely country vacation, except that we had no time to enjoy it.

We were constantly on the go. One day I would drive Ike up to the front, where he would visit the commanders and talk with the men. The next day we would fly to Portsmouth, and I would drive him to London to confer with the PM or to SHAEF at Bushey Park. Once in a while we would find time to visit the cottage for an hour or two. We would stroll around, and Ike would inspect the vegetable garden. We often returned to Shellburst with an armful of marrows or some beans. Ike had planted corn, but it was very disappointing. The English climate did not seem to agree with it.

We were rarely alone even in the car. An aide always accompanied the General when he visited the command posts at the front, and when we popped over to London, we usually took along a number of staff members. That handful of July days after my return from Washington when we had felt so close and loving now seemed like some long-ago, half-forgotten dream. These days we had to be content with fleeting caresses and glances. Ike would squeeze my hand under the breakfast table, or I would look up into the rear-view mirror to find him watching me. Now and again when we were free from observation, he would put his arm around my shoulders and draw me to him, but these little intimate moments were rare, and dangerous. Or so I felt. I had become coldly aware of the virulent gossip about us in Washington and did not want to add any fuel to that fire. If it had not been for Ike's habit of scribbling little messages on scraps of paper that he tucked into my hand almost every day, I might have felt lonely – even though we were always together. I would have loved to do the same thing, but the Supreme Commander could not simply tuck a bit of paper away in his pocket. It would be found by Mickey when he took care of the General's clothes. Nor could he read a message, tear it up and throw it away the way I did. There were always eyes watching the General. I told him once, 'If I ever write you a love letter, you'll have to tear it up and swallow it.'

'You don't have to write to me, Kay,' he said. 'Every time you look at me I see a love letter in your eyes.' He would say beautiful things like that when I least expected them, and they always meant a lot because he was usually so reticent.

This lack of privacy was not as frustrating as one might think. There were priorities, and our personal affairs – and those of everyone else involved in this mammoth war – were very far down on the list. We knew that we loved each other, and that was enough for now. Nor did we have time to fret about what might have been. The events of those days – the rapid Allied advance from the Normandy beaches across France and across the Rhine – are all part of history now. What amazes me today is how very routine it seemed at the time. The extraordinary was quite commonplace. We knew nothing else except this high-pressure, high-stakes world of war.

Paris was liberated on the twenty-fifth of August, 1944, and the next day Ike and I left his apple-orchard headquarters early in the morning for the five-or-six-hour drive to Chartres, where General Bradley had established his headquarters in a barnyard almost in the shadow of the great cathedral. As we drove through the French countryside, Ike was struck by the mounds of German equipment littered everywhere. 'We certainly caught them with their pants down,' he kept saying with great satisfaction.

The mood at Chartres was jubilant. There were almost as many journalists as soldiers there. Many of the correspondents had been in Paris the previous day, and several jeeploads of American and British newsmen were going back that afternoon. I asked Ike if it would be all right if I went along with them, since he would be spending the rest of the day conferring with General Bradley.

'Absolutely not,' he said brusquely. 'And that's an order. You stay right here, Kay.'

I acted a bit like a spoiled child and said something petulant about its not being much fun for me to sit around in Chartres all day with nothing to do. It was inexcusable – the only time I ever presumed on our relationship.

'Listen,' Ike said, 'it's too dangerous. I don't want you to go anywhere that I can't guarantee your safety. Hold your horses. You'll get to Paris one of these days.'

I was already ashamed of myself, and apologized. He patted my cheek and said, 'I know. I want to see Paris myself.'

It had absolutely nothing to do with my outburst, but the next thing I knew, Ike and General Bradley were making plans to visit Paris the following day to pay their respects to General de Gaulle. Ike invited Monty to accompany them, but Monty, who would never share the limelight with anyone if he could help it, sent back a short, snippy message declining the honour. Ike snorted. Then he laughed. 'It's just as well,' he said. 'The less I see of him, the better it is for my blood pressure.'

That night as we were driving over to Bradley's trailer for supper, Ike said, 'Well, I told you that you'd get to Paris, didn't I? Wouldn't you rather go with me than with that mob of correspondents?'

'Of course,' I said. 'Being able to see Paris with you . . . well, I didn't think it would be possible. For the two of us together, I mean.' We had a marvellous evening. Bradley and Ike got along very, very well, almost like brothers. We had dinner. Very simple it was. Just rations and a bottle of wine. We played a little bridge, talked a bit. That was all. We had a lot of evenings like this during those 300-some days before the surrender – innocent, high-spirited and very simple good times. Tooey Spaatz would always bring his guitar along when he came to dinner. Georgie Patton would have a store of new anecdotes. This was the kind of relaxation that Ike liked most.

The drive to Paris the next morning took a very long time, since the security people did not want us to go through Versailles, where there was still a lot of sniper activity. But we eventually got there, and as we drove along the Champs-Élysées towards the Arc de Triomphe, it was like a dream coming true. Paris was free. There were happy crowds lining the Avenue, and as Ike and Bradley got out to pay their respects to the Unknown Soldier, they were practically mobbed. A couple of dozen MPs had to throw themselves into the crowd to free Ike and clear a path so that he could get back to the car. He kept his grin, but as I moved slowly away in first gear, he said, 'My God, I didn't think I'd get out of that alive.' Bradley had fled to a jeep that roared away with its three-star passenger, but not before his face was smeared with lipstick.

On the way back to Chartres, Ike talked about the year he had spent in Paris when John was little. 'We lived on the Right Bank near the river, and I often used to walk up to the Arc de Triomphe with John,' he said, 'but nobody gave me a second look in those days.'

After the liberation of Paris, events seemed to race as if they were in some speeded-up newsreel. Ike kept moving Shellburst forward to keep up with the advancing armies. In early September, our advance headquarters was in Granville, a fishing port, where Ike had a house with a picture-postcard view of Mont-Saint-Michel, the ancient Benedictine abbey that, when the tide was high, rose like a magic island in the bay.

The day we set up headquarters there, Ike flew to Chartres to see Bradley. That evening we were starting to worry because he was late. The weather was bad. But when we called Bradley's HQ, we were told that the Supreme Commander had left and was planning to be home for supper. We were about to pull out all stops when a jeep stopped in front of the house. In the front seat was a wet, tired general who could barely walk. Two GIs put their arms around him and lifted him out of the jeep, into the house and up to his bedroom, where Mickey had him stripped, washed and in bed with a hot-water bottle in minutes. We asked no questions, just rushed about to make him as comfortable as possible.

Then we all sat around while he ate his supper from a tray and told us what had happened. His plane had conked out, and the only available replacement was a little L-5, a one-passenger plane with a limited range, designed for liaison work. Visibility was so bad that the pilot could not find the airstrip. And the plane was almost out of gas. They gambled that the local beach had not been mined and set the plane down on the sand. As Ike and the pilot were tugging and hauling to get the plane above the tide line, Ike slipped and twisted his knee. By the time they had walked across the salt marshes to the road, he was in agony. The pilot practically had to carry him the last few yards. What the GI driver of that jeep thought when he was flagged to a stop that rainy night by an Air Force pilot and a four-star general, I'll never know.

Ike was in real pain. His knee was swelling up, and he could not seem to find any position in which he was comfortable. It turned out to be quite a serious injury. A doctor was flown over from London the next day. He ordered Ike to stay in bed until the swelling went down. A few days later, he came back and put Ike's knee in a plaster cast. He told him to stay off his leg for at least a week. Ike stayed off it for about two days. That leg gave him trouble for months. He was often on crutches or used a cane around the house. But never in public. He would rather die than appear handicapped in any way in front of the men. Nevertheless, the pain was so much at times that every once in a while Ike would have to give up and go to bed for three or four days.

This accident turned out to have a silver lining of sorts, because it allowed the two of us quite a bit of time together that we would not have had otherwise. I would go to the office in the morning, take care of things there and then go to the house to have lunch with Ike and go over anything that might have come up. Afterwards we just sat and talked. We might hold hands or kiss, but always very hastily. One never knew who would walk in.

A few weeks later, Shellburst was moved forward again – to Versailles this time. This was more of a formal headquarters than the previous ones. Ike took over the Hôtel Trianon. His office there was so large that he had it partitioned off to make a separate office for me. There was a permanent feeling about the whole set-up. Telek and Caacie had joined us – and Caacie was pregnant again. I was living with the WACs again in a flat above what had once been the stables of Louis XV. And Ike was in a handsome mansion that had been hastily vacated by its previous tenant – Nazi Field-Marshal Karl Rudolf Gerd von Rundstedt.

Once again we were immersed in the social whirl of VIP's, but I was no longer the star-struck individual I had been in Algiers. I now shared Ike's view that while most of our visitors were charming or brilliant or powerful or all of these things, they were also a nuisance. They took precious time away from the business at hand. And yet, for one reason or another, they were entitled to hospitality and cordiality, so we managed to entertain all of them – from Fred Astaire and Bing Crosby to Madeleine Carroll and Katharine Cornell, from Anna Rosenberg and Bernard Baruch to Prince Bernhard of the Netherlands and a gaggle of Mexican generals.

Ike was always a warm and gracious host, but nevertheless it was a burden. The groups of Congressmen and politicians who kept trooping up to the front were the heaviest burden of all. More than anything else, they wanted to have their pictures taken with General Eisenhower. That really used to irritate him. Once he grumbled, 'The fellow who said that politics is too important to be left to the politicians knew what he was talking about.' 'But who else would want to bother?' I asked. He was always so vehement about not wanting to have anything to do with politics in any way whatsoever that I never dreamed that one day he would be running for office himself.

Ike insisted on visiting as many command posts, talking to as many officers and men as he could and generally leading a nonstop, sixteen-hour-a-day life. We drove to Brussels and Luxembourg, to Nancy, to Aachen. Every place. Whenever our armies advanced, he would go to the front to inspect the situation. And when we could not drive, he flew. It was not unusual for him to have meetings in three countries in a single day.

In October, I finally became a WAC. I was commissioned a second-lieutenant. Ike pinned on the gold bars himself in a little office ceremony. Now that I was a WAC and an officer, I could no longer drive the General. With winter coming on, I did not mind a bit. As it turned out, I still travelled with Ike almost everywhere he went. And even though I was no longer his driver, I continued to breakfast with him and we still drove to the office together. The only difference was that now I sat in the back with him instead of in front behind the wheel.

Just before Christmas, Ike was told that he was getting a fifth star. Things had suddenly taken a turn for the worse. The Germans had counter-attacked in the Ardennes and hit us at our weakest point. Our casualties were high, and we were retreating. This was the action that became known as the Battle of the Bulge. For that reason, there was practically no notice taken of Ike's fifth star around headquarters. But it meant a tremendous amount to him. There was a kind of glow about him for days after it had been made official. To Ike, becoming a General of the Army, the highest rank, was like being made a knight of some immortal round table.

Around the same time, he called me into the office. 'Kay,' he said, 'I've been talking to the PM about you.' Then he broke into a great grin. 'You've got a medal for yourself. The PM says you're going to be awarded the British Empire Medal.'

I had never imagined that I would get a medal – any kind of medal. The thought had never crossed my mind. Medals were for people who had done something extraordinary, not for a woman who had spent most of the war behind a steering wheel. When I said as much to Ike, he leaned back in his chair and said, 'I don't think you realize how valuable your services have been. I do. And so does the PM. If I were you, I'd just say "Thank you" and stop arguing.' I took his advice and immediately wrote to the PM telling him how surprised I was and how humbly appreciative.

Within weeks, the situation in the Ardennes was under control and the tide had turned in our favour once more. This was enough to encourage Ike to move his advance headquarters closer to the front. This time Shellburst was established in Reims, the city of champagne. It was pretty grim, not the kind of place one would associate with champagne. Headquarters was in a dismal red-brick schoolhouse where we could hardly hear ourselves think because it was on the main convoy route and the trucks continually pounded by, but Ike loved it. The proximity of Versailles to Paris had made him nervous.

In Reims, Ike promoted me to first-lieutenant and – even more exciting – made me his official aide. I was the first woman five-star aide in history. I glowed over the promotion every bit as much as Ike glowed over his fifth star. There was a special aide insignia – five stars on a blue shield topped with an eagle – that had been newly created. I wore it very proudly. I was no longer a kind of super girl Friday. I was now a first-lieutenant and aide to General of the Army Eisenhower, the Supreme Commander. When Ike told me about the promotion, I asked him, 'Is this part of your master plan?' and he said, 'You bet it is.'

The victories were coming thick and fast. Although there was still fierce fighting, it seemed as if we gained new ground every day. Ike was travelling so much that he said he often did not know where he was when he woke up in the morning. His knee flared up and gave him a lot of trouble. He had a series of colds, one of which turned into the flu. A cyst on his back was making him excruciatingly uncomfortable, so one day he had to go to the dispensary to have it cut out. It was a minor operation, but the wound was deep and required a number of stitches. Ike complained that there was not one part of his body that did not pain him. And his temper was truly vile.

If Butch had still been living with him, he might have been able to help Ike relax, but he was now on temporary duty with the Public Relations Division of SHAEF, which badly needed his expertise. And Jimmy Gault, who was now the live-in aide, could not talk as frankly to the General as Butch used to. Butch and Ike, after all, had been friends for many years before the war.

Beetle and I were very much worried. The General's physical and emotional condition was worse than we had ever known it. The two of us were forever having talks about Ike's state of mind and state of health. Beetle was positive that he was on the verge of a nervous breakdown. Finally a solution presented itself. A very rich American let it be known that he would be honoured if the Supreme Commander would make use of his villa on the Riviera. The only problem was how to get Ike to agree to use it. It took four days to convince him that he needed a rest. Beetle was very straightforward, told him that he was pushing himself too hard and that he would have a breakdown if he did not take some time off. Ike started to get angry, but Beetle said, 'Look at you. You've got bags under your eyes. Your blood pressure is higher than it's ever been, and you can hardly walk across the room.'

It was true. When Ike was out in public, he pulled himself together by sheer willpower and looked healthy and vigorous and exuded his usual charm. But the moment he got back to the office or the house, he slumped. And every time he had to take more than twenty or thirty steps, that knee put him in agony. Suddenly Ike gave in. And in the middle of March off we went to the Riviera.

The villa, Sous le Vent, in Cannes was the most luxurious place I had ever seen. We were told that more than three million dollars had been poured into it. Nothing that contributed to comfort was lacking. General Bradley came along with us, and Ruth Briggs and Ethel Westermann and a couple of others. It was a supersecret visit, and Ike did not leave the grounds of the villa at any time. That was no hardship. He was so run down that he could not have left it. For the first couple of days, all he did was sleep. He woke up long enough to eat and move from his bedroom to the terrace. He would eat lunch on the terrace, with two or three glasses of wine, and shuffle back to bed again. After forty-eight hours of this, he began to look somewhat human, but he had had us all very seriously worried.

The others did a bit of sight-seeing, but except for one trip to Monte Carlo, I stayed close to Ike. As he started to feel better, we would sit on the terrace all day long, looking out over the Mediterranean, chatting lazily, drinking white wine and sunbathing. One afternoon, I suggested that we might play bridge that evening, something we had not done during this little vacation. Ike shook his head. 'I can't keep my mind on cards,' he said. 'All I want to do is sit here and not think.' He was really blue. 'I just can't concentrate,' he complained. 'My mind is fuzzy.'

'Well, you know, you're simply exhausted. You can't push yourself the way you have and not feel it,' I told him.

'I suppose,' he said, 'but the way I feel now, I don't think I'll ever be able to concentrate on anything again.'

'Oh, that's silly,' I said. 'You don't want to think that way.'

He sighed. 'I've been thinking that way ever since we got here.

Why don't you tell me one of your Innis Beg stories? Maybe that will get my mind off myself.' He often asked me to tell him about things I had done when I was growing up in Ireland, especially at the end of a day that was more exasperating than usual. The little stories I remembered about my brother and sisters seemed to entertain him. I thought it was a good sign that he suggested this.

'Well,' I said, 'I'll tell you about once when I felt the way I think you're feeling now. My sister Evie and I used to ride bareback a lot. Once we were racing each other around the house and my horse stumbled. I sailed right over his head and landed on my head in the field. That really hurt, but we were always falling and we never paid any attention unless something was broken. I was a little dizzy when I picked myself up, but I was all right. That night, though, I woke up sick. The governess scolded me. She said I'd made a pig of myself eating green apples.'

'Huh,' said Ike. 'I bet you had a concussion.'

'Probably, but we didn't know anything about concussions. I went around with a headache for a few days, feeling pretty vague and out of it. But then I was as good as new.

'Did *you* ever fall off a horse?' I asked him.

'Oh, sure,' he said, 'but I never fell on my head.'

'I used to fall off a lot when I was first allowed to go hunting. I used to take too many chances. I really wasn't so very fond of hunting, chasing after a poor little fox. But I loved the hunt balls. They were the first dances I ever went to. Everybody would go. All ages. The men would wear their pink coats. I wore the same blue dress three years running. It didn't bother me. In the country we weren't so very fashionable, and I had no call for dancing dresses.

'I don't think I've ever had a dress I liked so much. Not even those beautiful creations from Worth. I used to think that the blue matched my eyes, but what I liked best about it was the ruffles at the bottom. I loved the way the ruffles flounced about when we did the gallop.'

'The gallop?' Ike asked lazily. 'What's that?'

'Oh, it's the most enormous fun. Everyone is in a circle holding hands and then you go around and around, then you reverse and go around again. Here, I'll show you.'

I got up and pretended I was holding two partners by the hand and

31. The Conquering Hero: General Eisenhower returns home

32. Towards the Presidency: On the steps of Columbia University Eisenhower gives
the famous victory wave and the smile that carried him to the White House

33. Kay Summersby Morgan, 1908-1975

started singing 'la-la, la-la, la-la, la-la,' and prancing around as if I were a fifteen-year-old dancing the gallop. Ike started laughing. It was the first time he had really laughed since we had arrived in Cannes.

'You should go on the stage,' he said. 'That's the funniest thing I've seen in years.'

I collapsed, out of breath and very proud of myself that I had got him out of his blue mood. That night after supper he said, 'Goddamnit, I'm tired of going off to bed every night while the rest of you do God knows what. How about staying home and playing a little bridge with the old man tonight?' It was a good evening. We won. There was nothing fuzzy whatsoever about his concentration on the cards. By the end of the week, he was so much better that it was hard to believe what a wreck he had been. Just getting some sleep and staying off that bum leg had probably been the very best medicine he could have had.

Back in Reims, everything continued to go well. We had crossed the Rhine. The Germans were on the run. They were demoralized, and many of them were surrendering. There was still scattered hard fighting, but there was no longer any doubt about the outcome.

Then one day there was terrible news. President Roosevelt was dead. This shook us all. Everyone was devastated by the loss. Especially that he had died before victory was completely within our grasp. He had seemed so very vital when I had seen him in Algiers that I could not believe he was dead.

Things were happening so fast now that there was little time to mourn. There was talk of surrender. Yes, they would. No, they would not. Then we heard that Hitler had killed himself, and the atmosphere at headquarters turned into what I once described as 'one grand happy mess'. Now we knew it was just a matter of days before the Germans surrendered. But how those days dragged on!

The Germans let it be known that they were ready to surrender, but the German generals stalled and dragged their feet, holding out for concessions – none of which they were granted. Finally, after several false starts, General Alfred Jodl, the German Chief-of-Staff, and Admiral Hans Georg von Friedeburg signed the surrender papers in the War Room that had been set up in our schoolhouse headquarters at Reims. At 2:41 in the morning of 7 May, the Germans finally surrendered – unconditionally.

Ike was alone in his office, where he had been since midnight, pacing up and down. I was at my desk in the outside office. And Telek was at my feet. We heard the Germans come marching down the hall, after having signed, at about three o'clock. They marched into my office, straight past me and into the Supreme Commander's office, where they stopped, clicked their heels and saluted. All I could feel was a cold hatred for these men who symbolized for me the evil that we had been fighting, the evil that we had conquered. Butch and I stood in the doorway of Ike's office and watched.

The Supreme Commander's voice was cold. 'Do you understand the terms of the document of surrender you have just signed?' I turned to my desk and wrote down his words in the diary. He continued. 'You will get details of instructions at a later date. And you will be expected to carry them out faithfully.'

That was all. He stared at them. They saluted, turned and left. Telek growled from under my desk.

Suddenly the office was full of people. The photographers rushed in to take pictures. Just as suddenly, it was empty again. Ike sighed, 'I suppose this calls for a bottle of champagne,' he said. There was no triumph in his voice, none of the elation he had shown when the photographers were there. Now he was alone with his wartime family. We drove back to the château where he lived in Reims – there were about ten or twelve of us – and drank champagne and discussed the events of the last few hours until dawn showed through the window. It was a sombre occasion. No one laughed. No one smiled. It was all over. We had won, but victory was not anything like what I had thought it would be. There was a dull bitterness about it. So many deaths. So much destruction. And everyone was very, very tired.

Chapter 26

'Let's take in a show,' the General said a few days after VE-Day. 'Something light. A comedy or a musical. I'd like to go to London. Everyone else has celebrated VE-Day. I think we should too.'

'Grand,' I said. 'When do we leave?'

'As soon as possible.'

John was in Reims for a few days then, and one Tuesday morning, Ike, John, Jimmy Gault, General Bradley and I took off for London. Jimmy had brought along eighteen bottles of the very best champagne obtainable in Reims. When he declared it at Northolt Airport, the customs officials raised a collective eyebrow – the duty would be sky high. 'It's for General Eisenhower's private VE party,' Jimmy said. That was all that was needed. The customs officers forgot they had ever seen or heard of those eighteen bottles.

We went straight to Telegraph Cottage. It was a glorious day. Ike and I inspected every corner of the place. His golf clubs were still in the closet. 'Goddamnit,' he said, 'I'd like to try that thirteenth hole again.' We walked down the little path to the golf course and played a couple of holes. We were pretty rusty. It had been more than a year since either of us had swung a golf club. On the way back, we passed our favourite rustic bench. Ike took my hand. 'Come on, let's just sit here for a few minutes.'

That bench held lots of memories for us. Some happy. Some sad. We had done a lot of talking, sitting here hidden from the house by the shrubbery. This was the place where a long time ago Ike had told me about a great tragedy in his life: the death of his firstborn son, Icky, from scarlet fever. Ike still mourned him. We had shared many confidences here.

Now Ike asked, 'Do you remember what we talked about the day you brought Telek back from the kennels last summer?'

'About having a baby?'

He nodded. 'I want to do something about that. If I can.' He turned to me and took me by the shoulders. 'Would you like it as much as I would?'

It was my turn to nod.

'Are you sure?'

'Yes, darling. I am very sure.'

'Then I'm going to try my damndest,' Ike said. 'That's all I can say. But I want you to know I'm going to try.'

Actually, I was not too sure what he was talking about. Did he mean – could he have meant that he would try to get a divorce? I don't know. I want to think so. He was not a man to make careless promises. He always weighed his words. He was always discreet. But he was very much elated on this personal, very private VE-Day celebration of his, and I think that a lot of things had been going through his mind in the days since the Germans had surrendered. I think he realized that he had to face up to making decisions about the rest of his life. We had come to the end of the life we had shared for so long. Or almost to the end. The tunnel of war had opened on to the light of a world that would soon be at peace. There were a lot of adjustments to be made.

There was no more time to talk. Lunch was served, and then it was time to leave for London. I didn't want to leave, and I said so. 'We'll be back,' Ike said. The car was waiting. I took one last look around the house and started down the walk. 'Kay,' he called, 'can you come here a minute?' I went back into the house to see what he wanted. 'Come here,' he said, stretching out his arms. 'You've never given me a victory kiss.'

The next item on the celebration agenda was a buffet supper in General Bradley's suite at the Dorchester. Ike had invited my mother to spend the evening with us. John was there, and a friend of mine, a very pretty girl who was in the WRNS, was there as his date. Jimmy Gault and his wife were there. And a couple of other dear, close friends. We had a marvellous time, and the champagne seemed to evaporate.

Then we were all off to the theatre to see *Strike a New Note*. It was just what Ike had wanted – an amusing revue.

A box had been reserved for the General at the theatre. John and his WREN sat on Ike's right and I on his left. General Bradley and my mother sat behind us. I had been dubious about sitting beside the General in such a public place and had suggested that I sit in the second row with my mother, but Ike said, 'Come on, Kay. This is where I want you.'

We settled ourselves very quietly, but people recognized the General and the word got around in seconds. There were cheers, and everyone clapped and whistled. I don't think Ike had realized how fabulously popular he had become. He was a bit surprised and very, very much pleased. When the audience started shouting, 'Speech! Speech!' he spread out his arms to quiet them and then, standing very relaxed with his hand on the rail of the box, he said a few words. He told the audience how pleased and happy he was to be back in England.

'It's nice,' he told them, 'to be back in a country where I can *almost* speak the language.' They loved it and cheered some more. It took a long time for the house to quiet down so that the curtain could go up. It was all tremendously exciting. None of us had had any idea that we would be caught up in this kind of heady welcome.

Afterwards we went to Ciro's for dinner. It was quite a while afterwards actually, because such a crowd had gathered outside the theatre that it was ages before we could move. Finally, the police told the driver to release the brake and they simply pushed the car along slowly until it was through the worst of the crowd. Ciro's was marvellous fun. We had a big table against the wall, and as soon as we were seated, the orchestra played 'For He's a Jolly Good Fellow,' and Ike grinned as if someone had given him the key to the city. Then it was more champagne, and our little party talked excitedly about the welcome the General was receiving. He turned to me. 'Kay,' he said, 'would you like to dance?' Of course I would. No question about it. We got up and walked out on to the floor. And then – I was in his arms. In his arms in public for the first time. I smiled at him and said, 'If anyone here tonight could guess how much I love you, they would not believe it.' 'I would,' he said. Then he concentrated on his dancing. A good thing, too. As we circled the floor, a story that Ike had told me long before floated into my mind. I could not help laughing. Ike wanted to know what was so funny. 'I'm thinking of how you told me they put you in the awkward squad at West Point because you couldn't march in time with the band.'

'You mean I'm not in time with the music?'

'Well, not quite.' It was hard to tell what step we were doing or what beat Ike was listening to. We were sort of hopping around the floor. But I didn't care. He had asked me for the first dance. That was my personal victory celebration. After Ike had danced with the other women in our party, we spent most of the rest of the evening talking and dancing together. It was heaven.

Supreme Headquarters was moved to Frankfurt about a week later. No more makeshift advance headquarters for us now. No more camouflaged buildings. No more tents, no more schoolhouses. Now we were in the immense I. G. Farben building, which was a small city in itself. It was very elegant – lots of marble and fountains and indoor flower gardens, great curving staircases and very luxurious offices. Several tennis courts could have been fitted into Ike's office. Bouquets of fresh spring flowers were placed in our offices every day. Mine was like an anteroom to his. We had a little window installed high in the wall between the two offices so that I could stand up and look in and see what was going on. That way if Ike seemed bored or restive, I could go to his rescue with a message just as I had at Bushey Park.

Life in the aftermath of war was very strange. There were dozens of celebrations and scores of honours bestowed on the Supreme Commander. He was always flying off somewhere to be given a medal or a degree or some other token of appreciation. There was one honour that meant more to the General, that stirred him more deeply, than any of the others. More than the Order of Victory bestowed on him by the Russians, an imposing platinum trinket studded with diamonds and rubies that was valued at a hundred thousand dollars. More than the Compagnon de la Libération given him by the French. Even more than the Order of Merit presented by King George VI, one of the most cherished awards of the British Empire and the first to go to an American. The one act of recognition of his services that meant more to him than all of these was the Freedom of the City of London, which was bestowed on him in an extremely moving ceremony in the ancient

Guildhall in the City of London, the historic structure that I had shown Ike when I took him and Mark Clark sight-seeing more than three years before.

For three weeks Ike had been working in Frankfurt on the speech he would deliver. And it turned out to be another victory for him. I don't think that he had ever realized until he delivered the Guildhall speech just how directly he could speak to people's hearts. He had worked hard on the text. One night he sat down in his house in Bad Homburg, on the outskirts of Frankfurt, and drafted a first version. I typed it for him. He spent night after night polishing and re-polishing until he thought it was right. He asked me to time him while he read it, because he wanted to keep it down to a certain time – ten minutes, I think it was. It was much too long, so he cut a bit here and a bit there; he also added a bit here and a bit there. He would call me into the office time and time again and say, 'Let me read you this version,' and I would sit with my eye on the clock. 'That took so many minutes,' I would say. And he would sigh, 'That's still too long. I guess I'd better whack away at it some more.' He finally got it down to the right length, and then that evening he polished it a bit more and took out a few more words. He handed me the final text in the morning and asked me to type a clean copy.

'You won't have to read this speech,' I said. 'You know every word of it.' When I gave him the final typewritten copy and his original with all the hen-track additions and deletions, he said, 'You know, this means a lot to me. It's exactly what I believe. I'd like to give you the manuscript. I know you believe these things too.'

I shook my head. 'No,' I said. 'This speech will be part of history. Someday historians will treasure that document. It should stay with all your important papers.' I was quite serious; but today, in a selfish way, I regret that I did not accept this generous gift. It would have meant so much to me over the years to be able to look at it now and again and relive that time. But I know I did the right thing. At least, I suppose I did. Now that I am older, it becomes harder and harder to know what the right thing is. Was it right to balk this generous gesture? To deprive Ike of the pleasure of making a gift? As he pointed out very often, he had little to give me. I don't know. Does it mean so much to have those few sheets of paper tucked away in the archives? I don't know. My refusal was a kind of rule-book conditioned response. I had the selfish gratification, at least, of having acted unselfishly.

Everything the General said in the Guildhall speech stirred my emotions. It was a generous tribute to the British and a testimony to how two proud and independent peoples can work together. It was a very human speech. He started off by saying that 'Humility must always be the portion of any man who receives acclaim earned in the blood of his followers and the sacrifices of his friends.'

And he spoke most movingly of the relationship between the English and the Americans. 'Kinship among nations,' he told the audience in the Guildhall, 'is not determined in such measurements as proximity, size and age. Rather we should turn to those inner things – call them what you will – I mean those intangibles that are the real treasures free men possess. To preserve his freedom of worship, his equality before law, his liberty to speak and act as he sees fit, subject only to provisions that he trespass not upon similar rights of others – a Londoner will fight. So will a citizen of Abilene. When we consider these things, then the valley of the Thames draws closer to the farms of Kansas and the plains of Texas.'

I listened intently as he spoke. He was very simple and open. There was an unpretentiousness about him that somehow seemed to lend his words extra weight. It was as if I were hearing the speech for the first time. I looked around at the others gathered in this ancient chamber. There were tears rolling down the cheeks of many of these English who prided themselves on their reserve.

Afterwards the General crossed to the Mansion House, where a luncheon was given in his honour. He and Winston Churchill came out on the balcony looking over the square, which was completely jammed with cheering people. The PM waved his arms about for silence and then gestured towards Ike, who leaned over and spoke to the crowd. Just a few words, but enough to provoke them to wild cheers.

'Whether you know it or not,' he said. 'I've got just as much right to be down there yelling as you do. You see,' he told them, 'I'm a citizen of London now too.'

Such a roar went up that it brought tears to my eyes. Ike and the PM stood there for a few minutes before they disappeared inside. The

General had a busy day. After the luncheon, he called upon Queen Mother Mary at her particular request. He had tea with the King and Queen and Princess Elizabeth at Buckingham Palace. And he had dinner at 10 Downing Street with the PM and some of the most distinguished men in England.

We flew back to Frankfurt for a day, and then it was off to Paris for more honours. Then he left for the United States. He was the Americans' hero, after all, and they wanted to honour him.

We had discussed this trip. After my appearance with the General at our own victory celebration in London, the gossip had become a factor to be reckoned with. The fact that my mother had accompanied us seemed to add fuel to the fire. There was plenty of gossip around headquarters, too. Butch had understood our special relationship for some time now, but he never said a word. And the WACs with whom I lived were discretion personified. But for everyone else, or so it seemed, Ike and I were the number one topic of conversation.

'How about it?' Ike asked. 'Would you like to go? There's plenty of room in the plane. I'm going to be busy, but you liked New York. This might be a good time for you to get to know it better.'

'No,' I said, without hesitation. 'It would be a mistake.' He didn't argue the point.

When Ike went off to the States in his Flying Fortress, I went off to the Riviera in his C-47 to spend a couple of weeks at the Hôtel du Cap d'Antibes. Every morning I rushed out to buy the papers to read all about the General's triumphal tour through the United States. While I was having a marvellous lazy time in the sun, Ike was shuttling back and forth across his native land, charming his fellow citizens with that grin and the truly simple niceness of his personality. He was a national hero. There had been no one like him, one writer stated, since Abraham Lincoln.

When he came back to Frankfurt, he was still very much the conquering hero. He was fêted in Luxembourg, Belfast, Brussels, Amsterdam. In Warsaw, Prague and Moscow. He was showered with gifts, everything from yards of lace to antique swords, but the loveliest of all was an exquisite cigarette case from General de Gaulle. It was fabulous. Platinum and gold with five sapphire stars on it. The clasp was a cluster of more sapphires. Inside the case, *Charles de Gaulle* and the date had been engraved in General de Gaulle's own hand-writing. I caught my breath when Ike showed it to me, it was such a fantastic work of art.

All these honours began to depress Ike. 'It's hard,' he said, 'going to city after city and trying to be natural about these things. It makes me feel like an actor. I want to tell them that it's a waste of time, but I know that it isn't. Ceremonies are important. But goddamnit, Kay,' he groaned, 'I was never a man who liked ceremonies.'

Ike was not always the guest of honour. He was host at two marvellous parties in Frankfurt that he gave at my suggestion. It had dawned on me that many people who worked at SHAEF did not know the General at all. A lot of the young officers used to ask me, 'What's the General like? What's he really like?'

'You ought to give a party for the lower-ranking officers,' I told him. 'Half the people at headquarters have never seen you.'

He was honestly surprised and exclaimed, 'What would they want to see me for?'

'They just want to look at you,' I told him.

And they did. The parties went down like hot cakes. He asked all the officers at headquarters with the rank of major and below, and made a point of saying something to every single person. They were simple affairs, just cookies and soft drinks, but everyone had a good time. And Ike made a great hit. He was very unassuming and made it easy for people to feel comfortable with him. He would wander from group to group and smile and say a few words. That grin of his! He had a bit of the actor in him. He knew how to turn on in public.

'That was an excellent idea of yours,' he told me afterwards. 'I think it was very, very useful.'

He was much more relaxed in Frankfurt than I had ever seen him. We were a small colony of conquerors, and we stuck together much as we had done in the early days at Telegraph Cottage. He often came to the WAC house for supper and bridge. This was something he would never have done before. I remember one evening we all sat on the floor and played bridge until four in the morning. He had a really good time. He loved things like that which were a bit childish and very informal. He trusted us completely. None of the WACs ever said a word about the General's being at the house on any of these occasions. If the word had got out, then he would have been expected to accept invitations to all the generals' houses for dinner. And that was the last thing in the world he wanted.

John was stationed nearby, and he used to come to Frankfurt several times a week for dinner. Ike enjoyed sitting around with him and talking. The three of us used to play with the dogs a lot. Telek had sired several litters since Versailles, with the result that there were seven or eight puppies – and none of them trained – tumbling about the house. They were adorable. Every night when we came home from the office, Ike would say, 'Well, it's puppy time,' and the whole scampering tribe would be let loose in the living-room, running here and there, poking their noses into everything, rolling around on the rug and just being puppies. Once Ike scooped them all up into his lap. I was heart-broken that there was no camera to record the scene.

We played bridge and we went riding a lot, almost every afternoon. But Ike was growing restive. His old cronies, the ones who had been so close, were gradually leaving. Tooey Spaatz had gone back to Washington, so there were no more nights of playing bridge and singing old songs to Tooey's guitar accompaniment. Omar Bradley also had gone back to Washington, to head the Veterans' Administration. Ike missed him a lot. He was an old-shoe kind of friend. The two of them used to replay old Army football games until everyone else was bored blind. They would go over a game play by play, man by man, happily analysing every minute. They seemed to have total recall. Ike was very lonely. Georgie Patton was still around, but he was in the doghouse again and Ike had to be fairly discreet about seeing him. They were still good friends, of course, but it was not politic for the Supreme Commander to spend much time with him.

Ike's spirits picked up during the Potsdam Conference, when he flew to and from Berlin almost every day. Towards the end of the conference, President Truman came to Frankfurt. Among other things, Ike spoke with him, as I reported earlier in this book, about my becoming an American citizen. 'I think it's going to work out,' Ike told me. 'There should be no difficulty. You've got to write a letter to Byrnes about yourself.' He outlined the information that my letter to the Secretary of State should contain and said that he would send a covering letter along with it.

I wanted very badly to be an American citizen. There was no other way that I could see for me to stay with Ike. It would be ridiculous to expect that the American Chief-of-Staff in that holy of holies, the Pentagon, could have a personal aide who was a British subject. And it was definite at this time that Ike's next post would be Washington and that he would take over from General Marshall as Chief-of-Staff. It was only a matter of time. And Ike kept saying that it would probably happen sooner than we thought.

Even with the prospect of change* in front of him, Ike was restless. 'This place is getting on my nerves,' he said. Frankfurt *was* utterly depressing. There was rubble everywhere, and the scars of war were much more visible here than any place else we had been. Neither of us felt comfortable living the life of conquerors. And after thinking of the Germans as the enemy for so long, we found it difficult to think of them otherwise. Frankfurt was a most unsettling place to live.

'Well, why don't we get away for a while?' I proposed. There really was not such a great deal of work at SHAEF that needed his daily attention. John, who was spending the evening with his father, thought it was a good idea. The upshot was that Ike laid on a trip to the same villa, Sous le Vent, where he had gone to rest when he was near total collapse in Reims. Several of us accompanied him, and Ambassador Harriman and Kathy dropped in for a couple of days. For the first time in all the months I had known him, the Ambassador threw off his cold diplomatic air and joined in all our holiday fun. What he wanted to do more than anything else was play croquet, but the rest of us voted him down and the Ambassador cheerfully accepted the verdict. Ike was able to take advantage of all the vacation activities this time. We went swimming and roared around in a speedboat. We even went out to a couple of nightclubs and restaurants. It was a marvellous few days, when we concentrated on doing just what people do on vacation. Ike and I even managed to have a few hours to ourselves now and again. Our last afternoon there, the two of us were lying on the terrace, sunning ourselves. Ike slept a little and I simply lay there, enjoying doing nothing.

* To be candid, it was a prospect that he did not relish. In my diary for 17 May I had written: *This morning E. got a very secret message from General Marshall – Relative: (1) Bradley being given a job in Washington to do with returning veterans of this war – (2) Marshall is going to try very hard to get out of his present job. In about 2 months he's going to ask the President to release him and then E. would have to become C/S (Chief-of-Staff). Confidentially, E. would loathe the job.*

'Where is everybody?' he asked when he woke up. 'I think they went down to the beach,' I said. 'I don't know. Or maybe they're napping, too.'

'It's nice here,' Ike said. 'Whenever we're together like this, it seems so right, the way things should always have been. But perhaps . . .'

He never finished the sentence. But he kept using those two words, 'but perhaps,' more and more often in our private conversations. I felt it was his way of saying that if anything could be done so that we could be together, he would try to do it. It was also his way of telling me that he could make no promises, make no proposals – yet.

'It's too bad we didn't meet each other years ago,' I said. He nodded. 'I never thought anything like this would happen to me,' he said. 'You know, in the Army, sometimes you don't discover what it's like in the world outside – until it's too late.'

Ike worried a lot about his age. 'Twenty years is a big difference,' he often said. 'It's all right now, but what about ten years from now?'

'We can worry about that in ten years. Or twenty,' I would say. 'Age isn't going to change what we have.'

There was nothing said that afternoon that had not been said before, no looks exchanged that had not been exchanged before. But there was a new feeling of peace and oneness, a feeling that we had come through a lot together, that we could face anything together. At least, those were my feelings. I would swear that they were his too.

After that holiday in the sun, Ike started planning more brief vacations. We went on a fishing trip with Beetle. And we visited Mark Clark in Salzburg. Clark took us to see Berchtesgaden, Hitler's mountain retreat. I was very uncomfortable the whole time I was there. Ike had told me about the concentration camps he had inspected in horrible detail, and that was all I could think of while we were looking around this mountain-top hideaway.

There were always a lot of photographs taken when we made these trips. Previously I had always slid into the background out of camera range, but now Ike insisted that I stay with him. 'Come here, Kay. Where are you going?' he would say as I started to walk away when the photographers went into action. It was as if he had decided to cast discretion to the winds.

One day Ike started to make a list of all the decorations and other honours and gifts that he had received. 'Where's that cigarette case that De Gaulle gave me?' he asked. 'It's in the safe,' I told him.

'Let me see it.'

I unlocked the safe and drew out the fine leather box that held the cigarette case and put it in front of him.

He opened it. 'It's very pretty, isn't it?'

'Oh, it's fabulous. Absolutely fabulous!'

'I'd like you to have it, Kay,' he said, most unexpectedly. 'I'll never be able to give you anything like this, and I'd like to think of you having it. The sapphires match your eyes.'

He smiled at me, that loving smile, and I just did not know what to say. I would have loved that cigarette case. Really loved it. Not only because it was beautiful and valuable, but because it was a present from the man I loved devotedly. But I just could not accept it. I wanted to. I was dying to say, 'Oh, thank you. I'd love it. I'll always treasure it.' But I couldn't.

I looked at Ike and my face got red and I said, 'Ike, I can't take it. Please. I just can't. It wouldn't be right. I'd love it. But I can't.'

He sighed. 'I wish you would. It was a personal gift. I can see no reason why I can't give it to you, Kay, darling – please take it.'

'I can't,' I said. 'I just can't.'

'Okay.' He nodded. And we went on with the list of honours and gifts. I never had second thoughts about refusing this gift. It was too valuable, and if General de Gaulle were ever to learn that Ike had given me the cigarette case, I am sure he would have taken it as a personal insult. And unlike the manuscript of the Guildhall speech, it did not represent a shared experience or emotion.

I did accept another kind of gift a few days later. A gift of a week off. Ambassador Harriman and Kathy stopped off in Frankfurt and asked me to come back to Moscow with them for a visit. I asked Ike if I could go. 'Of course,' he said. 'No problem.' And so I had a week in Moscow, a city very few Westerners had seen at that time.

We stopped in Vienna, and I was very much excited at being able to tour the famous Spanish Riding School where the magnificent white Lipizzaner stallions are trained. Even though the school was not in operation at the time, it meant a lot to me just to see the great oval ring where they display their gaits. I would have loved to spend more time in Vienna. Despite some bomb damage, it was still a beautiful and romantic city. I kept thinking, Maybe, someday, Ike and I can come here together.

After Vienna, Moscow seemed drabber than drab. Even the tour of the Kremlin that Mr Harriman arranged for me was rather depressing. It all seemed very cold and forbidding, and the relics of Russian history that were displayed seemed to hint at a primitive, even barbaric past. But I'm no historian. To tell the truth, what interested me most was the occasional sight of a long black limousine rolling down a street in the Kremlin enclosure. I used to wonder each time I saw one if Stalin was inside. There was no way of knowing. Those Russian limousines were all equipped with curtains, which were always drawn.

It snowed while I was there, and that provided the most beautiful sight of my stay. St Basil's Cathedral in Red Square, with its gaily painted onion spires, was breathtaking in the snow. Like an illustration in a child's book of fairy tales.

Kathy took me everywhere, from concerts at the Bolshoi to a trip on the famous Moscow subway. It was the handsomest subway I have ever seen. What I liked most of all, though, was just walking around and looking at the people. They were as grey and sombre as their city. It was a fascinating experience, but quite oppressive. I told Kathy I didn't see how she had stood it all those months. Although she and her father had been warm and thoughtful hosts, I was glad, for my part, to be going back to Frankfurt.

It was 14 October when I returned. Ike's birthday. It was a very quiet celebration. He came over to our house for dinner. We had managed to get some steaks, his favourite food next to oysters, and of course, there was a cake and a few bottles of champagne. We all gave him small presents – a handkerchief, a card, a chocolate bar, things like that. And after dinner we played cards. As always when he came to the WAC house, he was the only man present.

The next day we went riding as usual. It was a beautiful golden day. Just crisp enough to make you feel wonderfully alive. Afterwards we went back to Ike's house. We showered and changed – I always changed there, since we so often went riding straight from the office and it would have been a waste of time for me to go back to the WAC house – and then we relaxed with a drink in front of the fire in our favourite room, the library. There was a big leather davenport there that you could just sink down into and feel very, very comfortable. We were sitting there, not saying much, and then Ike got up and closed the door. 'Come here,' he said, and I went right to him. 'I've got a surprise for you,' he said, as he gave me a lot of little kisses.

'Not a cigarette case, I hope.'

'No – a trip.'

'Where are we going?'

'You're going alone,' he said teasingly. He was doing his whole act of building up suspense, and delighting in it.

'Where am I going?'

'You really want to know?'

'Ike,' I was practically squeaking in exasperation, 'yes, I do want to know.'

'You're going to Washington.'

'Alone? Why am I going to Washington?'

He laughed. He loved this little game. Then he told me that it had been arranged for me to become an American citizen. I had to go to Washington to take out my first papers. I was terribly pleased. I had been worrying that it might not have worked out, although naturally I had not said anything to Ike about it. It would not have been appropriate. But I had thought a lot about what I would do if I could not go to Washington with Ike. Like very many other people, I would have to make a new life for myself, a peacetime life. It would not be easy. More than anything else, I wanted to stay with Ike, work with Ike – and dream of a time, a place when we would be free to love each other openly.

I should not have worried. Over the months, Ike had gone ahead step by step working towards that very end. He had arranged for me to become a WAC officer, although I was a British subject. And now he had arranged for me to become an American citizen. There would be no bar now, no impediment to my serving on his personal staff as an aide at the Pentagon. It was like a reprieve from heartbreak. I was going to be happy forever after.

'I told you I'd work it out,' he said. We were standing, our arms about each other, our faces close.

I kissed him. 'I know you did. And I'm very happy.'

We sat there on that sofa making daydreamy plans for the future, kissing, holding hands and being quite indiscreet for the rest of the afternoon. Never in all the time I had known him had I had to hold Ike back. He had always been very circumspect, but this afternoon he was an eager lover. The door was closed and I knew that nobody from the household would be walking in. This was quite a formal household in Germany, not like the villa in Algiers or the cottage. People did not burst into rooms here. A closed door would never be opened.

The fire was warm. The sofa was soft. We held each other close, closer. Excitedly. I remember thinking, the way one thinks odd thoughts at significant moments, Wouldn't it be wonderful if this were the day we conceived a baby – our very first time. Ike was tender, careful, loving. But it didn't work.

'Wait,' I said. 'You're too excited. It will be all right.'

'No,' he said flatly. 'It won't. It's too late. I can't.' He was bitter. We dressed slowly. Kissing occasionally. Smiling a bit sadly.

'Comb your hair,' he said. 'I'm going to ask them to serve supper in here.' When I came back from the bathroom, there was a small table in front of the fire, with a bottle of white wine in a cooler, some chicken and a salad. We drank and ate and talked. The door was closed again. It seemed as if Ike had decided that he no longer cared what anyone thought or said. It was strange after all our years of discretion, but there had been a lot of changes in our lives and I liked this change.

There was none of the embarrassment between us that we had felt that night so long ago in fogbound London. We were such a comfortable old couple by now that we were able to talk about what had happened. Or had not happened.

'It's not important,' I told him earnestly. 'It's not the least bit important. It just takes time. That's all. And I'm very stubborn. You've said so yourself.'

'I know you are,' he said, 'but I'm not sure that you're right.' There was no point in arguing with him, I thought. Only time would show him that he was wrong. We dropped the subject.

Two weeks later I left for Washington in Ike's Flying Fortress. Everything went smoothly in Washington, although the days seemed to drag on forever. On the return trip, I sat willing the plane to go faster. I was terribly anxious to get back.

There was a bit of a shock awaiting me when I arrived in Frankfurt. Ike was packing.

'I'm going to Washington tomorrow,' he told me. President Truman had asked General Marshall to undertake a special mission in China. That meant that Ike was needed to take over in the Pentagon immediately. 'It's just for a few weeks, though,' Ike told me. 'I'll be back, and we'll both be leaving for Washington around the first of the year.'

We had dinner together that night. People were coming and going all evening. The telephone kept ringing. The next morning we were at the office at six to take care of last-minute details. Then it was time for him to leave. We kissed each other good-bye there in the office. 'Hurry back,' I said, and jokingly added, 'I mean hurry back, *sir*' – and I saluted.

'Christ!' Ike said. 'If you ever expect to work in the Pentagon, you'd better learn how to salute.'

That very afternoon I asked one of the West Pointers at head-quarters if he would drill me in saluting just as if I were a cadet. He thought that was grand fun and really had me whipping off a very snappy salute. Every night before I went to bed, I practised in front of the mirror, eager to surprise Ike when he came back.

Chapter 27

The last entry in my office diary for 1945 was on Saturday 10 November. It read: *1:30. E leaves for Paris en route to US*. After that, the pages are blank. Ike never came back. I never showed off my snappy West Point salute. Nothing was ever the same again.

As I wrote earlier, you never know when something important is going to happen, and when it does, you often don't realize that it did until some time later. If I had known that I was saying a final good-bye to Ike that Saturday morning, that we would never talk again in our easy familiar manner, that our hands would never touch again, that our eyes would never meet again in the same meaningful way . . . if I had known . . . Well, I don't believe that it would have made any difference. The tears would have come sooner. That is all.

There was not much to do after the General left. Odds and ends to finish, files to sort out, decisions to be made about what should be sent to Washington and what should stay at SHAEF. Then we heard that he was ill – so ill that the doctors said that he would not be able to fly back to Frankfurt when he got out of hospital. One of those colds that he was subject to had almost turned into pneumonia, and everyone had had a bad scare. Telexes flashed back and forth between Washington and Frankfurt. We were notified that the General's personal staff should be ready to leave for the States in ten days. Almost immediately after that, a Telex came in from Washington saying that Lieutenant Summersby was dropped from the roster of those scheduled to leave for Washington. There was no explanation. No reason given.

For a moment I thought that Ike must have decided he wanted me to come on ahead of the group. Either that or he wanted me to stay behind for a few days to take care of some of his personal business. But no. There were no substitute orders. There were no messages for me at all.

I was stunned. It took nearly an hour for the truth to sink in. I was not going to Washington with the others. The General did not want me to come earlier – or later. I was here and he was there. I felt like throwing up. And I felt like crying.

With more self-control than I had ever thought I possessed, I left the office very quietly and went home to the WAC house. I went to my room, closed the door, lay down on my bed and stared at the ceiling.

What had happened? What had *happened*? There must be some mistake. I went over and over everything – everything Ike had said, everything I had said, everything we had done since VE-Day, everything we had done since D-Day, everything we had done and said since we first encountered each other – searching for a clue. *What had happened?*

Finally, I cried. And cried. It was midnight when I had cried myself out. I was a wreck. I felt weak. My face was puffed and red. You're a bloody fool, I told myself. Tears won't help.

I could not face the office the next morning. I was sure that everyone would be feeling sorry for me, and pity was the last thing in the world that I wanted. I remembered what Ike had said – 'activity helps' – and decided to go riding. It reminded me of the days I had spent at Sailor's Delight after Dick died, galloping recklessly along dusty Algerian tracks. It helped. The next morning I was back at work. I went through all the motions. I smiled a lot. I lunched with friends at the Officers' Club and made plans for a farewell party.

General Lucius Clay, the Deputy Military Governor, told me that he was very eager to have me work for him in Berlin. He had a post, he said, for which I was ideally qualified: running the VIP guesthouse in Berlin. 'Ike has told me how good you are with people.' I thanked him for asking me and said that of course, I would be delighted to take it on. General Clay said that there would be a promotion involved. I would be made captain after the first of the year. I thanked him for that, too. But truth to tell, nothing meant very much to me, neither the new post nor the promotion.

Any sneaking secret hope I might have had that the whole thing was some ghastly mistake was killed when I received a letter from the

General. It had been dictated. It was quite impersonal. He said that it had become impossible for him to keep me as a member of his personal official family. The reasons that he gave were that there would be opposition to anyone who was not a completely naturalized American citizen working in the War Department, and also it appeared that I would be discharged from the WACs promptly upon arriving in the United States, and there could be no question, he wrote, of a civilian's working in the War Department. I could not understand. It seemed to contradict everything that we had been talking about for so long. There was a handwritten postscript saying that he was in bed and taking medicine constantly. The postscript ended, *Take care of yourself and retain your optimism.*

I read and re-read that letter. I looked for hidden meanings. I looked for something personal. He had written that he was distressed because he could not come back to give me a detailed account of the reasons I could not come to Washington. I told myself, however, that I should not misinterpret this or read anything into it. The General was always very courteous.

I packed up my things, and Telek and I went to Berlin, where we stayed for almost a year. It was an interesting experience. I met many extraordinary men and women – and many pretentious bores and boors. And I got over the worst of the hurt. I began to think about the future and decided that perhaps my future lay in the United States.

The transfer to the States was easily arranged. I had a lot of leave, and since it seemed as if everyone I had worked with during the past three or four years was now in Washington, that was where I went. I had a marvellous few weeks there, catching up with old friends, making new ones and going to dozens of parties.

There was a rather amusing aspect to those parties in Washington. I was one of the very few people who knew every general – and every general's girl-friend. I would be at a cocktail party having a good time, talking to someone's wife – it was interesting meeting the wives of these men I had known so well; I liked most of them very much – about clothes, about my experiences in the war, and I would always try to remember some story about what the woman's husband had done that might interest her. Then I would see the husband hovering about looking nervous. Officers I had known for years would come up, absolutely white, and say to their wives, 'Dear, I think we'd better be getting along. It's late.' They would be terribly nervous. They shouldn't have been. I never said a word about the things I knew.

I was in and out of the Pentagon a lot seeing old friends. It would have been ridiculous not to say hello to the General. Besides that, I was absolutely dying to see him.

I took Telek along with me. It was a strange experience. The General stood up to greet me as I came into the office. I stooped and let Telek off his leash, and he ran straight to Ike after all those months and rolled over on his back, paws in the air, to have his stomach scratched. I could tell that Ike was very much affected. He got all red, and it was not just from bending over to scratch Telek's tummy. We chatted for a few minutes. Ike seemed concerned about my future plans. I told him that I thought I might stay in the WACs a bit longer to find out if I really liked the United States as much as I thought I did. And then I would probably look for a job in New York.

'Good, good,' he said briskly. 'That sounds sensible. If there's anything I can do to help you about the job, I hope you will let me know when the time comes.'

I thanked him. He had written a recommendation for me months ago that had been forwarded to me in Berlin. Addressed TO WHOM IT MAY CONCERN, it described my work during the war. The General said that my outstanding characteristic was 'reliability' and that I had an 'engaging personality'. I told him that I would not call upon him for help unless it was necessary, but that I appreciated his offer very much. And then I stood up and said, 'Good-bye.' He asked me to drop in again with Telek. 'Anytime,' he said. 'I can always find a few minutes.' And I did bring Telek back once or twice.

I soon got my new orders. I was sent as far from Washington, DC, as one could get and still be within the limits of the continental United States: California. I was assigned to a small public relations unit. It was terribly dull. I could never feel that anything we were doing had the least importance. Who needs this? I said to myself, and applied for my discharge.

I headed straight for New York. And the first thing I did was go shopping. I think I wore a rut in the sidewalk as I trotted back and forth on Fifth Avenue from Saks to Bonwit's to Bergdorf's. After seven years in uniform, I found the idea of wearing clothes that made me look feminine very exciting. There was an exhilarating feeling of freedom in waking up in the morning and realizing that I had a choice of what to wear. I had saved quite a bit of money while I was a WAC and really indulged myself. I bought a couple of tweed suits and some sweaters – practical things. Some long dresses. Pairs and pairs of shoes. What I remember best was a smashing black satin suit and a hat from Sophie with a drooping feather on the side.

For the first time since I had been a very young woman in London, I spent my days sleeping late, having my hair done, lunching with friends, going to cocktail and dinner parties and dancing all night. Weekends, I would visit friends in the country and play bridge and golf. In my spare time, I worked on my book *Eisenhower Was My Boss*. I was happy.

Then one day I picked up the paper and saw that General Eisenhower had been appointed President of Columbia University and would be moving to New York. I had thought I was completely over the affair. I was having a very good time and had two quite attentive men friends, one of whom I was to marry a couple of years later. But that newspaper story – well, my hands were shaking when I finished reading it. I started thinking and dreaming about Ike all over again, love-sick as a young girl. There was nothing I wanted more than to see him and talk with him. I was obsessed with the idea. I missed him bitterly.

I started haunting Columbia University. I would take the subway up to 116th Street, go through the iron gates and walk around the University. I soon learned where his office was in the Low Library and where his house was. Finally, one spring morning, only a few weeks after he had been installed at Columbia, I ran into the General as he walked through one of the gates leading on to the campus. He was very much surprised to see me. And I acted surprised too. I had a story ready. I told him I was there to look up the sister of an English friend of mine who was in the graduate school. I am afraid that he did not believe me. He looked very much bothered, and after a few minutes, he said, 'Kay, it's impossible. There's nothing I can do.' He sounded terribly distressed.

I looked at him. There were tears in my eyes, but I tried to smile. 'I understand,' I told him. And I did. We had had a fabulous relationship, but it was over. Completely over.

After that, I thought, What's the good of forcing an issue and up-setting him when nothing can be done? So I made a determined effort to put him out of my mind. And I more or less succeeded. One gets over everything. Time really does heal the wounds.

A few months after that encounter, I learned that the General was going to speak to the Fellowship of United States-British Comrades. I made up my mind to attend the meeting. It was at the Seventh Regiment Armoury on Park Avenue, probably the most chic armoury in the world. I sat far back in the audience, since I did not want to call attention to myself. The General looked fine. It was the first time in my life I had seen him in formal civilian clothes. White tie. He wore them well, but to my mind he never looked as marvellous in anything as he did in his uniform. As soon as he had finished speaking, I slipped out. There was a reception afterwards, but I still did not trust myself to go up, shake his hand and say the conventional empty words. I had the feeling that if I were to touch him, I would cry. The few times we had met in the Pentagon I had carefully avoided shaking hands with him by bending down to unsnap Telek's leash. I just did not think I could bear it.

I discovered after that evening that the gossip about us was still as virulent and wildfire contagious as ever. Even the very proper *New York Times* in its report on the General's speech made a point of noting that I had been in the armoury and had left without speaking to the General. When I read it, I wondered what Ike would think when he read it in his copy of *The Times*.

My book was published that fall and was quite a success – so much so that a lecture tour was set up that took me to forty states. This was when I really got to know the United States. At first I had a marvellous time, but it was a lonely and exhausting way of life – going from hotel to hotel and living out of suitcases for weeks at a time. After several months, I decided that enough was enough. I wanted to go home. And I did – home to New York.

Thanks to the book and the lecture tour, I had no pressing financial worries. I resumed my giddy social life. Telek and I went out almost every night. He was checked in all the best cloakrooms in town: the Stork, '21', El Morocco, the Copacabana – everywhere that people went to have a good time. The hat-check girl would say, 'Are you sure he'll be all right?' And I'd assure her, 'He won't move.' And he never did. I would say, 'Telek, sit down and stay.' And he would. Sometimes he would stretch out and sleep. Other times he would just sit there, very alert, cocking his head and observing life in the cloakroom.

I went to England to spend the summer with my mother, and we read in the papers that General and Mrs Eisenhower were in London for a visit. Mummy was quite excited and said, 'We should ask them for tea or drinks. The General was always so very hospitable.' So I wrote a note to the Dorchester, where they were staying, saying that my mother and I would be very pleased if the General and Mrs Eisenhower could come by for drinks one afternoon.

There was no reply.

A few days later, a very charming young major appeared at Mummy's. He introduced himself and said, 'Well, I came around because General Eisenhower asked me to take you out for a drink.' I said, 'Oh, that would be lovely.' We talked, and it turned out that we had several mutual friends. Finally, he said, 'Kay, it's impossible. The General is really on a tight leash. He is not his own master.' He was a terribly understanding man and told me a bit about how the General was always surrounded by political people who practically dictated his every move. The General had obviously sent him to tell me that there was nothing he could do.

I was not particularly upset by this. If anything, I felt rather comforted that the General had cared enough to send this major around to see me. To me it was his way of letting me know that I still did mean something to him, although there was nothing he could do about it. And I had realized long ago that nothing could ever come of it. Nothing. Nothing. Nothing.

I wrote the General when I got married to Reginald Morgan, and he sent me a very sweet note wishing us happiness. From that time on, there was no contact whatsoever between us. I did write him when my mother died, but he never responded to that letter. I followed his activities on television and in the newspapers. When he was elected President, I was so proud of him! That man, who had always described himself as a simple country boy, was President.

I tried to watch all his press conferences on television. He really did not handle them very well, although he had been highly skilled with the press when he was Supreme Commander. I think the difference was that during the war he could tell the journalists what he thought they should know; he did not have to tell them what they *wanted* to know. Sometimes when I was watching him I would think, Oh my goodness, he's absolutely livid. I could see that temper flaring up. After all, he had spent his whole life in the Army, where his word was a command. This was something different.

When I heard about his illnesses I worried, and I felt very sorry for him at times. I remembered how he had told me once, 'All my life I've just worked. That's all I've done. That's all I do.' He was a man who had never had much fun in his life, but there were times when he was President that I thought he was probably having a bit more fun that he used to. When I would read about his going shooting quail with his rich friends or playing golf, I'd say to myself, He must be enjoying that. I truly think he was.

But somehow, there were always memories coming back to haunt me. I'd hear that old favourite song of mine, 'I'll See You Again,' and think of the time he had played the phonograph record to surprise me. It was a rather sweet sadness. But there was one time that was very bad. That was when Telek died.

That Scottie was seventeen years old when death finally caught up with him. One morning he staggered as he got up, and fell down. He tried to get up again, but just could not manage. I knew what this meant. He had been treated for various old-age ailments for a couple of years now. The vet had told me I must expect this.

I picked Telek up, put him in my lap and talked to him. I told him how much he had always meant to me, how much I had loved him. I told him that he was an important part of my life, that when I was sitting at home and he was curled up at my feet, I never felt alone. I talked to him about Ike. I told that poor tired Scottie how much Ike had liked him. I reminded him of how he used to ride in the car with us, of how he had visited Buckingham Palace, of how President Roosevelt had held him, of all the adorable scampering puppies he had sired. I suppose it was a bit silly, but Telek knew that I was loving him. I let my voice and my memories surround him. I wanted him to feel comfortable, loved and secure. Then I put him on my bed, buckled his little tartan coat around him and carried him out to a taxi and to the veterinarian.

'Please put him to sleep,' I said, and burst out crying.

Such a gallant little dog. Such a faithful, loving friend. It hit me very hard. It was not just Telek's death I was mourning. He had been my last link to Ike, the man I had loved more than anyone else in my life. And I was grieving for my own loss. From now on there would always be something missing in my life: the spirit, the gaiety, the devotion of a small dog named Telek.

I could never get used to the idea that the General was getting old. I always saw him as he had been in 1945. Then I would see a picture of him in the paper and think, Oh God, I can't believe it! With each of his illnesses, he seemed to shrink a little. During his final illness, my heart ached for him. It was so cruel. I felt relieved when he died. He had suffered too long. Far too long. And I had had the feeling that he had craved the peace of death.

And that is the story of the Eisenhower affair.

Do I regret anything? No, truly not. I cried a lot of foolish tears. I was hurt. But I have no regrets for what was. It was all perfect. A few regrets, perhaps, for what might have been. But it could not have been.

The General was a very ambitious man, and while I think he might have been happy if somehow we could have found a way to spend the rest of our lives together, I do not think that he would have been able to respect himself if he felt that he had gained a measure of personal happiness by giving up the privilege of serving his country.

That is why when I read about the letter that the General was supposed to have written to General Marshall saying that he wanted to marry me, everything seemed to fall into place and make sense. It may have been all right for King Edward VIII to turn his back on his empire for the woman he loved, but with the General, duty would always come first. He told me once that if there are two paths a man can take, both of them honourable, then all things being equal, he should take the path along which he will do the most good, inflict the least hurt. And that, I believe, is what he did.

So let there be no more whispers. No more speculation. This is what happened. All that happened. We were two people caught up in a cataclysm. Two people who shared one of the most tremendous experiences of our time. Two people who gave each other comfort, laughter, love.

Now that I am very close to the end of my life, I have a strong sense of being close to Ike again. It is almost as if he were looking over my shoulder as I write. Laughing now and then. Saying, 'Christ, I'd completely forgotten about that.' Or 'Oh, that was a great day. Didn't we have a good time that day!' Right now, he's saying, 'Goddamnit, don't cry.'

In my heart will ever lie
Just the echo of a sigh,
Good-bye.

FROM *Bittersweet*
by Noël Coward

1641 1 in 4 business premises sell liquor and beer. At corner of Whitehall and Stone Street, 1st official tavern is *At the sign of the Wooden Horse*. When serving in the militia, its owner had been sentenced to carry a pitcher of beer and a sword while riding a sharp-spined wooden horse on parade. ● James Bronck, a Dane who had arrived in July 1939, purchases 500 acres between the Harlem River and the Aquahung River, soon known as Bronck's River; hence borough's name.

1642 Religious dissenters from Massachusetts settle Gravenzande (Gravesend).

1643 Population of colony (Manhattan and surrounding farms) 400-500. ● *February* Near Fort Worth a lethal attack by Mowhawk warriors means 100s of Algonquins flee to New Amsterdam area and congregate at Pavonia and Corlaer's Hook. ● *February 25/26* Dutch soldiers make cowardly night attack, butchering 80 Algonquin men, women and children in their sleep in Pavonia, plus 40 in Manhattan. They march to Fort Amsterdam with the severed heads. 100s of Native Americans and many settlers will die in the Year of our Blood. ● Maspeth settlers kill 3 Marechkawiecks and steal 2 wagons of corn. When Kieft offers a truce, they reply, "Are ye our friends? Ye are merely corn thieves." 11 tribes from Long Island and Hudson valley unite against Dutch. ● French Jesuit, Father Isaac Jogues, arrives as town's 1st Roman Catholic priest – after rescue from burning at the stake by Mohawk Iroquois Indians.

1642 State House

1644 *February 25* 1st Free black community begins with 11 black slaves freed and given plots of land to farm (children still enslaved). Freed slaves include Manuel Gerrit (*see* Hanging spectacle 1641).

1641 *April 11* Drinking on Sunday during church hours is outlawed. Residents ignore this (a stronger law is passed 15 years later). ● Army detachment investigates theft of a pig, stolen by Dutch criminals en route to Delaware. Kieft's troops think Raitan Indians guilty and attack them, launching Governor Kieft's War, a struggle between Europeans in the northeast and various local tribes – tribes that are often at war with one another. 11 tribes attack the small settlement in Manhattan. Native Americans of Long Island, Hackensack and Westchester, once friendly, kill isolated farmers and take wives and children as captives. In September, when Raritan Indians attack Dutch settlements along Hackensack River and on Staten Island, the Dutch abandon these. ● *September* Annual live-stock fairs to begin in Manhattan.

1643 Town established. Services are held in St. Nicholas Church, a brewery and boatbuilding shed are erected, and a gabled inn serves visitors. ● *October* Native Americans attack Anne Hutchinson's home near Pelham Bay (killing all except her daughter who is carried off) and then destroy Throgmorton's settlement. Moody's settlement stoutly resists another attack. Kiefts War will last almost 2 years and destroy many villages and farms.

1641 Hanging spectacle
City's 1st public hanging.in Hanover Square: Dutch West India Company slaves who had killed a slave are threatened with torture if they do not name killer. All confess, assuming company will not want to lose 9 slaves. Governor Kieft orders them to draw straws. Gerrit loses. Many come to see this huge man hang but when the ladder is pulled away, both ropes break and he falls to the ground in agony. Gerrit is released. 3 years later he is emancipated and becomes one of the earliest landowners in Greenwich Village.

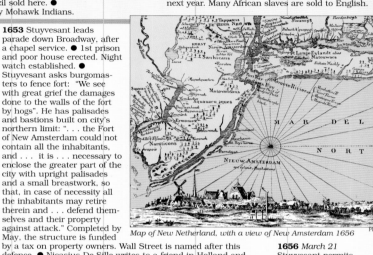

Along the waterfront, Old New York 1600s

1642 October Englishman John Throgmorton settles 35 households at Throg's Neck, where East River meets Long Island South. ● Dutch and Native Americans sign treaty, in Jonas Bronck's home, to end war. Sadly, fighting still continues for 2 years.

1642-44 Under threat of Native American attacks many settlers return to Holland. Manhattan's population drops from 300 to 100.

1641 Kieft states: "A great deal of bad seawant (wampum) . . . imported from other places – is in circulation, while the good, splendid seawant is out of sight or exported, which must cause the ruin of the country."

1641 New Council of Twelve is chosen by male heads of households to advise Director General.

1644 On official listings, city has:
1 baker
1 blacksmith
1 brewer
1 clerk
1 cooper
1 hog dealer
1 magistrate
1 minister
1 skipper
1 surgeon
1 weaver
2 millers
2 wheelwrights
4 shoemakers
4 tailors
10 carpenters
19 servants
38 farmers.
The minister earns the most at 1,000 florins; a shoemaker earns 65 florins, a carpenter's boy only 25 florins ● English settlement of Hempstead. ● 1 sheriff in New Amsterdam.

1645-57 Indian Wars documentation vanishes when General Governor's papers lost in a shipwreck.

1646 Public order maintained by a sheriff attorney. Guard watches out for Native Americans. If raids imminent, a paid nightly foot patrol (captain + 8 men) warns residents with rattles. Patrol controls unruly sailors, drunkards and prostitutes and keeps a fire watch. ● *June 25* Creoli convicted of sodomy for 2nd time and sentenced to be hung and his body burned. 10-year old Manuel Congo, caught with him, is flogged. ● All waterfront from Newtown Creek to the Gowanus cultivated.

1645 *October 10* Flushing receives charter from Governor Kieft. ● *December 19* As a reward for resisting Indian attacks, Gravesend receives patent. 16-acre square faces common (still part of Brooklyn's street plan, at MacDonald Avenue and Gravesend Neck Road). Charters grant, ". . . free liberty of conscience according to the custom and manner of Holland, without molestation or disturbance from any magistrate . . . or ecclesiastical minister that may pretend jurisdiction over them."

1652 Midwout (Flatbush) founded.

1650 *September 29* Peter Stuyvesant and New England colonies sign Treaty of Hartford: boundary set between English and Dutch on Long Island at western edge of Oyster Bay; in Connecticut line runs north from Greenwich Bay.

1647 *September 27* Kieft leaves aboard *Princess*, with 400,000 guilders (Dutch West India Company lost 500,000 guilders during his tenure). Ship sinks in Bristol Channel and many die, including Kieft and Revd. Bogardus.

1646 Father Jogues, writes: "On the island of Manhate, and in its environs, there may well be four or five hundred men of different sects and nations . . . English, Puritans, Lutherans, Anabaptists. . . . When anyone comes to settle . . . they lend him horses, cows [and] give him provisions, all of which he returns as soon as he is at ease; and as to land, after ten years he pays to the West India Company the tenth of the produce which he reaps." 1st cargo of slaves from Brazil sold here. ● Father Isaac Jogues attacked and martyred by Mohawk Indians.

1652 Jan de la Montagne sets up 1st Latin school. ● Daily firing of guns causes complaint. Law proclaims city off-limits to hunters and gun firing – or guns to be forfeited and fines imposed. ● Law requires drivers of wagons, carts and sleighs to walk in the city, leading horses (except on Broadway, where they can gallop, run, and ride vehicles). Fines are £2 (Flemish) for a 1st offence, and double for a 2nd.

1651 *March* Deed of Sale for Stuyvesant's purchase of the Company's farm in New Netherland, ". . . a dwelling house, barn, hayrick, land, six cows, two horses and two young Negroes".

1647 During Indian raids many houses and wheat-filled barns had been burned. Fort in disrepair and equipment broken. ● 17 taphouses now. ● Peter Stuvyesant plants 1st apple orchard, on his Bowery farm. Apples and tree grafts are shipped upstate via Hudson River. New York will become renowned apple producer. Upstate residents are called "appleknockers". Boys and men pick apples while women and girls below trees collect them in baskets. ● Sanitationists believe infectious disease is caused by vapors from stagnant water, open sewerage, rotting food, animal carcasses and dirty living conditions. Reformers try to improve sanitation for moral reasons. Contagionists believe disease is carried on ships and can be controlled by quarantine.

1649 *February* Manuel the Spaniard liberated. He promises to pay, "three hundred Carolus guilders within . . . three consecutive years . . . in seawan [wampum], grain or such pay as is current."

1647 *May 11* Peter Stuyvesant, former Governor of Curaçao, made Director General. He says: "I shall govern you as a father his children, for the advantage of the chartered West India Company, and these burghers and this land." Stuyvesant permits 1st election in New Amsterdam. 18, "most notable reasonable, onest and respectable" men selected: 9 will form advisory council.

1649 Van der Donck leads discontent over administration of colony, and is arrested.

1650 Peter Stuyvesant tries to establish exclusive rights of Dutch church but fails.

Peter Stuyvesant

1642 English settlement of Newtown: Revd. Doughty has charter to settle head of Newtown Creek and calls settlement Maspeth. ● 3 Long Island villages join to form Breukelen. Town's 1st inn, *The Stadt Herberg* (City Tavern) is built at 71-73 Pearl Street, overlooking the Great Dock and East River. Government officials conduct business on the upper floors, within easy reach of bar. ● Director General Kieft and Dutch Reformed congregation build a grand stone and timbered church in fort. Sly Kieft asks for contributions to the building fund after the 5th round of drinks at a wedding reception! St. Nicholas Church serves as a refuge during Indian raids and sur-vives for 99 years but blocks the wind from nearby windmills, creat-ing flour shortages. Earliest ferry between Manhattan and Long Island (Fulton Street to Peck Slip).

Trading with Native Americans

1649 1st wharf constructed at Dock Street, between Whitehall Street and Coenties Slip.

1648 Stuyvesant orders building of 1st pier – at Schreyer's Hook on East River, south of State Street – town's only landing point until 1649. ● *September 18* To protect merchants, visitors barred from conducting business on shore unless New Netherland residents for 3 years and had built, "a decent dwelling, each according to his circumstances and means" in New Amsterdam.

1645 Maspeth reestablished, renamed Middleburgh.

1646 Dutch settlement of Breuckelen.

1649 Charles I's execution at Westminster, London

1653 In England, Cromwell declares war on Dutch Republic. ● *February 2* New Amsterdam receives city charter separating it from province of New Netherland, ending direct control by West India Company.

1654 *May 7* Coney Island bought by Dutch West India Company for 15 fathoms of sewan, 2 guns and 3 pounds of powder.

1653 Stuyvesant leads parade down Broadway, after a chapel service. ● 1st prison and poor house erected. Night watch established. ● Stuyvesant asks burgomasters to fence fort: "We see with great grief the damages done to the walls of the fort by hogs". He has palisades and bastions built on city's northern limit: ". . . the Fort of New Amsterdam could not contain all the inhabitants, and . . . it is . . . necessary to enclose the greater part of the city with upright palisades and a small breastwork, so that, in case of necessity all the inhabitants may retire therein and . . . defend themselves and their property against attack." Completed by May, the structure is funded by a tax on property owners. Wall Street is named after this defence. ● Nicasius De Sille writes to a friend in Holland and describes oysters so large they had to be cut into portions. He also says: "They all drink here, from the moment they are able to lick a spoon. The women . . . entertain each other with a pipe and brazier; young and old, they all smoke. The country suits me exceedingly well. I shall try not to leave it as long as I live." ● New Amsterdam residents erect 13-foot log wall from the East to the West Rivers, with a land gate at Broadway and a water gate at Pearl Street. It will be torn down in 1699 to allow city to grow. ● Peter Stuyvesant writes to New Netherland Company about, "the raising of the Parliament's flag by some English freebooter . . . their immigrating and having favors granted . . . [must] . . . be restricted henceforth, that we may not nourish serpents in our bosom, who finally might devour our heads".

1653 to **1667** Studt Huys serves as City Hall.

1650s Weighbridge built at East River wharf. Bridges built across canal.

1653 English towns on Long Island object to taxation policy as they are not represented in New Netherland government. ● *February 7* Limited self-government granted. 1st sitting of Court of Schout, Burgomasters and Sheriffs at Stadt Huys. ● *December 10* Delegates from Breuckelen, Midwout, Amersfoort, Gravesend, Vlissingen, Middleburgh, and Heemstede idemand laws "resembling as near as possible those of the Netherlands", and claim Director cannot protect them from Indians.

1651 Commonwealth Parliament threatens Dutch sea trade with Navigation Act. Goods imported into England or English colonies must be carried on English ships, or ships from the country that produced the goods.

1652 1st Presbyterian Church of Newtown.

1653 Adriaen van der Donck is 1st to practice law in colony.

1652 Cornelius van Werckhovn buys Bensonhurst from Native Americans for 6 hatchets, 6 knives, 2 scissors, 6 combs, 6 shirts, 2 pairs of shoes and 6 pairs of socks.

1650 Dutch bakers become confectioners and sell sugarplums, sugar wafers and macaroons.

1654 Town's 1st inn. *Stadt Herberg* is renamed Studt-Huys or City Hall.

1652 Dutch establish settlement of Beverwyck.

1653 Dutch settlement of Midwout established.

1656 *March 12* Governor Stuyvesant and Takapausha (chief selected by Massapege, Maskahuong, Secataug, Meracock, Rockaway and Canarsee sachems) sign treaty. ● Captain Frederick de Konigh completes 1st full survey of city. It has 120 houses and 1,000 residents.

1655 *February 15* West India Company grant permission for Jews to live and trade in New Amsterdam. Stuyvesant still refuses to let them own property or trade freely. In June, Stuyvesant is again ordered not to hinder Jews.

1654 *August/September* 1st Jewish settler, Jacob bar Simson, arrives from Amsterdam in *Pereboom* (Pear Tree). On ship he had served as a guardian for 25 orphans sent as young settlers by Dutch West India Company. 2 weeks later, 23 Spanish and Portuguese Jews arrive from Brazil and bar Simson joins them for first Rosh Hashanah service in America in a private house on corner of what will be Broad Street and Mill Lane. Thus begins Congregation Shearith Israel, oldest existing Jewish congregation in New World. ● *September* 23 Jewish traders and merchants arrive from West Indies. Stuyvesant opposes their staying but permission granted by company directors in Amsterdam.

1655 *September 15* 1st cargo of 300 slaves from Africa arrives. 3 more slave ships follow next year. Many African slaves are sold to English.

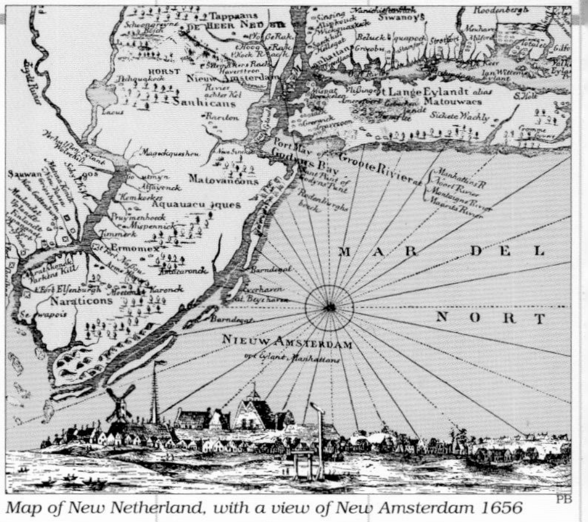

Map of New Netherland, with a view of New Amsterdam 1656

1654 *July* Council pass an act to control ferrymen on Manhattan: "the inhabitants are waiting whole days before they can obtain passage, and then not without danger, and at an exorbitant price." Act sets rates and a service from 5 am. to 8 pm. in summer and 7 am. to 5 pm. in winter, except, "when the windmill hath lowered its sail in consequence of storm." ● *July 18* On the wall of the Stadt-Huys a proclamation "announces" Peace, Union and Confederation has been reached between English and Dutch. August 12 to be a day of thanksgiving. ● Dutch West India Company to Stuyvesant, "The consciences of men ought to remain free and unshackled. This . . . has always been the guide of the magistrates in this city; and . . . people have flocked from every land to this asylum. Tread thus in their steps, and we doubt not you will be blessed".

1656 *March 21* Stuyvesant permits English group to settle Rustdorp. *September* 12 Food is sold in 1st public marketplace, on Saturdays near Whitehall and Pearl Streets. *October 26* 1st price-fixing law: all bread makers must bake white and coarse bread at least twice a week. Prices fixed at 8 stivers for a double 2lb. white loaf (1 stiver = about 2 cents) and 14 stivers for a double 8lb. coarse loaf. Single loaves cost half this. ● Directed at Lutherans, Quakers and Jews, religious meetings not in line with Reformed Church doctrines are banned. Also, £1 (Flemish) fine is levied on anyone found working on the Sabbath, with a £2 fine for playing bowls, card games, boating, sowing, mowing, fishing, hunting, tennis, dancing, gambling, cricket, building, tavern visits, parties, playing ninepin and cart-riding on Sabbath. Tavern keepers are charged 6 guilders per tavern and 3 guilders per customer (1 guilder = 50 cents) for serving on Sundays.

Miller at work 1656

1655 *August 6* 1st sales tax imposed, applying only to slave trade – 10% on purchase price of each slave carried beyond jurisdiction of New Netherland. ● *September 15* Stuyvesant leads soldiers against Swedes along Delaware River. ● Peach War begins. A Native American woman who steals peaches is shot and killed. Over 1,500 Native Americans attack Dutch who drive them back to their canoes, but then Staten Island, Hoboken and Pavonia are attacked. In 3 days, 100 Dutch die, 150 are captured for ransom, and 28 farms destroyed. 70 captives soon return but others are held for nearly 2 years.

1655 Van Borsum obtains 3-year lease to operate a ferry across East River and to build a tavern on Long Island side.

1643-1715 France - Louis XIV's reign
1642 Dutch discover New Zealand
1642-46 English Civil War
1644 China - End of Ming dynasty (began 1368)
1649 Charles I of England beheaded
1648 Expansion of Atlantic slave trade
1652 Capetown, South Africa, founded
1652-54 1st Anglo-Dutch War
1656 Pendulum clock invented
1655-60 Poland Russia and Sweden at war

The European settlers here were Dutch farmers and tradesmen who founded Flatlands on Jamaica Bay. In 1642, Manhattan was reached by sailboat and rowboat and in 1643, Lady Moody from New England founded Gravesend.

By 1834, Breuckelen town had become the 3rd largest city in the U.S. Steam ferries ran a regular service from 1814 and by 1872, made 1,200 crossings daily. The waterfront was a bustling center, with vast warehouses. Brooklyn Bridge was completed in 1883 and Brooklyn became an N.Y.C. borough in 1898.

Today there is a renowned Museum of Art (1897) with 1.5 million objects, including works by Monet and a splendid Botanical Garden that opened in 1911. Wyckoff House built in 1652, may be the oldest house in N.Y.C., named for a 1600s servant who became a rich farmer and magistrate (his descendants lived here until 1902). The oval Grand Army Plaza (1870) has a triumphal arch, 80 feet (24 m.) high, with a fine horse bronze chariot group and sculptures.

Triumphal arch (1870) at the Grand Army Plaza

Brooklyn Public Library and one of its inscriptions

THE BROOKLYN PUBLIC LIBRARY THROUGH THE JOINING OF MUNICIPAL ENTERPRISE AND PRIVATE GENEROSITY OFFERS TO ALL THE PEOPLE PERPETUAL AND FREE ACCESS TO THE KNOWLEDGE AND THE THOUGHT OF ALL THE AGES

One of the rollercoasters at Coney Island

Above: *Nathan's where the hot dog was created May 30 1920*

Left: *The Parachute Jump now closed*

Below: *Wonder Wheel*

Coney Island
Public bathing and carousels arrived in 1884, followed by horse racing, boxing, dance halls, brothels and gambling and, from 1897, amusement parks – Steeplechase Park, Luna Park, and Dreamland. In 1923, a boardwalk led from Brighton Beach to Sea Gate but fewer came. In 1964, Steeplechase Park and its Parachute Jump closed, but there is talk that the jump will be resurrected by 2004. The Wonder Wheel, Cyclone roller coaster and B & B Carousel survived and New York Aquarium arrived in 1955.

Coney Island facts
- The named comes from the *konijn* (wild rabbits) here.
- By 1907, visitors mailed an average 250,000 postcards from here every weekend.
- When the subways arrived in 1920 there were a million visitors a day in summer.
- Steeplechase Park burned down in 1944 and Dreamland in 1911.
- One couple lived in a house below the Thunderbolt roller coaster for 40 years.
- Frankfurters and hot dogs were launched here in 1920.

Bay Ridge
Bought by the Dutch West India Company from the Nyack Indians in 1652, this was called Yellow Hook for the color of its clay; until the yellow fever epidemic of 1848-49. In time, it became a wealthy suburban retreat. Bay Ridge was the setting for the film *Saturday Night Fever*; several scenes were filmed at a local nightclub.

Bedford-Stuyvesant
Here, in the largest black neighborhood in N.Y.C. are the Brooklyn Children's Museum (built 1899) and the Boys High School (1891) attended by Isaac Asimov and Norman Mailer.

Brighton Beach
In the 1800s, the racetrack made this a center of thoroughbred horse racing. In the 1970s, 30,000 Jews settled here, then Russians with many nightclubs and bookstores.

Broadway Junction and Gowanus
Known as Jamaica Pass in colonial times, in 1776, during the Battle of Long Island, the British used it as a passage to Gowanus, and trapped and defeated colonial troops here. Gowanus was settled in 1640, but grew in the 1840s when the Gowanus Canal arrived. 12-blocks on Smith Street had 23 taverns: it was so rowdy it was called the Gashouse District.

Brooklyn Heights
Canarsee Indians first lived here. By 1642, its farms were served by ferries and the village of Brooklyn thrived around the ferry landing. General Putnam withdrew his troops here after the Battle of Long Island, while Washington had his H.Q. and evacuated his troops over the foggy river in August, 1776. Steam ferries began scheduled crossings in 1814, streets were laid out and by the 1820s, the area bustled with tradespeople, seamen, merchants and ships docked at the wharves below.

Brownsville
In 1910, this was a Jewish slum, with sweatshops but no sewers or paved streets. The first U.S. birth control clinic opened in 1916 but 9 days on, was shut by the vice squad.

Bushwick and Canarsie
Bushwick is one of the original 6 towns here, a farming community set up in 1660. Many Germans arrived after 1840 and there were over 11 breweries in Brewer's Row. Canarsie was a quiet fishing and farming area until the 1870s, when Germans, Dutch, Scotch and Irish arrived and, in the 1920s, Italians and Jews. Many made their living fishing oysterbeds in Jamaica Bay.

Carrville and Clinton Hill
Free black farmers, laborers, and craftsmen came to Carrville in the 1830s. An African free school was set up and Citizens Union Cemetery in 1851 (black burials were often segregated). Many fine mansions in Clinton Hill predate the Civil War; others were built by rich industrialists. The magnificent 1874 home of oil executive, Charles Pratt, is now part of St. Joseph's College.

Cypress Hills and Eastern Parkway
20,000 veterans, many from the Civil War, are interred in over 18 cemeteries in Cypress Hills as well as Houdini, Mae West, and Edward G Robinson. In 1866, Eastern Parkway was the first 6-lane parkway in the world with promenades, equestrian paths and superb 19th-century houses.

Fort Greene
The first European settler (and first Italian in Brooklyn) was Peter Alberti, who in 1639 ran a tobacco plantation. The area is named for General Greene, who oversaw the fort building in 1776. During the Revolution, colonial prisoners were held in ships moored in the bay as the British had too little space in the jails. Starvation and disease led to 11,500 deaths: corpses were dumped in trenches on the riverbank but washed ashore until they were reburied in 1792. A shipyard opened here in 1791, followed by the Brooklyn Navy Yard. In the 1840s, many free blacks worked as shipbuilders and soon more than half the black population of Brooklyn lived here. In 1848 Olmsted and Vaux designed Washington Park, renamed Fort Greene Park. The Prison Ship Martyrs' Monument was built in 1908.

Kings Highway
A road following an Indian trail ran east from the Narrows; this linked small villages and was used by British troops during the Battle of Long Island. In the 1920s, Vitagraph, Warner Brothers and Ace films studios arrived and silent-movie stars built grand houses here.

Red Hook and West Brighton
Named for its shape and soil color, after years as a marshy, rural oasis, Red Hook became a tough, bustling place where Al Capone was a petty criminal before going to Chicago. In West Brighton, the network of narrow walks was once crammed with restaurants, hotels, carousels, roller coasters, and saloons.

Brooklyn Dodgers
This baseball team joined the major leagues in 1884. The name came from the skill of Brooklyn residents at dodging trolley streetcars. The team played at 2 stadiums in Brooklyn called Washington Park, and at Eastern Park in Brownsville, before moving to Ebbets Field in 1913 and to Los Angeles in 1957.

Brooklyn residents include:
W. H. Auden
Henry Ward Beecher
Clara Bow
Riddick Bowe
Mel Brooks
Al Capone
Anthony Comstock
Theodore Dreiser
George Gershwin
Woody Guthrie
Joseph Heller
Danny Kaye
Howard Lovecraft
Henry Miller
John D Rockefeller
Phil Silvers
Mike Tyson
Walt Whitman

The Bronx is named for Jonas Bronck, its first settler, who bought the area in 1639. It was part of Westchester County until 1898 when it was incorporated into New York City.

- This is the only part of the city belonging to the mainland. • Its highways, bridges, and railroads are the most heavily traveled part of the U.S.A.
- There are 11 colleges and universities. • It has more parkland than any other borough (24%).
- It has been home to Edgar Allan Poe, Theodore Roosevelt, Mark Twain and Toscanini.

Little Italy in the Bronx; the great variety of food, cafés and bars create a Continental atmosphere

Right: *Duke's head stone*

Above: *The Ellington patch in Woodlawn Cemetery*

The Yankee Stadium
The Metro travels above the cars on 233 Street

Bronx Park, the entrance to the Zoo, and the Botanical Garden

Bedford Park
This was named after Bedford, England, which also inspired its Queen Anne architecture. Many buildings built in the 1930s used art deco style. Residents include William Fox, founder of the film company that became 20th Century Fox.

Bronx Terminal market
A cold-storage warehouse was built here by the 1920s. The market became the city's main wholesale distribution center for ethnic foods. In 1935, Mayor La Guardia prohibited the sale of artichokes there to stop organized criminals inflating their prices.

Bronx Zoo
The Bronx Zoo project was launched in the 1890s. Workers landscaped the grounds and constructed buildings to house the animals in what is now the largest urban zoo in the U.S. at 265 acres, with 6,500 animals.

City Island
At the north-eastern tip is a causeway that links the island to High Island, first called Minnewits. Local residents earned an income from fishing and clamming, and from 1830, in a salt works. In the 1800s, marine pilots lived on the island, boarding steamships to guide them through the treacherous Hell Gate. The island became a center for sailmaking and for building and anchoring yachts. 5 yachts designed here won the America's Cup. Today it is home to North Wind Undersea Institute, a marine museum.

Clason Point
The first inhabitants were Siwanoys, whose village was one of the largest on the Bronx shoreline. Known as Cornells Neck after a 1654 farmer, it was later named for Isaac Clason, a wealthy merchant in the 1800s. It has been home to a military academy, dance halls and bathing piers.

Co-op City, Baychester
Where once cucumber and strawberry farms and a pickle factory had flourished, in 1968-70, Co-op City became one of the largest housing projects in the U.S. 60,000 lived here in 15,372 apartments.

Eastchester
Anne Hutchinson built a house here in 1642 after fleeing Puritans in New England (the Hutchinson River is named for her) but she was killed by Wiechquasgeck Indians.

Thomas Pell claimed the area in 1654 as part of a purchase from the Siwanoy Indians and in 1665 sold a large part to English farmers.

Fieldston and Fleetwood
Game was abundant in Fieldston and deer were seen until 1908. Known for its rural peace and large houses, this has become one of the wealthiest areas.
From 1870-99, Fleetwood was the site of Fleetwood Park Racetrack, a trotting track attended by Ulysses S. Grant, and John D. Rockefeller.

Jerome Park and Kingsbridge
Stock speculator, Leonard Jerome (grandfather of Winston Churchill), opened the Jerome Park Racetrack in 1866 with facilities for trap shooting, sleighing and ice skating. It closed in 1889 to make room for the Jerome Park Reservoir. In 1917, the Kingsbridge Armory was built, one of the largest in the world.
In 1693, King's Bridge was the first to connect Manhattan with the mainland over Spuyten Devil Creek. The strategic site of Kingsbridge saw many battles during the Revolution. In the 1860s, the Johnson Iron Foundry made munitions for the Union Army.

Locust Point and Marble Hill
Locust Point is named for the locustwood trees here, valued because they resisted rot. Marble Hill, above the Harlem River and site of an 1800s marble quarry, was severed from Manhattan by the Harlem River Ship Canal in 1895. Before World War I the canal was filled in, leaving Marble Hill on the mainland: residents were listed in both the Bronx and Manhattan telephone directories. The neighborhood grew in the 1920s.

New York Botanical Garden
This is one of the oldest and largest in the world with 250 acres, 40 acres of forest and 28 special gardens. Wiechquasgeck Indians inhabited the land thousands of years before Europeans. A turtle petrograph they inscribed can be seen here.

Spuyten Duyvil
Its name dreives from Dutch *spuit den duyvil* (in spite of the Devil) describing the strong flow of double tides. It grew in the 1800s with the completion of the Hudson River Railroad. In Henry Hudson Memorial Park, a statue of Hudson 16 feet (5m.) tall stands on a column 100 feet (30 m.) high.

Throgs Neck
The name comes from John Throckmorton, an Englishman who in 1642 settled a colony in here – driven out by Indian uprisings. Fort Schuyler, built 1856, was an active military installation until 1932 and then became the campus for New York State Maritime College. In 1961, the Throgs Neck Bridge ended its isolation.

University Heights
This was called Fordham Heights at the time of the Revolution. The area was renamed University Heights after New York University moved here from Greenwich Village in 1894. Since 1973, it has been used by Bronx Community College.

Woodlawn cemetery
Here are buried F.W Woolworth, Roland Macy, Herman Melville and Duke Ellington.

Yankee Stadium
Completed in 1923, here were seen Babe Ruth and Joe DiMaggio (who married Marilyn Monroe in 1954). Rebuilt in the 1970s, it can seat 54,000.

PEOPLE & HISTORICAL EVENTS

1658 *March 4* Village of Harlem receives charter.

1660 *March 6* Dutch make treaty with tribes on Long Island, Staten Island and across Hudson. Esopus and Raritan do not sign until July 15 and Esopus is attacked again in 1663.

1657 *August 6* Newly arrived Quakers preach wildly in the street. ● *August 9* Robert Hodgson addresses a group at 1st Quaker meeting in Heemstede. He is brought to New Amsterdam and sentenced – a 600 guilder fine or 2 years chained to a wheelbarrow, working with African slaves. Denied food, he is hung by his hands with weights on his feet and severely beaten. Stuyvesant's sister intervenes and Hodgson is deported to Rhode Island.

1663 *February 5* 1st recorded earthquake. ● Flood in spring and a smallpox epidemic.

1664
English-Dutch Conflict
January Under Duke of York's authority, Captain Scott visits English towns on Long Island. With 150 men, he marches on Dutch towns. ● *January 14* Stuyvesant sends a commission to Jamaica. Scott tells Dutch that Charles II has given New Netherland to his brother. ● *February* Stuyvesant relinquishes English towns on Long Island, in Westchester, and in Connecticut valley. ● *March* King

Charles II issues letters of patent granting area from Connecticut to Delaware, including New Netherland, to his brother, James, Duke of York. ● *May 16* Native Americans from Hudson Valley, Long Island, Staten Island and New Jersey sign another peace treaty. ● *August 26* 500 soldiers arrive in 4 English men-of-war that anchor in narrows off Staten Island. Colonel Nicholls captures Island. ● **English rename New Amsterdam, New York.** ● *August 30* Nicholls demands that Stuyvesant surrender province. With the fleet anchored opposite

the fort and threatening all with its guns, and troops landing near Breuckelen, citizens urge Stuyvesant to surrender peaceably. Dutch relinquish colony. ● *September 4* Soldiers land at Gravesend and march across Long Island to the Ferry. British frigates approach city. ● *September 6* Final surrender of New Netherland to British force. 2 days later Stuyvesant signs articles of capitulation declaring. "The Dutch here shall enjoy the liberty of their Consciences in Divine Worship and Church discipline." The English land. ● *September 15* Revd.

Drisus writes to Amsterdam: "We have been brought under the government of the King of England . . . there arrived . . . four great . . . frigates well-manned with sailors. They were provided with a patent . . . to . . . take possession of this province . . . If this could not be done in an amicable way . . . everything was to be thrown open for the English soldiers to plunder, to take it by assault, and make it a scene of pillage and bloodshed . . . We were not a little troubled by the arrival of the frigates." ● Population of city at time of conflict: 1,500.

1670 *April 13* Lenape Indians sign treaty giving Staten Island to English for 60 barrels of shot, 400 fathoms of wampum, 50 knives, 30 axes, 30 hoes, 30 kettles, 30 boots, 30 shirts, 8 coats and 1 keg of powder. To mark the surrender of rights, they hand over a clump of dirt and a twig from every kind of tree growing on Island – except ash and hickory, as they retain the right to make baskets from these.

1673 *January* Rider sets out on the new Boston Post Road to take 1st inter-colonial post between New York, Hartford and Boston. ● *February 9* Treaty of Westminster ends Dutch-Anglo war. Dutch surrender New York to English in exchange for Caribbean Islands, Curaçao and Demerara (captured by English during war) and Surinam. ● *July 30* Brief restoration of Dutch rule. 1,600 armed men in 23 Dutch vessels arrive off Sandy Hook. 5 warships under Captain Bencke and Evertsen attack Fort James, which resists for an afternoon until deputy governor, Captain Manning, surrenders. 600 troops land elsewhere on Manhattan, welcomed by 400 armed Dutch burghers. 2nd Dutch rule begins, with city renamed New Orange; they hold it for 15 months.

1667 *February 19* Peace of Breda confirms English possession of New York but colony is unaware of this until June. ● *July* News of Treaty of Breda reaches city (*see* February 19) ● Settlers grow vegetables and fruit trees. Native Americans and settlers catch deer, fox, bear, beaver, trout, oysters and perch.

New York, 1665

1664 Richard Nicolls takes over from Stuyvesant as Governor. ● *Gideon* arrives with cargo of 153 male and 137 female slaves from Guinea, 40 destined for Stuyvesant's farm.

Peter Stuyvesant tearing up the letter demanding the surrender of New Amsterdam, 1664

Surrender of Fort Amsterdam, 1664

LIFESTYLE

1657 Stuyvesant prohibits refuse disposal in streets but this is largely ignored. *April 11* Thursdays declared market days.

1658 *October* Unofficial police force of 4 men earn 24 stivers a night for patrolling from 9pm. to 6am. – called the Rattlewatch as they carry wooden, hinged-clapper devices to sound an alarm. ● Over 100 English ship captains petition Oliver Cromwell: "The Dutch eat us out of our trade at home and abroad; they refuse to sell us a hogshead of water to refresh us at sea, and call us 'English Dogs'. They will not sail with us but shoot at us . . ." ● Livestock fair for lean cattle in May and for fat cattle in October. Cattle driven across the river for 25 stivers a head; unsold animals ferried back free.

1658-60 Matron, Dr. Varravanger, establishes 1st hospital for those without families to care for them.

1659 An occasional ominous warning to wrongdoers is a tarred corpse, known as the "field bishop", left hanging in public. ● *June* Alexander Carolus Curtius opens a Latin school but after 2 years is dismissed – for accepting beaver pelts from pupils and failing to maintain discipline. ● *August* Raritan Indians kill a Dutch family at Maspeth Kill. By September, First Esopus War engulfs entire Hudson Valley.

1661 1st free public school opens in Brooklyn, near Fulton and Hoyt St. ● English describe Manhattan as:" . . . seated between Engld And Virginia, commodiously for trade . . . [it] hath good air, and is healthy, inhabited with several sorts of Trades-men and marchants and mariners". ● *February* Henry Townsend hosts Quaker meetings in Rustdorp (Jamaica). Stuyvesant sends soldiers to watch. ● *July 4* Citizens of Breucklyn petition Stuyvesant to subsidize schoolmaster's salary. Provincial council agree to pay 50 guilders in wampum per annum. He is also bell ringer, grave-digger, reader, chorister and town clerk.

1662 Flower gardens and fruit farms tended by 75 Dutch West India Company employees. Settlers plant and sow little, as trade is priority. Poorhouse near main canal is overseen by church deacons. Broadway is lined with small homes. A wall separates city from farms beyond. ● John and Hannah Bowne invite Quakers to use their home for worship. Bowne arrested and fined.

1663 *June 7* Hudson settlement, Esopus, attacked again (*see* 1660), 21 killed and 45 captured.

1664 *February* Stuyvesant forbids Breuckelen people to harvest crops until tithes are collected, or they will be fined 100 guilders. The lands had been granted with a 10-year tax exemption, after which 10 per cent of produce is due. ● Atlantic seaboard communities view Manhattan, with 1/3 of its taverns as the "capital of the devil". ● Frequent epidemics are seen as divine judgement. In hot weather, wealthy flee city. Moralists blame the poor for living in filthy conditions but others suggest better farm management, food distribution and production, street cleaning and waste disposal. New public health laws made.

1665 English victory brings harsh laws. Any public assembly of more than 3 Africans or Native Americans is considered illegal. Curfews are set for them. ● English jury system, trial by jury of 12 peers. ● Burial ground set aside on west side of town near Hudson River and windmill. ● *October 2* Witchcraft trial of Ralph and Mary Hall, accused of causing the deaths of a man and child by, "detestable and wicked arts". The court finds evidence against Mary but insufficient "to take away her life." Ralph is released.

1669 *May 3* Governor Lovelace grants John Archer permission to settle 16 families on the Maine, near a wading place – 1st settlement at Fordham.

1670 Many settlers move north to less crowded territory in Manhattan above what is now Canal Street.

1672 *February* Peter Stuyvesant dies and is buried in a vault in a chapel on his estate (now at St Mark's Church in-the-Bowery). His bust is in graveyard.

1673 *September 17* New Dutch Governor, Anthony Colve, arrives.

1676 *October 11-13* Dankers and Sluyter walk circumference of Staten Island.

1676 Captain Billopp receives patent to settle Staten Island's southern tip.

1679 *December 8* Council prohibits enslavement of Native Americans: ". . . that all Indians here have always been and are, free, and not slaves, except such as have been formerly brought from the bay or other foreign parts . . . But after the expiration of . . . six months, all that shall be brought here from those parts and landed, to be as free as other Indians."

1678 1st Anglican preacher in New York, Charles Wolley, arrives as chaplain to Governor.

COMMERCE

1657 Pilgrim

1660 *June 2* 1st Post Office opens.

1663 *November* Provisional assembly petitions Stuyvesant and West India Company for free trade between English and Dutch colonies. ● *January 9* Bowne deported on *Gilded Fox*. He secures right of religious freedom from Dutch West India Company in Amsterdam and returns. ● *April 16* Directors of Dutch West India Company write to Stuyvesant: ". . . The consciences of men ought to be free and unshackled so long as they continue moderate, peaceable, inoffensive, and not hostile . . . allow everyone to have his own belief, so long as he behaves quietly

Van Courtland's Sugar House used as a prison by the British in the 1670s

1670 Long Island towns reject Governor's order to contribute to Fort James' repair. 2 years later, when war between English and Dutch erupts, Lovelace asks each town to contribute to fort maintenance but then squanders these funds. ● *Blue Boar Inn* opens, city's 1st suburban tavern. ● Settlers use beaver, otter, musk and skins from Native Americans; beef, pork, wheat, butter and tobacco from Long Island; and malt, fish, cider, apples, iron and tar from Virginia.

1675 Annual fair for grain, produce and cattle begins near Brooklyn Ferry.

1666 *April* Governor Nicholls tries to impose new taxes on Long Island towns, but they resist and assault his agents. Nicholls permits towns to pay their own bills directly instead of via his administration, thus keeping self-imposed taxation.

1677 1 pump near fort is only water source. 6 public wells are dug. 10 wells will be created by 1700.

1681 Recalled to England, Major Andros does not renew import duties of 1677. Merchants pay to rate.

1679 Taverns serve excellent food and drink: good cider and mead, bean-and-bacon soup, roasted lamb, salad, young peas, sweet tarts, curds and cream, mulberries and currants.

POLITICS & RELIGION

1657 *December 27* Flushing citizens sign remonstrance protesting against Stuyvesant's intolerant policy towards Quakers.

1659 French Church founded.

1662 1st Presbyterian Church of Jamaica. ● *September 21* Stuyvesant bans public worship unless Dutch Reformed service. ● *December 14* Council threaten to transport John Bowne, "if he continues abstinate and pervicacious, in the first ship ready to sail . . ."

. . . Such have been the maxims . . . by which . . . the oppressed and persecuted from every country have found among us an asylum from distress. Follow in the same steps, and you will be blessed". ● Bowne's House becomes a national shrine to religious freedom.

1664 *April 10* At Provincial assembly meeting Stuyvesant appeals to representatives for supplies to check English threat, but they refuse to act. ● *December 6* Governor Nicholls grants freedom of worship to Lutherans. ● *February 28 - March 1* 34 delegates from Long Island and Westchester meet at Hempstead and adopt Duke's laws, similar to New England law but without demands for religious conformity.

1668-73 Colonel Francis Lovelace is Governor. ● Cornelius Steenyck serves as mayor 1668-70 (and again 1683-84). A prominent merchant, he uses his position to help Dutch.

1669 Hempstead, Jamaica, Flushing, Newtown, Gravesend, Eastchester and Westchester demand right to elect their own legislators. Lovelace Governor states he has no authority to allow this.

1673 Jew and Quakers no longer persecuted.

1674 *October 31* Major Edmund Andros arrives and Governor Anthony Colve, departs. King James instructs Andros: "You shall permit all persons of what Religion whatsoever, quietly to inhabit within the precincts of your jurisdiction . . . Provided they give no disturbance . . . nor do molest or disquiet others in the free exercise of their religion."

Major Edmund Andros

1680 Religions include Church of England, Presbyterians and Independents, Quakers, Anabaptists and Jews.

CITY STRUCTURE & DEVELOPMENT

1657 Red Hook becomes part of Breuckelen ● Many streets have long names such as, "the path that Burger Jorisson made to go down the strand". Now streets are straightened, fences and lots improved, and main routes cobbled. Frame dwellings extend along East River at island tip.

1658 Homes near a brewery suffer dust and dirt. Residents demand city pave street but they pay cost. Brouwer Street is 1st cobblestone-paved street in Manhattan and is renamed Stone Street. ● New Amsterdam is 1st American city with formally named streets. A trail from northern tip of Manhattan through forests to southern tip is called Beaver Path (Native Americans used it to bring beaver skins in to trade.) Path is widened and becomes *Breede Wegh* – eventually Broadway.

1659 1st poet is Jacob Steendam. A clerk for Dutch West India Company, he sends *The Complaint of New Amsterdam to Her Mother* to the Netherlands and 2 years later, writes, *The Praise of New Amsterdam*.

1660 *August 12th* Amersfoort receives permission to build church. *October* Cortelyou completes a plan of city, the model for Castello Plan, oldest existing city map.

1661 Town now has 300 buildings. A windmill, stepped gables and main canal echo Holland. Tallest roof is on Governor Stuyvesant's home, which English later call Whitehall. There are gallows and a crane to shift cargoes. A smelly canal extends up from Broad Street to allow boats in at high water. ● Billou-Stillwell-Perine House, oldest on Staten Island, built (1476 Richmond Road). 54-inch girth black locust tree there dates from then and is oldest living thing on island.

1665 2nd Anglo-Dutch war. Trade with Amsterdam cut off.

1664 350 houses and a population of 1,500. ● Highest point is a 2-story windmill.

1670 Merchants' exchange: Dutch and English craftsmen, traders, importers, and merchants agree to meet on a canal bridge at Bridge Street on Fridays from 11 am to noon. Financial city launched!

1665 *June 12* New charter makes city congruent with Manhattan Island and imposes English system of Mayor, Aldermen and Sheriff, replacing Dutch schout, burgomasters, and schepens. ● *June 15* Thomas Willett is 1st mayor. For 150 years, mayor will be appointed annually by New York State's governor. Early mayors sit on Common Council but have limited powers.

1676 City's bolting monopoly gives exclusive rights to process and ship grain. Great Dock built on East River.

1680 *January* Coopers form association to raise barrel raise prices – so crucial to New York commerce that barrels are part of the city's official seal. Council fines coopers £2.10 each and discharges those in public employ.

CULTURE & ART

A map of New Amsterdam in 1661

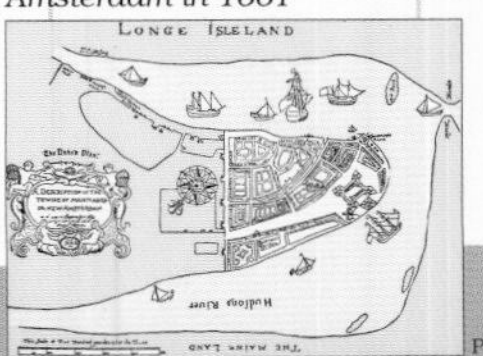

1665 *May 1* Wealthy upper class now has ample leisure time. Governor Nicholls sets up city's 1st racecourse on Hempstead Plains. He calls it Newmarket. He offers a silver cup for a race to be held each spring and autumn.

SPORT

1666 1st church in Brooklyn built at Fulton and Lawrence Streets.

1667 Houses are built of wood, or red, black or yellow brick (ship's ballast from Holland). They are 1, 2 or 3 stories high. ● *October* Governor Richard Nicholls grants a patent to Flatlands on October 4, Brooklyn on October 18, Flatbush and Bushwick on October 25.

1675 *November 23* Boundary between Flushing and Hempstead set at Little Neck.

1676 Canal through New York to Broad Street and Exchange Place, polluted with litter, is filled with fresh dirt to make 72-foot-wide Broad St.

1677 *November 20* City fathers order 1st insane asylum to be built.

USA & WORLD EVENTS

1662 Ireland – Boyle's Law
1660 Monarchy restored in England with Charles II

1659-61 Peace treaties in Europe: Peace of Pyrenees (France and Spain), Treaty of Copenhagen (Sweden and Denmark), Treaty of Kardis (Russia and Sweden)

1665 Isaac Newton's Law of Gravity
1665 & **1666** Great Plague and Fire of London
1665-67 Second Anglo-Dutch War

1667 Bacon's Revolt against Native Americans
1668 Triple Alliance: English, Dutch and Swedes against France
1669 Dutch painter Rembrandt dies (born 1609)
1670 France – Palace of Versailles built
1672 British – Newton's telescope
1673 Molière, French playwright dies (born 1622)

1679 British – Habeas Corpus act
1679 Father Hennepin reaches Niagara Falls
1680 British – Invention of the match
1681 Penn

1819 *May 31* Walt Whitman born in Huntingdon ● *August 1* Herman Melville born in Pearl Street.

1819 Rose Butler, thief, is last woman hanged on Washington Square gallows. ● Yellow Fever through summer ● Henry Fearon, *Sketches of America, London, 1819*: ". . . there is . . . a carelessness, a laziness, an unsocial indifference, which freezes the blood . . . shopkeepers . . . stand with their hats on, or sit and lie along their counters, smoking segars, and spitting in every direction, to a degree offensive to any man of decent feelings". ● 40 people stop slave catcher, John Hall, taking fugitive slave Thomas Harlett (jailed until he can be returned to his master).

1818 Quakers found Black Ball Line, 1st regular monthly packet service between New York and Liverpool. (*see also* 1821, 1878). ● **1818** *January 8* *James Monroe*, with room for 28, sails with only 8 passengers on board. Previously, ships had stayed in harbor until full. ● David Dunham, Father of Williamsburgh starts steam ferry to Manhattan. ● Henry Sands Brooks establishes men's clothing store in Manhattan.

1819 Depression: value of real estate and property in New York State drops from $315 million (1818) to $256 million. *March 26* 1st savings bank, the Bank for Savings of the City of New York. By December it has 1,527 accounts worth $153,378. ● Barrett & Tileston's dyeing and printing company set up on Staten Island.

1818 *February 18* Cadwaller D. Colden mayor ● African Wesleyan Methodist Episcopal Church, High Street, Brooklyn - split off from white congregation over slavery and racial equality issues - is Brooklyn's 1st black congregation.

1819 *November 1* Ordnance prohibits use, "of any private drain or sewer leading into any of the public common sewers ... for the purpose of carrying off the contents of privies or water closets".

1818 Revd. Peter I Van Pelt publishes 1st history of settlement of Staten Island.

1819 *August* With Cornelius Vanderbilt at the helm, paddle wheeler *Bellona* sails from Whitehall dock for a fishing trip –1st party boat.

1819 Brooklyn village adopts official street map.

1820 Only 518 slaves in city. ● Five Points, northeast of city hall, is most notorious district – with squalid, overcrowded dwellings and rowdy, licentious street life.

1820 Mercantile Library founded in Fulton Street to discourage young clerks from lounging on street corners or frequenting questionable places of amusement. ● General Society of Mechanics and Tradesmen found Apprentices' Library for young workmen (*see also* 1862). ● *May 25th* Park Theater (Park Row/Ann Street) burns down. ● Return of legalized thoroughbred horse racing.

1820 1st Unitarian Church, Chambers Street.

1822 New York now America's largest city.

1821 Bloomingdale Insane Asylum, 1st mental hospital in state, opens in Morningside Heights. ● Moving from rough alleyways and farmyards into saloons such as *Rat Pit* and *Kit Burn's Sportsmen Hall* near Bowery, fights are held between rats and dogs. City merchants now participate and bet.

1822 Yellow Fever outbreak, many evacuate to Greenwich Village. ● Alder Spooner publishes *Brooklyn Directory* at *Star* offices.

1821 Black Ball ships now sailing on 1st and 16th of every month (*see also* 1818, 1878). ● Competing with Black Ball Line, Red Star ships sail for England on 24th every month.

1822 Red Star Line now sails 4 vessels a month to Liverpool. ● Fulton Fish market opens at South Street Seaport. ● *February 28* City's 1st life insurance company, Mechanics' Life Insurance and Coal Company for life insurance, granting annuities, and to discover and work state's coal beds.

1821 *March 5* Stephen Allen mayor.

1822 *December 5* Presbyterian Church, Jamaica, opens Sabbath school for black children to prevent their ignorance of Bible; soon has 50 pupils.

1821 African Grove Theater for blacks only (Bleecker/Mercer Street). *Richard III* and *Othello* performed. ● *May 24* Whitestone Herald appears. ● *May 25th* New Park Theater opens, funded by John Jacob Astor and Jacob K Beekman. ● *January 4*

The Long Island Farmer published. ● Brooklyn Circulating Library founded with 800 volumes; annual subscription ● City is national center for horse racing until 1850. Wealthy residents form Jockey Club and build Union Course in Queens where most important races are held. ● Steamboat *Franklin* advertises fishing trips twice a week for $1.50, with dinner.

1821 Transporting ton of goods from Buffalo to N.Y. by wagon takes 3 weeks and costs $100.

1822 *July 25* Cornerstone laid for St. James Cathedral, oldest Catholic church in Brooklyn. ● St. Luke's Chapel of Trinity Parish on Hudson Street dedicated.

1819 Adams-Onis Treaty. U.S. acquires Florida from Spain

1820 Missouri Compromise: Missouri admitted as a slave state, while Maine admitted a free state

1821 Greek War of Independence

1823 *April 13* William Marcy Tweed born in Cherry Street

1823 *May* Sandy Hook Lightship anchored (*see also* 1828 and 1908). ● *August* Yellow Fever in Brooklyn. 19 reported cases, 10 fatal.

1824 Bread and Cheese Club founded. ● *July 3* Castle Clinton at Battery, originally a fort, reopens as Castle Garden – the Madison Square Garden of its day. It hosts "fanciful gardens," live concerts, fireworks, balloon ascents and scientific demonstrations. ● Terhune Brothers open Coney Island House – soon visited by Daniel Webster and P T Barnum. Coney Island will develop further after Civil War when 5 railroads connect it with rest of Brooklyn. Name derives from *konijn* (Dutch for rabbit: there were many wild rabbits there in 1600s).

1823 *March 26* New York Gas-Light Company incorporated to replace whale-oil lamps and light Broadway (*see also* 1825).

1824 *January 1* 326 vessels in harbor.

1824 *January 19* General William Paulding mayor.

1824 *November 20* Brooklyn Apprentices Library Association to create a library and provide, "maps, drawings, apparatus, models of machinery, tools and implements". ● Theaters open on Broadway and Bowery, actors arrive from U.K., seeking fame.

1823 1,217 vessels arriving at port. 1,097 boats are American. 91 British, plus Dutch, French, Swedish, Spanish and Portuguese vessels. 4,999 passengers. Goods arrive from America's sister states, European nations, West Indies and new South American republics.

1823 1st German neighborhood and commercial center from Pine Street to Pearl Street.

1824 *January 8* Entire streets of elegant brick buildings rise on former marshland.

1825 200 police officers in city. ● Cooper Club (or The Lunch) formed. ● Law bans liquor sales in Queens County courthouse. Sheriff builds a shed against building and takes orders through the window.

1826 Trying to stop slave catchers taking fugitives, crowd surrounds City Hall and attacks police with stones and sticks.

1825 Martin Van Buren helps set up Democratic Party in city.

1826 Philip Hone mayor.

1825 *July 4* Marquis de Lafayette lays cornerstone for Brooklyn Apprentices Library Association

Marquis de Lafayette

PB

(*see* 1824 November). ● *November 29* 1st Grand Opera: Rossini's *Barber of Seville at Park Theater*. ● Harlem Library founded as private circulating library. ● New York Trotting Club formed. Racing course built on Long Island.

1826 Bowery Theater opens (Canal /Hester Streets) 1st rival to Broadway. ● *January 19* National Academy of Design founded. Samuel Morse 1st president.

1825 *November 4* 363-mile long Erie Canal opens. De Witt Clinton's speech: ". . . it will create the greatest inland trade ever witnessed. . . . New York will . . . become the granary of the world, the emporium of commerce, the seat of manufactures, the focus of great moneyed operations".

Erie Canal Locks

PB

1825 *June 11* Cornerstone laid of Fort Hamilton, built to guard Narrows (completed 1831). ● *May* 1st gas pipeline laid by New York Gas-Light Company up Broadway from Bowery to Canal Street.

1826 Old potter's field becomes Washington Military Parade Ground, soon renamed Washington Square.

1827 Gangs meet at Bowery to brawl, target-shoot, drink and carouse. Many have tattoos. Chichesters Gang, mainly apprentice butchers, sport long sideburns. ● Abolition of slavery in New York State. ● *July 4* Last black slaves in New York freed. Revd. William Hamilton of African Zion Church declares: "This day has the State of New York regenerated itself. This day She has been cleansed of a most foul, poisonous and damnable stain." Black minister, Paul Williams, declares, "The freedom to which we have attained is defective, the rights of men are decided by the colour of their skin." ● Northern Dispensary opens, with free medical care for poor.

1827 *Journal of Commerce* founded. By 1828, it runs news schooners to intercept arriving vessels and scoop latest news. ● New York Merchants Exchange, H.Q. of New York Stock Exchange board, opens on Wall Street, supplanting Tontine Coffee House as commercial center.

PB

Stock Exchange

● Samuel Rust invents Washington hand press, making printing more efficient. Steam-driven presses arrive a few years later. ● Throgs Neck Lighthouse in operation (*see also* 1934).

1827 *March 16* 1st black-owned and edited newspaper in world is *Freedom's Journal*, launched by John B. Russwurm, 1st black American to graduate from college. ● After threatening to sell library, New York Historical Society gains $8,000 from state.

1827 City opens public park at Greenwich Village, now Washington Square Park. Once a marsh near an Indian settlement, site was used as a potter's field and for public hangings. Remains of 10,000 people still buried here (*see also* 1889, early 1900s and 1960s). ● John and Peter Delmonico open restaurant on William Street. After 1835 fire, they rebuild (Beaver/William Streets). Today's 8-story, cast-iron and steel-frame building dates from 1891. ● Village of Williamsburgh incorporated

1829 1st Hotel opens on Coney Island. ● City extends to north at Canal Street.

1828 John Jacob Astor purchases City Hotel ($101,000). ● Speciality shops sell baked foods, meat, fish, dairy goods, spirits, coffee and tea. ● *July 14* City buys 147-acre island in East River from Blackwell family for £32,500, to build prisons, asylums, workhouses and hospitals. Prisoners work in island quarries.

1829 Brooklyn Sunday School Union stages Protestant Sunday School Parade, initiating Anniversary Day (*see also* 1898, 1959). ● Robert Alexander Young publishes *Ethiopian Manifesto*, attacking slavery and proclaiming coming of a black messiah.

1828 Prince's Bay Lighthouse is lit on Staten Island; will not be extinguished until August, 1922. More lighthouses at Fort Tompkins and Navesink Highlands.

1829 *January 31* Seamen's Bank for Saving incorporated. ● Sandy Hook Lightship discontinued (*see also* 1823 and 1908).

1828 James Kent founds New York Law Institute.

1829 *December 29* Walter Bowne mayor.

1829 Bryant now Editor of *New York Evening Post*. ● *Freedom's Journal*, black-owned newspaper, folds.

1828 Delaware and Hudson Canal complete. With new railroad, this opens Pennsylvania coalfields to N.Y. market. ● Broadway extends north to 10th Street. Common Council order opening of 14th Street (Bowery to North River). ● New Utrecht Dutch Reformed Church (18th Avenue/83rd Street). A replica of Revolution liberty pole stands on front lawn.

1830-40 With more industrialization; city population rises from 240,000 to 391,000.

1832 *May 30* Returning to N.Y. after many years, Washington Irving honored at public dinner.

1830 Manhattan Gas-Light Company will supply rest of Manhattan. 1st private residence to use gas is 29 East 4th Street, now Old Merchants' House landmark. ● Renting of property increases. ● 1 death per 39 inhabitants. ● Fortress prison, the Tombs, built on site of old Collect Pond.

Visiting the Tombs PB

1831 Reformers believe poverty arises from misfortune, not moral failure. N.Y. is 2nd state to outlaw imprisonment for poverty. ● Theater prices and fares adapt to working-class needs.

1830 Manhattan Gas-Light Company incorporated; $500,000 to light homes and streets. Will merge with New York Gas-Light Company to become Consolidated Edison. ● *March 16* Just 31 shares change hands at stock exchange – all-time low.

Mid 1830s Equal split between N.Y. Whigs and Democrats.

1831 *April 18* University of the City of New York incorporated as secular institution.

1830-60 Astor family create an exclusive neighborhood (until 1890s) in what is now Times Square (7th Avenue and Broadway). ● Stagecoach journey from New York to Boston takes 11/2 days. ● 1st street railroad line, the New York and Harlem, with branch line to Hudson. 2 horses draw cars with 2 benches. ● *October 18* Cornerstone laid of Northern Dispensary (Waverly Place/ Christopher and Grove Streets)

1832 *July 2 – August 3* Cholera epidemic: 3,513 New Yorkers die, mostly poor immigrants.

1832 English actress, Fanny Kemble, great hit in Park Theater play. ● 1st student attends University of the City of New York, Washington Square

1832 Construction of Colonnade Row starts – stylish homes with marble façades and Corinthian columns. ● Clinton Avenue (named for DeWitt Clinton) laid out in Brooklyn. ● Union Square formally named. ● Erie Railroad chartered to lay a track from New York to Lake Erie, to take, "property or persons by the power of steam, or of animals. . . ." Capitalized at $10 million, it will cost $23.5 million. ● New York to Harlem Line extends to Prince Street. ● *November* 1st N.Y. railroad journey. ● America's 1st horse-drawn streetcar runs on tracks from Prince Street to Union Square; 250 horse-drawn cars and 200 hackney coaches carry passengers. On November 14, horsecars run between Prince and 14th Streets.

1831 1st Horse-drawn carriage, called an omnibus. ● **1831-33** *April*: city's 1st railroad incorporated, New York and Harlem Railroad to lay tracks along 4th Avenue from 23rd Street to Harlem River with a branch line on 125th street to Hudson and permission to extend to 14th Street. ● *December 17* Gramercy Farm set aside as a park with 66 housing lots. Park is fenced, planted and deeded to houseowners.

1830 Indian Removal Act and Black Hawk War

1834 *April 8* Brooklyn receives city charter.

1833 Vast disparity between lives of wealthy and those in slums. ● Anti Slavery Society of New York founded at Chatham Street Chapel. Threat of mob violence so 1st public meeting cancelled.

1834 *July 7-11* Anti-abolitionist riots. St. Philip's African Episcopal Church, Centre Street, destroyed.● *August* Stonecutters riot against convict labor at Sing Sing cutting marble for N.Y.U. building, Washington Square. 27th New York Regiment camps for 4 days on square to control protest. ● Cholera strikes again.

1833 General Trades Union of New York set up.

1833 *December* N.Y. opposes Brooklyn's application to become a city (*see also* 1834). ● Wealthy Australian priest leases 2nd Street church to St. Nicholas Kirche, 1st German parish. ● *January 2* Gideon Lee mayor.

1834 *February 13*, The Star *reports that Brooklyn inhabitants value their independence from N.Y.*: "They would consider an association . . . under a common government, as . . . surrender. Between New-York and Brooklyn, there is nothing in common . . . unless it be the waters that flow between them. And even those. . . however frequently passed, still form . . . an insurmountable obstacle to their union" (*see also* 1833). ● *April 8* 3 days of voting: closely contested elections marred by riots. Mounted troops control mobs who fight in streets, contesting 1st direct election for mayor. Democrat Cornelius Lawrence wins narrowly but Whigs take Common Council.

1833 Nation's 1st school for blind children. ● *September 3 The Sun* appears: entirely new – small, easy to read and only a penny.

1834 *July 17* New York University graduates 1st class. ● 1st issue of *New Yorker Staats-Zeitung*. Circulation of 2,000 1st year; grows to 55,000 by 1872.

1833 *June 1* Cornerstone laid of Marine Pavilion, Far Rockaway. 160-room hotel will cost $43,000. ● Horsecars run from City Hall to Murray Hill.

1834 N.Y. and New Jersey settle boundary dispute over Hudson River and harbor. Line set at river's midpoint but N.Y. has the islands. ● Brooklyn & Jamaica Company begin railroad from Jamaica to foot of Atlantic Avenue. ● Long Island Railroad incorporated (Cornelius Vanderbilt a stockholder). ● Tompkins Square opens. ● St. Joseph's Roman Catholic Church (Washington Place) consecrated. ● New Brighton develops on Staten Island. ● New York & Harlem Railroad extends streetcar line from Madison Square to 86th Street.

The familiar image of New York is of skyscrapers but these soar above a whole landscape under the city, upon which they are largely dependent.

From the early 1800s, science and engineering advanced into the 1930s to create a vast network underground that grew to include power cables for subway, telephone and telegraph systems, steam pipes for district heating, plus gas and sewage disposal pipes. Below all this ran the subway tunnels, and some 500 feet (152 m.) down, the City Tunnel carried drinking water.

Under the city are:

•

32 million miles (51 million km.) of utility lines.

•

22 tunnels.

•

443 miles (713 km.) of subway tracks.

•

Gas mains and steam pipes that could reach across the U.S.A and back 3 times.

•

230 miles (370 km.) of subway, used by 3.5 million each day.

•

80,500 miles (129,524 km.) of electricity cable.

After much research, it was decided to create a system with the shortest possible distance between street and subway – this would be more efficient than, say, the London Underground. So, instead of expensive deep tunneling, the streets were dug up Above: *6th Avenue in January, 1928 and* below: *six months later: the riveted steel girders which will support the traffic are in place over what will be the four-track subway*

Water supplies
English soldiers dug the first shallow wells in 1666. In 1677, the first public well was by the old fort at Bowling Green. In 1776, when the population had reached 22,000, a reservoir was built between Pearl and White Streets. Water from Collect Pond and nearby wells was sent through hollow logs laid in the principal streets. By 1800, profits from water sales founded the Bank of the Manhattan Company (today's Chase Manhattan Bank).

The city's water supply system is one of the most extensive in the world, each day delivering 1.4 billion gallons of water to 8 million city residents. Croton, Catskill and Delaware watersheds cover nearly 2,000 sq. m. (5,180 sq. km.).

Reservoirs
The city's first water tunnel was completed in 1842 with an aqueduct to carry water from the Old Croton Reservoir. It provided 60 million gallons per day. The *New Croton Aqueduct* arrived in 1890. Water tunnels connect to a 6,000-mile (9,654 km.) underground network of mains. It now provides about 10% of the city's drinking water.
The Catskill System
The Catskill System was launched in 1915, with more reservoirs and a tunnels by 1928. It delivers about 40% of the city's water.
The Delaware System
Work began here in 1936 but was interrupted by litigation and then by World War II. It was completed by 1967. 19 reservoirs and 3 lakes store 580 billion gallons. It provides about 50% of the city's water.

The 85-mile (137 km.) long Delaware Aqueduct is listed in *The Guinness Book of Records* as the longest tunnel in the world.

Water tunnels
City Tunnel No. 1 stretches 18 miles, from a reservoir in Yonkers. It has been in continuous use since 1917. *Tunnel No. 2* went into service in 1938. It has been in continuous use ever since and is 20 miles (32 km.) long. *Richmond Tunnel* runs 5 miles (8 km.) under Upper New York Bay to supply Staten Island. *Silver Lake Storage Tanks* are the world's largest underground storage tanks; each holds 50 million gallons. *Water Tunnel No. 3* Construction began in 1970 to improve service and pressure to outlying areas and allow repair of tunnels 1 and 2. "Sandhogs" instal air ducts 70

stories down while a tunnel boring machine allows workers to excavate an average 70 feet (21 m.) per day, more than 3 times the rate with explosives.

Water Tunnel No. 3
This tunnel is the largest construction project in the city's history. It will extend 60 miles (97 kms.).

Manholes
There are 750,000 manholes. Plumes of steam from manhole covers began in 1882, when a central steam-heating system was installed.
In 1935, some boys pulled an 8-foot (125-pound) alligator from a sewer and out of a manhole on 123rd Street.

DP

Gas and cables
Ancient deposits beneath the Gulf of Mexico provide gas piped 1,800 miles (2,896 km.). The city has a 32 million-mile (51 million-km.) phone system. Wires were laid below ground after overhead lines snapped in 1888's Great Blizzard.

Elephants
Once a year, a herd of elephants passes through the closed Queens-Midtown Tunnel into Manhattan, when the circus arrives.

Maps
Today's engineers who work underground use maps and mechanical drawings (some over 100 years old) that are closely guarded. If they fell into the wrong hands, infiltators could bring New York to a halt.

Atlantic Avenue Tunnel
This was built in 7 months in 1844. The last train ran in 1859. In 1861, the tunnel was sealed up and forgotten but in the 1980s, Bob Diamond made it his mission to rediscover the "fabled" tunnel. This took years of research. He now organises occasional tours there, as do the Transit Museum.

Sewers
When sewage levels drop late at night, workers operate but still must beware slippery surfaces and lethal or explosive gases.
Raw sewage from Upper West Side used to be dumped untreated into the Hudson. Now New York sewers are

among the world's cleanest; the contents are usually about 99% water.
In the North River sewage treatment plant, bacteria consume suspended solids and dissolved material, then settle on the tank bottom. The sludge is collected and baked at 95°F. (30°C.) for 3 weeks in huge tanks and then dried to become biodegradable pellets, sold as organic fertilizer. The water left is now at least 65% clean and can be pumped into waterways.

Glaciers and bedrock
Some of the bedrock under New York formed 450 million years ago in the Atlantic Ocean. When the protocontinents of North America and Africa collided, they pushed the rock to its present location. Glacial soil was propelled in front of a great glacier to cover parts of the bedrock and became rich topsoil – unsuitable for supporting skyscrapers but used in Central Park and for reclaiming shoreline in lower Manhattan. Bedrock appears at the surface from Central Park through Midtown, where skyscrapers stand on solid rock. This descends and appears again below Canal Street, where the World Trade Center was built.

Subways
In 1870, A.E. Beach obtained a permit for a pneumatic tube to carry mail below street level, and then built the first subway under Broadway – in secret until a reporter exposed the operation. When it opened, in 1 year 400,000 passengers rode 312 feet (95 m.) for 25 cents.

1870 The first subway had a 120-foot (37 m.) waiting room with a fountain, settees, frescoes, aquarium and a grand piano.
1918 97 died in an accident in Brooklyn when, during a strike, an inexperienced motorman took a curve at 7 times the advised speed.
1946 Subway system had a record 8,872,244 passengers.
1965 In a 13-hour blackout, 800,000 people were trapped in subways and trains.
1989 A new $868 million subway line opened under the East River.
2001 System covers 233 miles (375 km.) and has 468 stations.

Earthquakes
New York lies on several faultlines. There are faults at 125th Street and at Dykeman Street – so earthquakes do occur. 100s of chimneys collapsed in 1884, when a 5.5-Richter scale earthquake hit the harbor. In 2001, a city earthquake measured 2.5 on the Richter scale.

Steam ships and ferries

Named after the ferry landing on Arthur Kills, the *New Blazing Star* to New Jersey was established in 1757, creating a short route to Philadelphia. *The Savannah* was the first oceangoing steamship, built in 1819 in New York. She used sails as well as steam. She left Savannah for St. Petersburg but the owners declared bankruptcy, and she was converted into a sailing ship – lost off Fire Island in 1821. *The Berkshire,* built in New Jersey in 1913, was the largest steamboat on the Hudson River and worked as a night boat. At 4,500 tons and measuring 422 feet (128 meters) by 50 feet (15 meters), she operated between the city and Albany until 1937.

Street parking

Limited curbside parking (at set times to one side of the street) was imposed in 1950 to ease street cleaning. It began on Lower East Side but was soon used in all Manhattan, the Bronx, Brooklyn and Queens. Fines rose until, by 1991, they exceeded $100 million. On more than 10,000 miles (16,000 km.) of street, motorists move their vehicles each morning from one side of the street to the other – except on Wednesdays, Saturdays and 32 "suspended" holidays.

Malbone Street crash

In 1918, because of a strike, untrained dispatchers were working on November 1 when a rush-hour train, heading for Brooklyn, jumped the track near Malbone Street Station

(now Prospect Park). It had reached a speed of over 30 miles (48 kilometers) an hour where the speed limit was 6 miles (10 kilometers) an hour. 97 were killed immediately and 5 died later.

Elevators: vertical transport

In 1853, the first safety elevator was developed by Elisha Graves Otis in Yonkers, New York. It created a stir when he demonstrated this in 1854 at New York's Crystal Palace Exhibition. In 1857 the first passenger elevator was installed in a Broadway store. Suddenly, hotel rooms in upper stories could command high rates, high rise apartments became desirable and skyscrapers could be built. Often passenger traffic was overseen by a "starter" who stood in the lobby and gave orders to the operators. In 1945, when a B-25 bomber collided with the Empire State Building, an elevator dropped to the bottom of its shaft but the operator survived.

Flight and airports

JFK Airport
This is 15 miles (24km) south of Manhattan in Queens. In 1942, construction started on 1000 acres of marshy land on the site of Idlewild golf course – after which the airport was first named. Dedicated as New York International in 1948, it became John F. Kennedy International Airport in 1963. About $60 million was spent on its construction. It covers 5000 acres, generates $6.6 billion and 207,000 jobs.

Newark
16 miles (26km.) south-west of Manhattan in New Jersey, the airport was built on 68 acres of marshland and opened in October, 1928. It soon became the world's busiest commercial airport. During World War II it was used by the Army Air Corps. Newark Liberty International Airport (EWR) was launched in March, 1948. It covers some 2,027 acres.

La Guardia
In Queens, 8 miles (13km.) east of Manhattan, it was first occupied by Gala Amusement Park in 1929. It was built into a 105-acre private flying field. A new airport was dedicated October, 1939. In 1947, it was leased to the Port Authority, and renamed La Guardia Airport. A new Central Terminal Building opened in 1964 and was enlarged in 1967 and 1992.

Trains

Pennsylvannia Station
This is at 7th Avenue/34th Street. Today's station (built 1963-65) is underground, hidden below Madison Square Garden. The original masterpiece was built in 1910 and covered 12 acres. Its general waiting room was based on the Roman Baths of Caracalla.

Grand Central Terminal
This is at Park Avenue/42nd Street. The original Grand Central Depot was built here in 1871, and replaced with a new station in 1913. Its vaulted ceiling depicts the Zodiac and constellations: 2,500 stars are lit with electric light bulbs. The station houses over 100 stores and restaurants, including the famous, splendid Oyster Bar.

The New York Bus System

There are 3,500 to 3,700 buses, 3000 bus shelters and 19 bus depots where buses are stored and maintained. Buses recieve an an inspection every 3,000 miles. The Transit Authority pays deli's $50 to allow busdrivers to use their washrooms en route.

The interior of Grand Central Terminal

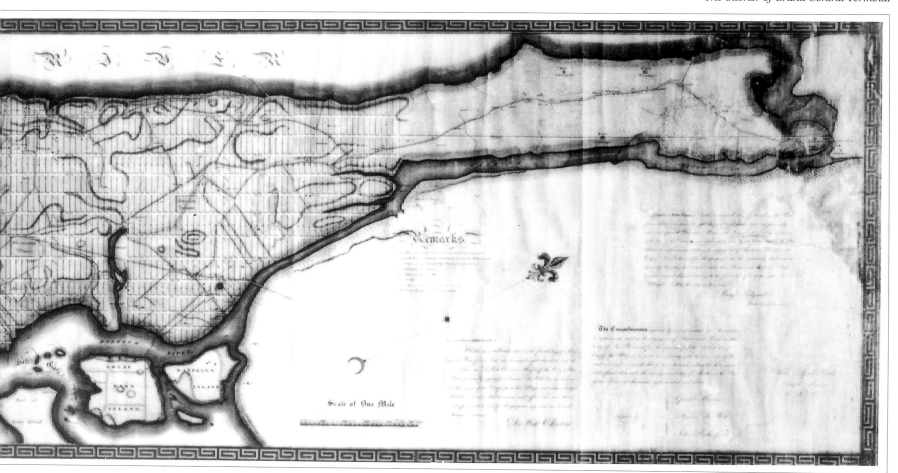

HISTORICAL EVENTS

1835 *June 21* Nativists and Irish fight in Five Points Riot. ● *December 16* City's most devastating fire evokes demands for reorganization of volunteer fire force or its replacement by a paid force, and introduction of horse-drawn engines with steam pumps. 17 blocks around Hanover Square destroyed. Water freezes in the fire hoses. 700+ buildings destroyed. Fire razes 20 blocks south of Wall Street and east of Broadway. Financial loss estimated at $20 million. 1,900 firemen fight blaze for 19 hours. 23 of city's 26 insurance companies go bankrupt afterwards.

1836 *March 2* Hudson and East Rivers, frozen solid through February, begin to thaw.

1837 Samuel Morse sends 1st telegraph message, from New York University.

Samuel Morse PB

1837 *February 13* Flour Riot: a hungry crowd, facing a hard winter and high prices, break into on Washington Street warehouses to steal flour and grain. Mayor and constables pelted with stones and ice. ● *April 15* Village of Flushing incorporated.

1839 *April 12* Astoria village incorporated.

1838 Baltimore slave, Frederick Douglass, escapes to N.Y.C. Publisher of *North Star*, he will help organize black regiments during Civil War and devote his life to civil rights and equality for blacks and women (*see also* 1835). He writes, "The flight was a bold and perilous one; but here I am . . . walking amid the hurrying throng and gazing upon the dazzling wonders of Broadway. The dreams of my childhood and the purpose of my manhood were now fulfilled. A free state around me and a free earth under my feet! What a moment this was to me!"

1840 More than 24,000 Germans live in city. 100,000 more arrive in next 20 years. German neighborhood develops east of Bowery, north of Division Street, and over to East River.

1830-39 200,000 Irish arrive.

1842 *January 24* Charles Dickens arrives for celebrated American visit

1843 *October 13* 12 young Germans found fraternal order of B'nai B'rith to assist new immigrants.

1844 54-year-old President John Tyler marries 24-year-old Julia Gardiner. Her father, a close friend of Tyler's, has recently died when a cannon exploded on a warship, the President narrowly escaping. Widower Tyler has 7 children; he will have 7 more – and live to be 72.

1845-70 Growing trade with Latin America and Caribbean; Latin American community surges. By 1870 increases from 508 to 2,062, many from Spain, Cuba, and Spanish-speaking West Indies. Expands further when U.S. acquires Puerto Rica.

1848 Brooklyn fire destroys 8 blocks and 200 buildings.

1846 Judge rules Georgia's laws do not apply in N.Y.; anti-slavery activist Louis Napoleon secures release of George Kirk, runaway slave and stowaway from Georgia.

1848 *March 29* John Jacob Astor dies, richest man in U.S., worth $25 million. ● *October 5* Frederich Hecker, hero of failed German revolution, arrives to huge welcome.

1850 *June 9* Henry Steinway, wife and 5 sons follow son Charles from Germany.

1849 *May 7* Irish workers and nativists disrupt *Macbeth* at Astor Place Opera House. On May 10, 10,000 protest about English actors. Militia open fire: 22 die and 150 injured. ● *May 14* Cholera in Five Points. 1,000 die in temporary hospitals; many more die at home. ● Brooklyn Gas Light Company provide coal gas for streetlights; lamplighters hired. ● St. Vincent's, 1st Catholic hospital, opens.

LIFESTYLE

1835 Committee of Vigilance founded to help runaway slaves (including Frederick Douglass –*see* 1838). ● Public executions banned in city.

PEOPLE

1836 15,825 passengers arrived in May. Philip Hone's diary says, "All Europe is coming across the ocean . . . They increase our taxes, eat our bread and encumber our streets, and not one in twenty is competent to keep himself."

1837 Now 17 daily papers in New York. Insufficient hotels for great number of visitors.

PB

1838 2 Tombs prisons complete: a women's prison and courtyard for hangings; male prison has 150 cells in 4 tiers (*see also* 1840, 1902 and 1970). ● Workers building Croton Aqueduct strike for higher wages.

1839 Poorhouse planned on Staten Island (will be Farm Colony). ● 1839 Robbins Reef Light, Bayonne operates (*see also* 1883).

1841-46 Robert E Lee post engineer at Fort Hamilton.

1840 Black sailors found Colored Seamen's Home. ● 1840s Coal, cheaper than wood, used as fuel. ● Irish riot when contractors try to reduce laborers' wages from $1 to 75¢ a day.

1842 *Spring* Protestant mob marches to Mulberry Street, threatening St. Patrick's Cathedral. Bishop's premises attacked and other dwellings hit by stones and brickbats. Military arrive to protect Cathedral. ● *October 14* Croton Reservoir on 42nd Street opens with a grand parade. Aqueduct's underground canal runs 32 miles to Harlem River Valley, crossing river in pipes 1,450 feet long. Water flows to a reservoir holding 150 million gallons in 35 acres – in what will become Central Park at 86th Street. Philip Hone's diary: "Nothing is talked or thought of in New York but Croton Water. . ." ● *October 18* American Institution's annual fair at Castle Garden. Morse and Samuel Colt demonstrate using electric current to detonate a mine to blow up a brig.

John Tyler PB

1844 Large numbers of Irish immigrants and economic depression. Gangs fight fierce fist, club and gun battles.

1845 *October 16* 1st detective agency in USA at 48 Centre Street. Few cities have a police force so criminals who flee N.Y. are rarely caught. Agency hunts offenders in other cities too. More agencies follow but some work with thieves! Wealthy hire detectives to check out children's suitors and for marital investigation. ● Immigrants, factories and tenements increase, so do race and class tensions and gambling. Mayor Havemeyer organizes a day-and-night police force of 800 men, nicknamed "star police" after their star-shaped badges. Fixed salaries mean some police take bribes from illegal businesses. Mayor also introduces garbage collection and health inspectors. ● Philip Hone diary: "Overturn, overturn, overturn! is the maxim of New York.... The very bones of our ancestors are not permitted to lie quiet a quarter of a century. . . . Pitt's statue no longer graces Wall Street, the old Presbyterian Church has given place to the stalls of the money-changers".

1847 New York Academy of Medicine founded

1848 Society for the Relief of Worthy Aged Colored Persons opens Colored Home (First Avenue /64th Street – *see also* 1898).

1850 New York City police now wear uniforms. ● 6,000 gambling houses in city; 1 gambling house to every 85 residents. About 25,000 men (1/20 of population) rely on gambling for livelihood.

POLITICS & RELIGION

1835 *Spring* City authorized to build Croton Aqueduct ● *October 29* William Leggett and Democrats try to take control of Tammany Hall. Loyal Tammany men extinguish lights. When insurgents light candles with newly-invented matches, or 'locofocos' (Latin for 'self-generated fire') – group is called the Locofocos. They oppose paper money issued by banks and imprisonment for debt.

1836 John McDowell organizes Magdalene Society to help prostitutes. ● Philip Hone sells his home near City Hall: ". . . all the dwelling houses [downtown] are to be converted into stores. We are tempted with prices so exorbitantly high that none can resist."

1837 *January* The Panic: Financial turmoil after President Jackson's bank war. 100s of businesses bankrupt and millions of dollars lost. Depression will halt economic development until 1843. ● *May 10* Run on New York banks: all but 3 suspend specie payments. ● Charles Lewis Tiffany establishes Broadway firm.

1838 *April/May* New York/Europe steamship service: in April, *Sirius* arrives from Cork and Brunel's *Great Western* from Bristol. On May 7 *Great Western*, 1st steamship in regular transatlantic service, sails from Battery, Pier 1.

1840 Strong supporter of slavery, Fernando Wood, elected to Congress. ● *September 21* Bishop Hughes requests funds for Catholic Schools. Common Council reject appeal, 15-1.

1841 *April 13* Robert H Morris mayor.

1842 Broadway brewery is 1st in U.S.A. to produce lager.

1843 Upper West Side area (59th to 110th Streets) is all farmland. Region is called *Bloemendael* (vale of flowers). ● Bankers and merchants found New York Association for Improving the Condition of the Poor.

1848 Book-publishing industry flourishes, with publishing houses such as D. Appleton; Dodd, Mead; E.P. Dutton; Harper & Brothers; Henry Holt; Doubleday, Page; Charles Scribner's Sons; and G.P. Putnam's Sons.

1849 Schaefer's brewery moves to Park Avenue.

1850 *March 4* Long Island Railroad in receivership.

1849 New city charter: mayor and aldermen to serve for 2 years, not 1. ● *April 10* Caleb S Woodhull – 1st mayor elected for 2-year term.

1850 Gangs rife, (including child gangs) especially in Five Points area. Revd. Pease opens Five Points Mission with Sunday School: day school and employment bureau follow. ● *November 5* Ambrose C. Kingsland elected mayor. ● Honest mayors try to veto corrupt franchises for railroad lines being granted through bribery of Common Council (called The Forty Thieves). Common Council overrides vetoes.

COMMERCE

1836 Stock Exchange awaits completion of Merchant's Exchange to hold 3,000 merchants and bankers.

1837 3rd county courthouse opens, Richmond Town ● *April 11* Whig Aaron Clarke elected mayor.

1839 Cunard Line U.S. HQ moves to N.Y.

1840 *November* Thomas Cole exhibits *The Voyage of Life*, commissioned by Samuel Ward (father of Julia Ward Howe who wrote *The Battle Hymn of the Republic*. ● Manhattan's 1st indoor bowling alley opens.

1842 *February 14* 2,500 attend 'Boz Ball' honoring Charles Dickens who records his caustic impressions of city in *American Notes*. ● Edgar Allan Poe's horror stories include *The Mystery of Marie Rogêt*, based on N.Y. murder case. ● *December 7* New York Philharmonic (originally Philharmonic Society) holds 1st concert, performing Beethoven's 5th. ● *November* PT Barnum meets midget Charles S Stratton (2ft 1ins tall) weighing 15 pounds. Renamed General Tom Thumb, he puts him on show in 1843.

1844 Hokey-Pokey men sell home-made, hand-dipped ice cream from small wagons, pulled by goats.

1843 *Rainbow*, one of 1st clipper ships, built in East River shipyard.

1844 Samuel F B Morse and partners incorporate Magnetic Telegraph Company.

1846 *April 14* Andrew F Mickle mayor.

1847 Henry Ward Beecher minister of Plymouth Church, Brooklyn Heights.

1848 *April 11* William F Havemeyer elected mayor again.

1846 *June 19* New York Knickerbockers, 1st baseball club, play a cricket team in 1st recorded baseball game. Knickerbockers lose 23-1.

1836 Presbyterians found New York Theological Seminary.

CULTURE & ART

1835 *May 6* 1st edition of J. G. Bennett's *New York Herald*: "We shall support no party – be the organ of no faction . . . endeavour to record facts . . . stripped of verbiage . . . just, independent, fearless, and good tempered." ● *Long Island Democrat* founded in Queens. ● Washington Irving and others form St Nicholas Society. ● 1st pleasure crafts built in city – soon top U.S. location for sailing.

1836 *October* Thomas Cole exhibits *The Course of Empire* at National Academy of Design. ● Minstrel shows launched with variety-show songs and dances – highly popular in next decade.

1837 Gothic revival New York University building, Washington Square, dedicated. One original finial remains. Samuel F.B. Morse is faculty member. N.Y.U. still on site. ● *Richmond County Mirror* launched, 1st newspaper printed on Staten Island.

1838 Saloons are political magnets during elections when politician saloonkeepers need gangs' allegiance. Gang members steal ballot boxes and intimidate supporters of rivals.

1839 *April 9* Isaac L. Varian mayor.

1841 *Spring* Walt Whitman, printer's apprentice and ex-school teacher seeks work as a writer and reporter in N.Y. ● *April 10* 1st issue of Greeley's *New York Tribune*.

1844 *October 28* Religious cult, the Millerites, believe world will end today. They wear ascension robes and close shops. ● *December 21* 122-year-old Quaker Meeting House, Maspeth, burns ● *April 9* James Harper mayor.

1845 33 German Jews establish Temple Emanu-El, 1st Reform congregation. ● *April 8* Democrat William F Havemeyer elected mayor.

1849 *March 12 Brooklyn Freemen* becomes *Brooklyn Daily Freemen* (*see also* 1848). ● 1st Jewish newspaper; weekly *Israels Herald* lasts 3 months.

1847 Herman Melville writes *Mardi*, *Redburn* and *White Jacket* and starts *Moby Dick*. ● Artistic and literary Century Club founded.

Jenny Lind PB

1848 Public school opens in Flushing. Village pays Flushing Female Association $75 per pupil to educate "colored" children (*see also* 1814). ● *January 27* Free Academy opens (23rd Street/ Lexington Avenue)

1850 P.T. Barnum signs contract worth $187,500 to bring Swedish operatic soprano, Jenny Lind, to city. Her 1st concert in September at Castle Garden has a 5,000 audience and receipts of $17,864. ● *Harper's New Monthly Magazine* begins as general-interest magazine promoting Harper's books. ● 1st billiard table made in city. Within 50 years 13 billiard manufacturers are based here

1838 Poor grocer Lorenzo da Ponte, dies. 1st professor of Italian at Columbia College, he wrote librettos for Mozart operas, including *Don Giovanni*, *Cosi fan tutti* and *The Marriage of Figaro*. ● Brooklyn City Library incorporated; 57 gentlemen take out 1st subscriptions on February 2.

Horace Greeley PB

1842 *May* Federal Hall demolished to make way for Doric marble United States Custom House in Wall Street. Greek Revival style preferred 1828-45 as war with U.K. makes English architecture unpopular.

1843 1st Ward School opened, 1st without Protestant Bible in curriculum – helps Catholic minority.

1845 *January 29 New York Evening Mirror* publishes *The Raven* by Edgar Allan Poe. ● Wealthy control thoroughbred racing. Harness racing becomes popular with middle class. ● *September 3* Knickerbocker Club founded. It sets baseball rules, field dimensions and number of players and innings at 9.

1836 *April 18/ May 3/ December 1* Brooklyn and Jamaica Company run 1st train from Atlantic Avenue to Jamaica. 1st accident on May 3, when train hits a cow and next train cannot stop. In December, Long Island Railroad lease line for 441/2 years. ● *April 18* 1st passenger train from city to Greenport. Long Island Railroad is nation's 3rd oldest railroad and largest commuter railroad to date. ● *April 28* Brooklyn City Hall cornerstone laid but soon financial panic stops work until 1846. ● *May 31* 600-room Astor House opens on Broadway (Vesey/ Barclay Streets) at site of John Jacob Astor's home.

1837 Construction begins of dam, aqueducts, and reservoirs to provide city's water. ● New York & Harlem Railroad opens at Madison Avenue and 26th Street. 4th Avenue Tunnel (34th to 42nd Street) built: streetcars every 15 minutes – fare 25¢. ● St James Roman Catholic Church at 32 James Street completed: parish of future governor Al Smith.

The entrance to . . .

BS BS

CITY STRUCTURE & DEVELOPMENT

1835 South Ferry runs from foot of Atlantic Avenue to Whitehall Street. ● Ramon de la Sagra writes, "Everywhere they are building houses . . . constructing superb hotels, opening large squares, and . . . laying out new streets and embankments."

John Draper PB

1839 *December* John Draper, of N.Y. University, makes 1st known portrait photograph.

1841 Jesuits establish St John's College, now Fordham University. ● *October 26* 1st issue of *Brooklyn Eagle* (folds 1955). ● *Winter* American Museum (Broadway / Printing House Row) opens.

1840 Halls of Justice (called the Tombs like the prison), complete (*see also* 1838, 1902, 1970s). ● Rail journey to Boston via Boston Post Road takes 1/2 a day.

1844 Edgar Allan Poe edits *Broadway* Journal. In time he will edit 5 magazines and contribute to over 30. ● New York Yacht Club founded. Its annual regatta soon attracts great press coverage and many spectators.

1839 Site acquired for Mount Morris Park. ● 2nd Trinity Church taken down after snow damage. ● 1st Catholic parish founded on Staten Island, St. Peter's. ● Brooklyn's street map takes grid beyond old village. ● Octagon Tower, Blackwell's Island, complete.

1841 New York & Harlem Railroad bridges Harlem River, taking service to Westchester.

1838 Green-Wood Cemetery, Brooklyn, commissioned (completed 1839). Cemetery covers 478 acres and today has 500,000 interments.

1842 Samuel F. B. Morse supervises laying of telegraph cable between Manhattan and Governors Island. ● Croton Aqueduct, costing $12,500,000, completed after 7 years. Water flows into Murray Hill Reservoir (site of New York Public Library).

1844 *July 27* Long Island Railroad (LIRR) reaches Greenport, connecting with Vanderbilt's steamer *New Haven*. ● New York and Harlem Railroad reaches White Plains.

1845 First Presbyterian, Manhattan's oldest Presbyterian congregation, consecrates new home (Fifth Avenue/12th Street). Wrought iron fence along Fifth Avenue is from original site at Wall and Nassau Streets. ● *July 19* Fueled by a saltpeter explosion, fire near Whitehall and Broad Streets destroys 345 buildings ($10-million worth).

1846 *January 26* 1st telegraph between New York and Philadelphia. Line to Washington complete in June.

1847 *May 10* Madison Square Park opens.

1848 High Bridge, with Croton Aqueduct over Harlem River, complete. ● St Joseph's, oldest Catholic church on Staten Island, built.

1849 St James Episcopal congregation in Newtown (Broadway/ 51st Avenue) build new church. ● Brooklyn City Hall complete.

1850s In Soho cast-iron commercial buildings will be popular for 50 years in world's largest area of cast-iron structures. Expensive skilled stonecutters no longer needed as iron designs (such as leaves for a capitol) can be ordered from a catalog and bolted onto brick façades. ● Bishop John Joseph Hughes buys land for St. Patrick's Cathedral.

USA & WORLD EVENTS

PL

1835 Samuel Colt introduces revolver

1838 Oberlin College 1st to admit women black students

1842 Webster Ashbun Treaty reduces border dispute between U.S. and Canada

1845-47 Irish potato famine

1846 U.S. Congress declare war on Mexico

1848 Mexican-American war ends

776 British cut down liberty pole (*see also* 1766, 1770 and 899) after they occupy city. Today, a replica stands west of City Hall. ● *January* Washington sends General Charles Lee to N.Y. He secures East River with forts on both banks from Battery to Hell Gate. Lee surrounds Brooklyn Heights. ● *April 13* Washington's army arrives in N.Y. His engineers extend Lee's line ne mile south and east of Heights. Fort Washington erected at Manhattan's northern end. ● *June 29* 100 British warships under General Howe sail into Staten Island harbor, warmly reeted. Soon nearly 500 vessels anchor – with 10,000 British ailors and 32,000-strong army. This huge force takes over 6 weeks to disembark and occupy positions. ● *July* Loyalists capture 1,300 of Washington's soldiers in Brooklyn's Flatbush area. Rest retreat to Brooklyn Heights and escape by crossing East River at nightfall. ● *July 4* Declaration of Independence adopted without N.Y.'s agreement. ● *July 9* General Washington assembles his troops for a reading of Declaration of Independence. ● *July 9* British warships gather in harbor. Declaration of Independence read to large crowd of troops and civilians on Commons. ● *July 12* Admiral Richard Howe, General Howe's brother, arrives with reinforcements. ● *July 16* Another public reading of Declaration of Independence. Citizens and soldiers march to Bowling Green and seize bronze statue of George III. Its head is set on a pole at *Blue Bell Tavern* (Broadway/181st Street). Loyalists send it to England later. The other 2 tons of British lead will be melted down to make 42,088 American musket balls. ● *August 22* With 15,000 men, Howe crosses Narrows and lands at Gravesend Bay. On August 26 he leads 10,000 troops through Jamaica Pass. ● *August 27* Outnumbered American forces driven back at dawn to Lee's 1st line of entrenchment on Heights. Battle of Long Island: fierce fighting but 25,000 British regulars defeat Washington's volunteers. ● *August 29* Lee's 9,000 troops escape to Manhattan during night, ferried over in small boats, with stores and equipment – as British discover next day! ● *September* Washington retreats to Harlem. British control Manhattan, Staten Island, Long Island and southern Westchester County. ● *September 6* *Turtle*, 1-man submarine, tries to sink British flagship *Eagle*, off Bedloes Island, by boring holes through its hull but cannot pierce iron. ● *September 11* Benjamin Franklin, John Adams and Edward Rutledge meet Lord Howe. British offer full pardon to repentant rebels, but this is declined. ● ***September 12, 1776 – November, 1784* N.Y. under British military occupation**
● *September 15-16* Howe attacks across East River with 5 frigates. Sir Henry Clinton's division is rowed across Newtown Creek in 84 boats. British troops push west and north. One story claims Mary Murray invites General Howe and staff for tea, delaying them while Washington's army reaches Upper Manhattan. Americans fight well in Battle of Harlem Heights. ● *September 19* Major Nicholas Fish to John McKesson: "A Cannonade from the Ships . . . seemed to infuse a panic thro' the whole of our troops . . . the enemy landed without the least opposition. . . these dastardly sons of Cowardice . . . fled in the greatest Disorder . . .". ● *September 22* British hang 21-year old Captain Nathaniel Hale (Yale graduate and Revolutionaries captain) as a spy. Hale's friend, William Hull, will set his last words as: "I only have one regret that I have but one life to lose for my country." ● *October 15* American soldiers attack British near St. Andrew's Church. ● *October 16* Washington evacuates city, leaving 2,000 troops to defend Fort Washington. ● *November 16* Washington tries to reclaim city but General Howe defeats him at Fort Washington. He withdraws. 2,800 soldiers captured plus equipment and cannons.

William Howe PB

1776 Most Jews, unwilling to collaborate with British Army occupation, leave for Philadelphia. ● *November* Loyalists and slaves flee to city as war rages.

1777 38,000 Loyalists in city form British militia but are never deployed.

1776 British army occupies city and polices residents, but many still keep their own voluntary police force. ● 3000 prostitutes shipped across from Liverpool.

1776 There is little time for sport – now seen as an English influence and, by some, as a violation of the Sabbath, like drinking. Police records suggest only a few colonists worry about alcohol violation! ● Slave, Bill Richmond, trounces 3 ruffians who pick a fight with him. His owner, the Duke of Northumberland, takes him to England and he becomes a professional boxer at 42. He runs a boxing school, teaching Lord Byron and Tom Molineux – who will become American's heavyweight champion.

1777 Artisans and independent craftsmen compete with merchant imports. They unite to protect their trade, and instigate riots.

Benjamin Franklin PB

1776 *May 10* Continental Congress instructs all Colonies to establish republican state governments.

1777 *April* New constitution for New York State.

1776 *August 29* Printer John Holt publishes last edition of *New York Journal*, then leaves city.

1776 *September 21* American patriots rebel. 2 fires in Manhattan destroy 493 buildings including 30% of city's houses and Trinity Church.

1777 Battles of Princeton, Brandywine, Germantown, Orinsky, Bennington and Saratoga. British Capture Fort Ticonderoga

December Independence

1778 *March 16* British attack 100 Americans near King's Bridge, killing 40. ● *July 23* Bulk of Lord Howe's army leave Staten Island. ● *August 22* General John Sullivan and 1,500 soldiers raid island. ● *November* Americans land at Bloomingdale and burn home of Loyalist General, Oliver De Lancy.

1779 *July* 600 American troops recapture Stony Point on Hudson. Evacuated British troops from here, and Rhode Island, crowd into city.

1780 *February* Upper bay freezes. British soldiers drag cannon 5 miles across harbor from Battery to Staten Island. ● *March 5* American prisoners, "wilfully, maliciously and wickedly" burn prison ship, *Good Hope*, in Wallabout Bay.

1782 When Lord Cornwallis surrenders at Yorktown, most British soldiers have withdrawn to N.Y.C., last British stronghold.

1781 Associated Loyalists create board of directors, including Benjamin Franklin's son, William, and refugees from revolutionary areas. They make raids across Hudson River for 4 months but disband when 1 captain hangs a prisoner he had agreed to swap.

1780 1,000s of Loyalists and slaves flood into N.Y., seeking refuge. British offer to emancipate any slave loyal to Crown.

1781 *September 26* George III's 3rd son, future King William IV, arrives in N.Y.

1782 Sir Guy Carleton evacuates British troops and Loyalists. On October 6, 1st convoy of Loyalists sails to Nova Scotia. Many flee to Britain. Black Loyalists who cannot escape are re-enslaved.

1778 Collect Pond on Lime Sheel Point fills with litter and fish vanish (*see also* 1808).

1779-80 Coldest winter in city's history.

1780 Former Virginia slaves take up British promise of freedom, camping near Broadway and Barclay Street. Many die of smallpox and are buried in nearby African Burial Ground.

1781 *March 26* New York loyalty oath begins: "I, ----, do hereby solemnly without any mental reservation of equivocation whatsoever, swear and declare, and call God to witness [or, for Quakers, 'affirm'] that I renounce and abjure all allegiance to the King of Great Britain".

1779 *January* Supplies arrive from Ireland and Nova Scotia. Flour shortage has made prices soar. ● Tory lawyers banned from practise.

1782 All city residents – and entire southern district – pay tax towards war costs.

1780 *HMS Hussar* hits Pot Rock and sinks in Hell Gate. They say she carried a cargo of gold, never found.

1781 Effingham Lawrence forms 1st pharmaceutical firm in city, which survives into 20thC as Schieffelin & Company. ● *May 28* City market regulations issued. ● *August 30* Bull baiting at Thomas McMullan's tavern.

1778 *February* New York is 2nd state to ratify Articles of Confederation. ● *March* Tories in New York disfranchised.

1781 *September* Provincial records, removed in November 1775, return to city.

1780 *March 21* Major General James Robertson last English Governor.

1778 *August 3* Cruger's Wharf burns. 60 buildings destroyed.

1780s De Lancey farms sold and become a grid of blocks and lots north of Division Street to East River. ● Travel from New York to Boston by horse takes 4-6 days.

1783 Treaty of Paris: U.S. now independent. ● *April 8* Royal proclamation, read at City Hall, ends hostilities. ● *November 25* Last British troops sail, having nailed a Union Jack to a greased flagpole – soon taken down! Washington makes ceremonial entry into city.

British Fleet leaving N.Y.

PB

● *November 29* 2 earthquakes. ● *November* It is said that George Washington, travelling through the Bronx, cried, "Surely this is the seat of the empire!" originating name, the Empire State (*see also* 1951). ● *December 4* George Washington bids farewell to his officers at city's Fraunces Tavern: "With a heart full of love and gratitude, I now take leave of you; I most devoutly wish that your latter days may be as prosperous and happy as your former ones have been gracious and honorable."

1785 New York named U.S. capital.

1783 *December 8* Occupation of Long Island ends as troops leave Jamaica. Washington writes that harbor, "was finally cleared of the British flag". ● *November 30* Black Brigade, a regiment of escaped slaves and free blacks, leaves Staten Island for Nova Scotia on *HMS L'Abondance*. 4,000 blacks sail for Canada. ● 100,000 N.Y. loyalists go into exile. ● *January* American soldiers and sailors released from prison ships in Wallabout Bay.

Prison ship PB

1783 *January* 11,500 patriots had perished in war. Many interred in Fort Greene Park crypt. ● *November 25* Evacuation Day will be celebrated as a holiday in NY for decades, with parades and patriotic dinners. ● *December* Peace treaty celebrated with a firework display. ● *December 4* 7 years' occupation ends: British troops leave Staten Island. Forests and livestock depleted; many buildings in ruins. ● *December 8* Residents place 13 candles in their windows to celebrate independence.

1783 *April* Governor Robertson sails home.

1783 *April 3* Writer, Washington Irving born.

1786 Most 1784 law measures persecuting loyalists repealed. "Rich when they left this City they have returned poor . . . to heaps of rubbish, and half-ruined houses–" Anon.

1786 *February 14* 1st city directory published.

1786 *February 15* Common Council seeks bids for a waterworks but gets only 3 offers.

1785 Samuel Ellis buys Ellis Island (Dutch settlers called it Oyster Island).

1787 *June 15* Mutual Assurance Company founded, 1st fire insurance company.

1784 *March* Bank of New York opens on Pearl Street. ● *February 22* *Empress of China* sails for Canton; China trade begins. ● *February* Bank of New York organized by Alexander Hamilton and others. It will open June 9 with $500,000 capital. ● John Jacob Astor arrives, seeking agents to represent family's musical instrument workshop. He enters fur trade.

PB

John Jacob Astor

1785 O'Reilly invents electric tattoo machine, a modification of Edison's electric engraving pen, and opens 1st mechanized tattoo shop in bawdy Bowery area. ● Wheat costs 75c a bushel.

1784 *May 12* Law bans loyalists (who had held office, served in army, abandoned state or joined British) from voting or holding office. 70% N.Y. residents lose voting right.

1784-1789 1st post-revolutionary N.Y. mayor – James Duane.

1785 Democratic organization, Tammany Hall, formed. ● *January 11* 1st Congress meeting, in City Hall. ● New York Manumission Society founded by Quakers and Anglicans hoping to stop slaves being kidnapped and sold.

1786 Columbian Order of Tammany Society founded. ● *November 4* St. Peter's, 1st Catholic Church, consecrated 2 years after repeal of anti-papist law.

1787 *May* 1st Methodist Society on Staten Island.

1784 King's College reopens as Columbia College.

Columbia College PB

1786 1st circus in city features horsemanship feats and a clown.

1785 *February 23* City's 1st daily newspaper *New York Morning Post and Daily Advertiser.*

1787 African Free School, city's 1st black school, founded. ● *October 27* Alexander Hamilton, James Madison and John Jay publish Federalist Papers in newspapers. ● Erasmus Hall High School, Brooklyn (2nd oldest public school in U.S.) 1st U.S. public school building designated a landmark. School deeded to Brooklyn in 1896.

1785 *March 31* Site chosen for new county courthouse at Queens (dedicated 1789). ● Presbyterian Church, Wall Street, restored. British had used it as a military hospital.

1787 Common Council plans to lay out new streets, funded by levies on house or lot owners affected.

1788 Owners of lots facing public slips must pay for paving of nearby streets. Most streets remain unpaved outside commercial center.

1784 India Act: East Indian Company cannot interfere in native affairs

1786 Annapolis Convention: Virginia invites states to discuss trade relations

1786 Shay's Rebellion demands relief from taxes and debts but farmers submit to state militia

1787 Constitution of the United States approved. 39 delegates, from 12 of 13 states, sign document

1788 *September* New constitution: N.Y.C. to be capital of new New York state, and temporary capital of nation.

1789 *April 30* FIRST PRESIDENT OF U.S.A. In Federal Hall, overlooking Wall Street, George Washington is inaugurated as 1st President of the United States. He is sworn in, after borrowing a Bible at the last minute from a nearby Masonic Lodge. ● *May 27* Martha Washington arrives to a 13-cannon salute at Battery.

Washington PB

1788 Tavern-keepers who permit card-playing, billiards, shuffleboard, gambling, dice games or cock-fighting may be fined or imprisoned. ● *April 13* Mob marches on New York Hospital, after rumours that medical students steal cemetery cadavers for dissection. Doctors are taken to safety in jail but 2 are hit by rocks. Citizens defend jail and fire on rioters. 5 die.

1789 *October 22* 2 black slaves burn home of Flushing's town clerk, destroying town records (*see also* September 1790). ● *November 3* District Court (later Southern District Court) meet for 1st time in Exchange Building – 1st federal court.

1788 *July 23* Trade guild members march to support Constitution ratification. Banner on model frigate *Alexander Hamilton* proclaims, "This federal ship will our commerce revive/And Merchants and shipwrights and joiners shall thrive".

1788 *September 17* Common Council permits federal government to use City Hall (now Federal Hall). $65,000 spent refurbishing it.

1789 *April 6* 1st Congress meet at Federal Hall. ● Alexander Hamilton is 1st secretary of treasury in new federal government. His policies help businesses and establish city as financial center. ● *April 23* Washington, President-elect, arrives at Battery.

Hamilton

PB

1789-1801 Richard Varick is mayor.

1789 Mutiny on *The Bounty*

1789 Washington inaugurated

1789 French Revolution begins 1789 France is 1st European government to give Jews full civil rights

1789 Judiciary Act. Government and Federal court system created. Department of the Army, State Department, Treasury Department and Post Office authorized

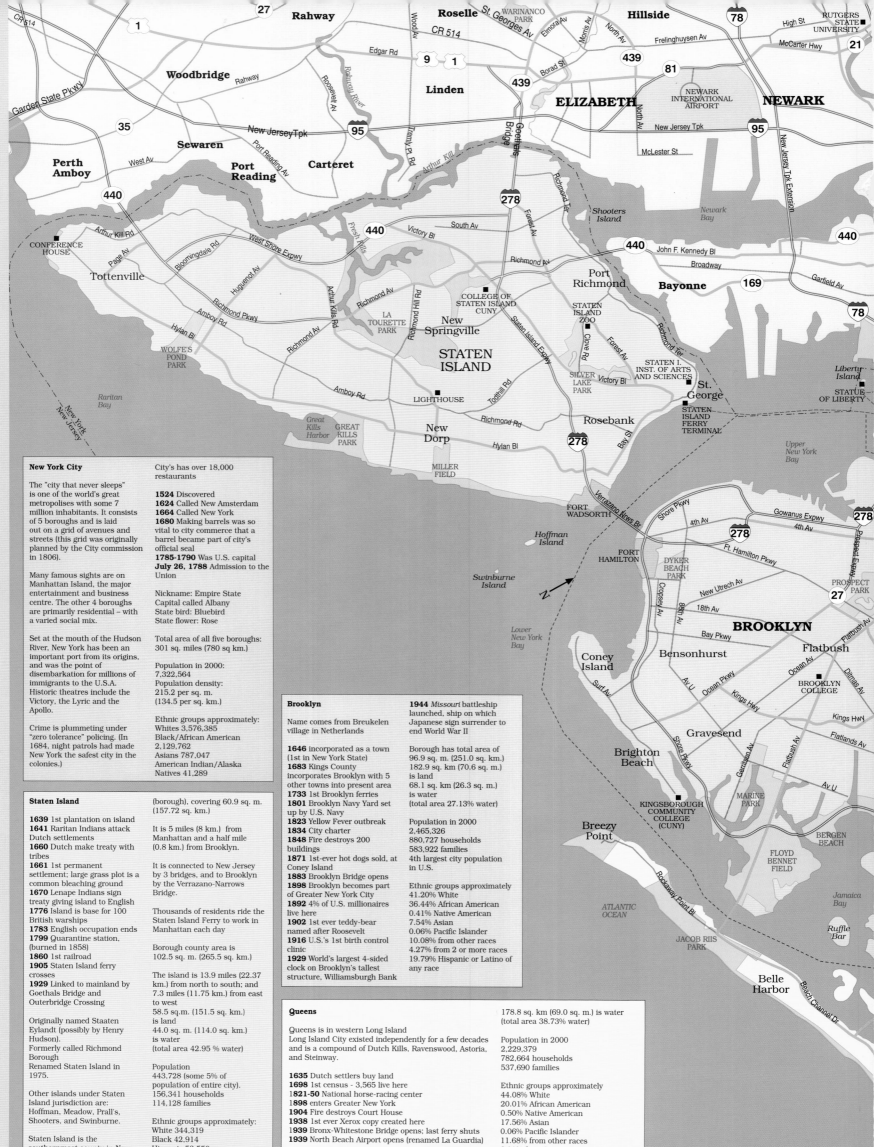

New York City

The "city that never sleeps" is one of the world's great metropolises with some 7 million inhabitants. It consists of 5 boroughs and is laid out on a grid of avenues and streets (this grid was originally planned by the City commission in 1806).

Many famous sights are on Manhattan Island, the major entertainment and business centre. The other 4 boroughs are primarily residential – with a varied social mix.

Set at the mouth of the Hudson River, New York has been an important port from its origins, and was the point of disembarkation for millions of immigrants to the U.S.A. Historic theatres include the Victory, the Lyric and the Apollo.

Crime is plummeting under "zero tolerance" policing. (In 1684, night patrols had made New York the safest city in the colonies.)

City's has over 18,000 restaurants

1524 Discovered
1624 Called New Amsterdam
1664 Called New York
1680 Making barrels was so vital to city commerce that a barrel became part of city's official seal
1785-1790 Was U.S. capital
July 26, 1788 Admission to the Union

Nickname: Empire State
Capital called Albany
State bird: Bluebird
State flower: Rose

Total area of all five boroughs: 301 sq. miles (780 sq. km.)

Population in 2000: 7,322,564
Population density: 215.2 per sq. m. (134.5 per sq. km.)

Ethnic groups approximately:
Whites 3,576,385
Black/African American 2,129,762
Asians 787,047
American Indian/Alaska Natives 41,289

Staten Island

1639 1st plantation on island
1641 Raritan Indians attack Dutch settlements
1660 Dutch make treaty with tribes
1661 1st permanent settlement; large grass plot is a common bleaching ground
1670 Lenape Indians sign treaty giving island to English
1776 Island is base for 100 British warships
1783 English occupation ends
1799 Quarantine station, (burned in 1858)
1860 1st railroad
1905 Staten Island ferry crosses
1929 Linked to mainland by Goethals Bridge and Outerbridge Crossing

Originally named Staaten Eylandt (possibly by Henry Hudson).
Formerly called Richmond Borough
Renamed Staten Island in 1975.

Other islands under Staten Island jurisdiction are: Hoffman, Meadow, Prall's, Shooters, and Swinburne.

Staten Island is the southernmost county in New York State
It is 3rd largest county

(borough), covering 60.9 sq. m. (157.72 sq. km.).

It is 5 miles (8 km.) from Manhattan and a half mile (0.8 km.) from Brooklyn.

It is connected to New Jersey by 3 bridges, and to Brooklyn by the Verrazano-Narrows Bridge.

Thousands of residents ride the Staten Island Ferry to work in Manhattan each day

Borough county area is 102.5 sq. m. (265.5 sq. km.)

The island is 13.9 miles (22.37 km.) from north to south; and 7.3 miles (11.75 km.) from east to west
58.5 sq.m. (151.5 sq. km.) is land
44.0 sq. m. (114.0 sq. km.) is water
(total area 42.95 % water)

Population
443,728 (some 5% of population of entire city).
156,341 households
114,128 families

Ethnic groups approximately:
White 344,319
Black 42,914
Hispanic 53,550
Asian 25,071
Native American 1,107

Brooklyn

Name comes from Breukelen village in Netherlands

1646 incorporated as a town (1st in New York State)
1683 Kings County incorporates Brooklyn with 5 other towns into present area
1733 1st Brooklyn ferries
1801 Brooklyn Navy Yard set up by U.S. Navy
1823 Yellow Fever outbreak
1834 City charter
1848 Fire destroys 200 buildings
1871 1st-ever hot dogs sold, at Coney Island
1883 Brooklyn Bridge opens
1898 Brooklyn becomes part of Greater New York City
1892 4% of U.S. millionaires live here
1902 1st ever teddy-bear named after Roosevelt
1916 U.S.'s 1st birth control clinic
1929 World's largest 4-sided clock on Brooklyn's tallest structure, Williamsburgh Bank

1944 *Missouri* battleship launched, ship on which Japanese sign surrender to end World War II

Borough has total area of 96.9 sq. m. (251.0 sq. km.).
182.9 sq. km (70.6 sq. m.) is land
68.1 sq. km (26.3 sq. m.) is water
(total area 27.13% water)

Population in 2000
2,465,326
880,727 households
583,922 families
4th largest city population in U.S.

Ethnic groups approximately
41.20% White
36.44% African American
0.41% Native American
7.54% Asian
0.06% Pacific Islander
10.08% from other races
4.27% from 2 or more races
19.79% Hispanic or Latino of any race

Queens

Queens is in western Long Island
Long Island City existed independently for a few decades and is a compound of Dutch Kills, Ravenswood, Astoria, and Steinway.

1635 Dutch settlers buy land
1698 1st census - 3,565 live here
1821-50 National horse-racing center
1898 enters Greater New York
1904 Fire destroys Court House
1938 1st ever Xerox copy created here
1939 Bronx-Whitestone Bridge opens; last ferry shuts
1939 North Beach Airport opens (renamed La Guardia)

Total area: 178.3 sq. m. (461.7 sq. km.)
109.2 sq. m. (282.9 sq. km.) is land

178.8 sq. km. (69.0 sq. m.) is water (total area 38.73% water)

Population in 2000
2,229,379
782,664 households
537,690 families

Ethnic groups approximately
44.08% White
20.01% African American
0.50% Native American
17.56% Asian
0.06% Pacific Islander
11.68% from other races
6.11% from 2 or more races
24.97% Hispanic or Latino of any race

90 1791 1796 1799 1801 1804 1807 1809 1812 1816 18

1790 *February* New York no longer federal capital.

PEOPLE

1790 City's 1st official census: Population of 33,131 is 2nd only to Philadelphia. Inhabitants include English, Dutch, African, Scottish, Irish, German (2,500), French and Welsh. 3,470 are African-Americans (2,369 of these are slaves). ● Saratoga hero, General Horatio Gates, moves in from Virginia after freeing his slaves. Horatio Street named for him.

PB
Horatio Gates

LIFESTYLE

1790 *September 2* slaves who burned Vanderbilt's home convicted; young Sarah reprieved, but Nelly hanged (*see also* 1789 October). ● Street gangs of young apprentices and journeymen (linked by neighborhoods, streets, and trades) fight over territory and harass pedestrians. ● *February 1790* Supreme Court convenes in Exchange Building.

COMMERCE

1790 *July 31* 1st patent issued in city (and nation) – to Samuel Hopkins of Philadelphia for a process to purify potash to make soap. Signatories include President Washington.

POLITICS & RELIGION

1790 *January 8* President Washington addresses both houses at opening of Congress at Federal Hall. ● *July* At a private dinner, Thomas Jefferson and Alexander Hamilton agree that Jefferson will support Assumption Bill (federal payment of state's Revolution debts), while Hamilton and Robert Morris will secure northern support for a national capital along Potomac. ● *August* Grand banquet honors Creek sachems. Treaty between Creeks and U.S. settles territorial disputes. *August 30* President and Mrs Washington leave city for final time.

CITY STRUCTURE & DEVELOPMENT

1790s Regular grid pattern of civic land laid out. ● 2nd Trinity church erected ● Old fort at Battery demolished. ● 1st sidewalks of brick and stone, scarcely wide enough for 2 people, on Broadway.

1794 *May 27* Cornelius Vanderbilt (Commodore) born on Staten Island. A ferryman, he will build a fleet of steamships, create New York Central Railroad and be worth over $100 million when he dies in 1877.

1791 New York Hospital, city's oldest, opens. ● *August to October* Yellow Fever epidemic; many flee to Greenwich Village.

1794 Bellevue Hospital opens on Murray estate along East River. ● Yellow Fever recurs, brought by British frigate. 732 die.

1792 *May 17* 24 merchants and auctioneers meet under a buttonwood tree (68 Wall Street) to found New York Stock Exchange which will open at 22 Wall Street (*see also* 1865 June).

1793 John Jacob Astor now most important American fur merchant.

1791 *October 24* Aaron Burr takes seat as N.Y.'s senator.

Aaron Burr
PB

1792 2nd courthouse in Richmondtown opens. (1st was destroyed during Revolution).

CULTURE & ART

1791 *Charlotte Temple, A Tale of Truth* by Susanna Rowson is 1st best seller - until 1852 when *Uncle Tom's Cabin* outsells it.

1792 *May 1* New school, Union Hall Academy, Jamaica.

1795 New York Society Library moves to Nassau/Cedar Streets.

1798 *January 13* Last performance at John Street Theater. ● *January 29* Park Theater opens on Park Row, near Ann Street.

1792 Common (City Hall Park) enclosed.

1793 Tontine Association, founded by merchants, completes $43,000 building (Wall/Water Streets). ● 17 buildings in Fulton, South and Front Streets built – now oldest row of houses in Manhattan and called Schermerhorn Row after chandler who built them as counting houses for shipping merchants.

1794 *City Hotel* opens, filling entire block.

HISTORICAL EVENTS

1796 *November* Albany replaces New York as state capital.

1796 Archibald Gracie is 1st president of Insurance Company that becomes Stock Exchange; his home on East River will become mayor's official residence – still Gracie Mansion.

1797 Newgate Prison opens. ● 2nd almshouse opens. **1798** Yellow Fever outbreak in August. Epidemic kills 2,000.

1796 *July* John Fitch sails experimental 18-foot steamboat with screw propeller around Collect Pond but idea not taken up.

Fitch's Steamboat
PB

● Tontine Coffee House (Wall/Water Streets corner) is New York Insurance Company's H.Q. (forerunner of New York Stock Exchange). 21 board directors, who assign values to ships, slaves and houses, form a "tontine": each receives a profit share that increases as others die.

1797 Dollar, dime and cent adopted by N.Y. for public use. ● Ironworks and soap factories, tallow chandlers, glue, starch and vellum makers pollute city. Law stops larger manufacturers fouling air south of Grand Street, west of Mulberry, or east of Hudson River. Soap and candle makers protest and are exempted if they operate inoffensively. Small, family concerns still pollute.

1796 City's 1st black church founded, African Methodist Episcopal Zion Church. ● Chief Justice John Jay elected Governor.

1798 *July 2 Memoir of the Utility and Means of Furnishing the City with Water from the River Bronx* presented by Dr J Browne. Common Council orders surveys.

1799 *December 14* George Washington dies. Memorial service on 31st.

1799 New law states children born to slaves after July 4 will have bonded servant status: men to serve until 28, women until 25, after which they are free. ● Staten Island quarantine station confines new arrivals with infectious diseases like Yellow Fever.

1799 *April 7/May 1* Manhattan Company founded. It creates city's 1st water supply system. Reservoir at Chambers Street. ● *September 1* With $2 million in capital, Manhattan Company opens bank – origin of Chase Manhattan Bank. ● *September 21* Bank of New York opens a Greenwich Village branch: Bank Street named after this.

1800 City's 1st exclusively black church, African Methodist Episcopal Zion Church (Church/Leonard Streets), organized by Peter Williams, a slave who stayed when his owner left U.S. Bought by church elders, he works as sexton and undertaker, pays back his price (£40) and becomes a businessman and property owner. His son is 1st black ordained in Episcopal Church. ● Republicans win New York State. ● Jefferson elected.

Jefferson
PB

● *February 15* Governors Island ceded to government as military base and harbor fortification.

1800 Park Theater popular for live entertainment.

1799 St. Mark's Church in-the-Bowery consecrated; on site of chapel at Peter Stuyvesant's farm. St. Mark's Episcopal Church, the Bowery (10th Street/Second Avenue) built. Now 2nd oldest church in Manhattan. Peter Stuyvesant is buried in churchyard; his great grandson sold church to Episcopal Church for $1.

1800 Alexander Hamilton buys the Grange, 30 acres uptown. He transplants 13 gum-tree saplings from Mount Vernon in Washington's memory. ● Population 60,515; includes 3,333 free blacks and 2,534 slaves.

1801 U.S. Navy sets up Brooklyn Navy Yard at Wallabout Bay. ● *June 1* Captain Randall bequeathes 20-acre estate near Washington Square for Sailors' Snug Harbor, for aged and worn-out sailors. Produce for residents to be grown on estate. ● *August 10* Haitians fight to prevent white Haitian refugee selling her slaves.

1803 Police force (about 76) called leatherheads wear leather helmets, light street lamps, firewatch, and control crime and grave-robbing. Graveyard watchmen are ill-paid so work as laborers by day: 120 are fined for sleeping at Potter's Field cemetery. ● *July to November* Yellow Fever: 6,000 die.

1800-1815 John Jacob Astor invests $695,000 and sells property worth about $200,000. ● Real estate values rise.

1800 Wheat costs $210 a bushel.

1803 New York exports goods worth $3,100,000.

801 *August 24* Edward Livingstone mayor. ● John Hays autocratic high constable; governs a small force for nearly 50 years, makes numerous arrests and disperses rebels.

1803 *October 29* DeWitt Clinton mayor.

1801 *November 16 New York Evening Post*, founded by Alexander Hamilton. It remains city's oldest newspaper.

1802 American Academy of Fine Arts founded. ● Thoroughbred horse racing banned. Harness races still allowed.

1801-02 Where Rockefeller Center is now, Elgin Garden is city's 1st botanical garden, funded by Dr. Hosack (who attended Alexander Hamilton after his duel with Burr. 20 acres offer relaxation; medical students can study therapeutic plants. Only Channel Gardens remain today.

1803 *May 26* Mayor Livingston lays cornerstone for City Hall: will cost $500,000 when built (1812).

1806 *April 24* Napoleonic Wars: British warship blockades harbor and attacks sloop off Sandy Hook.

1804 Samuel Wood opens 1st used-book store (Pearl Street). ● *July* In a duel, Vice President Aaron Burr shoots Alexander Hamilton (founder of financial sector). He dies next day and huge crowds attend his funeral. He is buried in Trinity Churchyard (*see also* 1801 Elgin Garden).

PB
Hamilton/Burr Duel

1805 Free smallpox vaccine now available. Physicians and public health officials want compulsory vaccination.

1806 Medical Society of Richmond County launched.

1805 *January* Havemeyers build sugar refinery on Vandem Street (in 1860 it moves to Williamsburg).

1804 *November 20* Hosack and Pintard found New York Historical Society.

1805 Park Theater purchased by John Jacob Astor and John Beekman. ● 1st free state schools. On February 19, Quaker Thomas Eddy establishes Free School Society. It runs all public schools until 1853, aiming to improve cleanliness and order.

1804 John Jacob Astor buys Vauxhall Gardens. Senator Mason writes that 700 buildings have been built in 12 months, with Broadway the best street in America.

1806 City Commission plans simple, rectilinear grid of agricultural holdings, houses, rights of way, waterways, hills and marshes – but Broadway survives.

1808 In his journal *Salmagundi*, Washington Irving refers to city as Gotham.

Washington Irving
PB

1807 Charles Wiley launches bookshop in Reade Street. Backroom Den is meeting place for William C. Bryant, James F. Cooper, and Samuel Morse.

1808 *May 26* Prison-ship martyrs' bones entombed against Brooklyn Navy Yard.

1808 *January 9* Embargo Act curtails trade with Europe. Common Council opens a Soup House and funds public works to help unemployed seamen and cartmen. ● Bowery and Broadway's "lofty and well built" homes are finest in city.

1807 *August 17* Robert Fulton launches his 1st steamboat, the *Clermont*. It travels up Hudson, reaches Albany in 34 hours, and will be in service for 7 years. ● New York exports $16,400,000 of goods.

Robert Fulton
PB
Fulton's Clermont

PB

1808 *May 8* Hook and Ladder Company established.

1807 *December 22* President Jefferson's foreign trade embargo shuts down port (repealed 1809). ● *March 16* Marinus Willett mayor.

1808 *February 22* DeWitt Clinton mayor for 2nd time.

1807 *May 2* Dr. S.L. Mitchill publishes *The Picture of New-York or The Traveller's Guide through The Commercial Metropolis of the United States.*

1808 *May 31* 1st permanent circus, *Pepe and Beschard's*, at Broadway and Worth Street.

1807 *April 3* Common Council plan,"leading streets and great avenues, of a width not less than 60 feet, and . . . public squares . . . to ensure a free and abundant circulation of air among said streets".

1808 Manhattan's Collect Pond is drained for buildings which later become slums.

1811 *May* Fire (Chatham and Duane Streets) destroys 100 buildings.

1809 Steamship route to Philadelphia, via Raritan River.

1810 16 year-old Cornelius Vanderbilt borrows $100 from his mother, buys a 2nd-hand sailboat and starts a ferry service to Manhattan. ● *September 25* Business is brisk; imports flow into warehouses and stores. In a single day 5 ships arrive from Liverpool. ● Steamboat *Raritan* starts regular scheduled trips (Manhattan to Amboy).

1811 World's 1st steam ferry, *Juliana*, between Manhattan and Hoboken.

1809 A Catholic receives Tammany Hall nomination for political office in N.Y. ● Abolition and discrimination issues: black members leave Trinity Church and form St. Philip's Episcopal Church. ● Long Island Star publishing in Brooklyn.

1810 *March 5* Jacob Ratcliffe mayor.

1811 *February 6* DeWitt Clinton mayor for 3rd time.

1809 *February 17* William Elliot publishes the *Observer*, 1st Sunday newspaper; it lasts 6 months.

1811 Fifth Avenue 1st appears on Commissioner's plan, running north from Washington Square to Harlem River. Broadway merges with Bowery. One well-connected landowner has Broadway's route moved northwest at 11th Street and disrupts neat grid. ● Castle Clinton at Battery, and Castle Williams on Governors Island, completed. ● West Road becomes Sixth Avenue.

1812 *June 18 to 1815* Congress declare war with Britain.

1814 Emperor Napoleon's brother, Joseph Bonaparte, buys huge acreage for him in N.Y. State. Later, his nephew, Joseph, will build several houses in city for his art collection and as a potential refuge for him.

1815-1915 33 million people immigrate to U.S. from all over world. 75% arrive at New York port.

1813 Burials below Canal Street prohibited. ● *September 2 U.S.S. Chesapeake* officers killed when frigate captured by *H.M.S. Shannon*.

1815 *December* Board of Health recommends residents be protected against smallpox.

1812-15 War disrupts commerce. British warships blockade harbor and Long Island Sound.

1814 *April 15* Village of Jamaica incorporated. ● *May 8* Steam ferry *Nassau* makes 1st trip from Brooklyn to Manhattan.

1812 1st Tammany Hall erected (Nassau/Frankfort Streets – *see also* 1868).

1815 *March 6* John Ferguson mayor. ● July 10 Jacob Ratcliffe mayor. ● Governor Daniel buys land on Staten Island for Tompkinsville with streets named after his children – Arietta, Minthorne and Hannah.

1814 *February 7* Flushing Female Association founded to improve "the situation of the poor children of Flushing . . . growing up in danger of being led into vice and immorality." School opens April 1 with 19 pupils.

1815 New York African Free School opens. St. James Parish of Trinity Church starts Sunday School for black children in Bloomingdale.

1812 Federal Hall torn down. Bookstore occupies spot for 30 years. ● City Hall complete – front and sides faced with Massachusetts marble.

1813 Bridge and dam built across Harlem River at 155th Street.

1814 *July 15* Fort Stevens completed in Astoria at Hell Gate.

1815 *May 4* Dedication of St. Patrick's Cathedral, Prince Street. Irish immigrants had founded parish in 1809.

1816 *January* Common Council allocate $1,000 for free smallpox vaccinations. ● New prison near Bellevue Hospital replaces Newgate Prison, Greenwich Village.

1817 2 private marine baths for swimming anchored off Battery.

1816 *April 12* Village of Brooklyn incorporated. ● 135-berth *Chancellor Livingston* starts overnight service to New England.

1817 Formation of New York Stock and Exchange Board.

1817 Steamboat *Nautilus* runs from Whitehall Street to Tompkinsville.

1817 *June 11* President James Monroe visits city.

Monroe
PB

1817 *August 5* Bloodgood Haviland Cutter, Long Island Farmer Poet, born in Little Neck. ● Brooklyn Public School opens: 190 whites and 45 blacks in segregated classes

1816 Survey for Manhattan's street grid complete up to 145th Street. ● *March 31* Richmond Turnpike Company to construct road from Tompkinsville to Travis, shortening journey to Philadelphia.

1789-95 French Revolution

1793 Louis XVI guillotined

1804 Napoleon Emperor of France

1805 Battle of Trafalgar

1807 Slave trade abolished in U.K.

1814 Stevenson's steam engine

90 1791 1796 1799 1801 1804 1807 1809 1812 1816 18

82 1688 1692 1695 1700 1705 1710 1720 1728 1730 17

1683 *November 1* Governor Dongan divides province into 10 counties: New York, Kings, Queens, Richmond, Suffolk, Westchester, Dutchess, Orange, Ulster and Albany. ● *December 6* Governor Dongan grants new charter.

1684 Native Americans sign over lands in Flushing and Whitestone.

1686 *April* King James II signs Dongan Charter, confirming New York's rights to harbor. Manhattan and Brooklyn boundary set on Brooklyn side of East River, at low-water mark.

1693 Long Island renamed Nassau in honor of William of Nassau, Prince of Orange and King of England. ● 192 cannons installed at Battery.

1698 Population of New York province 18,067. 1st census: 4,937 live on Manhattan; 2,017 in Kings; 3,565 in Queens (including Nassau); 727 in Richmond; 1,063 in Westchester; Blacks – free and slave –14% of population.

1685 New York now a royal province when Charles II dies and Duke of York becomes James II. ● King James tells Dongan not to interfere if French send an expedition from Quebec to exterminate Native Americans but Dongan warns tribes. He also negotiates with them (and nearby colonies) to establish New York's boundaries and creates charters for city and Albany.

1697 *May 6* King William III charters 1st Trinity Church for an annual rent of "one peppercorne". It faces Greenwich Street, on Hudson River shore, with a large tract of land. 6 Jewish families and nonconformist Protestants also help building fund.

William III/William of Orange and Mary

1688 New York incorporated into Dominion of New England.

1712 *April 7* Newly arrived African slaves revolt, lighting fires and killing white people who try to control blaze. 6 slaves killed; 19 captured and executed. ● Population of city 5,840.

1730 City residents play billiards.

1710 2,500-3,000 Germans, fleeing religious persecution, arrive to make tar for British Royal Navy. Some stay, some go to the Catskills; most go to Pennsylvania.

1718 517 slaves imported.

1719 *July 13* Governor Hunter sails to England.

1723 City population 7,248.

Above: *Slave auction*

Edward Hyde (Lord Cornbury) a cross-dresser

Colonial slave market, 1731

1685 Takapausha and Paman, the sagamore of Rockaway, sell Rockaway Neck to New York merchant, Captain Palmer, for £30. They claim this land had not been included in 1643 sale. ● Dutch Reformed Church led by honest Dominie Hendrik Selijns, popular among merchants.

1695 Politician entrepreneur Robert Livingston (1654-1728) is, "a literate man in a society just verging on literacy".

1701 Captain Kidd hanged in London.

1702 (Governor 1702-08) Arrival of new Governor, Edward Hyde (Lord Cornbury) – cousin of English Queen Anne, former army officer and MP, and a cross-dresser: a New York Historical Society portrait shows him in a fine blue gown, holding a fan (*see* 1703). ● 1st lawyer in Queens, Samuel Clowes, arrives in Jamaica as county and court clerk. ● 165 slaves imported from Africa.

1687 *August 23* Although his claim is disputed, Palmer sells Rockaway Neck to Richard Cornell who starts a settlement.

1692 *August 30* Governor Benjamin Fletcher arrives.

1688 *August 11* Major Andros, appointed by James II, arrives to govern New England, New York and New Jersey. ● King James fires Dongan, who retires to his 5,100-acre estate in Staten Island. ● William and Mary replace King James. Dongan takes refuge in New England and eventually returns to England, becoming Earl of Limerick. ● In name of William of Orange, Jacob Leisler leads a rebellion. He seizes control of Fort James and power in New York.

1696 Captain William Kidd sails from New York on *Adventure*, with a commission from British East India Company to fight pirates – but turns pirate himself. He visits New York in 1691 and marries a wealthy widow with a fine home on Wall Street (*see also 1701*).

1703 City census: population 4,375; 818 family heads (less than half with Dutch origins). ● Governor Lord Cornbury, out on Broadway in a dress, rouge and perfume, arrested by patrolling watchman who thinks he is a prostitute.

1717 Robert Blackwell marries stepdaughter of Captain Manning, and gains Blackwell's Island (now Roosevelt Island).

Jacob Leisler's house

1689 *August 16* Committee of Safety appoint Leisler commander in chief of province until William and Mary can send replacements from England. Leisler assumes governor's role with ease and manages to keep peace in turbulent times. ● William of Orange is invited by Protestants in England to invade their country. James II abdicates and flees.

1697 Street lighting arrives. At a shared cost, every 7th householder must, ". . . in the dark time of the moon, cause a lantern and candle to be hung out of his window on a pole." ● Dr. Bullivant writes: "The Dutch seeme not very strict in Keepeing the Sabath, you should see some shelling peas at theyr doors children playing at theyr usuall games in the streetes & ye taverns filled."

1708 *February* William Hallett, his wife, and 5 children axed to death at home near Hell Gate. 2 slaves involved are executed.

1717 William Burgis publishes *A South Prospect of ye Flourishing City of New York.*

Sailors' hot lunches cooked on open fireplace

1730 Promissory notes legal. Commerce graduates from barter towards credit-based economy.

1691 *May* An enemy of Leisler persuades new guard that Leisler is a rebel, traitor and murderer. Leisler and his son-in-law, Milborne, are convicted of treason. Sloughter refuses to agree a death sentence but, while drunk at a party, signs death warrant. On *May 16*, the only governor of New York ever to be hanged, is led to gallows at Broadway and Chambers Street. Crowd weep, shriek and plead for mercy but Leisler and Milborne are hung, drawn and quartered, and buried without ceremony at foot of gallows.

1698 *October* Parliament issues posthumous pardons to Leisler and Milborne. Their disinterred bodies lie in state for 2 days, then a full funeral service is held (*see also* 1691).

1702 Yellow Fever outbreak: 570 deaths.

1716 Free blacks right to own land ends.

1703 Wealthy English and Huguenot merchants live on Queen Street, Bridge Street, Waterside (renamed Dock Street) and Pearl Street. ● 1st Anglican school for blacks. ● 1st sewer: open trench on Broad Street, later bricked over.

1729 1st Richmond County courthouse (Richmond/Arthur Kill Roads).

1728 *May 28* Mayor's Court commits Edward Williams and Susannah Hutchins, ". . .for their Entertaining Negro Slaves on Thursday night last in their dwelling house."

1695 Scavengers employed to remove garbage. Residents ordered to sweep streets in front of their homes or risk a fine. City is remarkably clean until mid-1700s.

1709 Trinity Church establishes charity school for poor children. ● Lectures, animal shows, bear baiting, cockfights and rat killings held in taverns. All-male clientele drink porter, ale, rum, brandy and Madeira. Hot lunches cooked on fireplace; dinners are cold. Sailors find work through the *Sign of the Pine Apple*, near East River docks.

1728 *May 6* Jamaica Fair opens for sale of merchandise and horses. ● Schermerhorns run ships between New York and Charleston, South Carolina, and bring back rice and indigo. ● Banned from city center, tanners relocate near Collect (from Dutch *kolch*, a small pool). Pond is soon polluted (now Foley Square).

1683 Dongan Charter divides province of New York into 6 Wards. Closest to harbour and inhabited by English and French, Dock Ward is richest. Poorest is North Ward, where 78% of the inhabitants are Dutch.

1695 Mr. Smith begins ferry service from Maiden Lane to Long Island. Farmers sell wares there; it is called Smith's Valley.

1700 Commercial and residential areas intermingle. ● *April 9* Common Council bans gatherings of more than 3 slaves on Sundays.

1684 From 1684-89, a night patrol of 45 men make New York safest city in colonies.

1691 *April 24* Common Council ban sale of liquor to slaves without their masters' consent. Slaves barred from taverns on Sundays.

1701 Wampum no longer currency.

1708-15 150% increase in locally owned ships helps artisans, shopkeepers and innkeepers.

1730 1st sugar refinery near City Hall, Wall St.

1686 Currency from any country is welcome and Dutch coins continue to circulate long after New Amsterdam is New York.

1691 New Lieutenant Governor, Richard Ingoldsby, and new Governor, Henry Sloughter, sent from England. Jacob Leisler surrenders fort to new Governor.

1694 Wharf built at Wall and Pearl Street.

Trapper 1699

1701 City Hall

1711 Meal Market, for hire or sale of slaves, set up at end of Wall Street, near East River.

1713 *April 2* 1st ferry between Manhattan and Staten Island.

1720 *September 17* Governor William Burnet arrives. He bans trade between Albany and Montreal, helping N.Y. trade and strengthening ties with Iroquois. ● 1st shipyard opens. ● Strong contacts in Britain help establish trade and credit so N.Y.'s richer business residents are of English rather than Dutch descent.

1721 215 ships clear city ports, carrying an annual 7,464 tons.

Peter Schuyler

1689 *October 14* De la Noy is 1st mayor elected by popular vote.

Fur trade decreases **1699**

1709 1st paper currency boosts commerce.

1714 64 vessels and 4,330 tons clear N.Y. City ports.

1722 N.Y. develops trade with British West Indies and takes large share of Chesapeake tobacco trade away from Boston and British carriers.

1682 A convert to Catholicism, Duke of York appoints Colonel Dongan, a Catholic Irishman, as Governor. He arrives in April with a Jesuit priest. The mostly Protestant population is wary but his fairness, honesty and politeness soon win support. Duke instructs Dongan to ensure a generous measure of political and religious liberty. ● Dongan creates a Charter of Liberties and Privileges that allows a popularly elected General Assembly, forbids taxation without Assembly consent, establishes trial by jury, and grants freedom of worship to all Christians. When Duke becomes King James II in 1685, he signs charter but never returns it.

1696 Mayor draws up list of 10 Roman Catholics in city. ● *May 11* Reformed Protestant Dutch Church obtains royal charter confirming its rights and privileges.

1705 St Andrew's founded, 1st Anglican church on Staten Island.

1707 Visiting Irishman, Revd. Mackemie, is 1st Presbyterian clergyman to preach in city. He is arrested but acquitted.

1728 *April 15* John Montgomerie new Governor.

1729 1st *Committee of Grievances in the Practice of Law in New York.* Many complaints lodged but little changes.

1700 *August 9* Act orders Jesuits and popish priests to leave before November 1 or face imprisonment or death.

1709 *May 6* Lord Lovelace dies. Lieutenant Governor Ingoldsby new Governor. ● *May 6* Peter Schuyler is President of the Council (will be re-appointed twice before 1720).

1730 1st synagogue on Mill Street, near Wall St.

1683 *October 17* 1st provincial assembly meet. On October 30, it approves *Charter of Libertyes and Privileges Granted by His Royal Highnesse to the Inhabitants of New Yorke, and its dependencies* granting freedom of conscience to all Christians and affirming that only legislature can impose taxes and duties. *October 30* 1st Catholic Mass in New York.

1702 Society for the Propagation of the Gospel founds St. George's Parish, Flushing.

1698 *March 13* 1st service held in newly built Trinity Church. C. of E. members no longer worship at Dutch Reformed Church. ● *April 13* Richard Coote, Earl of Bellomont, appointed Governor.

1712 Anglican church built in Richmondtown. ● Governor Hunter orders all slaves must have religious instruction. ● *December 12* New laws limit slave access to liquor and permit masters to punish them: ". . . no Negro, Indian, or Mallatto, that here after be made free, shall enjoy, hold or possess any Houses, Pands, Tenements, or Hereditaments in this colony."

1694 *November 24* 1st meeting in Flushing's Quaker Meeting House. Quaker meetings still held here today.

1728 1st Hebrew School founded

1713 Revd. John Sharpe donates collection of English and Latin books to city to found public library. They will comprise core of New York Society Library.

1684 *February 5* 1st meeting of Court of General Sessions of the Peace for the City and County of New York. ● *February 14* 6 aldermen and 6 assistant aldermen meet as Common Council. ● *October 13* 1st election of aldermen, councilmen, assessors and constables by city's freemen.

1691 *July* New York's 1st autopsy when Governor Sloughter dies. After claims that he has been poisoned, or committed suicide in remorse over Leisler, 6 doctors examine body at New York's 1st autopsy and pronounce death due to alcohol poisoning.

1708 *December 18* Lord John Lovelace is Governor.

1714 *August 1* Governor Hunter's play *Androborus* 1st drama published in English colonies.

1725 *October 16/ November 8* City's 1st printer, William Bradford at 81 Pearl Street creates 1st New York newspaper, *New York Gazette*, on gray, dirty-looking paper. Text often borrowed and may be incorrect. ● Epitaph on William Bradford's tombstone: *Being quite worn out with old age and labor he left this mortal state in the lively hopes of a blessed immortality. Reader, reflect how soon you'll quit this stage. You'll find that few attain to such an age. Life's full of pain. Lo, here's a place of rest. Prepare to meet your God then you are blessed.*

1695 20 Jewish families in Manhattan have a synagogue called *Shearith Israel* (Remnant of Israel) on what is now South William Street. City's 1st rabbi is Saul Brown.

1671 Federal Hall

1686 *May 29* James II writes to Dongan, ordering that Assembly, with recently granted *Charter of Libertyes and privilidges* be disallowed.

CULTURE & ART

1699 Governor grants Richard Hunter permission to stage plays but there is no record of these productions or where they took place. Generally, plays were enacted in makeshift quarters.

1685 Cocclestown founded on Staten Island (later renamed Richmondtown).

1693 Kings Bridge, first to span Harlem River, built at Spuyten Duyvil (now Kingsbridge Avenue). ● 1st permanent pavement in Wall Street.

1701 New City Hall replaces Stadt Huys – will be renamed Federal Hall.

1712 1st Presbyterian Church, west of City Hall.

1722 City's 1st Presbyterian Church completed on Wall St.

1729 1st Jewish Synagogue in city.

1699 *August 9* Foundation of new City Hall on Wall Street is laid with stones from old bastions.

1704 Lord Cornbury appoints commission to lay out Kings Highway from river to Flatbush.

1719 Fraunces Tavern built as a fine home for prosperous merchant Stephen de Lancy, who gave city its first clock (*see also* 1762).

1692 Salem Street

William Penn

1705 Royal gift of land (Broadway to Hudson River and Fulton to Christopher Street) makes Trinity one of richest U.S. parishes.

1690s Town's 1st inn, *The Studt-Huys* (or City Hall), now fallen into disrepair, is sold to a merchant and soon demolished.

1708 Governor's House built on Governors Island – apparently paid for by taxes meant for harbor fortifications.

1730 Cocclestown on Staten Island renamed Richmondtown.

Governor's House today

1696 Trinity Church built at Broadway and Wall St.

Founds Pennsylvania

1692 Witch trials in Salem

1697 Czar Peter the Great visits Europe

1700s Agrarian Revolution

1728 Bering discovers Straits

1733-35 War of Polish Succession

2 1688 1692 1695 1700 1705 1710 1720 1728 1730 17

The first settlement here was by the Dutch in 1636 near Flushing Bay. Gradually towns like Newtown emerged – under English control by 1664. The area was named for Queen Catherine of Braganza, wife of Charles II.

During the Revolution, allegiance was divided and when the English captured Long Island in 1776, many patriots fled. Arbitration Rock ended a 1660-1769 dispute over the boundary between Brooklyn and Queens. Many Greeks moved here after the 2nd World War, and by the 1980s were the largest Greek community outside Athens.

Today it is New York's largest borough, 37% of the territory. It covers about 120 square miles (311 sq. km.) and is almost as large as Manhattan, the Bronx, and Staten Island combined. It is home to La Guardia and Kennedy Airports.

Above: *The Shea Stadium in Corona Park opened in April 1964 as the new home of the New York Mets. The stadium seats 55,101 and has also hosted the New York Yankees plus the New York Jets and New York Giants football teams. Special events have included rock concerts by the Beatles in 1965 (which 53,275 watched) and the Who in 1982 (which drew 70,346)*

Above: *The National Tennis Center in Corona Park*

Below: *Unisphere. This large, hollow, stainless steel globe was built as the symbol of the 1964-65 World Fair. It is 120 feet (35 m.) tall and 900,000 pounds (400,000 kg.) – the largest globe in the world*

Native Americans

Matinecock Indians were the first Bayside residents. Far Rockaway was inhabited by Canarsie Indians, who named the area Reckouacky (place of our people). They sold it in 1685 to John Palmer. Little Neck was originally inhabited by Matinecock Indians, an Algonquin tribe. Maspeth is named for the Mespat Indians, who lived at Newtown Creek headwaters. Ridgewood was home to Mespachtes Indians.

Sport and racetracks

Jamaica Racetrack: this thoroughbred racetrack operated from 1903-59. A gate of 64,670 on Memorial Day 1945 was a state record. *Centerville (Eclipse) Race Course* was popular in the 1850s and 60s. *Queens Country Jockey Club* opened a racetrack in 1894. *Sunnyside* is named for a roadhouse catering for visitors to the Fashion Race Course in Corona during the 1850-60s. *Shooting:* Belleaire was bought in 1899 by the secretary of the National Pigeon Shooters Association, who built a grandstand and casino here. Shooting events included the Grand American Handicap.

Alley: mills and store

Land at the head of Little Neck Bay was given a royal grant in 1673. The first grist mill arrived 1691, a 2nd mill in 1752, and a wool mill in the 1820s. A country store operated 1859-1920. In 1926, the mill was destroyed by fire.

Astoria

This was developed in 1839 by a fur merchant and named for fur trader John Jacob Astor. In the 1800s, a tract of land was bought by piano maker William Steinway who set up factories and a town with a church, library, kindergarten, and public trolley line. In the Kaufman Astoria Studios, Rudolph Valentino, the Marx Brothers, and Paul Robeson made films. The Museum of the Moving Image is here.

Films and theater

King Charles I issued patents for *Bayside* in 1644. During the American Revolution it was settled by Quakers but by the 1930s, sportsmen and film stars lived here, including Pearl White and James J. Corbett. *Beechhurst* also attracted many theater folk, including producer Arthur Hammerstein. In *Glendale* in the 1920s, there were silent-movie studios.

Queens County Farm

This museum in Bellerose has a working chicken coop and other barnyard animals.

Berlin and Broad Channel

Promoted as Berlinville in 1871 so it would appeal to German immigrants, all the streets were named after German cities. **Broad Channel,** the only inhabited island in Jamaica Bay, first consisted of a few fishermen's shacks and could be reached only by boat. In 1880, a fishing platform was built across the bay from Queens to the Rockaway Peninsula. A hotel and saloon opened, visitors rented boats and baymen continued to fish and dig for clams.

Dutch Kills and Elmhurst

Dutch Kills was an important road junction in the American Revolution and the British set up camps here from 1776-83. **Elmhurst,** called Newtown in 1652, was renamed in 1896 to avoid association with the foul smells of Newtown Creek.

Flushing

This town was begun by English settlers who received patents for it from Governor Stuyvesant in 1654. The name is derived from Vlissingen, a Dutch village. After the Civil War, many wealthy New Yorkers built elegant houses. It became a commuter suburb when trolley lines were extended (1888-99) and the railroad electrified.

Howard Beach

In the 1890s, William Howard, a Brooklyn glove manufacturer, operated a goat farm on meadowland near Aqueduct, as a source of skins for kid gloves.

Little Neck

The best known resident in the 1800s was Bloodgood H. Cutter, a wealthy, eccentric poet. In the 1850-60s, oystermen ran sloops and schooners, catching clams and oysters.

Long Island City

This low-lying area flooded easily so in colonial times there were few roads or settlers. Railroad terminals were built in the mid-1800s and a ferry to Manhattan began 1859. From 1874-80, the swamps were drained and the land filled.

Queens Village or Brushville

In colonial times this was called the Little Plains as it marked the edge of a treeless plain. Thomas Brush set up a wheelwright and blacksmith shop here in 1824. A tavern, general store, and tobacco-curing warehouse followed and the hamlet was soon called Brushville. In 1854, it changed to Queens Village.

Onderdonck House (below)

This is the only surviving Dutch farmhouse in the Ridgewood area, once tilled by Dutch farmers, and was built in 1731 in Dutch Colonial Style. It was lived in by his descendants up until 1905.

Above: *Races and religions here are too numerous to list. A Sikh Center is set across the street from the Temple Gates of Prayer*

Left: *A lady chooses cloth at a shop in Steinway Street, Astoria.* Below: *Bustling Main Street, Flushing*

Staten Island

This island in New York harbour is 160 sq. miles (55 sq km.), and lies south of Manhattan, between New Jersey and Brooklyn. When Europeans first lived here in 1630, it was inhabited by Aquehonga Indians who attacked the white settlers for 30 years until the Dutch West India Company granted land to the French and Oude Dorp (old town) was set up. Here, during the American Revolution, Conference House hosted talks between Benjamin Franklin, John Adams, Edward Rutledge and Lord Howe.

Native Americans

Places like Annadale in Raritan Bay were once inhabited by Raritan Indians – hence the name of the bay. The first European settlers on the island were attacked by Aquehonga Indians. Lenni Lenape Indians lived in Arrochar while Tottenville was first inhabited by Delaware or Lenape Indians – whose burial sites are near Ward's Point.

Homeport-Stapleton

This U.S. Navy base operated 1990-94, with berths for battleships, destroyers, cruisers, and reserve frigates. More than 4,000 worked here.

Quarantine riots

In 1857, Tompkinsville and Castleton residents attacked the quarantine station on Seguine's Point where sick sailors and immigrants were kept – but were restrained by police. Then, in 1858, when yellow fever victims arrived, locals mobbed the station again, burning the buildings down. One hospital worker was shot and patients were dragged out and beaten. Marines and police quelled the violence and many rioters were arrested.

Chinese Scholar's Garden, shipped from China in 40 containers and assembled by 40 Chinese laborers who made the mosaic (below) *from their beer bottles*

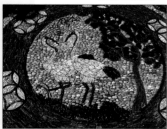

Sailors' Snug Harbor

This prototype retirement home was created through the bequest of Robert R. Randall, who had made a fortune in the maritime industry (and possibly piracy). A home for "aged, decrepit, and worn-out sailors", it opened 1831 with room for 27, but by 1900, housed 1,000.

Richmond Town

This was first named Cocclestown after the local shellfish. Here New York's only restored village and outdoor museum has the oldest elementary school in the U.S. and a General Store and Post Office – with their shelves filled!

Tompkinsville

The oldest village in eastern Staten Island, this was a landing where early explorers replenished water supplies and was known as the Watering Place. A village was created here in 1815 by Daniel D. Tompkins, who built a dock and initiated a steam ferry service to New York in 1817.

The Staten Island Ferry that has carried people to Manhattan every day, free of charge, since 1810 _{BS}

Staten Island's famous

- *Aaron Burr* (Port Richmond Hotel)
- *Giuseppe Garibaldi* (Rosebank) The Italian patriot lived here in the 1850s while in exile.
- *Frederick Olmsted* (Eltingville)
- *Cornelius Vanderbilt* (Stapleton)
- *William Vanderbilt* (New Dorp)

Midland Beach

In 1900, this was a fine summer resort. Summer bungalows and a pier were built, as excursion boats brought in visitors.

Fox Hills

The first 18 hole golf course on the Island opened here in 1900. During the first World War the largest army hospital in the U.S.A. was built here; it was used during the 2nd World War as an army training base and for prisoners of war.

West New Brighton

The area was originally the site of a hunting lodge built in the late 1600s by Governor Dongan on his Manor of Castleton. It was also called Factoryville – after the brick buildings and smokestacks. In 1936 the former estate of the Barrett family became the site of the *Staten Island Zoo*.

Charleston

The area is rich in clay and from 1850s to 1927, a brick factory operated here. The old clay pits can still be seen at Clay Pit Ponds State Park.

Silver Lake

Home to Silver Lake Park, in the late 1800s, the park area was popular for boating, fishing, picnics and ice skating. The lake supported a thriving ice-harvesting business.

Stapleton

Land was acquired from the Vanderbilts and, in the 1800s, streets were laid out by entrepreneur William Staples and Minthorne Tompkins, son of Vice President Tompkins. The two established a ferry service to Manhattan and advertised their newly created village from 1836.

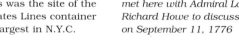

Howland Hook

Ferries ran from here to New Jersey 1736-1961. In the mid 1990s this was the site of the United States Lines container port, the largest in N.Y.C.

Conference House was originally _{CS} the home of a loyalist, Colonel Billop. Benjamin Franklin, John Adams and Edward Rutledge met here with Admiral Lord Richard Howe to discuss peace on September 11, 1776

Place names

- *Arrochar*
  Named after a village in Scotland from which its first European settler came.
- *Blazing Star*
  This village is named after a local 17th-century tavern. Naval officer, Billopp, given land here in 1678, was the first European settler in Tottenville. In 1778 a ball was held in Blazing Star where Captain Billopp (great grandson of the first settler) was captured by Americans.
- *Bull's Head*
  The name derives from a fierce bull on the sign of a tavern where Tories met. In the graveyard lies Ichabod Crane, whose name was borrowed by his friend Washington Irving for *The Legend of Sleepy Hollow*.
- *Chelsea*
  During the Revolution the town was known as Peanutville because the villagers stored nuts for ferry passengers here.
- *Dongan Hills*
  Named for Thomas Dongan, an Irish aristocrat appointed governor of New York in 1682 by the Duke of York.
- *Elm Park*
  A doctor who moved to the area in 1805 planted his estate with elm trees, giving the area its name.
- *Fort Hill*
  Here earthen redoubts were built by the British during the American Revolution.

- *Huguenot*
  The area was settled during the 17th and 18th centuries by Huguenots who built a church of serpentine rock.
- *New Dorp*
  Settled by the Dutch about 1671 as Niewe Dorp (new town), ten years after Oude Dorp (old town).
- *Old Place*
  Called Dover by the English, in the 1800s, the beach area became a summer resort and South Beach amusement park was built.
- *Prince's Bay*
  Named for the English prince who anchored his ship here during the Revolution.
- *St. George*
  In the 1880s, Erastus Wiman consolidated local ferry lines and rail routes and renamed the area for George Law, an investor whose land he needed for a ferry terminal.
- *Sandy Ground*
  Settled in the 1830s as the first free black community in New York State, it was known as Little Africa before being renamed after its poor soil.
- *Todt Hill*
  Called Yserberg (iron hill) by Dutch settlers, for the iron in the local serpentine rock.
- *Westerleigh*
  This area of woods and farmland developed in 1887 when Prohibition Park opened. Local streets were named for prohibitionists.

HISTORICAL EVENTS

1731 3-month smallpox epidemic kills 100s – 5 to 8% of city's 10,000 inhabitants. Smallpox innoculation 1st used in city.

1732 Smallpox kills 549.

1738 *September 28* 1st volunteer fire company: "30 strong and sober men".

1740 Ferry between Bay Ridge and Staten Island.

1747 Ferry from Manhattan to north shore of Staten Island.

1756 Seven Years' War begins. British make N.Y.C. their H.Q.: city prospers.

1757 William Smith's *History of New York* published in London.

1757 Governor Hardy sails for England, leaving Lieutenant Governor De Lancy in charge. ● New York Purse horse-race in Jamaica.

1764 British rank N.Y.C. 2nd in importance only to Philadelphia. Its population is 7th within 13 colonies, with 25,000 inhabitants in area below City Hall. It is wealthier than Boston.

1765 British pass Stamp Act mandating use of stamps on all legal and commercial documents. On October 7, Stamp Act Congress meets at Federal Hall. 9 of 13 colonies protest against stamp tax. Until act repealed, N.Y. merchants agree to support Boston's boycott of British goods. They petition George III, House of Commons and House of Lords. Throughout colonies many small merchants and artisans call themselves Sons of Liberty and commit to action. ● *October 23* Stamps arrive on *Edward*. The next day placards threaten anyone distributing or using stamp paper, "Let him take care of his house, person and effects." ● *October 31/November 1* 200 merchants meet at *City Arms Tavern* on Broadway and vow to resist hated law. ● *November 1* Offices close, flags fly at half-mast and black crepe hangs from gaming tables. 2,000 angry sailors, artisans, apprentices and free blacks, led by Sons of Liberty, march to Royal Governor's Bowling Green – to burn Lieutenant Governor Colden's effigy and his carriage and sleigh. They also attack Major James's estate; he had trained Fort George guns on city.

1766 *May* Sons of Liberty destroy a theater. ● *May 20* News arrives that Parliament repealed Stamp Act in March. Sons of Liberty erect 1st pole on the Common, dedicated: "To His most Gracious Majesty, George the Third, Mr Pitt and Liberty" ● *August 10* British soldiers cut down liberty pole. Sons of Liberty try to raise another the next day but soldiers attack them with bayonets. ● *August 12* Sons of Liberty successfully raise liberty pole again.

1770 Mid-January Hatred between British soldiers and Sons of Liberty highlighted when British cut down Liberty Pole on their 3rd attempt. ● *19-20 January* Battle of Golden Hill: Sons of Liberty with clubs and cutlasses fight British troops at William and John Streets. One American killed and several wounded. ● *February 6* Another Liberty Pole, on private land across from Common, is inscribed, "Liberty and Property".

1774 *April 22* Boston Tea Party: Dressed like Indians, Sons of Liberty board merchant ship, *London*, and throw tea into harbor.

Boston Tea Party

1775 *April 23* News of British defeat at Lexington and Concorde reaches city. Celebrating mob breaks into Arsenal on Hudson river and steals 600 muskets

PEOPLE

1731 Slave market at foot of lower Wall Street ● *February 11* Governor Montgomerie presents new city charter with jurisdiction up to King's Bridge. He dies in July and is replaced by Rip Canam.● Night watch created, with a constable and 8 citizens, but citizens unwilling to serve. ● *November 18* "All Negro, Mullatto and Indian slaves that are let out to hire within this city to take up their standing, in order to be hired, at the Market House at the Wall Street Slip, until such time as they are hired. . ." ● *November 27* 2 fire engines arrive from England.

1736 *March 10* Governor Cosby dies. George Clarke holds office until 1743.

1738 *June 28* Quarantine station set up at Bedloes Island, named after 1st owner, Isaac Bedloe.

1746 African immigration peaks at 20.9% of city residents.

1750 Trade with Irish ports brings skilled Irish merchants and Irish indentured servants. City's rigid penal code means few are Catholic.

1754 George Washington writes after his first battle: "I heard the bullets whistle, and, believe me, there is something charming in the sound." When this letter appears in England, George II remarks, "He would not have found the sound so charming if he had been used to hearing more."

LIFESTYLE

1735 1st almshouse. ● *August 4* Libel trial of Zenger, successfully defended by John Chambers and Andrew Hamilton, who receives freedom of city in 5.5 oz. gold box, for, ". . . his defence of the rights of mankind and the liberty of the press." (*see November 1733*).

1736 Public Work House and Home of Correction, with 6 beds, is 1st municipal hospital for lunatics and paupers, on Lower Broadway where City Hall is now.

1742 Iron plantations: Ancram Works on Livingston Manor and Stirling Ironworks in Orange County. ● *October 22* After June plot and arrests, 14 African slaves burnt at stake, 18 hanged, and 70 sold. 3 whites executed. 20% of city inhabitants are slaves but black population decreases over next 15 years.

1743 Phila Franks, from prominent Jewish family, scandalizes city by secretly marrying Oliver DeLancey.

1741 *June 11* Led by illegally enslaved Spanish Catholics, Negro Plot (great slave conspiracy) begins in taverns used by slaves on Sundays. Many false accusations lead to arrests of 26 whites and 160 slaves.

1746 Local Hand-in-Hand Fire Company saves valuables during a fire, while a bucket brigade passes water from a public well to a hand-pumped engine that directs it at flames.

Hand in Hand fire co. PB

1750 Prostitution restricted to areas near Trinity Church, St Paul's Church and City Hall Park.

1754 Politicians and businessmen seal deals at *Merchants' Coffee House* (Broad Street) and *Black Horse Tavern* (Exchange Place/William Street) ● Drovers and butchers settle cattle prices at *Bulls Head Tavern*, the Bowery.● Charter granted for foundation of King's College, renamed Columbia College (1784) and Columbia University (1896).

Black Horse Tavern PB

1752 Merchant's Exchange built at foot of Broad Street.

1759 1st dedicated jail built.

1760 Increase in riots, prostitution, thefts and assaults, due to overcrowding and maritime trade bringing more sailors. Medical practitioners must now be examined and licensed.

1762 1st paid police force.

1764 Mail service between New York and Philadelphia jumps from once a every two weeks to twice a week.

1766 1st St. Patrick's Day parade.

1768 *April 5* 20 merchants set up New York Chamber of Commerce in Fraunces Tavern.

1770 Most laundry done by washerwomen. ● Visiting cards establish social contact and visits. ● 4 years after its commission, to celebrate repeal of Stamp Act, bronze statue of George III in Bowling Green affirms loyalty to British Crown. ● *September 7* At public expense, white marble statue of William Pitt in Roman garb erected near Wall and William Streets in gratitude for repeal of Stamp Act.

1773 British soldiers housed on Bedloes Island in harbor. ● Slaves in Jamaica jailed, suspected of conspiracy against whites.

1774 Paid constabulary of 20 night watchmen.

COMMERCE

1763 End of Seven Years' War: NYC's prosperity diminishes; merchants' turnovers halve.

1764 *July 11* 1st lighthouse on Sandy Hook. ● Monthly packet service now between New York and London. ● Ferry service between Paulus Hook (Jersey City) and Manhattan.

1764-65 British Government tries to raise revenues with tax on sugar, paper and legal documents. N.Y. merchants outraged by Sugar Act which gives British control over U.S. sugar market.

1765-75 Rural communities flourish but economy and imports depressed by curtailed smuggling and short supply of currency. ● Ranelagh opens on northern edge of town: *Concert of Musick* held weekly.

1768 *October 30* John Street United Methodist Episcopal Church, 44 John Street, dedicated.

1769 *September 11* Governor Moore dies; Lieutenant Governor Colden assumes office again.

1772 David Hunt begins manufacture of hand-pumped fire-fighting apparatus.

1773 *May 5* George III signs act giving East India Company monopoly of tea trade in American colonies.

1774 City builders (mechanics) work for masters. They lead resistance against British, forming Committee of Mechanics, which will launch unions and trade societies

1775 Printers and stationers, Bowne & Company, open at 39 Queen Street (Pearl/Fulton Street corner). It is oldest New York company still doing business under original name

POLITICS & RELIGION

1732 *August 1st* New Governor, Colonel Cosby, regards colonies as English offshoots and enforces trade laws. He grants patronage, land tracts, contracts and judicial appointments to counteract assembly power.

1744 *May 3* Below Collect, skinners, leather dressers and curriers banned from using noxious vats – and hatters and starch makers from pouring waste into street. Garbage disposal regulated.

1752 1st Moravian church.

1755 *September 2* Sir Charles Hardy is Governor.

1753 *October 12* Sir Osborn commits suicide 5 days after becoming Governor. Lieutenant Governor De Lancey succeeds.

1758 First College degrees granted.

1761 *October 19* New Governor, General Robert Monckton, arrives.

1763 *June 25* Governor Monckton goes to England. Lieutenant Governor Colden assumes office again.

1764 *January 10* Boundary dispute between Newtown and Bushwick settled at Arbitration Rock. (In 2000, Rock will be unearthed below Flushing Avenue near Onderdonk House, Ridgewood.)

1765 *November 13* New Governor, Sir Henry Moore, arrives amid Stamp Act crisis.

1766 *October 30* Consecration of St. Paul's Chapel on Broadway, oldest church in Manhattan. 1st Methodist services held in Philip Embury's home on Barrack Street (Park Place).

1767 Methodist congregation rent space on William Street.

1768 Dedication of Presbyterian Brick Church (Nassau/Beekmans Streets).

1770 *October 18* John Murray, Earl of Dunmore, Governor.

1771 *July 8* New Governor, Sir William Tryon.

1772 Governor Tryon makes provincial assembly provide his salary out of general revenues, rather than from assembly allocation.

1774 Now 16 churches: 3 Presbyterian, 3 Anglican, 1 Huguenot; others for Anabaptist, Moravians and Methodists, German Reformed, German Lutheran and Dutch, plus 1 Quaker meeting house and 1 synagogue.

CULTURE & ART

1731 In City Hall, 1st public library opens with 1,642 volumes. Collection began when Revd. John Millington from England bequeathed 1,622 volumes to the Venerable Society for the Propagation of the Gospel in Foreign Parts.

1732 *December 6* 1st New Theatre in Maiden Lane, 1st theater, seats 400. 1st production is Farquhar's *The Recruiting Officer*.

1733 *November 5* Supported by wealthy merchants, J.P. Zenger publishes *New York Weekly Journal*, criticizing Governor Cosby. Zenger arrested for libel and sent to City Hall jail. His wife runs newspaper until his acquittal (*see 1735 August*).

1734 Jacobus Roosevelt buys Beekman's Swamp, drains it and lays out streets. ● St. James Episcopal Church built in Newtown.

1736 1st public concert. Musicians play a harpsichord, violin and German flute at *Todd's Tavern.*

1737 1st dancing master arrives.

1743 *September 22* Governor George Clinton arrives.

1746 Smallpox outbreak. Provincial assembly moves to Greenwich and then Westchester.

1750 English visitor James Birket remarks: "Neither their Streets nor houses are at all Regular Some being 4 or 5 Story high and Others not above two ... many of 'em Spacious Genteel Houses. Some are built of hewn stone Others of English & Also of the Small white Hollands Brick, which looks neat but not grand. . . The Streets are very Irregular & Crooked & many of 'em much too Narrow ... [but] well paved which adds much to the decency & Cleanliness of the place & the Advantage of Carriage."

1753 Trinity Church damaged by fire. Marriage, baptism and burial records lost. ● Merchant, Robert Murray, builds farmhouse near area that will become known as Murray Hill.

1754 *April 8* Opening of New York Society Library, 1st founded in City Hall (*see 1731*). Additional books from Revd. John Sharpe.

1756 An English Naval Officer writes: "The nobleness of the town surprised me. ... I had no idea of finding a place in America, consisting of near 2,000 houses, elegantly built of brick, raised on an eminence and the streets paved and spacious, furnished with commodious quays and warehouses, and employing some hundreds of vessels in its foreign trade and fisheries . . ." ● New regular stagecoach service from New York to Philadelphia takes 3-days. Soon a round trip takes only 5 days.

Travel by Stagecoach PB

1761 1st streetlights: whale-oil lamps lighted at public expense.

1762 Fraunces Tavern bought by black West Indian, Samuel Fraunces: will become famous for wining and dining (*see also 1719*).

1766 *New York Journal* published.

1767 Kings College establishes College of Physicians and Surgeons. ● John Street Theater opens.

1768-79 Captain Cook's voyages to Pacific

1769 Spain establishes settlement in California

1768 Samuel Francis's wax figure exhibition at Vauxhall Gardens.

Dunmore's Seal

1772 New York Society Library, city's oldest, has charter from George III.

1774 Printer John Holt replaces royal arms on *New York Journal* with logo "Unite or Die" and a dismembered snake – soon to be a coiled snake

1771 *June 13* Royal charter for New York Hospital, founded to care for lunatics plus smallpox and syphilis sufferers

1770 Merchant and privateer Thomas Randall, and others, found Marine Society – origin of Sailors Snug Harbor.

1772 Alexander Hamilton studies at King's College (now Columbia University). He will be captain of a city artillery company in American Revolution and will serve as lieutenant colonel on George Washington's staff.

Battle of Lexington

1774 *October 19* Governor Tryon flees to sloop-of-war *Halifax*, taking city records – not returned until 1787.

CITY STRUCTURE & DEVELOPMENT

1733 *March 12* 1st Common Council authorizes, "enclosure of Bowling Green for the ornament of the said street as well as for the Recreation and Delight of the Inhabitants of the City." Annual rent for this 1st public park is one peppercorn.

1734 *February 11* Volunteer police force replaced by paid night watch (3-12 men) policing 10,000: this will be replaced by another citizens' watch a year later.

1733 1st Brooklyn ferries.

1741 Handel composes *The Messiah*

1775 Winding creek connecting Harlem River on east with Hudson River on west is northern boundary of Manhattan. Dutch called creek *Spuyten Duyvil* (in spite of the devil) after a settler drowned trying to warn northern settlements that British were coming. He couldn't find a boat, and tried to swim across while drunk. (Creek rerouted 1895

USA & WORLD EVENTS

1740 First Silesian War

1733-35 War of Polish Succession

1748 Treaty of Aix-la-Chapelle ends War of Austrian Succession

1763 Treaty of Paris ends French and Indian War in America and Seven Years War (Europe, Asia, Africa)

1765 Watt builds steam engine

1767 New law: all roofs must be covered with tile or slate.

1851 *May 5* hilip Hone dies t home (Broadway/Great ones Street). ● *December 6* Hungarian patriot Louis Kossuth ands at Castle Clinton and nakes great American tour.

1851 New York uvenile Asylum et up. ● Fifth Avenue attracts isitors and ecomes fashionable abode.

1851 Suffragist Amelia Bloomer writes: "Men ... are defrauding us of our just ights by crowding us out of every lucrative employment, and subjecting us to virtual slavery."

1851 *September 18* 1st issue of *New York Daily Times* – price 1 penny. ● Commodore John C Stevens, founder of New York Yacht Club, wins Royal Yacht Squadron's regatta around Isle of Wight, England, in the *America*, thus starting Americas Cup. ● *June 3* Knickerbockers are 1st baseball club to wear uniforms – white shirts, blue pants and straw hats.

1851 *May 15* Parade along Broadway and Bowery celebrates completion, after 17 years, of Erie Railroad from Piermont on Hudson River to Dunkirk, Lake Erie. Next day, steamer *Erie* makes inaugural run. ● New York Central & Hudson Railroad finished along Hudson into Westchester ● Hudson River Railroad tracks laid on Upper West Side – previously farmland and small Dutch cottages. ● *May 5* Mayor Kingsland proposes public park, "The establishment of such a park would prove a lasting monument to the wisdom, sagacity and forethought of its founders." On June 21, State Senator Beekman authorizes city to buy Jones Wood, 150 acres along East River, from 66th to 75th Street. ● Most Holy Redeemer, stone church on 3rd Street, completed as center of growing German Catholic community.

1850 California becomes 31st state

1852 *July 28* Landscape architect A.J. Downing dies in steamboat accident. ● Louis Napoleon frees 8 slaves brought into city when their master stops en route to Texas. Judge Paine rules slaves are free once in N.Y. Pro-slavery merchants compensate owner for loss of property.

1852 10,000 homeless children on city streets. ● People's Washing and Bathing Establishment opens on Mott Street.

1852 N.Y. Custom House provides about 80% of federal government's revenue.

1852 Jacob A Westervelt elected mayor.

1852 *Uncle Tom's Cabin* by Harriet Beecher Stowe is bestseller.

PB
Harriet Beecher Stow

1852 New York merchants commission bronze equestrian statue of George Washington, for south end of Union Square. ● *January 31* Founding of Brooklyn Atheneum and Reading Room. Building (Clinton Street/ Atlantic Avenue) finished April, 1853. ● *June 30* YMCA opens reading room. ● Union Bay Boat Club founded, renamed Brooklyn Yacht Club in 1861.

1852 *January* Special Commission on Parks recommends a central park, roughly coinciding with present boundaries (*see also* 1851). ● Broadway buildings are usually 5-6 stories high, with marble, cast-iron and stone decoration. ● 148 miles of sewers now. ● 225-acre Lutheran Cemetery established in Middle Village. ● Flushing Railroad receives charter 3 March: construction begins in April. In September, directors select Hunters Point for terminal. ● New workhouse with 221 cells on Blackwell's Island replaces older one at Bellevue. ● St Mark's Roman Catholic Church to be built on Staten Island; completed 1858.

1853 *July 14* World's Fair at Crystal Palace.

1853 *November 9* Stanford White born at East 10th Street.

1853 Formal training for police and officers, now armed with nightsticks. ● Tenement House Report by R.M. Hartley: "Crazy old buildings – crowded rear tenements in filthy yards, dark, damp basements; leaky garrets, shops, outhouses and stables converted to dwellings, though scarcely fit to shelter brutes – are the habitations of thousands . . . in this wealthy city." ● Otis demonstrates steam-powered passenger elevator. ● Charles Brace launches Children's Aid Society. ● A really good meal comprises clam fritters, colonial carpet-bagger steak stuffed with oysters, Indian pudding and chocolate icebox cake. ● In taverns people meet, socialize, eat, are entertained or find employment – some receive mail here. Long, narrow bars replace tables. Free lunches served to factory workers. In evenings, men play cards, billiards, and shuffleboard or read newspapers provided. ● Board of Education takes over 9 colored schools.

1853 *March* Steinway and Sons established on Varick Street with 10 workers. 1st piano sells in September.

1853 *Uncle Tom's Cabin* opens at National Theater: runs for over 300 performances. ● 17-year-old Samuel Clemens (Mark Twain) starts work in a printing company's composing room. Later he states: "Make your mark in New York and you're a made man." ● *New York Clipper* founded, a weekly that popularizes baseball and boxing. ● 7 trotting tracks in metropolitan area; clubs in city for cricket, yachting, rowing, gymnastics, target shooting and racquet sports.

1853 St Nicholas Hotel (Broome/ Spring Streets), one of finest buildings in city, has 600 rooms, over 1,000 guests, and employs 322 people. ● Crystal Palace, glass and steel exposition hall, at Reservoir Square (later Bryant Park) from 1853 until fire in 1858. ● Group of African-American farmers and laborers develop Seneca Village at rock-strewn area in upper Manhattan – with 2 schools, 3 cemeteries, and 3 churches. 250 inhabitants, 2/3 black, 1/3 Irish. ● Five Points Mission rises, on site of notorious Old Brewery. 5-story brick structure, with schoolrooms, chapel and apartments.

1853 U.S. gain parts of Arizona and New Mexico

1854 319,000 immigrants arrive.

1854 *November 13* Extract from diary of George Templeton Strong: "Met . . . a most emphatic and truculent demonstration. Solid column, eight or ten abreast and numbering some two or three thousand, mostly young men of the butcher-boy and prentice type. . . We may well have a tremendous riot and carnage here at any moment." ● Rising disorder and street violence. *New York Times* states: "The streets at night are infested with ruffians. . . They hang around corners… They move about in gangs, men and boys together, abusing and sometimes hitting the quiet passerby." ● Common Council bann steam locomotives below 42nd Street – construction of Grand Central Terminal possible now.

1854 Otis Elevator Company established in Yonkers.

OL

1854 *November 7* Democrat Fernando Wood mayor – voted in by immigrant German and Irish. Innovative, shrewd and corrupt; his 2 terms of office see many scandals.

1854 Bowery Ampitheatre reopens as Stadtheater, presenting German-language melodrama, farce and popular entertainment ● Opening of Academy of Music at 14th Street and Irving Place ● *January 9* Astor Library, Lafayette Place, opens with 80,000 volumes. ● *May 4* National Racing Federation buys land in Corona for race course. Flushing Railroad, along Newton Creek to Hunters Point, opens in time for 1st races in June.

1854 *July 3* Brooklyn City Railroad Company run Brooklyn's 1st horsecar line. ● India House, 1 Hanover Square, complete. ● St. George's Episcopal Church dedicated in Flushing.

1854 U.S. Treaty with China

1854-1856 Crimear War

1855 City has highest city population in hemisphere – 622,924. ● *January 1* Brooklyn annexes Williamsburgh and Bushwick.

1855 Elizabeth Jennings, a black woman horsecar when she refuses to leave ends segregated public transport ● Homeless camp in alleyways and courtyards. 40,000 men are out of work in city.

1855 Castle Garden, one-time fort and concert hall, made official immigration center. ● Some 10,000 Irish immigrants crowd into Five Points, rough district north of city hall.

1855 Union Course Tavern on 78th Street in Woodhaven opens – oldest bar in Queens. Will become the Nier Hotel in 1891. ● White longshoremen strike for higher wages. When blacks replace them, brawls erupt on docks. Strike is settled and white workers regain jobs. ● 600,000 residents in city. 1,200 police fight crime, direct traffic, find lost children, settle domestic disputes, walk drunks home, and find the homeless shelter.

1856 Bellevue Hospital 1st in U.S. to use hypodermic syringes. ● *December* Blackwell's Island smallpox hospital opens. ● *June 1* Revd. Beecher holds a slave auction in church, to highlight its ills. Calling a woman to the front, he says: "This is a market-able commodity. Such as she are put into one balance and silver into the other." *New York Times* says: "The most stoical and the most refined shed tears like rain."

1855 Brooklyn to purchase stock in Nassau Water Company (which acquired Brooklyn Water Company), giving city control over its water supply.

1856 Brick Church on Beekman Street sold by trustees for $270,000.

Walt Whitman
PL

1855 *July 5* Walt Whitman's *Leaves of Grass* on sale in city bookstores.

1856 *January 21* Staten Island Historical Society 1st meet.

1855 Old Tontine Building (Wall and Water Street corner) taken down. ● *March 23* Mayor Wood vetoes measure to reduce Central Park's boundaries and saves park. ● *April 10* Railroad companies and City of Brooklyn agree to reset Atlantic Avenue tracks, which impede wagons and endanger pedestrians.

1856 Julius Kroehl builds cast-iron fire watch tower in Mount Morris Park. ● *July 4* Dedication of equestrian statue of George Washington in Union Square Park. ● Ferry road renamed Flatbush Avenue.

W.J. Worth monument

DP

1857 *April* Otis installs 1st passenger elevator with automatic safety devices in E.V. Haughwout's new cast-iron store. Steam-powered, it rises 40 feet a minute and costs $300 to build. ● *November 19* Fierce fire on Jamaica Avenue burns church and surrounding blocks.

1857 *Peleponnesos*, city's 1st Greek restaurant, opens. ● Joseph Gayetty makes 1st roll of toilet paper in world. Cream-colored hemp, it costs 50 cents for 500 sheets and is advertised as, "Gayetty's Medicated Paper – a perfectly pure article for the toilet and for the prevention of piles." ● Police officers authorized to carry service revolvers. ● *February 17* Peter Cooper founds Cooper Union for Advancement of Science and Art. ● 12 architects form Society of Architects. Later 11 others join them and launch American Institute of Architects. ● *17* State-run Metropolitan Police District set up to replace locally controlled Municipal Police. Rival police departments riot on City Hall steps. Courts order Municipals disbanded. ● Rival street gangs, Dead Rabbits and Bowery Boys, brawl on Bowery – finally quelled by militia. ● 1,000s of unemployed laborers hold hunger meetings in Tompkins Square. ● City close to municipal civil war. State legislature rewrites city charter and strips mayor of power. ● German Dispensary provides medical care to Lower East Side immigrants.

Central Park

DP

1859 Central Park, 1st urban park in U.S.A., opens. 400 horses helped clear land and move one billion cubic feet of earth from former swamp. 3,000 Irish laborers created park with 36 stone arches and bridges. It covers 840 acres, with 185 acres of lakes and ponds. Soon over 4 million trees will be planted. Reservoir holds 1 billion gallons of water. Conservatory Gardens cover 4 acres .

1857 *August* Panic of 1857: banks suspend specie payments until December. ● Extracts from George T. Strong's diary: Panic is very dreadful in Wall Street . . . failures are multiplying . . . October 10th Affairs are worse than ever . . . People's faces in Wall Street look fearfully gaunt and desperate . . . October 22nd . . . Walking down Broadway you pass great $200,000 buildings . . . that have gone up two stories and stopped, and may stand unfinished and desolate for years . . . November 10th – This financial crisis has thrown thousands of the working class out of employment . . .

1857 *December 1* Daniel F Tiemann mayor.

1857 Brooklyn Mercantile Library Association founded. ● Columbia College moves to 4th Avenue. ● 100 baseball teams in city. Players form National Association of Baseball Players with clear rules and codes. ● 1st national chess tournament held in city as part of First American Chess Congress. Winner is 20-year-old Paul Morphy from New Orleans.

PL

1857 *May* Institution for the Deaf and Dumb moves to Washington Heights. ● *October 1* Seneca Village torn down and inhabitants vanish. City condemns area, ready for reconstruction for Central Park works. ● Olmsted (co-designer of winning design for Central Park) appointed its Superintendant. ● Obelisk at Fifth Avenue marks grave of only public figure buried under Manhattan streets – General W.J. Worth, hero of Mexican wars.

1857 *April 28* Central Park commissioners adopt Olmsted and Vaux's Greensward plan. ● *August 15* Cornerstone of St Patrick's Cathedral laid. ● New York Times building begins on site of old Brick Church, Beekman Street.

1857 Indian Mutiny

PL

1858 *October 5* Crystal Palace exhibition hall burns down.

1859 *Spring* Thaddeus Lowe, inventor, sails above Central Park site in his new hydrogen-filled observation balloon, *The City of New York.*

PB

1858 *October 27* Theodore Roosevelt born at 28 East 20th Street. ● 1st recorded Chinese immigrant, Cantonese Ah Ken, opens cigar store on Park Row.

1859 *November 23* William Bonney, Billy the Kid, born at 70 Allen Street. At 16, he will kill a man in a street brawl and head west.

1858 *September 1* To stop infectious diseases arriving, Staten Islanders burn Quarantine Station – rebuilt on Hoftman and Swinbourne Islands. ● *March 15* Police Department founds Marine Division (Harbor Patrol). 12 5-man boats defend docks and ships against thugs.

1859 Five Points area now infamous – worst slum in USA. ● *April 28* 300,000 celebrate Brooklyn's new water system.

1858 *May 1* Hewitt and Cooper acquire Flushing Railroad, in receivership for a year. ● *October 27* Rowland H. Macy opens a small, fancy dry goods store on Sixth Avenue, taking $11.06 on 1st day. In just over a year, sales total $90,000. Red star symbol derives from the tattoo Macy had when on a whaling ship.

1859 Dime Savings Bank incorporated April 12. On June 1, it opens at Montague Street Post Office, with 90 accounts worth $1,892.

1858 Fifth Avenue Hotel, Madison Square, opens – favorite meeting place of Republican leaders.

1858 *April* Broadway Theater demolished. ● Columbia College establishes law school. ● USA's 1st official skating rink opens in Central Park South. In 1 year some 60,000 pairs of ice skates are sold in city. In 1859 rink is sex segregated – until 1870.

1859 Astor Library enlarged. ● St. Francis Academy (later St Francis College) opens.

1859 *April* Ferries run between Hunters Point and 34th Street. ● *November 4* Great Hall at Cooper Union opens. ● George Templeton Strong describes Central Park: ". . . lakes without water, mounds of compost, piles of blasted stone, acres of what may be greensward hereafter but is now mere brown earth; groves of slender young transplanted maples and locuts, undecided between life and death . . . dirt carts, derricks, steam engines . . ."

1859 Darwin publishes *Origins of Species*

1860 *October 12* Prince of Wales, future Edward VII, visits, honored by a grand ball at Academy of Music.

1861 *February 19* Lincoln visits city. Crowds gather outside Astor House; Whitman admires his "perfect composure". ● *April 20* 250,000 rally in Union Square to support Northern cause.

1861 *April 12* **Civil War breaks out.**

1860 Population 813,669: about 1/4 Irish born. ● *November* Abraham Lincoln elected President of U.S.

Abraham Lincoln
PB

1860 Henry Ward Beecher holds 2nd slave auction at Plymouth Church, raising $1,007 in cash and jewelry to buy a 9-year-old girl's freedom.

1861 Patriot Orphans' Home founded.

1860 *April* LIRR agree not to use steam engines between East New York and ferry; Brooklyn pays railroad $129,801.80 compensation. ● *August 30* Grand opening of Steinway's $150,000 factory Park Avenue.

1860 *February 25* Abraham Lincoln arrives, hoping to bolster his slim chances of winning election. ● *February 27* At Daguerrian Gallery, Abraham Lincoln sits for a formal portrait, having traded in his beaverskin hat for a silk top hat. Later he speaks at Cooper Institute. ● George Opdyke mayor.

1860 *June 14* 1st issue of *New York World.*

1860 *April 23* Staten Island's 1st railroad runs from Eltingville to Vanderbilt's Landing; reaches Tottenville June 1. ● Commissioners appointed to lay out streets and avenues north of 155th Street. ● Banzer's Cypress Hills Park, with 5-acre lake, dance hall, bowling alleys and shooting galleries opens.

1861 *May 9* Forced out of Brooklyn, LIRR open a Hunters Point terminal. ● Gothic gatehouse complete at Green-Wood Cemetery.

1860 Garibaldi takes southern Italy and stengthens Italian unity

1862 *Monitor*, 1st ironclad warship, launched from Novelty Iron Works, Brooklyn.

1863 President Lincoln makes Emancipation Proclamation. ● Governor Seymour sends 20,000 to block Robert E Lee at Gettysburg, depleting city garrison. ● Conscription Act causes bloodiest riots in U.S. history.

1862 *January 24* Edith Newbold Jones (Edith Wharton) born. ● Nathaniel Gordon hanged, only man in U.S. executed as a slaver.

1863 Irish longshoremen fight to drive black longshoremen from docks for 3 days, believing black workers will lower wages. Irish strike in June; Federal troops protect black strikebreakers.

1862 Racial incidents plague city. Irish men try to burn down a Brooklyn tobacco factory where black women and children work.

1863 *February 1* Police department's Marine Division launches 1st steamer, *Seneca.* ● *February 5* George T. Strong writes: "We are in a ... deadlock of contradiction, I fear; the North cannot be defeated and the South cannot be conquered." ● 12,000 troops quartered in New York, many at Union Course and Centerville Course race tracks.

1862 United States Custom House, Wall Street, made branch of independent treasury system.

1863 Macy launches annual clearance sales.

1863 William "Boss" Tweed dominates city politics, using his law practice to extort money. He will be elected to state senate. With others, he siphons $30-200 million from city.

1862-64 Fernando Wood mayor.

1863 Democratic Party rally opposes Lincoln's war conduct and calls for negotiations with Confederacy. ● *December 1* C.G. Gunther elected mayor.

1862 Apprentices' Library for young workmen open to working women. ● William Cammayer builds 1st enclosed baseball park.

1863 Long Island Historical Society set up. ● Popular blood sports include cockfighting, ratting (pitting man against rat), dog fighting, bull baiting, gander-pulling and bear baiting.

1862 *June 7* Flushing Town Hall cornerstone laid with mementos including a Bible, Thanksgiving Sermon, silver coins, local merchants' cards, list of county fair prizewinners.

1863 Central Park's northern boundary extends from 106th to 110th Street. ● 1st horsecar lines on Staten Island. ● 1st horsecars into Bronx from 129th Street and Third Avenue.

1862 Mighty Russian Five formed

The streets of present-day New York were planned out as early as 1806-11 with a rectilinear grid overriding all bar Broadway. The evolution of transport has been rather more unpredictable as invention spearheaded the flow from horse traffic to elevated railways, the motor car and air traffic.

The growth of New York City

1797 The format of the city's future growth was already being set by the repeated pattern of street line to river.

1780s The DeLancey farms had been sold and New York was becoming a grid of city blocks and small lots.

1790s The area below Division Street was laid out in a regular pattern. The city had expanded northwards in overlapping grids. City Surveyor, Goerck, had laid out larger pieces of civic land on a regular grid pattern.

1806 The city requested the state legislature to appoint commissioners to make a plan for the development of the whole island. This took four years to complete. A simple rectilinear grid was to be extended across all the existing rights of way, over agricultural holdings, waterways, marshes, hills and houses.

The historic road of Broadway alone survived the plan. Today it remains distinct on the maps and creates interesting street angles and buildings such as the Flatiron.

The approach was a tidy and economic lay-out of regular-shaped plots between right-angled street junctions. It was rightly assumed that straight streets would encourage the city's economic development and that corner lots would prove a sought after and valuable asset. Space was allocated for a military parade ground; Hudson Square was planned.

1811 The plans included no large-scale groups of rowhouses, and few public buildings of any size, except the City Hotel. Private dwellings were small and simple. Park land had been given scant attention.

At that time such factories as existed were only small artisans' workshops.

Current ships were small and so even shipyards were granted relatively little space.

In this, the city's embryonic development,

The last checker cab vanished in 1999

PL

Facts and figures

- There are 12,700 traffic lights in the city. Each light bulb lasts for about 333 days. The average daily traffic volume is 2.3 million vehicles.
- 271,503 people in the city share driving and vehicles in a car pool. Some 765,151 drive to work alone.
- At least 10,000 vehicles per day head onto First Avenue.
- 80,000 people were held up in cars in 1997, when a parade on 6th Avenue lasted for 3 hours. 10,000 extra pounds of carbon monoxide were produced by the 15-minute delay.
- The advertising budget for New York's custom license plates is $2 million. 2.5 million pairs of license plates are made annually.
- 72% of drivers use seat belts in New York. (The figure for the U.S. is 67%.)

important focus points – whether vital buildings, leading institutions or overall viewpoints – were not given great consideration. The aim was to create a regular road system and the Commissioners had no brief to redesign and rebuild the city: New York was not being redesigned – only its thoroughfares.

Paving

Streets in New Amsterdam were first paved in 1658 when cobblestones were laid along Stone Street. By 1876 there were 299 miles (481 km.) of paved streets in the city. Asphalt pavement was introduced during 1884.

Parkways

An innovative network of landscaped parkways was launched with the Bronx River Parkway and in time included Westchester and Long Island. The best known are the Grand Central Parkway, the Henry Hudson Parkway and the Hutchinson River Parkway.

Yellow taxis

- There are 12,053 licensed cabs in New York City.
- 200 million million people use city cabs each year.
- The average age of a cab is 4 years.
- The average number of fares a driver picks up each day is 30.
- Cab drivers drive an average 12 hours per day, cover 141 miles, and earn $190 in fares and tips.
- Round yellow lights to the left of the license plate on the bumper are "trouble lights". From 1994 all city cabs were required to have them in order to alert police and pedestrians if help was needed.
- The number of new licenses granted each year ranges from 400 to 1,000s.
- Less than 50% of new cab drivers survive 5 years.
- In 1968, city cabs had to be "painted yellow, or any shade thereof".
- Chevrolet Caprice and Ford Crown Victoria were the most commonly used cars in 1997.
- In 1975, illuminated advertisements appeared on taxicab roofs.
- In 1999, the last surviving checker cab was removed.
- A driver refusing to make multiple stops on request can be fined $200 – $500.
- Over 90% of new cab driver applicants are immigrants. 50% of new cab drivers are from Pakistan or India. 10.5% are American born. (The figure for the whole of the U.S. is 67%.)

The Commissioners' Plan of 1811 – the historic road of Broadway alone survived this plan

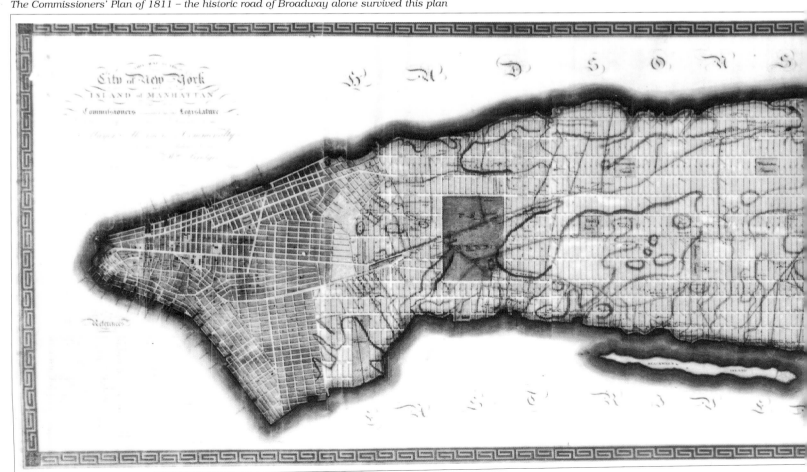

Central Synagogue
1870
652 Lexington Avenue
Designed by Henry Fernbach
Domed minarets 122 feet (37m) high

Fine example of Moorish Islamic revival architecture.
Twin towers represent the columns on Solomon's temple.
Fine stencilled interior was inspired by the Alhambra Palace in Spain.

St. Bartholomew's Church
1919
Park Avenue (50/51st Streets)
Architect: B.G. Goodhue.

Built on the site of a brewery, this beautiful ornate Byzantine-style church has a fine entrance portal that was moved from the first St Bartholomew's on Madison Avenue. The sculptures are by Daniel Chester French and Philip Martiny.

American Standard Building 1924
40 West 40th Street (Fifth/Sixth Avenues)
21 stories
Height: 338 feet (103 m)
Floors: 23
Architects: Raymond Hood and André Fouilhoux

This municipal landmark near Bryant Park is an important Gothic design by Raymond Hood who went on to design the Rockefeller Center. Its black brick façade is decorated with gold and terracotta and its tower rises to an ornate golden crown. It was designed and constructed in just 13 months. Built originally for a heating equipment company and called the American Radiator Building, it is now a luxury hotel.

Temple Emanu-el 1929
Fifth Avenue and 1 East 65th St.

One of the largest synagogues in the world.
Seats 2,500 in main sanctuary.
Built on site of Mrs William Astor's palatial home.
Brilliant stained-glass windows and mosaics.

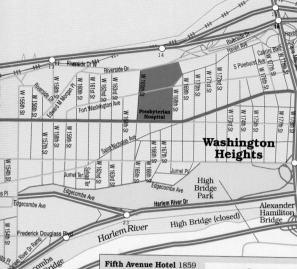

Hotel Plaza 1907 (with additions in 1921)
5th Avenue (59th Street) Cost $12.5 million.
20 floors, 88.4m (290 feet) high, 1,098 guest rooms

Built in French Renaissance style, with steeply sloped gables, running balconies, and pepperboxes. Hotel Plaza fronts Great Army Plaza and Central Park from where its limestone façade and green mansarded roof can be seen.
The city's very first taxis were launched here to take home party-goers.
The hotel claims, "Nothing Unimportant Ever Happens at the Plaza."

Carnegie Hall 1891
154 West 57th Street (Seventh Avenue)
1964 Made a national landmark

In Italian Renaissance style, New York's first great concert hall claims to have the best acoustics in the world. Tchaikovsky was guest conductor here on the hall's opening night. The building was financed by steel magnate Andrew Carnegie.

Fifth Avenue Hotel 1859
23rd Street

Offered, "unprecedented extravagance".
Elevator was described as, "a little parlour going up by machinery".
It was replaced by the Toy Center.

Tribune Building 1875
Nassau and Spruce Streets
Spire 260 feet

The *Tribune* newspaper was the main organ of Republican opinion and in the 1850s had a 200,000 circulation.
The building was one of the tallest in the city in the 1870s.
In 1886 the *Tribune* was the first newspaper to install Mergenthaler's slug-casting linotype machine which revolutionised typesetting.

Metropolitan Museum
1,000 Fifth Avenue (80th/84th Streets)
Founded 1870: occupied current site since 1880
Architects: Vaux, Mould and Hunt

The original central building has had many wings added to make it the largest museum in the western hemisphere.
It welcomes over 6 million visitors a year.
Museum houses 3.3 million treasures.
Library holds 150,000 books.
The building incorporates the ancient Egyptian Temple of Dendur built by Roman Emperor Augustus in 15BC.

United Nations
Built 1949-50
First Avenue (at 46th Street)

This 18-acre site is not on U.S. territory.
It is an international zone and even has its own stamps and post office.
John D. Rockefeller Jnr. donated 8.5 million dollars for the purchase of the site.
North and south façades are clad in Vermont marble.
Flags of all the member nations fly outside.

Trump Tower 1983   725 Fifth Avenue
68 stories 657 feet (202 meters)

This multi-purpose building is home to stores, restaurants, offices and luxury apartments. In its opulent lobby is a 5-story high waterfall. Its builder and owner, Donald Trump, has a 53-room penthouse here.

New York Yacht Club
44th Street
Architects: Whitney Warren and Charles Wetmore

The building has an ornate exterior and equally extravagant interior with a "stern gallery" dining room overlooking the main entrance.
19th-century financier, P. Morgan became commodore of the club in 1897. "If you have to ask how much it costs, you can't afford it," was his view of yachting. His wealth is reflected in the interiors of the clubhouse he commissioned with its grand model-display room, fine dining room, grille room, bedrooms for overnight visitors, chart room, library, and display room for the ornate silver bottomless urn that is the America's Cup trophy – relinquished to Australia in 1983.

1871 Grand Central Depot created by Cornelius Vanderbilt

The Oyster Bar Restaurant

Grand Central Terminal
Built 1903-1913
5th Avenue (58th and 59th Streets)
Covers 48 acres.

180 buildings were demolished to allow the station to be built and 2.8 million cubic yards of earth and rock excavated.

Built in elegant Beaux Arts style.
Nearly 500,000 people pass through every day.
Has 10,000 panes of glass.
The zodiac design on the ceiling shows over 2,500 stars with major constellations lit.
The double sweep entrance staircase is modeled on Paris Opera House.
The Oyster Bar is its most famous eatery.

General Electric Building, Rockefeller Center
1931-33
850 feet (259m)
570 Lexington Avenue

Art Deco/Gothic style.
Crown at top is designed to suggest radio waves.
Designed in materials and colors that are compatible with St. Bartholomew's Church behind.
One block north is where Marilyn Monroe stood over the grating with her skirt billowing in *The Seven-Year Itch*.

Crystal Palace Fire
42nd Street (bounded by Croton reservoir, 40th Street and Sixth Avenue)
1853-1858

Created for the *Exhibition of the Industry of All Nations*, and later used for special events and celebrations, the building was supposedly fireproof. However, on October 5, 1858, the wooden part of the structure caught alight and the iron skeleton collapsed in the ensuing heat. The building was destroyed in less than 15 minutes but the 2,000 people inside all escaped alive.

Map labels: The Little Red Lighthouse · George Washington Bridge · Henry Hudson Pkwy · Riverside Dr · Riverside Dr · Fort Washington Ave · Presbyterian Hospital · **Washington Heights** · **Fort George** · part of Washington Heights · Yeshiva University · Fort Tryon Park · The Cloisters · Inwood Hill Park · **Inwood** · **Marble Hill** · New York University · Subway Yards · Sherman Creek · Broadway Bridge · University Heights Bridge · **The Bronx** · Washington Bridge · Alexander Hamilton Bridge · Washington Bridge · Harlem River · High Bridge (closed) · High Bridge Park · Harlem River Dr · Macombs Dam Bridge · Yankee Stadium · Bronx County Court House

EVENTS

1865 *April 14* Abraham Lincoln assassinated.

1866 Atlantic telegraph cable links N.Y. and London for 1st time.

1865 *April 24* Train taking Lincoln's body passes through city en route from Washington DC to Illinois. President's body escorted to City Hall by 7th Regiment (1st few New Yorkers to march to war). 20,000 mourners pay respects.

1865 *March 30* Metropolitan Fire District established. Paid fire fighters replace volunteers in New York and Brooklyn.

1866 Metropolitan Health w enacted after alarm over rising typhus cases. Tenement inspections are first sanitary code in any U.S. city.

1864 *Journal of Commerce* and *New York World* publish forged document created by a stockbroker speculator – both papers suspend publishing for 2 days.

1868 Statue of Abraham Lincoln in Union Square dedicated.

1867 *December 27* At St Nicholas Hotel, Broadway, Mark Twain is introduced to future wife, Olivia Langdon.

1867 *May 14* City's 1st tenement house law requires light, air, fire escapes, sanitation, running water in house or yard, at least 1 window and no cellar habitation. ● 1st hospital in Bronx (West Farms), St Barnabas Hospital for Chronic Diseases. ● American Institute of Architects organized. ● Ticker-tape machines arrive.

1868 Protective Order of Elks begins in a room above a saloon on Delancy Street.

1867 Astral Oil Works founded in Greenpoint to refine kerosene (a Brooklyn-born word).

1868 *November 30* New York Stock Exchange and Open Board issue new regulations banning sale of fraudulent securities. The 2 exchanges merge in 1869. ● Membership of New York Stock Exchange now saleable– seats can cost $4,000. (see also late 1980s). ● East New York Savings Bank founded.

1869 *Herald* sends reporter Henry Morgan Stanley to find Dr. David Livingstone in Africa.

1870 Licorice-flavored Black Jack and chewing gum invented.

1870 Mayer introduces sugar wafers, popularized by Nabisco.

1869 Bellevue is 1st hospital in U.S. to offer a hospital-based ambulance service. ● *January 25* Merchant seamen strike for higher rates and advance pay before a voyage. Strike fails but gives rise to New York Seamen's Association.

1870 *July 12* 5 killed at 1st Orange Parade (marking Battle of the Boyne). ● Metropolitan Police District abolished. ● Fire-alarm boxes replace manned watch-towers.

1871 *July 12* Violence erupts at Orange Parade. 2 militiamen die; 24 wounded. 31 rioters and bystanders killed; 67 wounded. ● Frédéric Bartholdi sets sail for N.Y. to find a suitable site for Statue of Liberty.

1872 *January 6* Ned Stokes, who loves mistress of Jim Fisk (notorious financier and swindler) shoots and kills Fisk on Broadway Central Hotel staircase.

1873 *June 17* Bones of prison-ship martyrs, heroes of American Revolution, moved to crypt in Fort Greene Park.

1871 *July 10* To stop unruly riders and run-away carriages in Central Park, police department establish mounted unit.

1873 Harlem annexed to N.Y.C.

1874 Westchester towns, Kingsbridge, West Farms and Morrisania, annexed to N.Y.

1873 An estimated 100,000 children aged 5–14 years work in factories. ● *November* Boss Tweed convicted on 204 counts of fraud, sentenced to 12 years on Blackwell's Island.

1875 *February* Giant amputated hand appears on Madison Square (part of Statue of Liberty). French plan to present to New Yorkers if they will pay for pedestal.

1875 *March 15* Archbishop John McCloskey made cardinal (see also 1864).

1876 Charles Looff's carousel with hand-carved animals launched at Coney Island. In 1880 he opens a carousel factory in Brooklyn.

1877 *May 11* Alexander Graham Bell demonstrates telephone at St. Denis Hotel (Broadway) speaking to his assistant in Brooklyn.

A.G. Bell
PB

1878 *April 12* Boss Tweed dies in Ludlow Street Jail cell.

1878 On summer Sundays, 50,000 visit Coney Island.

1875 1876 Blackwell Island smallpox hospital becomes nursing school residence.

1876 *December 5* Fire at Brooklyn Theater, Washington Street, claims 295 lives.

Roller-coaster at Coney Island
BS

1880 69 Greek residents in city. ● Communities of Italians and East European Jews increase.

1879 New Tenement House Law restricts proportion of lots built upon. ● Telephone exchange opens on Nassau Street.

1880 *December 19* After electric streetlight on Broadway illuminates advert until 11:00 p.m., Ladies Mile on Broadway (14th to 26th Streets) is lit with electric arc lights by Brush Electric Illuminating Company. Meanwhile, Thomas Edison perfects light bulb, hoping to supply light to homes and stores, and sells stock in Edison Electric Illuminating Company.

1878 Bell Telephone Company publishes 1st telephone directory, with 252 listings but no numbers. For $20 a month, operator connects subscribers to named individuals.

1879 Staten Island Water Supply Company incorporated.

1880 *February /March* Varnishers at Steinway & Sons strike for restoration of wages lowered during 70s depression. William Steinway convinces Pianoforte Manufacturers to enforce a lockout. By March 25, they back down. Even Steinway offers 10% raise.

1881 Ulysses S Grant goes into partnership with Ferdinand Ward who runs firm. William K. Vanderbilt tries to rescue Grant with a personal loan of $150,000 but Ward cashes check and disappears.

1882 *September 4* Thomas Edison turns on lights at Broad and Wall Streets in office of his wealthiest customer, J. Pierpont Morgan.

1881 Charles Brush installs electric lights in Union Square and Madison Square (see 1880).

1882 *September 4* Edison Illuminating Company opens 1st underground electric system in U.S., with power for Stock Exchange, Times and Herald offices, etc. Electricity discharging onto streets makes streetcar horses hop (the "Pearl Street trot").

1883 *November 26* Statue of George Washington dedicated at Federal Hall on Wall Street. ● 1st sliding fire pole appears at 209 Elizabeth Street, made of splinterless brass.

1883 *December 12* Conrad Poppenhusen (industrialist and benefactor of College Point) dies.

1883 Chinese Consolidated Benevolent Association founded to help community and combat prejudice. They ship bodies to China for burial and mediate Tong Wars. ● *March 26* Alva Vanderbilt holds costume ball, described in Press as social event of the century, "probably never rivalled in republican America and never outdone by the gayest court of Europe."

1883 John D Rockerfeller moves Standard Oil Trust H.Q. from Cleveland to Broadway. ● Robbins Reef Light rebuilt (see 1839)

1883 City's 1st Chinese newspaper, *Mei Hua Shin Pao*. ● Emma Lazarus publishes sonnet *The New Colossus* to help faltering fund-raising campaign for Statue of Liberty pedestal. ● Washington Heights Library now open to all (see also 1868). ● Opening of Metropolitan Opera House, Brooklyn Bridge and Dakota Apartments (72nd Street/Central Park West). ● Joseph Pulitzer buys *The World*. Within 4 years he will own morning, evening and Sunday papers with 250,000 circulation, widest in U.S. ● *October* Romanesque-revival Metropolitan Opera House dedicated (Broadway/39th Street). ● New York Giants founded. ● *May 14* At Madison Square Garden, John Sullivan batters Englishman Charlie Mitchell. Police captain "Clubber" Williams stops fight in 3rd round. ● Polo Grounds complex used for Giants and Metropolitans baseball games.

POLITICS & RELIGION

1865 *December 5* John T. Hoffman mayor.

1866-71: Corrupt Common Council ring control Tammany Hall, municipal and county government, judicial system, governorship and Board of Audit (see also 1870).

1865 *December 5* John T. Hoffman mayor.

1867 *Harper's Bazaar* founded (see also 1867 1913, 1929). ● *May 6* At Great Hall, Cooper Union, Mark Twain delivers a "Serio-Humorous Lecture" at his 1st public appearance in city (tickets 50¢ each).

1868 Society of Tammany moves to Union Square. ● Thomas Coman mayor.

1869 *December 1* A.O. Hall, member of Tweed Ring, elected mayor.

1870 *February 1* 1st meeting of Ass. of the Bar of New York. ● New York City Women's Suffrage Association formed. ● *July* William Steinway purchases 35-acre farm in Astoria for his piano works. ● 500,000 lbs of opium a year arrive in U.S.

1869 *Harper's Weekly* published. Tweed complains about a cartoon depicting Tweed Ring: "I don't care a straw for your newspaper articles, my constituents don't know how to read, but they can't help seeing them damned pictures."

1872 *December 5* William Havemeyer mayor.

1871 Tweed arrested; will be sentenced to 12 years in prison.

1874 *November 3* William H Wickham elected mayor; will take office 1875. ● When Mayor Havemeyer dies suddenly, Samuel Vance covers last weeks of his term.

1876 Yudishe Gazeten founded, world's 1st Yiddish-language daily newspaper. ● *March 27* 1st edition of *Long Island City Star* ● Richard Fox, now editor of *National Police Gazette*, makes it popular weekly.

1876 E.F. Farrington, master mechanic, 1st to cross river on unfinished Brooklyn Bridge with a steam-driven traveller rope. ● Austin Corbin incorporates New York & Manhattan Beach Railway, opening his fashionable Manhattan Beach Hotel a year later. ● Elevated trains run over Sixth Avenue. ● Department of Parks pay $1,500 for small Swedish schoolhouse that becomes home to Marionette Theater in Central Park.

1876 *September 24* Explosives in tunnels under East River blow up dangerous Hell Gate reefs.

1876 *July 19* Queens County Bar Association founded at Garden City Hotel ● *November 7* Smith Ely elected mayor.

1876 *September 24* Queens County Courthouse in Long Island City dedicated.

1878 Adolph Douai founds *New York Volkszeitung*, Socialist Labor Party organ. ● *November 5* Edward Cooper elected mayor

1877 *December 22* American Museum of Natural History opens in Victorian Gothic building.

1877 LIRR trains run into new Flatbush Avenue terminal, 17 years after Brooklyn banned steam railroads within its limits. ● Tower and Home Buildings, Alfred White's model tenements for worthy poor, completed in Brooklyn. ● A decade after his death, statue of Fitz Greene Halleck dedicated on the Mall, Central Park – only American on Literary Walk.

1880 *November 2* 1st Irish Catholic mayor, William R. Grace, elected with help of Tammany Hall.

1879 *May 31* Opening of Madison Square Gardens, built by William Vanderbilt at 26th Street and Madison Avenue. Sporting hall features boxing matches and champion, John Sullivan, draws massive crowds.

1880 Opening of Metropolitan Museum of Art in Central Park facing Fifth Avenue (81st-84th Streets).

1879 Original St. Patrick's Cathedral on Prince Street downgraded to parish church. On May 25 new St. Patrick's Cathedral (Fifth Avenue) dedicated, 11th largest church in world and city's largest. ● *June 9* New York Elevated Railroad makes 1st run up Ninth Avenue (Columbus) from 53rd Street and features nerve-wracking S-curve at 110th Street.

1881 *September 20* Vice President Chester Arthur sworn in as President at 123 Lexington Avenue. A 17-foot bronze statue of him stands in Madison Square Park.

1881 Columbia University's Graduate School of Architecture established.

1882 *November* Franklin Edison elected mayor.

1882 Oscar Wilde appears at Chickering Hall, near Union Square.

1881 Carnegie Hall opens.

1881 *February* Cleopatra's Needle, a gift from Egypt to US, is set on a pedestal behind Metropolitan Museum of Art. A newspaper reports that the 219 1/4 tons of stone, are rotated into place, "as easily and delicately as if it were the minute hand of a lady's watch."

Fitz Greene Halleck
DP

COMMERCE

1868 *July 3* 1st elevated line along Greenwich Street. It runs 1/2 a mile between Dey and Cortlandt.

1867 352 churches in Brooklyn.

1867 Brooklyn's Prospect Park complete.

1869 *September 24* On 1st Black Friday, J. Gould and J. Fisk try to corner gold market but flee when financial crisis hits Wall Street and their fraud is discovered. ● F.W. Woolworth's "five and dime" stores develop. ● Bloomingdale opens.

1870 Backed by Commodore Vanderbilt, 1st female-owned brokerage house opens on Wall Street. ● Tiffany & Company open on Union Square near fashionable shopping area.

Bloomingdales
DP

1872 New record real estate price reached when Philadelphia banker, Drexel, pays $348 a square foot for a Wall Street building.

1873 *September 18* When Jay Cooke & Company (brokerage that underwrote Northern Pacific railroad) closes its doors, plummet on N.Y. Stock Exchange. ● *September 20* N.Y. Stock Exchange closes trading floor for 1st time in its 81 years.

1874 American Linoleum Manufacturing Company opens at Long Neck, Staten Island, soon known as Linoleumville.

1875 Williamsburgh Savings Bank, a golden-domed cathedral of finance, opens (Broadway/Driggs Street) ● Macy's motto appears: *We will not be undersold.*

1876 *September 24* Explosives in tunnels under East River...

1874 *January 13* Building depression. 7,000 workmen and families gather in Tompkins Square to protest appalling conditions. Battalions of mounted police ride down demonstrators. ● 90,000 unemployed and homeless – many starving – 900 New Yorkers had starved to death, 3,000 infants left on doorsteps, and some 100 corpses dumped. ● 60% of reported deaths in summer are children under 5.

1878 1st telephone exchange service: Metropolitan Telephone and Telegraph Company's central switching office opens in Manhattan for 271 clients (see also 1896). ● Black Ball shipline across Atlantic folds.

1877 *April 4* Queens County Courthouse in Long Island City dedicated.

1877 LIRR trains run into new...

1880 Opening of Metropolitan Museum of Art...

CULTURE & ART

1865 Atlantic Yacht Club set up in Brooklyn.

1866 *April* Long Island City Star launched; will become Long Island Star (folds 1968).

1867 *December 27* At St Nicholas Hotel...

1869 *June* Brooklyn Bridge designer dies after a ferry knocks him against a waterfront piling. Now his son, Washington Roebling, oversees construction.

1870 Metropolitan Museum of Art founded. 1st gift is a Roman sarcophagus. Museum now owns 3 million pieces.

1871 *April 20* New York Elevated Rail Road Company now run a steam locomotive, pulling 3 passenger cars, on Ninth Avenue elevated line. ● After 10 years, and millions of dollars lost through corruption, Tweed Courthouse (New York County Courthouse) complete in Chambers Street. ● Grand Central Depot opens on 42nd Street.

1872 1st "el" line on Greenwich Street: trains run every 2 minutes ● Washington Roebling, crippled after working in Brooklyn Bridge's western caisson, still oversees operations through a telescope from a nearby room, with his wife instructing workers and site managers.

1873 *January 1* Central Railroad runs from Flushing to Floral Park. A.T. Stewart builds and leases line to serve his new suburb, Garden City. ● Building of St. John the Divine Cathedral starts. John D. Rockerfeller gives $500,000 to project. When complete it will be largest in world: 601 feet long; its 177-foot high nave seats 10,000.

1872 *December 5* William Havemeyer mayor.

1872 Metropolitan Museum of Art opens (681 Fifth Avenue).

1873 Metropolitan Museum of Art moves to Douglas Mansion on 14th Street (see also 1872). ● *New York Daily Graphic* publishes 1st news photographs.

1875 *July 21* George Templeton Strong dies.

1875 Rapid Transit Commission empowered to lay out routes and assign franchises. ● Prospect Park & Coney Island Railway open.

1874 Town Survey Commission extends Brooklyn's street grid across rural towns. ● Work begins on railroad tunnel under Hudson River between Hoboken and Greenwich Village.

1878 Opening of "ell" (elevated) on Sixth Avenue. Ninth Avenue el extends northwards. Night-time services on Manhattan el. On August 26, Third Avenue el runs from South Ferry to 42nd Street. ● Post Office at lower end of city complete.

1878 Opening of Coney Island's Brighton racetrack.

1880 *August 26* 1st trains roll over new trestle across Jamaica Bay to Rockaways. 65,000 passengers in 1st week.

1880 Chinese Treaty: U.S. can limit, restrict, or suspend, but not prohibit it entry of Chinese into U.S.

CITY STRUCTURE & DEVELOPMENT

1866-1868 Loew footbridge relieves Broadway congestion. ● *January 24* Olmsted and Vaux submit plan for Prospect Park.

1864 1st systematic sanitary survey of New York.

1866 Hell Gate Brewery opens, will stretch from 91st to 94th Streets. ● New York Yacht Club sponsor 1st transatlantic race. ● 1st race meeting of American Jockey Club in N.Y.

Elevated Railroad
PB

1865 High Bridge Park opens.

1870 *November 15* New York Elevated Rail Road Company launched and 1st Manhattan "el" in operation. ● A.E. Beach secretly builds subway under Broadway. Subway opens February 28 but soon Boss Tweed orders subway to shut as he supports elevated railway.

USA & WORLD EVENTS

1865 Lincoln assassinated

1867 U.S. purchase Alaska for $7 milion

1876 Custer and 256 men killed at Battle of Little Big Horn

1881 Alexander II of Russia killed

1883 Modern American Pendleton Civil Se

1883 *May 24* 6,016-feet long Brooklyn Bridge opens, spanning East River. Designed by builder-engineer John A Roebling and his son, Washington. When someone yells that the bridge is collapsing 12 pedestrians are trampled to death in ensuing panic!

J A Robeling

1882 Financial problems halt construction of railroad tunnel under Hudson River. Hudson & Manhattan Railroad Company finish tunnels – now part of the PATH system (Port Authority Trans-Hudson Corporation). PB

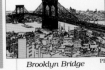
Brooklyn Bridge
PB

...st 10 ...im- ...ose ...-Richter ...rthquake ...rbor. 2 ... under ...nhattan, at 125th Street and Dykeman Street, but no building regulations here to lessen earthquake damage.

1884 Coney Island's 1st rollercoaster opens. ● Montefiore Home for Chronic Invalids open (Avenue A/84th Street – *see also* 1889). ● US's 1st bacteriology laboratory at Bellevue Hospital.

1884 Wallabout Market in Brooklyn created for Long Island farmers.

1884 Harvard graduate Samuel Brearley founds Brearley School for girls. ● *May 8* Board of Trustees of St Francis Monastery receive charter for St Francis College. ● Brooklyn Grays (ancestors of Dodgers) form as an American Association team who play at Washington Park. HQ is Old Stone House, scene of heroic fighting in Battle of Long Island.

1884 Opening of *The Dakota*, city's 1st luxury apartment building. ● Chelsea Hotel, 222 West 23rd Street complete, but as apartments (becomes a hotel in 1905). ● Reservoir Square (Sixth Avenue/42nd Street) given current name, Bryant Park, to honour William C. Bryant, poet, newspaper editor and advocate of public parks (*see* 1847, 1853-58). ● 3 large parks authorized in Bronx (Van Cortlandt, Bronx and Pelham Bay) and 3 smaller parks (Crotona, St. Mary's and Claremont) and 3 parkways. ● Madison Avenue Bridge over Harlem River opens.

1886 *October 28* Statue of Liberty finally unveiled. Pedestal, designed by Richard M. Hunt, paid for by 1,000s of ordinary citizens' nickels and dimes.

Statue of Liberty PB

1885 Robert E. Odlum jumps off Brooklyn Bridge for a bet: dies from internal bleeding 45 minutes later. ● *January 27* Jerome Kern born in Manhattan.

1885 Hotel St. George opens in Brooklyn Heights – will become city's largest.

1886 *June 19* Bowery Bay Beach amusement park opens. Renamed North Beach in 1890, it closes in 1920s. La Guardia Airport there today. ● 1886 University Settlement founded, 1st settlement house in America, originally the Neighborhood Guild. Eleanor Roosevelt volunteers here.

1885 Goldman, Sachs & Company founded. German immigrant, Marcus Goldman, opens Pine Street office to trade in promissory notes. His son-in-law Samuel Sachs had joined him in 1882 and his son Henry joins now (*see also* 1914).

1886 *May 5* New York Stock Exchange enjoys 1st million-share day.

1886 *November 2* Abram S Hewitt elected mayor.

1886 Illustrator Charles Gibson sells his 1st drawing to *Life magazine* for $4. His Gibson Girls prove very successful. ● *Richmond County Advance* begins as a weekly newspaper (renamed *Staten Island Advance* 1918).

1885 Villard Houses, built for financier Henry Villard, finished on Madison Avenue at 51st Street. 6 brownstone mansions resemble a Renaissance palazzo. ● Pier A, fire Department's Marine Division H.Q., completed (West Street near Battery Park). ● DeVinne Press Building on Lafayette Street completed, a Romanesque gem.

1886 *February 23* Ferry between St. George and Whitehall Street. Staten Island Rapid Transit Railroad Company starts service from South Beach to St. George – named after George Law, owner of waterfront property promised "canonization" if he relinquished ferry landing rights! ● *September* 778 buildings under construction on Upper West Side (59th-110th Streets). ● Using fireproof materials, brick and terracotta, Potter Building rises on Park Row where World Building burned.

1888 Blizzard PB

1888 *March 12* Worst winter storm of century. Blizzard and high winds last 54 hours. 12 freeze to death. ● Falling overhead power lines cause city's 1st blackout – lasts 3 hours.

1887 *March 8* Henry Ward Beecher, minister of Plymouth Church, dies.

1889 *November 14* Nellie Bly, reporter for the *World*, challenges Jules Verne's fictional *Around the World in 80 Days*. She completes trip in 72 days, 6 hours, 11 minutes and 14 seconds, visiting Verne in Paris on the way and arriving back January 25, 1890.

1887 Doctors perform 1st cesarean section in Bellevue hospital.

1888 City's last execution: convicted murderer, Daniel Lyons, hanged in County Jail (the Tombs) just before law bans executions.

1889 Washington Square Monument in Washington Square Park is made of wood. It will be re-created soon in marble.

1887 Bloomingdale's department store opens (59th Street/Third Avenue) – soon expands to Lexington Avenue.

1889 *July 8* Charles H Dow and Edward D Jones publish 1st edition of *Wall Street Journal* at 15 Wall Street: 2¢ a copy.

1887 *April 17* 1st Emmanuel Baptist Church, a French Gothic Church designed by F.H. Kimball dedicated in Clinton Hill (*see also* 1881).

1888 *November 6* Hugh J Grant mayor

1887 Gracie Mansion, official Mayor's residence, acquired by city for Museum of the City of New York.

Gracie Mansion DP

1887 Square mile of New Utrecht town named Bensonhurst. Benson family own 4 farms there.

1889 Washington Bridge opens over Harlem River at 181st Street.

1891 *September 28* Novelist Herman Melville dies at 104 East 26th Street, having lived in obscurity for 28 years.

1890 1st moving picture shows in city. ● Madison Square Gardens built by Stanford White, biggest building in U.S. devoted entirely to entertainment.

1891 After long campaign by Women's Temperance Union, N.Y. hires 1st female officers as police matrons.

1891 James Stillman president of National City Bank, city's 12th largest commercial bank (*see also* 1909).

1891 *February 6* Judson Memorial Baptist Church, Washington Square, has 1st services. Romanesque Revival, with stained-glass windows by John LaFarge, completed 1892.

1890 2nd Madison Square Garden opens June 16 (Madison Avenue/26th Street).

Madison Sq. Garden PB

1891 Population expanding and city commited to public education ● C.B. Snyder is Board of Education's architect – for 31 years. He designs stately Collegiate Gothic school buildings.

1890 *December* 349-foot World (Purlitzer) Building, the world's tallest, completed. City will have world's tallest building until 1974 (*see also* 1955). ● Photographers and artists see Flatiron building as N.Y. icon.

Flatiron building DP

1891 Name skyscraper 1st applied to tall buildings. ● *January 10* Century Association's home (7 West 43rd Street), designed by Stanford White, dedicated.

1892 *January 1* Ellis Island immigrant station opens. 15-year-old Annie Moore from County Cork is 1st down gangplank (*see also* 1900).

Ellis Island DP

● *September 27* Antonin Dvořák arrives. Mrs J. Thurber (founder of National Conservatory of Music, 1885) persuades Dvořák to be director (*see also* 1894).

1892 City's last cholera outbreak claims 100 lives. ● Backed by Vanderbilts, Clara Spence founds Spence School. ● Fordham Branch of Bellevue Hospital opens (*see also* 1899). ● *The Tribune* names 4,047 American millionaires; 27% live in New York, 4% in Brooklyn.

1892 *December 28* Dynamite explosion in Steinway Tunnel: 5 die. Lawsuits ruin New York & Long Island Railroad, later acquired by A. Belmont.

1892 *November 8* Thomas F Gilroy elected mayor.

1892 City's 1st Arabic newspaper, *Kawkab Amirka*. ● *January* Walt Whitman announces in *New York Herald* that, after almost 40 years, *Leaves of Grass*, his revolutionary book of poems, is complete. ● *August 27* Fire damages Metropolitan Opera House. Season cancelled. Carrère & Hastings redesign interior. ● *October 21* Anton Seidl conducts Metropolitan Orchestra and a 100-voice chorus in world premiere of composer's *Te Deum*, written for occasion.

1892 *October 21* Soldiers' and Sailors' Memorial Arch dedicated in Brooklyn's Grand Army Plaza. ● *December 27* St. John's Day: cornerstone laid for Cathedral of St. John the Divine (110th Street/ Amsterdam Avenue). In 1887, Bishop H.C. Porter had the intent to rival St. Patrick's. ● 1st trolleys on Staten Island, from Port Richmond to Meier's Corner. ● Columbus Monument, Columbus Circle, dedicated Columbus Day.

Columbus Statue DP

1893 Sprague installs 1st electric elevator in Postal Telegraph Building. ● *August 23* Hurricane and floods. Storm washes away Hog Island (Rockaway).

1894 Brooklyn annexes New Utrecht, Gravesend and Flatbush.

1893 *September 4* Moses Baline arrives at Ellis Island on *Rhyland*. His 5-year-old son, Israel, will become Irving Berlin.

1893 Lebanon Hospital (founded 1890 by Jewish philanthropists) opens with kosher kitchen in former convent. ● Faber factory produces famous pencil with its yellow shaft.

1894 *March 27* 300 women at Astoria Silk Works strike over working hours (8.30 am - 10.30 pm).

1894 New state constitution grants city greater home rule. ● McKane, political boss of Coney Island (Sodom by Sea) convicted of election fraud and sent to Sing Sing. ● *November 6* William L. Strong, elected mayor, appoints Theodore Roosevelt as police commissioner ● Police corruption investigated. Witness describes nightlife district above 14th Street as the Tenderloin.

1893 World premiere of Dvořák's *New World Symphony*. ● Color printing 1st used by the *World*, and leads to color comics in Sunday paper. Most popular is *Hogan's Alley*. ● Andrew Carnegie made a trustee of New York Free Circulating Library. ● Architect Richard Morris Hunt and others found Municipal Art Society: "To make us love our city, we must make our city lovely."

1894 *March 9* New York Philharmonic gives world premiere of Victor Herbert's *Cello Concerto;* Herbert is soloist. In audience, Antonin Dvořák is inspired to compose his own concerto.

1893 Metropolitan Life Insurance Building at One Madison Avenue complete. ● Statue of Nathan Hale dedicated in City Hall Park on Evacuation Day. Stanford White designed base.

1894 Metropolitan Traction Company's 8-story Cable Building, designed by McKim, Mead & White, completed (Broadway/ Houston Street). Powered by basement machinery, cable cars go from Bowling Green to 36th Street.

1895 All territory west of Bronx River annexed to New York. In June, City annexes villages of Wakefield, Eastchester and Williamsbridge, the town of Westchester, and parts of Pelham.

1895 Crazy Butch is a notorious young criminal who had been stealing for years. Butch teaches other youngsters how to steal and creates the Squab Wheelmen. One would crash a bicycle into a pedestrian and scream at victim until a crowd gathered. Squab Wheelmen would then pick pockets. Butch even trained his dog, Rabbi, to snatch purses.

1895 10,000 people can shop in James McCreery & Company store (Sixth Avenue/23rd Street). ● Electric streetlights reach 42nd Street. ● *October 19* N.Y.U.'s campus in Bronx dedicated. ● Construction begins on large amusement parks on Coney Island. ● *April 26* New York Zoological Society chartered (*see also* 1993). ● *May 4* Washington Memorial Arch (Stanford White – architect; MacMonnies – bas-reliefs) dedicated. Donations total $178,000 including $4,000 raised at a benefit concert by pianist Paderewski at Metropolitan Opera House in 1892.

1895 Staten Island Chamber of Commerce founded. ● William Randolph Hearst purchases the *Journal*.

1895 *May 23* New York Public Library founded, consolidating Astor Foundation, Lenox Foundation and Tilden Trust, with 360,000 volumes and $3.5 million in real estate holdings. Dr John Billings is 1st director (*see also* 1886). ● *April 18* Under architect John Carrère, Fine Arts federation of New York founded. ● Political bosses sponsor boxing matches and ensure police cooperation (severe legal restraints on boxing in 1890s).

1895 Straightening of Harlem River cuts off Marble Hill community from Manhattan. Later Spuyten Duyvil Creek is filled in, fusing neighborhood to Bronx. ● 3rd Macombs Dam Bridge completed, a 415-foot swing bridge designed by A.P. Boller. ● *May 5* Dedication of new home of First Presbyterian Church of Newtown (founded 1652).

1896 *January 20* Nathan Birnbaum (George Burn) born Lower East Side ● *June 4* LIRR president Austin Corbin dies in carriage accident.

1896 An estimated 25,000 opium users in city. ● *March 8* Ballington and Maud Booth found Volunteers of America. ● *March* 30.5 inches of snow, most recorded for any month. ● *April/May* Edison's vitascope shows moving pictures at Koster & Bial's Music Hall. W. Heise sets up tripod in Herald Square to show them. ● *May 30* Soldiers' and Sailors' Monuments, Hillside Avenue, Jamaica, dedicated. ● *August 29* Opening of Midland Beach resort, Staten Island. ● 1st bagel in city.

1896 *May 26* Dow Jones Industrial Index begins, closing at 40.94. Of original 12 companies, General Electric is only one still included. ● New York Telephone organized – absorbs Bell operations for city. ● Brooklyn Rapid Transit Company (BRT) formed, uniting surface, elevated and streetcar lines in Brooklyn. ● Massive Siegel-Cooper Department Store opens (Sixth Avenue/18th Street).

1896 Adolph S Ochs takes over *New York Times*. 8 years on, he moves it to Broadway's Times Tower. ● *March 19* Long Island City Public Library has charter – will become Queens Borough Public Library. ● Cosmopolitan Race, 2nd automobile race in America, staged along 30-mile route from Kingsbridge to Irvington-on-Hudson and back.

1896 *April 1* Real estate developer, Meyer, wants to dissociate community from maladorous Newtown Creek. Post Office is persuaded to change Newtown to Elmhurst. LIRR renames station next year. ● Bohemian National Hall finished at 321 East 71st Street. ● 21-story, 312-foot American Surety Building (Broadway/Pine Street) finished. Company had paid $1.5 million for site. John Jacob Astor IV complains that its cornice extends 3 feet over his lot and Company have to pay him $75,000 a year (about $900 per office) for infringement on his property. ● Crime spot, Five Points intersection at Baxter, Park, Worth, Mulberry and Dandy Lane, renovated as a park.

1897 *February 22* Citizens' Union founded.

1897 Arctic explorer Robert Peary arrives on the *Hope* with 6 Greenland locals, including 7-year-old boy – Minik. 20,000 people pay 25¢ each to see exotic visitors on ship. They are then "exhibited" at Museum of Natural History and live in basement. 1 returns to Greenland; 3 others die of TB, including Minik's father, whose bones are kept by Museum.

1897 Hotel Waldorf and Astoria Hotel (Fifth Avenue/33rd Street) open as single Waldorf-Astoria Hotel, largest in world (*see also* 1893, 1929).

1897 New York and Staten Island Electric Company incorporated.

1897 New home of German Evangelical Lutheran Church of St Paul, 315 West 22nd Street, finished. ● *May 2* Governor Frank S Black signs Greater New York's charter. ● *November 2* Tammany candidate Robert A Van Wyck elected 1st mayor of Greater New York.

1897 *October 4* Columbia University and Barnard College move from Madison Avenue /49th Street to Morningside Heights (Broadway/116th Street). New campus modeled on Athenian agora. ● *June 2* Brooklyn Museum, originally Institute of Arts and Science, opens. ● Spring Construction begins on New York Public Library. ● Richmond County Country Club (founded 1888) moves onto Dongan Hills estate. New golf course built.

1897 *April 27* President William McKinley dedicates Grant's Tomb on edge of Morningside Heights, overlooking the Hudson. 90,000 Americans had made donations towards mausoleum. (Former president, Ulysses S. Grant, died 1885).

William McKinley PB

PB *Tomb of General Grant*

1898 *January 1* **Greater New York created**, merging 5 boroughs to form world's 2nd-largest city. *New York Times* reports: "With the crash of cannon and the roar of exploding bombs, the flag of 'Greater New York' was officially unfurled over City Hall at midnight – and the second city of the world came into existence." In March, J. DeWitt Warner writes, "Today there are no new worlds to find. Upon us is the responsibility never before laid on a people – building the world's capital for all time to come." ● Queens enters Greater New York.

1899 *January 1* 1 year after creation of Greater New York had split Queens County, Hempstead, North Hempstead and Oyster Bay form Nassau County.

1898 *September 26* George (Jacob) Gershwin born at 242 Snediker Avenue, Brooklyn.

1899 *September 9* Henry H. Bliss 1st automobile fatality – struck by a car after stepping off a streetcar at 74th Street (Central Park West). ● Chinese Exclusion Acts passed by U.S. Congress bar Chinese immigrants from naturalization. Chinese are 1st ethnic group to be excluded from U.S. ● Bronx Zoo opens.

1898 *September 13* Board of Aldermen ban sale of tobacco products to children under 18. ● Life expectancy in city less than 50 years. ● Shantytowns in Central Park, Harlem and West Side 40s. Uptown shantytowns called the Goats.

1899 *July 20* Newsboys strike. In less than 2 weeks, Joseph Pulitzer and William Randolph Hearst have to abandon attempt to raise wholesale price of their papers. ● *December 16* Brooklyn Children's Museum opens.

1898 Charles De Kay founds National Arts Club, having previously founded Authors' Club and New York Fencers' Club. ● Emil Paur music director of New York Philharmonic. ● Municipal Art Society erect monument at Fifth Avenue/70th Street to architect Richard Morris Hunt.

1899 *February 6* Tottenville Free Library organized.

1898 *July 2* $5 million 2.3 mile Harlem Speedway (155th Street to Dykeman Street) opens, designed for carriages so elite can show off prized horses (*see also* 1919). ● New Third Avenue Bridge over Harlem River.

1899 Third Avenue trolley line electrified. ● Long Acre Square, once a thriving commercial center and site of W. H. Vanderbilt's American Horse Exchange now has high-end discreet brothels, dubbed "silk hat brothels". ● Automobiles banned from Central Park.

... begins ... Reform Act forms basis for today's U.S. Civil Service

1885 Louis Pasteur injects against rabies

1887 1st motor car engine and 1st gramophone ● Ethiopian Italian war

1890 Eiffel Tower built

1892 Carnegie Steel Works strike

1893 Revolt in Hawaii

1893 U.S. credit shortage panic: 15,000 businesses, 74 railroads and 600 banks fail

1895 1st Sino-Japanese war

1898 Spanish American war

1899-1902 Boer wars in Africa

Citicorp Center 1978
Lexington Avenue
(53rd/54th Streets)
Architects: Hugh Stubbins
and Associates
48 stories

The Citicorp Centre is a
distinctive shape in the
Manhattan skyline because of
the way the top is sliced off at
a 45° angle – this was meant
to act as a solar panel but has
never been used as such. The
building sits on four pillars
with a central column and is
sheathed in white aluminium.
It incorporates St. Peter's
Lutheran Church, a popular
venue for organ recitals and
jazz vespers.

F.F. French Building 1927
551 Fifth Avenue (45th/46th Streets)
Architects: H.Douglas Ives, Sloan and
Robertson
Height: 429 feet (130.4m) 38 stories

Inspired by Babylonian palaces and
temples, the building has richly decorated
faience polychromed panels on its russet,
terracotta brick façade.

Columbia University
Today's building begun 1897
West 116th Street

Founded 1754 as King's College in World Trade
Center /Ground Zero area.
Present site is where Bloomingdale Insane
Asylum once stood.
50 Nobel laureates studied here.
Famous students include Isaac Asimov, Joan
Rivers and James Cagney.

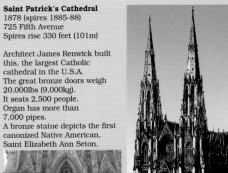

Saint Patrick's Cathedral
1878 (spires 1885-88)
725 Fifth Avenue
Spires rise 330 feet (101m)

Architect James Renwick built
this, the largest Catholic
cathedral in the U.S.A.
The great bronze doors weigh
20,000lbs (9,000kg).
It seats 2,500 people.
Organ has more than
7,000 pipes.
A bronze statue depicts the first
canonized Native American,
Saint Elizabeth Ann Seton.

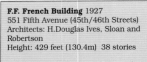

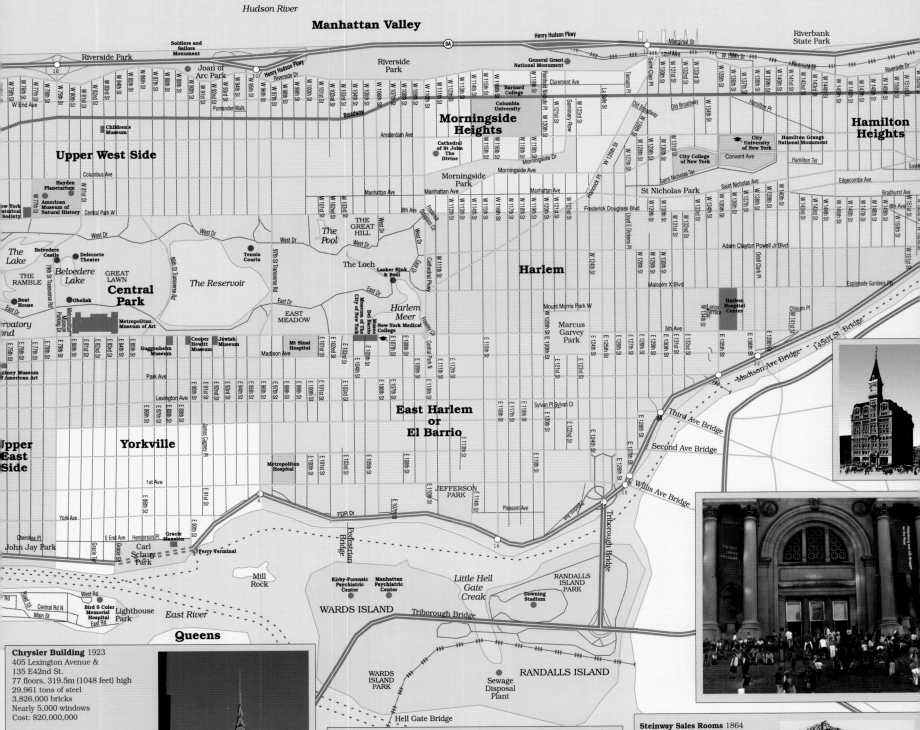

Chrysler Building 1923
405 Lexington Avenue &
135 E42nd St.
77 floors, 319.5m (1048 feet) high
29,961 tons of steel
3,826,000 bricks
Nearly 5,000 windows
Cost: $20,000,000

Walter P. Chrysler, owner of the
automobile company, decided to build
a monument to his achievement that
would be higher than the Eiffel Tower,
then the highest in the world.
To ensure it was taller than Forty Wall
Street Building, also under
construction, a spire was secretly
assembled within its crown and then
raised into place on top of the Chrysler,
once it was finished. This was a short-
lived victory, however, as the Empire
State Building claimed the title of the
tallest building within 12 months.
The tower is decorated in Art Deco
style, and its base has a frieze inspired
by car profiles as well as gargoyles that
resemble 1929 Chrysler car hood
ornaments; the upper ones are eagles.

Met Life Building 1963
(originally Pan Am Building,
its name changed in 1981)
Park Avenue (45th Street)
59 storys, 807 feet
(246m) high

Built in International style in
glass, cement and granite,
the shape is meant to
resemble the wing of an
aeroplane.
Its impact on the view of
Grand Central Station has
been much criticised.
The rooftop heliport was
abandoned in 1977 after an
accident showered debris
onto the streets below.

Steinway Sales Rooms 1864
East 14th Street

The Steinway factory created pianos
with the reputation of being the
finest ever made.
Between 1870 and 1873, in northwest Queens, William Steinway built
a spacious factory and an entire
town with church, kindergarten,
library and trolley line.
William Steinway became so
influential that when he died in
1896, the mayor ordered all the city
flags to be flown at half-mast.
In 1926 the company created 6,000
grand pianos.
During World War Two, instead of
pianos, the company made troop-
carrying gliders.

Academy of Music 1853-54
14th Street (Irving Place)
Seated 4,000

First opera house to succeed in New York, this was also the venue for many balls and receptions, including one for the Prince of Wales's visit in 1860. It closed in 1885 after the new Metropolitan Opera House attracted greater audiences.
Consolidated Edison Building replaced it on the site.

Woolworth Building 1913
223 Broadway
Tower is 60 stories
(729 feet)
Built at a rate of 1½ stories a week

Lavish and elegant, the building has vaulted mosaic ceilings, arches, gargoyles, and iron and bronze ornaments.
Frank Woolworth paid for the building with $13.5 million in cash. He had 1,000 stores around the world and a fortune of $65 million.
A gargoyle in the lobby, hugging a model of the building, depicts the architect, Cass Gilbert. F.W. Woolworth is also depicted – counting his money!
This was New York's tallest structure until 1930.
It has never had a mortgage.

United States Courthouse
1936
40 Centre Street
(corner of Pearl Street)
31 stories

Foley Square is the heart of the Civic Center. All the municipal, state and federal buildings are grouped in this area, built in austere, classical style.
Among them stands a building that resembles a classical temple; its tower is topped with a pyramidal golden roof. This, the U.S. State Courthouse, is a definitive landmark.
It was designed by Cass Gilbert and finished by his son, Cass Gilbert Jnr. after his father's death.
There is a shooting gallery for FBI agents in the basement.

Flatiron 1902 (formerly Fuller Building)
Entire block on 5th Avenue and Broadway (23rd St.) 22 floors, 87m. (285 feet) high

This is New York's oldest skyscraper.
It has exuberant Gothic and Renaissance detailing. It was first known as the Fuller but was soon nicknamed the Flatiron as it was thus shaped to fit its triangular site.
The architecture, based upon classical Greek columns, divides into 3 parts, the base in buff limestone with copper-clad windows, the main structure in pale-colored bricks and terracotta with undulating oriels, and the capital of arches and columns – all topped by a projecting cornice and balustraded roof.

Its rounded prow creates the illusion of a free-standing colossal column.
The expression, "Twenty-three skiddoo" derived from the drafts created by its height that fluttered ladies petticoats, so that constables had to "skiddoo" any men who peeked!

New York Times Building 1888
Printing House Square
(Park Row, Nassau and Spruce Streets intersection)

This handsome structure was the second Times building in the site and was considered a great engineering feat as it was built around the original building where the newspaper's business continued as usual throughout this process.
Its builder, David H King, was also responsible for the Statue of Liberty pedestal.

New Post Office 1875
City Hall Park
(demolished 1938-39)

This building was erected at what was then the city's busiest intersection. It was lacking in facilities and its extravagant opulence was thought by many to be an eyesore.

Bowery Savings Bank
1923
110 East 42nd Street

Designed like a Roman basilica.
Ornamentation includes a rooster to symbolise punctuality and a squirrel for thrift.
Its vast magnificent banking room interior is now used for private events with fine catering.

HISTORICAL EVENTS

PEOPLE

LIFESTYLE

COMMERCE

POLITICS & RELIGION

CULTURE & ART

CITY STRUCTURE & DEVELOPMENT

1900 Fire-damaged Ellis Island immigrant station replaced.

1901 *September 14* Theodore Roosevelt President

Roosevelt PB

1900 *August* riots: 3,500 citizens later protest over police brutality. ● Al Capone in Five Points Gang. Hell's Kitchen Riot. Blacks attacked.

1901 Jewish immigrants are skilled workers – butchers, carpenters, shoemakers, tailors.

Early 1900s Washington Square Park made a parade ground.

1901 John D. Rockefeller Snr establishes Rockefeller University as center for medical education and research. 16 of faculty will win Nobel Prizes – for isolating antibiotics, demonstrating DNA's hereditary transmission and preserving whole blood, making blood banks possible.

1900 International Ladies Garment workers union founded.

1900 1st Jewish congressman, Goldfoggle, elected to represent N.Y.

1901 November 5 Seth Low, anti-Tammany candidate, elected mayor.

1900 *May 4* Newtown High School opens.

1901 Andrew Carnegie funds 65 public library branches. Free Circulating Library merges with New York Public Library, becoming nucleus of branch system.

1900 *March 24* Mayor R. Van-Wyck breaks ground at City Hall for city's 1st IRT subway. Construction debris dumped on Governor Island will double its size.

1901 *October1* Construction of Manhattan Bridge starts.

1900 Electric lights replace gas on Broadway.

1902 *January 8* 2 trains collide under 55th Street near Grand Central. 15 die. State legislature forces railroad to switch from steam to electricity. ● Theodore Roosevelt lets his name be used by Brooklyn candy store owner – Teddy Bear born.

1902 O. Henry (William S. Porter) moves to city and writes about Tenderloin brothels and bars.

1903 Police begin fingerprinting felons

1902 1st electric train runs over Second Avenue elevated. ● Algonquin Hotel opens. Alan Jay Lerner writes *My Fair Lady* here.

Algonquin Hotel DP

1902 *July* I.R.T. (Interborough Rapid Transit Co.) operator of 1st city subways, formed by financier, Belmont. ● Philip Morris, British tobacco and food processor firm, opens 1st U.S. branch on Broad Street. ● Macy's moves 20 blocks north to Herald Square after 43 years on Sixth Avenue.

Macys

1902 November 2 George B McClellan elected mayor.

1903 Lyceum Theater opens. ● Enrico Caruso gives 1st performance at Metropolitan Opera as *Rigoletto*.

1902 Police row boats now all replaced by steamers. ● 20-storey, 300-feet Fuller Building (Broadway/Fifth Avenue) complete — called Flatiron Building because of its shape. ● *New York Times* built on 43rd Street. Long Acre Square renamed Times Square.

Flatiron Building

1903 All 4 Manhattan elevated lines now electric. ● Williamsburg Bridge opens.

1904 *November 26* Fire virtually destroys Queens County Court House. ● Excursion steamer *General Slocum*, catches fire with 1,335 passengers aboard for a picnic. As steamer passes 125th Street, a boy notices smoke on bow and tells a ticket-taker – who ignores him. Fire in paint storage locker spreads to consume lower deck. Empty sand buckets, useless fire hoses and ripped life jackets mean 1,021 die and 124 are injured. 2 thieves breaking rocks on Riker's Island seize a rowboat to save 15 lives before guards arrive. Steamboat inspection system is revised.

1904 W. H. Reynolds opens Dreamland. This most lavish Coney amusement park costs $3.5 million and has a million lights with 100,000 bulbs on a 375-foot tower. ● *Strand*, new 3,000 seat movie theater, opens (Broadway/47th Street). *New York Times Tower* opens with a fireworks display. 1st New Year's Eve celebration in Times Square.

1905 Fashionable N.Y. centers now on 58th Street and Fifth Avenue. ● *April 12 Hippodrome*, city's largest arena, opens on Sixth Avenue.

1905 William Entenmann's bakery moves to Bay Shore, Long Island (*see 1898*).

1904 City mayoral term extends from 2 to 4 years.

1905 *November 7* Amid blatant fraud, democrat George B McClellan re-elected as mayor after a vicious fight with political rival and newspaper magnate William R. Hearst. McClellan's government is efficient and honest. He expands city's water supply and tries to expand subway system.

1904 Joseph Pulitzer initiates Pulitzer Prize with $16,500 donation to Columbia University. ● Geore M. Choen's *Give My Regards* to Broadway.

1905 Photographers Alfred Stieglitz and Edward Steichen open "291" gallery.

1904 *October 27* Manhattan's 1st electric-powered subway by I.R.T. opens, from City Hall to 145th Street – takes 26 minutes, fare 5¢.

1905 1st crossing of Staten Island ferry.

1907 Agreement between U.S. Department of State and Japan to end direct migration.

1906 *September* Ota Benga, 23-year-old Belgian Congo Pygmy, is displayed in Bronx Zoo cage. Outraged black clergy insist he must have freedom of zoo grounds but he continues to sleep in primate house. He is finally sent to a Brooklyn orphan asylum and then to a Virginian seminary. He commits suicide in 1916. ● Architect Stanford White shot by his mistress's husband on roof of Madison Square Gardens which he had built in 1890.

1907 Scott Joplin moves to Manhattan. He publishes more than 20 works, including his opera*Treemonisha*.

1906 *June 30* Happyland amusement park opens at Staten Island.

1907 *July 30* Horse-drawn omnibus has final run along Fifth Avenue – replaced by gasoline-powered buses. ● *October 1* 1st metered taxicab. ● 800-room *Plaza Hotel* opens (Central Park South). ● Colony Club established for Society women. ● Illuminated time ball on New Year's Eve in Times Square.

1907 J.P. Morgan's $30 million loan spares city financial panic. ● *October* Proctor & Gamble open 77-acre Port Ivory complex on Staten Island; it will close 1991. ● Paris jeweler Cartier opens at 712 Fifth Avenue, 1st commercial building there.

1906 St. John's College now a university. ● E.W. Scripps founds United Press.

1907 Pierpont Morgan Library completed for J. P. Morgan's collection of books and manuscripts. ● *January 22* Metropolitan Opera stages U.S. premiere of Richard Strauss's *Salome* – thought so scandalous it is not repeated until 1934. ● 1st of *Ziegfeld Follies* staged in N.Y. ● Scott Joplin sets up office in West 29th Street to compose and arrange ragtime.

1906 Irving Berlin, a singing waiter at a Pell Street café is paid 37¢ for his 1st published song.

1906 Streets laid out for development in Forest Hills, Queens.

1907 United States Custom House dedicated at Bowling Green. ● Motor buses replace last horse-drawn public transport. Metered taxi cabs appear.

1909 *September/ October* Hudson-Fulton Celebration of 2 key events – Henry Hudson's discovery of Hudson River (1609) and launching of world's 1st steamboat service on river (1807). On 2 October over a million incandescent bulbs illuminate bridges, skyscrapers, ships, civic buildings and monuments. ● *September 29/ October 4* Wilbur Wright takes off from Governors Island for 1st flight over water and buzzes Statue of Liberty. On October 4 he flies above American fleet in Hudson River.

Wilbur Wright PB

1908 *February* Chief Joel Skidmore – last Canarsie Indian and officer in Kings County Supreme Court 1827-1907 dies aged 97.

1909 John D. Rockefeller is world's 1st billionaire.

1908 *January 10* 3 firemen die in blaze that destroys Parker Building. Fire hoses substandard. Fire department's own H.Q. not fireproof and telegraph system inadequate. Fire commissioner resigns.

1909 Police lieutenant Petrosino murdered while investigating someone from Sicily. Many suspect murder linked to organized crime.

1909 National City Bank now nation's largest (assets of $334 million a 10-fold increase since 1890).

1908 Isadora Duncan appears at Metropolitan Opera House, dancing barefoot on empty stage. ● Brooklyn Academy of Music opens.

1909 *Amsterdam News* launched – nation's oldest continuously published black newspaper.

1908 47-story, 612-foot Singer Building (Broadway/Liberty Street) completed, world's tallest for a year. ● Subways expand to Brooklyn and Bronx.

1909 700-foot Metropolitan Life Tower opens at Madison Square supplanting Singer Building as world's tallest. Tower is modeled after San Marco campanile, Venice. ● Completion of Manhattan and Queensborough Bridges.

Queensborough Bridge DP

1911 *March 25* Triangle Shirtwaist factory fire (Washington Place/Greene Street) kills 146 women, mostly Italian and Jewish, in less than 15 minutes. Many jump from 10th-floor windows rather than burn. Owners had locked exits but escape prosecution. In June, Factory Investigating committee forms. 36 new regulations made in 4 years.

1910 545,000 Italian residents in city. By 1914, Italian immigrants had sent $750 million to Italy. ● 41% of city's population are immigrants. ● Mayor William J Gaynor shot by discharged dockworker.

1911 *April* Record 11,745 immigrants on one day at Ellis Island.

1910 Manhattan's population reaches 23 million. ● Bohemian Hall opens in Astoria – city's last beer garden.

1911 1st black police officer, Samuel Battle, hired in city. ● Bellevue opens nations' 1st ambulatory cardiac clinic.

1910 New York Theological Seminary moves to Morningside Heights.

1910 Morris Park Racecourse burns (*see 1890*). ● W.E.B. Du Bois to edit *Crisis*, 1st magazine devoted exclusively to black writers' work. ● Premier of Puccini's *Girl of the Golden West* at Metropolitan Opera.

1911 New York Public Library completed ● At Tompkins Square, 10,000 witness finals of 1st interpark athletic contests. ● Polo Grounds (157th Street at Harlem River) razed by fire. Replaced with new concrete structure.

1910 Madison Avenue Bridge over Harlem River replaced. ● Opening of Long Island Rail Road Tunnel.

1911 *September 8* Pennsylvania Station opens, designed by McKim, Mead & White after Rome's Caracalla baths. Penn Tunnels bring newly electrified Long Island Railroad (LIRR) into station. ● *July 18* Board of Aldermen abolish tolls on Queensborough Bridge.

1912 *April 14* Bound for New York,*Titanic* hits iceberg and sinks. "Mrs Straus declared she would not leave her husband. They were standing arm in arm as the last boat left . . . she clung to him, and they went down arm in arm." 3 New York millionaires perish – Isidor Strauss, Benjamin Guggenheim and Colonel John Jacob Astor III whose 20-year-old son inherits $87 million.

Titanic PL

1912 Edna Ferber, Sinclair Lewis, Dorothy Parker, J.D. Salinger and Anaïs Nin live and write on Upper West Side.

1913 Vast women's suffrage parades.

1912 Investigation of police corruption reveals payoffs involving saloons, gamblers, and prostitutes. Police Lt. Charles Becker and 4 accomplices convicted of murder and sentenced to death.

1913 Salvation Army's largest, oldest shelter opens at 225 Bowery; holds 2,235. Original purpose was to be a bed and breakfast hotel for railroad and merchant marine retirees.

1913 J.P. Morgan & Company build at 23 Wall Street. Skyscrapers now being erected in Lower Manhattan but Morgan Bank want an unmarked, small, white marble H.Q. The lack of a name on exterior shows that those wealthy enough to bank there need no introduction.

1913 *November 4* John P Mitchel elected mayor, with 355,888 votes. At 34, he is youngest to win this office.

1912 *October 5* Dodgers lose to Giants in their last game in Washington Park, home field since 1898.

1913 More than 1/4 of a million visit 69th Regiment Armory modern art show. ● World's 1st movie palace, Regent Theater, built (116th Street/Seventh Avenue) ● 1st crossword puzzle published.

1912 *July* New York Connecting Railroad, begin building Hell Gate Bridge. When joined above East River in 1915, arms are only 5/16 inch apart.

1913 Woolworth Building completed – tallest in the world. ● New Grand Central Terminal opens at midnight. Ceiling shows constellations reversed. Professor Jacoby of Columbia provided sketch but claims artist put design on floor instead of holding it above his head. Charles Gullbrandsen, who worked on original and repainted it in 1944, said it was, "decoration, not a map".

1914 On New Year's Day, Bronx becomes state's 62nd county. Last Alderman Murphy is 1st Democratic Party county leader, operating from his saloon near Borough Hall until he dies (1922).

1915 *June 24* City's official flag and seal unveiled; marks 150th Anniversary of English taking New Amsterdam. ● May *Lusitania* sails from Pier 54; a German U-Boat sinks her off Ireland. 1,198 perish, including 128 Americans.

1914 Bomb squad created after terrorist attacks. ● *December 8* N.Y.P.D. appoint 1st black officer, Samuel Jesse Battle. ● Seamstress Mary P. Jacobs makes 1st brassiere.

1915 Typhoid Mary finally discovered after vanishing in 1910. Implicated in over 50 typhoid fever cases and 3 deaths, she spends rest of her life in prison.

1914 Federal Reserve Bank of New York receives over $99 million in commercial bank deposits on opening day.

1914*Watch Your Step* is Irving Berlin's 1st Broadway Show.

1915 Irving Berlin's *Stop, Look and Listen* features 1st shadow dance, in which a woman stripteases behind backlit sheet. ● Colonel Ruppert and Colonel Huston buy Yankees for $460,000. Team wear legendary pinstripes for 1st time.

1914 Municipal Building complete.

Municipal Building PB

1915 Brooklyn Garden's Japanese Garden opens, designed by Takeo Shiota. ● *June 22* 1st subway through Queensboro Tunnel between Grand Central and Queens. Service reaches Queensboro Plaza November, 1916.

1916 Over 8,000 children are victims of city's worst polio epidemic; 2,362 die.

1917 Eddie Cantor (singer and comedian) joins *Ziegfeld Follies* at $400 a week. ● *April 1* Scott Joplin dies – buried in St Michael's Cemetery, Astoria.

1916 *April 29* Cloak, Suit and Skirt Manufacturer's Protective Association begin lockout. 60,000 garment workers idle until August. ● Washington Memorial Arch: Hermon A MacNeil's statue *Washington in War* complete. ● Margaret Sanger opens nation's 1st birth control clinic, but is soon jailed.

1917 Motor patrol cars with radios introduced to police department. ● Wartime curfew 1 am. ● Steel net strung underwater across Narrows to stop German U-boats. ● German boats in New York Harbor taken over by Customs. ● 15,000 blacks march down Fifth Avenue to protest East St Louis race riots.

1916 Florentine neo-Renaissance palazzo fortress built for Federal Reserve Bank of New York – based on 15th-century Florentine banking family's Palazzo Strozzi. ● *October 17* Battleship *Arizona* commissioned at Brooklyn Navy Yard.

1917 Jamaica Bay closed to oystering by court order. ● Jeweler Cartier moves into 52nd Street mansion. Morton Plant reputedly sells building to him in exchange for a 2-strand pearl necklace for his wife.

1917 Edward Johnson, Republican from Harlem, is 1st black elected to state legislature. ● *November 6* Democrat John Hylan elected mayor.

1916 Term "Ashcan School" 1st coined by cartoonist Art Young for realist artists.

1917 German opera cut from Metropolitan's Opera's repertory for duration of war.

1916 *July 25* Zoning Resolution, 1st in U.S. to regulate size and use of buildings and protect against industrial and commercial invasion.

1917 *July 26* Final run of last horsecar line from Broadway to Ninth Avenue. ● New Catskill Aqueduct joins Croton system. ● Opening of Hell Gate Bridge.

1917-18 Deaths in World War from all boroughs: 7,446. ● 1st regular airmail route in U.S. set up between New York and Washington DC.

1919 *May 8* Navy's NC-4 flying boat leaves makes 1st transatlantic crossing; arrives May 31 in Plymouth, England.

1918 Fomer mayor John P Mitchel now in Army Air Corps. On July 6, he falls out of an open cockpit plane during a training flight. Garden City military airfield renamed in his honor. ● Flu kills 12,000 in New York (20 million people worldwide).● 102 die when BRT train derailed.

1919 *December 21* Russian-born Emma Goldman stripped of citizenship for opposing American participation in war) and with 248 others, deported.

1918 Mayor Hylan disbands Confidential Squad, investigating police corruption. New police commissioner, R. Enright, banishes Lewis Valentine, dedicated Squad member, to distant post. ● 97 die in Brooklyn subway accident when, during transit strike, inexperienced motorman takes curve at 45 m.p.h. instead of 6 m.p.h.

1919 Federal government buys Vanderbilt estate in New Dorp for a military airfield, named for Captain J. E. Miller, 1st American aviator killed in action. ● Trinity Church no longer requires parishioners to rent pews.

Trinity Church DP

1919 Philip Morris (tobacco and food processing) becomes publicly traded firm.

1918 Washington Memorial Arch: Sterling Calder's*Washington in Peace* completed. ● Official Directory of the City of New York published, listing agencies and public officials with addresses and salaries. In 1984 renamed *The Green Book*.

1919 St. Thomas Choir School opens, 1st church-affiliated boarding school for choirboys. ● New York Daily News – city's 1st tabloid. ● Theater rehearsals long and unpaid. Poorly paid actors often stranded after traveling roadshows. Just before curtain-up, actors throughout city strike. Equity secures 8-performance week and closed shop. ● Sun newspaper moves into A T ● Stewart's 1846 marble palace (Broadway/ Chambers Street). ● Sunday baseball legalised. ● Harlem Speedway open to automobiles.

1918 Tsar Nicholas II and family murdered in Russia

USA & WORLD EVENTS

1901 President McKinley assassinated

1901 Queen Victoria dies (reigned since 1837)

1903 Wright Brothers aeroplane flies

1905 *Theory of Relativity* published by Einstein

1906 San Francisco earthquake and fire kill 1,000

1908-27 Henry Ford's Model T built (15 million made)

1912 Captain Scott's ill-fated South Pole expedition

1914 Panama Canal opens

1914-18 War in Europe

1915 *Lusitania* sunk by a German submarine

1917 US declares war on Germany

1918 Armistice signed in Europe

1919 US Seaplanes cross Atlantic

1920-1933 Prohibition

Prohibition –Eighteenth Amendment – effective nationally, renders sale, consumption, transport and manufacturing of alcoholic beverages illegal. Congressman Fiorello La Guardia denounces it as unenforceable and discriminatory toward immigrants and workers. City becomes leading site for illegal alcohol, rumrunners or bootleggers, speakeasies and blind pigs.

1920 *September 16* A horse-drawn cart filled with dynamite causes explosion in Wall Street, kills 33 and injures 400 outside J. P. Morgan's H.Q. Only 1 person in bank injured. Incident unsolved. Pockmarks still visible in stone.

1920 Police department hire 1st black policewoman, Lawon R. Bruce.

1920 *May 30* At Coney Island, 150-foot high Wonder Wheel opens plus Nathan Handwerker's *Nathan's Famous*, selling hot dogs, beer, malteds and hamburgers at a nickel each.

BS

● 1st traffic light installed (42nd Street/Fifth Avenue).

1920 Frances Steloff opens Gotham Book mart (West 47th Street).

1920 $150,000 spent in 1916 alone by suffragist organizations, Tammany Hall's backing, and women's role in World War I help win voting rights for women in Nineteenth Amendment to U.S. Constitution.

1920 *The Little Review* publishes James Joyce's *Ulysses* in instalments – is fined $100 in an obscenity suit lead by New York Society for Suppression of Vice.

1920 *May 31* Hero Park in Tompkinsville dedicated, honoring 144 Staten Islanders killed in World War I. ● Prohibition means *Knickerbocker* Hotel on Broadway becomes an office building. Parrish's Old King Cole mural in bar is removed – now in St Regis Hotel.

1920 Prohibition begun

1920 Gandhi leader of Indian Independence Movement

1920 Women's Suffrage

1922 *June 15* Great Fire in summer homes at Beach 59th Street and Larkin Avenue; 400 buildings burn.

1921 *October 25* Newspaperman William Barclay "Bat" Masterson – gunslinger, gambler, lawman – dies at his typewriter. ● 30% of city population is Jewish.

1922 F Scott Fitzgerald and Zelda (married in St Patrick's Cathedral, 1920) move to 6 Gateway Drive, Great Neck. In the "nifty little Babbit house," as Zelda called it, he writes *The Great Gatsby*.

St Patrick's Cathedral PB

1921 Town hall opens (West 43rd Street).

1922 Harlem's Cotton Club opens with black entertainers performing for a mostly white audience.

PL

Cotton Club

1921 *April 30* Port of New York Authority created to develop port facilities. Territory extends 20 miles in all directions of Statue of Liberty. ● *August 31* Prince's Bay Lighthouse, in operation since 1828, extinguished.

1921 *November 8* Mayor Hyland re-elected.

1921 *Shuffle Along* by *Blake and Sissle* opens – 1st Broadway revue with all-black cast. ● Dempsey-Cartier heavyweight championship at Madison Square Garden is 1st million-dollar gate.

1922 *February* 1st issue of Reader's Digest published by DeWitt Wallace and Lil A. Wallace from basement room under a Greenwich Village speakeasy. By 1970 monthly sales will reach 17 million copies.

1921 US Bureau of the Budget restricts spending of government funds

1921 Modern Turkey founded

1921 Washington Naval Convention

1924 World War I, "red scare" and fear of new wave of arrivals leads to immigration quota system favoring Nordics from U.K. and Germany. Limit of 150,000 for countries outside Western Hemisphere discriminates against Italians, southern and eastern Europeans, and excludes Asians.

1923 Elkan Naumberg donates limestone bandshell on Bethesda Mall, Central Park. Irving Berlin, Duke Ellington, John Philip Sousa and Grateful Dead will perform here.

1924 *December* Typhoid outbreak: Health Commissioner closes all shellfish beds in harbor. ● Harlem Renaissance: Writers and artists arrive to join artistic and literary movement. Magazine *Opportunity* and meetings bring together prominent black writers and white publishers. Many writers launched.

1923 Clothing workers open independent labor bank, Amalgamated Bank of New York.

1924 Huge Federal Reserve Bank at 33 Liberty Street opens, designed like a Florentine palazzo. 80 feet below Nassau Street vast vaults contain gold reserves.

1923 *March 23* 1st issue of *Time Magazine* has 32 pages and sells for 15¢ Circulation of 1st issue 9,000 copies. ● Museum of the City of New York founded:in Gracie Mansion. ● 1st professional soccer league in U.S., American Soccer League, includes an N.Y.C. team. ● Yankee Stadium opens in Bronx

1924 *July 8* Municipal radio station WNYC-Am goes on air. ● Hearst founds tabloid newspaper *The Mirror. Herald* and *Tribune* merge as *Herald-Tribune*. ● Jazz focus moves from Chicago to New York with Louis Armstong and lax prohibition.

1923 Police department take control of taxi licensing after complaints about dirty, dangerous, uninsured cabs used for holdups, bootlegging and burglaries. 16,000 licensed cabs in city. ● City starts to dismantle old elevated railways.

1924 *June 7* 120-foot Eternal Light Memorial dedicated in Madison Square Park. Topped with a glowing star, it honors Americans who fell in World War I.

1922 Tutankhamun's tomb discovered

1923 Klu Klux Klan exposed

1925 Robert Moses begins 40-year career as city's master builder.

1926 In Kaufman's drug-store Lenox Avenue, Congressman Fiorello La-Guardia undermines Prohibition by demonstrating how to make beer. ● *August 6* 19-year-old Gertrude Ederle of Manhattan is 1st woman to swim English Channel, cutting 2 hours off previous record. She has ticker-tape parade up Broadway's Canyon of Heroes. Aquacade built for 1939 World Fair will be named in her honor.● When film star Rudolf Valentino dies crowds throng streets. ● Magician, Houdini, dies in escape routine on Halloween.

1925 Luciano-Costello gang pays $10,000 to Police Commissioner's office to allow their gambling interests to remain unmolested

1926/1928 George McLaughlin appointed to clean up police department. Lewis Valentine returns to head Confidential Squad but his vigor creates problems for Mayor Walker. In 1928 police commissioner Whalen will demote Valentine and disband unit.

1925 Steinway & Sons move into Steinway Hall showroom (111 West 57th Street). Façade depicts Brahms, Liszt, Chopin, Mozart, Schubert, Grieg and Bach.

Steinway Hall DP

1926 *November 2* Robert F. Wagner elected to 1st of 4 terms in the U.S. Senate.

1925 Tim Mara forms New York Giants football team. Over 70,000 fans watch them play Red Grange and Chicago Bears at Polo Grounds in December.

1926 *May 26* New York City Board of Higher Education launched. ● Long Island University founded.

1925 B.R.T. (Brooklyn Rapid Transit Company becomes B.M.T. (Brooklyn-Manhattan Transit Corporation). ● Steam railroad on Staten Island switches to electric. ● Women become taxicab drivers; Taxicab Commission formed.

1925 Baird + others invent television

1927 *June 13* 750,000 pounds of ticker tape and paper greet Charles Lindbergh to celebrate solo flight across Atlantic.

Charles Lindbergh PB

● Bell Telephone Laboratory sends television pictures from N.Y. to Washington and 1st telephone service between N.Y. and London.

1927 Mae West spends 10 days in a Roosevelt Island workhouse, fined $500 for giving a lewd performance in Broadway show *Sex*.

1928 In memory of John P Mitchel, a memorial is dedicated in Central Park plus a flagpole before 42nd Street library.

1927 Police department launches Air Service Unit with small airplanes. ● *June 26* Cyclone roller coaster opens in Coney Island: 105-second ride with 90-foot, 68° drop.

Roller Coaster

PB

1928 1st animated electric sign in Times Square.

1927 Yeshiva University founded in Washington Heights. ● *Showboat* opens on Broadway. ● 1st talking movie *The Jazz Singer.*

1928 Silent-screen star Harold Lloyd makes *Speedy*, a comic dash through city featuring Babe Ruth. Buster Keaton makes *The Cameraman*. ● *November 18* Walt Disney's *Steamboat* Willy at *Colony Theater* introduces Mickey Mouse.

1927 *November 12* Holland Tunnel opens, named for chief engineer Clifford Holland, 1st tunnel in world specifically designed for automobiles. Next day 51,748 vehicles use it. Tolls: 50¢ for cars, 25¢ for motorcycles, $1 for trucks and buses. Ventilation system designed by engineer, Ole Singstand.

1928 *October 1* Newark Airport opens – soon U.S.'s busiest

1927 Transatlantic radio telephone service inaugurated

1927 Lindbergh solo flight over Atlantic

1928 Earhart is 1st woman to fly across Atlantic

1929 on *October 14* Borough's official flag 1st raised at Borough Hall.

1930 17% of city population is of Italian descent; 25% of immigrants in 1930s are Jews escaping Nazism. ● *August 6* After emptying 2 bank accounts and selling $16,000 in stock, Judge Joseph Crater, implicated in Tammany scandals, disappears for ever.

1929 *October 24* Police department founds Air Service Division (later Aviation Unit) at Glenn Curtiss Airport, with 4 flying boats, 12 pilots and 24 mechanics – 1st such unit in U.S. ● Morrisania Hospital opens, 1st public hospital in Bronx.

1930 Rikers Island dump closes: island had grown from 80 to 400 acres, with 4 cranes, 15 miles of track, 12 engines and 30 flat cars to move garbage from scows.

1929 *October 24* (Black Thursday) Stock market crashes.On Tuesday 29, 16,410,030 shares change hands.

1929 *November 5* Mayor Walker reelected.

1929 *November 9* Museum of Modern Art opens (Fifth Avenue/57th Street). 43,000 visit in 1st month to view works by Cézanne, Gauguin, Seurat and Van Gogh. Abby A. Rockefeller is treasurer. In 1932 Nelson Rockefeller joins board.

1930 *April 22* Board of Higher Education create Brooklyn College, consolidating branches of Hunter College for women and City College for men.

1929 Glenn Curtiss Airport opens at North Beach. ● Brooklyn's tallest building, 512-foot Williamsburgh Bank, complete and crowned by world's largest 4-sided clock.

1930 *January 22* Workers dig foundations for Empire State Building. An average 3,000 men worked on building every day. Framework is complete 25 weeks after 1st steel column riveted. ● Brooklyn has trolley coaches (rubber-tired buses attached to overhead wires). ● 77-storey art deco Chrysler Building finished, tallest in world then,

PB

1929 Stock Market crash

1930 Gandhi leads revolt in India

1930 Particle accelerator, Cyclotron (atom smasher) invented

1930 Flash bulb introduced

1931 *December 13* Winston Churchill forgets cars drive on the right here and, looking wrong way, is hit by a car on Fifth Avenue. Once recovered, he resumes his lecture tour, speaking about Anglo-American cooperation and the coming conflict with Communism.

Winston Churchill PB

1931 After removing rivals, Masseria and Marazano, Charles "Lucky" Luciano takes over as boss of all bosses, controlling a 5-family syndicate.

1931 Schwarx Toy Bazaar now uptown at 745 Fifth Avenue.

1931 Waldorf-Astoria Hotel opens (Park Avenue.

DP

Waldorf-Astoria Hotel

IF *Christmas trees have been placed in the Rockefeller Center for over 70 years*

1931 On Fifth Avenue builders begin Rockefeller Center's and launch city tradition by placing a decorated Christmas tree on site in December.

1931 Whitney Museum of American Art opens. ● C F. Jenkins opens 1st television station in N.Y. C.B.S. starts experimental TV station. ● College basketball games, to benefit city Relief Fund, are a sell out at Madison Square Garden. ● On Christmas Day, Metropolitan Opera's performance of *Hansel and Gretel* is 1st radio broadcast of a complete opera.

1931 *May 1* Empire State Building on Fifth Avenue, with 102 floors, is world's tallest building. Construction estimated at $50 million but is $5 million under budget and ready 6 weeks early. Depression means it is only half rented until after World War II, so is nicknamed Empty State Building. ● George Washington Bridge and Bayonne Bridge open.

Empire State Building DP

1932 *June 26* Father Francis Patrick Duffy dies. He received a Distinguished Service Cross as chaplain of 69th New York Regiment during World War 1, then served a Hell's Kitchen parish.

1933 Severe economic problems in black neighborhoods: murder rate there rises to 35.1 per 100,000 residents compared with citywide average of 4.3. ● Prohibition repealed. Beer flows again a minute after midnight on April 7.

1932 *April 29* Depression worsens. Board of Estimate allocate $5 million for immediate relief 11% of population, receive public or private charity. ● 17 shantytowns in Central Park.

1933 1st electric billboard in Times Square, a steaming A & P coffee cup. signs for Kool and Camel cigarettes follow, with famous smoke rings (used 1941-66).

1933 Fiorella LaGuardia begins 3 terms as mayor.

1933 R.C.A. Building, Rockefeller Center, opens.

1932 Tiffany Studios bankrupt. Founded in 1837, firm peaked in early 1900s with its popular multicolored leaded-glass lamps.

1932 Tammany corruption investigated.

DP

1932 Little Red Schoolhouse moves to Bleecker Street. ● Radio City Music Hall opens – world's largest indoor theater, seating 5,874. ● Vaudevillian Jack Benny begins 23-year career in radio

1933 *March 2* King Kong, starring Empire State Building in its screen debut, opens in N.Y.

PB *King Kong topiary*

1933 *July 15* Grand Central Parkway open from Kew Gardens to Nassau County.

1933 Roosevelt is President ● Hitler Chancellor of Germany

1935 *February 9* Boys find 125-pound, 8-foot alligator in a sewer on 123rd Street near East River. They drag it out manhole and kill it with snow shovels. Decades of city sewer stories ensue.

1934 *January 1* Mayor Fiorella La Guardia appoints Robert Moses city's 1st Parks Commissioner. Chief Inspector Valentine Lewis tells commanders, "Be good or be gone. . . There is no room . . . for parasites and drones." He is made Police Commissioner in September. In 4 years, he fires 221 officers. 70 others commit suicide.

1934 United States Supreme Court stops ocean dumping. Soon 90 dumps and landfills open. ● 10 lawyers found Women's Bar Association of New York: 1st president, Hilda Ginsburg Schwartz – later a judge.

1935 21,000 homeless live in city shelters. ● *March 19* Harlem riots. 16-year-old Lino Rivera is caught stealing a penknife; he escapes in struggle but rumors spread that he is killed and rioters loot stores on 125th Street. 75 arrested; 57 civilians and 7 police officers injured.

1935 Bettmann, Jewish refugee, arrives with 25,000 pictures, launching 5-million image Bettman Archive.

1934 Throgs Neck Lighthouse (1827) decommissioned.

1935 Bronx Terminal Market opens.

1934 Nelson Rockerfeller has a Diego Rivera fresco he had commissioned destroyed because Lenin is depicted therein.

1934 Apollo Theater changes ownership: blacks are allowed in audience. Bessie Smith sings the blues on opening night.

1935 Babe Ruth reties from baseball. ● Hayden Planetarium (built with federal funds and $150,000 donation from banker Charles Hayden) opens at American Museum of Natural History.

Museum of Natural History DP

● Monroe College founded in Bronx.

1935 Parks Department unearth stones and reconstruct Old Stone House, Third Street, in Park Slope.

1936 Riker's Island penitentiary opens. ● *July 9* 106° – highest recorded temperature in city.

1936 Former mayor Jimmy Walker marries longtime mistress Betty Compton (divorced 1941).

1936 *February 7* Welfare Island jail closes; $12 million Rikers Island facility opens. ● *June 10* Staten Island Zoo opens.

1936 American Labor Party founded. In 1937, 5 A.L.P. members on City Council. ● *November 3* Voters approve a new charter. It abolishes Board of Aldermen. New City Council to be elected by proportional representation; office of deputy mayor and City Planning Commission set up.

1936 *December 3* John Hogan and Elliott Sanger form Interstate Broadcasting Company and turn Hogan's experimental W.2.X.R. into W.Q.X.R., 96.3 FM. From a room above a Long Island City garage, Hogan broadcasts his own classical records to radios within a mile. In 1944 when *Times* buys W.Q.X.R., it has largest audience of any classical station. ● *Life* Magazine founded. ● Joe DiMaggio joins New York Yankees who will win 7 pennants and 6 World Series by 1943 and be dubbed the "Bronx Bombers". ● *June 19* German heavyweight boxing champion Max Schmeling defeats Joe Louis in 12 rounds at Yankee Stadium. ● Berlin Olympics: American officials have to replace Jews, Glickman and Stoller, for 400-meter relay. Star athlete Glickman becomes New York sports announcer, calling games of Knicks, Jets, Giants and local colleges. ● Skating rink at Rockefeller Center opens on Christmas Day. A 12-year-old girl and with an 88-year-old man skate exhibition waltz . Omero C Catan, "Mr First" is 1st paying patron. ● Astoria Pool opens in time to host Olympic swimming and diving trials and Downing Stadium in time for track and field trials.

1936 Vanderbilt mansion in New Dorp demolished. ● *July 11* Opening of Triborough Bridge (25-cent toll) and Grand Central Parkway to Kew Gardens. 11 million vehicles cross in 1937 (55 million by 1996).

Triborough Bridge DP

1935 Radar invented

1935-36 Abyssinian War

1936-39 Spanish Civil War

1936 Oil found in Saudi Arabia

1936 Edward VIII abdicates – George VI becomes British king

1936 Revolt in Japan

It was the invention of the lift by Otis in 1852, together with new building techniques using industrial steel, that made skyscrapers possible.

Building in pyramidal style from the 1920s onwards meant that light was not restricted from surrounding buildings and also reduced winds created at street level.

In the late 1920s members of the native Canadian Caughnawaga tribe were employed as scaffolders because they had no fear of heights.

Battery Maritime Building 11 South Street Built 1907
This was the terminal for the ferries to Brooklyn from 1909-38 (and prior to that was where Dutch Colonial ships set sail for Holland). Fronted by distinctive arches 300 feet (91m.), it has scrolled columns and Beaux Arts latticework and rosettes. The steel and ironwork frontage has been painted green to look like copper. Today's tall towers, including One New York Plaza, rise behind this piece of history.

Statue of Liberty National Monument

County Courthouse 1871
City Hall Park
Now known as the Municipal Court Building

The County Courthouse is famous not for its architecture but for the infamous dealings of Tammany Hall and its control over city politics and finances – and for the length of time taken to build the Courthouse. William Marcy Tweed and his Ring made this the most expensive public building in the U.S. then, with a final bill of $12million, 3/4 of which was fraudulent and lined the pockets of Tweed and his associates.

Governors Island Support Center

Empire State Building 1929
Fifth Avenue
(33-34th Streets)
102 floors
1,454 feet (443.2 m) high plus antenna 204 feet (62 metres)

Built at a rate of 4 storys a week.
6,500 windows.
73 elevators.

1,860 steps.
Faced with 10 million bricks.
Completed in 1 year and 45 days (one month ahead of schedule).
Observation deck on 86th floor is visited by 3.5 million people a year.
A B25 US bomber crashed into the 79th story in heavy fog in 1945.
Suicide barrier was erected

in 1947 after 12 suicides. Since then 6 determined people have still managed to kill themselves.
Couples can marry in the Empire State Building on Valentine's Day.
In an annual event, contestants race up 1,860 steps to the 102nd floor, occasionally in less than 10 minutes.

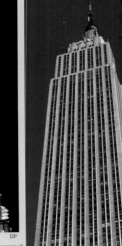

Empire State Building colors

Red, black and green
January's 3rd Monday – Martin Luther King Jr. day
Green
17 March – St. Patrick's Day
22 April – Earth Day
Red, white and blue
National holidays
February's 3rd Monday – President's Day
May – Armed Forces Day
May's last Monday – Memorial Day
June 14 – Flag Day
July 4 – Independence Day
September's 1st Monday – Labor Day
November 11 – Veterans Day
Red
February 14 – Valentine's Day

Yellow and red
Spring (March-April) and Easter Week
Blue, white and red
May 4 – Anniversary of Israel's Independence
December – First day of Hanukkah
Blue
May's 3rd Monday – Policeman's Day
Red, yellow and green
June 10 – Portugal Day
Yellow and green
September 7 – Brazilian Independence Day
Purple and white
Late June – Gay Pride
Purple, brown and white
June – Osteoporosis Day
Red, white and green
October's 2nd Monday –

Columbus Day and discovery of America
Blue and white
March 25 – Anniversary of Greek Independence
October 24 – United Nations Day
Red and yellow
October-November – Autumn
Black, yellow and red
November 10 – Anniversary of German reunification
Pink and white
September – Breast Cancer Day
Green, white and orange
August 15 – Indian Independence Day
Red and green
December 14 to January 7 – Christmas Holidays
Unlit
December 1 – Aids Day

Madison Square Garden
Garden 1 1879-90
Garden 2 1890-1925 at Madison Square, Madison Avenue
Garden 3 1925-68 at Eighth Avenue, (49-50th Streets)
Garden 4 1968 at Seventh Avenue (33rd Street)

P.J. Barnum's earliest circus shows were held in the first Garden in the Great Roman Hippodrome – an arena made from converted railroad sheds.
Garden 2's tower was the 2nd highest structure in the city.
The architect of Garden 2, Stanford White, was murdered on the building's roof by jealous multimillionaire, Harry Thaw.
It was in the present building that Marilyn Monroe sang *Happy*

This picture depicts Garden 2

Birthday to you to President Kennedy in 1962.
Today's building is 10 stories high and covers 8 acres.
1.6 billion cups of beer, 1.2 million cups of soda and 180,000 hot dogs are sold annually here now.

Ellis Island National Monument

The buildings listed on the wheel at the front of the book section are pinpointed on this map.

Cooper Union 1859
Cooper Square
(Astor Place/Seventh Street)

This old iron-framed building was one of the earliest free educational establishments, financed by Peter Cooper whose fortune had been made in iron and who made the first rails for railroads. It was one of the first colleges to admit women students. Abraham Lincoln spoke here in February, 1860, at the launch of his presidential campaign.

Statue of Liberty 1886
Liberty Island (formerly Bedloes Island) Commissioned 1871 and finally dedicated. Height from ground to torch tip 305 ft 1 in. (92.99 m.)

This projected 1875 design changed: the final pedestal is different and Liberty faces the city – not out to sea as originally devised.
The statue's framework was designed by Gustav Eiffel of Eiffel Tower fame.

Trinity Church
Broadway at Wall Street
Parish founded 1697
Present building erected 1846
280 foot (86m) steeple

Tallest structure in New York until 1860s.
William Kidd attended this church.
A school for Indians and black slaves was held here in early 18th century.
Buried in the 2 1/2 acre churchyard are: Statesman Alexander Hamilton, William Bradford who founded the first New York newspaper, Francis Lewis who signed the Declaration of Independence, John Jacob Astor and Robert Fulton, the boat inventor.

Harrison Street
These restored Georgian houses hidden amongst the soaring 20th-century towers of Tribeca create a brief illusion of past times.

Wall Street Area Buildings
1 MLIB
2 Irvin T Co
3 NY Stock Ex
4 Bankers Trust
5 Equitable
6 Marine M B
7 40 Wall Street
8 OneChaseMan Plaza
9 Federal Reserve Bank
10 Bank of NY
11 City Bank FT
12 60 Wall Street

Republic National Bank

New York Stock Exchange 1865 14-16 Wall Street
Present home and entrance is on Broad Street (since 1903).

In 1792, 24 brokers signed an agreement under a buttonwood tree at 68 Wall Street and so founded the basis of the New York Stock Exchange. This neo-Classical façade has fine sculpted figures; winged Integrity protects Science Industry, Invention, Agriculture and Mining.
100 million transactions take place each day on the busy trading floor.

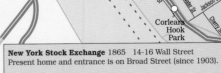

Map labels:
Hudson River
Jersey City Ferry
Battery Park City
North Park
North Cove Yacht Harbor
3 World Financial Center American Express
Rector Park
World Trade Center (in Memory)
Tribeca
SoHo
Alternative Museum
Federal Office Building
Woolworth Building
Civic Center
City Hall
Foley Square
Chinatown
Columbus Park
Chinese History Museum
Castle Clinton National Monument
Battery Park
US Custom House
Financial District
Battery Maritime Building
Wall Street
Municipal US Court Building
Bowery
Two Bridges
Upper Bay
Staten Island Ferry
Brooklyn Battery Tunnel
478
Ferry Terminal
Governor's Is Ferry
South Street Seaport
Bayonne Ferry
Brooklyn
Brooklyn Bridge
Manhattan Bridge
Lower East Side
Tenement Museum
Seward Park
Rutgers Park
Corlears Hook Park

Ethnic publications in city	
Haitian	3
Irish	2
Polish	2
Chinese	6
Russian	25
Swedish	1
Lithuanian	1
Norwegian	1

Elmhurst in Queens is home to people from 99 different countries. Newspapers in Polish, Arabic, English, Sanskrit, Gujarati, Spanish, Korean, Chinese, Greek, and Bengali can be found at one grocery store.

Chinese

In 1858 the first recorded Chinese immigrant, Cantonese Ah Ken, opened a cigar store on Park Row. In 1866, a second Cantonese, Wah Kee, arrived – from San Francisco, to open a vegetable and curio store in Pell Street. Over the next decade, many Chinese settlers arrived but in 1899 a Chinese Exclusion Act barred Chinese immigrants from naturalization, the first time an ethnic group had been excluded from the U.S. In 1965, the Immigration Reform Act allowed many Chinese families in the city to be reunited. Chinatown boomed as garment factories supported its economy, and by 1980 the Chinese population in the city was the biggest in the U.S.

Other Communities

Poles
Most Poles are Catholic and celebrate strong national traditions in the Pulaski Day parade on October 5.
Greeks
In Astoria, Queens, there is a strong Greek community.
Armenians
Many live in the Bronx.
Also . . .
Many Haitians, Latin Americans, Japanese, Koreans and Indians have settled in New York since the 1960s.

Ellis Island

In 1808, New York State purchased Ellis Island from Samuel Ellis's heirs and Ellis Island immigration center was launched January 1st, 1892. 2,250 immigrants were processed there on its first day of operation.
In 1897 fire razed the wooden buildings but by 1900, a new fire-proof structure was complete – to accommodate half a million annual immigrants. This too proved inadequate when the number soon reached over a million a year. The island was enlarged with landfill. The main structure was extended, a third floor added and 33 extra buildings raised.
In the huge registry room, health inspectors and officials checked each individual, refusing entry to criminals, mental defectives, contract laborers, the impoverished, and any suffering from contagious ailments or eye infections. None the less, 99% of the hopeful immigrants were granted entry in less than 8 hours. One-third of these took a ferry to the Battery and stayed in New York. The rest boarded trains for destinations throughout the U.S.
Marriages were held on Ellis Island because women were not allowed to leave the island with any man not related to them, including fiancés.
16 million immigrants had passed through the compound by 1924, but then mass immigration was stopped and immigrants were screened before leaving home. Ellis Island was used instead to detain those being deported. 145,000 immigrants returned home during the Great Depression. In World War II, 2,000 German sailors were interned at Ellis Island after being caught in Allied ports. The island was proclaimed a national monument in 1965, by which time 71% of immigrants to the U.S. had passed through Ellis Island, including Bob Hope, Irvine Berlin and Isaac Asimov.

Population increase in New York City	
1642	300
1664	1500
1703	4,375
1764	25,000
1800	60,515
1840	391,000
1855	622,924
1860	813,669
1900	3,437,202
1940	7,454,995
1950	7,891,957
1970	7,867,760
2000	7,322,564

Population facts in 1900
• 22% of the population were Irish by descent or birth.
• 25% (748,882) of the population was of German descent.
• 7,500 were Latin Americans. 50% were from the Caribbean.
• 6,321 Chinese residents lived in Chinatown.

DP

EI

Above: *Genuine immigrant baggage from the Ellis Island museum*
Right: *Queuing for the Ellis island ferry, circa 1910*
Below right: *Ellis Island Immigration Center today*
Below: *Many immigrants settled in cramped and squalid tenements*

PB

DP

HISTORICAL EVENTS · PEOPLE · LIFESTYLE · COMMERCE · POLITICS & RELIGION · CULTURE & ART · CITY STRUCTURE & DEVELOPMENT

1937–1938

1938 *September 20* Hurricane of '38, the Long Island Express, cuts new channels through barrier islands. ● *October 22* Chester Carlson produces 1st xerox photocopy in his Queens workshop.

1938 *July 17* Douglas Corrigan plans flight to California and takes off at 5.15 a.m. into cloud. 28 hours, 13 minutes, and 3,150 miles later he lands and asks in Dublin airport, "Where am I?" Wrong Way Corrigan becomes a folk hero, celebrated with a Broadway ticker-tape parade.

1937 N.Y.P.D. introduce 2-way radios in patrol cars. ● *October 23* Ward's Island Water Pollution Control Plant is city's 1st to treat sewerage.

1938 Passenger regulations, *No Smoking*, *No Spitting*, *No Littering*, posted in subways.

1938 Topps Chewing Gum Company to make baseball cards and chewing gum called Bazooka.

1937 Anne Farley of Bronx is city's 1st woman to serve as a juror.

1938 38,000 Communist Party members in N.Y. (80,000 in nation.)

1937 Guggenheim Museum founded. ● *Look* magazine founded.

1938 *January 16* Benny Goodman and sextet perform 1st jazz program at Carnegie Hall. Count Basie appears.

1937 *December 22* 8,216-foot center tube of Lincoln Tunnel opens. Omero C. Catan, "Mr First", pays 1st toll.

1938 597-foot radio antenna installed atop Brooklyn Tech. – now highest structure in Brooklyn.

1939–1940

1939 *April 30* World's Fair, *Building the World of Tomorrow* opens at Flushing Meadow. Roosevelt's address is 1st televised presidential speech but only a few technicians see it on experimental station. ● Columbia University team of physicists split atom.

1940 *July 4* Bomb explodes at British Pavilion at World's Fair; kills 2 bomb squad members.

1939 *May 20* 1st televised event at Madison Square Garden – part of a 6-day bicycle race. ● Police department's Aviation Unit reactivated, with 6 pilots and 6 mechanics. Anonymous donor gives 2 new engines, enabling city to order new planes. ● 6-level parking garage at 10 Rockefeller Plaza opens, 1st parking garage in a city office building.

1940 1st air-conditioned taxi, a 1940 Packard. ● 1st blood bank opened by Dr. Drew – not allowed to donate his own blood as he is black.

1940 Tiffany & Co moves to 57th Street/Fifth Avenue.

1939 *July 22* Jane M. Bolin is 1st black woman in nation appointed a judge. ● 22,000 drawn to a Nazi Americanism rally.

1940 Existence of Murder Inc. revealed: syndicate enforcement arm executes contracts on "bums".

1939 *May* Batman makes debut in *Detective Comics no 27*. The Caped Crusader protects Gotham City, modeled on N.Y.C. ● Rockefeller Center opens.

1940 *February 28* 1st televised basketball game, broadcast live from Madison Square Garden.

1939 *April 29* Bronx-Whitestone Bridge opens for easy access to new airport and World's Fair. Clason Point-College Point Ferry shuts down same day, last ferry serving Bronx and Queens.

1940 United States Custom House on Wall Street made a museum; dioramas depict Washington's inauguration. ● Midtown tunnel opens.

1941–1942

1942 Times Square blacked out during war.

Times Square

DP

1942 *February 9* During refit as a troop ship, liner *Normandie* burns in Hudson River. 1 death; 128 injured. ● *June 12* 4 German saboteurs captured after landing on Long Island.

1941 *November 12* Abe "Kid Twist" Reles falls 6 floors to his death from *Half Moon Hotel*, Coney Island, despite police stationed outside his door. He was to testify against the boss of Murder, Inc. Lucky Luciano claims police were paid $50,000 to push him out. Locals say: "The only law Kid Twist could understand was the law of gravity."

1941 Long Island *City Star-Journal* exposes house in Ridgewood as Nazi Bund H.Q. 1941 ● After attack on Pearl Harbor, Navy closes Woolworth's Building observation deck with its views of harbor and Navy Yard. It never reopens.

1942 Wartime: lights dim on Broadway. ● Army buys Paramount Studio, Astoria, for Signal Corps Photographic Center

1942 Rockefeller Center has 3 Christmas trees, 1 with red ornaments, 1 with white, 1 with blue.

1941 Diamond Dealers Club moves to 47th Street – handles 80% of all diamonds entering U.S.

Diamond Center DP

1941 Adam C. Powell, Jr. 1st black City Council member; 1st black member of Congress, for Harlem.

1941 *March* Vast mural by Spanish Jose M. Sert unveiled on lobby ceiling, 30 Rockefeller Plaza.

1942 *December 30* Frank Sinatra makes solo debut at *Paramount Theater* – an "Extra Added Attraction" with Benny Goodman Orchestra. ● La Guardia is 1st mayor to move into Gracie Mansion.

1941 Construction begins for international airport in Idlewild, Queens.

1942 *June 30* Last ferry between Manhattan and Brooklyn (Bay Ridge to Battery).

1943–1944

1944 *January 1* Battleship *Missouri* launched at Brooklyn Navy Yard. In 1945, Japanese will sign surrender on her foredeck, ending World War II.

1943 Mass migration of blacks fleeing South's poverty and racism; riots in Harlem. ● *February 1st* Having lived in West Avenue for 17 years, Rachmaninov becomes U.S. citizen but dies in March.

1944 Columbus Day Riot when Sinatra appears at *Paramount Theater*.

1943 Pap test for cervical cancer named after its "inventor", Papanicolaou (New York Hospital). ● *February* Bronx campus, Hunter College, turned over to Navy; 80,000 train there. ● *August 1* Riot in Harlem after policeman shoots black soldier. 6 killed. ● *August 30* 20 women became Port Authority's 1st female toll collectors at George Washington Bridge and Lincoln and Holland Tunnels.

1944 Organized crime leaders like Frank Costello (rich from slot machine network and rigged judicial appointments) and Joe Adonis (controls drug trade and Brooklyn docks) use wealth to dominate Tammany Hall and enter politics: close network of politics and crime.

1944 Black leader Adam Clayton Powell elected to Congress.

Adam Clayton Powell PB

● Worried about communist influence in Labor Party, Alex Rose and others found Liberal Party.

1943 *December 11* City Center open: 1923 Mecca temple acquired by city through tax foreclosure in Great Depression but now home to New York City Ballet and City Opera. ● New musical *Oklahoma* (Rodgers and Hammerstein) opens. ● *A Tree Grows in Brooklyn*, by Betty Smith, published. ● *September* W.N.Y.C.-F.M. on air.

1944 *January 18* 1st jazz concert at Metropolitan Opera House (Louis Armstrong, Billie Holiday, Benny Goodman). ● *On The Town* opens on Broadway.

1945–1946

1945 *Saturday July 28* B-25 bomber, in dense fog, crashes into 79th floor of Empire State Building. Minor structural damage, 14 killed and 26 injured. ● War ends. Times Square celebrates V-E Day on May 8 and V-J Day on August 15 when 1,000s jam square. At 7.03 p.m. news zipper on Times Tower declares: "Official Truman announces Japanese surrender".

End of WW II PL

1946 *February 14* United Nations select New York City as H.Q.

1945 Penicillin introduced; venereal disease brought under conrol. ● Sixth Avenue renamed Avenue of the Americas: New Yorkers never adopt name.

Avenue of the Americas

PB

1946 Bronx-born Bess Meyerson 1st Jewish contestant crowned Miss America.

1945 *November 6* William O'Dwyer elected 100th mayor.

1946 Land for United Nations in Turtle Bay bought by Rockefeller for $8.5 million: "If this property can be useful to you in meeting the great responsibilities entrusted to you by the people of the world, it would be a source of infinite satisfaction to me and my family." City to pay $5 million to help clear cattle, slaughterhouses, shanties and tenement houses, and resettle 270 residents. Street and waterfront rights to U.N. Grounds do not come under national, state, or city laws. U.N. has own police force, fire department and postal service, and employs 6,000.

1946 1st performances of Ballet Society. Reformed 1948 as New York City Ballet.

1946 Holocaust Memorial (Riverside Park) honors Warsaw Uprising and concentration camp victims. ● *December 23* N. Y. subway system has record 8,872,244 passengers.

1947–1948

1947 *December 26* 26.4 inches of snow in 24 hours halts city. ● *September 18* Parade along Queens Boulevard in Kew Gardens celebrates Greater New York's Golden Jubilee.

1948 *August 12* Due to be put on a plane for Soviet Union, Russian schoolteacher Oksana S Kasenkina jumps to freedom from 3rd floor of Soviet Consulate. She is made a U.S. citizen in 1954. ● Ed Sullivan hosts his 1st television show.

1947 Police department's Aviation Unit is 1st U.S. department to have helicopters.

1948 State legislature agree to fund city colleges. State University of New York established. ● C.B.S. television broadcast New Year's Eve live from Times Square.

1947 *September 20* Fiorello La Guardia dies.

1947 *A Streetcar Named Desire* by Tennessee Williams. ● *April* Dodger manager Durocher suspended, for mixing with gamblers. Jackie Robinson makes major-league debut at Ebbets Field, 1st African-American to play in major baseball league. 14,000 blacks attend. ● *April 27* Babe Ruth Day retires: his no.3 uniform is retired too!

1948 1st Tony Awards presented. ● *The Naked City* hits big screen. ● *June 13* Babe Ruth's last appearance at Yankee Stadium, for ballpark's 25th anniversary. He dies August 16. 1,000s of fans pay last respects to his body, laid out at Stadium.

1947 City's 1st fully air conditioned office building opens (445 Park Avenue). ● *June 1* Port Authority take over New York International, La Guardia and Newark Airports.

1948 *July 31* President Truman dedicates New York International Airport (Idlewild), the "front door" of the United Nations and largest commercial airport in world: "As the Statue of Liberty symbolized freedom to those who came here by sea, the New York International Airport should symbolize America's devotion to peace, among those who come by air." O. C. Catan,

1949–1950

1950 Greater New York (with surrounding suburbs) largest metropolis in world: 124 million people.

1950 Census reports 56% of city's population is foreign-born, or of foreign or mixed parentage. ● Severe drought. City hires meteorologist W. E. Howell as a rainmaker for $100 a day. He seeds clouds in Catskills. By February 1951, reservoirs are 99% full; drought declared over. Dr. Howel reckons he has increased rainfall by 14%.

1949 *August* Police and members of American Legion attack outdoor performance by Paul Robeson in Peeksville, claiming he and his audience are communists. ● Charlie "Bird" Parker performs at Birdland on Broadway and at Carnegie Hall.

DP *Carnegie Hall.*

1950 *Your Show of Show* on air, a 90-minute comedy program starring Sid Ceasar and Imogene Coca – runs until 1954. Comedy writers include Neil Simon, Mel Brooks, and Woody Allen.

1949 *November 8* Mayor O'Dwyer re-elected; Robert F Wagner Jr. elected Manhattan borough president.

1950 Robert Moses appointed to head Slum Clearance Committee.

1949 Arthur Miller's *Death of a Salesman* opens. ● *April 7* *South Pacific* opens at *Majestic Theater*: runs for 1,900+ performances into 1954.

1950 *Guys and Dolls* opens on Broadway.

1950 Castle Clinton, the Battery, designated national monument. ● May 25 Brooklyn-Battery Tunnel opens. To make way for Manhattan entrance, Little Syria demolished. ● December Port Authority Bus Terminal opens. ● United Nations Secretariat Building opens. ● Last trolley crosses Brooklyn.

United Nations DP

1951–1952

1951 Ethel Merman (born Astoria 1909) wins 1st and only Tony award for *Call Me Madam.*

1951 Trial of Julius and Ethel Rosenberg in U.S. District Court. Convicted of espionage in March, they are executed in electric chair at Sing Sing in June, 1953. ● Albert Anastasia takes over Gambino crime family after murder of Philip Mangano.

1952 *January 14* *Today Show* broadcast for 1st time from N.B.C. Studios, Rockefeller Center. ● Civilian Complaint Review Board created to address police brutality.

1952 New York's Franklin National Bank issues 1st credit card.

1951 Impellitteri succeeds O'Dwyer as acting mayor but fails to win Democratic support.

1952 Links between organized crime and city politics end as district leaders directly elected.

1951 *October 1st Honeymooners sketch on Cavalcade of Stars*. Later *The Honeymooners* moves to C.B.S. On October 15, *I Love Lucy* goes on air – set in Manhattan but filmed in Hollywood. ● Rumors that college basketball games at Madison Square Garden rigged. City College of New York win both N.I.T. and N.C.A.A. championships. District Attorney Frank Hogan discovers players are deliberately reducing margin of victory for point shaving. 32 players from 7 schools arrested. Devastating effect both on games and Madison Garden finances.

1951 *April 19* Port Authority begin helicopter flights to Idlewild from roof of H.Q. Heliport No 1, Pier 41, East River, opens June 27. ● Opening of Lever House, Park Avenue, designer G. Burnshaft – city's 1st "glass box" office.

1952 Lever Building (designers Skidmore, Owings & Merrill) complete. Lever House is 1st of many International Style office buildings on Park Avenue. ● *June 11* New York Heliport No 2 opens at Pier A, Battery.

1953–1954

1953 *August 24-September 5* City's longest heatwave: 12 consecutive days above 90°F.

1953 *November 9* After a night's drinking at *White Horse Tavern*, 39-year-old Welsh poet, Dylan Thomas, dies.

Dylan Thomas MJ

1954 Leona Baumgartner city's 1st female health commissioner. Salk vaccine against polio given to 94% of city schoolchildren (by 1962). She oversees formation of Poison Control Center (1955) and fluoridation of city's water supply (1965).

1953 *November 10* Con Edison's Astoria power plant opens. ● 8,000 private busline drivers begin 29-day strike for a contracted 5-day, 40-hour week.

1954 Bronx doo-wop group, the Chords, are 1st black pop group to break into top 10 with *Sh-Boom but gold record* goes to Crewcuts, a white group that covered hit. ● Ellis Island immigration station closes, abandoned to vandals.

Ellis Island DP

1953 Mayor Robert F. Wagner begins 1st of 3 terms.

1953 Ralph Ellison's *Invisible Man* wins National Book Award.

1954 *April 12* Bill Haley and the Comets record *Rock Around the Clock* at Decca's studio (West 70th Street).

1953 Construction begun on Albert Einstein College of Medicine, Bronx. Einstein permits University to use his name only if school open to all.

Albert Einstein PB

1954 *June 22* Brooklyn Queens Expressway opens with triple-deck roadways and Brooklyn Heights Esplanade.

1955

1955 *March 12* Aged 34, Charlie Parker dies of cirrhosis of liver. ● *December* Several on trial for distributing anti-war leaflets in City Hall Park and refusing to go into shelters in civil defense drill. Sentenced to 5 days in jail or a fine, Hennacy says, "As a Catholic, I twice refused to take part in air-raid drills in accordance with the practice of Saint Peter, who was arrested twice for speaking on the street, and he and all the Apostles said to the state that they should obey God rather than man." Judge suspends sentences.

1955 1,392-bed Bronx State Hospital for mental patients opens, last such institute in state.

1955 McDonald's Corporation founded. ● Philip Morris introduce Marlboro Man.

1955 Mayor Wagner creates Commission on Intergroup Relations.

1955 *The Village Voice* founded as weekly alternative paper. ● Marian Anderson 1st black singer to perform at Metropolitan Opera. Robert McFerrin is 1st black singer to receive a contract there, appearing in Verdi's *Aida*. ● *Brooklyn Eagle*, founded 1841, folds. ● Stanley Kubrick produces and directs *Killer's Kiss*, grade-B thriller. Unlike most films shot in city then, all pre-and post-production also done in N.Y. ● *The Honeymooners* brings working class New York to televisions nationwide. ● Brooklyn Dodgers finally win a World Series, defeating Yankees. ● *September 21* At Yankee Stadium boxing champion Rocky Marciano defeats Archie Moor. ● Elston Howard 1st black player on New York Yankees team.

1955 World (Purlitzer) Building demolished for Brooklyn Bridge approach. ● Subway and bus systems now under Transit Authority.

PB *Subway Train*

● *April 18* Governor Harriman signs Limited-Profits Housing Companies Law: state subsidizes over 140,000 apartments in city. Co-Op City in Bronx is largest. ● *October 13* 1st section of Long Island Expressway open. ● *October 16* L.I.R.R.'s last steam locomotive makes final run from Jamaica to Greenport. ● 1st 'Walk/Don't Walk' sign installed. ● *November 5* "Mr First", O. C. Catan, leads way when Major Deegan Expressway opens. ● *December 15* Tappen Zee Bridge opens. "Mr First" there. ● Demolition of Third Avenue "el".

USA & WORLD EVENTS

1939-45 World War II

1940 Battle of Britain

1941 Japanese attack Pearl Harbor

Penicillin first used

1945 Germany surrenders; Atomic bomb on Hiroshima; Japan surrenders

1946 1st electronic computer

1951 1st color T.V. broadcast

1953 Mount Everest climbed

1954 McCarthy witch-hunts

1955 First McDonalds restaurant in Illinois

Mirage unveiled

U-2 spy plane tested

56 1957 1959 1961 1963 1965 1966 1968 1970 1971 19

1956 *July 2* 2 thorium explosions shake plant in Bayside. Atomic Energy Commission claim there is no radiation hazard outside building and contamination confined to 1 part of a laboratory, that no one would suffer from exposure unless in room during blast or straight after. ● Nike guided-missile battery installed on Hart Island. *Times* says:"The modern Nike represents a triumph of electronic science, a winged messenger of death to the attacker and a symbol of ultimate victory over aggression." 24 Nike batteries ring city.

1956 Soul singer James Brown wins amateur night competition at *Apollo*.

1956 20 volunteers help public school teachers under School Volunteer Program –1st in U.S. ● *April 26* McLean Trucking Company introduce containerization.

1856 Company abandon Faber's pencil factory in Brooklyn.

1956 John Marchi elected to state senate from Staten Island; later reelected into next millenium – longest serving U.S. state legislator.

1956 Joffrey Ballet Company founded with 6 dancers. ● Eugene O'Neill's *Long Day's Journey into Night* opens - so painfully close to his real life he did not want it staged until he had died. ● Yankees beat Dodgers in Subway Series.

1956 *April* New York *Coliseum*, Triborough Bridge and Tunnel Authority's $35 million convention center and 26-story office tower, open. 44 buildings demolished include *Majestic* Theater and Gotham National Bank. ● *September 26* Port Authority's West 30th Street Heliport, Manhattan's 1st commercial heliport, opens.

Heliport DP

Suez crisis

1957 *January* Mad Bomber, George P. Metesky, arrested. With a grudge against Consolidated Edison (who had dismissed him) he planted 47 pipe bombs over 16 years, causing many injuries. His reply to an open letter in *Journal-American* helped identity him. He is sent to a mental institution. ● Ed Sullivan hosts Elvis Presley.

1958 *September 20* While signing copies of his book in a Harlem store, Martin Luther King Jr. is stabbed.

Martin Luther King PB

1957 *October 25* Albert Anastasia gunned down in Park Sheraton Hotel barbershop. A member of Murder Inc., responsible for 500 murders, he worked for Luciano and Costello. Gambino takes over. ● Closure of City Hospital on Blackwell's Island.

Blackwell's Island. DP

1958 1 death in fire at Museum of Modern Art. Original façade with curved marquee destroyed.

1958 Nabisco moves out of Manhattan bakery.

1957 *December 30* Mayor Wagner signs law banning racial discrimination in private housing.

1958 *August 1* 194,418 Jehovah's Witnesses throng Yankee Stadium, Polo Grounds and nearby sites.

1957 Althea Gibson, honoured with a ticker-tape parade, is 1st black world champion tennis player. ● 14-year-old Bobby Fischer wins U.S. Chess Championships. ● *West Side Story* opens ● Dodgers move to Los Angeles.

1957 *April 7* Last trolley goes over Queensboro Bridge with 125 passengers and trolley enthusiasts. ● *November 26* 29-story Tishman Building at 666 Fifth Avenue is world's largest aluminium-clad skyscraper. ● Aquarium from Castle Clinton reopens in Coney Island.

1957 Sputnik launched

1958 Microchip invented

1959 *February 3* American Airlines flight crashes into East River, killing 66.

1960 *December 16* 2 planes collide above Staten Island, killing 129 passengers and crew and some on ground. ● *December 19* 50 workmen die as aircraft carrier burns while being built at Brooklyn Navy Yard.

1959 Vincent Astor dies. His widow gives $200 million to city institutions over next 38 years.

1960 Over 66% of nation's well-known artists live and work in N.Y.C.

1959 *May 14* President Eisenhower turns 1st shovel at Lincoln Center groundbreaking. Robert Moses had offered 53-acre slum clearance site to Metropolitan Opera and Philharmonic in 1955. 1,000s of families and many businesses evicted.

Lincoln Center DP

1960s Washington Square Park closes to traffic; fountain bcomes public meeting place.

1960 *October 28* John F Kennedy campaigns. He speaks for 30 minutes to 15,000 people, apologizing to, "any Republican commuters who have been caught unwittingly in this crowd," and then boards Brooklyn ferry. He addresses 200,000 in garment district.

John F. Kennedy PL

1959 Opening of Frank Lloyd Wright's Solomon R. Guggenheim Museum on Fifth Avenue.

1960 City buys Carnegie Hall – a National Historic Landmark by 1964. Main hall seats 2,804.

1959 San Juan Hill, largely African-American neighborhood, razed for construction of Lincoln Center ● Seagram Building inspires zoning law revisions to encourage building of towers on open plazas.

1960 *January 17* Diesel buses replace 138 trolley coaches on 5 Brooklyn routes.

1959 1st shots of moons' far side

Castro seizes power in Cuba

1960 Lasers invented

1962 *March 1* American Airlines 707 crashes in Jamaica Bay. 95 die

1961 Political and economic turmoil in Middle East: Arabs and Israelis move to N.Y. ● *May 19* President Kennedy's birthday celebrations in Madison Square Garden. Marilyn Monroe sings, "Happy Birthday, Mr President".

Marilyn Monroe DG

1961 *April 9* Folksingers scuffle with police over music ban in Washington Square. ● City University of New York forms.

1962 *November 27* 278 women in police force now. Court rules they can take departmental sergeant examinations. In 1965, Shpritzer, who had brought suit to court, and Schimmel made sergeants. In 1972, Schimmel made 1st woman captain.

Woman Police Officer PL

1961 Mayors given authority to prepare capital budget (previously done by City Planning Commission), to alter operating budget and reorganize municipal offices.

1962 *February* Wall Street lawyers and brothers-in-law, J.D. Mahoney and K. O'Doherty, found Conservative Party.

1962 Summe Good reviews for Bill Cosby's stand-up comedy at *Gaslight Café*, Greenwich Village. ● Philharmonic Hall opens but has poor acoustics until redesigned in 1976. ● New York Mets baseball team forms. Loses 120 games this season. Yankees win series again.

1961 *January 11* Throgs Neck Bridge opens. Clearview Expressway to take traffic from bridge to Belt Parkway but community opposition blocks highway. 500 homes moved or demolished.

1961 Berlin Crisis: building of Wall

Gagarin 1st man in space

President Kennedy inaugurated

Cuban missile crisis

1964 10-year-old Al Sharpton (later protest leader, politician and state senate candidate) ordained. Aged 4, he toured as a "wonder boy preacher". ● *May 4* General Douglas MacArthur dies: spent final years in Waldorf-Astoria suite.

Waldorf-Astoria DP

1963 Revd. Lynn L. Hageman founds Exodus House in East Harlem; innovative drug treatment center rehabilitates heroin addicts through abstinence, group therapy and spiritual counseling.

1964 1st black precinct commander, Lloyd Sealy, appointed. ● Riot in Harlem when police lieutenant shoots 15-year-old after he lunges at him with knife. Riots in Bedford Stuyvesant 5 days later: 1 death, 118 injured, 465 arrested. ● *September 19* City's 1st gay rights demonstration at Whitehall Street Induction center, protesting military's dishonorable discharge of homosexuals.

1964 February 9 73 million watch Beatles on Ed Sullivan Show; also shown is a scene from Broadway's *Oliver*, with future Monkee, Davy Jones, as Artful Dodger. l New York State Theater, home of New York City ballet and City opera opens. ● *Funny Girl* opens, musical starring Barbra Streisand. l C.B.S. purchase 80% of Yankees for $11.2 million. l Riot at Madison Square Garden after basketball championship: this does not return until 1989. ● Polo Grounds destroyed. ● New York Mets baseball team moves to Shea Stadium.

1963 *December 24* New York International Airport renamed John F. Kennedy International Airport.

J.F.K. Airport. DP

● Opening of Pan Am Building, Park Avenue. ● Pennsylvania Station demolished. Outcry – Landmarks Preservation Commission set up.

1964 *April 16* New $36 million terminal and $1.6 million control tower at La Guardia Airport. ● Verrazano Narrows Bridge links Brooklyn and Staten Island.

1963 President John F. Kennedy assassinated

1964 Beatles visit America

1965 *February 21* Malcolm X assassinated at Audubon Ballroom on 165th Street by Black Muslims.

1965 Hart-Cellar Immigration Act. Equal quotas of 20,000 for Eastern hemisphere countries. For 1st time limitations on emigration from Western hemisphere. Immigration Reform Act generates new wave from Asia, Africa, Latin America and Caribbean. Chinese families in city reunited.

1965 New York Stock Exchange: electronic display replaces tape stream from historic stock ticker.

Stock Exchange PL

1965 1st newspaper vending machine, on Bronx street corner. ● *October 4* Sherman Billingsley closes world-famous Stork Club.

1965 City has industrial workforce of 1 million and manufacturing payroll of nearly $3 billion. ● Garment factories support economy of Chinatown.

Chinatown DP

1965 *October* Pope Paul VI visits World's Fair, holds a mass in Yankee Stadium, and addresses U.N.

1965 New York Philharmonic offers free park concerts. ● *August* 1st rock concert in a ballpark: Beatles perform to capacity crowd at Shea Stadium. ● Bobby Fischer not allowed to go to Cuba for Chess Tournament. His moves are relayed by telex – he finishes 2nd.

1965 Original Pennsylvania Station demolition completed to create new station to house offices and Madison Square Garden. ● Port Authority Trans-Hudson Corporation launch air-conditioned trains in mass transit system. ● 3 new Staten Island ferries – John F. Kennedy, Gov. Herbert H. Lehman and American Legion. 294-foot boats carry 3,500 passengers and 45 cars. ● 13-hour blackout hits Manhattan, Bronx and Brooklyn. 8000,000 people trapped in subways, trains, and elevators.

1965 Vietnam War escalates

1966 *June 30* U.S. Army leave Governors Island, base since 1790s. Rear Admiral Stephens accepts island for Coast Guard (there for 30 years). ● *July 21* 11-year-old Eric Dean shot by sniper in East New York's racial tension. Mayor Lindsay rushes to neighborhood to defuse situation.

1967 *August 23* Ambrose Lightship decommissioned: now part of South Street Seaport Museum. ● Oscar Wilde Bookstore, Christopher Street, 1st dedicated to gay and lesbian literature.

Oscar Wilde PL

1967 *From July 23* Off-duty policeman intervenes in Harlem street quarrel and shoots man who attacks him with a knife. 1,000 police and Mayor Lindsay arrive. 34 arrested, 36 injured and 2 killed by police bullets. On Labor Day, a detective jumps from his car in Brownsville to stop a mugging and shoots young thug. Both men are black, but rumors that cop is white triggers 4 nights of violence.

1966 Newspaper strikes.

1967 Muriel Siebert is 1st woman to buy a seat on New York Stock Exchange; hers is 1st woman-owned brokerage firm since 1870.

1966 Yankees fire broadcaster Red Barber when he has television camera scan 1,000s of empty seats at Yankee Stadium during a game.

1967 *Electric Circus discotheque* at 19-21 St. Marks Place has psychedelic lights and circus acts. Visitors dress as they like, dance, sit, think, "tune in and turn on". ● Demonstration against New York Athletic Club (N.Y.A.C.) accuses them of sponsoring black athletes but denying them membership.

1966 Rikers Island Bridge to Queens complete. Only way to prison had been by ferry from Bronx. ● Singer Building (Broadway /Liberty Street) is tallest building ever demolished.

1967 Singer Building (Broadway/Library Street) is tallest building ever demolished

1966 Kashmir crisis

1967 1st heart transplant

1969 *November 10*: Bombs explode at R.C.A. and G.M. buildings and a Chase Manhattan Bank. December 21: bombs explode at Banco de Credito, Woolworth's and Commonwealth of Puerto Rico's office.

1968 Carlo Gambino is leading organized crime figure in city.

1969 Al Sharpton, aged 15, made youth director of "Operation Breadbasket". He spends 2 years leading boycotts and demonstrations over employment of black workers.

1968 Over 400 arrested in Harlem after assassination of Martin Luther King Jr., despite Mayor Lindsay's attempt to calm crowds.

1969 *April 22* Black and Peurto Rican students, wanting student body to reflect racial makeup of high schools, padlock gate at City College. In July, Board of Higher Education announces policy of open admissions, starting 1970.

1969 *January 16* City issue municipal bonds worth $140,380,000 at 5.702%, highest rate since 1932. On 29th a $30.1 million housing bond issue withdrawn. By July 15, $146 million bond issue rates 6.156%.

1968 1st black woman in Congress, Shirley Chisholm, represents Brooklyn; will be 1st woman to run for President

1969 Comptroller Procaccino wins Democratic primary. In Republican primary, State Senator Marchi defeats Mayor Lindsay by 6,000 votes. Procaccino campaigns, saying: "We must stop coddling the criminals and pampering the punks. The do-gooders and bleeding hearts must stop handcuffing the police." In November, Lindsay reelected on Liberal line with 42% of vote.

1968 Studio Museum in Harlem founded. ● 5 major national tennis championships consolidated into U.S. Open, held at West Side Tennis Club, Queens. ● New Madison Square Garden seats 20,000 ●

1969 Woody Allen directs 1st complete feature film called *Take the Money and Run.*

1968 2nd Pennsylvania Station finished – busiest train station in North America.

1969 Moon landing

R. Kennedy killed

Concorde flies

1970 *March 6* 3 members of S.D.S. die in explosion at 18 West 11th Street, 1840s rowhouse they used as a bomb factory. They planned to blow up Columbia University library. 2 survivors go into hiding.

1970 *January 4* Subway fare rises from 20¢ to 30¢ and new, larger token introduced. Subway use declines. ● *March* Explosions rock corporate H.Q. of I.B.M., Mobil, and G.T.E. Explosion in East Fifth Street tenement kills 1 and injures 1 black radical who had set off bomb in Electric Circus. ● *April 25th Times* runs story detailing police corruption. Mayor Lindsay appoints Wall Street lawyer, Knapp, to head commission to investigate. ● 15,000 join 1st Gay Pride march, then rally in Central Park's Sheep Meadow. ● *August* Executive order bans age and sex discrimination in city employment. Women's Strike for Equality marks 50th anniversary of women's suffrage with a march up Fifth Avenue. ● 1st Earth Day celebrated in Central Park.

PL

1970 Racketeer Influenced and Corrupt Organizations laws (R.I.C.O.) hamper organized crime and make it easier to prove conspiracy and to prosecute organizations rather than individuals. Prosecutors allowed to seize assets of criminal organizations and can impose stiffer penalties. ● *August 10* Women win legal right to drink at *McSorley's Old Ale House* (15 East 7th Street), bastion of male exclusivity since 1854. ● Bronx resident Herman Badillo is 1st Puerto Rican Congressman.

1970 *September 13* 1st New York City Marathon in Central Park. N.Y. fireman Gary Muhrcke wins making 4 6-mile laps in just over 2.5 hours. 127 runners start; 55 finish.

1970s Castle Clinton restored: serves as ticket booths for Statue of Liberty and Ellis Island ferries. ● Tombs prison replaced again (Egyptian-inspired prison replaced 1902) but name endures. Halls of Justice completed. ● World Trade Center's 1st buildings open – part of New York Port Authority's urban renewal plan.

1971 Big Apple now City's promotional logo.

1971 Al Sharpton forms National Youth Movement (*see also* 1969). ● *June 28* Italian-American rally at Columbus Circle: reputed mafia boss J.A. Colombo, head of Italian-American Civil Rights League, shot by black gunman, J.A. Johnson, who is gunned down. Colombo never recovers.

1971 Illegal artist-residents of SoHo warehouses win zoning victory to keep homes and studios. ● 1st gay rights bill introduced in City Council; it does not pass. ● *May* Gay Activist Alliance moves into Firehouse – center of gay activism until 1974 arson destroys it. ● Palisades Amusement Park in Fort Lee closes. High rise apartments built. ● Governor Rockefeller urges blocking of new District Council contract, with generous pension plan. Municipal workers open drawbridges (causing gridlock) and sewer lines, fouling harbor and beaches.

1971 *February 11* Mayor John Lindsay switches from Republican to Democrat ready for a presidential run. ● *March 2* Board of Education terminates contracts of 3,500 teachers due to lack of funds.

1971 *June 13/July 1* *Times* starts printing 1967 Pentagon Papers. Nixon administration tries to stop this: Attorney General Mitchell writes, ". . . publication of this information is directly prohibited by the provisions of the espionage law" but on July 1, Supreme Court affirms paper's right to publish.

Richard M. Nixon PL

● *March 2* City acquires Yankee Stadium and announces $24 million modernization. In 2 years costs soar to $110 million. ● New York Cosmos soccer team forms as part of North American Soccer League, which moves H.Q. to Manhattan. ● *March 8* Smokin Joe Frazier defeats Muhammad Ali to win heavyweight crown at Madison Square Garden.

1971 Bogardus Building, Washington Street, razed. Thieves take 2/3 of cast-iron panels. Landmarks Preservation Committee store remaining panels in locked warehouse but they are stolen too!

1971 Idi Amin seizes power in Uganda

6 1957 1959 1961 1963 1965 1966 1968 1970 1971 19

Above: *Health officers examine steerage passengers for signs of disease at Quarantine Point in the bay near Staten Island (1887).*
Above right: *Immigrants secure certificates of naturalization (1868).*

would commence. St Patrick's Day is still an occasion to make merry in New York and the Irish parade is one of the city's largest.

The flow of immigration

As the mid-19th century drew to a close, millions of refugees, mostly from Europe, arrived in the U.S., hoping to escape famine, wars, economic and political repression, and religious persecution. Irish, English, Germans, Swedes, Jews, Italians and Slavs had to endure a long, uncomfortable voyage in crowded ships.

Immigration 1851-1924		
Peak		
Year	From	Number
1851	Ireland	4.72 m
1882	Germany	6.98 m
1882	Scandinavia	2.53 m
1888	U.K.	4.90 m
1907	Italy	5.29 m
1907	Austro-Hungary	4.32 m
1913	Russia	3.37 m
1924	Canada	4.11 m

Jews

The initial immigration was of Sephardic Jews in the 17th century, but from 1870 Jews from eastern Europe began arriving in vast numbers, fleeing pogroms and poverty. Many settled on the Lower East Side in squalid tenements – in what soon became the most densely populated district in the world. By 1894, the population reached 986 people per acre.
Usually banded together in

national groups, they all shared religious ideals and rituals, while eking out meagre wages earned in sweatshops or tiny, crowded rooms, serving the garment industry. Others worked in small retail shops and factories or became pushcart vendors, hawking their wares on the streets. Soon synagogues and religious schools sprang up. A Yiddish theater was founded and Jewish book publishers and newspapers flourished. By the 1920s, immigration was restricted. Gradually, with families and trades established, the Jews moved to better neighborhoods. The collapse of the Communist block in 1989 created a new wave of Russian Jews.

Hispanics

Immigrants from Puerto Rico flocked to east Harlem, *El Barrio,* from 1921-24. The Cubans arrived in the 1960s, and by 1990 numbered 900,000 (over 10% of the population).

The Germans

The first Germans arrived in about 1710. By 1790 they made up 10% of the population. 70 years on, there were 118,000 in the city, many shopkeepers living in Deutschlandle, east of the Bowery, between Houston and 12th Streets.

The Italians

Many southern Italians who came to New York in the late 19th century lived in Lower East Side apartments so close together that sunlight never

penetrated the lower windows or yards. With over 40,000 people crowded into 17 blocks, disease was rife; but the Mulberry Street Little Italy area remained lively with a strong atmosphere of Italy which it still retains today. Many of the Italians who arrived in the 20th century came with the intention of returning to their homeland. Often single men emigrated alone, but later decided to stay and would then bring over their families.
By 1930, Italians numbered 1,070,355. Many of these worked alongside Jews in the garment industry.
In the 1930s, the *Caffè Roma* on Mulberry Street was the haunt of Italian actors, such as Migliaccio, a performer of Neapolitan folk songs who appeared in Bowery theaters.

Above: *A procession of immigrants on the streets of New York (1873).*
Below: *The San Gennaro festival in Little Italy.*

Early Dutch Settlers trade with Native Americans.

English Governors of New York 1664-1775

	Appointed
Richard Nicolls	September 8 1664
Colonel Francis Lovelace	August 17 1667
Major Edmund Andros, Knight	November 10 1674
Anthony Brockholles, Com. in Chief	November 16 1677
Sir Edmund Andros	August 7 1678
Anthony Brockholles, Com. in Chief	January 13 1681
Colonel Thomas Dongan	August 27 1682
Sir Edmund Andros	August 11 1688
Francis Nicholson, Lieutenant Governor	October 9 1688
Jacob Leisler	June 3 1689
Colonel Henry Sloughter	March 19 1691
Major Richard Ingoldsby, Com. in Chief	July 26 1691
Colonel Benjamin Fletcher	August 30 1692
Richard Coote, Earl of Bellomont	April 13 1698
John Nanfan, Lieutenant Governor	May 17 1699
Earl of Bellomont	July 24 1700
William Smith, as eldest Councilor present	March 5 1701
John Nanfan, Lieutenant Governor	May 19 1701
Edward Hyde, Viscount Cornbury	May 3 1702
John, Lord Lovelace	December 18 1708
Peter Schuyler, President of Council	May 6 1709
Richard Ingoldsby, Lieutenant Governor	May 9 1709
Peter Schuyler, President of Council	May 25 1709
Richard Ingoldsby, Lieutenant Governor	June 1 1709
Gerardus Beekman, President of the Council	April 10 1710
Brigadier Robert Hunter	June 14 1710
Peter Schuyler, President of Council	July 21 1719
William Burnet	September 17 1720
John Montgomerie	April 15 1728
Rip van Dam, President of the Council	July 1 1731
Colonel William Cosby	August 1 1732
George Clarke, President of the Council	March 10 1736
Admiral George Clinton	September 2 1743
Sir Danvers Osborne, Baronet	October 10 1753
James de Lancey, Lieutenant Governor	October 12 1753
Sir Charles Hardy, Knight	September 3 1755
James de Lancey, Lieutenant Governor	June 3 1757
Cadwaller Colden, President of the Council	August 4 1760
Major General Robert Monckton	October 26 1761
Cadwaller Colden, Pdt. of the Council	November 18 1761
Major General Robert Monckton	June 14 1762
Cadwaller Colden, Lieutenant Governor	June 28 1763
Sir Henry Moore, Baronet	November 13 1765
Cadwaller Colden, Lieutenant Governor	September 12 1769
John Murray, Earl of Dunmore	October 19 1770
William Tryon	9th July 1771
Cadwaller Colden, Leiutenant Governor	April 7 1774
William Tryon	June 28 1775

European explorers. In 1524, explorer Da Verrazano was impressed by the beauty of the people, but by the next year Portuguese captain Gomez was using them as slaves. In 1600, their skills in pottery were noted plus their use of stone, bone, copper and antler to make fishhooks, knives, drills, needles, whistles, choppers, scrapers, awls and pestles. It was 1626 when Peter Minuit purchased Manhattan from the Algonquin chiefs and wives for 60 guilders (about $30).

The Europeans arrive

Navigator Adriaen Block explored the waterways on behalf of Dutch merchants. In 1613, his ship was destroyed by fire and his crew camped on Manhattan. Their rough huts were the first European settlement here.

Dutch and English rule

In 1609, the Dutch East India Company sent Henry Hudson to seek the Northwest passage. He found instead the Hudson River and by 1613, the colony of New Amsterdam was set up with two forts. The Dutch held sway here until the English arrived and seized the town, renaming it New York in 1664. Bar for a brief re-occupation by the Dutch, New York remained an English colony until American Independence in 1783.

Native Americans

5 tribes of central and western New York, led by Hiawatha, formed a Confederacy of Five Nations in 1570. These were the Mohawk, Oneida, Onondaga, Cayuga and Seneca. For 150 years they would oversee waterways and fur trade, and act as go-between for the interior tribes and seacoast traders. A unifying element, they controlled warfare. The Iroquios and the resident Algonquin tribes of the Lower Hudson Valley and Long Island were the first point of contact for

African Americans

In 1890, there were only 24,000 African Americans in New York but by 1940 there were 460,000, 6% of the population. By 1990, African Americans numbered more than 2 million.

African Free Schools

In the 1700s, the first African Free School taught boys and girls reading, writing, arithmetic, grammar and geography. In 1797, trustees added an evening school for adults. The schoolhouse burned down in 1814 and another one was built in William Street and another in Mulberry Street in 1820. By 1834 blacks taught in 5 of the 7 schools – which became part of the public school system in 1847.

African Burial Ground

When Trinity Church received its charter in 1697, it declared that Africans could no longer be buried in its churchyard. In 1991, a burial ground north of Wall Street, used from 1712-94, was discovered when preparing the site for a new office building. 390 human remains were excavated, 92% of African origin, with 600 burial artefacts, including shroud pins, trade beads, coins, and copper jewelry. The total number of interments may be as many as 20,000. A pavilion area has been made where 200 undisturbed burials remain underground and the site has been designated a national historic landmark.

The Irish

By 1790 Irish settlers were as numerous as the Dutch had been. Famine, poverty and religious repression meant many more arrived from the 1820s to the 1850s. By 1860 the Irish made up 25% of the city population. Special occasions in Ireland were traditionally marked with hill bonfires and these remained an Irish tradition in the city until the 1920s. On the eve of an election, fires blazed, bars would lay on buffets and revels

Above: *An Iroquois Indian.* Below: *Passengers queue for food on a crowded immigrant ship.*

PEOPLE

1972 *April 7* Mobster Joey Gallo gunned down in *Umberto's Clam House*, Little Italy. ● Charles Atlas dies. Born Angelo Siciliano, he began bodybuilding after a bully kicked sand in his face at Coney Island. He took his new name from statue at *Atlas Hotel*, Coney Island. He posed for *Dawn of Glory memorial* (Jamaica Avenue), for *Washington in Peace* (Washington Square Arch) and *Civic Virtue* (City Hall Park and then Queens Borough Hall). ● F.B.I. director, J. Edgar Hoover, dies

HISTORICAL EVENTS

1973 *February 10* Liquid natural gas facility on Staten Island explodes: 40 die. ● DC-10 airplane crashes after colliding with gulls on take-off and burns at Kennedy Airport.

1973 Elizabeth Connelly elected to New York State Assembly, 1st woman elected on Staten Island. ● *May* Duke Ellington dies aged 75; he had lived in N.Y. since 1923. ● Petit walks tightrope between twin towers of World Trade Center – he becomes artist-in-residence at St. John the Divine Cathedral.

1973 *May 8* Rockefeller drug laws mean imprisonment for even small amounts of illegal drugs; plea bargains eliminated. Prison population swells. ● Roosevelt Island (formerly Blackwell's/Welfare Island) takes present name.

LIFESTYLE

1972 Local police to fight organized crime more vigorously. F.B.I. works closely with Drug Enforcement Agency. ● Federal prosecutor Giuliani executes mob crime leaders, powerful in city's heroin trade. ● Television reporter, Rivera, exposes deplorable conditions in Staten Island's Willowbrook Developmental Center for retarded. Lawsuit over dirt and overcrowding (6,000 in space for 4,200). ● False report leads police into mosque (Lenox Avenue). Officer Philip Cardillo killed. ● After pilot program 1st N.Y.P.D. female officers patrol. Numbers increase after height restrictions eliminated.

Roosevelt Island DP

1974 *Saturday Night* Live premier. ● City Planning Commission make Sunnyside Gardens, Parkchester, Fresh Meadows and Harlem River Houses "Special Planned Community Preservation Districts".

1973 New York Stock Exchange registers 1st 200 million share day.

1973 Syndicate controlled by George Steinbrenner buys New York Yankees for about $10 million. ● Secretariat shatter track record by 2.6 seconds to win Belmont Stakes and capture Triple Crown.

COMMERCE

1972 *November 14* Dow Jones closes at 1,003.16, breaking 1,000 for 1st time.

1974 *October 31* South Street Seaport Museum acquires 1911 4-masted, steel-hull *Peking*. ● *1974-76* Yankee Stadium renovated. Cost estimate $24 million but over $100 million spent.

CULTURE & ART

1972 Newport Jazz Festival moves to N.Y. ● *Ms Magazine* launched.

CITY STRUCTURE & DEVELOPMENT

1972 *January 5* Subway fare increases to 35¢.

1974 Sears Tower, Chicago (1,4 feet) is world's tallest skyscraper, 1st time since 1890s not in Manhattan. When television antenna added to Tower One, World Trade Center, it regains title at 1,730 feet.

1973 U.S.A. withdraws from Vietnam

1972 President Nixon meets Brezhnev and visits China

1975 *April 8* Borough of Richmond becomes Borough of Staten Island.

1976 *July 4* Parade of tall ships highlights bicentennial celebrations on Hudson River. PB

Tall Ships

1976 *October 15* Crime boss Carlo Gambini dies of cancer. His cousin Paul Castellano takes over.

1975 *January 24* Puerto Rican terrorist organization plant bomb in *Fraunces Tavern*: kill 4, injure 53. ● Illuminated advertisements appear on taxicab roofs.

1975-76 Fiscal crisis: city services and jobs severely cut. ● Top of Empire State Building illuminated.

1975 Elimination of fixed commissions for stockbrokers. ● *October 30* City faces bankruptcy and appeals to President Ford for loan guarantees. *Daily News* prints his rebuffal: "Drop Dead."

1976 D.O.T. system replaces ticker-tape.

1975 Elizabeth Ann Seton is 1st American-born saint and 1st New Yorker canonized by Catholic Church. She founded Sisters of Charity, 1st American order. Her shrine is a 1793 house on State Street.

1976 Queen Elizabeth II visits and receives 279 peppercorns – symbolic back rent – from Trinity Church, one for each year, as in 17th-century charter.

1975 Brazilian soccer star Pele signed to New York Cosmos. He draws huge crowds and team moves to Yankee Stadium.

1976 *September 28* Yankee Stadium: heavyweight champion Muhammad Ali wins unanimous decision over Ken Norton.

1975 Pier A at Battery Park designated a landmark and saved from demolition.

1976 17,000 attend Sailor's Snug harbor opening. ● Roosevelt Island tram launches Swiss cable car. ● World Trade Center's twin towers open.

World Trade Center PL

1974 President Nixon resigns

1978 *December 11* Hooded gunmen led by "Jimmy the Gent" Burke burst into J.F.K. terminal to steal $5.8 million – never recovered. In time gang members murdered. Burke convicted – not for heist, but for basketball point-shaving and killing drug dealer who owed him $250,000.

1977 *August 11* David Berkowitz arrested after year of murders and maiming of young couples. He sent notes signed "Son of Sam" to *Daily News* columnist. Will be convicted of 6 murders in 1978.

1977 Bronx Zoo has Wild Asia exhibit. Zoological Society begin Mountain Gorilla Project in Rwanda.

Mountain Gorilla PL

1977 *July 13* 25-hour blackout in heatwave: great looting and arson. 4,000 arrested. Bushwick devastated.

1978 Telephone company abandon change place-named exchanges to digits. ● Salvation Army's shelter at Bowery, haven for mental health sufferers.

1977 London's Christie's auction house opens NYC branch at 520 Park Avenue.

1978 *August 8* At City Hall desk used by George Washington, President Carter signs legislation for federal guarantees of bonds issued by city and Municipal Assitance Corporation.

1977 *Saturday Night Fever*, based on N.Y. magazine article, hits big screen. ● *1977* Rupert Murdoch buys *Village Voice, New York Magazine* – and *Post*, transforming it into conservative tabloid. ● National Tennis Center opens near Shea Stadium; replaces Forest Hills Stadium as U.S. Open site.

1977 Citicorp complete with distinctive slant-roofed tower.

1978 *April 12* Final Rockettes appearance planned as Rockefeller Center Inc. is to close Radio City Music Hall but $2.2 million state grant saves music hall and Rockettes.

1979 *January 26* Nelson Rockefeller (70-year-old 4-time governor of N.Y. and former Vice President) dies after a heart attack while working late at his town house.

1980 Now over 16 million immigrants in N.Y. ● *December* John Lennon fatally shot in front of Dakota apartment building where he lived. Dakota's switchboard had received some 25 calls a day from his fans.

1979 *April - June* 88-day tugboat strike: sludge and garbage pile up. Health emergency declared.

Tug Boat PB

1979 *December* L.I.R.R. trainmen 10-day strike. President Carter invokes Railway Labor Act, ordering them back to work for 60 days. ● *February* Guardian Angels, volunteer patrols of young men and women in red berets and T-shirts, aim to reduce crime on streets and subways. ● Puerto Rican terrorist maimed when device he is assembling explodes. ● *1980* After lawsuit, fire department hire 42 women.

1979 Philip Morris, largest industrial corporation in city, move H.Q. to Park Avenue/41st Street. ● City able to sell its notes in the bond market for 1st time since fiscal crisis in 1975. ● Christie's East auction house opens at 219 East 67th Street.

1979 Norman Mailer's *The Executioner's Song* wins Pulitzer prize. ● Greta Waitz wins N.Y. Marathon in world-record time of 2.27.33. Bill Rodgers wins men's race for 4th year running. 1st Marathon televised.

1980 Central Park Conservancy founded to raise funds for restoration in park. In 1998, Parks Department award them contract to manage Central Park. ● Building starts of AT & Ts postmodern World H.Q. tower with Chippendale profile.

1979 Southern Rhodesia becomes Zimbabwe

1979 Militant students seize U.S. Embassy in Teheran

1977 President Carter pardons draft evaders

1981 New York Central Labor Council hold Labor Day parade (1st for 13 years) to support striking air traffic controllers fired by President Reagan.

Ronald Reagan PB

1982 *February 22* Thelonius Monk's funeral at St Peter's "Jazz Church" (Lexington Avenue). Defining jazz, Monk said, "New York man. You can feel it. It's around in the air."

1981 *January 30* 2 million spectators watch ticker-tape parade for Iran's American Embassy hostages. ● AIDS virus identified. G.M.H.C. founded by 6 gay men.

1982 800,000 protest nuclear arms in Central Park. ● Fax machines replace bicycle messengers.

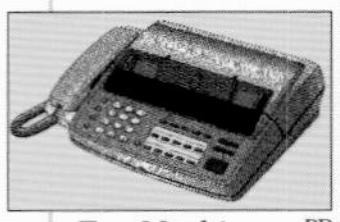

Fax Machine PL

1983 City has spent 5 years and $12 million renovating Central Park's Wollman Memorial Rink. Donald Trump takes over and reopens rink in a few months.

1983 Economic boom: property prices skyrocket. ● *December* Phelps Dodge shuts down century-old copper refinery in Maspeth, Newtown Creek.

1982 Loft (Multiple Dwelling) Law legalizes studios and homes artists created in SoHo and Tribeca lofts – landlords must bring spaces up to code.

1981 *New York Native* launched, 1st to write about "gay plague" AIDS. Circulation peaks at 20,000. ● Simon and Garfunkel perform to half a million in Central Park.

1982 11,000 athletes compete in New York City Games. Visitors to Gay Games spend $400 million.

1981 Battery Park City built on landfill left over from World Trade Center construction.

1982 Battery Park designated part of Harbor Park, group of historic waterfront sites.

1983 Lever Building designated a landmark.

1981 Reagan shot

1982 Falkland Islands War

1984 Mayor proclaims Kander and Ebb's *New York, New York* as city's official song.

1985 *December 16* Mob boss Paul Castellano (Gambino family leader) and underboss, Bilotti, shot outside Sparks Steak House (East 46th Street). John Gotti ordered hit and is now family leader with Salvatore "Sammy Bull" Gravano underboss.

1984 *May 17* Legislation introduced to allow Staten Island to secede from city. ● Benjamin Ward is city's 1st black police commissioner.

1985 *May 7* Vietnam veterans receive belated Broadway ticker-tape parade. ● Helen Hayes and Morosco Theaters demolished. Landmarks Preservation Commission designate remaining Broadway theaters.

1985 *Crains New York Business* releases 1st issue.

1984 *March 19th* At St. Patrick's Cathedral, John O'Connor made 8th archbishop. ● 1st female vice-presidential nominee of major party, Queens Congresswoman, Geraldine Ferraro.

St Patrick's Cathedral DP

1985 Mayor Koch reelected for 3rd term.

1984 Liberty Cup, sponsored by Harbor Festival Foundation, founded as annual race. ● *September 6* Jets play 1st game at Giant Stadium in Meadowlands.

1985 Isamu Noguchi Garden Museum opens in Long Island City. ● New York Cosmos leave soccer league and disband.

1984 Philip Johnson's AT & T (now Sony) building joins skyline.

1985 Demolition of S Klein on Union Square, city's 1st discount department store.

1984 Indira Ghandi murdered

1984 AIDS breaks out

1981 Reagan shot

1985 Gorbechav new Soviet Leader

1986 Statue of Liberty centennial celebrations.

Statue of Liberty PL

1986 Police stop erratic car on Grand Central Parkway and find Queens Borough President Manes with self-inflicted knife wound. Later he plunges a knife into his heart and dies. He is implicated in cable television franchise bribery. Parking Violations Bureau investigate his colleague.

1987 Judge F.X. Smith, (a City Council president) convicted of bribery in cable television franchises.

1986 Jacob K. Javits Convention Center covers 4 blocks on 38th Street and 11th Avenue. Now city's largest convention center: it can hold 85,000 people and 6 simultaneous events.

1987 *March* AIDS Coalition to Unleash Power stage 1st demonstration. 250 arrive at Wall Street to protest high price of medication and demand more research.

1986 Schwarx Toy Bazaar moves across street to 767 Fifth Avenue.

1987 Dow breaks 2,000. Market peaks at 2,722.42 on August 25. On October 19, Dow drops 508 points. Stock market crash next day as 608 million shares (worth $21,000 million) traded. Dow-Jones Industrial Average declines by over 500 points. New special controls implemented.

1986 Socrates Sculpture Park opens on abandoned site next to sculptor Di Suvero's studio (East River, Astoria). Made city park 1998.

1987 *July 1* All-sports radio W.F.A.N. on air. 10 years later it is highest-grossing station in U.S. and radio home of Mets, Jets, Knicks and Rangers.

1986 *New York Coliseum* closes – demolished 1999.

1986 Chernobyl nuclear disaster

Space shuttle *Challenger* explodes

1987 Reagan and Gorbechav sign treaty, ending Cold War

1989 Queen of Mean, Leona Helmsley, sentenced to 4 years in prison for tax evasion. ● *December 1* Choreographer Alvin Ailey dies of AIDS.

1988 Central Park Zoo busy when it reopens after $35 million, 4-year refurbishment. ● 25% of New Yorkers live below poverty line. ● Accusations of police brutality in Tompkins Square riots. ● Many violent deaths at Bloody Angle in Chinatown.

1989 Recycling made mandatory in city. ● Citicorp Tower completed in Hunters Point.

Citicorp Tower

Late 1980s Seats for membership of New York Stock Exchange sell for $1,1 million. ● Children's bank opens at Schwarx Toy Bazaar. *Miracle on 34th Street* and *Big* filmed here.

1989 *May 3* Staten Island Homeport dedicated. 1st ships are guided-missile cruiser *Ticonderoga* and destroyer *Hayler*.

1988 President Reagan and Soviet premier, Gorbachev, hold summit on Governors Island.

1989 David Dinkins city's 1st black mayor.

Mikhail Gorbachev PB

1988 *New York Press* new free alternative weekly. *Our Town* and *West Side Spirit* free in city. ● Lower East Side Tenement Museum set up.

1989 Tom Wolfe publishes *Bonfire of the Vanities*. ● Juma Ikangaa wins New York City Marathon's Men's Division at 2:08:01.

1989 *October 19* New $868 million subway line under East River. "Train to nowhere" terminates at 21st Street, Long Island City, with a stop at Roosevelt Island, 1st subway station there: access to Manhattan no longer only by tram.

1989 Berlin Wall comes down

Earthquake in San Francisco

1990 City census. 18,087,000 residents; over 90 languages spoken. ● Huge oil spill from Exxon pipeline into Arthur Kill.

1991 18th-century African burial ground near Foley Square uncovered by building workers. 100s of skeletons taken to Howard University. Building redesigned to allow reburial and a memorial.

Nelson Mandela

1990 *June 21* Nelson Mandela honored at Yankee Stadium and has ticker-tape parade up Canyon of Heroes.

1991 City Councilman Guillermo Linares is 1st Dominican elected to U.S. public office.

1990 Federal court of Appeals overturns district court decision affirming right of homeless to panhandle on subways. Judge F. X. Altimari rebukes lower court for setting rights of beggars over those of passengers and upholds state law banning loitering to beg in terminals. ● New records: 2,245 murdered in year; 365 killed by motor vehicles. ● *March 25* Arson at Happy Land Social Club in Bronx kills 87, mostly Hispanic immigrants.

1991 *August 19* 3-day race riot in Crown Heights after Hasidic driver accidentally kills 7-year-old black child. Jewish student stabbed to death by Nelson (sentenced to over 19 years). 43 civilians and 152 officers injured. 7 years on, Price has 21-year sentence for violating civil rights and inciting mob. ● Last surviving automat closes.

1991 *April 17* Dow breaks 3,000 for 1st time

1990 David Dinkins, New York's 1st black Mayor, takes office.

1991 *February 12* Former mayor Robert F. Wagner dies.

1990 Ellis Island reopens as immigration museum. ● Neil Simon's play *Lost in Yonkers* opens – wins Tony Award. ● New York Yankees have won a record 22 World Series and 33 American League pennants. ● Over 20,000 entrants in N.Y.C. Marathon – now has prize money, television contract and corporate sponsors.

1990 Lincoln Tunnel world's busiest with 40 million vehicles a year.

1991 5 die as train crashes into Union Street Station when motorman drunk.

1990 Germany united

1990 Nelson Mandela freed

1990 Channel Tunnel: French and English bore holes meet

1990-91 Gulf War after Iraq attacks Kuwait

1989 Formal end of U.S.S.R.

992 Mob boss otti convicted n felony charges nd murder: iven a life sentence.

1993 Staten Island votes in favor of secession from New York City in referendum.

1994 Jacqueline Kennedy Onassis dies at Fifth Avenue home; Central Park's reservoir named for her.

1993 *June 6* reighter *Golden Venture*, carrying 286 llegal Chinese immigrants, goes aground ff Rockaways. Some drown trying to wim ashore. Many deported. Others pend years in immigration facility.

992 City's 1st elephone dial-a-arlor opens. *September 8 Jew York 1* Jews broadcasts over city 24 ours a day. ● *December 2* Radio station WQEW-AM goes n air. ● 68 of ity's 75 police recincts report decrease in elonies. ● *January 1* ubway fare ises from $1.15 o $1.25. ● *ugust 25* After years of renoation and conicts with homeess, anarchists nd squatters, ompkins quare Park eopens. 3 days ater, 75 activists efy midnight urfew. 21 rrests.

1993 Asbestos banned and removed from public buildings, including schools. ● Some 100,000 people attend West Indian Labor Day Festival parade in Brooklyn. ● *February 26* Bomb explodes in parking garage below World Trade center. 6 die; over 1,000 injured. Muslim terrorists convicted. ● *December 13* Police seize 424 lbs of pure heroin ($240 million street value) at 201 West 57th Street apartment. ● Bethesda Mall bandshell threatened with removal but Court of Appeals overrules this. ● *December 7* Jamaican immigrant, Colin Ferguson, fires pistol on L.I.R.R. train as it pulls into errillon Avenue station: kills 6, ounds 19. Carolyn McCarthy, widow f a victim and mother of wounded, lected to Congress 1994, ousting epublican who opposes gun control. erguson convicted 1995.

1994 Tourism strong – 28 million visitors. ● *September* Biggest theft at Tiffany's: $1.9 million of jewelry stolen. ● *June* Salvation Army's shelter at 225 Bowery closes. ● *Summer* Northern Boulevard shelter for homeless women closes; emergency men's shelter opens.

992 *September* udge Mollen nvestigates allegations of coruption and rug trafficking y Harlem and 3edford-Stuyesant police. lis 1994 report ill recommend ndependent agency to comat corruption.

1994 Guided-missile cruiser sails from Staten Island for last time June 27. $300 million base closes August 31.

1993 City officeholders terms limited. ● Giuliani defeats Dinkins to become city's 1st Republican mayor in 28 years.

1994 New York City Council members make $66,572 worth of cellular phone calls. One member's calls cost $6,678. ● Rudolph W Gulliani is 1st Republican mayor since 1965.

992 *Angels in merica* brings IDS epidemic o Broadway tage. ● Lisa ndieki wins ew York City arathon's omen's ivision.

1993 Borough of Manhattan Community College chess team win Pan American Intercollegiate Chess Tournament, beating Harvard in finals. – and in 1994.

992 *April 21* edesigned ryant Park pens.

1994 New York Rangers win Stanley Cup.

1994 *February 24/ April 5*, After 14 years of repair, all Queensboro Bridge lanes reopen. In April, inbound outer roadway closes for reconstruction.

Queensboro Bridge DP

1995 City's Fourth of July fireworks display computerized. 10,000-20,000 firework shells fired each year; 2,000+ light bulbs used on barges.

1996 *January 7 and 8* Blizzard halts city with 21 inches of snow. Record 75.6 inches of snow 1995/96 winter.

1995 *January 31* Broadway director George Abbott dies, aged 107.

1996 Joseph Mitchell dies. He wrote for *World-Telegram, Herald Tribune* and *New Yorker*. His work is collected in *Up in the Old Hotel* and *My Ears Are Bent*.

1995 *June 5* J train slams into rear of M train on Williamsburg Bridge, motorman dies, 50 passengers injured. Motorman had run a red signal but signal spacing and poor brakes contribute.

Williamsburg Bridge DP

1996 Water sampling stations set up around Manhattan. State law requires city to test water supply at least 480 times a month.

1995 Proliferation of multimedia businesses in Silicon Alley (23rd Street /Tribeca). 10,000 people in city work in new media.

1996 Chrysler, who had used New Yorker since 1939, drop longest continuous nameplate. ● *October 14* Dow closes at 6,010. It had doubled in only 5.5 years.

1995 *October 7* Pope John Paul II takes mass at Giant Stadium, Aqueduct racetrack and in Central Park before 125,000.

1996 Mayor Guilliani credited with city's great comeback.

1995 Tickets for Barbra Streisand's show at Madison Square Garden cost up to $350. Ticket scalpers charge $300-$350 per ticket for $125 seats. 65,000 tickets sell in an hour.

1995 Chelsea Piers renovated and open as sports and entertainment complex. ● *October 5* First Lady Hillary Clinton dedicates Eleanor Roosevelt Monument (72nd Street/Riverside).

1997 *February 23* Palestinian, Ali Abu Kamal, shoots 7 people, 1 fatally, on observation deck of Empire State Building. Deck reopens 2 days later with heavy security.

Observation Deck of Empire State Building PL

1997 *July 1* Duke of Ellington Memorial dedicated in Central Park. ● 1997 183 McDonald's restaurants in city.

1997 40,000 N.Y.C. police force is largest in city history. Prison population growing. City's crime rate drop is treble national average. 25 American cities have higher crime rate. ● *May 5* News zipper around Times Tower in Times Square dismantled. 1,000s of 30-watt bulbs are replaced by digital zipper with 235,000 light-emitting diodes that go into operation July 29. ● AIDS has claimed 60,000 New Yorkers but with new treatment, annual death toll drops 48%.

Times Square DP

1997 *February 13:* Dow closes at 7,022.44. July 16: Dow closes at 8,038.88. ● Mayor Guiliani reelected

1997 Museum of Jewish Heritage opens at Battery Place – a monument to Holocaust. ● New York Public Library is 2nd largest public library in U.S. Over 6 million volumes in city's main branch and 7,883,330 volumes in overall system. Annual 5,842,590 reference inquiries handled by Brooklyn Public Library. ● Disney's musical *Lion King* opens in renovated home of *Ziegfeld's Follies*.

New York Public Library DP

1997 *April 1* Supreme Court rules that N.Y. owns only original 3 acres of Ellis Island. Other 24.5 acres belong to New Jersey. To keep main building under single jurisdiction, N.Y. granted 5 acres. ● Metrocard introduced.

1998 Centennial celebrations of Greater New York's consolidated 5 boroughs. ● *January 2* Chaos on Fifth Avenue: water-main break creates 30-foot crater, 10 feet deep. Traffic held up for over a week in Flatiron district. Parked car partially swallowed into hole and a gas fire rages.

Flatiron DP

1998 *March 31* Former congresswoman Bella Abzug, dies. Famous for her liberalism, feminism, large hats, and saying, "Agree with me or I'll make you deaf".

1998 628 murders this year, fewest since 1964. ● 4,000-5,000 street fairs each year in city. Upper West Side's Greenflea market has 350 vendors and 10,000 visitors. ● *June 6* Darrel K. Harris sentenced to death for murdering 3 people while robbing a Brooklyn social club. 1st application of state's restored death penalty (last execution 1963). ● *June 24* City Council grant benefits to municipal employees' partners, regardless of marital status or sexual orientation. ● *July* City shuts down sex shops and strip clubs, defined as a public nuisance. ● *December 27* Radio station WQEW-AM goes off air at midnight after *Times* sells station for $40 million to Disney for a children's station.

1998 Corruption and election fraud follow District Council 37's 1996 contract ratification vote. ● Ellis Island divided between New York and New Jersey as legal battle ends.

1998 Shelley Taylor-Smith wins swimming race around Manhattan for 5th time.

1998 *October 1* Grand Central terminal celebrates 85th birthday after $200-million restoration.

Grand Central terminal DP

1999 *July 16* John F Kennedy Jr., wife, and sister-in-law die when private plane plunges into water off Martha's Vineyard. ● West Nile virus outbreak. 31 confirmed cases and 7 die.

1999 *February 4* police officers hunting serial rapist fire 41 shots at street peddlar Diallo, in Bronx. Officers indicted but acquitted. ● *March 6* Judge McGill of New Jersey rules that Hartz Mountain Industries cannot build 16-foot towers that would block view of Manhattan skyline from Lincoln Tunnel entrance, writing, "The views in question are a world-class amenity . . ." ● Pentagram designs *The New York Century* for Museum of the City of New York. ● *December 31*: New Year's Eve City hosts great new millennium celebration at Times Square. ● *June 25* Rochelle T "Rocky" Jones fire department's 1st woman Captain.

1999 *March 1* Recordmart, Times Square subway mezzanine, evicted after nearly 40 years by developers of skyscraper above. ● *March 30*: Dow closes at 10,006.78. 24 trading days later, closes at 11,014.69.

1999 *August 15* 40,000 gather in Central Park to hear Dalai Lama. ● *June* Iman El Hajji Izak-El Mu'eed Pasha is N.Y.P.D.'s 1st Muslim chaplain (40,000 officers; 102 Muslim).

1999 *April 8* Bronx Museum of Art opens permanent exhibit of works by African American, Asian American and Latin American artists. ● *February 18* New York Philharmonic performs 13,000th concert. ● International Jazz Museum to open in city.

1999 On old Penn Central Railroad Yards, 1st 2 towers by Donald Trump (son of Fred Trump) open. Jimmy Breslin writes: "I don't see what right people have to buy the sky. If you did that in a movie I'd tell you to sit down." ● Last surviving Checker cab removed.

Checker cab PL

2001 *January:* Earthquake in city measures 2.5 on the Richter scale. ● *September 11* Muslim terrorists highjack 2 airliners and fly them into World Trade Center. 1st plane hits Tower One at 8.45 am. 2nd hits Tower Two at 9.03 am. Extreme heat causes towers to collapse. Nearly 3,000 people die, including 343 fire-fighters, 23 police officers, 37 Port Authority police officers, and other emergency personnel. 5 other buildings in World Trade Center complex also collapse.

New York grieves DP

2000 *May 31* Jazz great mambo King, Tito Puente, dies. 1,000s watch his funeral procession.

2000 *March* Undercover officer Vasquez shoots Haitian, Dorismond, who objects to questions about drugs. At funeral, 1,000s of mourners confront police in riot gear. 27 arrests. 23 officers and 7 civilians injured.

2001 *November 12* American Airline jet crashes soon after take-off in Rockaways, Queens. All 260 passengers and crew die, and 5 people on ground.

2001 *September 17* Trading on Wall Street resumes but with highest 1-day drop in history.

2000 *May 3* Cardinal John O'Connor dies aged 80; succeeded by Bishop E.M. Egan.

2001 *July 30* Harlem welcomes former president Clinton who moves into his 125th Street office.

Bill Clinton PB

2000 Eltinge Theater reopens as multiplex cinema

2001 New $22 million home of American Museum of Folk Art opens (45 West 53rd Street). ● St John's University win N.C.A.A. Fencing Championship.

2000 *September 12* 10 lanes of Queensboro Bridge finally open, including pedestrian and bicycle lane.

2002 *March 11* The Sphere, a burned, mangled relic from Twin Towers, is dedicated in Battery Park as sign of hope. ● *March 11 - April 13* Tribute In Light, 2 giant light rays beam out to fill void in night skyline for over a month, projecting nearly a mile into space, in memory of those who died.

2002 *September 11* One year after September 11, 2001, families stand in the pit amid swirling dust, as names of dead are read aloud. Bagpipers march from all corners of city to Trade Center site. Relatives leave a ring of personal shrines. Later, George W. Bush joins them. The mayor, surrounded by international leaders, lights an eternal flame. Parks in all 5 boroughs host candlelit concerts.

Bagpipers Ground Zero DP

2002 14 million visit Central Park each year – open 18 hours daily. Some 42 bald eagles and 11,000 hawks seen annually. One golden eagle spotted, and 20 raccoons live there. Strawberry Fields, 3-acre tribute to John Lennon, has 161 different species of plants from 150 nations. ● President Bush agrees to transfer Governors Island to state. ● Co-Op City with 50,000 residents may go private to raise monies. ● Major increase in homeless families. An old Bronx jail houses homeless for a while. ● *July* For 1st time in over 25 years, borough's welcome road signs change. Now they read: "How Sweet It Is!" and "Name it . . . We got It!"

Bald eagle PL

2002 Year of economic losses on Wall Street.

2002 *October 15* Sex scandal rocks Catholic church when 40 people claim abuse by clergy members (including a bishop) over 50 years in Brooklyn Diocese. ● In 1 year John Liu, 1st Asian elected to citywide office, has achieved many goals, including cleaning up downtown Flushing.

2002 May Department of Education H.Q. moves to Tweed Courthouse, by City Hall. ● *March 7* Liam Neeson leads celebrated cast in Arthur Miller's drama *The Crucible* about Salem witches.

Tweed Courthouse DP

2002 August 15 Musical *Hairspray* hits Broadway by storm. ● *October Movin' Out* music and dance, inspired by Billy Joel's music, makes exciting ballet. ● All-stars from New York win enthusiastic support but not the Little League World Series.

2002 Knicks fail to make the playoffs for 1st time since 1987. ● Yankees fail to make World Series: 1st time in 55 years. ● Giants and Jets make playoffs in same season for 1st time since 1986. Giants finish with a 7-9 record just 1 year after reaching Super Bowl. ● *December 19* Yankees sign Japanese power hitter, Hideki Matsui.

2002 On May 28, those who labored at Ground Zero take turns to cut last girder. On May 30, Ground Zero closes as an empty stretcher is slowly carried out, representing those never recovered. Final debris is trucked up ramp with last flag-draped girder. Workers had removed 1.7 million tons of debris.

2002 *September 17* Reopening of restored Winter Garden, St Paul's Chapel, after 8 months of tending to Ground Zero site workers. ● *December 7* new teams of architects unveil design plans for 16 acres of new World Trade Center.

2003 *February 17* Snow blankets U.S. east coast. ● *February 15* Huge crowds of anti-war demonstrators; 100,000 converge near United Nations to protest. ● *April* Iraqi envoy's son faces spy charge. ● *February 21* Massive explosion at Exxon Mobil oil plant on Staten Island. Blast starts huge fire.

Raccoon PL

2003 *February 19* German court jails Mounir Motassadeq, 28-year-old Moroccan, for helping 9/11 suicide hijackers.

2002 *August* State Supreme Court Justice Victor Barron given prison sentence for taking $100,000+ bribe over a lawsuit settlement. ● *August 29* Former City Councilman Rodriguez sent to prison for 5 years for taking $50,000 cash and over $1 million in property for supporting construction of Red Hook supermarket. He says: "Politics is a tough business, and sometimes there are many, many, many temptations out there." ● *September 18* Spraying for West Nile virus returns as a man succumbs to deadly virus. At New York Hospital, Queens, Dr. Rahal finds that alpha-interferon, a protein injection, lessens symptoms. ● *September 23* Lamont Branch wins freedom after 13 years in prison for murder. His brother admits to crime. ● *December* Couple robbed and beaten at isolated Long Island Railroad station in Flushing Meadows Park. Woman is gang raped. 6 men face charges. ● *December 5* After 13 years, charges dropped against 5 convicted men who served time over racially charged Central Park jogger case.

2003 Wall Street: 10 brokerages reach a deal with regulators over charges of bamboozling investors during 1990s. ● *April* American Airlines staff vote to accept a pay cut to help company stave off bankruptcy. ● *January 29* AOL TW posts loss of nearly $100 billion AOL Time Warner post 2002 as largest annual loss in U.S. corporate history. ● *January 27* Dow Jones dips below 8,000. ● *March* Stocks soar to best gains of year on 13th. By 21st, Dow rises for 8th consecutive session.

2003 *March 8* Broadway shows closed by strike. ● Raiders silence Jets 30-10 in playoffs and return to A.F.C. Championship.

2003 *February 26* Spire design by Daniel Libeskind chosen for New World Trade Center. ● New piers planned to be built in Brooklyn for the new larger cruise ships.

2003 *January* European Union against military action in Iraq. Anti-war protests sweep world. ● *February 1* In Texas, space shuttle and crew lost on re-entry. ● *March - April* President Bush warns Saddam Hussein he has 48 hours to leave Iraq. ● *March 19* U.S. and U.K. launch 3-week war. Their troops enter and control cities including Baghdad. Saddam Hussein disappears.

The future
2017 By 2017 there will be no unsold cemetery plots in city.

2 Riots in Los eles

1994 Nelson Mandela president of S. Africa

l War in former oslavia

1993 ATF assault on Koresh's H.Q. in Waco, Texas

1995 Israeli P.M. Rabin assassinated

Truck bomb explodes in Oklahoma

1996 Taliban capture Afghanistan

1997 U.S. *Pathfinder* transmits images from Mars

1998 U.S. embassies bombed.

1998 Peace agreed in Northern Ireland

1999 President Clinton impeached

1999 War in Kosovo

1999 Global warming an issue

1999 Floods in India

2000 Concorde crashes near Paris

2001 Terrorist attacks on Pentagon and Flight 93

2002 North Korea admits to developing nuclear bomb

2002 Human genome deciphered

2002 Tensions increase between U.S.A. / U.K. and Iraq

2002 Civil War in Angola

THE TIMELINE HISTORY OF
NEW YORK CITY

INTRODUCTION

In an exposé of high life and lowlife in New York City after the Civil War, Junius Henri Browne wrote: "New-York is the City of the time to come. The sea that washes its shores is murmuring of its greatness; the breezes that fan it are whispering of its beauty; the stars that shine over it are silently predicting its excellence."

The city has known dark days, and has had more than its share of terrible fires, civil conflict and

hardship. It has also known things which few other cities have experienced: a sense of absolute superiority, of size and great wealth, and profound influence over a nation which spanned a continent.

Within living memory New York has become the dominant city in the world. For a long time it has not been the largest city in the world nor does it have the tallest skyscraper, yet it remains the richest in possibilities.

There is for New York, a natural language of superlatives – biggest, tallest, richest, most diverse – and extremes. There are half-truths in many of these claims, and a fair sprinkling of exaggeration. Nonetheless it is true that New York will never just be another large city, with the usual range of problems which urban life creates.

The outsized ambition of the city, its cultural riches and its historical complexity, makes a

Timeline which unfolds across 14 feet, supported by a world of facts and images and presented in a colorful and informative way, a wonderfully appropriate invitation: "Welcome to New York. There is a lot to check out here."

Eric Homberger
author of THE HISTORICAL ATLAS OF NEW YORK CITY
Professor of American Studies
University of East Anglia
Norwich UK

Contents

How to use this book

This book provides a unique combination of timeline and conventional book pages to create a highly informative document – one that presents all the events, great and small. It covers the history and culture of New York City in a way that is both clear and accessible.

The Timeline
Each page can be turned over or the whole timeline can be folded out to create a continuous 14 feet to be viewed.

Streams
The information in the timeline is separated out into various "streams":
Historical events
People
Lifestyle
Commerce
Politics and religion
Culture and art
City structure and development

U.S.A. & World events
The narrow stream at the bottom of the chart shows what was happening in the rest of the world and the U.S.A. at the same time as New York developed.

Factfinder
In order to help trace information, the Factfinder links events and personalities to dates and places. Thus it acts as a useful summary of events as well as an index to lead the reader to the appropriate date on the chart.

Special subjects
The Timeline has space for only very brief information on any one subject or event. In order to compensate for this, additional historical material is in the book and on the reverse of the timeline.

The wheel
100 buildings of New York: Turn the wheel 360 degrees and find information on each one, plus facts and figures about the highest buildings in Manhattan. One side of the wheel shows the date each structure was built, the height and the number of floors – while the addresses and architects can be found in the slots on the reverse.

Maps
There are fold-out maps of the Rivers, Central Park and Buildings in Manhattan – each one contains an exceptional amount of highly interesting information.

Acknowledgements and copyright details are on page 38 inside back cover of the book

To find a specific item in the timechart, refer to the Factfinder on page 73.

The streams vary in size as the events or changes require. This in itself is a reflection of the pattern of history and culture – and shows for example, the surge of new settlers that arrived in the 1640s.

The names of the streams are repeated on every other page to help readers follow the flow.

A stream of World Events runs through the entire timechart so that the reader can see, for example, when New Amsterdam was just a few wooden structures and a windmill, the Taj Mahal was being built in India.

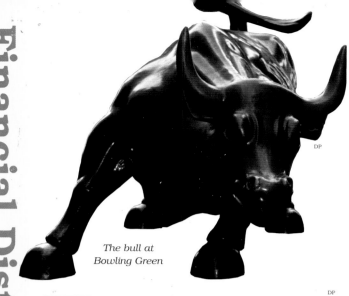

The bull at Bowling Green

Above: *City Hall*   Below: *Castle Clinton*

The financial area is an evocative mix of colonial buildings, narrow streets and towering skyscrapers. Fortunes have been made and lost here. Meanwhile, laws and the organisation of the city have been created and upheld in the fine Civic Center

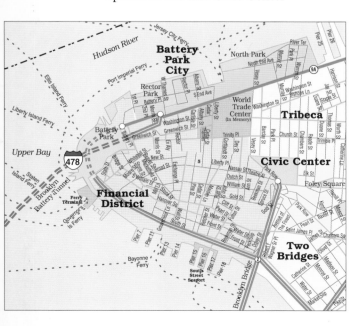

New York Banks

There are about 1,319 bank branches in New York City. The only black-owned bank is the Carver Savings Bank on 25th Street near Lenox Avenue.

> **Approximately 40% of the world's monetary gold is stored in the city.**

The *Federal Reserve Bank* of New York is the largest of 12 in the Federal Reserve System, and is the banker for the U.S. government. The city branch holds the world's largest store of gold valued at $117 billion, twice the value of the gold at Fort Knox. 12,000 tons of gold (700,000 bricks valued at $153,000 each) is kept 5 stories underground in a vault – accessible only by elevator. Security can seal off the building within 30 seconds. When one country pays a debt to another, the bullion simply moves from cell to cell.

Landmarks and museums

The area's rich history can be explored at the *Museum of American Financial History*, former law office of first Secretary of the Treasury, Alexander Hamilton. Other monetary landmarks include The *New York Stock Exchange* and the *Mercantile Exchange*, which trades in gold and precious metals, the *Federal Reserve Bank* and *Trinity Church*, where Alexander Hamilton is buried. *Tontine Coffee House* was built in 1793 at the corner of Wall and Water Streets. In 1796 it became the H.Q. of the New York Insurance Company, precurser of the Stock Exchange. Values were assigned to houses, slaves, and ships to form a tontine – each member received a share of the profit that increased as other members died. Archibald Gracie was its first president and his home on the East River became the official mayoral residence.

Wall Street

This small street runs along the original northern edge of New Amsterdam where, in about 1653, a small wooden wall was built to protect against attacks by Native Americans, New Englanders, or the British. The British demolished this in 1699, but the street became the site of the New York Stock Exchange and is synonymous with high finance. At noon on 16th September 1920, a terrorist bomb exploded beside J P Morgan and Company at 23 Wall Street, killing 33 and injuring more than 400. Scars from the explosion remain visible in the stonework. A statue of Washington at the steps of *Federal Hall* marks the first ever presidential oath taken at this spot in 1789. The fine classical building was raised 1834-1842. By contrast,

The New York Stock Exchange, floor (above) *and exterior* (left)

Battery Park City epitomises the new New York, built in the 1980s on 92 reclaimed acres (37 ha.) by 50,000 workers at a cost of $4 billion. Despite the loss of the World Trade Center towers, it remains an impressive architectural mix.

Castle Clinton

1808-11 A single tier fort with 28 gun-mountings was built to protect the harbor from invasion. It never saw combat.
1823 Given to the city and converted into Castle Garden, a center for entertainment.
1830 Aeronaut, Charles Durant, launched his balloon flight here.
1850 Singer Jenny Lind presented by P T Barnum.
1855 Reclaimed by city and used as an immigration station.
1896 Converted into New York Aquarium – here till 1941.
1950 Designated a national monument.
1970s Restored and now has ticket booths for Statue of Liberty and Ellis Island ferries.

Civic Center and Seaport

Here in the gracious Civic Center, overlooked by the grandeur of the Woolworths

Building, are many fine municipal structures that include the New York County Courthouse, United States Courthouse, the Municipal Building, Criminal Courts Building, Surrogates Court (Hall of Records) and City Hall. In the 1880s, this was the heart of the newspaper industry and is still the center of the city's police department. St. Paul's Chapel on Broadway dates from the 1700s and claims the pew where George Washington knelt in prayer after his inauguration. Nearby, the bustling *South Sea Seaport* dates from the 1800s and still has ship owners' and merchants' houses in Schermerhorn Row, built in 1811. The Titanic Memorial lighthouse on Fulton Street was raised in 1913 in memory of those who died. *Fulton Fish Market* first opened in 1821. There are many oyster bars here with clam chowder for sale. Historic ships can be seen from Pier 17.

Right: *17 State Street*
Below: *Pier 17, its cafés and bars*

Engraving of I.M. Singer & Co.'s Sewing Machine Factory at Center and Elm Streets, 1853, showing sophisticated steam-powered equipment.

SoHo and Tribeca are today havens for artists, inspired by the splendid cast-iron architecture in these areas. Much of this was threatened with demolition in the 1960s but has, thankfully, been saved and now is being restored. Soho was once refered to as "Hell's Hundred Acres" because its crowded slums were constantly razed by devastating fires, rebuilt and razed again.

Chinatown is a thriving mix of the Orient and America, where even the banks have pagoda-style features. Exotic shops sell Chinese food and artefacts while in Columbus Park men play board games on the site of a dire 19th-century slum.

This 120-year-old enclave has a population that has been as high as 150,000 – the largest gathering of Chinese outside China's mainland – but is now about 80,000. Of the estimated 300,000 Chinese in New York, about half live in Chinatown but this is changing as a flow of Chinese are moving to Astoria.

SoHo
"SoHo" is an acronym for the area South of Houston Street. Until the late 1700s, it was largely rural and cut off by marshland. With the filling in of the Collect Pond and the paving of Broadway to Astor Place, the area became the most populous ward, with a large freed-slave population. Retail emporiums like Tiffany's, elegant hotels, theaters and music halls arrived and Broadway became an entertainment center – and also one of the largest red-light districts in the city.

Shops, cast iron and hats
As the entertainment district moved up to 14th Street, the residential areas in SoHo diminished, to be replaced by prestigious grocers, textile merchants and furniture stores. Needing space and attractive shop fronts, the store owners commissioned new cast-iron "palaces" with façades reminiscent of Venice. Initially, architects tried to give the cast iron the appearance of stone, by covering it with paint and sand, but then, as its popularity grew, they began to exploit the properties of cast iron, creating decorative new motifs. One block, between Broome and Spring streets, has 13 cast-iron façades.
By the early 20th century, the district was a millinery center with felt hat makers, and fur and feather processors. Then came light manufacturing and warehousing.

SoHo streets
Greene Street, named after the Revolutionary War hero, General Greene, is still cobblestoned, and has the largest number of cast-iron buildings in the world, as well as some fine bishop's crook lampposts.
Broome Street is named for John Broome, the city's first alderman and a lieutenant governor. He initiated the lucrative China tea trade by imported the first two million pounds of tea.
Here the Gunther Building has unusual curved windowpanes and a splendid roof cornice. The protruding pedestal blocks on both sides of the Gunther Building plaque once supported life-size statues. The diminishing heights of each floor create an illusion of rather greater height.
The "ou" in Houston St is pronounced "ow" because the street was named for William Houston, a Georgian delegate to the Continental Congress and this was how he pronounced his name.

SoHo today
SoHo is now a center of creativity, popular with artists and sculptors, and has many galleries. However, rising rents are driving the less affluent and younger artists to less expensive neighborhoods. There are still sweat shops employing Chinese immigrant labor at subsistence wages.

Singer Building
Isaac M. Singer was a humble laborer, repairing an early sewing machine when, in just 12 hours, he devised his simple revolutionary sewing machine model. He had to borrow $40 to complete the prototype and apply for his 1851 patent. He went into partnership, founded the Singer Manufacturing Company and launched an industrial empire.
The ornate skyscraper that bore his name was 612 feet (186.5 m.) tall. It was completed in 1911, after zoning laws limited the height of new buildings to make them relative to the area they covered and the street frontage – thus establishing setbacks and terraces. This was the tallest building in the world for 18 months.

Museums
SoHo is home to some excellent museums that include the New Museum of Contemporary Art, the Guggenheim Museum of SoHo, the Alternative Museum, and the Museum for African Art. New York City Fire Museum, housed in an old fire station, has 17th-century firemarks and fine old fire engines.

Points of interest
The *St Nicholas Hotel* on Broadway was once used as an H.Q. for the Union Army.
The first Otis steam-powered safety elevator was installed in the *Haughwout Building* on Broome Street. Haughwout, a specialist in tableware, commissioned this building, one of the first cast-iron masterpieces.
The Holland Tunnel, built in 1927 to link Manhattan with New Jersey, is close to the site of what was once a park built by Cornelius Vanderbilt and then a railroad depot (demolished 1936).
The federal-style *Ear Inn* in Spring Street, originally stood on the edge of the Hudson. As port traffic grew, the river was filled in up to West Street to make room for more docks. The house became a distillery, then during Prohibition, a brothel and speakeasy.

Tribeca
Originally known as Lower West Side, Tribeca's new name

Tribeca can claim the first skyscraper in the U.S., the Woolworth Building.

Even the banks have an oriental style . . .   . . . and the streets are full of Chinese lettering

derived from "Triangle Below Canal". In 1705, Queen Anne gave the land here to Anthony Lispenard and Trinity Church parish. When the lands were later sold off, the streets were given the landowners' names.

Fruit and factories
From 1850-1920, the western end of Tribeca was a trading center for wholesale fruit, vegetables and dairy products; it has Romansque Revival warehouses and factories, many built of brick. Its eastern section has Italianate commerce palaces with marble façades. As steamship traffic grew, docks spread along the river banks and much of the produce landed here was taken to Washington Market.

A place to live
Today Tribeca has become a residential area. There are fine, small cast-iron buildings along White Street while Harrison Street has a pleasing row of Federal style townhouses.

Lobby tiles and mosaic
The Western Union Building occupies an entire block on Hudson Street. Its lobby

Playing traditional Chinese games in Columbus Park

has orange, brick walls and above, a superb glazed tile ceiling that curves into a basket arch.
The Art Dec AT&T building on Sixth Avenue has a huge tiled map of the world in its lobby and allegories are depicted in mosaic on the ceiling.

Gang warfare
The Dead Rabbits and Plug Uglies gangs once terrorised the streets of Chinatown. Liu Shih's monument to Confucius stands in Confucius Plaza. Close by is Doyers Street. At the end of the 1700s, this street was used as a cart lane for a distiller, Anthony H Doyer, and was named for him. A hundred years later, the area was called the Bloody Angle as so many violent gang fights and ambushes were perpetrated here. In the 1920s, the Tongs secret organisation held sway. The Hip Sing and the On Leong used to battle here for control of local criminals.

Chinese settlers
Seamen from a Chinese junk *Kee Ying* arrived in New York in 1847. They were followed by Chinese coolies who came to work on the transcontinental railway to California and settled in this area, then owned by John Mott and Joshua Pell. Others set out to work in the gold mines out west but moved to New York when the mines' yield dropped.

Statue of Lin Ze Xu who fought against drugs

Some 2,000 people a month arrived in 1965 after the easing of restrictions on immigration from the Far East. The immigration reform of 1986 failed to stem the flow as illegal immigrants were still smuggled

A Chinese Clubhouse in 1874, depicting opium smokers and Chinese sailors gambling with dominoes. The first Chinese settled in New York in 1858 and by the 1880s, the city's Chinese population was about 700.

in – at a charge of up to $50,000 dollars per head.

Chinatown today
Today there are throngs of people, and many small shops selling cheap watches, scarves, vegetables and fish. The streets are lined with ramshackle buildings, bright pagodas, and inscriptions in Chinese characters. Apart from tourism, a strong clothing industry has also developed.
New York police statistics would seem to indicate that Chinatown is the safest part of the city – but this is only because no-one dares report any crime. Power is stil in the hands of organized Mafia-like gangs.

Temples and statues
The heart of Chinatown lies immediately north of the Civic Center. There is a Buddhist temple in Pell Street and another in Mott Street, surrounded by restaurants and souvenir shops.
Edward Mooney House, one of the oldest buildings in Manhattan, dates from about 1785. Opposite this is Confucius Plaza with a statue of Confucius presented by the Chinese community in 1976. In Chatham Square, the Kim Lau memorial, was erected in 1962 to commemorate Americans of Chinese descent who fell in the war. Here, too, is a statue of Lin Ze-Xu, a hero of the Opium

Wars. This was raised in 1997, the year in which the British colony of Hong Kong was handed back to China.

Irish bars
In the 1800s, Doyers Street and Pell Street had many Irish bars. A Chinese restaurant is still called its original Irish name of *Pell's Dinty*.
The post office occupies the site where one of the most popular bars, *Callahan's* used to stand. Scantily dressed waitresses and singers attracted customers. Al Jolson and Irving Berlin used to work here.
At 70 Mulberry Street is the small *Museum of Chinese in the Americas* where much can be discovered about the history and culture of Chinese in the West.

Imported goods for the Chinese

41

This area is a fascinating mix of ethnic groups and their vibrancy has had an impact on the neighborhoods. Here the streets have witnessed dire poverty but great hope and determination, too.

Little Italy
Today the Italian population of Little Italy is only some 5,000 but the atmosphere is still Continental, especially during the Feast of San Gennaro in September when the saint's shrine and relics are paraded through the streets.
Mulberry Street is full of Italian restaurants and stores and during the San Gennaro

celebrations, many stalls sell Italian homemade pasta, sausages, breads and pastries. On a more sombre note, in 1972, Mafia boss, Joey Gallo, was shot in *Umberto's Clam House* during a family dinner. The area was shown in both the *Godfather I* and *Godfather II* films about the Mafia.
The former *Police Headquarters Building* in Centre Street, erected in 1909 in the Baroque style of a French town hall, was funded in part through bootlegging pay-offs by liquor merchants to the police in Prohibition times. It has now been restructured as a luxury apartment block.
On the corner of Grand and Mulberry streets, is the Banca Stabile, a family-run Italian bank set up in 1865 to help immigrants. Tickets for transatlantic crossings could be bought here.

San Gennaro Celebrations
In September, when the festival is on in Little Italy, the streets are closed to traffic and full of stalls selling Italian food and fare, clothes and souvenirs. Mulberry Street is the focal point of the festivities and is where the patron saint of Naples has his parade. The celebrations last for ten days from noon to midnight each day when the streets are crowded with visitors.

The streets have to be cleaned at least on Mondays and Thursdays! At festival times, there are barbecues on the street

Lower East Side and the Bowery
After Broadway, the 17th-century Bowery (Bouwerie means farm) is New York's 2nd oldest street and follows the line of an old Indian trail. Peter Stuyvesant, the last Dutch governor, purchased the land and built an approach road to his estate. The Bowery lay outside city limits until the extension of New York in the 1800s, when it became a residential street for wealthy New Yorkers, such as fur dealer, Jacob Astor.
In 1826, the Great Bowery Theater opened, along with music halls, other theaters, and beer gardens, but then the area declined. Entertainment moved to Broadway and business to Fifth Avenue. The Bowery became disreputable with many

Lower East Side population
This are now some:
40% Puerto Rican and Spanish speaking
30% Chinese
15% Jewish
10% Black
5% others (Indian, Ukrainian, Polish, Albanian, and Italian)

Knickerbocker Baseball Club
This was formed in 1842 to play the precursor of modern baseball. In 1845, members of the club competed against each other in Manhattan before moving to the Elysian fields in Hoboken, New Jersey. The Knickerbockers remained an amateur social and athletic club until they disbanded in the mid-1870s.

Two Bridges
This small area is set between The Brooklyn and Manhattan bridges, built 1870-83 and 1901-09, respectively. The approach to the Manhattan Bridge has a fine colonnade based on St. Peters in Rome and promenades (shown left in 1900, and below today).

homeless, beggars and alcoholics. It still has soup kitchens and doss-houses, including a Men's Shelter, offering free beds and meals in what was once a Y.M.C.A. This historical area has aways been popular with immigrants and has welcomed Dutch, Irish, Black, Jewish, Italian, Chinese, German and Latin American families. During the 1870s, the Lower East Side was called "The Big Onion": every time a layer was peeled away, there was another nationality hiding underneath.

By the late 1800s, the Bowery had become a place for the homeless and spoored many illegal activities. In 1884, it accounted for 27% of arrests in New York and had 82 bars, an average of 6 per block.

By 1910, thousands of Jews lived here, many working as street vendors. Hester Street was very busy, especially on Thursday evenings when women came to buy provisions for the Sabbath. In Essex Street at the heart of the old Jewish business district, many came to eat gherkins at the famous Guss's Pickles store, still operating today.

Lower East Side
New immigrants from many nations now occupy some of these neighborhoods of low-rise buildings, but the old flavor remains. Composer Irving Berlin grew up here. He once said, "Everybody ought to have a Lower East Side in their life."

Tenement Museum
This museum on Orchard Street is housed in a former tenement building from 1863, that would once have been "bursting at the seams" with immigrant families. Several apartments simulate living conditions then.

The Educational Alliance
This Broadway building, first erected in 1891, was known as the Hebrew Institute and was a social, educational, cultural, and intellectual center for the residents of Lower East Side.

Its classes in English and citizenship helped train newcomers and sped up their assimilation into the American neighborhood. Its classes were later used as models for the New York City Board of Education's citizenship program. There was a free library – at a time when no public libraries existed in the city. Clothing and food were given to the needy, and children were taught Jewish religion and history. There were free Sabbath and High Holy Day services for the poor and summer camps for the children.

The Alliance expanded to offer free courses in art, music, philosophy, drama, science, and vocational skills. It now holds classes for children whose parents work during the day and is active in community projects, and in helping senior citizens. The original East Broadway building was modernized in 1970-71 and renamed the David Sarnoff Building.

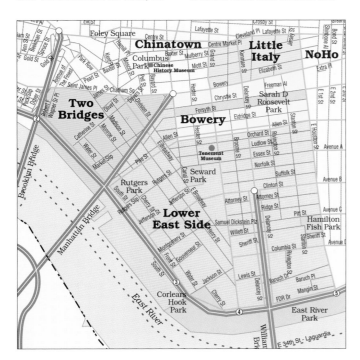

Elegant fire escapes grace many buildings here and were a legal requirement by the early 1920s

New York is ever a city of contrasts and this is very evident in these areas. Chelsea has been home to the rich and famous – but in the late 1800s was an area of tenements and poverty.

Similarly, the Garment District, now dominated by fashion houses, was once full of brothels and gambling dens – while Greenwich has been an area of prosperity and fine Georgian houses, as well as a backdrop to demonstrations and gay riots.

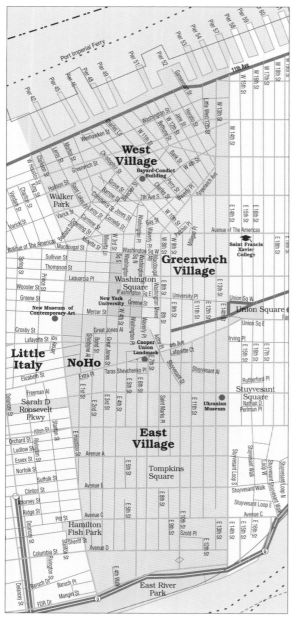

During his visits to the city, Dylan Thomas drank at the White Horse Tavern and stayed at the Chelsea Hotel

Greenwich Village

Canarsie Indians called this swampy, wooded area Sapohanikan and set up a trading post here. Later, during the Dutch period, tobacco farming dedeveloped. Governor Van Twiller seized 222 acres for a private plantation and in 1696, his "wooded farm" was renamed Greenwich Village by the English.

Through three centuries, Georgian, Federal and Greek Revival houses were built. Greenwich became prosperous, centered around the shipping industry. In the 1820s, Lower Manhattan residents fled here to avoid cholera and yellow fever. At the foot of Christopher Street stood Newgate Prison from 1797 to 1829.

Greenwich street pattern reflects old boundaries and streams, and does not conform to the city's grid. Here are New York University and Washington Square Park – in the 1960s, a scene of Anti-War movement. At the *Stonewall Inn*, the first gay rights riot took place in 1969.

Today the Halloween costume parade and the Gay Pride March draw thousands. The area has ever been a bohemian haven for artists and writers. Washington Square Park remains a forum for oratory, demonstrations, fashion parades and music of all kinds.

Northern Dispensary

This clinic opened in 1827 to provide low-cost or free health care for the local residents. In 1831, it moved to a triangular building by Christopher Street.

White Horse Tavern

This tavern, built in 1880, is one of the few timber-framed buildings left in the city. It was a speakeasy during Prohibition and a seamen's bar until the late 1940s. It was frequented by Welsh poet, Dylan Thomas, during his visits to New York. In 1953 a room was dedicated to his memory.

NoHo

The name is short for "North of Houston". Here were the botanic gardens that John Jacob Astor bought to develop the area which became known as Astor Place. More recent

residents have included Keith Richards and Cher.

East Village

Here Cooper Union offered free education when it was built in 1859 and has the oldest auditorium in New York. In the 1960s, many writers, artists and musicians moved here from Greenwich in search of cheaper housing. The area saw a rise in drug-related problems in the 70s and riots in the 80s. In 1990, police evicted the homeless from Tomkins Square Park, leading to more marches and violence.

Top: *The Cooper Union*
Middle *and* bottom: *Interior and exterior of the General Post Office*

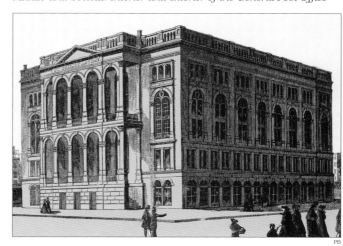

Some famous Greenwich Village residents

- W. H. Auden
- Alexander Calder
- E.E. Cummings
- Jimi Hendrix
- Edward Hopper
- Fiorello La Guardia
- Sinclair Lewis
- Herman Melville
- Eugene O'Neill
- Edgar Allen Poe
- Katherine Anne Porter
- Margaret Sanger
- Mark Twain

Chelsea

Chelsea was named by Captain Clarke, a retired English Naval Officer who bought land here in 1750 and called it after the Chelsea Royal Hospital in London. In 1822, his grandson, Clement Moore, wrote *A Visit from St. Nicholas*, while he was driving in a sleigh, back for Christmas dinner.
He is buried in Trinity Church Cemetery, Riverside Drive; each Christmas a candlelight procession of children lays a wreath on his grave.

Chelsea grows

By the 1830s Chelsea had changed from farmland to city suburb. In the 1870s, when 9th Avenue El (the city's first overhead railway) arrived, so did music halls, theaters, department stores, dray wagons and horse-drawn omnibuses. The *Haymarket* became the most-raided den of vice in the city's history.
Soon the motion-picture industry was working in silent movie studios in vast, barnlike buildings. By the end of the 1800s, however, department stores drove wealthier residents uptown. Warehouses sprang up and tenements housed poor immigrants. Chelsea was left a depressed district, until the Els vanished and New Yorkers rediscovered the area, buying up and restoring the spendid town houses. The Historic District of Old Chelsea is now a quiet residential area.

General Post Office

Completed in 1913, this fine edifice was inspired by the original Penn Station whose designers, McKimm, Mead and White were commissioned to undertake this building, too.

Chelsea's yellow cabs

Swarms of yellow cabs emerge from their compounds, west of Tenth Avenue at 5.00 p.m. as cabs change over from day to night shift.

Chelsea Hotel

Guests at this famous hotel (opened on 23rd Street in 1884) have included Dylan Thomas, Jack Kerouac, Tennessee Williams, Mark Twain, and Brendan Behan. Edgar Lee Master wrote a poem called *The Hotel Chelsea*.

Hell's Kitchen

This area was farmland and forest until the 1700s when a glass bottle factory arrived. By the late 1800s, there were warehouses, slaughter houses, gangs and some of the worst slums in the city. The name may derive from a local gang called this in about 1870. There are still warehouses, Irish bars and tenements.

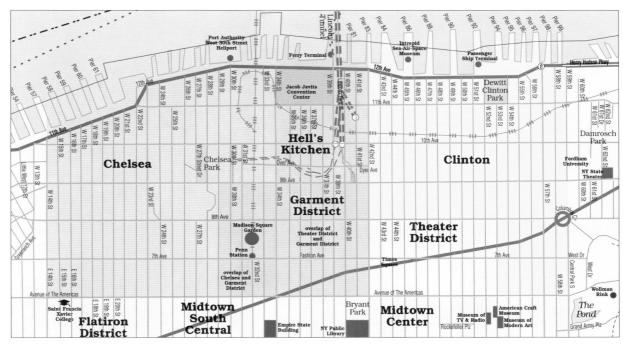

DP

DP

Madison Square Garden

This concrete cylinder stadium has seating for 20,000 spectators and hosts many major sporting and musical events. It is home to the New York Knickerbockers basketball team and the New York Rangers hockey team (*above*).

Garment District

In the 1880s-90s, this area was filled with dance halls, bordellos, gambling parlors and nightclubs, and so was known as the Tenderloin District: the name refers to extortion payments made to the police.

Macy's and the fashion area

Macy's, the world's largest department store, grew from a small store in 1857, opened by a whaler. It expanded under Nathan and Isidor Straus. The latter was lost on the *Titanic* and is commemorated in a plaque by the main entrance. Later the brothels and gambling dens were replaced by stores as this bcame a fashion area. It is now the center of the U.S. "rag trade" where 7th Avenue is known as Fashion Avenue. The Fur District is at the southern end of the Garment District. The Flower District, around 6th Avenue and West 28th Street, is bright with floral displays – and very lively when florists pack their vans in the early morning.

Clinton

In 1959 this name was given to a neighborhood by the Hudson River, bounded by 42nd and 59th Streets and originally part of Hell's Kitchen.

Waterfront

Today the waterfront is home to the Circle Line tours, the Intrepid Sea Air Space Museum and the Jacob Javitts Convention Center.
The latter opened in 1986, has 16,000 panes of glass and a lobby high enough to absorb the Statue of Liberty.

DP

Top: *Statue of sewing machinist*
Above: *Wall advertising in the fashion area. Macy's star logo was inspired by a tattoo on the whaler who set up the original small store*

DP

Left: *One of the aircraft on the U.S.S. Intrepid at the Intrepid Sea Air Space Museum complex on Pier 86*

DP

Times Square is not a square at all. It is made up of two triangles created by Broadway crossing 7th Avenue. This was once an area for horse trading, blacksmiths, thieves and pickpockets.

Top: 1983 illuminated sign advertising New York as the Apple

Left: Also 1983, huge 3-dimensional sign

Below: A 1985 advertisment for Camel cigarettes carried a health warning.
The 1972 advertisment for Winston cigarettes had smoke continually puffing out from the mouth and carried no health warning

Left: George M. Cohan, 1878-1942, composer who wrote, Give my Regards to Broadway. *Right: Duffy Square, the north triangle of Times Square, is named after Father Duffy, a chaplain in World War II: 1938*

The New York Times Tower

The new Times headquarters officially opened on New Year's Eve, 1904, with a fireworks display that launched the first New Year's Eve celebration in Times Square. This was so successful that Times Square immediately replaced City Hall Park as the favorite site for New Yorkers to ring in the New Year.

1907 The first illuminated "time ball" was dropped on New Year's Eve.
1928 The first animated electric sign appeared in Times Square advertising.
1938 A statue of Father Duffy, chaplain to the 69th New York Regiment during World War 1 and a priest in Hell's Kitchen parish, is dedicated in the Times Square triangle, renamed Duffy Square.
1933 Douglas Leigh instals the first electric billboard, a steaming A & P coffee cup.
1941-66 Signs for Kool and Camel cigarettes, with their famous smoke rings, were installed, and then for Pepsi-Cola and for Super Suds detergent (showing 3,000 illuminated bubbles a minute).
1935 *Olympia Theater* was demolished.
1942 Times Square was blacked out during the war.
1945 As the war ended, Times Square celebrated V-E Day on May 8 and V-J Day on August 15 when 1,000s jammed the square. At 7.03 p.m. the news zipper on Times Tower declared: "Official Truman announces Japanese surrender".
1995 An old mains pipe ruptured and leaked for 8 hours under Times Square, causing $1 million damage.
1997 In May the news zipper around Times Tower was dismantled. 1,000s of 30-watt bulbs were replaced by digital zippers with 235,000 light-emitting diodes that would go into operation on July 29.
1999 On New Year's Eve, the city hosted a great millennium celebration at Times Square.

Sunday afternoon crowd listening to a Navy band.
The screen shows an aircraft carrier as the Navy are also recruiting.

Theatres arrive around Times Square

Previously, theater impresarios had believed that Long Acre would always be dominated by crime, drugs, and prostitution. However, with the arrival of the *New York Times*, the square developed a lively atmosphere and many new playhouses opened. Prostitutes still worked by the Times Tower, but the once $2-dollar streetwalkers now charged more, dressed well and often also worked a showgirls at the new dance halls on "Soubrette Row". By 1905, making a success on 42nd Street had become part of the great American Dream. Meanwhile, as the *New York Times* blossomed, William Hearst's publishing empire declined and he retaliated with strong editorials against bootleggers and show business entrepreneurs, Still he could not displace the *New York Times* that became the city's, and nation's, major newspaper.

Manteo Sicilian Marionette Theater

In 1923, the Manteo family built life-size marionettes and opened a theater on Lower East Side, later moving to Little Italy. They performed 394 episodes through 13 months of nightly performances to complete one long saga. After Aggrippino Manteo's death, the title of Papa Manteo passed to his son Miguel, who led the troupe until his death in 1990. The family have performed for the Festival of American Folklife at the Smithsonian Institution and the Staten Island Institute of Arts and Sciences. This is the last surviving company of its kind in North America.

Radio City Music Hall

The largest and most famous theater in the U.S. is in the Rockefeller Centre in an opulent Art Deco interior with 5,874 seats. It opened in December 1932. 3 large elevators on a vast stage create fast scene changes and dazzling effects: whole choruses can rise through the floor. In 1979, the interior was declared a landmark and restored. The theater has hosted the Grammy Awards, the Moscow Circus, an annual Christmas show, and concerts by Michael Jackson, Frank Sinatra, Liza Minnelli, and Shirley MacLaine. The Rockettes, 36 bejeweled dancers, arrived in 1933.

Theatres on or near Broadway today include:	
Ambassador	219 West 49th Street
American Airlines	227 West 42nd Street
Booth	222 West 45th Street
Broadhurst	235 West 44th Street
Broadway	681 Broadway
Brooks Atkinson	256 West 47th Street
Circle in the Square	1633 Broadway
Cort	138 West 48th Street
Ethel Barrymore	243 West 47th Street
Eugene O'Neill	230 West 49th Street
Ford Center	214 West 43rd Street
Gershwin	222 West 51st Street
Helen Hayes	240 West 44th Street
Imperial	249 West 45th Street
John Golden	252 West 45th Street
Longacre	220 West 48th Street
Lunt-Fontanne	205 West 46th Street
Lyceum	247 West 46th Street
Madison Sq. Garden	Seventh Ave/34th St
Majestic	247 West 44th Street
Marquis	1535 Broadway
Martin Beck	302 West 45th Street
Marquis	1535 Broadway
Minskoff	200 West 45th Street
Music Box	239 West 45th Street
Nederlander	208 West 41st Street
Neil Simon	250 West 52nd Street
New Amsterdam	214 West 42nd Street
Palace	1564 Broadway
Plymouth	236 West 45th Street
Richard Rodgers	226 West 46th Street
Royale	242 West 45th Street
Roundabout	1530 Broadway/45th Street
Shubert	225 West 44th Street
St. James	246 West 44th Street
Studio 54	524 West 54th Street
Virginia	219 West 48th Street
Walter Kerr	1634 Broadway
Winter Garden	245 West 52nd Street

Theatres off Broadway include:	
Astor's Playhouse	100 7th Avenue
American Jewish	307 West 26th Street
Astor Place	434 Lafayette Street
Circle in the Square	159 Bleeker Street
47th Street	304 West 47th Street
Joyce	175 8th Avenue
Kaufman	534 West 42nd Street
Lucille Lortel	121 Christopher Street
Mitzi E. Newhouse	Lincoln Center
Players	115 MacDougal Street
Playhouse 91	316 East 91st Street
Radio City Music Hall	1260 Sixth Ave 50th St.
Sullivan Street Playhouse	181 Sullivan Street
Union Square	100 East 17th Street
Variety Arts	110 Third Avenue
Vivian Beaumont	150 West 65th Street
Westside Theatre	407 West 43rd Street

During the early 1900s, Second Avenue had several Yiddish theaters.

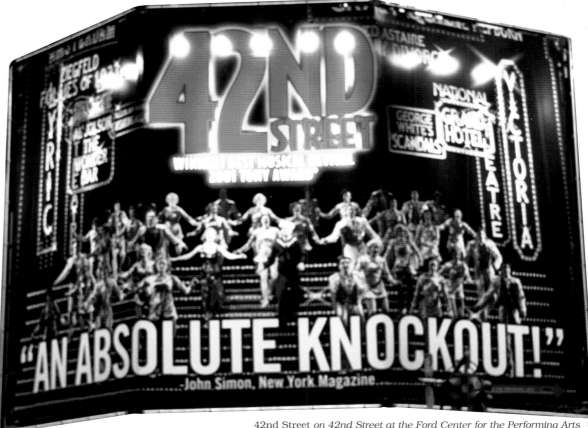

42nd Street on 42nd Street at the Ford Center for the Performing Arts DP

DP

On May 18, 2003, *Les Miserables* musical, based on Victor Hugo's 1861 novel, ended a 16-year run on Broadway with its 6,680th performance and ticket sales of $410 million since its opening in 1987. It is the 2nd-longest running show there, after *Cats*. One person paid $18,750 for a ticket for the final performance and, in its final week, the show grossed $853,505.

Cats opened at the Winter Garden Theater in October, 1982, and by 1997, had been seen by an estimated 8 million people (50 million worldwide), injecting some $3.12 billion into the New York City economy, using 231 actors, and outlasting 2 presidents (Reagan and Bush). By February, 2000, when its closure in June was announced, the longest-running production in the history of the city's theatre had been in performance for nearly 18 years with estimated takings of almost $400 million.

Cats, *the longest ever running show in New York* PL

Thoroughly Modern Millie DP

PL

Above: *The ever-changing illuminations of Times Square*
Below: *The Announcements of significant events*

Mounted police in Times Square

DP

Roxy Theater
This famous movie theater opened in 1927 on 50th Street and Broadway. It cost about $12 million and seated over 6,000. It even had its own infirmary – and a power plant that could have lit a city of 250,000. It was razed in 1961.

Construction starts	1920
Open to traffic	1927
Number of tubes	2
Number of traffic lanes	4
Length between portals north tube	8,558ft (2608m)
south tube	8,371ft (2551m)
Maximum depth, mean high water to roadway	93ft 5in (28.47m)
Supply and exhaust fans	42
Cost of original construction	$54,000,000

In the 1990s it cost $100 million to convert the rusting steel buildings into a 6-block, 30-acre sports complex. From **Pier 59** to 62 facilities include bowling, aerobic studios and Manhattan's largest cardiovascular and strength training facility.

Lincoln Tunnel

Construction starts	1934
Open to traffic center tube 1937; north tube 1945	south tube 1957
Number of lanes	6
Max length between portals (center tube)	8,216ft (2,504m)
External diameter	31ft (9.45m)
Maximum depth, mean high water to roadway	97ft (29.5m)
Cost of original structure	$75,000,000

In the 1990s it cost $100 million to convert **Pier 59** to a 4-story golf range, with 52 driving stalls on 4 levels surrounded by 15-story-tall netting. A 200-yard (182.88 m.) Sports Center, 150,000-sq. feet (13,935 sq.m.) running the length of 3 football fields, has a 1/4 mile (0.4 km.) indoor running track, 3 basketball/volleyball courts, volleyball court, a 46-foot (14 m.) rock-climbing wall, a 6-lane swimming pool, 2 outdoor sun decks, a spa and a boxing ring. **Pier 61** houses the Skating Club of New York, the second oldest in U.S. with 2 rinks for hockey and figure skating and seating for 1,800.

During its construction, "sandhogs" enter air locks; then the doors at each end are sealed. Air pressure climbs until equal to the next lock they must enter. Men must work fast because they can cope with the pressure only for brief intervals. Their time is limited to half an hour in the morning and half an hour in the afternoon, with five hours rest in between. The Lincoln Tunnel is the first major tunnel completed without a single fatality.
• On August 3, 1935, a hydraulic engineer from the New Jersey crew is pushed by his feet through an opening to meet the New York crew.
• The Lincoln Tunnel carries some 120,000 vehicles per day (40 million a year) and is the busiest motor vehicle tunnel in the world.

1910: the 1st piers open. At the height of sea travel, there are 9 piers and luxury White Star and Cunard liners, like the *Lusitania* and *Mauretania*, dock here. At a less salubrious level, immigrants board ferries for Ellis Island and World War soldiers depart.

Life-Saving 1877
Lifeguard rushes out with a life preserver on a rope anchored to the shore to help a swimmer in distress.
In 1926, 19-year-old Gertrude Ederle of Manhattan was the first woman to swim the English Channel. In 1995, 20 swimmers raced around Manhattan. Shelley Taylor Smith swam 28.5 miles in a record 5 hours, 45 minutes, 25 seconds.

Between **Piers 61** and **62** the 70,000 square-ft. Field House includes a 23,000-sq.ft. (2,136.7 sq.m.) gymnastics training center (largest in city), 2 basketball courts, 2 indoor soccer fields, lacrosse, martial-arts, 4 batting cages, dance studios, and a rock-climbing wall.

The Piers
Piers 53, 54 or **56**
Steamers from New York sailed from here. Cunard's brochure on 20 April, 1917, advertises sailings with excellent connections from England for:
India every week
Japan fortnightly
Australia weekly
China fortnightly

Rangoon every week
South Africa every week
Egypt every few days
South America every week
Deckchairs or rugs can be rented on board and cost of dollar each for the voyage.
Pier 54 Old Cunard pier (opposite 13th Street).
Here the *Titanic* survivors disembarked on April 19, 1912.

Sailed 1936- 67 (crossed Atlantic 1,001 times)
During World War II, she was painted gray for camouflage and nicknamed The *Gray Ghost*. Hitler offered a $250,000 reward and the Iron Cross to any submarine captain who could sink her. • Carried: 765,429 military personnel, Winston Churchill to conferences 3 times, wounded back to U.S., 12,886 G.I. brides and children – and sailed a total of 569,429 miles (916,407 km.).

Queen Elizabeth
Gross Tonnage	83,673 tons
Dimensions	987.4 x 118.6 feet (300.94 x 36.14m.)
Number of funnels	2
Number of masts	2
Service speed	29 knots
Built in	Glasgow, Scotland
Passengers	823 1st class
	662 cabin class
	798 tourist class

This was the largest liner ever built when she was launched in September, 1938. She went into wartime service in 1940 and by the end of the war had carried over 750,000 troops and travelled

500,000 miles.
She made her first passenger voyage to New York October, 1946 by 1951 had made her 100th Atlantic crossing. Her final crossing was in 1968.
She was first sold to a group of U.S. businessmen for £3,250,000, then to a Hong Kong shipping group for a £5 million refit to turn her into a university. On January 9 1972 fires spread through her – the work of an arsonist and went down near Kowloon. She appeared later, albeit scuttled, in a James Bond movie.

Queen Mary
Length	1,019 feet. (311 m.)
Beam	118 feet (35.97 m.)
Draft	39 feet (12 m.)
Officers and Crew	1,174
Passengers	1,957
Gross Registered Tons	81,237
Speed	28.5 knots
Portholes	over 2,000
Rivets	over 10 million
Rudder	140 tons
Number of Decks	12
Boilers	27
Built in Scotland	1930-1934

QE2
Original Cost	£29 million
Length	963 feet (293.5 m.)
Beam	105 feet (32.03 m.)
Draft	32 feet (9.87 m.)
Passenger Decks	13
Total Crew	1,015
Passengers	1,820 (1976)
Gross Registered Tons	70,327
Speed	28.5 knots
Built in Scotland	1965-1969

Customs check 1879
Travel became ever more popular in the 1800s and customs officers ever more vigilant as they checked baggage for any items subject to duty upon return from Europe.

Roosevelt Island (Welfare Island)
147 acres (59.5 hectares)
2 miles (3.2km) long
800ft (244m) wide at its broadest

1637 Island bought from Algonquin Indians and called Hog Island (Dutch raise pigs here). **1666** British reclaim island from Dutch. It is granted to Captain Manning, sheriff of New York, and known as Manning's Island. In 1673 he is sentenced to life imprisonment on island for relinquishing Fort James to Dutch without a shot being fired. **1686** Manning's stepdaughter renames island after her husband, Robert Blackwell. **1796** Blackwell house built – oldest structure here today. **1828** City purchases island and builds mental institutions, hospitals and prisons. **1842** Charles Dickens visits island and lunatic asylum. **1872** Convict laborers build 50ft (15.2m) tall lighthouse **1921** City renames Welfare Island. **1927** Mae West serves ten days in jail here. **1968** Island a training facility for city's Fire Department. **1973** Renamed Roosevelt Island. **1976** Tramway service opens. **1989** Subway service begins. **1970s-80s**: 3,200 residential units and stores constructed. **2068** Ownership of Roosevelt Island will revert to City of New York.

Queens-Midtown Tunnel
Construction starts	1936
Open to traffic	1940
Length between portals south tube	6,272ft (1,911.7m)
north tube	6,414ft (1955m)
Number of traffic lanes	4
External diameter of tunnel	31ft (9.45m)
Maximum depth, mean high water to roadway	86ft(26.2m)
Supply and exhaust fans	46
Fresh air per minute	2,889,000ft3 (81,807.8m3)
Cost of original structure	$52,758,000

In November 1939, ahead of schedule, "sandhogs" digging from Manhattan and Queens at a rate of 140ft (42.7m) per month, hole through successfully. • There were no deaths from "the bends" – only the second major tunnel to claim this. • It was largest non-Federal project of its time. • President Roosevelt is 1st to drive through.
• Today it takes 80,000 vehicles daily.

Swimming Pool 1870
This public bath was at the foot of Charles Street on the Hudson River, where 200 swimmers could be accommodated. Each visitor was allowed a 30-minute session for his "public hygiene and recreation".

Williamsburg Bridge
Type of bridge	Suspension
Construction starts	1896
Open to traffic	1903
Length of main span	1,600ft (487.68m)
Number of subway tracks	2
Height of towers	310ft (94.5m)
Length of each of 4 cables	2,985ft (909.83m)
Total length of wires used	17,500ml (28162.75km)
Weight of cables and suspenders	4,344tons (4,413,504kg)
Cost of original structure	$24,200,000

Brooklyn Bridge took twice as long to build as Williamsburg Bridge. • Built in 7 years, this is longest, heaviest suspension bridge in the world then – and 1st made entirely of steel. It is the 2nd bridge made over the East River.

Queensboro Bridge
Type of bridge	Cantilever (multi-span)
Construction starts	1901
Open to traffic	1909
Length of western main span	1,182ft (360.3m)
Length of eastern main span	984ft (299.9m)
Number of decks	2
Number of traffic lanes 10 (4 upper; 6 lower)	
Height of towers	350ft (106.7m)
Total structural steel used	50,000tons (50,800,000kg)
Cost of original structure	$20,000,000

Scott Fitzgerald in *The Great Gatsby* states: "The city seen from the Queensboro Bridge is always the city seen for the first time, in its first wild promise of all the mystery and beauty in the world."
• It architect said, "It looks like a heap of scrap metal." • Final link is completed in 1908. • Bridge opens to the public in March 1909, marked by a

Roosevelt Island Bridge
Type of bridge	Vertical lift
Construction starts	195
Open to traffic	195
Length of main lift span	418ft (127.4m)
Number of traffic lanes	
Clearance over	closed 40ft (12.2m)
mean high water	open 100ft (30.5m)
Height of towers	170ft (51.8m)
Cost of original structure	$6,500,00

Early **1950s**: Serves 230,000 cars per year and is only public connection here. **1952** in March construction begins of new vertical-lift crossing to island. **1954** Lift span is raised into position. This takes 2 days. **1955** Originally called Welfare Island Bridge. • Roosevelt Island Bridge still has rare Whitestone-style lightposts with cuplight fixtures.

spectacular 2-hour fireworks display.• 50 died in its construction. • **1930** a 4-cab elevator service between lower deck of Queensboro Bridge and Welfare Island is introduced – carrying 230,000 cars a year by 1950s.

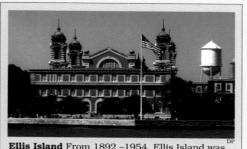

Ellis Island From 1892 –1954, Ellis Island was the US immigration depot. Nearly 17 million people were "processed" through to disperse in the greatest wave of immigration ever known. In the 1920s, 700 worked there – doctors, nurses, interpreters, watchmen, workmen and clerks. Half of America's population can trace its family back to the island. In 1990 it was restored at a cost of £156 million and is today a national museum.

Holland Tunnel This trans-Hudson rail tunnel opens in 1910 and is then longest underwater tunnel in the world • It is named after its designer and chief engineer, Clifford Holland. • Holland dies just 1 day before construction crews from New York and New Jersey sides meet. • Construction workers, called "sandhogs", are aware of danger and say: "Think twice, you only live once." • 13 workers die during construction. • On a good day, the "sandhogs" move some 40ft (12.19m) forward. • Tunnel incorporates revolutionary 2-duct system – since adopted by vehicle tunnels worldwide.• Ventilator fans and airshafts circulate clear air with 42 blowing fans and 42 exhaust fans. • It takes about 90 minutes to completely change tunnel's air. • 115,000 tons (116,840,000kg) of cast-iron steel and 130,000yd³ (99,388m³) of concrete line tunnel.

Battery Park The park rose on landfill from 18th-19th century building (just as Battery Park City rose on soil excavated for the World Trade Center). Castle Garden was an entertainment hall for over 30 years (singer Jenny Lind was presented here by Barnum in 1850), a federal immigration center, (1855-90) and an aquarium 1896-1941.

Circle Line This excursion boat line began in 1945 when several other lines merged. At first converted troop carriers circled Manhattan Island clockwise; now the boats go the other way, as guides point out historic and architectural landmarks. From mid-March until December ends, some 590,000 passengers enjoy a "boat's eye view" of Manhattan.

Manhattan Bridge The Canal Street entrance has a fine arch with flanking colonnades. • The bridge is made of steel and has 2 levels.

Type of bridge	Suspension
Construction starts	1901
Open to traffic	1909
Length of main span	1,470ft (448m)
Number of decks	2
Number of traffic lanes	7 (4 upper, 3 lower)
Number of subway tracks	2
Height of towers	322ft (98.15m)
Clearance at center	135ft (41.15m)
Length of each of 4 cables	3,224ft (982.67m)
Cost of original structure	$31,000,000

ns likely that
. Cornbury,
ld this mansion
1 on high ground
cture was greatly
mes since.

Heliports The Police department's Aviation Unit was the first U.S. one to use helicopters in 1947. In 1951, the Port Authority began helicopter flights from Pier 41. By 1954, there were heliports at the Battery, on 34th Street at the East River, at the bus terminal on 8th Avenue and at the foot of Wall Street.

1884 P.T. Barnum demonstrates bridge strength by parading over with a herd of 21 elephants.
1885 Robert E. Odlum is 1st to jump off bridge; he does not survive.
1895 Clara McArthur is 1st woman to jump. She fills her stockings with 20 pounds of sand to keep her feet first – and survives.
1974 Jimmy Weber imitates Spiderman scampering up and down cables 120 feet (36.58 m.) high.

Map labels: Ellis Island Ferry, and Ferry, Hudson River, Jersey City Ferry, Port Imperial Ferry, Battery Park City, North Cove Yacht Harbor, North Park, North End Ave, River Ter, Murray St, Park Pl, West St, Hoboken Ferry, Port, Pier 40, Holland Tunnel, Pier 34, Pier 32, Pier 25, Pier 26, Renwick St, Watts St, Desbrosses St, Vestry St, Laight St, Hubert St, NYC Fir, Rector Park, W Thames St, Albany St, Rector St, S End Ave, Battery Pl, World, Castle Clinton National Monument, Battery Park, Ferry Terminal, US Custom House, 478, Battery Tunnel, Ferry Terminal, Financial District, Governors Is Ferry, Bayonne Ferry, Pier 7, Pier 11, Gouverneur Ln, Old Slip, Hanover, Water St, Pearl St, Fletcher St, Front St, Fulton St, South St, Bank, Ferry Terminal, Pier 13, Pier 14, Pier 15, Pier 16, Pier 17, Pier 18, South Street Seaport, Beekman St, Peck Slip, Dover St, Robert F Wagner Sr Pl, Saint James Pl, Chinese, Two Bridges, Catherine St, Brooklyn Bridge, Manhattan Bridge, Front St, South St, Water St, Jackson St, Lewis, Corlears Hook Park, East River P, Cherry St

Events and celebrations

First New Year celebrations

The first rooftop New Year celebration at One Times Square was a fireworks display in 1904 to celebrate the *New York Times* new building and the renaming of Longacre Square as Times Square.

The Times Square Ball

The first ball lowering was on December 31, 1907. In 1942 and 1943, this celebration was suspended due to the wartime dimout and instead, the crowds in Times Square gathered for a minute of silence, followed by chimes from an amplifier truck. The original New Year's Eve ball weighed 700 lbs (318kg.) and was 5 feet (1.5m.) in diameter. It was made of iron and wood, decorated with 100 25-watt light bulbs.

The ball was refurbished in 1948 and 1995. It is a geodesic sphere, covered with about 500 Waterford crystal triangles. The exterior is illuminated by 168 halogena crystal light bulbs, exclusively engineered to enhance the crystal.

The ball interior is illuminated by 432 bulbs (208 clear, 56 red, 56 blue, 56 green and 56 yellow), and 96 high intensity strobe lights which create bubbling bursts of color.
The exterior has 90 rotating pyramid mirrors that reflect light back into Times Square. The lights and mirrors are computer controlled to produce a dazzling kaleidoscope effect. Each New Year, 72 of the crystal triangles are replaced with a new design.

TC

Up to a million people have watched the lowering of the ball each New Year's Eve:
85% come in from outside New York City.
35% are from abroad.
37% are aged 19-25 years.
21% are aged 26-35 years.
4% are over 50 years old.

300 million watch the celebrations on television. Typically, the total cost of the festivities is about $385,000, as in 1996, when the revenue they gained for the city was about $48.5 million.

4 garbage trucks are used to clean up afterwards.

> The *Times* posted election returns on the world's first moving sign in 1928

Above: *Governor Smith (left) and Mrs Smith in conve* *Governor Whitman in the Reviewing Stand as the tr* Right: *March past of the 369th Regiment, after Worl*

Below: *Times Square at midnight as the new millen*

Events and parades

1760s The first St. Patrick's Day parade was held.
1788 A great parade and a banquet for 5,000 celebrated the ratification of the American constitution.
1824 The Marquis de Lafayette, French hero of the American Revolution, was greeted by several parades and a lavish ball.
1865 A march of several thousand soldiers through Manhattan celebrated the end of the Civil War.
Late 1800s Ticker tape parades began in the Financial District.
1920s Macy's department store launched their colorful Thanksgiving Day parade.
1996 A ticker tape parade marked the New York Yankees baseball victory.

Annual para

Late winter in Chinatown dragons ente
February Bla – African Am throughout c State Buildin
March 17 St Fifth Avenue green clothes
March 25 Gr Day – dancin
Easter The E glorious hats
Late April to Blossom Fest Botanic Gard
May Martin Day Parade.
Mid May Nin Festival with and food.
June Puerto Parade.
• Museum M

Verrazano Narrows Bridge

From 1964 to 1981, the main span of the Verrazano-Narrows Bridge is the world's longest suspension bridge. • Bridge is named after the Italian explorer who discovered New York Harbor in 1524.• Made up of 26,000 tons (26,416,000kg) of steel, the two towers support 4 cables, each 7,205ft (2196m) long and 36ins (0.91m) in diameter, with 61 strands of 428 wires apiece, totaling 143,000 miles (230,130km) in length. The upper deck opened in November 1964. Some 12,000 men worked on the bridge, with as many as 1,000 working on site at peak times.

Type of bridge	Suspension
Construction starts	1959
Open to traffic	upper deck 1964
	lower deck 1969
Length of main span	4,260ft (1,298m)
Number of decks	2
Number of traffic lanes	12 lanes (6 upper; 6 lower)
Height of towers	693ft (211m)
Number of cables	4: each 7,205ft (2,196m)
Total number of wires per cable	26,108 wires
Total length of wires	143,000ml (230,130km)
Cost of original structure	$320,126,000

DP

Statue of Liberty

Height from ground to tip of torch	305ft 1ins. (92.99m)
Height of statue	151ft (46.05m)
Length of nose	4ft 6 ins (1.48m)
Thickness of copper skin	0.093ins (2.37mm)

Concept initiated by French immigrant Edouard de Laboulaye • Sculptor: Frédéric Auguste Bartholdi (statue may have been modeled on his mother). **1885**: Shipped from Paris to America in 214 crates on the frigate *Isère*. • **1886**: Dedicated October 28: then the tallest statue in the world. • **1933**: Made a national monument.

• **1956**: Bedloe's island renamed Liberty island.

• **1986**: Restoration for centennial celebration on July 4. Smaller scale replica erected in Paris.

Cost of upkeep of the bridges
$91,000,000 spent on repair and upkeep of New York's bridges each year

Statue of Liberty National Monument

Ellis Island National Monument

PB

PB

Liberty Is

Upper Bay

Staten Island F

Jersey City Ferry

Brooklyn Battery Tunnel

Construction starts	1940
Open to traffic	1950
Length between portals	9,117ft (2,778.9m)
Number of traffic lanes	4
Operating headroom of tubes	11ft 9ins (3.58m)
Supply and exhaust fans	53
Fresh air per minute	4,150,000ft³ (117,628m³)
Cost of original structure	$90,568,000

It is longest continuous underwater tunnel for motor vehicles in North America.
It is used by 59,000 vehicles a day.

Governors Island Support Center

DP

Brooklyn P

Governors Island Mansion It see British governor of New York, Lor appropriated funds in order to bu on Governors Island in 1708, place to the northeast. The original stru altered in 1749 and again many ti

Brooklyn Bridge

The construction To help the descent of the caissons (in which workers clear silt under the riverbed), dynamite is used for 1st time in bridge construction. • Bridge designer, John Roebling, checking a tower site, has his foot crushed against the pier by a ferry and dies of tetanus. His son, Washington, takes over as chief engineer but is paralysed after working at depth. His wife, Emily, studies mathematics and bridge engineering, and directs the construction from then on, her husband watching through a telescope from a bedroom window. • Laborers in the subterranean foundations are paid $2.25 per day to work with hammers, drills and chains. Fires, explosions, and changes in air pressure kill 20. • Several workers above ground die after being hit by falling masonry or falling themselves. One worker instinctively holds on to his wheelbarrow as it slides from a high plank, and plunges to his death.

PB

Type of bridge	Suspension
Construction starts	1870
Open to traffic	1883
Length of main span	1,595ft 6ins (486.31m)
Width of bridge	85ft (25.91m)
Number of traffic lanes	6
Height of towers	276ft 6ins (84.28m)
Total length of wires	14,060 miles (22,626.76km)
Total weight of bridge	14,680 tons (14,914,880 kg)
Cost of original structure	$15,100,000

*rsation with
oops march by.
d War I.*

MM

nium begins

RS

Rockefeller Christmas Tree
- First Christmas tree plugged in at Rockefeller in 1933.
- Tallest Rockefeller Plaza Christmas tree was 90 feet (27m.) used in 1948.
- 65 trees were on display through 1997, with an average weight of 7.5 tons.
- 5 miles (8km.) of Christmas lights are used on each tree.
- The tree is taken down on January 8. It is then ground into 3 tons of mulch to make ground cover at a Boy Scout camp in New Jersey.

Color schemes have included:
- Monochromatic blue (1938)
- White (1934 and 1939)
- Black light during the war (1945)
- Clear bulbs (1950s and 1960s)

IF

...les and celebrations include:

Chinese New Year
. when traditional
rtain the crowds.
ck History Month
erican events
ty. • Empire
g Run-up.
. Patrick's Day.
celebrates with
. flowers and beer.
eek Independence
g and food.
aster Parade with
on Fifth Avenue.
May Cherry
ival in Brooklyn
en.
uther King Jr.

th Avenue Street
music, dance

Rican Day

le Festival.

Mid-June Gay and Lesbian Pride March
June-July Jazz Festival in various venues.
• American Crafts Festival in Lincoln Center.
July 4 Independence Day – celebrated with Macy's incredible firework display over the East River.
July Lincoln Center Festival with dance, opera and performing arts.
July-August Mostly Mozart Festival in Lincoln Center.
August Harlem Week with art, music, films and sport.
• Out-of-Doors festival: free performances by the Lincoln Center.
September Richmond County Fair in historic Richmond Town.• West Indian carnival in Brooklyn.• Brazilian festival between Times Square and

Madison Avenue.• New York Film Festival at the Lincoln Center.• San Gennaro festival in Little Italy.• Von Steuben Day Parade – German American celebration in Upper Fifth Avenue.
October Greenwich Village Halloween Parade. • Columbus Day Parade on Fifth Avenue.
• Pulaski Day Parade on Fifth Avenue.
November Macy's Thanksgiving Day Parade.
Early December Tree lighting ceremony at Rockefeller Center.
December Messiah Sing-In at the Lincoln Center.
• Hanukkah Menorah at Grand Army Plaza, Brooklyn, and Festival of Lights.
New Year's Eve Fireworks in Central Park and Times Square celebrations.• Poetry in St Mark's Church.

Riverside Park is a long narrow strip of land between Riverside Drive and the Hudson River, extending from 72nd street to 158th street. Prehistoric glaciers left rocky outcroppings and steep bluffs on the site and before European settlement the rough terrain was only sparsely populated by American Indians. **1846**, the Hudson River Railroad was built along the shoreline. Between the end of the Civil war (President Grant's tomb is in the park) and 1875 the land between the tracks and the bluffs was acquired by the city and plans for a park were commissioned from Frederick Law Olmstead, the chief designer of Central Park. His plan (with numerous modifications) was implemented between 1875 and 1900. • Between **1934** and **1937** a plan known as the West Side Improvement was executed along the Hudson riverfront to double the size of Riverside park to include the West Side Highway and the railroad tracks (which were covered by a promenade). As such the park is split in half by the West Side Highway, the main north-south freeway on the west side (it's East side counterpart is the FDR drive which runs along the East River). • The soldiers and sailors monument at 89 St is a 1902 memorial to the dead of the Civil War designed by French sculptor Paul DuBoy and architects Charles and Arthur Stoughton. • Riverside Park is Manhattan's most spectacular waterfront park, stretching four miles from 72nd to 158th Streets along the Hudson River. Since 1875, the landscapes of Frederick Law Olmsted have offered escape from the city and opportunities for people of all incomes to relax, play and socialize in tranquil settings. His design for Riverside Drive made it one of the most beautiful boulevards in the world, affording views of the Hudson River along its serpentine route.

George Washington Bridge

". . . the most beautiful bridge in the world. Made of cables and steel beams, it gleams in the sky like a reversed arch. It is blessed. It is the only seat of grace in the disordered city... innumerable vertical cables, gleaming across the sky, are suspended from the magisterial curve. . ." *Le Corbusier*

This is the only bridge across the Hudson in N.YC. **1931** George Washington Bridge is longest suspension bridge in world, twice the length of any contemporary span. Bridge is ready 8 months ahead of schedule and initially called Hudson River Bridge. The soaring towers contain over 43,000 tons (43,688,000kg) of steel. • Diameter of 4 great cables is 4ft (1.2m). • Each steel rope suspended from cables contains 107,000 miles (172,195m) of wire. • 12 lives lost during construction. **1942** *The Little Red Lighthouse and the Great Gray Bridge* by Hildegarde Swift features the tiny lighthouse next to the Manhattan tower. **1946** Bridge is increased to 8 lanes **1959** Construction of 6-lane lower level begins, to alleviate traffic growth. **1962** August: Lower deck and new approach roads complete – cost $20 million. **1963** Bus terminal, with room for 200 buses and over 10,000 people, connects to upper level of bridge. • New Jersey tower stores a U.S. flag, the largest free-flying flag in the world at 60ft by 90ft (18.3 by 27.4m), with 5ft

---

Hudson River Steamboat 1813

Hudson River

Manhattan Valley

Riverside Park

Riverside Park 1880

Pier 57
Old White Star Line pier
Piers 59 and **60**
where the *Carpathia* deposits the *Titanic* lifeboats.
Pier 61
former White Star Line pier where the *Lusitania* docked.
Piers 88 and **90**
Old United States Line piers.
Pier 88
plaque commemorates the diving school founded at this spot in May 1942 on the wreck of the *Normandie*.
Piers 88, 90 and **92**
Cruise ship berths where transatlantic liner *QE2* docks.
The Titanic
On April 17 1912 the *Titanic* is expected to arrive at Pier 60, which with Pier 61, has been enlarged for the great ship.

On April 15th only the *New York Times* dares to admit that the unsinkable ship had sunk. 2,228 on board, only 705 survive. To meet them are 10,000 at the Battery and 30,000 near Pier 54. 1st-class passengers are driven in their carriages to luxury hotels. The 174 3rd-class passengers are taken to a reception center at Jane West Hotel.

Gracie Mansion is one of the oldest surviving wood structures in Manhattan and the only surviving 19th-century country home. **1799** Prosperous merchant Archibald Gracie builds a country house. **1823** Gracie in financial difficulties; house bought by Joseph Foulke. **1857** House owned by Noah Wheaton. **1896** City of New York appropriates estate with 11 acres (4.455 hectares) of grounds into new Cark Schurz Park. Gracie Mansion is restored and becomes first home of the Museum of the City of New York and then is later is run by Parks Department. **1942** Fiorello H. La Guardia moves into house – now official residence of mayor. Successive mayors live here from now on. • **1966** House enlarged to include grand ballroom and two reception rooms. **1981** Gracie Mansion Conservancy set up to preserve, maintain and enhance Gracie Mansion. **2002** Interior and exterior restored. House transformed into the People's House with greater public access. Also accommodates visiting officials and dignitaries, such as Nelson Mandela.

Intrepid Sea-Air-Space Museum The museum on the World War II aircraft carrier *U.S.S. Intrepid* (commissioned 1943) has many excellent exhibits, including an Apollo space capsule, and over 25 aircraft. Its 600,000 annual visitors can also explore destroyer *U.S.S. Edson* and the submarine *U.S.S. Growler*. The museum was conceived by Zachary Fisher, who spent $24 million of his own money to save the Intrepid from being sent to the scrap-yard.

Pedestrian Bridge The Wards Island Bridge over the Harlem River (built 1951) connects East 103rd Street to Wards Island with its park, hospitals and stadium. The first known bridge to what was then called Great Barn Island was built in 1807 by Milledolar and Ward, to help their cotton business there. A storm destroyed all but the stone piers of this wooden drawbridge in 1821.

The Randalls Island Poorhouse
1875 Outside in the snow, a line of men wait for dinner at the poorhouse on Randall's Island. The needy were catered for on Blackwell's (now Roosevelt) Island, too, with almshouses for men, women and the elderly, hospitals, a workhouse and a lunatic asylum.

To locate a pier number add 41 to the street number.

Madison Avenue Bridge

Type of bridge	Swing
Construction starts	1907
Open to traffic	1910
Length of main span	300ft (91.4m)
Number of traffic lanes	4
Cost of original structure	$2,200,000

The old Madison Avenue Bridge opened November 1884. • New Madison Avenue Bridge begins in October 1907, opens to traffic on July 18, 1910.

Macombs Dam

Near today's Yankee Stadium. • A Bronx park and a nearby drawbridge have been named after dam. **1813** Dam built by Robert Macomb to power a mill. It blocks boats' passage. **1838** Riverside residents charter a coal barge and pay crew to break through dam with axes. Dam owner sues for damages but

Rail Metro North Bridge

Type of bridge	Vertical lift
Construction	started 1954
Opened to traffic	1956
Main lift span	340 ft. (103.6m.)
Number of railroad tracks	4 tracks
Clearance open	135 ft. (41.15 m.)
high water closed	25 ft. (7.62 m.)
Height of towers	170 ft. (51.82 m.)

Third Avenue Bridge

Type of bridge	Swing
Construction starts	1893
Open to traffic	1898
Length of main span	300ft (91.4m)
Number of traffic lanes	4
Cost of original structure	$4,000,000

Willis Avenue Bridge

Type of bridge	Swing
Construction starts	1897
Open to traffic	1901
Length of main span	304ft (9.14m)
Number of traffic lanes	4
Cost of original structure	$2,500,000

Willis Avenue Bridge features a draw span that can swing perpendicular to the approach roadways. When this is open, Harlem River vessels can travel through 2 channels, each 108ft (32.9m) wide. When closed, the bridge allows 25ft (7.62m) of

Triboro Bridge

Triborough Bridge is a complex structure with 3 long-span bridges, several smaller bridges and viaducts, plus 14 miles (22.5km) of approach highways and parkways.

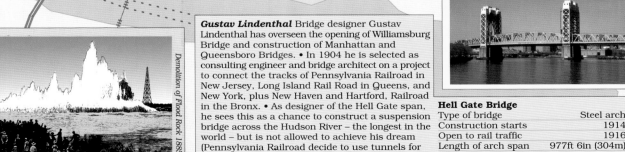

Hell Gate The name derives from Dutch *Hellegat* (hell channel). A narrow strait between Astoria and Ward's Island, it is hazardous with powerful tides and many rocky outcrops. It has been widened and deepened over the years but is still difficult to navigate. 100s of ships have sunk here. **1612** Adriaen Block makes first reported passage. **1780** British frigate *Hussar* sinks, carrying gold and silver for city's military paymasters – treasure still sought by divers. **1876** U.S. Army Corps of Engineers blast underwater rocks in world's largest controlled explosion at time. **1917** New York Connecting Railroad Bridge (Hell Gate Arch) is one of the finest steel arch bridges in world. It joins Bronx and Queens and makes direct rail link to New England. **1936** Triborough Bridge opens for traffic and connects Manhattan, the Bronx, and Queens. Like Hell Gate Arch, it passes over Wards Island and Randalls Island, once separated by Little Hell Gate Creek.

Gustav Lindenthal Bridge designer Gustav Lindenthal has overseen the opening of Williamsburg Bridge and construction of Manhattan and Queensboro Bridges. • In 1904 he is selected as consulting engineer and bridge architect on a project to connect the tracks of Pennsylvania Railroad in New Jersey, Long Island Rail Road in Queens, and New York, plus New Haven and Hartford, Railroad in the Bronx. • As designer of the Hell Gate span, he sees this as a chance to construct a suspension bridge across the Hudson River – the longest in the world – but is not allowed to achieve his dream (Pennsylvania Railroad decide to use tunnels for rail traffic across the Hudson and East Rivers). However, Hell Gate is still the longest steel arch bridge in the world in 1916.

Hell Gate Bridge

Type of bridge	Steel arch
Construction starts	1914
Open to rail traffic	1916
Length of arch span	977ft 6in (304m)
Number of railroad tracks	4
Height of towers	250ft (76.2m)
Cost of original structure	$20,000,000

Strawberry Fields
This place of contemplation is named after the Beatles song; it was created in 1985 as a tribute to John Lennon who lived and died (shot in 1980) nearby at the Dakota Apartments. Its 3 acres (1.2 hectares) are planted with 161 species from 150 different countries.

Ice Skating
In 1858 The Lake opened for public ice skating. Along with sleigh riding, this soon became extremely popular, with more people visiting Central Park in winter than in summer. On Christmas Day 1859, for example, 50,000 people visited the park, most of them skaters. The sport became especially popular with couples as it was one of the few acceptable ways for men and women to hold hands in public. By the 1950s, there was such a huge demand for guaranteed seasonal skating that the Wollman Rink (1950, *right*) and the Lasker Rink (1966) were built.

Turtle Pond
Below Belvedere Castle, this stretch of water was originally part of the huge Croton Reservoir. This was partly filled in with city rubble in the 1930s, creating the Great Lawn and, on the southern end, a shallow pond called Belvedere Lake. It has since been renovated, reshaped and renamed Turtle Pond (after some of its occupants). It is home to fish, frogs, dragonflies, waterfowl and herons – as well as turtles.

Seneca Village
Many poor farmers had lived in shacks and even caves in a rock-strewn area (east of today's Eighth Avenue, between 82nd and 86th Streets) in what would become a vast squatter camp. As houses were built, the hamlet flourished and grew to include 2 schools, 3 cemeteries and 3 churches. Some 250 poor immigrants, (Irish, blacks and American Indians) were living here when the city bought the land in the early 1850s. Squatters were forced from their homes and left to set up camp elsewhere; landowners were paid a meagre sum and then evicted. By October 1, 1857, the buildings had all been torn down.

Upper West Side

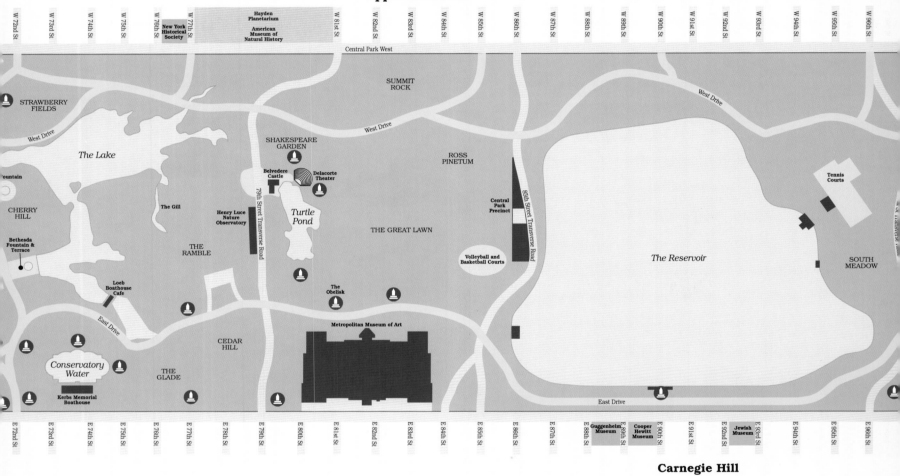

Carnegie Hill

Bethesda Terrace
Both the fountain and the sculpture *Angel of the Waters* were designed by Emma Stebbins in 1873 (mid-Park/73rd Street). The ornamental Terrace was designed by Calvert Vaux and Jacob Wrey Mould and overlooks the lake, the Ramble's wooded shores and Bethesda Fountain.

Conservatory Water
Famous model boat pond modelled on smaller Parisian counterparts. Visitors can watch radio-controlled regattas, children with their small wind-powered sloops, or rent their own miniature boat.

Hans Christian Andersen
This sculpture by Georg Lober (1956) depicts Andersen reading a book with the little Ugly Duckling at his feet. His other creations include *The Snow Queen* and *The Emperor's New Clothes*. Andersen was in love with Swedish singer Jenny Lind who sang to an audience of 5,000 at Castle Garden in 1850.

Alice in Wonderland
Statue group shows Lewis Carroll's famous character Alice with the Mad Hatter and the White Rabbit. Lewis Carroll (1832-98) was the pen name for English author and mathematician Charles Lutwidge Dodgson who wrote *Alice in Wonderland* (date uncertain) and *Through the Looking-Glass* in 1872.

Cleopatra's Needle (The Obelisk)
This 3,500-year-old Egyptian obelisk was presented to the city by the Khedive Ismael Pasha in 1869. 77-feet (23.5 m) high, it was originally situated at Heliopolis in Egypt, erected by Tuthmosis III.

Metropolitan Museum of Art
Founded in 1870, the present building opened in 1902. This is the largest art museum in the U.S.A. and the third largest art in the world. It contains 300 exhibition rooms, 3.3 million works of art and 100,000 exhibits.

The Great Lawn
The Lawn was not part of the original park design: at the time the site contained the 33-acre rectangular Croton Reservoir which held 180 million gallons of drinking water piped in from the Croton River in Westchester County. A 1917 plan for a new water tunnel retained the older receiving reservoir nearby (now the Jacqueline Kennedy Onassis Reservoir) but rendered the Croton Reservoir obsolete. From 1931 the Croton Reservoir was filled in with rubble such as the stones from the building of Rockefeller Center, and a 13-acre oval lawn was created in the reservoir's place. 8 ballfields were added in the 1950s. The Great Lawn has become the venue for some of the city's major outdoor events. Pope John Paul II led a papal mass here in 1995. Over 100,000 people have gathered for concerts by artists such as Paul Simon, Elton John and Pavarotti. In summer the New York Philharmonic and Metropolitan Opera each play two free concerts.

The Jacqueline Kennedy Onassis Reservoir
Completed in 1862 while the Park was under construction, the Reservoir covers 106-acres and holds over a billion gallons of water. It no longer provides fresh water to Manhattan residents but its overflow is vital for providing fresh water to the connecting *Pool, Loch,* and *Harlem Meer* in the northern part of the Park. The 1.58 mile track surrounding it is a popular route with thousands of joggers, especially in the summer when evaporation from the water surface cools the surrounding air. In 1994 The Reservoir was renamed after the former wife of President John F. Kennedy and the Greek shipping tycoon, Aristotle Onassis.

Type of bridge	Suspension
Construction starts	1927
Open to traffic	1931; lower deck 1962
Length of main span	3,500ft (1,066.8m)
Number of decks	2
Number of traffic lanes	14 (8 upper; 6 lower)
Height of tower	604ft (184m)
Total length of wires	107,000ml (172,195km)
Cost of original structure	$59,000,000

DP

George Washington Bridge

Little Red Lighthouse The Jeffrey's Hook lighthouse was erected in 1880 at Sandy Hook, and moved to its present location in 1921. It became known as "The Little Red Lighthouse" after being popularized in a children's book by Hildegarde H. Swift in 1942, when it symbolized the importance of small things in a big world. There was a public outcry at its proposed removal in 1951 but it was saved by its transfer to the City of New York: Parks & Recreation.

DP

The Little Red Lighthouse

Henry Hudson Pkwy
Riverside Dr

Alexander Hamilton Bridge

Type of bridge	Steel-arch
Construction starts	1960
Open to traffic	1963
Length of main arch	555ft (169.1m)
Height at center	151ft 6in (46.2m)
Number of traffic lanes	8
Cost of original structure	$21,000,000

This large arch design spans the deep, narrow valley that surrounds the Harlem River. • Its single main arch exceeds Washington Bridge (just north) by 45ft (13.7m).

Washington (Heights) Brid

Type of bridge	
Construction starts	
Open to traffic	
Length of main arches	5
Height at center	151
Number of traffic lanes	
Cost of original structure	

Riverside Dr
Haven Ave
Cabrini Blvd
W 160th St
W 177th St
Aud

Court of Appeals rules that federal government has jurisdiction over navigable waterways and that state should not have allowed dam to be built in the first place.

High Bridge Park
Harlem River Dr
High Bridge (closed)
Alexander Hamilton Bridge
Washington Bridge
Harlem River
Macombs Dam Bridge
Yankee Stadium

Macombs Dam Bridge

Type of bridge	Swing
Construction starts	1892
Open to traffic	1895
Length of main span	412ft (125.5m)
Number of traffic lanes	4
Cost of original structure	$1,800,000

DP

1814 First dam and bridge opens to traffic – The tides through its dam gates provide power for new industries along the river. • With growing traffic, the dam and bridge prove an obstacle to shipping. • Tolls are resented. • In **1839**, Lewis Morris, leading 100 men, forces his vessel through bridge and dam – tearing a hole in this. **1861** The second bridge – Cost overruns and construction delays plague second bridge, now renamed the Central

145 Street Bridge

Type of bridge	Swing
Construction starts	1901
Open to traffic	1905
Length of main span	300ft (91.44m)
Number of traffic lanes	4
Cost of original structure	$2,750,000

DP

This is the 3rd bridge here. • The first in **1797** is called Coles Bridge. • There is a 2nd in **1868**.

Work begins in April **1901** but construction is delayed by the simultaneous building of the IRT subway tunnel, running below the southern pier. • Rim-bearing swing bridge has 3 trusses. A 368-ton (373,888kg) turntable powers the central 1,177-ton (1,195,832kg) swing span. 2 roadways, each 27ft (8.2m) wide, run between each exterior truss and the central truss. There are also 2 sidewalks (9ft (2.7m) wide) along the exterior trusses.

DP

vertical clearance. • As the bridge is being built, the plans change to include greater boiler and dynamo power (with electricity rather than steam), incandescent lights, 4 pedestrian shelters, a better end-lift system, and cement rather than asphalt on both roadway and sidewalks.

Construction starts	1929
Open to traffic	1936
Cost of original structure	$60,300,000

Bridge is made up of:

East River Suspension Bridge

Length of main span	1,380ft (420.6m)
Number of traffic lanes	8
Height of towers	315ft (96m)
Total length of wires	10,800ml (17,380km)

Harlem River Lift Bridge

Length of main lift-truss span	310ft (94.5m)
Height of towers	210ft (64m)
Clearance of lift span	55ft (16.8m)
when raised	135ft (41.1m)
Number of traffic lanes	6

Bronx Kills Crossing

Length of main truss span	383ft (116.7m)
Clearance of truss span	55ft (16.8m)
Number of traffic lanes	8

High Bridge

Type of bridge	Masonry and steel-arch
Construction starts	1839
Open to traffic	1848
Length of main arch	360ft (109.7m)
Cost of original structure	$950,000

This 13-arch structure is New York's oldest surviving bridge. • It is originally built to carry the Croton Aqueduct. • A pedestrian walkway (now closed) is 135ft (41.1m) above the Harlem River valley. **1848** Roman-style bridge has 15 circular masonry arches, with pipes inside arch walls to carry water. **1860** 3rd pipe added. **1872** A watchtower equalizes water pressure. **1906** Still more water needed so new aqueduct opens. **1917** Original aqueduct inside High Bridge closes to eliminate risk of sabotage when U.S. enters World War I. **1927** Greater clearance needed over navigable channel below, so 5 of the 8 arches are replaced by

a single steel-plate girder arch with a clearance of 360ft (109.7m) – a $1 million project. **1949** Watchtower ceases operation as a pumping station.

At High Bridge a party board an excursion steamer about 1880

PB

The Carousel
The Park's first carousel was built in 1870 and is said to have been turned by a blind mule and a horse. Today's vintage 1908 carousel is the fourth on the site, and was found abandoned in the old trolley terminal on Coney Island. It is one of the largest in the U.S.A., with 58 hand-carved, painted horses. It has retained its appeal, with almost 250,000 riders a year.

Tavern on the Green
Famous elegant restaurant set among trees. Built in 1870 (as the Sheepfold) it was converted into a restaurant in the 1930s, with an opulent dining room and chandeliers. An outdoors dining area is surrounded by trees and topiary. Since 1970, the illuminated trees have marked the finishing line of the New York Marathon.

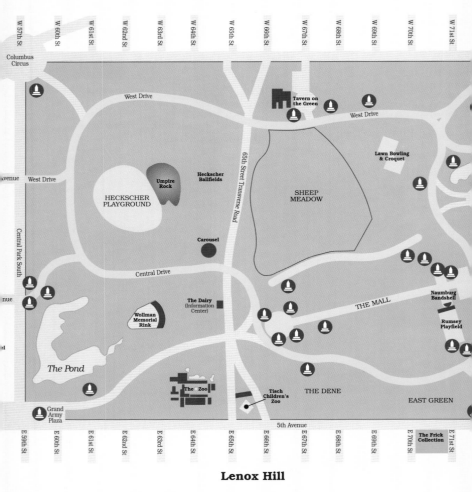

Lenox Hill

The Pond
Half of all Park visitors enter through nearby Grand Army Plaza and this picturesque, comma-shaped pond offers visitors and office workers an instant haven from the city. The lake is surrounded by grass lawns and benches; Gapstow Bridge (below), made from local bedrock, arches gracefully over the north east of the Pond. Recent enhancement works included shoreline and upland plantings, a waterfall, cascades, and a new island habitat for turtles and birds.

Heckscher Ballfields
Named after August Heckscher who was Parks Commissioner for six years from 1967. There are six fields in which baseball or softball can be played, and spectators can watch the games from the bleachers that surround the ballfields.

The Dairy
Originally where milk from the park's grazing cows was sold. The present Gothic Victorian stone building was built in 1870 and restored in 1979 when it became the Visitor Information Center.

Brief History of Central Park

This was the first landscaped public park in the United States. Many wealthy citizens who had travelled overseas admired the parks in European cities and felt their own home needed a public countryside area for recreation.

1853 State legislature authorizes the city to obtain 700 acres of land in central Manhattan. The swamps, bluffs, and rocky outcrops of the area had made it unsuitable for building development. People living or squatting here are simply ousted to make way for the park's development.

1857-1870 The first Central Park Commission wants the park kept out of the hands of locally-elected (mainly Democratic) office holders and becomes city's first planning agency.

1857 Central Park Commission holds the nation's first landscape contest and chooses the "Greensward Plan" by Frederick Olmsted (then the park's superintendent) and English-born architect Calvert Vaux. This aims to create a romantic, pastoral landscape with rolling meadows plus the more formal Mall and Bethesda Terrace. To retain sweeping views, roads for traffic are kept at a lower level. Separate carriage drives, pedestrian walks, equestrian paths and over 40 bridges are included in the plan.

1859 Park opens for public use.

1863 Park extended to 110th Street and reaches its current size.

1865 Park now has over 7 million visitors a year.

1859-69 Over half of the visitors arrive in rich carriages; middle-class locals flock here for winter skating and summer concerts; a ban on group picnics stops many German and Irish from coming; small tradesmen are not allowed to use their commercial wagons for family drives here; only schoolchildren with a note from their principal can play ball on the meadows.

1870 A new city charter restores park to local control and the mayor appoints park commissioners.

1880s Working-class New Yorkers campaign for concerts on Sunday, their only day off. Other popular attractions arrive, such as the Carousel, goat rides, tennis on the lawns and bicycling on the drives.

1871 Zoo is given permanent quarters.

Early 1900s Attendance reaches its all time high.

1927 Heckscher donates the first equipped playground on the south eastern meadow. Plans are laid for The Reservoir site to be naturalistically landscaped into the Great Lawn.

1934 Robert Moses is made responsible for all city parks. Helped by federal money, he creates 20 playgrounds, adds athletic fields to the North Meadow, renovates the Zoo, and realigns the drives for cars.

1950s & early 60s Benefactors add Wollman Skating Rink, Lasker Rink and Pool, new boathouses, and the Chess and Checkers house. Moses introduces permanent ball fields to the Great Lawn.

1960s Park commissioners, Hoving and Heckscher, encourage "happenings" and rock concerts.

1970s Fiscal crisis; general decline in maintenance.

1980 Central Park Conservancy for private fundraising set up; will restore the Sheep Meadow, the Bethesda Terrace, and Belvedere Castle.

1980 to 1996 Central Park Conservancy led by Elizabeth Barlow Rogers, also appointed the Central Park Administrator.

Central Park continues to be shaped by those who use it, whether they be joggers, roller skaters, sport and fishing enthusiasts, nature lovers or bird watchers. At present there are campaigns for further traffic restrictions.

Broadway

Seventh

Sixth Av

Plaza Hot

Henry Hudson Bridge

Type of bridge	Steel-arch
Construction starts	1935
Open to traffic	lower deck 1936 upper deck 1938
Length of main span	840ft (256m)
Number of decks	2
Number of traffic lanes	7 (4 lower; 3 upper)
Cost of original structure	$4,949,000

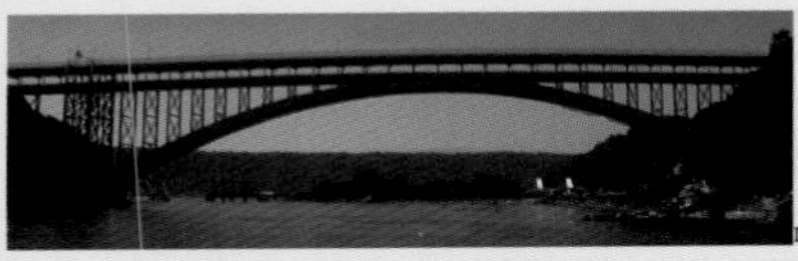
DP

1904 Henry Hudson Bridge is proposed by N.Y.C. to alleviate congestion on nearby Broadway Bridge and to be ready in time for the 300th anniversary of Hudson's voyage (made in 1609) when he navigated the river that bears his name. **1936** 30 years after it is proposed, bridge becomes reality as its high, steel arch rises from the cliffs on either side of the Harlem River. Its main span, a fixed plate girder arch, is the longest such arch in the world when the bridge opens on December 12. **1937** More than 17,000 vehicles per day pay 10¢ to cross the new bridge, despite close proximity of the free Broadway Bridge. **1938** 3-lane upper level is complete by July, and 7 lanes of traffic can cross.

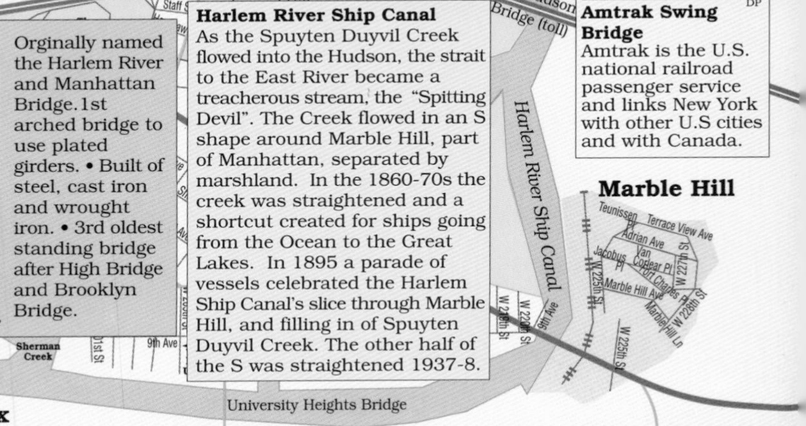
Amtrak Railway Swing Bridge
Henry Hudson Pkwy
Henry Hudson Bridge (toll)
Harlem River Ship Canal
Marble Hill
Teunissen Pl
Terrace View Ave
Adrian Ave
Jacobus Pl
Van Corlear Pl
Marble Hill Av
W 225th St
W 227th St
W 228th St
9th Ave
Sherman Creek
University Heights Bridge
9A
16
17

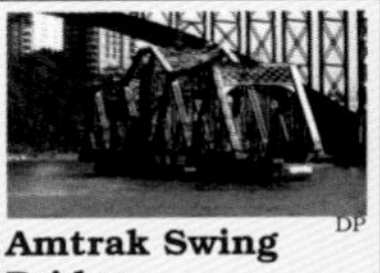
DP

Amtrak Swing Bridge
Amtrak is the U.S. national railroad passenger service and links New York with other U.S cities and with Canada.

...ge

	Steel arch
	1886
	1888
	...0ft (155.4m)
	...t 6in (46.2m)
	6
	$3,000,000

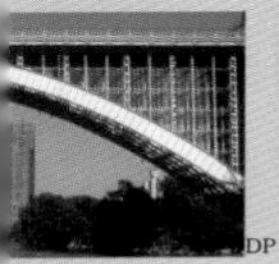
DP

Orginally named the Harlem River and Manhattan Bridge. 1st arched bridge to use plated girders. • Built of steel, cast iron and wrought iron. • 3rd oldest standing bridge after High Bridge and Brooklyn Bridge.

Harlem River Ship Canal
As the Spuyten Duyvil Creek flowed into the Hudson, the strait to the East River became a treacherous stream, the "Spitting Devil". The Creek flowed in an S shape around Marble Hill, part of Manhattan, separated by marshland. In the 1860-70s the creek was straightened and a shortcut created for ships going from the Ocean to the Great Lakes. In 1895 a parade of vessels celebrated the Harlem Ship Canal's slice through Marble Hill, and filling in of Spuyten Duyvil Creek. The other half of the S was straightened 1937-8.

The Bronx

Bridge. • It costs $50,000 but excessive traffic takes its toll on the wooden planking, and the drawstrings. At times, the dilapidated bridge is closed to traffic. **1895** The third bridge – The new iron bridge opens to traffic on May 1, at a cost of $1.8 million. Initially, steam power propels the draw mechanisms and the roadway is gas lit. **1904** Electricity replaces steam and gas power. • This is the bridge familiar to baseball fans on their way to the Yankee Stadium.

University Heights Bridge

Type of bridge	Swing
Construction starts	1903
Open to traffic	1908
Length of main span	267ft (81.4m)
Number of traffic lanes	2
Cost of original structure	$1,200,000

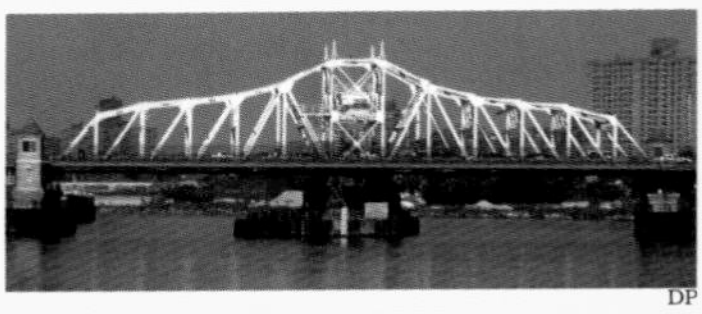
DP

In 1903 work begins on dredging and building center pier on which the draw span will rest. Although not complete, University Heights Bridge opens to traffic in January 1908. The electrical work is done by November. • Trolley service crosses it in 1910, and continues for 30 years.

Fordham Footbridge
In 1881 a wooden footbridge connects Manhattan with University Heights in the Bronx. It has a draw span of 32ft (9.75m) and bottom chords only 4ft (1.22m) above the Harlem River. This is no obstacle to vessels because the river is not yet navigable north of Sherman Creek. • Bridge is removed by 1895 when the new Harlem River Ship Channel permits vessels to travel from East to Hudson River. Several existing swing bridges are now reconstructed.

A to Z of New York Bridges

Bridge	*Date*	*Crosses*	*Links*
145th Street	1905	Harlem River	Manhattan-Bronx
Alexander Hamilton	1963	Harlem River	Manhattan-Bronx
B & O Railroad	1928	Arthur Kill	Staten Island-New Jersey
Bayonne	1931	Kill van Kull	Staten Island-New Jersey
Borden Avenue	1908	Dutch Kills	Queens
Broadway	1962	Harlem River	Manhattan-Bronx
Bronx-Whitestone	1939	East River	Bronx-Queens
Brooklyn	1883	East River	Manhattan-Brooklyn
Bruckner Boulevard	1953	Bronx River	Bronx
Carroll Street	1889	Gowanus Canal	Brooklyn
City Island	1901	Pelham Bay Narrows	Bronx
Cropsey Avenue	1931	Coney Island Creek	Brooklyn
Cross Bay-Veterans' Memorial	1939	Jamaica Bay	Queens
East 174th Street	1928	Bronx River	Bronx
Eastchester	1922	Eastchester Creek	Bronx
Flushing (Northern Boulevard)	1939	Flushing River	Queens
Fresh Kills	1931	Richmond Creek	Staten Island
George Washington	1931	Hudson River	Manhattan-New Jersey
Goethals	1928	Arthur Kill	Staten Island-New Jersey
Grand Street	1903	Newtown Creek	Queens-Brooklyn
Greenpoint Avenue	1929	Newtown Creek	Queens-Brooklyn
Hamilton Avenue	1942	Gowanus Canal	Brooklyn
Hawtree Basin (pedestrian)	1963	Hawtree Basin	Queens
Hell Gate	1917	East River	Queens-Wards Island
Henry Hudson	1936	Harlem River	Manhattan-Bronx
High Bridge	1848	Harlem River	Manhattan-Bronx
Hook Creek	1931	Hook Creek	Queens-Nassau
Huchinson River Park Extension	1941	Eastchester Creek	Bronx
Hunters Point Avenue	1910	Dutch Kills	Queens
Kosciuszko	1939	Newtown Creek	Queens-Brooklyn
Lemon Creek	1958	Lemon Creek	Staten Island
Little Neck	1931	Alley Creek	Queens
Macombs Dam	1895	Harlem River	Manhattan-Bronx
Madison Avenue	1910	Harlem River	Manhattan-Bronx
Manhattan	1909	East River	Manhattan-Brooklyn
Marine Parkway-Gil Hodges	1937	Rockaway Inlet	Brooklyn-Queens
Metropolitan Avenue	1933	English Kills	Brooklyn
Midtown Highway	1940	Dutch Kills	Queens
Mill Basin	1940	Mill Basin	Brooklyn
Ninth Street	1905	Gowanus Canal	Brooklyn
North Channel	1925	North Channel	Queens
Ocean Avenue (pedestrian)	1917	Sheepshead Bay	Brooklyn
Outerbridge Crossing	1928	Arthur Kill	Staten Island-New Jersey
Pelham	1908	Eastchester Bay	Bronx
Pulaski	1954	Newtown Creek	Queens-Brooklyn
Queensboro	1909	East River	Manhattan-Queens
Rikers Island	1966	Bowery Bay	Queens-Rikers Island
Roosevelt Avenue	1925	Flushing River	Queens
Roosevelt Island	1955	East River	Queens-Roosevelt Island
Stillwell Avenue	1929	Coney Island Creek	Brooklyn
Third Avenue	1889	Gowanus Canal	Brooklyn
Third Avenue	1899	Harlem River	Manhattan-Bronx
Third Street	1905	Gowanus Canal	Brooklyn
Throgs Neck	1961	East River	Bronx-Queens
Triborough	1936	East + Harlem River	Queens-Wards Island, Bronx Kills Manhattan-Randalls Island
Union Street	1905	Gowanus Canal	Brooklyn
Unionport	1953	Westchester Creek	Bronx
University Heights	1908	Harlem River	Manhattan-Bronx
Verrazano Narrows	1964	Narrows	Brooklyn-Staten Island
Wards Island (pedestrian)	1951	East River	Manhattan-Wards Island
Washington	1888	Harlem River	Manhattan-Bronx
Westchester Avenue	1938	Bronx River	Bronx
Whitestone Expressway	1939	Flushing River	Queens
Williamsburg	1903	East River	Manhattan-Brooklyn
Willis Avenue	1901	Harlem River	Manhattan-Bronx

Great Hill

...nsted and Vaux designed the ...ncourse with superb views of ... Hudson River and the ...isades. As the trees grew, ... view became obscured. In ... mid-20th century the Great ...l was turned into a sporting ...a but by the 1980s it had ...come a neglected ruin. The ...a was restored in 1993 as a ...ce for community leisure.

The open hilltop meadow is surrounded by fine English and American elms and is a popular location for picnics. The three-quarter mile soft surface oval track is much used by joggers. The site has also become known for the annual "Great Jazz on the Great Hill," event, a summer music concert sponsored by the Central Park Conservancy.

e Pool

...e small 2-acre Pool is a ...utiful — yet not so well-...own — landscape in the park. ...nsted and Vaux's original ...sign has survived here so that ...w grassy banks, willows ...nding over the water, and a ...shing waterfall all make it a ...aceful place to escape the ...stling City. Near the south-...st section of the Pool, a ...eam ripples into a ...uralistic boulder grotto.

Here a hidden pipe brings in water from the Reservoir to keep the Pool, the Loch, and Harlem Meer filled and all the cascades flowing. At a dramatic cascade by the bridge at the north-east corner, water gushes over a rocky dam and into the stream, which flows under Glenspan Arch and into a wooded ravine. Here, the trees change from willows and red maple to oaks, elms and maples.

PB

Horse-drawn carriages
The engraving shows carriages driving through the park in 1875, when servants rode inside the coaches while the employers enjoyed the view from above. Carriage rides continue to be a popular and romantic way to see Central Park, with many marriage proposals being made on the rides.

PBL

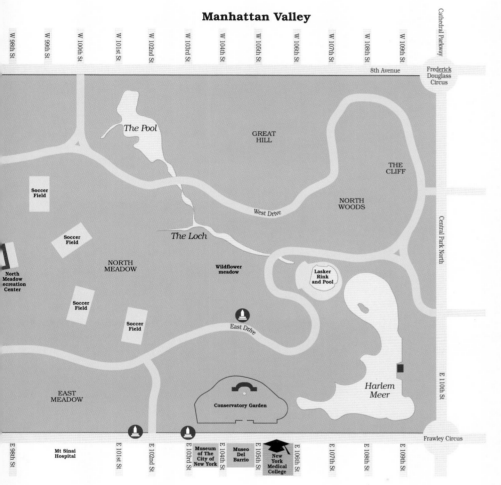

Manhattan Valley

W 98th St.
W 99th St.
W 100th St.
W 101st St.
W 102nd St.
W 103rd St.
W 104th St.
W 105th St.
W 106th St.
W 107th St.
W 108th St.
W 109th St.

8th Avenue

Cathedral Parkway

Frederick Douglass Circus

The Pool

GREAT HILL

THE CLIFF

NORTH WOODS

West Drive

The Loch

Central Park North

NORTH MEADOW

Wildflower meadow

Lasker Rink and Pool

North Meadow Recreation Center

Soccer Field

Soccer Field

Soccer Field

Soccer Field

East Drive

EAST MEADOW

Conservatory Garden

Harlem Meer

E 110th St.

Frawley Circus

E 98th St.
E 101st St.
E 102nd St.
E 103rd St.
E 104th St.
E 105th St.
E 106th St.
E 107th St.
E 108th St.
E 109th St.

Mt Sinai Hospital

Museum of The City of New York

Museo Del Barrio

New York Medical College

th Meadow

... the late 19th Century the North Meadow was used for ...nnis, croquet, school picnics and, in winter, snow-shoe ...lking. With its lush green lawn and 12 official ballfields, ... still the largest open space in Central Park today. There ... 7 baseball and 5 softball fields; in the fall these are ...verted into 6 fields for soccer or touch football.

PB

Harlem Meer

The 11-acre Harlem Meer has a natural shoreline surrounded by oak, bald cypress, beech, and ginko trees. Its dramatic rock landscape reflects Olmsted and Vaux's plan to retain rugged topography in the northern park. A swamp became the Meer (Dutch for *lake*) and the surrounding wooded areas were romanticized to include a planted ravine and a waterfall. Concrete and fencing was introduced in the 1940s, but the shoreline was restored in 1993 and given a miniature sandy beach. A cove in the south-east corner of the Meer has steps going down to the water's edge. Native plants, roses, hydrangeas, and irises cascade down the slope to the water's edge. Today the Meer offers fishing, tours, 2 playgrounds, plus exhibits, talks, jazz and dancing at The Charles A. Dana Discovery Center.

Conservatory Garden

The 6-acre Conservatory Garden is the park's only formal garden. Its name derives from a huge glass conservatory that opened in 1898. It was replaced in 1934 by the present garden which opened to the public in 3 years later. The Vanderbilt Gate (which originally stood before the Vanderbilt Mansion on Fifth Avenue) leads to an Italian-style garden where, in a walkway under the pergola, medallions name the original 13 states. In the classical French-style garden, Walter Schott's 1910 sculpture is called *Three Dancing Maidens* or the *Untermeyer Fountain*, after the family who presented it to the City in 1947. In the spring, 20,000 tulips bloom, replaced in fall by 2,000 chrysanthemums. In the southern English-style garden the bronze Burnett Fountain (installed in 1936) depicts Mary and Dickon from Frances Hodgson Burnett's *The Secret Garden*. In spring, the woodland slope here is filled with thousands of daffodils.

Christopher Columbus at Literary Walk

This Italian mariner and navigator (1451-1506) is said to have been the first European to sail across the Atlantic. This statue was sculpted in 1892 by Jeronimo Suñol and is based on one in Madrid. It depicts Columbus beside a globe, resting on a roped sea anchor. Although not an author, Columbus did write copious diaries.

DP

Pilgrim Fathers

In 1620, to escape religious persecution, the Pilgrim Fathers and families (102 in all) set out for Virginia in *The Mayflower* from Plymouth, England. One died on the voyage and one was born. They anchored off the coast of New England on December 16, 102 days after leaving England; they then landed in a wintry storm on a barren place since known as Plymouth Rock.

Frederick Law Olmsted 1822-1903
Designer of Central Park
"The time will come when New York will be built up, when all the grading and filling will be done, and when the picturesquely varied, rocky formations of the Island will have been converted into rows of monotonous straight streets and piles of erect buildings. There will be no suggestion left of its present varied surface, with the single exception of the Park. Then the priceless value of the present picturesque outlines of the ground will be perceived . . . The park should be an antithesis to its bustling, paved, rectangular, walled-in streets. The chief effect like that of music. . . cannot be fully given the form of words."

Diary of George Templeton Strong
Extract from June 11th, 1859
Improved the day by leaving Wall Street early and set off to explore the Central Park, which will be a feature of the city within 5 years and a lovely place in A.D. 1900, when its trees will have acquired dignity and appreciable diameters. Perhaps the city itself will perish before then, by growing too big to live under faulty institutions corruptly administered. Reached the park a little before 4, just as the red flag was hoisted – the signal for the blasts of the day. They were all around us for some 20 minutes, now booming far off to the north, now quite near, now distant again, like a desultory "affair" between two great armies... It promises very well. . . though now . . . "lakes" without water, mounds of compost, piles of blasted stone, acres of what may be greensward hereafter but is now mere brown earth... caravans of dirt carts, derricks, steam engines, these are the elements out of which our future Pleasaunce is rapidly developing. The work seems pushed with vigor and system. A broad avenue, exceptionally straight. . . with quadruple rows of Elms, will look Versailles-y by A.D. 1950.

Central Park – odd facts
- The parkland began as a swamp; 1 billion cubic feet (283,170 cubic metres) of earth was moved and 4 to 5 million trees planted.
- 3000 Irish laborers worked to create the park, and 400 horses cleared the land.
- Central Park is 2.5 miles (4 km) long and a 0.5 miles (0.8km) wide.
- It has 36 stone arches and bridges.
- 840 acres (340 hectares) include 185 acres (75 hectares) of lakes and ponds.
- The reservoir holds 1 billion gallons and is 40 feet (12 metres) deep.
- The Conservatory Gardens cover 4 acres (1.6 hectares).
- The park is visited by or is home to some 42 bald eagles, 11,000 hawks, 1 golden eagle and 20 racoons.
- Sheep last grazed in the park in 1933.
- Approximately 14 million people visit the park each year.
- The blasting out of the rocky ridges used more gunpowder than was fired at the Battle of Gettysburg.

Movies and television
Many movies and television shows have used Central Park as a setting. These include:

The Fisher King: scenes set in the Sheep Meadow and along park perimeter.

Balto: 1995 animated movie tells the story of Balto the sled dog. An animated version of the park statue also appears.

Ghostbusters: enormous marshmallow character terrorizes Columbus Circle.

Wall Street: a young stockbroker confronts an inside trader on Sheep Meadow.

When Harry Met Sally: Harry and Sally sip drinks in the Boathouse Cafe.

Hannah and Her Sisters (Woody Allen): Hannah and her sisters discuss the meaning of life as they stroll through the park.

The Single Guy: NBC's show begins with the main character sitting on a park bench.

The Indian Hunter
Sculpted in 1866, this is 1 of 4 statues created for the park by American sculptor John Q. A. Ward. Located outside the Sheep Meadow near the Mall, it depicts a young man in a loincloth clutching a bow and arrow in one hand while the other has a firm grip on the neck of his wild dog. The hunter leans forward, both he and his dog eager to begin.

DP

Balto
In 1925 the town of Nome in Alaska had a bad outbreak of diphtheria. Anti-toxin serum was taken by train from Anchorage, 1000 miles distant, to Nenana, still 667 miles away. In blizzard conditions 20 dogs traveled over the treacherous ice bound tundra. Lead dog Balto raced on to the stricken city in a record-breaking 5 days, 7 hours – and so saved many lives. This 1925 scupture is by Frederick George Richard Roth.

Seventh Regiment Memorial
This Civil War memorial is sculpted by John Quincy Adams Ward and stands on a grassy incline north of Tavern on the Green. It depicts a soldier standing heroically with hands resting on his rifle and pays homage to the 58 men of the Seventh Regiment who sacrificed their lives defending the Union during the American Civil War of 1861-65.

DP

Midtown, the business center of New York, was a center for Beaux Art and Art Deco – and home to the rich and influential such as J.P. Morgan, the Astors and Vanderbilts.

Gramercy and the Flatiron district developed in the 1800s into a fine residential enclave while Murray Hill has many opulent mansions and brownstones.

This area is home to Grand Central Terminal, the jewelry district including Diamond Row, the Rockefeller Center, Bryant Park and Radio City Music Hall. It has a wealth of exciting skyscrapers, including the Empire State, the Flatiron and Chrysler buildings.

PL

PB

Top: *The Chrysler Building, an Art Deco extravagance, built in 1930.*
Above: *The Empire State Building: when it was first built in 1932, its space was so difficult to rent that it was nicknamed the "Empty State Building".*
Right: *Pete's Tavern was a secret drinking place during Prohibition.*

Chrysler Building

This Art Deco skyscraper on Lexington Avenue was designed by William Van Alen, initially for the developer of Dreamland at Coney Island but it was then bought by the automobile magnate Walter Chrysler – hence the Chrysler radiator caps and the helmet top. The executive dining hall, the Cloud Club is on the 71st story, and displayed Chrysler's first tool kit. On completion in 1930, the building was briefly the tallest in the world.

Empire State Building

This was the tallest building in the world from 1932-1972. It was built in 1 year and 45 days and has 6,500 windows, 73 elevators, weighs 365,000 tons and is 1,454 feet (443m.) high. Its antenna adds another 204 feet (62m.).

Octagon Tower

This ruin on Roosevelt Island was built in 1839 as the New York City Lunatic Asylum. Its rotunda is surrounded by a spectacular flying staircase. The dome was destroyed by fire in 1982.

Pete's Tavern (below)

The oldest drinking place in continuous use in the city opened in 1864 near Gramercy Park. It once offered nightly lodging and stables for horses and was a favorite meeting place of politicians from Tammany Hall, a few blocks south. O. Henry lived nearby boarding house and spent hours at the tavern, where he wrote *The Gift of the Magi* (1905). During Prohibition, it was converted into a mock florist shop: the back drinking rooms were reached through a dummy refrigerator door.

DP

Below: *The "21" Club, a restaurant at 21 West 52nd Street*

DP

Below: *On Park Avenue, the glass skyscrapers Lever House (left) and the Seagram building (No. 375, right) reflect each other.*

DP   DP

Lever House

This skyscraper was completed in 1952 as the headquarters for the soap manufacturer Lever Brothers and was the first glass skyscraper on Park Avenue. It has 21 stories of metal and blue-green glass, and was designated a landmark in 1982.

Players Club

In 1888, its members came from the theater, music, literature, and the arts. Actor Edwin Booth purchased this 1845 Gothic Revival brownstone building, remodeled by Stanford White to resemble an Italian Renaissance palace. It has a

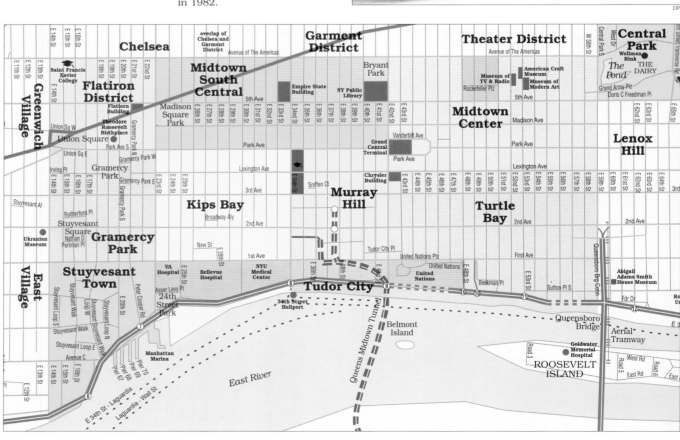

working library of theater history and Shakespeare quotations grace every wall.

United Nations
The center for this international organization borders the East River from 42nd to 48th Streets. In 1946, John D. Rockefeller Jr. donated 17 acres (7 hectares) of land in Turtle Bay and construction began the next year. The Secretariat Building is an imposing 39 stories with its domed General Assembly Hall, the Conference Building and the Dag Hammarskjöld Library. The grounds are not considered part of the U.S. and so are outside national, state or city law. In the mid 1990s, the U.N. employed some 6,000.

Flatiron building
This is one of the city's earliest skyscrapers, built in 1902 when it was the world's tallest building. The locals were terrified it would fall over in the strong winds that buffeted the intersection and raised ladies' skirts above their ankles.

New York Public Library
This is the epitome of the city's Beaux Art period, built on the site of the Croton reservoir. It cost $9million and opened in 1911. 88 miles (140km.) of shelves hold 7 million volumes. It houses Thomas Jefferson's handwritten *Declaration of Independence*, T.S. Eliot's typed copy of *The Waste Land*, a *Gutenberg Bible* and the first globe showing America (1519).

Above *and* above right:
The Flatiron Building has ornate decoration and gargoyles.

Right: *New York Public Library.*

Above: *The United Nations Building*
Below: *Radio City Music Hall. This Art Deco auditorium opened in December 27, 1932 and contained the world's largest indoor theater, seating 5,874. Spectacular shows followed, especially at Christmas with music, dance and the famous Rockettes as a major feature. In 1978, it was threatened with closure but a $2.2 million state grant saved Radio City Music Hall and the Rockettes*

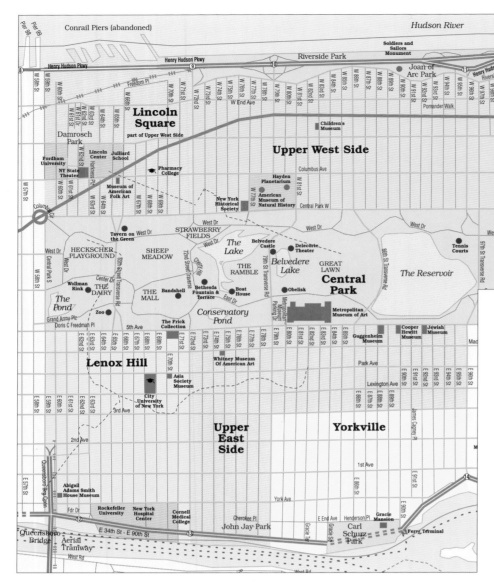

Conrail Piers (abandoned)　Hudson River　**Manhattan Valley**

Henry Hudson Pkwy　Riverside Park　Riverside Park

Soldiers and Sailors Monument

Joan of Arc Park

Lincoln Square
part of Upper West Side

Damrosch Park

Fordham University

Lincoln Center

Juilliard School

NY State Theater

Museum of American Folk Art

Pharmacy College

Hayden Planetarium

Upper West Side

Columbus Ave

Amsterdam Ave

Cathedral of St John The Divine

New York Historical Society

American Museum of Natural History

Central Park W

Manhattan Ave

8th Ave

THE GREAT LAWN

The Pool

The Loch

Lasker Rink & Pool

Tavern on the Green

West Dr

STRAWBERRY FIELDS

The Lake

Belvedere Castle

Delacorte Theater

Tennis Courts

West Dr

HECKSCHER PLAYGROUND

SHEEP MEADOW

THE RAMBLE

Belvedere Lake

GREAT LAWN

Central Park

The Reservoir

Wollman Rink

THE DAIRY

Bandshell

Bethesda Fountain & Terrace

Boat House

Obelisk

The Pond

THE MALL

Zoo

Conservatory Pond

Metropolitan Parking Dr

Metropolitan Museum of Art

Grand Army Plz

Doris C Freedman Pl

The Frick Collection

Lenox Hill

Whitney Museum Of American Art

Asia Society Museum

Cooper Hewitt Museum

Jewish Museum

Guggenheim Museum

City University of New York

Lexington Ave

Park Ave

Upper East Side

Yorkville

Queensboro Bridge

Abigail Adams Smith House Museum

Rockefeller University

New York Hospital Center

Cornell Medical College

John Jay Park

Carl Schurz Park

Gracie Mansion

Ferry Terminal

Queensboro Bridge

Aerial Tramway

The Dakota building

Famous Upper West Side residents include:
- Bix Beiderbecke
- Harry Belafonte
- John Coltrane
- James Dean
- F Scott Fitzgerald
- George Gershwin
- William Randolph Hearst
- Billie Holiday
- Harry Houdini
- Groucho Marx
- Bette Midler
- Dorothy Parker
- Sergei Rachmaninoff
- Richard Rodgers
- Babe Ruth
- J D Salinger
- P G Wodehouse

"Once you have lived in New York and it had become your home, no place else is good enough."
John Steinbeck

In this part of the city, homes range from the little wooden houses by York Avenue to Gracie Mansion, residence of many a city mayor, and the fortress-like Dakota Apartments where John Lennon lived and died. There are numerous museums, especially in Museum Row, and fine theatres and concert halls in the Lincoln Center that have replaced slums and tenements.

The Lincoln Center for the Performing Arts

Lincoln Square
Many Puerto Rican immigrants arrived in the city from the 1920s, at first to East Harlem, but then many settled in the West Side area too. One part was called "San Juan Hill" because of this. Sadly they often clashed with the dock workers who had been there for generations, a conflict that inspired Bernstein's *West Side Story* which was set in this area in the late 1950s. Lincoln Centre now stands on the area depicted.

Lincoln Center for the Performing Arts
This vital cultural center covers 15 acres of what was once slums. *The New York State Theater* (1964) seats 2,500 and has so many rhinestone lights and chandeliers, it is called the "little jewel box". *Metropolitan Opera House* has murals by Mark Chagall. Maria Callas and Luciano Pavarotti have performed here. *Lincoln Center Theatre* is, in fact, 2 theatres – the 1,000 seat Vivian Beaumont and the intimate 280-seat Mitzi E. Newhouse. Exhibits in the *New York Public Library for the Performing Arts* include original scores and playbills. *Avery Fisher Hall* (1962) is home to the New York Philharmonic Orchestra.

Upper West Side
Today this is home to about 250,000 people and has some 3,000 storefront business. In the 1600s the Dutch called it Bloemendael (Vale of Flowers) because of the flowery meadows. In due course, Bloomingdale Road would become part of Broadway. The Upper West Side became a popular residential area in 1879 when the El arrived.

The Dakota
This luxurious apartment house was built in 1884 by Edward Clark, heir to the

Singer Sewing Machine fortune, and creator of Clark's O.N.T thread. It is a veritable fortress and was the setting for the film, *Rosemary's Baby*. It has been home to Lauren Bacall, Leonard Bernstein, Judy Garland and Boris Karloff – who is supposed to haunt the building. Yoko Ono still lives here and John Lennon was assassinated outside.

Congregation Shearith Israel
This Spanish and Portuguese Synagogue is where the first Jewish congregation in the U.S. met in 1730. Inside are two millstones from an original Dutch mill on Mill Street.

Pomander Walk
This private row of 2-story cottages was based on the English village in Louis N. Parker's play *Pomander Walk*. The cottages have bright colored shutters while hedges and flower boxes line the street. There are old-fashioned lamp-posts and a small wooden sentry box. Famous residents have included Mary Martin and Humphrey Bogart.

American Museum of Natural History
- Opened in 1877, it is built in pink Vermont granite.
- It holds 36 million artefacts.
- Jewels and gems here are worth some $50 million.
- Here is the most complete barosaurus in the world.

Bloomingdale's store

Lenox Hill

Here is the most famous store in the city, *Bloomingdale's*, which in 1870 began as a humble store in a working class area. When the "els" vanished, the area went "upmarket" and so did the store.

The *Abigail Adams Smith Museum* is the house of president John Adam's daughter, a federal style building that became a country inn and is now a museum of period furniture.

Frick Collection

Henry Clay Frick (1849-1919), an industrialist, was an avid collector from childhood and his elegant mansion now houses many incredible works of art by artists such as Vermeer, Rembrandt, Holbein and Bellini.

Temple Emanu-El

This is the site of the oldest reform congregation in the city and is the world's largest Jewish house of worship.

Seventh Armoury Regiment

The huge inner hall of this brick fortress was large enough for military manoeuvres. This was the rallying point for the seventh regiment of the National Guard.

Upper East Side Museums

Just east of Central Park is Museum Mile – with the Guggenheim Museum's marvellous collection of modern art, the Jewish Museum, Cooper Hewitt National Design Museum (former home of industrialist Andrew Carnegie) and the Whitney Museum of American Art.

The Metropolitan Museum is set within Central Park bounds, fronting Fifth Avenue and has the most comprehensive collection of art in the world. For more facts and figures on museums *see page 37*.

East 93rd Street is where the Marx Brothers spent their childhood.

The Cherokee Apartments

This building was created in 1910-11 for relatives of TB patients. It features external staircases, large courtyards, and wrought-iron French balconies. The sloping driveways to the basement have deep grooves to prevent horses' hooves from slipping.

Wooden buildings

Between York Avenue and East 78th Street are two rural wooden dwellings, 450a and 450b, that once housed workers from a duck farm here in the 1850s.

Yorkville

This was a village in 1790 and later the location of many bierkellers and breweries, including Jacob Ruppert's brewery, which filled 3 blocks.

Henderson Place

Here there are fine Queen Anne buildings built on the site of a farm owned by John Jacob Astor. When he died in 1848, Astor was the richest man in America, worth $25 million. It is now named after John Henderson, who imported furs and made hats before moving into real estate and buying this property.

Gracie Mansion

This was built as a fine country manor in 1799. It is now the traditional home for the New York mayors and has been since Fiorello La Guardia moved in in 1942. Its famous visitors include Louis Philippe (later King of France), President John Quincy Adams and Washington Irving.

New York Hospital

The medical center here incorporates the city's oldest hospital. This was built when Dr. Samuel Bard of King's College (now Columbia University) begged King George III for a medical training school and somewhere to treat the "sick poor of the Colony" in 1769.

Gracie Mansion

Above: *The Metropolitan Museum of Art, early 1900s*   Below: *The Solomon R. Guggenheim Museum on Museum Mile*

The area north of 59th Street was called Muscoota (flat place) by the Native Americans. When the Dutch arrived and took over the southern part of the island, they left the Native Americans undisturbed in the north until one trader, Mynheer de Forest, ventured north and became the first European to set foot in Muscoota. He built a house, planted crops and was soon followed by more Dutch settlers. In 1643, the Indian Wars erupted after Governor Kieft tried to tax Native Americans. He also sentenced some to death and butchered 80 in their beds.

Many of the Harlem settlers were killed in the ensuing "Year of our Blood" but peace was restored when Governor Stuyvesant arrived. He built a town in Muscoota that he called Nieuw Haarlem, changed by the English in 1664 to Harlem.

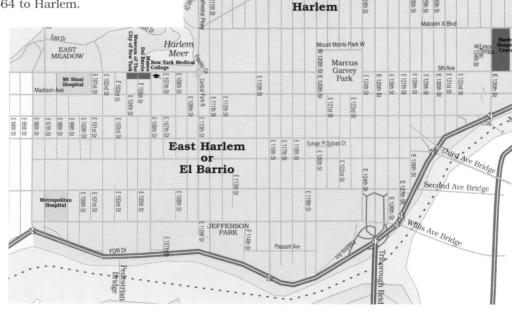

DP

DP

DP

DP

DP

Top left: *Churches are often created in converted buildings*
Far left: *Typical tenement block*
Left: *Striver's Road, named for the hard-working occupants*
Bottom left: *Archetypal row of Brownstone houses*

Harlem

In 1837, the New York and Harlem Railroad was built along Park Avenue. Harlem became a fine neighborhood with an opera house, gracious townhouses and apartments. In 1878-81 the elevated railroads reached into its midst. In the late 1880s, an influx of poor Blacks arrived in Harlem. Then hundreds of families moved here in 1906-10, displaced by the building of the first Pennsylvania Station. There was a large German population and many European Jews arrived too. By 1920, 200,000 blacks were living here. With a large number of black musicians, intellectuals and writers, Harlem developed through the 1900s as the mecca of Black American culture and politics and as a stong center for business and the arts. Harlem became the largest black community in the world – but many were victims of segregation. Black Muslims founded the Temple of Islam on Lenox Avenue where Malcolm X worked before setting up his own organisation.

In 1968, Harlem was the scene of rioting by black residents – but in the new millenium, it is flourishing once again.

Jazz in Harlem

In 1895, Thomas Edison's motor-driven phonograph was invented: this would contribute greatly to the popularity of jazz which became part of the Harlem scene. In the 20th century, legendary musicians such as Louis Armstrong, Duke Ellington and Bessie Smith lived and worked in Harlem, performing at the Cotton Club, the Savoy Ballroom, and the Apollo theatre.

Spanish Harlem

Spanish Harlem or El Barrio and has a strong Hispanic community and Latin American culture. La Marquetta street market here is a focal point.

Harlem Hellfighters

Two regiments from New York served with the French army during the First World War and became the 369th U.S. Infantry. All the enlisted men were black and the officers white. The 369th served 191 days combat in the war, longer than any unit in the armed forces. The first Croix de Guerre awarded to any Americans went to Corporal Johnson and Private Roberts of the 369th, and the unit also earned the Croix de Guerre as a unit citation – while the band helped to introduce jazz to France. In 1920 the unit built First Armory (142nd Street/5th Avenue). Unit commander, Colonel Davis, left in 1940 to become the first black American general. The unit also served in the Second World War, the Korean War and the Persian Gulf.

Schomberg Center

This research center into black culture is a branch of the New York Public Library and began through the black history collection of Arthur Schomberg, who sold his collection to the library in 1926 and then worked as a curator there.

Notable Harlem Residents

- William Borroughs
- Duke Ellington
- George Gershwin
- Allen Ginsberg
- Oscar Hammerstein II
- Jimi Hendrix
- Billie Holiday
- Scott Joplin
- Jack Kerouac
- Fiorella La Guardia
- Joe Louis
- Malcolm X
- Thurgood Marshall
- Thomas Nast
- Paul Robeson
- Norman Rockwell
- Charlie Parker
- Igor Ivan Sigorsky

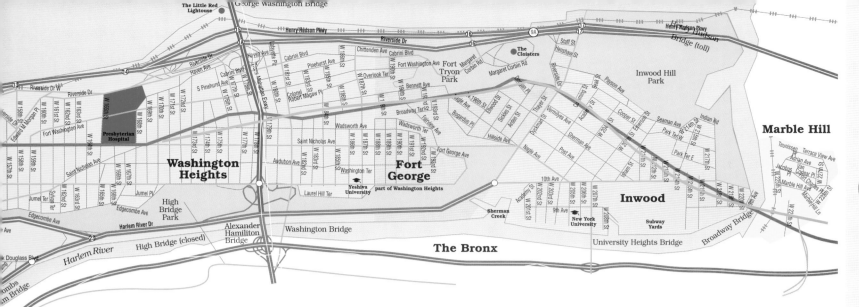

Morningside Heights
This was the site of a Revolutionary War battle in 1776 when patriot forces under George Washington defeated the British in the Battle of Harlem Heights. In this area Bloomingdale Insane Asylum was built in 1818, and an Orphan Asylum in 1838.

Columbia University
This was founded in 1754 as Kings College but the present campus was begun in 1897 on the site of the Bloomingdale Insane Asylum. Columbia has had 50 Nobel laureates and famous alumni include Isaac Asimov, J.D. Salinger, James Cagney and Joan Rivers. The Low Memorial Library, built in the shape of a Greek cross, has an exquisite Beaux Arts interior with a vast rotunda and dome. The Butler Library opposite is one of the largest in the nation, while the Avery Library holds the most extensive collection of architecture books in the U.S.

Cathedral of St John the Divine
Work began on the cathedral in 1892 but the largest cathedral in the world is still not finished; another 50 years' work is needed! The interior is over 600 feet (180m.) long and 146 feet (45m.) wide. Stone-cutting inspired by masonry from the Middle Ages has reintroduced ancient techniques to create wonderful Gothic features.

Riverside Church
Inspired by Chartres cathedral, this 1930 Gothic-style church has the largest carillon in the world, with 74 bells, and one of the biggest organs with 22,000 pipes. Here Martin Luther King gave his renowned sermon: "It is time to break the silence."

Grant's Tomb (right)
This was erected in 1897. Ulysees S. Grant was the commanding general of the Union forces in the Civil War. Over 90,000 Americans gave a total of $600,000 to create this 8.5 ton sarcophagus.

Hamilton Heights
Hamilton Heights and Sugar Hill developed in the 1880s along with the "el" line. Sugar Hill became a favorite of the elite with its fine stone houses set on a high hill and the area has been home to Thurgood Marshall, Count Basie, Duke Ellington, and Sugar Ray Robinson.

Washington Heights
This high, wooded area was home to the Wiechquaesgecks before the colonists moved north. During the American Revolution, many defences were erected here, including Fort Tryon, a colonial outpost seized by the British and named after the last English governor of New York colony.
Always an area of mixed nationalities and unrest, in February 1965, Malcolm X was assassinated, at the Audubon Ballroom – now part of a biotechnology research center.

Inwood
This is the northern tip of Manhattan and thought by some to be where Peter Minuit bought the island in 1626. Here are large sections of parkland and the last piece of primeval forest in Manhattan. The Cloisters – a section of the Metropolitan Museum of Art – was set up in 1938 in a medieval style building that houses European art treasures from the Middle Ages.

Dyckman House
This historic house in Inwood was built about 1785 by William Dyckman. There are period rooms including parlors and a colonial kitchen. It is the last remaining colonial farmhouse in Manhattan.

Right and below: Dyckman House, only example of the type of farmhouse built by settlers of Dutch origin up until 1850
Bottom: The Cloisters Museum

There are many fascinating museums and galleries in Manhattan and New York City boroughs – over 90 are listed here. The history of the city, fine art collections and other special areas of interest, including dolls and dinosaurs, can be explored.

Abigail Adams Smith Museum

This was the house of president John Adam's daughter, a federal style building that became a country inn and is now a museum of period furniture.

Adriance Farmhouse

Built 1772, this historic house is part of the Queens County Farm Museum. The first farm here was built in 1697. The present Dutch style property was a truck farm which opened as a museum in 1975.

Above: *The Cloisters* Below: *The Cooper Hewitt*

American Museum of Natural History

Founded in 1869, it houses over 30 million artifacts and specimens from every continent in over forty exhibition halls. It has one of the world's greatest and most diverse collection of dinosaur fossils in the world, the Hayden Planetarium, and the largest natural history library in Western hemisphere.

Brooklyn Museum

The second largest art museum in the New York state, its collection includes works from ancient Egyptian masterpieces to contemporary art.

Children's Museum of Manhattan

As well as fascinating exhibits, the museum offers art, music, video, storytelling and science workshops, toddler and pre-school activities, a television-production studio, and a 200-seat theater.

The Cloisters

Set in Fort Tryon Park, this is a branch of the Metropolitan Museum of Art. John D. Rockefeller financed the buiding that incorporates portions of five French monasteries and is devoted to European art and architecture of the Middle Ages. The garden has over 250 species and herbs cultivated in medieval times.

Cooper-Hewitt

The National Design Museum was founded in 1897 as the Cooper Union Museum for the Arts of Decoration.

The Eight

In 1907, a group of artists (Robert Henri, John Sloan, George Luks, William Glackens,

Everett Shinn, Arthur B Davies, Ernest Lawson and Maurice Prendergast) formed to promote new works and ideas and widened the opportunities for new artists to exhibit.

Ellis Island Museum of Immigration

This recreates the immigrant experience in the place where they arrived, with many photographs and exhibits.

Frick Collection

The mansion of industrialist Henry C. Frick (1849-1919) – an ardent art collector who left behind $30 million worth of works – has paintings by great European artists, fine French furniture and porcelain, Limoges enamels, Oriental rugs and sculpture.

Guggenheim Museum

Four museums make the Guggenheim an international foundation for "the promotion and encouragement and education in art and the enlightenment of the public" – established by copper magnate

The Guggenheim Museum

Guggenheim in the late 1920s. It houses a vast collection of 20th-century art.

Historic Richmond Town

A well-restored village on Staten Island that dates from the 1600s, with the oldest elementary school in the U.S., a general store, courthouse and tavern.

Intrepid Sea, Air, Space Museum

An aircraft carrier 900 feet (275 meters) long, has been converted into a museum at Pier 86. Launched in 1942, the *Intrepid* carried over 100 aircraft and 3,000 men. Opened in 1982, it recounts the history of the ship, has space exploration exhibits, aircraft and jet fighters displayed on deck, plus a submarine and battleship to visit alongside.

Metropolitan Museum of Art

This one of the largest and finest art museums in the world. Its collections include over 2 million works that span more than 5,000 years of

Submarine in the Intrepid Sea, Air Space Museum

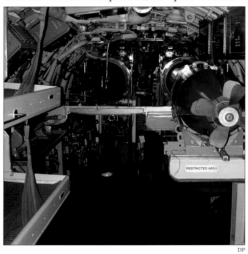

Metropolitan Museum of Art

National Museum of the American Indian

New York School
This group of abstract impressionist artists in the city were active in the 1950s and included Arshile Gorky, Franz Kline, Jackson Pollock and Mark Rothko.

New York Transit Museum
Visitors can explore 100 years and 700 miles (1126 km.) of urban infrastructure.

Nicholas Roerich Museum
This is a major center for viewing paintings by Roerich. Visitors can also see reproductions of his art and related books.

South Street Seaport Museum
Founded 1967 at the site of the original port. The 11-square-block historic district has stone-paved streets and 18th- and 19th-century buildings plus a fleet of historic vessels.

Statue of Liberty *(left)*
The Statue of Liberty, unveiled in 1886, has been restored for its 100th birthday. A gift from the people of France, she was sculpted by Frederic-Auguste Bartholdi who devoted 21 years to her. The interior frame was designed by Gustave Eiffel, who later built the Eiffel Tower. The Museum here has exhibits on immigration and on the design of the statue.

Whitney Museum of American Art
Founded in 1930 by sculptor Gertrude V. Whitney, this serves as a perpetual art gallery for living artists. Its collection of 20th-century American art is the most comprehensive in the world, with over 10,000 pieces.

history and culture, from prehistoric times to today. Founded in 1870, the first work of art donated was the Roman Sarcophagus from Tarsus. When J.P. Morgan's art collection arrived in 1913, it was valued at $60 million. The museum has 32 acres of floor space, a huge collection of American art and 24 period rooms. There are works by Leonardo, Raphael, Renoir and van Gogh, as well as an Egyptian wing with objects from the 16th century BC.

Museum Mile Festival
The Museum Mile stretches along Fifth Avenue from 82nd to 104th Streets with many museums and other fine arts institutions, One of the Mile's newest museums on the corner of 86th Street, is the, *Neue Galerie New York*, devoted to early 20th-century German and Austrian art and design. In June, Fifth Avenue is closed to traffic, the museums are open to the public, and the area is full of live bands, street entertainers and musicians, with many activities organised for children. This is one of New York's great cultural traditions and over one million people have now enjoyed this event.

Museum of the City of New York
This was established in 1923 to collect, preserve and present original cultural materials

related to the city's history and was originally housed in historic Gracie Mansion. It has a wonderful collection of doll houses and toys, and period rooms that include John D. Rockefeller's bedroom.

Museum of Modern Art
Founded in 1929, this has over 100,000 paintings, with works by Monet, Cezanne, Gaugin, Van Gogh, Toulouse-Lautrec, Rousseau, Picasso, Matisse, Chagall, and Dali. U.S. painters include Hopper, Shahn, Wyeth, and Pollock. There are sculptures by Rodin and Moore – some in the sculpture garden.

Museum of Television and Radio
This institution aims to collect and make available a fine collection of programs.

National Museum of the American Indian
Founded in 1916, the collection covers 10,000 years of Native American history, with jewelry, rugs and pottery. It is housed in the former U.S. Custom House (where frescoes depict both the first European explorers arriving and Greta Garbo disembarking from an Atlantic liner!).

New York Hall of Science
Hands-on, interactive science provides a fun learning experience for both children and adults.

Museum of the City of New York

Pierpont Morgan Library
This houses the book and art collection of leading financier J. Pierpont Morgan, plus porcelain, sculpture, and old-master paintings and drawings. Galleried tiers of bookshelves contain Morgan's books, added to by various curators. Here are the 12th-century Stavelot Triptych, a copy of the *Gutenberg Bible* (c. 1455), illuminated medieval and Renaissance manuscripts, music manuscripts, old bindings, rare children's books, and 9,000 prints and drawings that include works by Dürer, Leonardo and Michelangelo.

Salmagundi Club
Formed in 1871 by a group of artists and patrons, by the mid 1990s there were some 600 members. The club hosts exhibitions, lectures, demonstrations, and sketch classes and has a reference library. The building reputedly had the only remaining stoop on Fifth Avenue.

Studio Museum in Harlem
Dedicated to the art and artefacts of black America and other cultures of African origin, this collection grew until by 1991 it had over 10,000 items. The museum continues to provide studio space for artists.

Right: *Museum of American Financial History*
Below: *Museum of Jewish Heritage at Battery Place.*

Other museums include:

- Albany Institute of History & Art
- Alternative Museum
- American Fine Art Society
- American Folk Art Museum
- American Museum of the Moving Image (MOMI)
- Archives of American Art
- Artists Space
- Asia Society & Museum
- Audubon Terrace Historic District
- Bard Graduate Center for Studies in Decorative Arts
- Bronx Museum of the Arts
- Brooklyn Trolley Museum
- China Institute
- Con Edison Energy Museum
- Corning Museum of Glass
- Czech Center
- Dahesh Museum of Art
- Dia Center for the Arts
- Drawing Center
- Dumbo Arts Center
- Dyckman Farmhouse Museum
- El Museo del Barrio
- Federal Hall
- Forbes Collection
- Fraunces Tavern Museum
- Heckscher Museum of Art

- Hudson River Museum
- IBM Gallery of Science & Art
- Indocenter of Art & Culture
- International Center of Photography
- Isamu Noguchi Garden Museum
- Jacques Marchais Museum of Tibetan Art
- Japan Society
- Jewish Museum
- Liberty Science Center
- Liberty State Park
- Library & Museum of the Performing Arts
- Lower East Side Tenement Museum
- Lyman Allyn Art Museum
- Merchant's House Museum
- Micro Museum
- Montclair Art Museum
- Mount Vernon Hotel Museum
- Municipal Art Society
- Museum for African Art
- Museum of American Financial History
- Museum of American Folk Art
- Museum of American Illustration
- Museum of Arts & Design (was American Craft Museum)
- Museum of Chinese in the Americas, Chinatown

- Museum of Jewish Heritage, Battery City
- Museum of the American Piano
- Nassau County Museum of Art
- National Museum of the American Indian
- National Academy of Design
- National Jazz Museum, Harlem
- Neuberger Museum of Art
- Newark Museum
- New Museum of Contemporary Art
- New York City Fire Museum
- New York Hall of Science
- New York Historical Society
- New York Public Library
- Police Museum
- PS1 Contemporary Art Center
- Queens Museum of Art
- Rockwell Museum of Western Art
- Rotunda Gallery
- Scandinavia House: The Nordic Center in America
- Schomburg Center for Research in Black Culture
- Seventh Army Regiment
- Studio Museum in Harlem
- Temple Emanu-El
- Theodore Roosevelt Birthplace
- Vanderbilt Colony
- Yeshiva University Museum

This is a city full of splendid statues and monuments. The few depicted here are just a selection from over 2,000 in the city's public places.

American Merchant Mariner's Memorial
DP

Sir Walter Scott
DP

Robert Burns
DP

Angel of the Waters
DP

Duke Ellington Memorial
DP

Above: *Firemen's Memorial on 100th Street*
DP
Below: *Grand Army Plaza, Prospect Park, Brooklyn*

DP

DP

Atlas *(above)*

Set outside Rockefeller Center's International Building, this cast bronze by Lee Lawrie weighs 4,000lbs (1,800kg).

Battery Park memorials

Here the purchase of Manhattan from Native Americans is remembered on a flagpole – and the bravery of men at sea is movingly recorded in the American Merchant Mariner's Memorial for World War II seamen, unispired by a news photograph.

Central Park statues

The park is a veritable outdoor gallery of wonderful sculptures. These include literary figures such as Sir Walter Scott, Robert Burns and William Shakespeare, plus other renowned personalites like Beethoven and Columbus. Balto the Dog, an Indian Hunter, the Pilgrim Fathers, Alice in Wonderland and Hans Christian Andersen can also be found here, while the lovely Angel of the Waters (dedicated in 1873 to mark the opening of the Croton Aqueduct System some 30 years earlier) graces Bethesda Terrace. Jazz player, Duke Ellington, also has an impressive memorial. For more information, *see* pages 53-55.

Dogny Sculpture Project

In 2002, the American Kennel Club launched a project to place up to 300 life-size dog statues in public spaces throughout the city, especially in front of police stations, fire houses and parks, to commemorate September 11.

Firemen's Memorial

This is on 100th Street and is dedicated to New York's fire department: "soldiers in a war that never ends".

Grand Army Plaza, Brooklyn

In 1892, this robust Soldiers' and Sailors' Arch was set at the entrance to Prospect Park.

Grant's Tomb

This vast mausoleum contains the coffin of General Grant, America's 18th President.

Horace Greely

The founder of the *New York Tribune* rests on a cushioned chair in Greely Square *(below)*. Greely is also depicted near the Civic Center.

DP

Captain Nathaniel Hale

In 1776, the British hung 21-year old Nathaniel Hale (a Revolutionaries captain) as a spy. His friend William Hull set his last words as: "I only have one regret that I have but one life to lose for my country."

Jewish Memorial

This Riverside Park memorial *(below)* remembers the Warsaw ghetto and 6 million Jews lost in World War II.

DP

DP

Joan of Arc Monument

This fine Riverside edifice near West 93rd Street *(above)* was raised in 1915, the 500th anniversary of Joan of Arc's birth in 1412.

DP
Marquis de Lafayette

A French hero of the American Revolution, the Marquis visited New York in 1824 and is depicted in Union Square.

Abraham Lincoln

This statue in Union Square remembers President Lincoln, who delivered his "Right Makes Might" speech in the Cooper Union in 1860.

New York Herald

This clock used to crown the New York Herald building, demolished in 1921. Stuff and Guff chime the hours.

Mary Lindley Murray

A plaque in Park Avenue recalls how, at this site in 1776, Mary Murray invited British General Howe and his staff for tea, delaying them so Washington's army could reach Upper Manhattan safely.

DP

Theodore Roosevelt

America's 26th President sits astride a horse outside the Natural History Museum.

Lin Ze Xu

A statue in Chinatown remembers the 19th-century pioneer against drugs.

George Washington

Statues of Washington include the one that depicts him standing outside Federal Hall, and one of him on horseback in Union Square.

World War One monument

This memorial to the soldiers of World War I is at 28th Street and Ninth Avenue in Chelsea.

Major General Worth *(right)*

This hero of the mid-1800s Mexican Wars is the only public figure ever buried under the city streets – in Worth Square.

Statue of Liberty

- The statue is modeled after sculptor Bartholdi's mother.
- Its 350 pieces were shipped to the U.S. in 214 crates.
- When the wind speed is 50 m.p.h., the statue sways 3 inches (76 mm) and the torch 5 inches (127 mm).
- The crown spikes represent the 7 oceans or 7 continents.
- Her torch represents enlightenment.
- The chains underfoot suggest her crushing the chains of slavery.
- The statue weighs 225 tons.
- 354 steps lead to her crown.
- Her mouth is 3 feet (900mm) wide.
- Her index finger is 8 feet (2.4m.) high.
- 4.2 million visit Liberty and Ellis Islands each year.

New York Herald

Theodore Roosevelt

Left: *Monument to World War One in Chelsea*

Below: *Major General Worth's monument*

New York has inspired many movies, plays, musicals and books, proving an evocative setting for art, literature and drama. Some have drawn upon the slums and gangland; others have focused on finer surroundings like the Plaza Hotel and Dakota building.

Plays and musicals have included:
- *42nd Street*
- *Barefoot in the Park*
- *A Chorus Line*
- *Guys & Dolls*
- *Plaza Suite*
- *West Side Story*

Movies

An Affair to Remember
Deborah Kerr leaves a taxi on 34th Street and meets Cary Grant at the top of the Empire State Building (1957).

Balto
The 1995 animated movie tells the story of the sled dog whose statue is in Central Park.

Barefoot in the Park
Jane Fonda and Robert Redford are in Washington Square Park.

The Cotton Club
The movie's jazz and dancing scenes are set in Harlem.

The Fisher King
This features a magic ballroom scene in Grand Central Station and scenes in Central Park.

Gangs of New York
Depicts the violent rise of gangland power in the Five Points area and the political corruption in 1846 (2002).

Ghostbusters
This shows Sigourney Weaver's home at 55 Central Park West and Columbus Circle.

Godfather I and II
These films show Little Italy and the Mafia activities there.

Hannah and her Sisters
This Woody Allen movie shows the city including Central Park.

Killer's Kiss and **The Killer that Stalked New York**
Both films show Pennsylvania Station, the Concourse, and wonderful 1950s train shed.

King Kong
The film's climax is at the top of the Empire State Building.

Love Story
Scenes shot in Central Park.

Marathon Man
The film includes Central Park.

The Manchurian Candidate
The climax of this Frank Sinatra film is set in Madison Square Garden.

Miracle on 34th Street
This story about Santa Claus depicts the rivalry between the Macy's and Gimbel Brothers stores (1947).

Mo Better Blues
Many fine shots of the Brooklyn Bridge are included in this film.

Moonstruck
Both the Metropolitan Opera House and Brooklyn Heights feature here.

North by Northwest
This Hitchcock thriller shows the United Nations building.

The Palm Beach Story
Shots of Seventh Avenue, Pennsylvania Station entrance and an excellent replica of the train shed (1942).

Rosemary's Baby
Mia Farrow undergoes some harrowing experiences in the Dakota Building.

The Seven Year Itch
This Marilyn Monroe film has views of Pennsylvania Station, and the Concourse just before it was demolished (1955).

Sleepless in Seattle
The final romantic meeting takes place at the top of the Empire State Building.

Spellbound
Ingrid Bergman and Gregory Peck are escaping from the police in New York. The film has several scenes of Pennsylvania Station (1945).

Strangers on a Train
A Hitchcock thriller with scenes that focus around Pennsylvania Station, showing carriageways, the arcade and the Main Waiting Room (1951).

Sweet Smell of Success
This includes shots of the Brill Building on Broadway.

Tootsie
Dustic Hoffman had lunch in the Russian Tearoom.

Under the Clock
This movie has many scenes of the city, including Grand Central Station where Judy Garland meets Robert Walker, and Pennsylvania Station.

Wall Street
A story of a young stockbroker, the movie shows New York City scenes and Central Park.

West Side Story
This movie is set in the slums where the Lincoln Center has been built now – but begins with sweeping aerial shots of Manhattan.

When Harry Met Sally
This depicts Katz's Deli – and Central Park's Boathouse Café.

Year of the Dragon
There were many shots of Chinatown in this film.

Other movies include:
Annie Hall 1977
Breakfast at Tiffany's
A Bronx Tale 1993
The French Connection 1971
Manhattan 1979
The Man in the Grey Flannel Suit 1956
On the Waterfront 1954
Raging Bull 1980
Rear Window 1954
Taxi driver 1976

Books featuring the city include:

Paul Auster	New York Trilogy	Henry Miller	Crazy Cock
James Baldwin	Another Country	Joseph Mitchell	Up in the Old Hotel
Wilton Barnhardt	Emma Who Saved My Life	O. Henry	The Last Leaf
Saul Bellow	Seize the Day	Jacob Riis	How the Other Half Lives
Truman Capote	Breakfast at Tiffany's	Hubert Selby Jr.	Last Exit to Brooklyn
Caleb Carr	The Alienist	Betty Smith	A Tree Grows in Brooklyn
E.L. Doctorow	The Waterworks	Hildegard H. Swift	The Little Red Lighthouse and the Great Gray Bridge
J. P. Donleavy	A Fairy Tale of New York		
Dos Passos	Manhattan Transfer	Charlotte Temple	A Tale of Truth (1791)
Ralph Ellison	The Invisible Man	Edith Wharton	Age of Innocence
F. Scott FitzGerald	Tender is the Night	Walt Whitman	Leaves of Grass
Washington Irving	A History of New York	Thomas Wolfe	Bonfire of the Vanities

This hotel's telephone number was immortalised when Glenn Miller used it in his swing classic, Pennsylvania 6-5000

The elegant restaurant at Central Park's Tavern on the Green

New York offers 65,000 hotel rooms, restaurants with every imaginable cuisine and a dazzling variety of shops.

Algonquin Hotel

In the early 1900s, this was one of the few hotels to welcome solo females, including Irish actress Lady Gregory, who created a stir when she lit up a cigarette in the lobby. When 16-year old Tallulah Bankhead arrived in 1919 to study acting, her wild behaviour led owner Frank Caseo to say, "Either I can keep an eye on Tallulah or run this hotel. No man does both!" 10-year-old Ben Bodne began his career selling newspapers. Helen Keller and Annie Sullivan gave him 10 cents for a 2-cent paper, insisting he keep the change. Years laters, when Ben saw Helen and Annie lunching in the Oak Room, he reminded them of this. To Miss Keller's query, "What did you do with the 8 cents?" he said, "I bought the Algonquin." Famous visitors include John Barrymore, Robert Benchley, Douglas Fairbanks, Ella Fitzgerald, George S Kaufman, Angela Lansbury, Alan Jay Lerner and Dorothy Parker.

Savoy Ballroom

In 1926, this was described as the, "world's most beautiful ballroom." It sponsored dog races and so was called "the track", too. By the 1930s-40s, it promoted band battles and dance contests: many dances evolved, including the Lindy Hop. 250 big bands played here, including Duke Ellington's and Benny Goodman's.

Hotel lodgings (SRO's)

In the mid 1940s, cheap single rooms with communal bathrooms provided vital housing for the poor, especially around the Bowery. Residents were usually single men, often transient workers.

George Hotel

In 1884, this Brooklyn hotel had 2,632 rooms (the greatest number in the city), a ballroom, swimming pool, and rooftop dining and dancing.

Waldorf-Astoria

On Fifth Avenue two separate hotels were raised by feuding cousins: the Waldorf (1893), built by William Waldorf Astor on the site of his father's mansion, and the Asoria (1897), built by John Jacob Astor IV on the site of his mother's mansion. In time, the two buildings became a unit, but could still be sealed off from each other when family rows required. With 1,300 rooms, it was the largest, grandest hotel during the 1890s but in 1929 was demolished to make way for the Empire State Building. *Waldorf-Astoria II* then rose (Park and Lexington Avenues) opening 1931, with 1,410 guest rooms, including 106 tower suites. Famous residents include Herbert Hoover, Cole Porter, Douglas MacArthur, and Prince Ranier and Princess Grace of Monaco.

Windsor Hotel fire

In 1899, one of the worst hotel fires began when a guest threw a match out of the window, igniting the lace curtains. The staff's cries were drowned by the St. Patrick's Day Parade on Fifth Avenue but even when spectators noticed the fire and raised the alarm, low water pressure hampered the firemen. Many guests jumped from high windows. The hotel was destroyed; 33 died and 52 were injured, with property losses some $1 million.

Automats

Horn & Hardart's fast food, served in chrome-and-glass restaurants, led to the world's largest cafeteria-restaurant chain, serving 800,000 people a day. The first one in the city opened in Times Square in 1912, offering buns, beans, fish cakes, and coffee, each item costing 5 cents, and bought by dropping a nickel into a slot. By the 1930s, Automats offered full lunch and dinner and by the 1940s-50s, served more than 350,000 customers a day. Hot savory food was eaten in huge rectangular halls at lacquered tables. "Nickel throwers" in glass booths exchanged paper money for 5-cent pieces to operate the machines. Paupers and investment bankers might sit together at the same table, while founders Horn and Hardart lunched at the Sample Table to test for quality. After closing time, trucks carried surplus food to "day-old" shops which sold it at reduced prices. Its fresh-brewed coffee was known as the best in town. In the 1950s, Automats sold more than 90 million cups a year, and Irving Berlin's song, *Let's Have Another Cup of Coffee* became the company's theme song. Automats declined during the 1970s and 1980s when Burger King and McDonald's arrived – and the last city Automat closed in 1991.

Delmonico's

The oldest restaurant in the city opened in 1827 and, by 1831, was the best known in the U.S. Destroyed by fire in 1835 and 1845, it was succeeded by a 5-story hotel and restaurant on Broadway, and then Fifth Avenue. Its elegance soon attracted the city's elite. Famous culinary innovations included Baked Alaska, Eggs Benedict and Lobster Newburg. The first city debutante ball held outside a private home took place here in 1870. The restaurant closed during Prohibition, but reopened in the late 1920s and by 1982, had arrived at Beaver Street. Patrons include all the presidents since the 1830s, Charles Dickens, Queen Victoria, Oscar Wilde and Diamond Jim Brady.

Keens Chophouse

On West 36th Street, this grew from an actors' club into a popular eaterie for actors, playwrights, and producers in 1885. Regulars joined the Keens Chophouse Pipe Club, which, for a fee of $5, provided them with long-stemmed clay pipes, stored in racks above the tables. The club grew to 50,000 members, including Babe Ruth, Will Rogers, Enrico Caruso, and Douglas MacArthur. It was an all-male preserve until 1901, when actress Lillie Langtry sued them. The Langtry Room was named in her honor.

Maxwell's Plum

This restaurant and bar on First Avenue was a renowned "singles bar" with garish décor, Tiffany lamps, ornate mirrors, and stained glass. In the 1970s, it served 350,000 meals a year but it closed in 1988.

Oyster bars

From the 1830s, oyster bars were very popular in a city surrounded by rich oyster beds. In the 1840s, bars in Canal Street allowed patrons to consume as many oysters as they wished for 6 cents. Most liked their oysters raw, but fried, stewed, roasted, and scalloped ones were also enjoyed. By the 1850s, $6 million worth of oysters were eaten annually and local beds were eventually exhausted. Today, oysters are a rich man's luxury but the Oyster Bar at Grand Central Terminal remains one of the finest seafood restaurants.

Left: Advertisement at Grand Central's Oyster Bar

Cocktails
Both Manhattan and the Bronx have cocktails named after them, the latter created by a Waldorf-Astoria bartender in the early 1900s.

Lindy
Lindy's restaurant, opened in 1921 on Broadway, and immortalized New York-style cheesecake.

Lombardi's Pizzeria
The first pizzeria in the U.S. was opened in 1905 on Spring Street by Italian, Gennaro Lombardi. His brick-oven pizzas became an institution.

Tavern on the Green
This Central Park restaurant stands on the site of a sheepfold and opened in 1934. It has stained-glass windows, including one by Tiffany. The restaurant serves some 2,000 customers a day.

T.G.I. Friday's
This First Avenue restaurant and bar (1965-94) is regarded as the world's first "singles bar" and gave rise to 294 franchises throughout the world.

Shopping and store stories

Abercrombie and Fitch
When David Abercrombie began this in the late 1800s as an outdoor supply store, one of the first customers was Ezra Fitch, a wealthy lawyer who became a partner. In 1908, the store provided President Roosevelt with equipment for an African safari, including snake-proof sleeping bags. In 1917, the store moved to Madison Avenue.
A fly-casting pond was set up on the roof and a shooting range in the basement. Customers include Presidents Taft, Harding, Wilson, Hoover, and Eisenhower, Admiral Byrd, Charles Lindbergh, Amelia Earhart, King Hussein of Jordan and Katherine Hepburn – who rode a bicycle across the main floor.

Barnes and Noble
The book publishers and booksellers began in 1873 as wholesale book jobbers to supply schools, colleges, libraries and book dealers with new and used books. Their first store opened on Fifth Avenue in 1917. By the 1970s, Barnes and Noble had become one of the first U.S. discount retail booksellers and its Fifth Avenue bookstore is now said to be the largest in the world.

Bloomingdale's
This began as a dry goods store in 1872, known as the "great East Side bazaar". The store attracted more customers after the Third Avenue "el" arrived in 1879. By 1927, it occupied an entire block and offered "the best possible value for the least possible price" and has remained popular ever since.

Brooks Brothers
The first Brooks & Co store opened in 1818, "to make and deal only in merchandise of the finest quality." More stores and the flagship at Madison Avenue (1915) arrived as the chain spread. There are now 158 U.S. stores, plus outlets in Japan, Hong Kong, Rome and Milan. When he was assassinated, Abraham Lincoln was in a fine Brooks Brothers coat; Ulysses S. Grant had uniforms made for the Union officers and Theodore Roosevelt wore a Brooks Brothers uniform in his march up San Juan Hill. John F. Kennedy had a two-button suit for his inauguration. The Astors, Goulds, Vanderbilts and Rockefellers have shopped here and 5 generations of Morgans, including J.P., were attended by one salesman, Frederick Webb, who worked at the store for 65 years.
After his South Pole expedition, Admiral Byrd had Brooks make him a dress uniform for his first public appearance and aviator Charles Lindbergh wore a Brooks suit for his ticker-tape parade.
Other clients include Cary Grant, Gary Cooper, Douglas Fairbanks, Sr., Rudolph Valentino, Errol Flynn, Rudy Vallee, Clark Gable, Jack Dempsey, Fred Astaire, Jack Kerouac, Gene Hackman, the Lincoln Center Jazz Orchestra and Sir Paul McCartney. The Duke of Windsor wore their dressing gowns and Katherine Hepburn, one of the first female stars to don trousers, had them tailored here.

Christie's
The 1766 London auction house opened their first U.S salesrooms in Park Avenue in 1977, and in East 67th Street in 1979. One collection of contemporary art sold for $25,824,700 in 1988 and in 1990, a Van Gogh portrait for $82.5 million, the largest sum paid for any auction lot.

Hot dogs
Charles Feltman in Coney Island and Harry Stevens at the City Polo Grounds both claimed to have launched hot dogs. Nathan's hot dog stand on Surf Avenue in Coney Island, opened in 1916. By the early 1900s, the franchise had 62 U.S. outlets and in 1991, the original Surf Avenue stand sold 1.05 million frankfurters.

F. W. Woolworth
Formed as a 5 and 10 cent store in 1879 by Frank W. Woolworth, it sold essentials cheaply, and when it moved into the Woolworth Building, then the tallest building in the world, it had over 1,000 U.S. stores. By 1918, the firm made over $100 million in sales.

J. Levine and Company
A family business for 4 generations, it was once the largest manufacturer of Torah covers and Ark curtains in the U.S. and remains the main retailer of Jewish books.

Jahn's
The chain of ice cream parlors, begun 1897, were well known for extravagant dishes like the "Kitchen Sink", a vast portion of ice cream, fruit and syrups that serves 8.

Black, Starr and Frost
The oldest jewelers in the U.S. formed in 1801 and moved to New York in 1810. They sold porcelain, silver, paintings, bronzes and gemstones and exhibited at London's Crystal Palace Exposition of 1851.

Macys
1858-59: Rowland H. Macy opened a small fancy dry goods store. First-year sales were some $85,000.
1902: Macy's moved to Herald Square which by 1924, was largest store in the world, with its 7th Avenue addition. 10,000 people watched Macy's first Thanksgiving Day parade.
1935: Fred Lazarus, Jr., persuaded President Roosevelt to change Thanksgiving holiday to the 4th Thursday of November, to extend the Christmas shopping season and help the nation's business: 1941 Act of Congress fixes this.
1990-92: Bankruptcy threat with an $8 billion debt but after consolidation, a new public company emerged.
2002: Visited by approximately 30,000 visitors a day, Macy's Herald Square store is the third most visited site in the city, with 1 million square feet of selling space.

Marble Palace
The first department store in the world, a 4-story structure on Broadway opened in 1846. Eventually the Marble Palace occupied the entire block and was the largest store in the world by the 1850s.

Strand Books
The largest secondhand bookstore in the city, founded 1929 by Ben Bass, houses more than 2 million books, with over 45,000 of antiquarian interest. Now run by the founder's son, Fred Bass, its slogan is "8 Miles of Books".

Tiffany
These jewelers on Fifth Avenue began in 1837. After selling jewelry and silver from Europe, it began manufacturing gold items in 1848 and silver in 1851. As the business grew, it created elaborate diamond and enameled jewelry, and built a collection of rare gemstones. Capote's *Breakfast at Tiffany's* (1958), later made into a film, helped it become the most famous jewelry store in the U.S.

Zabar's
This gourmet delicatessen on Broadway began in 1939, and by the 1960s offered more than 7,000 foods. It now has over 30,000 customers a week.

Jazz came from New Orleans and the South but discovered a new life force in New York. The city is now a renowned center for all kinds of jazz, classical music and dance.

Arthur's Tavern on Grove Street

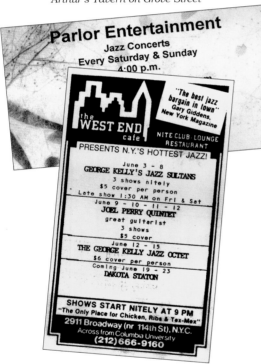

Above: *A flyer for the now-closed West End Cafe. Many such jazz clubs have closed in the city; many people now attend jazz sessions in private homes*

Below: *A fashionable crowd leaves slowly after a performance at the Metropolitan Opera in 1890*

Beer halls
Beer halls were a prominent feature of the city's German neighborhoods. There were also opulent halls where families could drink, eat, sing, dance and be entertained by music and drama.

Cotton Club Nightclub
Opening in 1922 at 142nd Street, this became one of the leading cabarets in Harlem. It did not admit black customers but engaged them as musicians and entertainers. Duke Ellington opened here in 1927. Other prominent performers include Louis Armstrong, Lena Horne and Ethel Walters.

American Museum of Natural History
Here on Fridays, the Sphere at the Rose Center for Earth and Space hosts jazz musicians; admission is included with the museum price.

Arthur's Tavern
On Grove Street since 1937, this is the longest continually run jazz club in the city.

Arturo's
Live jazz takes place nightly in an aromatic coal oven pizza shrine on West Houston Street.

Blue Note
Opened in 1981 on West Third Street, this is one of the world's most famous jazz clubs.

Cafe Creole
Subterranean MacDougal Street venue offers Cajun and Caribbean cuisine plus jazz.

Cleopatra's Needle
A Broadway venue with music from 9 pm to 4 am. and chances to see top national and international jazz giants.

The Garage
A Seventh Avenue two-tiered restaurant with an expansive oyster bar, it features aspiring jazz groups and living legends.

Guggenheim Museum
The rotunda hosts the Worldbeat jazz program, classic jazz and international music.

Iridium
On Broadway: top international artists play here.

Jazz Gallery
Hudson Street's 2nd-floor jazz art and artist showcase with concerts, Jazz Gallery performances and a Sunday series of concerts on the river aboard the ferry "Yankee" moored at Pier 25.

Blue Smoke and Standard
On East 27th Street, Blue Smoke is a barbecue restaurant on the ground level with a jazz and soul juke box, and the *Jazz Standard* below, featuring live music.

K'av'eh'az
Mercer Street: offers a coffee house and art gallery with jazz.

Knickerbocker Bar and Grill
University Place: Opened 1978 and often features legendary stars like Earl May.

The Lenox Lounge
On Lenox Ave with 1930s art deco. The Zebra Room has a baby grand piano, tiled floors and leather banqueted booths. Local jazz legends play here.

Louis
East Ninth Street cafe and wine bar that pays homage to Armstrong with live jazz solo piano on some nights.

Parlor Entertainment
Edgecombe Avenue: Harlem jazz – standards and original music provided by a roster of jazz legends and local talent, plus free cookies and punch!

Redeye Grill
Seventh Avenue: Jazz nightly, a Steinway piano, and a good menu. Local hero, Joel Forrester, performs original solo piano masterpieces.

Showman's
West 125th Street : A mix of genteel and earthy soul in this jazz showcase, which has been home to Sara Vaughan, Lionel Hampton, Duke Ellington, Eartha Kitt and Pearl Bailey since 1942.

Smoke
2751 Broadway: sometimes hosts big name acts.

St. Nick's Pub
St. Nicholas Boulevard: This has the best Monday night jam session in the city. Guest artists frequently stop by.

Sugar Hill Bistro
On West 145th Street, in Harlem's historic Sugar Hill area, this finely appointed restaurant offers a chance to catch jazz luminaries sitting in.

Village Vanguard
Seventh Avenue: Set up by Thad Jones and Mel Lewis over 33 years ago, it still has a big band tradition – an archetypal Greenwich Village jazz club

Brooklyn Academy of Music
Lafayette Avenue: BAMcafé Live has featured great artists from jazz, blues, afro-pop, Latin, r&b, and rock, plus the Sounds of Praise Sunday Gospel Brunch on some Sundays.

Up Over Jazz Cafe
Flatbush Avenue, Brooklyn Top jazz by the city's legendary players.

CBGB (& OMFUG)
(Country, Bluegrass, Blues and Other Music for Uplifting Gourmandizers). By the mid 1990s, this rock club was the best known in the U.S.

Irving Berlin
The famous song writer arrived from Russia in 1893 and began his career on Lower East Side as a street singer and singing waiter, and then in Tin Pan Alley, as a song plugger. He performed in revues and achieved his first real success with Alexander's Ragtime Band (1911). He wrote lyrics too but, as a self-taught pianist, was able to play in only one key – so his piano was equipped with a unique keyboard shifting device. His songs include *God Bless America, White Christmas, Puttin on the Ritz* and *Easter Parade*. Shows include *Annie Get Your Gun* (1946) and *Call Me Madam* (1950). He spent his last years as a recluse in a Beekman Place mansion.

George Gershwin
Brooklyn-born George Gershwin (with lyricist brother Ira) composed some of Broadway's most famous shows, including *Lady be Good, Funny Face* and *Girl Crazy*. His *Porgy and Bess* and *Rhapsody in Blue* have become classic musical creations.

Metropolitan Opera
In 1883, the Metropolitan Opera Company began as the Opera House opened. The City Opera was founded in 1944 by Mayor La Guardia to provide "opera for the masses". In the 1950s, conductors such as Leonard Bernstein increased public interest as did television broadcasts in the 1990s. Now major opera stars can ask up to $13,000 for a performance. There are currently 40 opera companies in the city. Enthusiasts line up for standing room tickets from 6.00 a.m. and about 150 admirers wait outside Luciano Pavarotti's dressing room after each of his shows here.

Steinway Hall
This concert hall was built by the piano makers in 1866. The lavish auditorium had superb acoustics and seated 2,500. Here Charles Dickens held readings in 1867 and Anton Rubinstein's made his American début in 1872.

Carnegie Hall and the Avery Fisher Hall are both world-famous music venues.

In 1638, a soldier was stabbed in a brawl outside New Amsterdam's fort. This was the colony's first murder. Today, the city prides itself on reducing crime.

Prisons

Bridewell
The first Bridewell Prison was built in 1734, the next in 1775. This was a rallying point for protests against the British and the jail held patriots and revolutionary soldiers.

Debtor's prison
Old City Hall attic was a debtor's prison until New Gaol arrived on Chambers Street in 1755. Debtors were imprisoned on suspicion of hiding assets and had to rely on family or friends to survive. After 1810, debtors could post bond and live on the "limits" – south of 14th Street. In 1831, New York became the 2nd state to stop imprisonment for insolvency.

The Tombs
The prison was first named after an Egyptian tomb. As the population grew, the decrepit Bridewell worsened but the new prison also proved inadequate and began to sink into the swampy landfill. Its deplorable conditions were banished by 1983 renovations and the new Tombs was linked by a bridge to a facility on White Street with the same warden and staff. Together they hold over 900 inmates.

Fort Apache
This 41st Police Precinct station is in the Bronx. The nickname arrived when crime, drugs, and arson peaked in the 1960s-70s.

Happy Land fire
87 died in an arson fire in March, 1990, at this Bronx's social club. It was started by Julio Gonzalez, who, after a quarrel, splashed gasoline through the front door – and only exit. Many inside were trapped and suffered smoke inhalation. More died than in any other fire since the Triangle Shirtwaist fire of 1911.

Lindbergh Kidnapping
In March, 1932, the 10-month-old son of aviator Charles Lindbergh, was taken from his home. The kidnapper lived in the Bronx, where he had two meetings with an intermediary, in St. Raymond's Cemetery. A $50,000 ransom was handed over but on May 12, the baby's body was found in a grave just a few miles from his parents' home. Bruno Hauptmann was arrested after trying to spend some of the marked ransom money at a filling station and was executed in 1936.

Mad Bomber
From 1940-56, George Metesky planted 33 homemade bombs. 5 were at Grand Central Terminal, 3 at Pennsylvania Station, 2 at Radio City Music Hall and 2 at the Port Authority Bus Terminal. 23 detonated before being found and 15 people were injured. He was arrested in 1957 and served 17 years in an asylum for the criminally insane.

Barrel Murder
In 1903, a man was found stabbed and nearly decapitated in an ash barrel on East 11th Street. This was part of a criminal syndicate's internal wranglings. Tomasso Petto was suspected but never convicted.

Murder Incorporated
In the 1930s, this criminal organization carried out 400 to 1,000 contract killings for an organized crime syndicate. 10 leaders included Lucky Luciano (the most powerful), Joe Adonis and Frank Costello, Louis "Lepke" Buchalter, and Albert Anastasia, known as the "Lord High Executioner". They disbanded in 1940 when some lower-ranking criminals were arrested: Abe "Kid Twist" Reles gave information that led to some prosecutions and executions, but before he was able to testify against Anastasia, he fell (or was pushed) to his death from a window of Coney Island's *Half Moon Hotel*.

Negro Plot
In 1741, there was an alleged conspiracy by black slaves to burn the city and murder whites. Several slaves were implicated in fires and robberies and the provincial supreme court charged 170 with conspiracy, mostly based on hearsay and circumstantial evidence. 31 blacks and 4 whites were executed, and over 77 people were banished.

NYPD
The current police force has 75 police precincts and some 38,400 police officers. The city spends $23,000 per cadet on training. Police recruits spend 8 days in firearms training at the academy and must qualify twice a year by scoring 80% on a target-shooting test. The city has 4,300 transit police – over 10% undercover. and about 155 arrests are made each year by subway police pretending to be drunk or asleep.

Gangs

Five Points Gang
This mainly Italian street gang formed in the 1890s, led by prize fighter Paul Kelly. A subgroup called the James Street Gang was led by Johnny "the Brains" Torrio. The Five Points gang used force on behalf of corrupt politicians and businessmen. Its major rivals were the Eastmans gang. Kelly's headquarters were at the New Brighton Dance Hall. By 1915, the gang's influence had dropped but several members became prominent in organized crime in Prohibition times, including Torrio, Al Capone, Lucky Luciano and Frankie Yale.

The Westies
An Irish-American gang, based in Hell's Kitchen, inspired by the 1800s street gangs. Violent crimes from the 1960s to mid-1980s were instigated, mostly from the West Side docks, and included gambling and drug dealing. Links with the Mafia led to internal rivalries and assassinations and the Westies disbanded after murder and racketeering convictions.

Gangs today
There are 125 city gangs. 6 gangs work the area of the Upper West Side. Chinatown has over 100 different Tongs or gang groups. There are about 40,000 members in the Gee How Oak Tin Association. About 3,000 teenagers pledge allegiance to a city gang. There are 200 in the Latin Kings and 200 in the Netas.

Rosenberg case
In this celebrated cold war court case, a husband and wife were accused of giving atomic secrets to the Soviet Union and convicted of spying. They were executed at Sing Sing Prison (Ossining) in 1953.

Trunk mystery
In 1871, a baggage master discovered a nude female corpse in a trunk at the Hudson River Depot. Jacob Rozenweig had attempted to perform an abortion on the 19-year-old unmarried pregnant woman, but when she died as a result, he tried to conceal the evidence by sending her corpse to Chicago. He was sentenced to 7 years in prison.

Corruption
The Forty Thieves was a corrupt group of politicians who controlled city government, extorting money from contracts, franchises, and legislation. Led by William M. "Boss" Tweed, the Tweed Ring controlled Tammany Hall, municipal and county government, the judicial system and the Board of Audit. In 1871, the *New York Times* claimed that the ring had defrauded the city of millions of dollars. The disgraced Tweed Ring was swept from power and Boss Tweed went to prison.

Crime reduction
Since 1994, violent crime in the city has decreased by 43% (27% in U.S.). Murder has dropped by 57%, forcible rape by 31%, robbery 54% and vehicle theft 57% down.

Visiting prisoners at The Tombs prison, 1870

A Five Points beer saloon in 1880. It was in haunts like this that New York's criminals found refuge from the police, who would rarely follow them there

William M "Boss" Tweed

New York Crime Statistics 1990 - 2000

Year	Population	Violent	Property	Murder	Assault	Robbery	Burglary
1990	17,990,455	212,458	932,416	2.605	92,105	112,380	208,813
1991	18,058,000	210,184	917,467	2,571	90,186	112,342	204,499
1992	18,119,000	203,311	858,178	2,397	87,608	108,154	193,548
1993	18,197,000	195,352	814,824	2,420	85,802	102,122	181,709
1994	18,169,000	175,433	745,845	2,016	82,100	86,617	164,650
1995	18,136,000	152,683	674,342	1,550	74,351	72,492	146,562
1996	18,185,000	132,206	619,250	1,353	64,857	61,822	129,828
1997	18,137,000	124,890	584,438	1,093	63,628	56,094	118,306
1998	18,175,000	115,915	536,287	924	62,023	49,125	104,821
1999	18,196,601	107,147	489,596	903	58,860	43,821	93,217
2000	18,976,457	124,890	483,078	952	60,090	40,539	87,946

A view from the South Tower with the top of the North Tower and up to Midtown

The World Trade Center created a focal meeting point for international trade and business. It epitomised the thrust of western ideals which is why it became a prime target for any opposed to these.

Facts and figures
10,000 worked at the site to build the twin towers.
The building of the towers used 200,000 tons (203,200,000 kg.) of steel, 425,000 cubic yards (319,808 cubic metres)of concrete, 600,000 square feet (55,740 square metres) of glass and 12,000 miles (19,311 km.) of electric cable.

plaza were opened officially. They will soon be the place of work for 500 businesses and 50,000 people with 200,000 daily visitors.

The 110-story twin towers eclipsed the Empire State Building as world's tallest. One World Trade Center was 1,368 feet (417 m.) high; Two World Trade Center was 1,362 feet (415 m.). The full complex of seven buildings was edged to the north by Vessey Street, to the south by Liberty Street, to the west by West Street and to the east by Church Street. An observation deck at the top of Tower 2 became a popular tourist attraction. Below the towers lay a vast underground shopping concourse. Several smaller buildings surrounded a huge plaza that was planned as a modern version of St. Mark's Square in Venice. A Gothic-style passageway encircled this.
Each tower had an area of 4 million square feet (371,600 square meters), and a base length of 400 feet (122 meters). It was constructed with load-bearing steel walls and had a system of local and express elevators.

Backdrop
1947 New York Governor Dewey proposed revitalizing lower Manhattan as a center of world trade.
1962 Minoru Yamasaki was engaged as the architect. The World Trade center complex was to be built as part of a massive urban renewal project by the Port of New York Authority.
1965 164 buildings were demolished.
1967 The city agrees to pay the Port Authority $6 million a year and workers excavate 70 feet (21 m.)down to the bedrock.
1968 The towers rise.
1970 The first buildings opened and tenants moved in.
1973 The twin towers were dedicated.
1974 Philippe Petit walked a tightrope between the two towers, 1,350 feet (411 m.) high.
1975 Owen Quinn parachutes down from the north tower's 110th floor.
1976 The World Trade Center's twin towers and the

1976 *King Kong* movie was remade with the World Trade Center in the final climax instead of the Empire State Building.
1977 George Willig, the "Human Fly" scaled the outside of the north tower.
1981 Battery Park City was built on landfill from the World Trade Center construction.
1988 The last building was completed.
1993 On February 26, a bomb in a truck exploded in a basement parking garage, below the World Trade Center. 6 people died and over 1,000 were injured. The towers were closed for weeks and several Islamic terrorists were convicted in 1994.

The tragedy of the events and aftermath of September 11, 2001, have made an indelible mark on the consciousness of the people of New York, the U.S.A. and the entire world that shared the shock with them.

It is believed it was the extreme heat that caused the steel cores of the towers to collapse. As hundreds of terrified bystanders fled from the falling buildings, from the smoke, flames and appaling dust, firefighters, police and rescue services ran towards it – and a massive rescue operation was begun that would continue for many long days. Five other buildings in the World Trade Center complex also collapsed and many surrounding structures were severly damaged.
September 13, 2001 Steel beams in a perfect cross were found in the rubble by a laborer and were raised as a symbol of hope.
March 22, 2002 Visible for miles, twin vertical light beams pierced the sky to echo the outline of the twin towers six months after the tragedy 9/11.
May 30, 2002 The last steel beam was ceremoniously removed, draped in the Stars and Stripes, at 10.29 a.m. – the precise time at which the South Tower collapsed. Some 20,000 people watched a small group of firemen carry an empty coffin out from Ground Zero to mark the end of the digging and clearing process. There were no speeches. The mayor and a few city officials stood to attention.

To quote Alistair Cook: *A sombre ceremony in downtown New York in the grand canyon created by the explosion and fall of the Twin Towers . . . marked the taking away, by the last band of workers, of the last grain of debris of the 1,800,000 tons (1,828,800,000 kg.) they had had to cart off since the dreaded 11 September.*
What is left now is, I should think, the largest hole anyone has ever seen in the middle of a great city. . . this landscape was finally bare as a dinosaur's bone.

September 11 2002

Led in by solemn, military bands, bagpipes and police, thousands gathered in the streets around Ground Zero for a day of vigil and remembrance. Here the names of all the victims were read aloud, their families laid wreaths, and vigils and services were held throughout the city to honor those lost. President Bush arrived in the afternoon and talked to many of the bereaved families.

On the first aniversary of 9 September 2001, the crowds stood and listened while every name was read out, and were given bottles of water, passed from the front and handed over heads

Memory graffiti   *One of many home-made shrines*

After the official ceremony the bands play for the crowd in the street

Daniel Libeskind's model with the 1,800 foot (560 m.) spire

This is one of four wreaths that bear the signatures of over 35,000 Federal employees of New York City. The three other wreaths were taken to Ground Zero on September 10, 2002 and placed in a special area on one of the private viewing platforms. Attached to each wreath was a note stating that these wreaths carried the condolences of the Federal employees of New York City to the families of the victims of September 11, 2001 as well as the Federal employees compassion for the Greater New York City community of which they are a part.

2002 December
Seven new teams of architects unveiled their design plans for 16 acres of the new World Trade Center.

February 26, 2003
The spire design by Daniel Libeskind was chosen for the New World Trade Center.

Left: Tee shirts with lost ones pictures and the dust still rising from Ground Zero, a year later

Rent commitments
May 2003 A company that rented 4 floors in the north tower (and lost 658 employees) are being sued for back rent of over $1 million.
Larry Silverstein, head leaseholder at the World Trade Center, still has to pay $116 million rent a year to the Port Authority and, under the terms of his lease, is obliged to rebuild the towers at some $8.2 billion.

The New York Police Department bagpipe band march in to Ground Zero, having been followed by thousands of of people through the streets to Ground Zero, early morning, on September 11, 2002

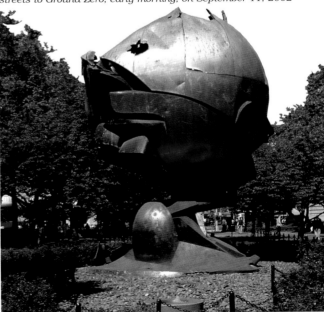

For three decades, this sculpture stood in the plaza of the World Trade Center. Entitled "The Sphere," it was conceived by artist Fritz Koenig as a symbol of world peace. It was damaged during the tragic events of September 11, 2001, but endures as an icon of hope and the indestructible spirit of this country. The sphere was placed here [Battery Park] on March 11, 2002, as a temporary memorial to all who lost their lives in the terrorist attacks at the World Trade Center. This eternal flame was ignited on September 11, 2002 in honor of all those who were lost. Their spirit and sacrifice will never be forgotten.

There are many squirrels in the city. Squirrels are numerous in Central Park but are especially friendly in Riverside Park and Madison Square

New York has a plethora of fascinating statistics, inventions, and snippets of history. Here are just a few . . .

Discovery and invention

It was pirate and explorer Giovanni da Verrazano who first sighted the natural harbour of New York in 1524.

In 1609, Henry Hudson sailed up the river now named for him. After discovering Hudson's Bay, but then trapped in ice, the crew mutinied. Hudson and his small son were cast adrift – and never heard of again. Just as new technology and steel made high buildings possible, Otis's invention in the 1850s of the elevator made living in skyscrapers desirable.

Light snow in Central Park gives the park a magical feeling. The 1888 blizzard, however, caused huge damage

In 1857, Joseph Gayetty of West 33rd Street manufactured the first roll of toilet paper in the world.

The first mechanized tattoo shop opened in 1875. Samuel O'Reilly invented the electric tattoo machine to insert ink into the skin, as a modification of Edison's electric engraving pen. In 1961, tattooing was banned in New York.

Alexander Bell first demonstrated the telephone in New York in 1877.

The first electric street lighting appeared in 1880.

Panic on Brooklyn Bridge, 1883

City facts and figures

There are over 18,000 restaurants in the city.

9 million people speak 80 languages here.

There are about 1,766 Protestant churches; 1,256 Jewish; 437 Roman Catholic; 66 Orthodox.

1,701 city-owned parks cover 28,312 acres (11,458 hectares).

New York is the largest city in the U.S. at 301 square miles (780 sq. km.) and the port of New York is the largest port complex on the East Coast.

Average daily traffic volume on the streets is 2.3 million. Traffic speed in the city is an average 5.3 m.p.h. (8.5 km.) Each year, about 1 billion people ride the subway and 80 women go into labor there. Every day, 340,000 people walk to work in the city.

26,400,000 lbs (11,975,040 kg.) of garbage are collected daily.

The city handles over 600,000 emergency 911 calls annually.

New York's steam heating system is the most extensive in the world and was instigated by Thomas Edison's company (Con Ed) in the 1890s.

City weather

In the 1888 March blizzard, 21 inches (53 cm.) of snow blocked city roads. Gales of 60 miles (96 km.) an hour piled up drifts two stories high and temperatures dropped to 5°F (15°C.). There was $20-25 million damage.

Usually snow removal costs about $9 million, but $50 million was spent in the winter of 1993/94.

Jamaica Bay and Lower New York Bay receive up to 2 inches more rainfall than midtown Manhattan; Brooklyn is the windiest borough; the Bronx and north and central Queens are the snowiest.

The surface of a city street on a hot day is about 150°F. (65°C.) – hot enough to cook an egg).

Buildings and bridges

In 1858, New York's Crystal Palace exhibition hall burned to the ground, just as the English Crystal Palace would in London, in 1936.

The New York Public Library at Fifth Avenue/42nd Street stands where the Croton Reservoir once held 660 million gallons of water.

In 1857, the site of St Patrick's Cathedral was sold to the church for just $1.

When the Brooklyn Bridge opened in 1883, somebody shouted that the bridge was collapsing. Although this was clearly untrue, in the panic that followed, 12 people were trampled to death.

In 1906, architect Stanford White was shot dead on the roof of Madison Square Garden – which he had built in 1890.

Sugar House prisons

Sugar houses were built during the 1700s to reduce the need to import refined sugar from Europe. Later the British used them as prisons for American soldiers during the Revolution. Many died in captivity here and were buried in nearby Trinity Church graveyard.

Animal facts

There were 120,000 licensed dogs in the city in 1997.

A portrait of a pet costs from $500 to $15,000.

Dog run in Madison Square Park

A pet funeral, including monument, starts at $1,000.

Pet massage therapy costs $60 per hour.

Gus (Central Park Zoo's polar bear) was seen by an animal psychiatrist at a charge of $50 per hour.

There are 2,000 members of the New York Turtle and Tortoise Society.

The city has the highest concentration of peregrine falcons in the world. 70% of the state's breeding population is in the city.

The city record for the number of stories a cat has fallen – and survived – is 46.

The "pooper-scooper" law was introduced in 1978.

The cockroach (or roach), a notorious pest in the city, is attracted to toothpaste.

Ferrets arrived in 1890 but were banned as pets in 1990.

In 1995, there were 260 reported rat bites in city. Ratio of rats to humans is 3:1. Squirrels are numerous in Central Park but are especially friendly in Riverside Park and Madison Square. Meanwhile, a new 54-story building on Lexington Avenue is not due to be finished until 2005, but a squirrel has already moved in on the 8th floor. One worker said, "Nah, I'm not giving out names. Next thing you know he gets an agent, the agent gets 60%, he goes to a bigger site." Another commented, "I've been trying to get him to wear safety goggles, but he refuses."

Haunted *Ye Waverley Inn*

Lights turn on and off, the fire rekindles itself, a man in a top hat and waistcoat appears in a mirror and something heavy is dragged up the back stairs.

Santa Claus

In 1897, Francis Church wrote a *Sun* editorial in answer to a child's letter asking, is there a Santa Claus?
"Yes, Virginia, there is a Santa Claus. . . Alas! how dreary would be the world if there were no Santa Claus! It would be as dreary as if there were no Virginias. There would be no childlike faith then, no poetry, no romance.... Thank God! he lives, and he lives forever. A thousand years from now, Virginia, nay, ten times ten thousand years from now, he will continue to make glad the heart of childhood."

Amusement arcades

At penny arcades in the 1880s, slot machines told fortunes, depicted oddities such as, "Life among the Head Hunters in Borneo", rated your prowess as a lover (on a scale from cold to hot) and depicted risqué scenes such as, "They Forgot to Lower the Curtain," and "Bare in the Bear Skins".

Death, burials and birth

In 1869, the city began using Hart Island for burials: a million interments had taken place by the mid 1990s. Each year, volunteer convicts from Rikers Island perform about 1,500 burials of the poor.

In 1702, some 10% of the city population died of yellow fever; in 1731, 5-8% died of smallpox; in 1832, 72 people died of cholera on July 18.
In the 1800s, many infants were abandoned in public places or put into almshouses.

In 1869, the Sisters of Charity began the New York Foundling Hospital for illegitimate infants.

Today in the city 48.4% of births are to unmarried women.

The first ever cesarean operation in America took place at Bellevue Hospital in 1887.

A woman who died in a chair in Barnes and Noble bookstore in 1994 was left for 4 hours – patrons assumed she was asleep. Even a group of mystery novelists passed her by.

In 1935, a rumor claimed Bette Davis has died, She retorted, "With a newspaper strike on, I wouldn't dream of it!"

Sorosis

One of the first women's clubs in the U.S. was launched n 1868, when the New York Press Club barred female reporters from a function honoring Charles Dickens' visit.

These six pages list a selection of people, places and major events from all the elements of *The Timeline History of New York City* – the Timeline itself, plus the various folding sections and book pages. With such a density of information, especially in the Timeline, this *Factfinder and index* can be only a brief survey of the numerous detailed entries but serves as a guide to the vast store of information in this book and to the story of New York City.